WORKERS' COMPENSATION

BENEFITS MANUAL

California Laws
Explained & Applied

By
GWEN HAMPTON, B.S.
Casualty Claim Law Associate

Published By
Workers' Compensation Co.
P.O. Box 11448, Glendale, CA 91226
(818) 247-8224

Workers' Compensation Benefits Manual
Printed 1997
2nd Printing 1998

DISCLAIMER

As is true of all other books on the topic of workers' compensation, this book is intended to be utilized in conjunction with reference to current statutory laws, case law, and opinion from legal counsel as appropriate. For this reason, the author and publisher hereby disclaim liability for any claim that may be alleged to arise from reliance upon information contained in this text.

Previous books
by
Gwen Hampton

Workers' Compensation: Mechanics of Administering Claims
© 1985
Workers' Compensation Claims Desk Book
© 1989
Workers' Compensation Claims Desk Book 2
© 1993

Internet: Locators:
Web Site: http://home.earthlink.net/~wcomp
E-mail: wcomp@earthlink.net

THE AUTHOR

GWEN HAMPTON earned a B.S. degree from the State University of New York College at Buffalo and a Diploma in Liability Law for the Claimsman from the American Educational Institute in New Jersey. She holds the professional designation of Casualty Claim Law Associate, is a Certified Self-Insurance Administrator, and a licensed Private Investigator.

Ms. Hampton's experience includes a management position with a national insurance company, the supervision of claim supervisors and examiners; appearances as a Hearing Representative before the Worker's Compensation Appeals Board; Information and Assistance Officer at the Worker's Compensation Appeals Board; Director of Investigations for a private investigation company; and Editor of *California Workers' Compensation Law and Practice 2d* by Judge Sheldon St. Clair. She has conducted private in-house courses for attorneys, physicians, insurance companies, self-insurance claims administrators, and employers. She has developed and instructed many courses on specialized areas of workers' compensation including one-day courses for the Insurance Educational Association (IEA), a semester course entitled "Workers' Compensation Litigation" for UCLA and many other courses that have been approved by the State Bar Association of California as providing basic and advanced workers' compensation legal specialization credits for attorneys.

Ms. Hampton has served on a California Workers' Compensation Institute (CWCI) study committee; as President and member of the Board of Directors of the Workers' Compensation Claims Association (WCCA); and on an educational subcommittee of the Los Angeles County Bar Association's Workers' Compensation Section. She presently instructs workers' compensation courses on a private basis and is the Manager of Discovery Investigations, a firm specializing in claim-related investigations.

EDITOR-IN-CHIEF

RUTH HINDMAN, J.D. earned a B.A. degree, cum laude, from U.S.C.; completed an English Literature course at Cambridge University, England; and obtained her Juris Doctorate Degree from Whittier College School of Law. Ms. Hindman's is a former Workers' Compensation Manager in Pacific Bell's Legal Department, a former Information and Assistance Officer with the Workers' Compensation Appeals Board, and a former Senior Claims Examiner for self-insured employers. She has had many years of experience with a variety of defense and applicants' law firms and has also served as an expert witness in civil litigation. She is currently employed with the law firm of Koszdin, Fields & Sherry.

TECHNICAL EDITORS

The technical editors of each chapter voluntarily devoted hours of personal time to the review of text material for technical accuracy.

[California System] **RONALD R. KOLLITZ:** Attorney at Law with the firm of Clopton, Penny & Brenner; former Presiding Workers' Compensation Judge; former Senior Attorney, WCAB Writs, Court of Appeal, Second Appellate District..

[California System] **RON FEENBERG:** Attorney at Law with Rose, Klein & Marias; former President of the California Applicant's Attorney's Association.

[Insurance & Self-Insurance] **CHERYL LAMBERT:** Vice President of Insurance Services, California Casualty Insurance Group; formerly the Manager of Workers' Compensation and Safety for Kaiser Permanente Medical Care Program.

[Jurisdiction] **OSCAR J. RIVERA JR.:** Attorney at Law with Sacks, Rivera & Zolonz; past Secretary of Southern California Workers' Compensation Defense Attorneys Association.

[Employment] **GEORGE C. ROTHWELL:** a Workers' Compensation Judge; former sole practitioner specializing in workers' compensation and L&H Act.

[Injury] **KEVIN PENDREY:** Claim Supervisor with Crawford & Company; Instructor of workers' compensation certification courses for the Insurance Educational Association.

[Statutes of Limitation] **THERESA MUIR:** Manager of Workers' Compensation for the Southern California Edison Company; former Vice President of Statutory Benefits, Carter Hawley Hale Stores, Inc.; an initial Trustee of the Self-Insurers' Security Fund; and past three-term President of California Self- Insurers Association (CSIA).

[Medical] **ROBERT DICKINSON:** Attorney at Law, with Taylor, Fabiano & Dickinson.

[Medical] **NORIN GRANCELL:** Attorney at Law with Grancell, Lebovitz, Stander, Marx & Barnes; Legal Advisor for the California Administrative Service Organizations (CASO).

TECHNICAL EDITORS
— Continued —

[Compensation Rate] **PHYLLIS I. RENEAU:** a Certified Self-Insurance Administrator and a private claims consultant; former Acting Claims Manager of Redwood Fire & Casualty.

[Compensation Rate] **ROBERT DICKERSON:** Pacific Region Claims Manager, Liberty Mutual Insurance Company; Instructor of college-level courses of instruction in workers' compensation laws.

[Temporary Disability] **RHONDA COOPER:** Vice President, Republic Indemnity Company of America; Instructor for the Insurance Educational Association.

[Permanent Disability] **MARK KAHN:** Regional Manager of the Division of Workers' Compensation; former Workers' Compensation Judge.

[Rehabilitation] **STEPHEN TESSLER, Ph.D.:** President of Tessler Counseling Group; past President of the California Association of Rehabilitation Professionals (CARP).

[Death] **BARBARA HESTER:** National Accounts Executive, Gates McDonald & Company; former Vice President of National Quality Control for HCM/Presidium, Inc.; two-term President of California Administrative Service Organizations (CASO).

Special recognition is extended to:

SHIRLEY HAMPTON JAMES, an Area Supervisor with the Division of Workers' Compensation and former Permanent Disability Rating Specialist, for editorial assistance with permanent disability rating and Uninsured Employer's Fund topics.

SUZANNE HONOR, Workers' Compensation Consultant with the Division of Workers' Compensation, for general editorial assistance.

SUSAN VAN WOLTZ SILBERMAN, Attorney at Law, for editorial assistance regarding rehabilitation benefits.

TABLE OF CONTENTS

CALIFORNIA CODES REFERENCED IN TEXT

BPC . . . . Business & Professional Code
CC . . . . . Civil Code
CCP . . . . Code of Civil Procedure
CR . . . . . Code of Regulations
GC . . . . . Government Code
HSC . . . . Health & Safety Code
IC . . . . . Insurance Code
LC . . . . . Labor Code
PC . . . . . Penal Code
RTC . . . . Revenue & Taxation Code
UIC . . . . Unemployment Insurance Code
VC . . . . . Vehicle Code

[1] CALIFORNIA SYSTEM

1.1 INDUSTRIAL REVOLUTION

The workers' compensation system we have today can be traced to the Industrial Revolution in the late 18th Century. Before this time, the workplace was comprised predominantly of trades, apprenticeships and guilds. Employers had small numbers of employees. Job-hopping was uncommon. Employees usually had one job per lifetime. Through a long course of training or apprenticeship, often years in duration, personal bonds developed between employers and their employees. It was not unusual for an employee to reside in the home of his employer. When an employee suffered a work-related injury, some employers felt a personal responsibility to care for the injured worker.

The earmark of the Industrial Revolution was the advent of factories and mass production. A large force of unskilled laborers was exposed to a variety of dangerous machinery. The need for a high volume of employees negated the potential for close personal relationships between an employer and its employees. Serious injuries occurred, and employers did not want to pay. Employers felt little personal responsibility towards the mass labor force. Unskilled injured workers were easily replaced with unskilled healthy workers. Employees who were removed from the labor force by injuries often became wards of society. In addition to an immediate loss of income, serious injuries often meant that employees could no longer find any employer willing to hire them.

1.2 EMPLOYER LIABILITY LAWS

In the early 1900's, employer liability laws were enacted in the United States. These initial workers' compensation laws were patterned after employer liability laws enacted in England and Germany in the 1800's. Negligence of the employer as well as the employee determined whether compensation was legally due to the employee. The employee had the initial burden of proving that the employer's negligence caused the injury. Once the employee met this burden, the employee then had to prepare against three special defenses, called common law defenses, that the employer could use to defeat a claim.

Common Law Defenses

Common law defenses were only utilized by an employer in cases where the employer was negligent in causing an injury. If the employer was not negligent, there was no liability for compensation or damages, so no further defense was necessary. There were three common law defenses.

     1. Assumption of risk.
     2. Fellow servant doctrine (or fellow servant rule).
     3. Contributory negligence.

Assumption of Risk. Certain dangers or hazards are an inherent part of any employment. Under the common law assumption of risk doctrine, the employee was presumed to have a free choice of jobs. If the employee chose to work in a dangerous occupation, the employee voluntarily accepted the risk of injury from known dangers. Potentially hazardous jobs usually paid more money. Thus, the employee put a price on his health by accepting higher wages and voluntarily exposing himself to a greater potential for injury.

If an injury occurred, the employer's defense was established by showing: the employee was injured by a predictable occurrence; the employee foresaw or should have foreseen the danger; and, the employee willingly exposed himself to the danger (there were limited exceptions that will not be covered here). For example, an employee who worked in a mine shaft assumed the risk of injury from inhalation of fumes in the mine. The employee who ran a wood lathe assumed the risk of an eye injury from flying wood splinters. An employee who worked with explosives could expect to be blown up or injured by flying debris.

Fellow Servant Rule. The negligence of a coemployee relieved the employer of liability under the common law system. If a fellow servant's negligence caused an injury, then the employer's negligence did not. The employer may also have been negligent, but the employer's negligence did not produce an injury in and of itself. "But for" the negligence of the coemployee, the employee would not have been injured. The employer was responsible for its own negligence but not for the negligent actions of others.

Suppose the employee was injured when a coemployee turned on a machine without realizing that the employee had his hand in it. The employer may have been negligent for not maintaining the machine in proper repair. However, the negligent action of the inattentive fellow servant was the direct cause of the injury. If a coemployee dropped a heavy item on another employee's foot, it didn't matter if the employer was negligent in directing the fellow servant how to properly grip the item. The fellow servant dropped the item. Therefore, the fellow servant, not the employer, caused the injury.

Contributory Negligence. Under the common law system, if the employee was negligent in any way, the employer did not owe compensation. The contributory negligence of the employee relieved the employer from any liability. This was true even if the employee was 1% negligent and the employer was 99% negligent. Employers had a right to expect that their employees would not be negligent or cause injuries to themselves. Where the employee's injury would not have occurred absent the employee's negligence, the employee could not obtain any recovery from the employer. The necessary requirement for the legal obligation of the employer was not present because the injury did not result solely from the employer's negligence.

Suppose the employee was placing a metal part onto a moving assembly line. The part slipped out of his hand causing a jam on the line, and a piece of metal flew out and hit him in the eye. Inadequate lighting provided by the employer may have been a contributing factor in the resultant injury. However, since the employee's negligent action also caused his injury, the employee was barred from any recovery. The employee would likewise be barred from recovery any time the employee accidentally dropped any work item on his foot, hit his hand with a hammer or slipped and fell on a substance the employee had spilled.

Advantages of Common Law System

From the employee's perspective, the common law system was advantageous in that employees could sue the employer in civil court. Employees could seek monetary damages for pain and suffering. Serious injuries could bring high awards. The employee's recovery could far exceed any actual expenses incurred by the employee. A major advantage to employers under the common law system was the fact that the employer could avoid payment to many injured employees. The costs, delays and hazards of pursuing litigation deterred many employees from pursuing any recovery. Litigation was simply too expensive for employees who sustained minor injuries. It was difficult for any employee to prove that the employer's negligence was the cause of the injury, and the three common law defenses gave the employer a way to avoid paying anything even when it was negligent.

1.3 EARLY CALIFORNIA LAWS

The common law system produced some harsh results. Negligent employers made profits while their injured employees were unable to support themselves or their families. There was some public outcry for the plight of those seriously injured workers who were not entitled to recover any compensation from their employers. Employers actively resisted any expanded financial responsibility for injuries to their employees. However, modifications of the common law system were gradually enacted in every state.

Roseberry Act. Effective 1911, the Roseberry Act abolished the common law defenses of assumption of risk and fellow servant rule, significantly modified the employer's defense of contributory negligence, and established a system of voluntary workers' compensation coverage in California. Employers could elect to come under the provisions of this Act but were not required to do so. If an employer elected coverage under the Act, its employees were entitled to the recovery of compensation without regard to negligence, and the employer owed benefits in limited amounts set forth in the Act. Willful misconduct of the employee barred the employee from the receipt of benefits. Willful misconduct of the employer, and certain other limited actions of the employer, provided the employee with the option of seeking workers' compensation benefits or filing a civil court action for damages.

Few employers elected to come under the provisions of the Roseberry Act. Absent elective coverage, the employer was not liable for damages unless the employee could establish the employer's negligence. Even with the elimination of common law defenses, this burden of proof was often difficult for employees. Thus, many injured employees still did not receive compensation promptly following a work-related injury.

Boynton Act. Effective 1913, the Boynton Act created a compulsory system of workers' compensation laws in California. Employers were required to cover their employees. Benefit levels were set by law. Employees could no longer seek damages from their negligent employers. Employees were required to accept workers' compensation benefits as a full discharge of their employers' liability for injuries. Employers were required to pay compensation for all work-related injuries (there were limited exceptions for special circumstances that are not covered here). Workers' compensation claims became subject to the jurisdiction of a special tribunal instead of the civil courts. This tribunal was originally called the Industrial Accident Commission (IAC). Since 1966, this tribunal has been called the Workers' Compensation Appeals Board (WCAB). This new compulsory system has advantages for both the employee and the employer as well as society as a whole.

W.C. Insurance & Safety Act. The Workmen's Compensation Insurance and Safety Act of 1917 incorporated most provisions of the Boynton Act and made further changes in California's workers' compensation system. Significant new provisions dealt with repercussions for an employer's failure to secure the payment of compensation (e.g. by insurance or self-insurance) and established the State Compensation Insurance Fund (see Chapter 2). This Act was codified in 1937 and serves as the foundation of the State Labor Code in use today albeit with significant modifications in subsequent years.

Advantages of Compulsory Laws

Under compulsory laws, the employer became liable for compensation to all injured employees, but its liability was limited to set amounts. The employer was not liable for damages or any payment for pain and suffering. Employers were not confronted with lawsuits for damages in amounts that could impair the employers' ability to continue in business. The employer paid for more injuries but in lower amounts. The employer realized financial savings by the elimination of civil liability and the high potential costs of defense and damages in civil suits.

Under compulsory laws, employees did not have to prove that an injury resulted from the employer's negligence or overcome the employer's common law defenses. An employee could receive compensation even if the employee's own negligence caused the injury. The provision of benefits was fairly automatic and immediate, since the employer's liability was clearly stated in the law. Employees were assured of compensation for all injuries whether serious or minor.

Society bore the burden of inequities of the common law system. Employers paid benefits to small numbers of injured workers. The employer could usually afford the costs of protracted litigation, but employees frequently became wards of society after an injury occurred. If damages were awarded, the employer passed this cost along to consumers. Society bore the cost of work injuries through the costs of public support programs for the needy, the higher costs of products and services, and the costs of financing the over-burdened civil litigation system.

Society still bears the cost of work injuries, but the cost is lower and better distributed. Employers automatically owe compensation to injured workers. If the employer contests a claim, the employer also incurs litigation expenses. The employer pays the initial cost for its workers' compensation program and then passes this cost along to consumers in the costs of its product. The employer can reduce the costs for its workers' compensation program by providing a safe place to work. Fewer injuries mean lower production costs, a better competitive position for the employer in the marketplace, and greater profits. Employers have a financial incentive to reduce the frequency and the severity of work injuries and to concern themselves with accident prevention. Society benefits from lowered production costs for employers that translate into lower costs for products and services in the marketplace.

Society also gains from an emphasis on rehabilitation rather than indemnification. Expeditious dissemination of fixed benefit amounts avoids the likelihood that injured workers will go uncompensated and thus rely upon public support programs. Immediate provision of medical treatment assists employees in an early recovery from the effects of their injuries and a prompt return to a productive role in society.

1.4 WORKERS' COMPENSATION REFORM ACT

The original compulsory workers' compensation system was a trade-off with employers and employees giving up their advantages under the common law system in exchange for new and different advantages. Since the enactment of the initial compulsory workers' compensation laws in California, employer and employee groups have routinely sought legislative attention to what they view as inequities between the rights of the parties under the existing system. Employee groups seek to increase benefit levels and extend the meaning of "injury" to cover more employees. Employer groups pursue, among other things, limitations on their liability for injuries and medical conditions that have only a tangential relationship to the employment. The basic trend in legislation has been, and continues to be, the extension of benefits to injured workers, but the 1990's brought sweeping changes in other areas as well.

1989 – Reform Act

The Workers' Compensation Reform Act of 1989 did not abolish the California workers' compensation system. The purpose of the "Reform Act" was to improve the existing system, not to replace it. All changes were incorporated into the existing system of workers' compensation laws rather than creating an entirely new system. However, alterations to the existing system were pervasive. Changes impacted nearly every aspect of the workers' compensation system including types and amounts of benefits; medical evidence and costs; funding and functions of State administrative, regulatory, advisory, and judicial agencies; penalties; statutes of limitations; dispute resolution procedures; and, forms and procedures in general.

The Workers' Compensation Reform Act of 1989 was not urgency legislation, so the changes contained in the bills passed by the Legislature did not take effect mid-year (e.g. on the date signed by the Governor and filed with the Secretary of State). Rather, the reform legislation first became operative on January 1st of 1990. However, some provisions of the reform legislation had operative dates other than 1/1/90. For example, the Reform Act amended LC4658 effective 1990 to increase the number of weeks of permanent disability benefits that would be owed to employees with 25% or more disability who had "injuries occurring on or after January 1, 1992."

1990 – Clean-Up Legislation

The Reform Act was followed a year later by supplemental legislation nearly as voluminous as the initial reform legislation. A portion of this later legislation that took effect in 1991 attempted to correct the multiple unintended errors (in grammar and content) in previously enacted laws as well as further implement reform of the California workers' compensation system. This subsequent legislation is commonly referred to as "clean-up" legislation.

1993 – Major Changes

Additional new laws affecting workers' compensation have been enacted every year since 1990 in an attempt to further amend and clarify the Reform Act. The most significant changes were those enacted in 1993 (many of which have mid-1993, rather than 1/1/94, effective dates).

The 1993 legislation established new limitations on the compensability of psychiatric and post-termination claims, the nature and extent of rehabilitation expenses, and the securing of medical-legal expenses. Additionally, the 1993 legislation created a presumption of correctness for the findings of the treating physician, changed the way in which permanent disability issues are tried, obligated the employer to provide reasonably available modified or alternative work for permanently disabled employees and included other procedural changes.

The Workers' Compensation Reform Act of 1989 marked the commencement of a new era and precipitated many changes. New forms and procedures have been developed, implemented and assessed. New and existing personnel continue to be trained and retrained. Time has to pass before the impact of new laws can be evaluated. Much that changed, changed more than once. The earmark of the reform era is change, then change again.

1.5 CALIFORNIA CONSTITUTION

State laws are created by the authority of the California Constitution as found in Art. XIV, Section 4. The Constitution provides for a complete system of workers' compensation including a delivery system made up of judicial and administrative bodies. The Labor Code contains the state laws, or statutes, enacted by the Legislature. State laws cannot exceed the authority granted by the Constitution. Therefore, a good starting point for understanding the workers' compensation system is a review of the basic provisions of the California Constitution.

1.6 PURPOSE OF WORKERS' COMPENSATION LAWS

The purpose of workers' compensation laws is to compensate workers for injuries or disabilities sustained in the course of their employment or their dependents in the event of death. To effect this purpose, the Constitution provides for enforcement of liability against the employer "irrespective of fault of any party." Negligence of the employer or employee does not affect the employer's liability to pay compensation. The expressed intent of the Constitution is to "accomplish substantial justice in all cases expeditiously, inexpensively, and without encumbrance of any character." This the Constitution declares "to be the social public policy of this State." The purpose of workers' compensation is to provide benefits to entitled workers, and obstacles to this goal are to be avoided so that benefits can be provided expeditiously.

1.7 LABOR CODE & AFFILIATED LAWS

Workers' compensation laws are merely a component part of a constitutionally created system providing for the "general welfare of employees." The Constitution not only grants the Legislature the right to "combine in one statute all the provisions for a complete system of workers' compensation," but the Constitution also addresses many other aspects of employment, the workplace, and employer liability such as minimum wages, health and welfare of employees, safety in places of employment, provision of insurance coverage by employers, and the regulation of such insurance coverage. Nearly all laws specifically enacted regarding work injuries are contained in the California Labor Code, but many sections of the Labor Code relate to other areas of enforcement of an employer's legal obligations to its employees.

Other California Codes also encompass workers' compensation topics within the specific area of law they otherwise address. For instance, the Insurance Code contains laws that regulate the business of selling workers' compensation insurance. Likewise, Section 7125 of the Business and Professions Code specifies repercussions for a licensed contractor who files a false statement that denies the existence of employees in order to avoid workers' compensation coverage for such employees.

Code of Regulations

The Code most closely affiliated with the workers' compensation provisions of the Labor Code is the Code of Regulations. (Note: it is rare for the name of a State code to be changed, but the former Administrative Code was renamed the "Code of Regulations" effective 1989.) Included in Title 8 of the Code of Regulations are the Rules and Regulations of the Administrative Director of the Division of Workers' Compensation and the Industrial Medical Council, the Rules of Practice and Procedure of the Workers' Compensation Appeals Board, and regulations promulgated by the Director of the Department of Industrial Relations governing the administration of self-insurance plans.

Unlike the Labor Code, the provisions of the Code of Regulations are not enacted into law by the Legislature. Rather, the provisions of this code are promulgated by administrative agencies and added to the Code of Regulations following public hearings that allow interested parties an opportunity to provide input on proposed changes. Statutory authority for the adoption of sections of the Code of Regulations (or changes to existing sections) is granted to the Administrative Director of the Division of Workers' Compensation in LC5307.3, the Workers' Compensation Appeals Board in LC5307, the Industrial Medical Council in LC139.2, and the Director of the Department of Industrial Relations in LC3702.10. (Note: see also GC11346.4 and GC11350-GC11351 regarding the applicability of the Administrative Procedure Act to the adoption of these regulations.)

Per LC5307.4, notice of public hearing dates and the proposed changes to rules and regulations of the Administrative Director or the appeals board "shall be provided to ... individuals who have requested notice thereof." This right to receive advance notice and provide input does not apply to "interpretive rules, general statements of policy, or rules of agency organization." Thus, the State is not required to hold a public hearing before issuing a policy statement regarding redistribution of staff within State agencies or curtailing service of documents where such service is optional rather than required under the provisions of existing laws.

The public is not entitled to ongoing notice regarding the creation of or changes to policy and procedural manuals developed by various State agencies. (Note: copies of some internal manuals are available upon request at the cost of duplication expense, e.g. the policy and procedure manuals of the Workers' Compensation Appeals Board and the Rehabilitation Unit). New policies or rules that do not require advance public notice are those that do not result in any financial repercussion or penalty for noncompliance by a person not employed by the State. Public notice is required by LC5307.4 for any proposed changes to administrative notices, forms, reporting requirements and time periods relative thereto.

1.8 ENFORCEMENT OF EMPLOYER'S LIABILITY

Article XIV, Section 4 of the California Constitution vests the Legislature with the power to enforce liability against employers to compensate "any or all of their workers for injury or disability, and their dependents for death incurred or sustained by the said workers in the course of their employment." The employer can purchase insurance coverage to protect itself against this liability. In fact the California Constitution establishes an insurance company, the State Compensation Insurance Fund (see 2.5). The Constitution provides for the regulation of "insurance coverage in all its aspects." In addition, the employer's right to self-insure its liability is also granted: "full provision for otherwise securing the payment of compensation." No matter whether the employer insures or self-insures, the Constitution provides for the enforcement of the employer's liability for workers' compensation.

1.9 LIMITS ON EMPLOYER'S LIABILITY

The purpose of workers' compensation benefits is to provide compensation as that term is defined in LC3207, meaning those benefits or payments that are conferred by the Labor Code upon injured employees or their dependents. However, the extent of compensation that is owed by the employer is limited by Article XIV, Section 4 of the California Constitution to "the extent of relieving from the consequences of any injury or death." A basic principle derived from this language is that an employee should not financially profit from a workers' compensation claim but only be fairly compensated for the injury. Compensation for an injury does not mean damages (that, per LC3209, are "contrasted with compensation"), nor payment for every financial loss that the employee may incur, nor the provision of payments that would constitute a monetary profit or reward.

The Constitution provides for the payment of awards to the State where the employee dies and leaves no dependents. Monies thus collected are designated to be used for the payment of "extra compensation for subsequent injuries beyond the liability of" the employer. This wording limits the employer's liability to the effects of an original injury. It is the basis for statute sections dealing with the topic of apportionment of the employer's liability. In addition, it is the basis for creation of the Subsequent Injuries Fund (see 10.52).

1.10 LIBERAL CONSTRUCTION OF STATUTES

Under the compulsion of LC3202, certain sections of the Labor Code "shall be liberally construed by the courts with the purpose of extending their benefits for the protection of persons injured in the course of their employment." This statute was enacted to effect the constitutional purpose of providing benefits to injured workers expeditiously and without encumbrance. Known as the liberal construction statute, LC3202 intends to eliminate unnecessary litigation by stating that the purpose of California's workers' compensation laws is to provide benefits. Where vagueness exists and multiple interpretations of statutory language are possible, LC3202 mandates that the employee, not the employer, will receive the benefit of a favorable interpretation.

1.11 PREPONDERANCE OF EVIDENCE

Section 3202.5 of the Labor Code directs itself to evidence on legal issues. In the legal arena, a party disputing a matter must meet "the evidentiary burden of proof by a preponderance of the evidence." This burden applies equally to the employer and the employee and (since 4/3/93) to "a lien claimant." Basically, a lien claimant is a person or entity who seeks to recover payment for a bill out of compensation awarded to an employee or dependent. A list of "liens which may be allowed" by the WCAB appears in LC4903. For instance, a lien claimant could be a physician who provided treatment or an attorney who provided legal services and now seeks fees out of compensation awarded to the employee.

The fact that LC3202 requires liberal construction does not mean that an injured employee can rely upon a construction of statute sections that defies the intended meaning of language in the Labor Code. All parties must establish the validity of their position by presentation of evidence. No party is relieved from the burden of proving the facts because of any vagueness in statutory language.

1.12 ADMINISTRATION & ADJUDICATION

The Constitution grants authority for the creation of an administrative agency that is given all "requisite governmental functions" to determine disputes or any other workers' compensation matter. The legislature is also granted the power to provide for the settlement of disputed claims by an industrial accident commission, by the courts, by arbitration, or by any combination of these alternatives. Additionally, the legislature may determine "the method and manner of trial of any such dispute, the rules of evidence and the manner of review of decisions rendered by" its designated tribunal.

A restrictive phrase of the Constitution dictates that review of "all decisions of any such tribunal shall be subject to review by the appellate court of this State." By this provision, the California Court of Appeal or the California Supreme Court has authority to overturn decisions of any lower court or workers' compensation tribunal. These provisions of the Constitution are the basis for the creation of the Division of Workers' Compensation, the Workers' Compensation Appeals Board and all of their component parts.

Construction Industry

Effective 7/16/93, LC3201.5 allows for exceptions to traditional methods of dispute resolution by the Workers' Compensation Appeals Board or the Division of Worker's Compensation. For union employees in the construction industry, LC3201.5 authorizes alternative dispute resolution systems to be subject to negotiation pursuant to collective bargaining agreements. Construction industry employers are permitted to establish an "alternative dispute resolution system governing disputes between employees and employers or their insurers that supplements or replaces all or part of those dispute resolution processes contained" within the Labor Code "including, but not limited to mediation and arbitration."

Employees can appeal decisions that are rendered through the employer's alternative dispute resolution system to the WCAB in the same manner as decisions of workers' compensation judges are appealed. Statutory provisions relating to alternative dispute resolution procedures for construction related employments are commonly referred to as "carve out" legislation. This term derives from the fact that LC3201.5 authorizes a portion of the normal duties of the State's administrative and judicial staff to be performed elsewhere (see 2.4).

1.13 DEPARTMENT OF INDUSTRIAL RELATIONS

Per LC50.5, the Department of Industrial Relations (DIR) has the overall responsibility to "foster, promote, and develop the welfare of the wage earners of California." This Department is divided into six functional units, the Divisions of: Workers' Compensation, Occupational Safety and Health (commonly called "Cal/OSHA"), Labor Standards Enforcement, Labor Statistics and Research, Apprenticeship Standards, and the State Compensation Insurance Fund. The areas of responsibility of each of these units are set forth in various sections of the Labor Code. The head of each unit is appointed to service by the Governor, who also appoints the person who serves as the Director of the Department of Industrial Relations.

1.14 DIVISION OF WORKERS' COMPENSATION

The Division of Workers' Compensation (DWC) is divided into judicial and administrative sections involved solely in the area of workers' compensation. (Note: prior to renaming in 1990, this Division was known as the Division of Industrial Accidents.) The judicial section of this Division is known as the Workers' Compensation Appeals Board (WCAB). This section is comprised of a nontrial entity in San Francisco that is staffed with commissioners and statewide WCAB district offices where judges perform their duties.

The nonjudicial functions of the Division of Workers' Compensation are assigned to various subdivisions or units. The Division includes a Disability Evaluation Unit, Rehabilitation Unit, Information and Assistance Unit, Audit Unit, and Claims Unit (claims filed against the Uninsured Employer's Fund and the Subsequent Injuries Fund are processed in the Claims Unit). The entire Division is headed by an Administrative Director (the "A.D.") who is appointed by the Governor. Each Unit is headed by a Manager who is appointed by the Administrative Director. The Medical Director of the Division of Workers' Compensation is appointed by the Industrial Medical Council within the Department of Industrial Relations whose members are physicians appointed under LC139 by either the Legislature or the Governor.

1.15 WCAB – JUDGES

Effective 1/1/94, workers' compensation "judges" were officially renamed "referees" by a change in LC27 (that continues to distinguish a "referee" who was previously entitled a "judge" from a "settlement conference referee" whose qualifications and duties relative to mandatory settlement conference proceedings are specified in LC5502). Notwithstanding the fact that the title "referee" became legally correct as a result of this legislative change, there has been no change in common practice — the title "judge" continues to be used by most "referees."

Trial-level judges are located at the various district offices of the Workers' Compensation Appeals Board (WCAB) throughout the State. Proceedings before a trial judge result in the issuance of formal findings, decisions, orders, or awards. These judges are experienced attorneys hired through the civil service examination process. Judges are provided the services of a secretary and a court reporter (although the increasing use of the less costly process of tape recording for certain administrative proceedings other than at the WCAB portends an end to historical transcription methods). Clerical support staff is also provided for each district office.

One judge at each WCAB location is designated as the "presiding judge." Some matters regarding the conduct of proceedings and enforcement of the WCAB Rules of Practice and Procedure are designated to be handled by a presiding judge instead of a judge. For instance, petitions requesting automatic reassignment of a regular hearing to another judge are routed to the presiding judge for action (per CR10453) as are requests for removal of arbitrators from an assigned panel (per CR10998). Besides special assigned duties, the presiding judge is the administrative supervisor of all the Workers' Compensation Appeals Board staff in a local office.

References to the term "referee" can be confusing. Judges used to be called referees before their title was officially changed to "judge" by LC27 in 1986 (although some Labor Code sections have not yet been "modernized" to reflect this change in title). Thereafter, as part of reform legislation, LC5502 created a new type of litigation proceeding called a "mandatory settlement conference" (for a trial period of 1991-1993). Section 5502 also specified that such conferences would be conducted by a "referee," basically defined as a person who meets the qualifications to become a judge but has a different title and duties.

Effective 1991, LC27 specifies that the term "referee" means "judge" when used in the Labor Code but distinguishes both of these terms from the "settlement conference referees" required by LC5502. Thereafter, a change to LC5502 effective 1/1/93 provides that settlement conferences can be conducted by either a judge or a "referee" (meaning here, per LC27, a settlement conference referee). This latter change enabled the State to best utilize staff and resources so it was not necessary to staff small district offices with both settlement conference referees and judges, and previously-hired settlement conference referees could be assimilated into vacant judge positions (since the qualifications for either position are now the same per LC5502, "settlement conference referees" have disappeared).

Ethical Standards & Enforcement

Per LC125.5, workers' compensation judges are required to "maintain membership in the State Bar of California during" their tenure. Per LC123.6, such judges "shall subscribe to the California Code of Judicial Conduct adopted by the Conference of California Judges" (until the Supreme Court adopts a Code of Judicial Ethics and, then, by that code, per CR9720.2). Administrative regulations regarding the establishment and enforcement of ethical standards for judges are set out in CR9720.1-CR9723, all of which took effect 12-1-95.

Per CR9720.1, the purpose of regulations regarding ethical standards is "to provide all parties with an independent, impartial investigation into allegations of misconduct by referees" (judges). A Workers' Compensation Ethics Advisory Committee that is established by CR9722 is charged with the duty of reviewing complaints and making recommendations to "the administrative director, the legislature and the public concerning the integrity of the workers' compensation adjudicatory process" (recommendations are due annually on February 15th). Information obtained by the committee that is not otherwise available to the public is held to be "strictly confidential from public disclosure (except from a judge who is "otherwise entitled to the information" by virtue of the performance of routine duties).

Unless the Administrative Director provides advance written approval pursuant to CR9721.2, workers' compensation judges are prohibited from accepting any item "exceeding five dollars in value, the cost of which is significantly paid for by" attorneys or other persons "whose interests have come or are likely to come before the" WCAB. Judges are specifically precluded from ownership or contingent types of financial interests in educational programs by CR9721.31, e.g. being paid per person or as a percentage of revenue (with the exclusion of certain income from certain publishers as specified in advisory A.D. Opinion No. 2; see below).

Any person can file a complaint with the Workers' Compensation Ethics Advisory Committee (CR9722.1). However, CR9721.32 charges judges with a duty to "initiate appropriate disciplinary measures" against their peers or any other individual upon becoming aware of improper conduct. Judges are entitled to be informed of the nature of complaints made against them and the outcome of any investigation that is conducted.

Upon a request, CR9723 provides that the Administrative Director of the Division of Workers' Compensation may issue an advisory opinion on the application of established ethics standards to any particular situation. Three such opinions were issued on January 22, 1997. Per A.D. Opinion No. 1, the ethical standards that apply to judges have been determined to also apply to the Vocational Rehabilitation Consultants and Auditors (whose duties are deemed, for this purpose, to be "quasi-judicial" in nature) and attorneys who are employed as the Division's staff counsel.

In A.D. Opinion No. 2, the above-mentioned employees who self-publish are required to submit and obtain advance approval for a plan that follows recommended safeguards to assure that the author-employee "is not aware of the identities" of book purchasers. Lastly, A.D. Opinion No. 3 sets out policies related to educational presentations including the acceptance and the waiver of fees for speaking and attendance, respectively.

1.16 WCAB – COMMISSIONERS

The term "WCAB" (and/or "Appeals Board") can refer to district offices that are staffed with judges or to the nontrial entity with the same name that has its office in San Francisco and is staffed by commissioners. WCAB commissioners review appeals of decisions originating from judges in district offices but have other special functions as well. The term WCAB is commonly used to mean both the initial trial level and the first appellate level of the litigation process. Ordinarily, the context in which the term WCAB is used makes it clear whether reference is being made to the WCAB whose members are commissioners or to a WCAB district office.

The WCAB is staffed by seven commissioners, secretaries (who can act as deputy commissioners), attorneys, assistants and clerical staff. Commissioners are appointed by the Governor, subject to the consent of the Senate, for six-year terms. Per LC112, five of the commissioners must be attorneys, and two members need not be attorneys. The Governor selects one of the commissioners to serve as the chairman of the WCAB.

The Chairman assigns appealed cases to panels of three commissioners on a random rotation basis. Occasionally, the Chairman will assign a case of import to the full panel of commissioners. Per LC115, a case may be reviewed "by the appeals board as a whole in order to achieve uniformity of decision, or in cases presenting novel issues." A decision rendered by a majority of a three-commissioner panel is called a "panel" decision; whereas, a decision concurred in by a majority of the members of a full panel is called an "en banc" decision. When all commissioners reviewing a case concur in a decision, the decision is referred to as a unanimous decision, e.g. a unanimous en banc decision.

Per LC110, when the term "appeals board" is used in the Labor Code, it means the board whose members are commissioners. In actual fact, the term appeals board is used throughout the Labor Code to refer to actions of judges as well as commissioners, because any action by a judge is considered to be an action of the "appeals board" unless the judge's action is reversed after an appeal. For instance, LC5702 provides that "the appeals board" may make its findings and award upon written stipulations of the parties, but judges routinely issue such awards. If no appeal is filed after an award issues, the decision of the judge has the same effect as if the award had been issued by the "appeals board" itself.

One of several distinctions in terms of authority for specific actions is found in the Rules of Practice and Procedure of the WCAB. In CR10301, "Appeals Board" is defined as "the commissioners and deputy commissioners" of the

WCAB. A listing of specific orders, decisions and awards for which jurisdiction is exclusively vested in the appeals board is set out in CR10340 and CR10342. For instance, LC5706 provides that the "appeals board may require an autopsy." However, CR10342 specifically restricts authority for directing an autopsy or exhumation to "the Appeals Board or a member thereof." Another distinction is found in LC5500.3 that mandates that "no local office of the appeals board or workers' compensation judge shall require forms or procedures other than as established by the appeals board."

1.17 ATTORNEYS & HEARING REPRESENTATIVES

An employee can litigate a claim and have disputed issues resolved by the WCAB without an attorney, in which case the employee is referred to as being "in pro per" (an abbreviation of the Latin phrase "in propria persona"). Most employees who litigate a claim choose to be represented by an attorney. Per LC4906, an attorney is required to provide an injured worker with an Attorney Fee Disclosure Statement (DWC Form 3). This form advises the employee, among other things, that the normal fee for an attorney's services is ~~9% to 12%~~ *15%* of the benefits awarded to the employee (with exceptions; see CR10775) and that the employee can obtain information regarding benefits from an Information and Assistance Officer within the Division of Workers' Compensation "at no charge."

Since 1990, attorneys are required to provide an Attorney Fee Disclosure Statement to the employee at the initial consultation and provide the employer with a copy that is signed by the attorney and the employee. Since 1991, LC4906 requires that a copy of the signed disclosure form shall be "sent to the employer" (or its insurer or claims administrator, if known) "by the attorney within 15 days of the employee's and attorney's execution thereof."

Any party can be represented by a nonattorney representative rather than an attorney in litigation proceedings before the WCAB. (Note: an employee can represent himself at all levels of appeal, but nonattorney representatives are not permitted to handle appeals to the civil courts, including the Court of Appeal and the Supreme Court.) An employee may prefer to be represented by a nonattorney spouse, friend or paralegal rather than by an attorney. Per LC5501, a nonattorney representative is required to "notify the appeals board in writing that he or she is not an attorney licensed by the State Bar of this state." Per LC4903, "no fee for legal services shall be awarded" by the WCAB "to any representative who is not an attorney" (exceptions apply prior to 1992).

Claims administrators commonly utilize "hearing representatives" rather than attorneys to represent their interests in litigation matters. A hearing representative may be employed full time in this capacity by a claims administrator; a claims person may make appearances in litigation proceedings in addition to claims administration duties; or, a claims administrator may utilize the services of a nonemployee hearing representative under a contractual arrangement. Companies exist that provide this service by properly qualified staff (usually persons with legal and/or claims administration knowledge and experience).

The Labor Code regulates fees of nonattorney representatives for employees and dependents, not employers. Per LC4903, the WCAB is statutorily precluded from awarding a fee for any services that are rendered by a nonattorney representative of the employee or the employee's dependents. It is these nonattorney representatives who cannot charge a fee nor be awarded a fee for their services.

1.18 WCAB PROCEEDINGS

Application for Adjudication

Per CR10400, "proceedings for adjudication of rights and liabilities before the" WCAB "shall be initiated by the filing of an Application for Adjudication, Compromise and Release Agreement or Stipulations with Request for Award" (see 1.20). In cases where the parties are able to resolve any disputes between themselves, the first document that requests WCAB review and decision may be one of the two types of settlement documents mentioned by title in CR10400. In other cases, WCAB proceedings are ordinarily initiated by filing an Application for Adjudication of Claim, although proceedings are not scheduled on the court's calendar until a Declaration of Readiness to Proceed is also filed.

Per LC5501, an "application may be filed with the appeals board by any party in interest, his attorney, or other representative authorized in writing." If the employee is represented by legal counsel, the employee's attorney completes the application form and submits it to the WCAB on the employee's behalf. Parties who have an interest in whether the employee is entitled to compensation or the extent thereof and who may also file an application to seek WCAB adjudication of a dispute include an insurer or a medical provider lien claimant. The term "applicant" ordinarily refers to the injured worker in litigation proceedings regardless of the entity that actually files an application. The term "defendant" ordinarily includes the employer and its worker's compensation insurance carrier or other claims administrator (both of whom are named in the caption section of the WCAB's application form).

One or more applications may be filed for the same claim. A new application form is required if a prior application form was dismissed, and a different application form is used if an injury results in death. If a case is later taken "off calendar" (meaning no specific date is scheduled for additional WCAB proceedings), the form used to request further WCAB proceedings is a Declaration of Readiness to Proceed.

Antifraud Statement

For 1994 or later injuries, LC4906 requires submission of an antifraud statement to the WCAB concurrent with the filing of an application for adjudication or an Answer form. In common practice, this statement is usually attached to any initial document that invokes WCAB jurisdiction, including a settlement (although not specifically required by CR10404) and regardless of the date of the injury. Separate antifraud statements are usually prepared for the signature of various entities involved in a claim rather than attempting to procure the signatures of multiple individuals on a single form.

The antifraud statement (or disclaimer) that is required by LC4906 must be in writing and signed under penalty of perjury by the "employee, the insurer, the employer, and the attorneys for each party." Each of these individuals is required to affirm that they have not personally violated LC139.3, which prohibits the offering or receipt of certain financial incentives relative to medical examinations. Some employers and employees may be reluctant or even refuse to sign the required disclaimer upon request. Such reactions usually result from a lack of understanding of what is actually being requested of them rather than any fraudulent action on their part. The antifraud statement is strictly limited to a denial of fraud relating to medical examinations.

Answer

Per LC5500, no "pleadings other than the application and answer shall be required." Per LC5501, a defendant is allowed 10 days after service of an application to file an answer with the WCAB. However, an answer is usually considered timely if filed within 6 days after service of a declaration of readiness to proceed as required by CR10480. Per LC5505, the purpose of an answer is to enable a defendant to "disclaim any interest in the subject matter of the claim in controversy" and to set "forth the particulars in which the application is inaccurate or incomplete, and the facts upon which he intends to rely" (see 6.29).

Adjudication Alternatives

Initial adjudication of claims is ordinarily conducted by a WCAB judge at a district office of the WCAB. However, if the employee is represented by an attorney, a final determination on other disputed issues may be made by a judge pro tempore, an arbitrator or a settlement conference referee. The common qualification of these individuals is that each must be an attorney. Since 1990, the use of arbitrators is mandatory for disputed issues that are specified in LC5275 (e.g. disputed insurance coverage; see 3.21). For 1994 or later injuries, arbitration is also mandatory under LC4645 and LC5275 for certain disputes regarding rehabilitation benefits (see 11.32). The parties can agree to voluntarily submit any other issues to arbitration "regardless of the date of injury." However, LC5270 specifies that all Labor Code sections pertaining to arbitration proceedings (LC5270-LC5278) "apply only in cases where the injured employee or dependent is represented by an attorney." Arbitration proceedings may be held at a district office of the WCAB or any location that is mutually acceptable to the parties.

Mandatory Settlement Conference

Per LC5502, mandatory settlement conference (MSC) proceedings are required for all injury cases except cases for which an expedited hearing or arbitration is required. The LC5502 requirement for a mandatory settlement conference applies to "all applications filed on or after" 1/1/91 "regardless of the date of injury." Per LC5502, mandatory settlement conference proceedings are required to be held within a maximum of 30 days after a Declaration of Readiness to Proceed is filed with the WCAB (and within 6 days of service of this document, CR10480 requires an Answer to be filed with the WCAB).

Conference proceedings are preliminary to regular hearings (commonly called "trials"). If disputed issues cannot be resolved at a mandatory settlement conference (MSC), then LC5502 requires that "the parties shall file a pretrial conference statement noting the specific issues in dispute, each party's proposed permanent disability rating, and listing the exhibits, and disclosing witnesses." Discovery closes "on the date of the mandatory settlement conference, except where a party can demonstrate that evidence "was not available or could not have been discovered by the exercise of due diligence prior to the settlement conference." (In actuality, it sometimes happens that neither party files a conference statement and/or the result of one conference is that the case will proceed to another mandatory settlement conference.)

Telephone Conferences

Effective 1993, LC3714 permits a new type of proceeding that can be conducted by a judge without the physical presence of any party to a case. Labor Code 3714 permits certain WCAB conference proceedings to be conducted as telephone conferences with submission of documentary evidence by facsimile machine but with formal filing and service required within 5 working days.

Telephone conferences will only be conducted in cases that involve the Uninsured Employers Fund, the Subsequent Injuries Fund or the Non-Dependent Death Unit as a party (and therefore involve the Claims Unit of the Division of Workers' Compensation). Such proceedings will be conducted at specified district offices of the WCAB for a two-year trial period that commences after the State has arranged for appropriate facilities and judicial resources. Full details of this pilot program are set out in LC3714.

EDEX System – Computer Access to WCAB Records

Since 1994, it has been possible to access certain information regarding the status of WCAB cases or lien claims through an electronic data exchange system that is referred to as the "EDEX" system. Available information includes verification of case filings, case numbers, lien filings, and the addresses of parties of record. The system enables automatic notification to subscribers who request notice of future events such as the filing of a WCAB case for a particular employee or receipt of settlement documents that may impact a lien claimant's rights.

Electronic access to WCAB case information is available only to approved subscribers, since the system includes safeguards to ensure compliance with applicable laws regarding privacy of information contained in public records. For further information, contact: Division of Workers' Compensation, EDEX Subscription, P.O. Box 420603, San Francisco, CA 94142.

Window Period vs. Nonwindow Period Cases

Effective 1994, the WCAB litigation process involves a two-track system. Distinctly different laws, forms, and procedures apply if an injury occurred during the period of 1990-1993, referred to as the "window period." Cases with injury dates during 1990-1993 are called "window cases," as opposed to "non-window cases."

Litigation procedures and some forms are relatively equivalent for nonwindow cases involving either pre-1990 or post-1993 injuries, although nuances do exist (not all of which are detailed herein). For window cases, filing of a claim form with the employer rather than filing an application with the WCAB operates to establish jurisdiction of the WCAB. For window cases, WCAB proceedings are requested by the filing of an application (not a declaration of readiness). A variety of pre-application discovery forms and procedures apply solely to window period cases. Other significant changes effective 1994 include repeal of a provision of LC5401 that allowed certain lien claimants to file an application for adjudication before a claim form was filed with the employer and a new requirement for filing of an antifraud statement (see above).

WCAB Sanctions

In any case where an Application for Adjudication of Claim was filed after 1993, LC5813 authorizes the WCAB to order a party and/or its attorney to pay "reasonable expenses, including attorney's fees and costs" that are "incurred by another party as a result of bad faith actions or tactics." The type of actions/tactics that may result in a penalty are basically described as those that "are frivolous or solely intended to cause unnecessary delay." The WCAB "in its sole discretion may order additional sanctions not to exceed" $2500. Also, any party can request a sanction against another party or its attorney by making a written application to the WCAB.

Per CR10561, penalty payments will not be ordered pursuant to LC5813 until "the alleged offending party or attorney" has been "given notice and an opportunity to be heard." This administrative regulation further describes a "bad faith action or tactic" as "one which results from a willful failure to comply with a statutory or regulatory obligation or from a willful intent to disrupt or delay the proceedings of the" WCAB. Also included is an action or tactic "that is done for an improper motive or is indisputably without merit."

Generally, actions that can be justified by proper motivations and common standards of conduct will not result in penalties or sanctions. Per CR10561, specific types of actions that can result in sanctions include: appearing late at a WCAB proceeding as a pattern of conduct or without a reasonable excuse; filing a legal document that is intended to cause an unnecessary delay; or, failing to comply with any of the WCAB's Rules of Practice and Procedure, "including an order of discovery," absent an acceptable reason.

Uniform Court Procedures

Per LC5500.3, the appeals board is required to establish procedures that are uniform for all district offices of the WCAB statewide. Uniformity is required for court forms and the time of court settings. This statute also specifies that no local office of the WCAB or any "worker's compensation judge shall require forms or procedures other than as established by the appeals board" (see 1.7).

1.19 LEVELS OF APPEAL

The parties have the right to appeal any final decisions including approval of settlement agreements (e.g. on the grounds of fraud or error) that are made by a referee, an arbitrator, a judge pro tempore or a judge. For instance, the decision of an arbitrator after mandatory arbitration of any issues specified in LC5275 will have the same final effect a decision of a WCAB judge, e.g. result in the right to appeal as explained below.

The first level of appeal is a request for review by the WCAB commissioners in San Francisco and is effected by filing a Petition for Reconsideration. An appeal from a decision of the WCAB commissioners is made to the Court of Appeal (for the appropriate district; see LC5950). At this level of appeal, the case first enters the civil court system. An appeal of a Court of Appeal decision is made to the Supreme Court of California. Appeals to either a Court of Appeal or the Supreme Court are effectuated by filing an application for writ of review. An appeal to the Supreme Court is ordinarily the final level of appeal, since workers' compensation is a state law and the California Supreme Court is the highest court in California.

On infrequent occasions, a workers' compensation case may be appealed to the U.S. Supreme Court. This would only occur if the case involved a legal issue relating to constitutional rights under the federal constitution. For example, it may be alleged that a state law violates a section of the U.S. Constitution such as the Equal Protection Clause. This occurs so rarely that it can usually be assumed that any reference made to the "Supreme Court" refers to the California Supreme Court unless specific mention is made to the United States Supreme Court.

1.20 LITIGATION FORMS – LISTING

A listing of the forms most frequently utilized in litigation proceedings for 1994 or later injuries is provided below as a convenient reference. Also shown are the sections of the WCAB Rules of Practice and Procedure that contain information pertinent to the use of the form such as filing and service requirements.

Filing refers to the provision of a document (ordinarily the original) to the WCAB for its file (see CR10390-CR10396 and CR10615). Service refers to the provision of copies of documents to other parties to a case either by mail or in person. Any form number below that refers to the Division of Industrial Accidents (DIA) easily identifies the form as one that existed before 1990 when the Division was renamed the Division of Workers' Compensation (DWC).

As a general matter, CR10392 requires that all documents that are filed with the WCAB "shall be on 8½ × 11 inch paper with two holes punched at the top and centered to fit" into the WCAB's file. Also, all documents "shall include in the heading the name of the injured employee and the" WCAB case number. If two or more medical reports are filed on the same day as an attachment to any WCAB form, CR10392 requires attachment of a transmittal letter that lists "each report by name of physician and date of report."

◦ **Answer:** used to respond to matters raised by an Application For Adjudication of Claim by specifying facts or issues that are disputed and defenses that will be raised; see LC5500, LC5505, and 10480 (WCAB Form 2).

◦ **Application For Adjudication Of Claim:** used to commence litigation against an employer or to initiate arbitration of a dispute. The WCAB assigns a case number when this document is filed, and this case number must thereafter appear on any other documents filed in the case; see LC5500, LC5501-LC5501.5, CR10400-CR10405, and CR10408 (DIA WCAB Form 1).

Application For Adjudication Of Claim (Death Case): serves the same purpose as a regular Application, but relief is sought for issues arising by virtue of the employee's death (e.g. burial expenses); see CR10408 (DIA WCAB Form 2).

Arbitration Submittal Form: a required attachment to an Application For Adjudication of Claim whenever arbitration of an issue is required by LC5275; see CR10995-CR10999 (WCAB Form 32).

Arbitration Submittal Orders: issued by a judge to require specific issues submitted for arbitration; see CR10995-CR10997 (WCAB Form 33).

◦ **Compromise And Release:** a type of settlement document whereby an employee receives a payment in addition to any compensation that is otherwise owed in exchange for releasing the employer from liability for future payments, as specified in the form; see LC5000-LC5005, CR10165.5 and CR10870-CR10886 (DIA-WCAB Form 15).

Compromise And Release (Dependency Claim): used to settle claims and release the employer from future liability for payments to dependents of the deceased employee; see LC5000-LC5005 and CR10870-CR10886 (DIA-WCAB Form 16).

◦ **Declaration Of Readiness To Proceed:** used to request a WCAB proceeding after an Application For Adjudication of Claim (regular or death case) has been filed with the WCAB; see CR10414-CR10417 (DIA-WCAB Form 9).

◦ **Employee's Claim For Workers' Compensation Benefits** form: provides written notice that an employee or dependent is claiming a work injury. Filing of a completed "claim form" with the employer tolls certain statutes of limitations until a claim is denied or else determined to be compensable; see LC5401-LC5022, LC5404.5, and CR10117-CR10121 (DWC Form 1).

◦ **Fee Disclosure Statement:** used by an attorney to provide notice to the employee of certain rights and to place the employer on notice of legal representation; see LC4906 and CR10134-10135.1 (DWC Form 3).

◦ **Notice And Request For Allowance of Lien:** used by a person other than the employee (or dependents in a death case) to request a determination to resolve a disputed claim for payment, e.g. used by a physician who provided medical treatment for a work injury; see CR10770 - CR10772 (DWC-WCAB Form 6).

Notice Of Dismissal Of Attorney: used after an application or a claim form has been filed and the employee wishes to represent himself. This form does not require the signature of the attorney being dismissed; see CR10774 (DIA-WCAB Form 37). Note: if an application has not yet been filed with the WCAB, the appropriate procedure is to have the employee to sign a withdrawal from a Fee Disclosure Statement (see LC4906).

Petition For Appointment Of Guardian Ad Litem And Trustee: used when the applicant entitled to compensation is a minor or incompetent; see CR10402 (DIA-WCAB Form 8).

Petition For Commutation Of Future Payments: used to request part or all of an award of compensation that is otherwise payable in installments to be paid in a lump sum; see LC5100-LC5105, LC4061, and CR10165.5 (DIA-WCAB Form 49).

Petition For Reconsideration: used to appeal a final decision of a judge, settlement conference referee, or arbitrator by requesting reconsideration by the Appeals Board; see LC5900 - LC5911, CR10352 and CR10840 - CR10869 (DIA-WCAB Form 45).

Petition To Reopen: used by the employer or the employee to request reopening of a previously closed WCAB file within five years from the date of injury; see LC5803 - LC5804 and CR10454 (DIA-WCAB Form 42).

Request For Dismissal: used by the employee to end litigation and close the court file without prejudice, thereby reserving certain rights to reopen the case; see CR10780 (DIA-WCAB Form 43).

Request For Expedited Hearing And Decision: used when a party is entitled to an expedited hearing pursuant to LC5502(b), that lists issues requiring expedited determinations; see CR10136-CR10137 (DWC Form 4).

Stipulations With Request For Award: used to settle an employee's claim based upon the written agreements of the parties. When signed by a judge, the third page of the form is an award of compensation that may or may not award lifetime medical benefits to the employee; see LC5702, LC4061, CR10165.5, and CR10496 (DIA-WCAB Form 3).

Stipulations With Request For Award (Death Case): used to settle claims with the employee's dependents; see LC5702 and CR10496 (DIA-WCAB Form 4).

Subpoena: used to command a personal appearance of a witness, usually at a deposition to be taken in an attorney's office or else at a proceeding at the WCAB; see CR10530 - CR10537 (DIA-WCAB Form 30).

Subpoena Duces Tecum: used to command the production of specifically described materials or records for inspection or review; see CR10530-CR10534 (DIA WCAB Form 32).

Substitution Of Attorneys: used after an application or a claim form has been filed to notify all parties that a previous attorney is no longer involved in a case and the name and address of the new attorney. This form requires the signature of the attorney who is being substituted out of the case; see CR10774 (DIA-WCAB Form 36).

⚬ **Third Party Compromise And Release:** used to settle a claim of injury where the employer has a right of subrogation or recovery and the employee has a right to receive workers' compensation benefits and a monetary recovery from a negligent third party; see LC5000-LC5005, LC3850-LC3862, and CR10870-CR10886 (DIA-WCAB Form 17).

1.21 INTERNET REFERENCE GUIDE - WEB SITES

Persons with internet access will benefit from the listing of web sites below which enable current information regarding California workers' compensation and affiliated laws to be fairly immediately located and obtained in written form. Most professional organizations in the workers' compensation field currently maintain an internet presence as does the State of California and many of its separate agencies and divisions.

   a. Find California Code:
       http://www.leginfo.ca.gov/calaw.html
   b. Bill Information: http://www.ca.gov/gov/official.html#laws
       http://www.leginfo.ca.gov, OR
       http://www.leginfo.ca.gov/bilinfo.html
   c. Search State Agencies:
       http://www.ca.gov/s
   d. California government Home Page:
       http://www.dir.ca.gov
   e. Find U.S. Codes, Bills and Regulations
       http://www.ca.gov/s/govt/govcode.html

(THIS PAGE LEFT BLANK INTENTIONALLY)

[2] INSURANCE & SELF-INSURANCE

2.1 SECURING PAYMENT OF COMPENSATION

Per LC3700, every employer is required to "secure payment of compensation." There is one exception, and that is the State of California itself. All other employers have two basic choices: insure or self-insure. The employer may select one of these two options for its entire liability, or the employer may self-insure a portion of its liability and insure the remaining portion.

2.2 INSURANCE ALTERNATIVES

Employers can purchase a workers' compensation insurance policy from any insurance company that is licensed to sell such insurance in California. Many private companies sell this type of insurance. The employer can also purchase insurance directly from the State's own insurance company, State Compensation Insurance Fund. The coverage provided by all workers' compensation insurance policies, public or private, is fairly standardized. Certain language is required in every policy. Basically, any insurance contract provides that the insurance company will assume the employer's liability for compensation under the provisions of the Labor Code.

2.3 LIMITED COVERAGE – BY LAW

Insurance companies cannot insure every liability of an employer. Under the Insurance Code, certain penalties are uninsurable risks. Under IC11661.5, an insurance company cannot sell insurance to protect the employer against its liability for the penalty assessed for illegally employing "persons under 16 years of age" (see LC4557). Per, IC11661.6, an employer cannot insure its liability for certain increases in late payments of indemnity benefits that are owed pursuant to LC4650 as a result of an employer's delay in properly forwarding notice of a claim to its insurer (see 9.16). Also, IC11661 prohibits the sale of insurance for the penalty assessment "for serious and willful misconduct of the employer or his agent" (see LC4553). It is permissible for an employer to purchase insurance to cover the cost to defend itself against a serious and willful claim, but not the cost to pay this penalty if it is determined to be owed to an employee. However, it may be difficult for employer to purchase this type of coverage since many insurers do not sell this optional coverage.

2.4 LIMITED COVERAGE – BY CONTRACT

Some limitations on coverage are made by endorsements to the insurance policy. The types of limitations are restricted by provisions of the Insurance Code. Copies of common endorsements are listed in Title 10 of the California Code of Regulations. This list is included in the *California Workers' Compensation Uniform Statistical Reporting Plan* published by the Workers' Compensation Insurance Rating Bureau of California (WCIRB) in San Francisco. Some approved types of endorsements are listed below.

a. Relatives of the Employer: no coverage for specified relatives if, at the time of injury, one of these relatives: "resides in the household of the employer" or the employer's spouse and/or "is a child under the age of 12 years." This endorsement is used only when the employer is an individual or a husband and wife.

b. Employees, Operations and/or Locations: no coverage under the insurance policy for those specifically named in the endorsement. For instance, coverage under the policy may exclude officers and directors who are the sole shareholders of a private corporation; employees of a liquor store owned by an employer who also owns a chain of florist shops; or, out-of-state locations where the employer also operates a business.

c. Liability of the Employer: no coverage arising out of "operations conducted jointly by said named employer with any other person, firm or corporation." This circumstance would constitute the creation of an employer identity that is different from the employer originally insured under the policy.

d. Medical Benefits: no coverage for medical benefits under LC4600. Use of this endorsement is referred to as an "ex-medical" or a "med-ex" policy. All other insurable liability for workers' compensation benefits is covered under the insurance policy. The employer must be legally self-insured for medical benefits in order to obtain this endorsement. Even so, the endorsement provides for monitoring and the assumption of necessary control by the insurance company to ensure an employer's compliance with statutory obligations.

The endorsements described above permit an insurance carrier to restrict the extent of workers' compensation insurance that it will sell to an employer, but they do not alter an employer's statutory duty to secure the payment of compensation for its employees. Some employers may have to purchase policies from more than one company in order to provide insurance coverage for all employees for whom workers' compensation coverage is required under the Labor Code.

Construction Industry.

Per LC3201.5, it is permissible for employers within construction-related industries to negotiate certain aspects of claims administration pursuant to a collective bargaining agreement. Per LC3201.5, collective bargaining agreements can provide for the establishment of such things as an alternative dispute resolution system (see 1.12), return-to-work programs, and the use of agreed lists of providers for medical treatment, examinations by Agreed or Qualified Medical Evaluators (see 7.75), or vocational rehabilitation services (see 11.11). Any such contractual provisions are subject to regulation by the Administrative Director of the Division of Workers' Compensation to ensure the employer's compliance with the provisions of the Labor Code (see CR10200-CR10204).

2.5 BUYING INSURANCE FROM THE STATE

When the first constitutional provisions on California workers' compensation were enacted, no insurance companies were licensed to sell this type of insurance in California. The State Compensation Insurance Fund (SCIF) was created to enable employers to meet the newly-created legal requirement that they secure the payment of compensation for their employees. For a short time, State Compensation Insurance Fund was the only company from which employers could purchase workers' compensation insurance. Other insurance companies soon became licensed, and State Compensation Insurance Fund presently does business in a competitive market with many other insurance companies.

State Compensation Insurance Fund is subject to the same state laws that apply to all other insurance companies. State Compensation Insurance Fund is merely an alternative choice for an employer who buys insurance. However, there are some distinguishing features between State Compensation Insurance Fund and private insurance companies.

The employees of State Compensation Insurance Fund are state civil service employees. State Compensation Insurance Fund is a nonprofit organization; profits are returned to policyholders in the form of dividends. Private companies have a right to refuse to sell insurance to any employer at their option, e.g. to a business with a history of recurrent layoffs or strikes. As a rule, State Compensation Insurance Fund cannot refuse to sell workers' compensation insurance when an employer is required by law to obtain coverage for its employees (an exception in IC11784 permits State Compensation Insurance Fund to decline to insure an employer that has inadequate safety or accident prevention standards). However, State Compensation Insurance Fund is not compelled to sell insurance for a lower price than private insurance would cost.

2.6 BUYING PRIVATE INSURANCE

Private insurance companies are profit-making operations (there are various exceptions such as mutual or reciprocal insurers). Their goal is to collect premium, process and pay claims, and to have some profit remaining. Premium costs vary from one insurer to another for a multitude of reasons. Most insurance companies offer competitive pricing on workers' compensation premiums, historically through the use of dividend or retrospective rating plans although the modern trend under the open rating system is for employers to achieve cost savings up front (see 2.12). Some companies offer a wide range of services including such items as quality claims administration, in-house rehabilitation staff, in-house safety and loss control expertise, and state-of-the-art reports and statistical analysis. Still other companies provide captive programs or otherwise allow the insured to retain some of its risks. These factors account for the variance in premium quotations from one insurer to the next.

2.7 REGULATION OF INSURANCE

Insurance companies must be licensed in order to sell insurance in California. Basic requirements include submission of a detailed application, payment of required fees, and filing of a bond (see IC11690 et seq.). A Certificate of Authority to transact the business of workers' compensation insurance is issued by the Department of Insurance. This Department, that is headed by the Insurance Commissioner, has authority to regulate most aspects of the business of insurance.

The financial condition of insurance companies is of particular interest to the Commissioner. Insurance companies are monitored through an ongoing system of required reports to ensure that adequate reserves are posted to claim files (meaning that sufficient funds have been set aside or held in reserve to pay incurred losses; see 2.24). State laws specifically relating to the business of insurance are located in the Insurance Code.

An insurer's ability to cancel an existing policy is greatly restricted by virtue of detailed requirements for advance notice, and cancellation is permissible solely for circumstances that are listed in IC676.8 (see 3.21). For these reasons, an employer wishing to purchase insurance can anticipate that a prospective insurer will exercise reasonable care in investigating pertinent facts prior to issuing a workers' compensation insurance policy.

2.8 SAFETY & LOSS CONTROL SERVICES

Amendments to the Insurance Code took effect 7/16/93 that impact all insured employers whether insurance is purchased from the State Compensation Insurance Fund or any private insurance company. Pursuant to IC11721, employers are entitled to the provision of loss control services without charge, except free services need not be provided where there is no significant risk of preventable hazards. Per LC6354.5, loss control services (as specified in IC11721) must be provided by personnel who are certified by the Director of the Department of Industrial Relations. Fees charged for this service replenish the Loss Control Certification Fund. However, LC6354.5 precludes insurers from charging any separately-stated premium for statutorily required safety and health loss control services.

Effective 1995, LC6354.5, requires each insurer to submit an annual "health and safety loss control plan" to the Director. This report will include a review of the insurer's loss control activities and explain the manner in which the insurer will target employers "with the greatest workers' compensation losses and the most significant and preventable health and safety hazards."

Labor Code LC6314.1 requires the Division of Occupational Safety to establish a program of inspections that targets "employers in high hazardous industries with the highest incidence of preventable occupational injuries and illnesses and worker's compensation losses." The costs of this program are payable from the Cal/OSHA Targeted Inspection and Consultation Fund that is created by LC62.7. Employers who have workers' compensation experience ratings of 125% or higher will be levied an assessment for this fund.

2.9 WCIRB – INSURANCE RATING BUREAU

The Workers' Compensation Insurance Rating Bureau (WCIRB) is a State-required rating organization and the only rating organization in California. It is a nonprofit and unincorporated association. All insurance companies that underwrite workers' compensation coverage are required to belong to the Workers' Compensation Insurance Rating Bureau and are assessed fees for their membership (See IC11750-IC11759.1).

The Workers' Compensation Insurance Rating Bureau works closely with the Insurance Commissioner's office compiling statistical records and generating reports. Records are maintained for each worker's compensation policy issued in the State on incurred losses, posted reserves, and claims' expenditures. This information is submitted by insurers under a mandatory reporting program called the "Unit Statistical Plan" that is published by the Workers' Compensation Insurance Rating Bureau as the *California Workers' Compensation Uniform Statistical Reporting Plan*. This plan is updated and reprinted on an annual basis and available for a fee (write to address shown in 2.10).

Reports submitted pursuant to Unit Statistical Plan are often referred to as "Unit Stat" reports or "Unit Stats"). The Workers' Compensation Insurance Rating Bureau utilizes this information to comply with its duty under IC11750.3 to "collect and tabulate information and statistics for the purpose of developing pure premium rates (see 2.11). The duties of the WCIRB as a rating organization are set out in IC11750.3. These duties include the development of pure premium rates, formulating regulations relative to insurance rating systems, inspection of risks to evaluate occupational classifications, and examination of insurance policies "to ascertain whether they comply with the provisions of law."

As of 1994, LC138.6 provides for the Workers' Compensation Insurance Rating Bureau to act in a consultative role with the Administrative Director of the Division of Workers' Compensation who is required to develop an information system. It is the Legislature's stated intent that this "information system be compatible with the Electronic Data Interchange System of the International Association of Industrial Accident Boards and Commissions." This information system is intended to measure the efficiency of the benefit delivery system and "provide statistical data for research into specific aspects of the workers' compensation program." The report to the Legislature that LC138.6 requires "on the development of this system and recommendations for any necessary legislative action" is available to the public upon request.

2.10 WCIRB – INSURANCE COVERAGE RECORDS

The Workers' Compensation Insurance Rating Bureau of California maintains records of all employers covered by workers' compensation insurance in California since 1958 including names of insurers, policy numbers, and effective dates of coverage. These records are available (for a fee) to insurance companies upon written request to the WCIRB at 525 Market Street, Suite 800, San Francisco, CA 94105. In the event an insurance company's records are lost or destroyed, WCIRB records can be obtained to verify whether or not insurance coverage for a particular employer was provided on the date of injury alleged by an employee.

Coverage information is routinely requested in cumulative injury or occupational disease cases where the date of injury that appears on claim documents is shown as a period of employment rather than a specific date (for an explanation of the relationship between the employment period claimed and the statute of limitations period, see 6.14). Per LC5500.5, the employer or employers who are liable for payment of compensation in such cases are those who employed the employee during the one year period "immediately preceding either the date of injury, as determined pursuant to Section 5412, or the last date on which the employee was employed in an occupation exposing him or her to the hazards of the occupational disease or cumulative injury, whichever occurs first." An insurance carrier may wish to verify that it had valid insurance coverage for a particular employer for this entire period of time and/or the identity of insurance companies who also had coverage for a portion of the period of liability in LC5500.5 and who are therefore jointly liable for a portion of the compensation payable to the employee.

2.11 WCIRB – INSURANCE PREMIUMS

Prior to 1995, the Workers' Compensation Insurance Rating Bureau published a manual that set out expected manual rates, that (with exceptions; see 2.12) generally established the lowest permissible levels for insurance premiums. The minimum rate law was repealed as of 1995 (by amendment to IC11750.3). Effective for policy inception dates of 1995 or later, an open rating system replaced the prior rating system.

The Workers' Compensation Insurance Rating Bureau continues to publish a rating manual. However, manual rates are advisory only and represent a "pure premium rate" (PPR). This term is defined by IC11730 to mean "that portion of the rate which represents the loss cost per unit of exposure, including loss adjustment expense" (not included is any amount representing profit).

Advisory rates are based upon data accumulated from claim payment information that is reported by insurance companies pursuant to the *California Workers' Compensation Uniform Statistical Reporting Plan* (see 2.9). This manual contains the pure premium rates that are published each year by the Workers' Compensation Insurance Rating Bureau (see IC11750.3). Generally, insurance premiums cannot fall below the expected pure premium levels (per IC11736; see exceptions in 2.12). This is because the expected advisory premium rates are a prediction of how much premium an insurance company must collect in order to pay anticipated losses. Advisory premium rates are based upon:

1. Occupational classifications: the types of work activities that are performed by employees are categorized according to the probability that any injury will occur and the probable severity (cost) of injuries that may be sustained, AND
2. Payroll: the total payroll for all employees in each separate occupational category covered under the policy.

Many occupations are listed by name in the *California Workers' Compensation Uniform Statistical Reporting Plan.* Those not listed are classified by analogy to one of the occupations that are listed. Each occupation is assigned a separate classification code and a corresponding pure premium rate. Multiplying the pure premium rate by each $100 of annual payroll for all workers in the same classification would produce a pure premium rate for this category of worker. Adding together the separate premiums for all occupational classifications for a particular employer results in a total annual amount of pure premium. Some examples of occupations, classification codes, and pure premium rates from the 1995 manual are shown below.

Occupational Classification	Code No.	Manual Rate
Clerical Office Employees	8810	.62 per $100
Insurance Companies, all employees	8822	.96 per $100
Hospitals, all employees	9043	2.41 per $100
Police Officers, not volunteers	7720	7.09 per $100
Furniture Mover	8293(2)	17.70 per $100

From an employee's perspective, entitlement to California workers' compensation benefits at the employer's expense is a right provided by State law, not a benefit provided by the employer. Consider, from the employer's perspective, the example of a policeman earning $40,000 a year. The advisory insurance premium for this one employee using the 1995 rates above would be $2836.00 each year ($40,000 ÷ 100 = $400 × 7.09), an overhead cost of approximately 7% of the employee's annual earnings. Most employees are unaware of how much money their employers pay for this insurance coverage, since LC3751 provides that "no employer shall exact or receive from any employee any contribution, or make or take any deduction from the earnings of any employee, either directly or indirectly, to cover the whole or any part of the cost of compensation."

The fact that IC11735 permits every insurer to develop its own "rates, rating plans, and supplementary rate information" in lieu of reliance upon State-approved pure premium rates is referred to as an "open rating" system. Per IC11735, an insurer is required to submit its proposed premium rates to the Insurance Commissioner's office at least 30 days prior to using such rates.

Prior approval of rates is not required, but IC11737 provides the Insurance Commissioner with authority to disapprove proposed rates that are unfairly discriminatory, may tend to create a monopoly, or may affect the insurer's financial solvency (if rates are disapproved, the Insurance Commissioner will specify interim rates to be used). All workers' compensation insurance rates and information related to rates are open to public inspection at reasonable times, and copies of this information are available to persons who provide payment of reasonable charges.

Employers may utilize pure premium rate information as a guideline, but other factors can significantly affect the premium that an employer may pay (for instance, the success of a return-to-work program or the employer's Injury and Illness Prevention Program that is required by LC6401.7). Employers can obtain information on open rating from their current insurers. For any policies that are new or renewed after 1994, IC11752.8 requires the insurer to provide a notice that explains "in easily understandable language the workers' compensation rating laws." Included in this notice shall be an "easily understandable ... summary of the changes in the rating laws enacted" in 1993 and 1994.

Pursuant to IC11752.6, the Workers' Compensation Insurance Rating Bureau is required to make "available, in writing, to" an insured employer "all policyholder information contained in its records upon request of the employer and after notice to the employer's insurer." Policyholder information includes "information relating to the employer's loss experience, claims, classification assignments, and policy contracts." Also included is "information relating to rating plans, rating systems, manual rules, and any other information that" impacts "the policyholder's pure premium rates." To facilitate the employer's right to information, IC11752.5 requires that a rating organization (e.g. the Workers' Compensation Insurance Rating Bureau) shall establish a "policyholder ombudsman." This individual is to be provided with appropriate staff and resources to enable the ombudsman "to provide prompt and complete service to workers' compensation policyholders of this state."

2.12 WCIRB – EXPERIENCE RATING PLANS

An exception to standard application of pure premium rates is the computation of premiums based upon experience modifications. Per LC11730, "experience rating" refers to "a rating procedure utilizing past insurance experience of the individual policyholder to forecast future losses by measuring the policyholder's loss experience against" that of other "policyholders in the same classification to produce a prospective premium credit, debit, or unity modification."

The Workers' Compensation Insurance Rating Bureau establishes the "ex mod" for a particular employer based on the actual frequency and severity of the employer's past claims. The established premium rate for an employer is unaffected by an "ex mod" of 100. A variance above or below 100 will result in an adjustment of the employer's established premium that is proportionate to the extent of the variance. For instance, the employer will pay 156% of its established base premium rate with an "ex mod" of 156 (and will thus owe an assessment to the State; see 2.8). Conversely, through good loss experience, an "ex-mod" of 86 will mean that the employer pays only 86% of its established premium rate.

There are two basic types of rating plans (presented simplistically here, but having many exceptions and alternatives). Prospective rating plans base premium on actual experience in prior years (per the *California Workers' Compensation Experience Rating Plan;* see 2.10). Under retrospective rating plans, both past and current loss experience affect the amount of premium. The employer pays an estimated premium subject to later adjustment after expiration of the policy term (as explained in the *California Workers' Compensation Retrospective Rating Plan*).

2.13 SELF-INSURANCE ALTERNATIVE – IN GENERAL

The reason for choosing self-insurance is financial. Insurance premiums include amounts for expenses other than the actual cost of paying claims. Overhead expenses are included for such items as rents and employee salaries. Charges may be made for special services, e.g. design, implementation, or use of integrated computer systems for loss reporting or tracking. Also, premiums include some additional amount that represents profit.

A self-insured employer must pay all claims and expenses necessitated by administration of a workers' compensation claims program. The difference between these costs and the cost of any insurance premium is the amount of potential savings to the employer. The larger this gap is, the more likely it is that the self-insurance option will save the employer money. A further consideration is the continued need for any services previously provided by the insurance company that must now be provided at the employer's expense. If an employer cannot pay claims more economically than an insurance company can, self-insurance is inappropriate.

Self-insurance is not feasible for every employer and is not a viable option for most small employers. The employer must meet stringent financial qualifications and comply with exacting record-keeping regulations. Financial ability to pay claims is required as well as the expertise to administer the California workers' compensation laws and the ability to maintain an adequate safety program. Self-insurance can save money as opposed to high insurance premiums, but the self-insurance alternative can also be expensive.

Effective 1994, LC3701 provides that either an individual employer or a group of employers (as a single entity) may obtain a Certificate of Consent to Self-Insure. Employers that conduct homogenous business endeavors may realize a cost advantage to self-insuring as a group whereas individual employers within the group may not otherwise qualify or financially benefit from self-insurance. Administrative regulations that have been adopted for the purpose of "authorizing and encouraging group self-insurance" pursuant to LC3702.10 are set out in CR15470-CR15481.

2.14 SELF-INSURANCE – QUALIFYING REQUIREMENTS

An employer wishing to become self-insured must submit an Application for a Certificate of Consent to Self-Insure to the Director of the Department of Industrial Relations. As a practical matter, a third party administrator or insurance broker will usually provide the employer with considerable assistance in the application process. In any event, a certificate will not be given unless, per LC3700, the employer can furnish satisfactory proof of these two items: the "ability to self-insure and to pay any compensation that may become due" under the Labor Code.

Proof of ability to self-insure includes proof under CR15353 of "an effective accident prevention program." This requirement should not prove difficult because every employer in California is required to "implement and maintain an effective injury prevention program" that "shall be written" and shall include all of the elements specified in LC6401.7 (see also LC6400-LC6408.) The employer must furnish the names, addresses, and telephone numbers of the individuals responsible for its safety program, the percentage of their time that is devoted to this activity, and evidence that the existing program is effective. The effectiveness of an accident prevention program is measured by its success in reducing the frequency and the severity of injuries in the workplace.

The employer must furnish proof that, per CR15452, it will "conduct the administration of" its "self-insurance program through the services of a competent person or persons." At least one competent administrator must be located at each office where the claims will be administered. Competency is ordinarily demonstrated by passing a written State examination described by CR15452 as "designed to test technical knowledge of workers' compensation law and claims administration." Persons who pass the State examination used to receive a brief letter notifying them of this fact, but the State currently provides a "Certificate of Achievement." All persons who have passed the State examination are customarily referred to as "certified self-insurance administrators" or as being "certified" (although some persons possess a letter instead of a formal certificate).

As proof of ability to pay compensation, a private employer is required to submit specific information regarding its financial condition and to post a security deposit. Instructions regarding the deposit of different types of security are set out in LC3701. Acceptable security is limited to a deposit of "cash, securities, surety bonds, or irrevocable letters of credit in any combination," and the employer "loses all right, title, and interest in, and any right to control, all assets or obligations posted or left on deposit as security." The State can, and will, liquidate the security deposit in the event the employer cannot or does not make required compensation payments.

The amount of the security deposit for each private employer is computed under LC3701 by multiplying set percentages times the total amount of "the private self-insurer's estimated future liability for compensation" (the dollar amount of the total reserves posted to all open claim files; see 2.24). The security deposit is comprised of two separate minimum amounts that are added together. A minimum of 125% is required to secure payments of compensation that may become due under the Labor Code. A separate minimum of 10% of estimated future liability for compensation is required to secure the payment for "all administrative and legal costs relating to or arising from the employer's self-insuring," e.g. fees of attorneys who represent the employer's interests in litigated cases and fees for services provided by private investigators. Per LC3702, the security deposit required of a private self-insurer shall in no event be less than $220,000.

Effective 1994, LC3701 enables coordination of security deposit requirements for employers who are self-insured under California workers' compensation laws and the federal Longshore and Harbor Workers' Act (L&H Act). Per LC3701, an employer who self-insures its liabilities under both state and federal laws can make a joint security deposit for its workers' compensation obligations. Affected employers will make appropriate modifications to their annual report form as detailed in LC3701 (see 2.15).

2.15 SELF-INSURED CLAIMS – ADMINISTRATION

Effective 6/30/94, a newly self-insured employer no longer enjoys the freedom to decide whether to self-administer its claims or to contract with a third-party claims administrator. Per CR15450.1, every private employer (except those who were self-insured prior to 6/30/94) is required to contract with a third-party claims administrator for the first three full calendar years of its self-insurance program. For private employers who become self-insured as a group, administration of claims by a third-party administrator is required for the "first five full calendar years of self-insurance."

Established self-insured employers have alternatives regarding administration of their claims. They can handle claims in-house or contract with an outside firm to handle their claims. When claims are handled by employer personnel, the employer is both self-insured and self-administered.

Some insurance companies provide claim adjusting services for self-insured employers as well as insured employers. There are other companies whose sole business is claims administration for self-insured employers. These companies are not insurance companies. Claims are administered on a contract fee basis versus collection of insurance premiums. A separate company that acts as a self-insured employer's claims administrator is most commonly known as a third party administrator (TPA), but such companies may also be referred to as adjusting agencies or as self-insurance administrators. The function such companies serve is to allow an employer to enjoy the financial benefit of being self-insured without the necessity to staff or maintain a claim department on the employer's premises.

The employer's involvement in claims administration can be total or limited. The options available for claims administration allow the employer to undergo a gradual transition to self-administration while enjoying the financial benefits of self-insurance. The transition may be from an insurance company to an adjusting agency to eventual in-house administration. The greatest cost savings are effected through good self-administration, but some employers may prefer to use an external claims administrator or adjusting agency.

2.16 REGULATION OF SELF-INSURANCE

Self-insured employers are regulated by the Office of Self-Insurance Plans within the Department of Industrial Relations. The administrative Rules and Regulations governing self-insurance administration are located in Title 8 of the Code of Regulations (CR15000-CR15481). All self-insured employers must be familiar with these regulations and adhere to them. Basically, a self-insured employer is required to satisfy all initial qualifying requirements on a continuous basis. For instance, the private employer's security deposit must be increased when estimated future liability for compensation increases.

The employer is required to notify the State of a variety of specific changes in status on an ongoing basis. These include changes in the employer's business such as the addition or deletion of employment locations or of any subsidiary operations. Notification is also required of any change of a designated claims administrator, e.g. the selection of a different individual, a change from one adjusting agency to another, or a change from an adjusting agency to in-house claims administration or vice versa (see CR15402 et seq.).

The State reviews claim file reserves and other pertinent financial information that are submitted each year in the Self-Insurer's Annual Report that is required by LC3702.2. This report is due on or before March 1 each year for private employers and October 1 for public employers. The claim file reserves of private self-insurers are also monitored through audits that are mandated by LC3702.6 to be conducted a minimum of once every three years to determine "the adequacy of estimates of future liability" established on claim files (see 2.24). Public employers are not subject to these routine cyclical audits, but the State can conduct special audits if good cause exists to evaluate the adequacy of claim file reserves. Audits under LC3702.6 are in addition to audits of claim files conducted by the Audit Unit of the Division of Workers' Compensation to determine the employer's compliance with its statutory obligations for the provision of benefits (see 2.26).

Subsequent to initially qualifying for self-insurance, the amount of an existing self-insured employer's security deposit is thereafter subject to computation under CR15210 as of 1/21/93. The minimum deposit that is specified in LC3701 (the greater of $220,000 or 135% of claim file reserves, to cover benefits and administrative costs) is, in effect, increased pursuant to CR15210. Based upon information presented in an employer's annual report, the employer's deposit must also include an amount that is computed as the average of estimated future liabilities (claim file reserves) for the preceding five years; this amount is required to be posted as an advance payment for future liabilities in the coming year.

Also pursuant to CR15210, the employer is entitled to reduce "the liability to be reported on individual claims due to any new documentation of specific excess insurance coverage not previously reported." Per CR15251, the employer may claim a credit against calculations of the employer's security deposit "for any claims exceeding the retention level of any specific excess insurance policy for which the carrier has accepted liability in writing."

Private self-insured employers pay the State's cost to regulate them. Per LC3702.5, such costs shall be borne by "private self-insurers" through payment of annual certificate or license fees that are based upon the number of employees and the number of locations where claims are administered. A chart of annual license fees appears in CR15230. This regulation also provides for additional user funding assessments when necessary to finance the cost of State regulation.

The employer will be invoiced on or before October 1 of each year for the total assessment owed and will have 30 days to pay without penalty (see 3702.9). Per LC3702.5, the State may also assess other fees when necessary "to cover the costs of special audits or services." Special audits include audits of claims that are administered at an out-of-state location and repeat or extended audits scheduled after problems are identified in a routine audit.

Self-insurance is a privilege, not a right. Per LC3702, the employer's Certificate of Consent to Self-Insure can be revoked at any time for "good cause." Some specific grounds that constitute good cause for revocation are financial problems affecting ability to pay compensation, violations of health or safety orders, failure or inability to fulfill required obligations, and dishonesty or unethical practices in administering claims. A pattern of under-reserving of claim files (see 2.24) or a habit of forcing employees to litigate in order to receive compensation due them, whether by intent or incompetence, are examples of practices that would constitute good cause.

2.17 REGULATION OF THIRD-PARTY ADMINISTRATORS

Third-party administrators are subject to regulation by the Office of Self-Insurance Plans pursuant to LC3702.1, but only "with respect to the adjustment, administration, and management of workers' compensation claims." This law specifically exempts insurance carriers from its provisions, but all other third-party administrators (or TPA's) are required to obtain "a certificate of consent to administer self-insured employers workers' compensation claims." This certificate is not a certificate of consent to self-insure but merely a permit to conduct the business of claims administration on behalf of self-insured clients. Per CR15450, a "Certificate to Administer" can be issued for "a period of 1, 2, or 3 years" and always expires June 30 unless reapplication for renewal is made before June 1.

Per LC3702.1, "a separate certificate shall be required for each adjusting location" (and CR15454 requires payment of a certificate fee for each separate office location where claims are adjusted). As a condition of receiving the required certificate, 3702.1 requires that "all persons given discretion by a third-party administrator to deny, accept, or negotiate a workers' compensation claim shall demonstrate their competency by written examination, or other methods" (see 2.14). Self-insured employers should also take an active interest in appraising the competency of the persons who adjust their claims since LC3702 provides that good cause exists for revocation of the employer's certificate of consent to self-insure when either the employer or its "agent in charge of administration" engages in any of several specifically prohibited claims practices listed in this statute (see 2.16 and 2.26).

2.18 REGULATION OF PUBLIC EMPLOYERS

Since 1979, the only employer in California that has been permitted to be "legally uninsured" is the State of California itself. The State is not required to secure its liability for payment of compensation by either insurance or self-insurance. Regulation of insurance companies as well as self-insured employers is conducted by State employees. The State of California is not however required to regulate itself. In essence, being legally uninsured for workers' compensation means not being regulated by the State.

Use of the term "legally uninsured" is incorrect in reference to a public employer other than the State of California (and has been since 1979). Per LC3700, public agencies that do not purchase insurance are deemed to be self-insured and subject to the same requirements for securing a certificate of consent to self-insure as are private employers. This mandate applies to public agencies that self-insure their individual liability. It also applies to "each member of a pooling arrangement under a joint exercise of powers agreement" (referred to as a "JPA").

There are many similarities and differences between public and private self-insured employers. All self-insured employers are required by 3702.2 to submit an annual report. However, public self-insureds are not required to pay an annual license fee under CR15230 nor to post a security deposit under LC3701. Private self-insureds are subject to routine audits of claim file reserves, but LC3702.6 authorizes the Office of Self-Insurance Plans to conduct "a special audit of any public self-insured employer to determine the adequacy of estimates of future liability of claims." (Note: prior to 1993, all self-insured employers were subject to routine cyclical audits of claim file reserves; and, prior to 1990, LC3702.6 authorized State audits of claims practices as well as claim file reserves.)

2.19 ILLEGALLY UNINSURED EMPLOYER

Where the Labor Code requires compulsory coverage, any employer that fails to secure its liability for compensation is an illegally uninsured employer. The employer may be unintentionally uninsured: its insurance premiums may lapse due to an oversight. Some employers intentionally fail to purchase a workers' compensation insurance policy in order to avoid the cost of the premium. Failure to meet this legal requirement can subject the employer to prosecution for a misdemeanor, large fines, certain employee remedies (discussed below) and even a jail sentence. Once the employer's omission is discovered, the costs of penalties for noninsurance will far exceed the amount the employer would otherwise have paid for insurance premiums. The law intentionally ensures this result.

2.20 REMEDIES AGAINST UNINSURED EMPLOYER

An injured employee can sue an illegally uninsured employer in civil court for damages. The employer is presumed to be negligent and cannot use any common law defenses. The employee may attach the property of the employer to satisfy any damages awarded, and the employee is entitled to have his attorney's fees paid by the employer (see LC3706-3728). The employee can also report the employer to the Division of Labor Standards Enforcement. This State agency can obtain a court order restraining the employer from operating its business unless, and until, it does obtain workers' compensation insurance.

In addition to a civil action or instead of a civil action, the employee can file a claim with the Workers' Compensation Appeals Board. The employee can be awarded workers' compensation benefits just as if the employer had insurance, plus attorney fees, plus the employer can be assessed a penalty that increases the benefits awarded by 10% (LC4554-LC4555). If the employer is not willing nor financially able to voluntarily pay the award, the employee's award is paid out of a special fund called the Uninsured Employers Fund. Per LC3716.2, the Uninsured Employers Fund "is not liable for any penalties or for the payment of interest on any awards" of the WCAB. However, the above-mentioned penalties will be paid to the employee if they are collected from the uninsured employer as a result of the Uninsured Employers Fund's collections efforts.

Certain penalties increase the amount of workers' compensation that the employer will pay to its injured employee. However, an illegally uninsured employer is also subject to a penalty assessment under LC3722 that is payable to the State of California (for deposit to the Uninsured Employer's Fund). The amount of this penalty assessment depends upon whether the WCAB determined that the employee's claim of injury was compensable or noncompensable. For compensable injuries, the penalty is $10,000 "per each employee employed on the date of the injury." For noncompensable injuries, the penalty is $2,000 for each person employed "at the time of the claimed injury." Per LC3722, the maximum amount of penalties that may be assessed, regardless of the number of persons employed on the date of injury (or claimed injury) is $100,000.

2.21 UNINSURED EMPLOYERS FUND

The Uninsured Employers Fund is part of the Claims Unit of the Division of Workers' Compensation. The term "UEF" is used to refer to the fund itself as well as the Unit that administers the fund. The Uninsured Employers Fund provides payments to employees of uninsured employers and then institutes collection procedures to recover its payments. Per LC4903.3, the Uninsured Employers Fund can advance benefits to an injured employee prior to any WCAB award. Per LC3716, once a WCAB award issues, the employee can request full payment of the award directly from the Uninsured Employers Fund. If the employee also filed a civil action against the employer, the Uninsured Employers Fund has a first lien right against any recovery otherwise payable to the employee. If no civil recovery was sought, the Uninsured Employers Fund will take action directly against the uninsured employer. Monies recovered are placed back into the Uninsured Employers Fund for future use.

The Uninsured Employers Fund pays compensation to employees only. It is not liable for contribution payments to insurance companies or self-insured employers. Per LC3711, the Uninsured Employers Fund does not owe payment of an uninsured employer's share of benefits in a cumulative injury claim where any liable employer has secured the payment of compensation by insurance or self-insurance. The Uninsured Employers Fund will pay benefits in a continuing trauma case if the only liable employer was uninsured or if all liable employers were uninsured.

2.22 EMPLOYER – DUTY TO REPORT INJURY

All employers, whether insured or self-insured, are required to comply with a LC6409.1 reporting requirement. Labor Code 6409.1 requires the filing of an Employer's Report of Occupational Injury or Illness (Form 5020) with the State Division of Labor Statistics and Research for each injury or illness that "results in lost time beyond the date of the injury or illness, or which requires medical treatment beyond first aid." It is rare for an injured worker to lose time from work for an injury that does not require any treatment beyond first aid (e.g. where an injury results in instant death). In most cases, the provision of medical treatment beyond first aid is the event that will precipitate the filing of the employer's report. For purposes of this reporting requirement, CR14001 mandates the use of the definition of "first aid" in LC5401 (see 6.7).

The State requires an Employer's Report to be filed whenever the employer has knowledge that an employee has either sustained or is alleging to have sustained an industrial injury or illness. The report is mandatory for admittedly compensable injuries as well as for cases where the employer denies liability for compensation and has notified the employee of this determination (see 6.9). Per LC6409.1, the employer is also required to file an amended report with the State if it subsequently learns that the employee died "as a result of the reported injury or illness" (not from unrelated causes). This requirement enables the State to more accurately determine the number of fatal injuries in any given year. (In any case that involves a serious injury or death, LC6409.1 also requires the employer to make an immediate report to Cal/OSHA "by telephone or telegraph.")

Labor Code 6409.1 requires a copy, but not the original, of the Employer's Report to be filed with the State. Modern communications between employers and their claims administrators often involve the transmission of information without transferal of original documents or hard copies of documents, e.g. the employer may submit its report to its claims administrator by facsimile machine, modem, or computer media such as a tape or diskette. It is also the State's intention that required reports can eventually be filed using computer media (which explains the anticipatory reference in CR14001 to the transmittal of reports by "use of computer media, prescribed by" the State "and compatible with" its "computer equipment").

Per LC6409.1, self-insured employers are required to file a copy of their reports with the State within a maximum period of five days of first knowledge of a claim. Insured employers are required by LC3760 to file "a complete report of every injury to each employee as specified in Section 6409.1" with their insurer who is then required by LC6409.1 to file a copy of the Employer's Report with the State "immediately upon receipt." Regardless of who files a copy with the State, the original of the Employer's Report should be kept in the claim file (retention of this document is mandatory per CR10101).

All employers should be aware of LC6412 which provides that the employer's report form is not "open to public inspection" and is not "admissible as evidence" in WCAB proceedings. An employer can make comments on the form and communicate confidential information to its insurance carrier or other claims administrator without concern that information in the form can be obtained by subpoena or in any manner produced or utilized as evidence against an employer "in any adversary proceeding before the" WCAB. However, an employer has ample motivation for ensuring the accuracy of information reported to the State and its insurance carrier. Since 1992, the employer's report (like the physician's first report; see 7.55) is one of the documents that is required to contain the antifraud clause set out in LC5401.7: "Any person who makes or causes to be made any knowingly false or fraudulent material statement or material representation for the purpose of obtaining or denying workers' compensation benefits or payments is guilty of a felony."

2.23 CLAIMS ADMINISTRATION – OVERVIEW

Claims for work injuries are processed by the employer's designated claims administrator after receipt of notice or knowledge that a work-related injury has occurred or is being alleged (CR10100.1). Ordinarily, notice is provided by receipt of a claim form that is forwarded by the employer. However, a claim form or knowledge of an alleged injury may also be received directly from the employee, an attorney, a medical provider or any other entity.

A work-injury claim generally refers to a claim for which some category of workers' compensation benefit would be payable if the claim was determined to be compensable (by the claimsperson or the WCAB). A claims administrator will assign a separate claim number to each work injury claim upon knowledge of the claim, and all documents relating to the same injury will be placed in a single claim file. A claims administrator is required to maintain an annual claim log that lists all work-injury claims by the date each was received and includes: the employee's name, the claim number, date of the injury, whether the claim is a medical-only claim or an indemnity claim, and an entry identifying each claim that has been denied (CR10103.1).

New claims are ordinarily reviewed by supervisory staff prior to assignment for handling by a particular claimsperson. Various titles that are used to refer to a claimsperson include claims administrator, claims examiner, claims adjuster, claims supervisor or case manager. A claimsperson will review available information, seek missing but necessary information, and arrange for the timely provision of (or the denial of) benefits.

Per CR10101.1, certain forms "or documentation of reasonable attempts to obtain the form" are required to be maintained in a claim file. Such forms include the employer date-stamped copy of a claim form (see 6.12), an Employer's First Report of Occupational Injury or Illness (see 2.22), a Doctor's First Report of Occupational Injury or Illness (see 7.55) and the "original or a copy of every medical report pertaining to the claim." Additionally, the claim file should include a copy of all notices or reports that are required by the Division of Workers' Compensation (e.g. benefit notice letters and medical reports), "a record of payment of compensation," a copy of any Application for Adjudication of Claim that is filed with the WCAB, and all orders or awards of the WCAB or the Rehabilitation Unit.

In any case where the employee is being paid less than the maximum compensation rate for workers' compensation benefits, CR10101.1 requires that the claim file include documentation of an investigation of the employee's earnings. Notes and documentation must also be maintained within a claim file regarding "the provision, delay, or denial of benefits, including any electronically stored documentation" (e.g. reference to the fact that a denial of a claim is based upon tape-recorded voice evidence or on film evidence).

✱ Per CR10102, closed claim files cannot be destroyed until expiration of each of the time periods that are listed below.
     1. Five years after the injury, AND
     2. One year after:
          a. The last provision of benefits, AND/OR

b. The finalization of the findings of a pending audit by the Audit Unit, AND/OR

c. All "compensation due or which may be due has been paid."

Occasionally, an employee who is entitled to compensation refuses to acknowledge correspondence or cash checks that are provided, or the employee may disappear without any forwarding address. Claim files cannot be destroyed where compensation is admittedly owed. Claim files will not be closed until all benefits due have been paid or the WCAB determines that the employer has no further liability for benefits (e.g. by approval of a Compromise and Release settlement or issuance of an Order of Dismissal of Claim).

On April 1st of each year, every claims administrator is required to file an annual report of inventory with the Administrative Director of the Division of Workers' Compensation. Per CR10104, a separate report is required for each adjusting location where claim files are administered. The report will identify a person who is responsible for coordinating any scheduled audits with the Audit Unit. The report will include the total number of claims administered at an adjusting location and separately identify the number of claims for each self-insured employer or insurer liable for the payment of compensation. Self-insured employers can comply with CR10104 by submitting a "copy of both sides of part three of the Self-Insurer's Annual Report, 'Liabilities by Reporting Location' in lieu of separately listing data for that entity." This report is utilized by the Audit Unit in selection and scheduling of audits of claim files pursuant to LC129 (see 2.26).

2.24 CLAIM FILE RESERVES – IN GENERAL

Reserves are monies set aside to pay claims. Reserves are posted to individual claim files by the claimsperson handling the claim. Closing a claim file means closing all reserves on the file; the reserve is reduced to zero when no further compensation will be paid. When a claimsperson is asked to state the reserve for a claim, the answer will be the total incurred, an amount comprised of the sum of compensation paid to date plus the estimated dollar value of future liability for payment of compensation (the outstanding reserve). The total outstanding reserves posted to all claim files of an employer represents the amount of money that must be set aside, or reserved, in order to pay all currently open claims to their conclusion. Outstanding reserves for an employer are in a constant state of flux as new claims are received and existing claims are paid and closed on a daily basis.

An insurance company's financial ability of to pay all open claims to conclusion is monitored through the reporting of claim file reserves under the *California Workers' Compensation Uniform Statistical Reporting Plan* (2.9), and the reserves of self-insured employers are reported to the State in the Self-Insurer's Annual Report form. Statistical data is thereby available that reveals average reserves for various types of claims. Reporting of reserves that consistently deviate from established averages will be suspect and may lead to on-site audits of claim files. Inflated reserves may indicate an inability to administer claims expeditiously or without unnecessary litigation. Unusually low reserves may indicate that less than full compensation is being paid on claims and/or financial weakness is being concealed. From a regulatory standpoint, under-reserving is a problem that can lead to revocation of an employer's Certificate of Consent to Self-Insure or an insurance company's Certificate of Authority to transact business in California (see CR15300-15301 and IC11550-11558).

Insurance companies and self-insured employers both have additional motivations for assuring the overall accuracy of reserves posted to claim files. Of prime concern are investment decisions that need to be based upon accurate reserves. When reserves are over-valued, money is set aside and designated for payment of compensation that could otherwise be used for a preferable purpose such as income-producing investments. When claim file reserves are understated, insufficient monies are allocated to pay all compensation that becomes due. If other monies are not readily available to make compensation payments when due, a potential consequence is the general insolvency of the employer or insurance carrier.

Insured employers may take an interest in monitoring the accuracy of reserves posted to their claims, especially those who have some type of experience modification rating plan (see 2.12). A common concern is that overly-high reserves will cause them to pay proportionately higher insurance premiums. Some employers go so far as to pay for an audit of claim file reserves conducted by an independent auditor. If an employer has sufficient knowledge of workers' compensation laws to appraise the propriety of reserves posted to its claim files, the employer may question the appropriateness of reserves on one or more claim files by telephone or at a meeting with insurance company personnel.

For claims with 1994 or later injury dates, LC3761 provides insured employers with the right to request written reports of reserve amounts established on claims including estimated costs for benefits and itemization of other anticipated claims expenditures. Also, LC3762 requires an insurer to "discuss all elements of the claim file that affect the employer's premium with the employer" and to "supply copies of the documents that affect the premium at the employer's expense." Requirements for such discussions are restricted to "normal business hours." The employer's access to claim file information continues to be restricted as to documents that are protected "under the attorney-client privilege, any other applicable privilege, or" a statutory prohibition from disclosure (e.g. where the insurer must maintain confidentiality of information accumulated as part of a fraud investigation; see IC1877-IC1877.5).

Neither LC3761 nor LC3762 apply to claim files involving injury dates prior to 1994. Regardless of the date of injury involved, nothing prohibits an insurer from establishing reasonable procedures concerning the frequency or depth of detail of its response to claims inquiries or from charging a fee for its services. Indeed, due to the open rating system for workers' compensation insurance premises since 1995, it is commonplace to negotiate premiums that reflect the level of servicing that the employer wishes to receive.

2.25 CLAIM FILE RESERVES – ESTABLISHING

There are five categories of workers' compensation benefits: medical, temporary disability, permanent disability, rehabilitation, and death benefits. All benefits except medical benefits are called indemnity benefits. All claims files will be one of two types: medical only or indemnity files. Medical only files (MO's) are those where no benefit other than medical benefits will be paid. Indemnity files are those where any other category of benefit will be paid in addition to medical benefits (all litigated cases are reserved as indemnity files.) Indemnity benefits that are payable to an employee, or a dependent in a death case, are wage replacement benefits that are intended to indemnify the recipient (at least partially) for a wage loss that is caused by an injury. However, indemnity benefits also include any nonmedical benefits that are owed on a claim such as vocational rehabilitation services (see example below).

Indemnity files are commonly referred to interchangeably as "lost time" cases despite the fact that this label is not correct in all instances. Employees with medical only claims may lose less time from work than the noncompensable waiting period for temporary disability indemnity benefits (see 9.12). Employees can receive permanent disability benefits and never lose time from work (occasionally an employee is willing and able to continue working in his regular job with an arm or a leg in a cast, or the employer will allow the employee to continue working performing modified duties).

Medical only files are commonly handled by claim assistants or medical only clerks. Generally, an experienced claimsperson reviews the first notice of claim and determines that the claim is compensable, the injury is minor, no indemnity is payable, and the claim requires a person to review and process medical bills only. Many medical only files are paid and closed upon payment of the first bill. Unlike indemnity files, the method of establishing reserves on medical only files varies from one claims facility to another.

Most companies do not require claimspersons to post any dollar reserve to medical only files. A reserve may be automatically established by a computer using a coding system based upon probable medical costs for the type of injury sustained, or reserves may be based upon an aggregate method whereby an average cost is used as the reserve amount for all open medical only claims. Sometimes a specific reserve is posted only after payments exceed a specified value such as $500 or after the claim has remained open for a set period of time such as six months. At these break-off points, a claimsperson may be required to convert the file to an indemnity file by posting an anticipatory reserve for indemnity benefits based upon the likelihood that indemnity benefits may become payable.

The total reserve on an indemnity file is comprised of separate dollar values for medical and indemnity benefits. The estimated value of compensation to be paid in the future is determined from a review of all information that is known, including information reported in writing and/or readily available by telephone. Reserves are established at the time a claim file is created. Thereafter, the claimsperson is responsible for reevaluating the posted reserve on a continuous basis and increasing or decreasing the total reserve upon receipt of any information that alters the previous prediction of the amount of compensation that will be paid on the claim by the time it is closed.

Accuracy in reserving requires a claimsperson to know the full extent of every category of benefit that is allowed under the Labor Code. From this potential pool of benefits, the claimsperson identifies those specific benefits that are owed or may become payable in the future. (Note: Code of Regulations 15400 requires a claims administrator for a self-insured employer to "set a realistic estimate of incurred liability for each claim file and ... adjust the estimate upon receipt of medical reports, orders of the Appeals Board, or upon the administrator's own evaluation of the claim based on other relevant information that indicates the current estimate of future liability needs to be adjusted.") Each company has general guidelines, but the appraisal of each specific benefit in terms of its actual cost potential on the claim is based upon the experience and judgment of the claimsperson.

For example, if the first medical report contains a statement that the employee may require vocational rehabilitation services, a minimal reserve will be set immediately for any of the statutory categories of rehabilitation benefits in LC139.5 that might realistically be paid on this claim (see 11.5). A reserve may be set for vocational rehabilitation maintenance allowance benefits and for vocational services (such as an evaluation of potential rehabilitation services by a counselor and perhaps a job analysis), but usually no monies will be set aside for additional living expenses. When it is determined that the employee is a qualified injured worker or that rehabilitation services are necessary, additional reserves will be added to cover anticipated costs for maintenance allowance benefits, training, mileage, and counselor or vendor services. Further revisions in reserves can become increasingly more precise, e.g. where the reserve designated for counseling is based upon knowledge of the counselor's hourly rate and the estimated number of hours of counseling that will be provided (subject to the fee schedule in CR10132.1).

Most claims facilities have devised reserve worksheets (on paper or in a computer where entries are displayed and entered on a screen) to assist the claimsperson in establishing accurate reserves. Worksheets usually contain headings for each major category of benefits, subheadings for each subcategory of a benefit (e.g. death benefits are further broken down into burial expense and dependency benefits), and a listing of specific items for which payment is frequently provided when a particular benefit is owed (such as X-rays, treatment and medication under medical benefits). Extra space is usually provided for claimspersons to list additional specific items on a case by case basis (e.g. penalties owed by the insurer that do not affect the employer's premium).

Detailed listings help the claimsperson to make ongoing appraisals of each component portion of the overall claim reserve and assist in prompt identification of the need to change a reserve during the progress of a claim. Indeed, computer programs are in use that prevent a claimsperson from making a computer-generated claim payment in excess of the current posted reserve for various subcategories of expenditures that a particular company has chosen to monitor in this fashion. Information from detailed listings is also used by many companies for statistical or accounting purposes. Detailed cost breakdowns also enable presentation of specific documentation to address concerns of an employer or its insurance agent regarding the accuracy of reserves posted to particular claim files.

2.26 CLAIMS PRACTICES – STATE AUDITS

Effective 1990, the Labor Code provides for auditing of an employer's compliance with its statutory compensation obligations. Audits of the claim files of an insured or self-insured employer may be conducted at any time (with advance notice) by Auditors who are employed within the Audit Unit of the Division of Workers' Compensation (who are also referred to as Workers' Compensation Compliance Officers).

The purpose of the audits, as stated in LC129, is to "make certain that injured workers" or their dependents "receive promptly and accurately the full measure of compensation to which they are entitled." To effectuate this purpose, the Audit Unit is mandated to "audit insurers, self-insured employers, and third-party administrators to determine if they have met their compensation obligations under" the Labor Code or "the regulations of the administrative director" (under the Code of Regulations).

Approximately half of all audits will be scheduled on a random selection basis, but priority audits will be scheduled in direct and fairly immediate response to knowledge or belief that improper claims practices are occurring. For instance, an imminent nonrandom audit is a predictable response when improper claims practices are identified by Information and Assistance Officers, Rehabilitation Consultants, or other State employees in the performance of their duties. The Audit Unit also identifies candidates for priority audits based upon a ranking system that considers the number as well as the type of complaints that it receives from injured workers or other entities involved in a claim, e.g. a medical or rehabilitation provider who complains of improper delays in payment of bills.

Per LC129, if an Auditor "determines that any compensation, interest, or penalty" that is due to an employee or dependent has not been paid, a notice of assessment will be issued that orders the amount due to be paid. A copy of the notice will be sent to the person entitled to payment. If payment is not made within 30 days after service of the notice, the employer will additionally be liable for attorney fees that are thereafter "incurred by the employee or dependents to obtain amounts due." Concurrently with a notice of assessment of unpaid compensation, interest or penalty under LC129, the employer will receive a notice of assessment of an administrative penalty under LC129.5 for its delay in providing amounts determined to be due (see 2.26). Note also that should the employer refuse or merely delay payment for more than 15 days after service of a notice of assessment under LC129, the employer can be assessed an additional administrative penalty under LC129.5 for its delay in the payment of the administrative penalty that was previously assessed!

The Labor Code does not specify the manner in which the employer may contest or appeal a notice of assessment of unpaid compensation, interest, or penalty. Rather, LC129 provides that a determination of a State auditor "shall not in any manner limit the jurisdiction or authority of the appeals board to determine the issue." The procedure for pursuing an appeal is set out in CR10952. There is one prerequisite to filing "an Appeal of Notice of Compensation Due" with the WCAB. First, the employer must file a timely objection (within 30 days of issuance per CR10105) "to a notice of intention to issue notice of compensation due." Failure to comply with this administrative prerequisite "may result in dismissal of the" employer's appeal before the WCAB. Once a notice of compensation due has issued, the employer has 15 days from receipt to institute an appeal under CR10952.

On April 1st of each year the State is required to publish a report of the results of "audits conducted pursuant to" LC129 "during the preceding calendar year." Per LC129, this annual report will identify by name of each insurer, self-insured employer, and third party administrator whose files were audited the "total number of files audited, the number of violations found by type and amount of compensation, interest and penalties payable, and the amount collected for each violation."

Per LC129, the only administrative penalties that will appear on the annual report will be ones that were assessed in an earlier audit that remain unpaid at the time of a later audit. Administrative penalties that are paid timely will not appear in the State's published report nor will administrative penalties that are assessed for any violations other than a late payment of compensation, interest or a penalty. For instance, an administrative penalty that is assessed pursuant to LC129.5 for failure to provide an employee with a timely notice of termination of payment of temporary disability benefits will not appear in this report.

2.27 CLAIMS PRACTICES – PENALTY ASSESSMENTS

Effective 1990, LC129.5 mandates the assessment of administrative and civil penalties for a variety of improper claims practices. Each occurrence of an improper claims practice constitutes a violation for which a penalty may potentially be assessed. However, penalties are only assessed when and if a violation is identified during a State audit of the employer's claim files. Per LC78, penalties collected "shall be deposited into the Workplace Health and Safety Revolving Fund" and used to fund grants for which employers or employee organizations may apply "to assist in establishing effective occupational injury and illness prevention programs." Proceeds from this fund are expended for grants to applicants only upon approval of the Commission on Health and Safety and Workers' Compensation at 30 Van Ness Avenue, Room 2122, San Francisco, CA 94102.

It is not necessary to list each improper claims practice that provides a basis for assessment of administrative penalties. Almost any and every noncompliance with a statutory requirement to provide notices, reports or compensation can be a basis for the assessment of an administrative penalty. For instance, failure to pay or appeal any notice of assessment of compensation, interest or penalty due under LC129 (see 2.26) within 15 days from receipt will result in assessment of an administrative penalty under LC129.5. Likewise, failure to pay or contest any notice of assessment of an administrative penalty under LC129.5 within fifteen days of receipt will result in assessment of an additional administrative penalty.

The amount of a single administrative penalty will vary according to the type of improper claims practice from $100 to a maximum of $5,000. (Effective 1/28/94, CR10111.1 sets out a schedule of penalty amounts for specific violations that applies to cases involving 1994 or later injury dates.) However, a finding of multiple separate violations and/or multiple instances of a particular violation during the same audit can result in a total assessment of administrative penalties in excess of $5,000.

A civil penalty differs from an administrative penalty in that the maximum monetary limit for a civil penalty is $100,000; the improper claims practices that provide a basis for the penalty must be "knowingly committed" and performed with such "frequency as to indicate a general business practice"; and, the administrative director cannot assess a civil penalty until a hearing has been held. Multiple civil penalties may be assessed as a result of a solitary audit or separate and unrelated audits. In the event that "a second or subsequent" civil penalty is assessed, the State certificate that is required to process claims at the particular claims facility (the separate certificates required of insurers, self-insurers, and third-party administrators of self-insurers' claim files) can be revoked after a hearing by the appropriate State agency (either the Insurance Commissioner or the Director of the Department of Industrial Relations). Any of the following claims practices can result in a civil penalty assessment under LC129.5:

1. Inducing employees "to accept less than compensation due."
2. Making "it necessary for employees to resort to legal proceedings against the employer to secure compensation due."
3. Refusing to "comply with known and legally indisputable compensation obligations."
4. The discharging or administering of "compensation obligations in a dishonest manner."
5. Administering claims in such "a manner as to cause injury to the public or those dealing with the employer or insurer."

Penalty assessments under LC129.5 apply solely to claims for injuries that occurred on or after 1/1/90, the effective date of this statute. However, other statutory provisions that also address the topic of improper claims practices are applicable regardless of the date of injury. For instance, LC5814 provides that when "payment of compensation has been unreasonably delayed or refused either prior to or subsequent to the issuance of an award, the full amount of the order, decision or award shall be increased by 10 percent." Labor Code 3702 provides a basis for the revocation of an employer's Certificate of Consent to Self-Insure should either the employer or its "agent in charge of the administration" of its compensation obligations engage in any of several specified claims practices (all of which are encompassed under LC129.5).

2.28 FRAUD – IN GENERAL

Fraudulent acts are known to have been committed by virtually every entity involved in workers' compensation claims. It is for this reason, the standard antifraud clause in LC5401.7 is required to appear on certain forms that are required to be completed by employees, employers, physicians and attorneys (see 2.22).

Examples of fraud on the part of insured employers include making intentional misstatements of payroll information in order to avoid full payment of premiums that are owed or misstating the facts of an employee's injury in an attempt to defeat the employee's claim (see IC11760and LC6410.5). Employers sometimes lie to obtain benefits for persons who are not covered under the employer's workers' compensation insurance policy (e.g. a business owner, relatives or friends). Other entities who may be proper targets of fraud investigations include providers of medical services, legal representatives and agents of either. Actions of claimspersons can also be fraudulent, e.g. accepting known fraudulent claims, denying known compensable claims, or intentionally discouraging injured workers from "claiming benefits or pursuing a claim" (see IC1871.4).

Per LC3219, effective 7/16/93, it is a felony to offer or provide any type of inducement (monetary or otherwise) to a claim adjuster. It is also a felony for a claimsperson to request or receive prohibited inducements. Specifically, LC3219 states that "any adjuster of claims for compensation, as defined in" LC3207 (see 1.9) "who accepts or receives any rebate, refund, commission, preference, patronage, dividend, discount, or other consideration, as compensation, induce-ment, or reward for the referral or settlement of any claim, is guilty of a felony." (Note: LC3219 also contains provisions that apply to medical providers and allow for divestiture of improper financial gains.)

Also effective 7/16/93, IC1871.5 provides for the divestiture, after a convic-tion, of all compensation that was received as a result of claim fraud (e.g. commission of any act that is prohibited by IC1871.4). The claims administrator would seek a recovery of monies paid by requesting the WCAB to issue an Order Directing Restitution (see 9.30). Effective 1994, the fraudulent activities of medical providers and attorneys can result in the assessment of civil penalties per LC3820. This statute provides that it is unlawful to "knowingly operate or participate in a service that, for profit, refers or recommends clients or patients to obtain medical or medical-legal services or" workers' compensation benefits (e.g. the operation of a referral service that profits from the solitary function of referring employees to other entities such as medical providers or attorneys). Effective 1995, PC803 provides that the statute of limitations for prosecution of a claim-related fraud commences upon the date of discovery of the fraud.

2.29 FRAUD – SPECIAL INVESTIGATION UNIT

Since 1992, insurance companies have been required by IC1875.20 to "maintain a unit or division to investigate possible fraudulent claims by insureds or by persons making claims ... against policies held by insureds." The internal unit established for this purpose is commonly referred to as a "special investigation unit" (SIU). Ordinarily, a Special Investigation Unit will be staffed with the insurer's own employees, although IC1875.21 allows an insurer the option of "contracting with others for that purpose." An insurer need not hire additional staff nor assign any of its existing staff to exclusive duties relative to fraud investigations. Rather, IC1875.23 permits an insurer to assign such duties to "employees whose principal responsibilities are the investigation and disposition of claims" (e.g. claimpersons or claim supervisors).

Activities of a Special Investigation Unit may be limited or broad in scope depending upon the size of a particular insurer and the availability of finances and internal and external resources. At a minimum, there must be a means for ensuring a review of claim files sufficient to identify all circumstances that are required to be reported to the Fraud Bureau (see 2.27). With sufficient staffing, funding, and outside resources, investigations of fraud can be nearly as complete as those conducted by law enforcement agencies. An intended goal of an investigation is to accumulate evidence that is sufficient to result in a conviction.

Some self-insured employers have established fraud investigation units on a voluntary basis. Self-insurers are victims of the same type of fraudulent acts (both internal such as actions of claimspersons or external such as medical billing fraud) and nothing prevents a self-insured employer from duplicating the antifraud efforts of insurers. It makes sense for self-insured employers to respond with equal vigilance and thereby experience cost savings that result from an active interest in identifying and resisting fraudulent claims. Besides, self-insured employers are subject to the same requirements for reporting fraud to the State as insurance companies.

2.30 FRAUD – REPORTING

The provisions of the Workers' Compensation Insurance Fraud Reporting Act (IC1877-IC1877.5) apply to insurance companies, self-insured employers, and third party administrators. Some confusion regarding application of the act to self-insured employers derives from the title of the act itself as well as the fact that the provisions of the act are found in the Insurance Code. However, "insurer" (for purposes of this Act) is defined in IC1877.1 as meaning any "insurer admitted to transact workers' compensation insurance in this state" and a self-insured employer or third-party administrator.

Reporting is required by IC1877.3 whenever an insurer "believes it knows the identity of a person whom it has reason to believe committed a fraudulent act relating to a workers' compensation claim." Such persons can include workers' compensation claimants, insurance company employees, legal providers, medical providers and employees of pharmacies. Reporting is also required when an insurer has knowledge of "a fraudulent act that is believed not to have been reported to an authorized governmental agency." Within 30 days from the date its duty arose under either of these circumstances, the insurer is required to notify both of these entities:

1. The Fraud Division (formerly the Bureau of Fraudulent Claims) of the California Department of Insurance (CDI), AND
2. The "local district attorney's office."

Pursuant to IC1877.3, all insurers (including self-insurers) are required to use a prescribed form "for purposes of reporting suspected fraudulent workers' compensation acts." There are actually two required forms for workers' compensation claims (different forms are required if suspected fraud involves property claims, automobile claims, or other types of casualty claims such as long-term disability claims). The form that details the suspected fraud and specifies all allegations and evidence in support thereof is the Suspected Fraudulent Claim form (CDI-FB-1). This form has a second page that provides identifying information such as addresses and telephone numbers for all persons or entities involved (CDI-FB-2). A supply of currently required forms can be obtained from the Fraud Division, State of California, Department of Insurance, 9342 Tech Center Dr., Suite 500, Sacramento, CA 95826.

The job of the claimsperson is to recognize and report suspected fraudulent acts. There is no requirement for the claimsperson to prove fraud — that is the job of the Fraud Division and the district attorney's office (and the purpose of the required reports to these entities). Once a matter has been referred to the Fraud Division, the claimsperson may receive inquiries from other entities such as law enforcement agencies. The insurer is required by IC1877.3 to release certain information to a "requesting authorized governmental agency," and IC1877.5 grants an insurer limited immunity from civil liability as a result of complying with its statutory reporting requirements concerning fraud.

To protect against the potential for civil liability, the greatest care should be exercised to avoid any referral that is based upon malice or any release of information that is not protected by the immunity provisions of IC1877.5. For instance, there is no immunity for a claimsperson who informs a physician's staff that bills are not being paid because the physician is suspected of perpetrating a fraud. Likewise, there is no immunity for the assistant to the personnel director who informs coemployees that the claim of a particular employee is being investigated for fraud.

[3] JURISDICTION

3.1 WCAB JURISDICTION – IN GENERAL

Jurisdiction of a court refers to the court's authority to act on a particular matter. A party who seeks legal relief must pursue redress through a court that has authority, or jurisdiction, to grant the type of relief being sought. The WCAB has jurisdiction over those matters that are specified in the Labor Code including jurisdiction over claims for compensation under the California workers' compensation laws. The WCAB has jurisdiction to decide if it has jurisdiction and may rule that it does not. This could be the case where an individual does not have a legal right arising out of the Labor Code, or the person comes under the jurisdiction of federal laws or the laws of some other state.

3.2 WCAB – EXCLUSIVE JURISDICTION

Per LC5300, the WCAB has exclusive jurisdiction over "the recovery of compensation, or concerning any right or liability arising out of or incidental thereto." No other court in California has this authority (the WCAB's jurisdiction to decide jurisdiction is concurrent, not exclusive, because a civil court also has jurisdiction to determine that the WCAB has jurisdiction over a matter that was filed incorrectly with the civil court). Physicians who object to the employer's denial of payment for services rendered to an injured worker must present their claims to the WCAB. Employees seeking California workers' compensation benefits must file their claims with the WCAB. Dissatisfaction with decisions rendered by the WCAB does not entitle a party to file a claim for a second opinion with some other court such as a municipal or superior court. Rather, proper recourse is an appeal of the decision of the WCAB to the civil appellate court.

3.3 CALIFORNIA vs. OTHER JURISDICTION

Workers' compensation is a state law, and the WCAB's jurisdiction is limited to matters arising out of California laws. Some workers in California are covered under the laws of another state or come under a federal law. Some workers are not covered under any workers' compensation law. The Labor Code specifies the circumstances that invoke the jurisdiction of the WCAB. Jurisdiction can exist over a person who lives, works, was hired, or is injured in California.

3.4 CONTRACT OF HIRE IN CALIFORNIA

Per LC3600.5, whenever an employee "has been hired" in California, the employee is "entitled to compensation according to the law of this state." The employee may work and reside in a different state. The employee has the right to claim benefits under California law solely on the basis that he was hired in this state.

A contract of hire is one that creates an employment relationship. The necessary elements of the contract are an offer and an acceptance. A contract exists when there is a mutual understanding that the employee accepts employment upon the terms offered by the employer. The contract arises at the time the understanding is reached. It is therefore necessary to identify the physical location of the parties at the time the contract was made.

If the final act that gave rise to the contract took place in California, then California has jurisdiction over a claim for compensation. For instance, a contract of hire over the telephone will be a contract of hire in California when the employee (offeree) was located in California at the time the employee uttered the final words of acceptance of the offer of employment extended by the employer (offeror). When the contract of hire is in writing, it is necessary to determine what final act gave rise to the creation of the contract, for instance the signing of, or receipt of, formal documents of employment.

The employee's regularly assigned work location may be in some other state, and the employee may never perform any work in this state. For instance, California jurisdiction has arisen where employees of national companies were required to come to the employer's home office location in California to sign a formal contract of hire. However, the employer need not have any employment location or representative in this state. A California resident might respond to a newspaper advertisement placed by an out-of-state employer who offers permanent employment in a different state. The employer's only contact with California may be due to the mere coincidence of the employee's residence in California at the time the employee sought to be employed in, and move to, a different state. If the out-of-state employer communicated entirely by telephone or entirely in writing, California's interest in the contract seems somewhat tenuous, but jurisdiction may still be exercised.

3.5 REGULARLY EMPLOYED IN CALIFORNIA

Per LC3600.5, California has jurisdiction over all employees who are "regularly employed in this State." This is true regardless of where the employee was hired, resides or is injured. The regular employment qualification clearly refers to any employees who work at one job site that has a California address. If the employee works solely at one California location, then no jurisdictional dispute would arise. In addition, California jurisdiction is clear when a person who is regularly employed in California is injured during a temporary work assignment in some other state. Per LC3600.5, such employees "shall be entitled to compensation according to the law of this state."

The employer may or may not have a regular place of business in California. An out-of-state employee with unique skills may be sent to a branch office in California to provide his expertise on a specific project. A national company without any business operations in this state may hold a business meeting for some of its countrywide employees at a California hotel or resort. The fact that the employer has an ongoing place of business in this state is not controlling on the issue of jurisdiction. Employees who travel to California to perform services for a temporary and specified period of time and are thereafter scheduled to return to a regular work location in another state are not regularly employed in this state.

It is possible that temporary assignments in California may be repeated with enough frequency to constitute regular employment in this state. For instance, a route supervisor or a regional director may spend 50 to 60% of his time at the employer's California offices. The jurisdiction of some other state may be undisputed whereas California jurisdiction is tenuous. However, the WCAB has jurisdiction to determine whether the employee meets the LC3600.5 requirement of being "regularly employed in this state." Should the WCAB determine that the employee's work assignments constitute regular employment within this state, California jurisdiction can be invoked even if the employee's injury is sustained while working in another state.

3.6 RESIDENT OF CALIFORNIA

A residence address in California is not sufficient in and of itself to invoke California jurisdiction. An employee is not entitled to receive California benefits just because his employer has a corporate location or address in this state. The employee may reside in California or he may merely maintain a mailing address in California while residing in a different state. Additional criteria are required before the employee will come under California jurisdiction for a workers' compensation claim.

Under LC5305, California jurisdiction covers some employees who are injured outside this state. There is a two-part requirement. The employee must be "a resident of this state at the time of injury and the contract of hire" must be "made in this state." It has already been made clear that a contract of hire in California is sufficient for California jurisdiction. LC5305 does not change, amend, or alter this basic criterion. The fact that the employee is a California resident will not give rise to California jurisdiction by itself; a contract of hire made in this state will. Sometimes the state where the contract was made is disputed. In such cases the fact of California residency may sway the WCAB in favor of California jurisdiction. This would appear to be the basic effect of the reference to California residency in the statute.

3.7 STATE vs. STATE JURISDICTION

California decides jurisdictional disputes based upon California laws. It is possible that more than one state will have jurisdiction over one injury because of the separate application of each state's own law. The employee may file a claim in California because the contract of hire was made here. The same employee may also file a claim in one or more additional states. These could be states where the employee resides or is regularly employed or was injured. California clearly has jurisdiction. One or more other states may also have jurisdiction. There is no California law that prevents the employee from filing a claim in multiple jurisdictions; however, the employee's recovery in another state can be credited against, or deducted from, the amount of any California benefits that may be awarded (see 3.10).

3.8 RECIPROCITY OF JURISDICTION

Per the authority of LC3600.5, California has an official agreement with a small number of other states that only one state's jurisdiction will apply to the same injury. Nevada and Oregon have had reciprocal agreements with California in the past. The Workers' Compensation Insurance Rating Bureau would be the proper source for an inquiry as to what states presently have such agreements (see 2.10). The reciprocity agreement coordinates the workers' compensation laws of the two states. The agreement is set forth in the law of each state under an extraterritorial jurisdiction provision that refers to the state's authority to accept jurisdiction for an injury that occurs in a different state. No state has reciprocity of jurisdiction with another unless that state also has a mutually reciprocal provision in its laws.

Reciprocity does not pertain to employees who were hired in California since California always has jurisdiction in such cases. Reciprocity pertains to a situation where the employee has an injury while working temporarily in a state that is not his normal place of employment. Reciprocity means that the state where the employee was temporarily employed has no jurisdiction. The home state retains jurisdiction. Each state retains jurisdiction over injuries sustained by its employees while they are working in the reciprocating state. If the employee filed a claim in the state where the employment was temporary, that state would not have jurisdiction according to the provisions of its own laws.

There is one further element to jurisdictional reciprocity. The employer must secure the payment of workers' compensation benefits under the law of the state where the employee is regularly employed. California will not deny jurisdiction to an employee who is injured in this state if the employer has not secured workers' compensation benefits in the home state. This is true even if both states have a reciprocal provision in their laws. The employer's coverage of the employee under another state's workers' compensation act is a prerequisite to a denial of California's jurisdiction.

The purpose served by reciprocal agreements is the elimination of concurrent filings in multiple jurisdictions. Reciprocity prevents the employee from electing jurisdictions and/or filing concurrent cases. It places jurisdiction with the state having the greatest governmental interest in the employee rather than the injury. Jurisdiction does not ensue from the employee's selective appraisal or comparison of benefits under the laws of different states. Rather, jurisdiction ensues from the provisions of state laws. Since reciprocating states have equivalent statutory provisions, each one knows in advance how the other will handle a particular situation.

3.9 RECIPROCITY OF PROCEEDINGS

There are occasions where a hearing on a California case will be conducted in a different state with the other state applying California laws to the matters in dispute. This may be necessary where the employee has moved to another state after an injury and, for some reason, is unable to attend a proceeding in California. Cross-examination of out-of-state physicians can be conducted in the same manner. In order for this to be done, the other state must agree to take on this extra work. Not all states will do this. Those that do usually require that California reciprocate. This type of reciprocity does not involve jurisdiction. One state has jurisdiction, and the other is willing to assist in a procedural way such as hearing witnesses' testimony. However, the foreign court will not decide the case.

When testimony is taken in another state, the law of the state having jurisdiction is applied. The referring state must advise the other tribunal of its laws. This does not amount to sending another state a copy of California's Labor Code. It requires specific explanation of statutory provisions that are pertinent to the matter at hand. The tribunal receiving this information is expected to read it and achieve an understanding of it before conducting a proceeding. Some states are not willing to take on this type of task. Those that do have usually had an opportunity to require this same assistance in the past.

Reciprocity may be limited to specific areas. Some states will hold a hearing. Others will not. Some states will provide a transcript of a proceeding free of charge. Others require a fee for this service. Others will not provide a transcript. The WCAB Policy and Procedure Manual contains a reciprocity directory for other states that designates what another state will or will not do and the cost involved. This list also contains a directory of telephone numbers and addresses for the workers' compensation tribunals in other states. A state's position on reciprocity is subject to change. It is thus wise to contact a particular state directly at the time a reciprocity question arises.

3.10 MULTISTATE AWARDS

Very few states have reciprocity of jurisdiction with California. It is thus possible for multiple states to have jurisdiction over the same claim and for multiple awards to be issued for the same injury. Through case law, a policy has evolved that limits the employee's recovery in multiple jurisdictions. The employee can claim workers' compensation benefits in different jurisdictions. The total amount the employee can collect from the employer is limited.

An investigation should be conducted to determine the nature and extent of benefits the employee was awarded by some other state(s). The employee may be entitled to a greater payment under California law for any category of benefits. For example, California law may provide:

a A higher weekly compensation rate for temporary or permanent disability or a larger maximum payment for dependency benefits.
b. Compensation for a type of disability that is not compensable under the law of the other state such as loss of sense of smell or a prophylactic work restriction.
c. Payment for a category of benefits that is not provided under the law of the other state such as rehabilitation benefits.
d. Payment of an expense that is not compensable in the other state such as medical-legal expenses or the cost of a specific type of treatment such as services provided by psychologists or acupuncturists.

A publication that is useful in comparing benefit provisions of different states is the *Analysis of Workers' Compensation Laws*. This annual publication is available for a fee from the Chamber of Commerce of the United States, 1615 "H" Street N.W., Washington, D.C. 20062. The employer will not be ordered to repay any benefits it has already paid to the employee. Under an award in a different state, the employer may have made payment for the full period of temporary disability at the rate of $400/week. The WCAB can order the employer to pay the difference (e.g. $90/week or whatever the difference may be) between the California weekly rate and the weekly rate in the other state. Likewise, the employee's recovery for each benefit area is limited to the difference between the full payment of benefits under California law and the amount of the payment that the employee has already received for the same specie of benefit.

3.11 CONCURRENT JURISDICTION – CALIFORNIA COURTS

Concurrent jurisdiction exists when more than one tribunal has authority to make decisions over the same employee for the same injury. This will occur when the employee has separate legal rights and remedies under different laws. Multistate awards are one example of concurrent jurisdiction. The WCAB can also have concurrent jurisdiction with a different California court, a civil court, or a federal court. It is possible for longshore and harbor workers to have concurrent remedies under state and federal compensation laws. The employee can have a civil remedy against a negligent third party and a concurrent right to file a claim with the WCAB. In limited situations, the employee may have a right to workers' compensation benefits and a separate civil remedy against his employer.

3.12 EXCLUSIVE REMEDY RULE

Compulsory workers' compensation laws established workers' compensation benefits as the employee's exclusive remedy against his employer. A basic trade-off between the parties was codified in the Labor Code. Employers became liable for compensation "without regard to negligence." Employees lost their right to sue their employers for civil damages to compensate them for the effects of a work injury.

Per LC3600, the employer is liable for compensation "in lieu of any other liability whatsoever." This provision is restated in LC3706 that provides that compensation is the "sole and exclusive remedy of the employee or his or her dependents against the employer." As final as this language sounds, exceptions exist. Labor Code 3600 refers to "specific exemptions to the employee's exclusive remedy " that are detailed in Labor Code sections 4558, 3602, 3706, and 3715 (see 2.20 regarding uninsured employers). Other exceptions exist due to concurrent rights of employees under other state and federal statutes (see 3.13).

3.13 CIVIL REMEDIES AGAINST EMPLOYER

The WCAB may lack jurisdiction over a claim for a work injury. If so, the employee's remedy is through the civil courts. Per LC3715, this will be the case for certain employees of homeowners. Per LC3352, other types of workers may also be barred from coverage under the Labor Code. Specific criteria must be met before any worker is entitled to workers' compensation benefits. If the conditions contained in LC3600 are not met, the worker has no entitlement to benefits. These sections pertain to persons who are excluded from coverage under the Labor Code. These workers have the right to seek civil remedies for work-related injuries. Per LC3602, the employer's liability will be the "same as if" the Labor Code "had not been enacted." This means the employer is liable only for damages but not for workers' compensation benefits (see 2.20).

Ordinarily when the employee is entitled to workers' compensation benefits, the employee is not also entitled to sue the employer for civil damages. Three specific exceptions to the exclusive remedy of LC3600 are listed in LC3602(b). The employee can sue the employer for civil damages in addition to workers' compensation benefits in any of the following situations:

1. **Assault by Employer.** The injury results from "a willful physical assault by the employer." For example, the employer intentionally punches the employee or strikes him over the head with a lead pipe.
2. **Fraudulent Concealment.** The employee's injury "is aggravated by the employer's fraudulent concealment of the existence of the injury" and/or "its connection with the employment." For example, the employer may be aware of side effects of chemicals used in the workplace but fail to inform its employees of the potential for injury, or the employer may require the employee to continue working with the chemicals after being notified that the employee has health problems that are known to result from this exposure.

3. Defective Product. The employee's injury "is caused by a defective product manufactured by the employer." The employer must first transfer the product to "an independent third person." The product must leave the employer's ownership and control. Thereafter, the third party provides the defective product for the employee's use, and an injury results. For example, the employer manufactures a defective automobile that it sells it to a car rental business. The employee rents this car while on a business trip and sustains an injury as a result of the defect.

Power Press Exception. An additional exception to exclusive remedy is stated in LC4558. The employee can sue the employer for damages if an injury is "caused by the employer's knowing removal of, or failure to install, a point of operation guard on a power press." Almost every term inside the quotation marks is separately defined in LC4558. Some additional criteria are also required as a prerequisite to a civil action. "The removal or failure to install" must have been "specifically authorized by the employer," and the employer must also have knowledge of the "probability of serious injury or death." If each and every qualifying factor can be proved, the employee will not be limited to the exclusive remedy of workers' compensation for a resultant injury.

Concurrent Civil Remedies. A variety of state and federal statutes enable civil suits against an employer by its employees, whether or not the employees have sustained work-related injuries. For instance, employees can sue their employer in civil court for libel, slander, false imprisonment or wrongful termination. Civil remedies can also derive from any type of alleged discriminatory behavior that is prohibited under state or federal law such as discrimination because of disability (see 11.35), age, gender, or reporting of the employer's violations of laws that were enacted for the protection of employees (under so called "whistleblower" laws). As a general rule, the exclusive remedy provisions of the Labor Code do not vacate concurrently applicable provisions of other state and federal laws that would provide a comparable, uninjured employee with a civil remedy. The Labor Code merely limits the financial recovery that the employer owes for a work injury alone.

3.14 EXCLUSIVE REMEDY – DUAL CAPACITY

An employment relationship may not be the only relationship between the parties; the employer may be operating in a dual capacity. Suppose a nurse is employed by a physician who renders treatment to her for an industrial injury. A physician-patient relationship exists. The physician is both a physician and an employer. Suppose the employee is an apartment manager. A landlord-tenant relationship exists. If the employer is a manufacturer and allows its employees to purchase its products on the premises, there is a seller-buyer (customer) relationship.

Work-related injuries can arise during a time that the employer is acting in some dual capacity. The employer's dual capacity does not give rise to dual civil and workers' compensation remedies. Per LC3600(a), "the fact that either the employee or the employer also occupied another or dual capacity prior to, or at the time of, the employee's industrial injury shall not permit the employee ... to bring an action at law for damages against the employer." The employee's right to a civil remedy exists only in those situations specifically stated in LC3602, 3706, 3715, or 4558.

The one statute pertaining to dual capacity is LC3602(b-3). This provision is set forth in great detail and applies solely to specifically-described situations where the employer is also a manufacturer, and the employee is an end user of its product. This statute does not apply to every situation where the employer happens to be a manufacturer. In those dual capacity situations that are not described in LC3602, if an employer-employee relationship exists at the time of injury, then the employee's sole and exclusive remedy against the employer is workers' compensation.

3.15 CIVIL REMEDIES AGAINST THIRD PARTIES

The employee may be injured by the negligence of a third party while the employee is acting within the course of his employment. If so, the employee has dual remedies. The employee may file a claim against his employer for workers' compensation benefits. Per LC3852, this claim "does not affect his or her claim or right of action for all damages ... against any person other than the employer." The exclusive remedy provisions of the Labor Code restrict civil actions against a negligent employer.

The employee's civil action arises out of a workers' compensation claim, but it is not a remedy against the employer. It is a concurrent or dual remedy arising out of an industrial injury. Some examples of potential third party targets for civil damages include:

a. The manufacturer of a defective product, e.g. a defective punch press, vehicle, ladder, or tool.

b. Anyone in the chain of distribution of a defective product, e.g. the warehouse where the defect was created in a product that was later used by the employee or a distributor who previously had the product under its direction and control.

c. A negligent provider of a service, e.g. the restaurant or hotel where the employee contracted food poisoning or the contractor whose employees made negligent repairs at the employee's workplace.

d. The individual whose negligence caused an injury, e.g. the negligent driver of an automobile or an irate customer who kicks the employee in the knee.

e. The employer of the negligent individual, e.g. the company that employs a negligent driver or the company employing a negligent loader-unloader at a delivery site.

f. The owner or lessor of property where a defect in the property results in injury, e.g. the owner of a delivery site where the employee slips and falls or the roof collapses.

3.16 SUBROGATION – CIVIL SUITS

Where the employer becomes liable for workers' compensation benefits as a result of the negligence of a third party, the employer has a right of recovery, also referred to as a right of "subrogation," against the negligent third party. This right is stated in LC3852. The employer can seek a recovery of any amount the employer pays or becomes obligated to pay as compensation as well as "all salary, wage, pension, or other emolument paid to the employee or to his or her dependents."

The employer's right of recovery exists both concurrently with and independently of the employee's rights. For this reason, the method by which the employer seeks its recovery is determined by whether or not the employee institutes a civil suit against the third party. If the employee files a civil suit, the employer can join in the employee's action. The document used to effect the joinder is called a Complaint in Intervention. It may also behoove the employer to file a lien in the employee's civil case for the amount of workers' compensation benefits it has paid. The employer's lien will not prevent the employee from settling a case directly with the third party, but a lien may protect the employer's right to recover monies it has paid in the event of a judgment in the civil suit in some circumstances.

It is not always in the employer's best interests to merely join in a suit that has been filed by the employee. There are several reasons why an employer would prefer to file suit in its own name by filing an original civil complaint. The amount of the employer's potential recovery from a third party can be reduced or eliminated by the employee's actions or inactions. The employee's suit could be dismissed for lack of prosecution, or legal theories relied upon by the employee's attorney may conflict with those that the employer would otherwise rely upon to establish the negligence of a third party.

An employee may choose not to pursue a civil remedy where one exists, preferring instead to seek only workers' compensation benefits. In this case, the employer has no choice but to file its own civil action against the third party. When the employer files suit in its own name, the employer does not seek any recovery of damages that the employee could recover if suit was filed in the employee's name such as recovery for the employee's pain and suffering. Per LC3853, "if either the employee or the employer brings an action against such third person, he shall forthwith give to the other a copy of the complaint." The purpose of this notification is to enable either party to join in the suit filed by the other party.

3.17 EMPLOYER CREDIT FOR CIVIL RECOVERY

Per LC3600, any amount for which the employer is liable as compensation is credited against the amount of damages awarded to the employee by a civil court for the same injury. The statutory credit provision applies regardless of whether the civil award is payable by a third party or the employer. The credit provision prevents a duplicate or double recovery of workers' compensation benefits where there is concurrent civil and WCAB jurisdiction for an industrial injury. Civil awards are not added to WCAB awards; receipt of civil damages by the employee satisfies the employer's liability for compensation in the same amount.

Per LC3856, the employer's credit does not apply against any portion of damages that a court orders to be paid as "litigation expenses incurred in preparation and prosecution of such action, together with a reasonable attorney's fee." The employer is entitled to a credit only for money that the employee actually receives, commonly referred to as the employee's "net recovery." If the employer pays compensation prior to a civil recovery, the employer does not owe additional compensation unless and until compensation becomes due over and above the amount of the civil recovery. If civil damages are awarded prior to any payment of compensation benefits, the employer does not owe compensation unless and until the amount of compensation otherwise payable exceeds the amount of the employee's civil recovery.

LC3600 has been interpreted to give the employer a credit when a civil case is settled out of court rather than by judgment. The amount the third party pays the employee, less attorney's fees and any incurred costs of litigation, is a credit to the employer. Instead of recovering this amount directly from the third party, the employer simply does not owe this amount of compensation to the employee.

Sometimes a joint settlement is worked out between an employee, his or her employer, and the third party. The WCAB form used for this purpose is a Third Party Compromise and Release. This form is submitted to the WCAB, because any release of workers' compensation benefits must be approved by a WCAB judge.

A third party settlement will be deemed adequate only if the employee's net recovery is equivalent to, or exceeds, the amount of compensation the employee would be entitled to receive if he only filed a workers' compensation claim. The employer and the third party may jointly contribute to the settlement amount, or the employer may waive its credit rights. In the latter case, the amount of any workers' compensation benefits previously paid is included in the total amount of the employee's settlement, but the employer waives its right to recover its previous payments from the negligent third party (see 3.18).

3.18 CREDIT RIGHTS – EMPLOYER NEGLIGENCE

Negligence is normally irrelevant in a workers' compensation claim, but the comparative negligence of the employer, if any, does affect the employer's credit rights in third party cases. If the employer's negligence was a causal factor in the employee's injury, the employer should not profit from its negligence. For this reason, where employer negligence is alleged, the percentage of comparative negligence of the employer will be determined by the jury in a civil proceeding, and the employer's credit for compensation will be reduced proportionately by the extent to which the employer was negligent. For instance, if the employer was found to be 50% negligent, the employer's credit would be subject to a maximum limit equal to 50% of the employee's net recovery in the civil suit. The employer may have paid compensation in excess of this amount, but it would be precluded from claiming a credit for any greater amount.

Problems arise where there is a question regarding employer negligence, but the employee settles a third party case out of court. In such cases, the percentage of the employer's negligence has not been determined by a jury and may be hotly disputed between the parties when the employer seeks to assert its credit rights. One solution to this dilemma is to request a WCAB hearing for the purpose of having a judge determine the percentage of the employer's negligence. This type of proceeding requires that a workers' compensation judge apply principles of civil negligence that are not ordinarily addressed in the WCAB forum. Understandably, some WCAB judges are reluctant to conduct such proceedings, and employers are reluctant to have their negligence determined in this forum.

Any dispute as to the percentage of the employer's negligence is commonly resolved by mutual agreement and encompassed within the terms of a Third Party Compromise and Release settlement agreement. The employer assesses the costs involved in obtaining a judicial determination of any negligence on its part as well as the likelihood of an adverse decision. This evaluation assists the employer in reaching a compromise under which the employer waives its right to any credit or accepts a reduced amount of credit for compensation.

There is a further alternative to obtaining a WCAB determination of the employer's negligence. The employer may agree to submit the matter to binding arbitration, e.g. through the American Arbitration Association. This alternative requires the acquiescence of the third party since any decision affects the amount it will pay.

3.19 STATE vs. FEDERAL JURISDICTION

Some employees in California are covered under the provisions of federal compensation acts (as set out in the United States Code). Below is a brief description of some of the various federal laws:
   a. Federal Employees' Compensation Act (FECA): for certain civil service employees of the United States government.
   b. Federal Employers' Liability Act (FELA): for employees of interstate railroads.
   c. Jones Act: for seamen on board vessels.
   d. High Seas Death Act: for death of a seaman.
   e. Longshore and Harbor Workers' Compensation Act (L&H Act): for the individuals described by its title.
   f. Defense Base Act: an extension of coverage under the Longshore and Harbor Workers' Compensation Act to certain employees on military, air or naval bases.
   g. Outer Continental Shelf Lands Act: an extension of Longshore and Harbor Workers coverage to employees whose work involves the natural resources of the continental shelf (land under navigable waters).

3.20 WCAB JURISDICTION FOR L&H ACT

It is possible for the WCAB to have jurisdiction over a Longshore and Harbor Workers' Act claim (a "L&H claim"). Authority for this is found in LC128. The WCAB is not required to do so but "may accept appointment as deputy commissioner ... to enforce" the Longshore and Harbor Workers' Compensation Act. If the WCAB chose to, it could provide such assistance by accepting jurisdiction and conducting proceedings. Benefits awarded would be those provided under the federal Longshore and Harbor Workers' Act.

The Workers' Compensation Appeals Board can have concurrent jurisdiction over a Longshore and Harbor Workers' Act claim. This could occur where a dispute arose as to whether state or federal law applied to the injury. Depending on the employee's duties and location at the time of injury, the employee may have dual remedies. It is not always clear which law applies. It is possible for the employee to receive concurrent, but not duplicate, state and federal compensation awards. Each award is a credit against any money paid by the employer under the other award.

3.21 WCAB JURISDICTION – INSURANCE CONTRACTS

The injury itself, or the employee's entitlement to compensation, may not be in dispute. The dispute may be limited to the issue of who is responsible to pay for compensation that is due, the employer or its insurance company. Disputes between employers and their insurers can delay the provision of benefits to deserving employees. By invoking WCAB jurisdiction, litigation proceedings can be effective in achieving the constitutional mandate to provide compensation expeditiously without encumbrance of any kind.

Disputes involving contracts between parties are ordinarily a matter for the civil courts, but the WCAB can, and has, accepted jurisdiction to resolve conflicts between the parties to a workers' compensation insurance policy. Authority for doing this is supported by various subsections of LC5300, as well as sections of the Insurance Code. Per IC11651, an insurer is liable for payment of compensation "for which the employer is liable, subject to the provisions, conditions, and limitations of the policy." The WCAB or an arbitrator (see below) can determine whether or not coverage is provided under an existing insurance contract. If so, the insurer can be ordered to pay benefits to the employee.

Since 1990, LC5275, provides that mandatory arbitration proceedings are required to resolve a disputed issue of insurance coverage with one exception. Per LC5270, arbitration is not required if the injured employee (or dependent in a death case) is not represented by an attorney. Labor Code 5271 permits the parties to mutually agree to the selection of any attorney to arbitrate a coverage dispute. If agreement is not possible, an arbitrator will then be selected in the normal manner from a list (or a panel) that is prepared by the presiding judge. Arbitration proceedings can be conducted at any time and place that is agreeable to the parties (rather than a district office of the WCAB). The parties are required to submit their evidence 10 days before arbitration proceedings, which are required to be held within 30 to 60 days after the selection of an arbitrator per LC5276. Per LC5277, the arbitrator is required to issue a Findings and Award within 30 days of submission of the case (any extension is by agreement only or else the arbitrator forfeits all fees and voids the arbitration proceeding). The costs of arbitration of an insurance coverage dispute will be borne equally by the employer and the insurer (or insurers). Per LC5277, the decision of an arbitrator can be appealed in the same manner as decisions of judges to the WCAB in San Francisco.

An insurance company can limit coverage under the policy to particular locations, operations, or employees. Thus, an insured employer can have some liability that is not covered under one insurance policy. The employer may have good reason to strenuously deny the existence of previously acceptable limitations on coverage. If there is no coverage under the policy, the employer can be faced with possible penalties and legal actions as an illegally uninsured employer (see 2.19). The issue for the WCAB or an arbitrator is whether the injured employee is entitled to coverage under the standard terms contained in the policy or whether coverage was limited intentionally by both the employer and the insurance company. The insurance company may have to pay benefits to an employee for whom no premium was collected or insufficient premium was collected. If so, the insurance company can thereafter file a civil action to recover unpaid premiums from the employer.

The employer may have obtained coverage by false representations where no coverage would have been provided if accurate information were known. For example, the insurance company may be able to document the fact that it does not sell insurance for certain high risk categories of employment such as blasting operations, all-night convenience stores, or ambulance drivers. Inaccurate information submitted by the employer may reveal an attempt to defraud the insurance company (and is prohibited by IC11760).

A mere misrepresentation of payroll is not an important issue to the WCAB or an arbitrator, since the insurance company was aware of the nature of the risk it insured. If premium was collected for the occupational classification that the employee comes under, it is difficult for the insurance company to deny coverage, but false representations of the nature of the employer's business operations are a different matter. The WCAB or an arbitrator is unlikely to endorse dishonest or fraudulent business practices by employers. Such employers are liable to be found to be illegally uninsured for specific employees even where an existing policy covers other employees.

A common coverage issue arises where the employer does not pay its premium. An employee subsequently has an injury and the employer claims "the check is in the mail," but the insurance company alleges a cancellation of the policy prior to the injury date. Per IC676.8, an insurer is required to provide a minimum of 10 days advance written notice of cancellation for failure to pay premium (30 days advance notice is required if notice of cancellation was based upon an employer's failure to comply with state or federal safety laws or there was a material change in ownership or business operations with a potential for affecting the anticipated frequency or severity of injuries).

The insurer is precluded by IC676.8 from canceling a policy within the required advance notice period if the employer "remedies the condition to the insurer's satisfaction." Coverage continues through the last moment of this grace period if payment is presented (or specified corrective action is taken). Most companies send cancellation notices via certified mail, return receipt requested. The receipt is very good evidence of an effective cancellation, since written documentation is always the best evidence in coverage disputes.

Where, for whatever reason, insufficient documentation exists, coverage issues are likely to be hotly disputed. Where coverage must be decided on the credibility of the parties, the trend is a decision in favor of the employer. From the WCAB's perspective, a decision in favor of valid insurance coverage for the employer has the desirable effect of a resultant prompt provision of benefits to the injured employee by the insurance company. Since the insurance company that becomes liable for payments in this manner has recourse through the civil courts to collect unpaid premiums, the WCAB or an arbitrator may not give the employer's misrepresentation regarding unpaid premiums the weight desired by the insurance company.

(THIS PAGE LEFT BLANK INTENTIONALLY)

[4] EMPLOYMENT

4.1 EMPLOYMENT – IN GENERAL

Employment is a necessary prerequisite to the receipt of workers' compensation benefits. An employment relationship must exist between a worker and an employer. The injured worker must be an employee as that term is defined in the Labor Code. The type of work engaged in must be a covered employment. Some types of employment are excluded from coverage under the workers' compensation law. Employees engaged in such work are excluded from entitlement to compensation. There are some exceptions to these basic principles, and these will be covered in detail.

4.2 EMPLOYMENT CONTRACT

An employment contract is defined by LC2750 as a contract "by which one, who is called the employer, engages another, who is called the employee, to do something for the benefit of the employer or a third person." This definition requires an action by both parties. The employer must engage a person to perform a service for its benefit. The employee must agree to perform the service under the direction and control of an employer.

An employee cannot create an employment contract by himself. If a stranger paints someone's house and then requests payment, there is no contract of employment. There was no understanding between the parties that an employment relationship would be created because the parties were unknown to each other at the time the service was performed. A person's willingness to accept employment is insufficient. A person is not an employee until the employer "engages," hires, or requests the person to perform a service for the employer's benefit. This is a voluntary and intentional action on the part of an employer that clearly relays an intent to engage a person in the employer's service.

The services rendered by an employee may benefit the employer directly or may provide a direct benefit to third persons who are not employers. If the employer owns a mattress factory, employees who make mattresses perform a service of direct benefit to the employer. A singer may be hired to sing for the benefit of patrons of a restaurant owner. The employer of a plumbing company may engage employees to perform plumbing work for the company's customers. Patrons and customers are examples of "third persons" who pay to obtain the services offered by a business·entity without creating any employment relationship between themselves and the person(s) performing services for their benefit.

After an injury occurs, the relationship of the parties is sometimes disputed. The employer may deny having any employees or any intent to create an employment relationship. The employer may have intended to engage an independent contractor (a self-employed person) rather than an employee. An injury may occur prior to some final act of formality; for instance, the employer may assert that the contract did not exist because a routinely required formal document had not yet been signed. The employer's position might result from an honest misunderstanding of the liberal interpretation that is given to the meaning of an employment contract; for example, a contract has been judicially determined to exist in cases where a job applicant is injured while performing try-out activities under the direction and control of an employer.

Employers can have self-serving reasons to deny the fact that a person was indeed in their employ. If the employer did not secure the payment of compensation, the employer could be liable for the fines and penalties assessed against uninsured employers. If the employer did not accurately report the number of its employees or their wages to its insurance carrier, the employer could be liable for retroactive premium charges. Regardless of the employer's reasons for denying employment status, the WCAB can determine that the facts support the existence of an employment relationship. An employment contract exists when the relationship of the parties is encompassed within the definition of an employment contract in LC2750.

4.3 CONSIDERATION

The LC2750 definition of employment contract makes no reference to payment or consideration for services performed. However, consideration is a necessary part of an employment contract, and it is often the major distinguishing element between an employee and a nonemployee where employment is disputed. In the absence of some type of consideration, there is no employment contract. Conversely, proof that consideration was provided can overcome an employer's denial of an employment relationship (see also 4.53).

Consider the reasons why employers engage and pay employees. Employers want someone to do something that benefits the employer. They can't do it themselves because they lack the knowledge or expertise needed. They may not want to do it themselves because they lack the time or motivation. They may require the assistance of others in order to complete a desired task. However, workers are unwilling to provide the desired services and come under the control of an employer without the provision of consideration in return for the services they provide.

Evidence of actual receipt, or promised receipt, of consideration by a worker supports the person's position that he was engaged to perform services under an employment contract. Consideration need not be money, but it must be something that has a monetary value, e.g. free rent provided to an apartment manager. Proof that no consideration was requested, offered or provided lends credence to an allegation that services were not rendered under an employment contract. For instance, holding a door open for someone does not create an employment even if the person requests you to perform this service for his or her benefit. Where services are rendered by a volunteer, a key element in identifying the absence of an employment contract is the absence of consideration.

The State Division of Labor Standards Enforcement enforces the legal requirement for employers to secure the payment of compensation for their employees. It is the position of this State agency that a person who is engaged in a business operation is not properly labeled as a volunteer when performing work normally performed by employees. For instance, if a family business requires a child to work in the business without pay, the absence of consideration does not negate the existence of an employment relationship. A contrasting situation would occur where services are rendered without pay to a charitable organization, and the intent of the parties is to have work performed by volunteers who want to offer their services without payment and who do not want to be employed.

4.4 EMPLOYER – DEFINED
The term employer has a distinct meaning for purposes of workers' compensation. In LC3300, several employers are listed by title:
 a. "The State, and every State agency"
 b. Each county, city, and district
 c. All public corporations and public agencies
 d. All quasi public corporations and agencies
 e. Public service corporations with employees

Additionally, LC3300 provides a broad definition that includes as employers "every person ... which has any natural person in service." This language immediately raises the question, "what is a natural person?" A "natural person" is simply a living, breathing, human being. Every employee is a natural person whereas an employer can be a natural person or a legally created person.

Partnerships and corporations are examples of legal persons. These employers are comprised of more than one person, such as partners or officers. The actions of the employer are the actions taken on its behalf by the individuals whom it so designates. Under the law, the employer's actions are considered as those of one legal person. Defining the employer in this way enables claims to be made against a corporation without the necessity to make a separate claim against each natural person who may own the corporation.

4.5 SPONSOR – NOT AN EMPLOYER
Per LC3301, persons sponsoring bowling teams are excluded from the definition of employer where the sole relationship between the parties is as sponsor and sponsoree. For example, a business may donate money to a local bowling team

as a goodwill gesture. The team members may or may not even be known to the sponsor. Under such circumstances, the sponsor is "excluded" from the definition of employer and need not secure the payment of compensation for the bowlers. However, the sponsor may do something that takes it out of the LC3301 exclusion and creates an employment contract. For instance, the sponsor may demand a service of benefit to it in exchange for a donation. The service may consist of wearing shirts containing a public advertisement for the employer's business. When a service is performed at the sponsor's request for consideration, the sponsor has exercised the type of control that is ordinarily exercised by an employer, thus creating an employment relationship.

Also excluded from the statutory definition of an employer is a private non-profit organization that sponsors a person whom the superior or municipal court has given a work sentence instead of a jail sentence. Private nonprofit organizations that provide a workplace are excluded from the definition of employer as long as they act "solely as the sponsor" of an individual sentenced to perform "services for the organization." (However, a person performing community services for a different entity, such as a public employer, in lieu of imprisonment or to pay off a fine is considered to be an employee of such entity.)

4.6 EMPLOYEE – DEFINED

Per LC3351, an "employee" is defined to mean "every person in the service of an employer under any appointment or contract of hire or apprenticeship." The agreement of the parties may be "express or implied, oral or written." Any such person is defined as an "employee" regardless of "whether lawfully or unlawfully employed." The component parts of the definition of employee are further explained in the following sections.

4.7 EMPLOYEE — IN SERVICE OF EMPLOYER

An employee must be engaged in the service of an employer. This part of the LC3351 definition of "employee" reiterates the LC2750 definition of a "contract of employment." Services must be rendered at the request of an employer and under the employer's direction and control. Although not specifically stated in the Labor Code, it appears that consideration must be provided in exchange for the employee's services, and the parties must intend to create an employment relationship.

4.8 EMPLOYEE — UNDER APPOINTMENT

Some government officials are appointed to their jobs. An example is the Administrative Director of the Division of Workers' Compensation. Per LC138.1, the Administrative Director is "appointed by the Governor, with the advice and consent of the Senate." The Administrative Director holds office "at the pleasure of the Governor," and the appointment may be withdrawn whenever the Governor chooses. When new Governors takes office, they will customarily replace previously appointed individuals with new appointees they select. Jury duty is another example of an appointee position. A person who is appointed to serve as a juror is deemed to be an employee of the appointing county for workers' compensation purposes.

4.9 EMPLOYEE — UNDER APPRENTICESHIP

Apprentices are persons hired to do a job they don't know how to do. They are paid to learn the job by doing it. An apprenticeship is a formal program for training a person to learn a trade. The employer provides on-the-job training possibly supplemented with outside schooling. The employee's wages increase at regular intervals as the employee develops additional skills and ability. Apprentices work for lower pay than fully qualified workers. The training and the experience received by an apprentice are deemed to be part of the consideration or pay provided by the employer. The State of California regulates apprenticeship programs through the Division of Apprenticeship Standards. Assistance from this agency may be solicited where the existence of employment under an apprenticeship is disputed.

4.10 EMPLOYEE — UNDER CONTRACT OF HIRE

Most employees are engaged under a contract of hire rather than under an appointment or apprenticeship. A generalized definition of a contract of hire is found in LC2750 (as explained in 4.2). In LC3351, additional details are provided regarding the creation of employment contracts. These details are discussed separately in text sections that follow.

Oral or Written

There is no requirement that a contract of employment be formalized in writing. A contract can be entirely oral. Many employees are hired verbally because most small employers do not usually have formal job applications or other formal employment documents. Written contracts constitute documentary evidence of the intent of the parties. However, the absence of a written contract is insufficient evidence to negate the existence of an employment relationship.

The existence of an employment contract may be disputed after a worker sustains an injury. If the contract was oral, the parties may hotly contest what was said, not said or intended by them. Even where a written contract exists, the parties may dispute its terms or meaning. However, the actual existence of an employment contract can be implied from the circumstances, as explained below.

Express or Implied

In an "express" contract, the details of the employment contract have usually been discussed and agreed upon by the employee and the employer, and the parties' intent to create an employment relationship may have been expressed orally or in writing. The existence of a contract of employment can be assumed in any case where the worker's status as an employee is not disputed by the employer.

Whether a contract existed may be disputed. However, a contract may be implied even when no express contract was made. An investigation is necessary to determine whether or not an employment contract does in fact exist. This fact can be ascertained by scrutinizing the actions and conduct of the parties involved and reviewing any written documents that may exist and statements from any available witnesses.

The parties to the contract may be the only persons aware of its terms or existence. Even so, certain reasonable inferences can be made or implied based upon the actions of the parties or the circumstances. The first thing to determine is the nature of the service that was rendered. Next, some inquiries should be directed to the parties. Affirmative responses to the following types of questions will support the existence of an employer-employee relationship:

    a. Is the service a type ordinarily performed by employees?

    b. Are there any coemployees who perform the same or similar services?

    c. Did the worker receive any consideration for his services?

    d. Was the employer aware that the service was being performed?

    e. Did the employer request the service to be rendered?

    f. Did the employer request this particular individual to render the service?

    g. Did the employer derive any benefit from the service?

4.11 EMPLOYEE – LAWFULLY OR UNLAWFULLY EMPLOYED

An employee can be either lawfully or unlawfully employed. Both terms, as used in the definition of employee in LC3351, refer to the creation of an employment relationship. The term "lawfully" is self-explanatory. The term "unlawfully" requires some clarification. There is an important distinction between being "unlawfully employed" and being employed in an unlawful employment. A prerequisite to definition as an "employee" is being employed in a lawful employment.

Persons engaged in unlawful employments are criminals, and they are not defined as employees under the workers' compensation laws. The term "unlawful employment" refers to a type of business that is illegal. For instance, prostitution is an illegal activity and an unlawful employment. Performance of the services requested by the employer constitute the commission of a crime. Bookies, "con artists," pimps, murderers, and other criminals are unlawfully employed in unlawful employments. Whenever the services that the employee was engaged to perform constitute the commission of a crime, the person is engaged in an unlawful employment. This situation is distinctly different from being "unlawfully employed" in a lawful employment.

Compensable injuries can be sustained by an employee who is "unlawfully employed" in a legitimate occupational endeavor. The type of employment and the employee's duties are legal. The term "unlawfully employed" refers to the legality of the act of employing the person. For instance, State laws prohibit employers from hiring illegal aliens and certain minors. If the employer hires such persons, the employer commits an illegal act. The employer is subject to legal actions, but the person's status as an employee is unaffected. By including "unlawfully employed" persons in the definition of "employee," these employees are entitled to compensation for work-related injuries and are not penalized by the illegal actions of their employers.

4.12 DEFINED AS EMPLOYEES – INCLUDED

The statutory definition of employee "includes" several categories of persons who are listed in LC3351. Special criteria or limitations apply to some persons who are listed, and the general definition of an employee is modified as it applies to these persons. Many categories of employees are not specifically mentioned. However, coverage under the workers' compensation laws is compulsory for any persons who meet the statutory definition of "employee" and are not specifically excluded from mandatory coverage by the provisions of the Labor Code.

4.13 ALIENS

An alien is someone who is not a United States citizen. The U.S. Department of Immigration monitors aliens who legally reside and work in this country. Some aliens are employed in this country illegally contrary to federal law. Employers who hire illegal aliens are subject to legal action. Regardless of whether they are employed legally or illegally, aliens are defined as "employees" by LC3351. They are entitled to compensation for work-related injuries.

After a work-related injury occurs, the employer may try (anonymously of course) to get the employee deported. The employer's ability to investigate a claim and determine its liability for benefits is seriously impaired, if not completely eliminated, after the employee leaves this country. However, once an injury has occurred, the employee's residence in another country does not relieve the employer from its liability to provide all compensation to which the employee would otherwise be entitled. Employers of illegal aliens may experience difficulty supporting any legal issues that require a judge to weigh the employer's credibility against that of the injured employee. A judge may be more receptive to reasonable information extended by the injured employee than information presented by an employer with questionable ethics.

4.14 MINORS

A minor is a person under 18 years of age. California has child labor laws that restrict the employment of certain minors. For example, it is illegal to employ a child under the age of 16 without a work permit that is issued by the State Division of Labor Standards Enforcement. Per LC3351, minors are defined as employees, and coverage is compulsory whether minors are legally or illegally employed. Minors are defined as employees when they are working in a place of business regardless of whether the employer is or is not a family member.

4.15 PRISONERS

Prisoners incarcerated in a county facility are not defined as employees. Per LC3351, the only prisoners who are defined as employees are those who are "incarcerated in a state penal or correctional institution." These prisoners are not covered 24 hours a day. They are only defined as employees and entitled to receive workers' compensation benefits for injuries they sustain "while engaged in assigned work."

4.16 PAID PUBLIC OFFICERS

Per LC3351, some elected and appointed public officers are "employees." These persons are employees if they are paid for their services. Public officials who receive no compensation would be volunteers rather than employees.

4.17 OFFICERS – PRIVATE CORPORATIONS

Per LC3351, officers and members of boards of directors of private corporations may or may not be employees. Some persons with these titles are not employees and are excluded from coverage under the Labor Code. When these persons are defined as employees, coverage under the workers' compensation laws may be compulsory or voluntary (see sections that follow). In all cases, in order to be defined as an employee, these persons must meet both of the following criteria:

1. The person must be rendering a service at the time of an injury, AND
2. The person must be paid by the corporation for performing the service.

4.18 OFFICERS – NO SERVICES RENDERED

Corporate officers who do not render any services to the corporation are not employees. An officer might simply put up money in exchange for a title and the prospect of a return on the money invested. This officer's status is that of an investor, not an employee. For example, an officer might receive stock dividends proportionate to the amount invested but not contingent upon the performance of any services. In order to set up a corporation, it is necessary to designate the identity of the officers of the corporation. Officers of private corporations such as a vice president or secretary-treasurer may accept a title without any real involvement in the business. Such persons are officers in name only. They do not perform any services for the corporation nor do they have any financial interest in the operation of the business.

4.19 OFFICERS – NOT PAID FOR SERVICES

Per LC3351, officers or directors who render services for a corporation are not defined as employees if they do not receive payment for their services. For example, the president of a private corporation may render services for the corporation but not receive any payment. The president might reinvest any income that is received from the business; there may not be any income if the corporation is losing money; or, the president may have sufficient income from other sources and not need a salary from the corporation.

A person may serve as a member of the board of directors of a private corporation for personal satisfaction or for the prestige derived from the position.

An officer or director may give a speech for the corporation and decline any payment for this service. The corporation may provide a token gift after the speech. This could be viewed as a form of payment for services. However, the speech was not contingent upon receipt of consideration. The gift is an after-the-fact act of gratitude. It did not motivate the performance of the service, and the service would have been rendered regardless of whether the gift was provided.

4.20 OFFICERS – SOLE SHAREHOLDERS

Officers and directors who render service for pay are "employees." A corporation employer is required to secure the payment of compensation for these employees. Per LC3351, there is one exception to this. If the officers and directors of a private corporation are the "sole shareholders," these employees are exempt from the compulsory coverage provisions of the law. These officers can elect to provide coverage for themselves, but coverage is not required.

When the officers and directors are the sole shareholders, these persons are usually personally known to each other and are probably relatives or close friends. A private corporation is not public, meaning that its stock cannot be purchased in the stock market. Stock is distributed internally to personally selected individuals. Due to the statutory exempting of such persons from compulsory coverage, the WCAB avoids jurisdiction over what may be purely family or personal matters.

If the corporate employer does not voluntarily provide workers' compensation coverage for its exempt employees, the exempted officers or directors can still recover compensation for work-related injuries by filing a civil suit against their employer. Assuming that a personal relationship between the exempt employees and the corporation, such severe action is unlikely to be taken unless there is a falling out between the shareholders.

"Sole shareholders" means that no other person owns stock in the corporation except for the officers or directors. If even one other person owns stock, the LC3351 exemption from compulsory workers' compensation coverage will not apply. The corporation will come under the requirements for mandatory coverage for all of its employees including employees who are officers or directors.

In privately held corporations, it is necessary to investigate the ownership of the stock in order to determine whether this exemption applies. In a family corporation, stock may be issued to a relative who is neither an officer nor a director. Failure to secure the payment of compensation for all officers who render services for pay can subject the corporate employer to penalties for being illegally uninsured (see 2.20). The remedy exists regardless of whether a relative or friend would choose to pursue it.

4.21 PARTNERS

Partners may be owners of a partnership or a limited liability company. In a limited partnership, a partner's liability for business losses is limited to the amount of capital that a particular partner has invested. A partnership may be created as an ongoing business enterprise, or a partnership may cease to exist after completion of a specific project.

Per LC3351, partners must meet two requirements in order to be defined as an "employee." A partner must be performing work for the partnership or a "limited liability company," and the partner must receive "wages irrespective of profits from the" business. Workers' compensation coverage is compulsory for working partners who are paid wages, and these partners will be entitled to compensation for work-related injuries they sustain.

A person may hire a group of "workers associating themselves under a partnership agreement" to perform "labor on a particular piece of work." This person should inquire as to whether or not the partnership has provided coverage for the working partners. If the partners obtained workers' compensation coverage for themselves, the person receiving the services is not their employer and is not required to provide duplicate coverage. However, per LC3360, if the partners do not have the required coverage, the partners are deemed to be employees of the person for whom the work is performed. This person is liable for workers' compensation coverage for these employees and will be illegally uninsured if coverage is not obtained.

General Partners. Per LC3351, general partners are defined as "employees" when they are "working members of the partnership." General partners manage the business affairs of the partnership. Instead of wages or salary, general partners sometimes receive a designated share of the profits or income of the partnership in return for services rendered. General partners can be covered by election, but worker' compensation coverage is not required. Absent an election of coverage under LC4150, general partners are not entitled to receive workers' compensation benefits for any injuries they sustain (see 4.31).

Limited Liability Company. Effective for 1997 or later dates of injury, LC3351 contains comparable provisions for working members of a "partnership or limited liability company." As a legal entity, a limited liability company may itself be a partnership or a private corporation. Where the employer entity is a limited liability company, coverage is elective for working members who are "managers."

4.22 TRUSTS

Effective 1997, LC3351 contains special provisions regarding businesses that are conducted as a trust. The provisions apply equally to businesses that are operated as a partnership, a limited liability company or a private corporation. Where such businesses are operated as a trust, "the persons holding the power to revoke a trust" as to the business being conducted "shall be deemed to be the shareholders of the private corporation, or the general partners of the partnership, or the managers of the limited liability company." Coverage is elective for such persons, shareholders, general partners and managers if they are injured while performing paid services for the employer entity.

4.23 WORKERS IN REHABILITATION PROGRAMS

An injured employee may receive on-the-job training as part of his compensation for an industrial injury. Ordinarily, the employer providing training is an employer of the worker receiving rehabilitation. The employee is entitled to workers' compensation benefits from the temporary employer if the employee sustains a new injury while working in the training program. Since the worker is not a perfect physical specimen to start with, some employers are reluctant to risk potential liability for a new injury. For this reason, some employers will not agree to provide a work site for employees seeking rehabilitation through on-the-job training.

In cases where rehabilitation is handled by the State Department of Rehabilitation, on-the-job training programs are encouraged. Per LC3351.5, compensation for an injury will be provided by the employer's insurance company in the same manner as it is provided for any regular employee of the employer, but the "department" will pay "the full amount of any additional workers' compensation insurance premium expense." If the employer's insurer collects premium for the employee, no cost is incurred by the employer. The benefits of this section apply only to rehabilitation provided through the State. If a private rehabilitation company arranges training, the new employer must secure the payment of compensation for the trainee as its employee.

4.24 NOT DEFINED AS EMPLOYEES – EXCLUDED

Certain persons who are employees are excluded from mandatory coverage under the provisions of LC3351. These persons are defined as employees, but they are not entitled to workers' compensation benefits unless coverage was provided voluntarily by an election. Other employees are excluded from compulsory coverage under the provisions of LC3352. Excluded employees meet the general definition of employee, but the Labor Code specifically states they are not deemed employees for purposes of workers' compensation coverage. Other persons are excluded from compulsory coverage under the Labor Code because they have a different status, and they are not engaged in an employer-employee relationship (e.g. an independent contractor).

4.25 VOLUNTEERS

A "volunteer" is a person who performs services without consideration and without any intent to create an employment relationship. Employees ordinarily work to earn money to support themselves. Persons who are able to volunteer their time without payment ordinarily do not need any income or have other sources of income. The motivating reason to perform the service is not "consideration."

If volunteers were defined as employees, some organizations would lose the services of many persons. The organization might not be able to afford the costs of providing wages or securing the payment of compensation for employees. It might therefore cut down on the number of persons providing services as well as the number of services the organization could provide. Charitable, religious, and nonprofit organizations often provide services that would otherwise be provided at public expense. Therefore, it is in the interest of social public policy to encourage the provision of such services by volunteers. This is the reason why volunteers are not classified as employees.

Volunteers can receive some form of payment, but it will differ from "consideration" paid to employees. Volunteers may be reimbursed for out-of-pocket expenses such as transportation, food, lodging, or minor incidental expenses that they incur while performing services. This is a dollar-for-dollar reimbursement of actual expenses whereas wages paid to employees are an inducement for the performance of the service itself. Most organizations that utilize the services of volunteers ordinarily reimburse volunteers for their out-of-pocket expenses so that it does not become costly for volunteers to give freely of their time.

Volunteers sometimes receive the free use of facilities such as a campground, lodge or recreational facility. The organization may charge a fee for the use of these facilities by nonvolunteers. The fact that the item has a monetary value and is not a direct expense reimbursement does not in and of itself classify the item as "consideration." The organization's intent is to display gratitude, not to create an employment relationship. Some volunteers may even refuse receipt of any item that would cause the organization to use its financial resources. They may insist on paying expenses that the organization offers to provide.

Although not defined as employees, volunteers can be covered for workers' compensation benefits by an election of coverage. Private nonprofit organizations can elect to cover volunteers pursuant to LC3363.6, and persons who perform voluntary service for a public agency may be covered by an election under LC3363.5. Absent an election, various subsections of LC3352 specifically exclude several categories of volunteers from the definition of "employee." Some of these are:

1. LC3352(b): person receiving "aid or sustenance only" from a "religious, charitable, or relief organization."
2. LC3352(c): volunteer "deputy clerk, deputy sheriff, or deputy constable" of a county or municipal corporation who is "appointed for his own convenience."
3. LC3352(d): volunteer at a camp or lodge "operated by a nonprofit organization."
4. LC3352(e): volunteer ski patrolman if payment consists only of use of ski tow or lift facilities, meals and/or lodging.
5. LC3352(g): volunteer athlete who is not a regular employee of the employer, and payment consists only of "use of athletic equipment, uniforms, transportation, travel, meals, lodgings" or other incidental expenses.
6. LC3352(i): volunteer for a "public agency or a private nonprofit organization. "
7. LC3352(j) and LC3352(n): volunteer official for intercollegiate or other "amateur sporting events" sponsored by public agencies or

nonprofit organizations if the only payment is a stipend "to cover incidental expenses."
8. LC3352(k): student athlete in "amateur sporting events" with designated sponsors if the only payment is the "use of athletic equipment, uniforms, transportation, travel, meals, lodgings, scholarships, grants-in-aid" or other incidental expenses.

4.26 WATCHPERSONS & SECURITY GUARDS

Watchpersons, watch guards, or security guards may be paid jointly by businesses occupying the same building or premises. Per LC3358, "watchmen for nonindustrial establishments" who are "paid by subscription by several persons are not employees." (Note: LC21.1 contains a statement of legislative intent that the use of "men" in the Labor Code shall be deemed to mean persons.) What is meant by "nonindustrial establishments"? The fact that all work-related injuries are also called industrial injuries does not mean that every place of work is an industrial establishment; in this context, the word industrial is merely used in a historical sense dating back to the origins of workers' compensation laws (see 1.1).

Considering the common usage of the terms "commerce" and "industry," a nonindustrial establishment would appear to be a commercial business as opposed to a manufacturing or industrial operation. Businesses that rent space in office buildings (e.g. highrise towers or shopping malls) are examples of nonindustrial establishments. Individual tenants may be assessed a proportionate share of payment to a watchperson for the entire premises. These tenants are not employers of the watchperson because such watchpersons are not defined as "employees."

When watchpersons do not fall under the terms of the above exclusion, they are employees of the persons for whom they perform a service. There is one exception to this. Some watchpersons are self-employed in their chosen occupation. These watchpersons may elect to obtain their own workers' compensation insurance policy. If they do so, persons who engage their services are not required to provide duplicate coverage. Thus, watchpersons may or may not be defined as "employees." Employers of watchpersons are liable for compensation unless the stated exclusion applies or the watchpersons purchased insurance to cover themselves.

4.27 CASUAL EMPLOYEES

A casual employee is someone whose work is not the same type of work as the trade, business, profession or occupation of his employer. Coverage for casual employees of a business enterprise is compulsory. Coverage for employees of occupants of residential dwellings is only compulsory under certain conditions as explained below.

Casual Business Employee. Business enterprises that employ any casual employees are required to secure the payment of compensation for all such employees. Failure to do so subjects the employer to a civil suit under LC3706-3708 and penalties for being illegally uninsured. There is no distinction between a casual employee and any other employee the employer may employ in its business.

Casual Residential Employee. The solitary statutory reference to casual employees is contained in LC3715 and pertains solely to employees of owners or occupants of residential dwellings. Such employees are commonly referred to as residential or domestic employees. In reference to these nonbusiness employees, LC3715 provides that certain casual employees are excluded from workers' compensation coverage. The exclusion requires that the worker first meet the definition of a "casual employee." The wording of the exclusion actually states who is covered rather than who is excluded. Casual workers are excluded unless they meet two criteria. Those casual workers who meet the criteria below are "employees," and their residential employers are required to secure the payment of compensation for them:

    1. The work to be performed will take 10 or more days to complete, AND

    2. The total cost for labor will be $100 or more.

4.28 RESIDENCE EMPLOYEES – OPTIONAL COVERAGE

Per LC3351, the definition of "employee" includes "any person employed by the owner or occupant of a residential dwelling." However, the employee's duties must not be "in the course of the trade, business, profession, or occupation" of the employer. Per LC3356, this means "any undertaking" the employer engages in "with some degree of regularity, irrespective of the trade name, articles of incorporation, or principal business of the employer." This language warns the employer that a judge will not be easily fooled. The employer's business is what it actually is, not what the employer says it is. Coverage is compulsory for all of the employer's regular business employees.

The provisions of LC3351 require that the employer must be either the owner of the property or a tenant who resides there, and the premises must be set aside for a residential purpose. If the owner or tenant operates a business out of a home or apartment, a determination must be made whether the services performed by a worker were in furtherance of this business as opposed to the maintenance and use of the premises for residential purposes. Further, if the employer is in the business of renting or selling residential property, persons hired to maintain such property may be business employees rather than residential employees under LC3351. In order to be defined as an employee under LC3351, a residential worker's duties must be "incidental to," or related to, one of these specific categories:

    a. Ownership or occupancy of a dwelling: this is simply contrasted with a connection to a regular trade or business activity of an owner or tenant.

    b. Maintenance of the dwelling: this refers to activities such as painting, carpentry, carpeting, plumbing or cleaning work. This type of work is performed in or on the building itself.

c. Use of the dwelling: this refers to activities such as mowing lawns, installation of sprinklers, gardening, pool cleaning, trash clean up. This catchall phrase could be construed to encompass many non-specified types of work.

d. Care and supervision of children: this refers to babysitters or other personal services such as a lifeguard for children in a backyard pool.

Some workers who are defined as employees by LC3351 are excluded from the definition of employee by LC3352. A residential worker is excluded from the definition of employee if:

1. The employer at the time of injury employed this worker for less than 52 hours in the previous 90 days, OR

2. This employer paid this employee less than $100 in the same period, OR

3. The worker is employed by "his parent, spouse, or child." These family members are excluded from the definition of "employee" by LC3352.

Coverage for domestic employees who meet the criteria of both LC3351-LC3352 is secured by obtaining an insurance policy containing comprehensive personal liability coverage, e.g. a homeowner's or renter's policy. Anyone who purchases such a policy has this coverage automatically regardless of whether they have any domestic employees or whether their insurance policy makes reference to workers' compensation. Per Insurance Code 11590, comprehensive personal liability insurance cannot be sold unless it includes such coverage.

If a residential employer does not have a homeowner's or renter's policy with comprehensive personal liability coverage, an injured residential worker who is defined as an "employee" (pursuant to LC3351-LC3352 as explained above) can file a civil action against the employer. If the employer does have comprehensive personal liability insurance, the employee's remedy is limited to compensation under the workers' compensation law.

4.29 RESIDENCE EMPLOYEES – MANDATORY COVERAGE

Per LC3715, coverage is compulsory for specific employees whose work involves a residence location rather than a business location. Employers of residential employees are required to purchase a workers' compensation insurance policy to cover the employees described below. These individuals are not covered under a homeowner's or renter's insurance policy if they sustain an injury before they have worked 52 hours or before they have earned $100 for the employer where an injured occurred. Their employers are required to purchase a standard workers' compensation insurance policy to cover them for work-related injuries.

a. A household domestic employee "who is employed by one employer for over 52 hours per week," e.g. a maid or cook.

b. A part-time gardener whose work for one employer "exceeds 44 hours per month."

c. Casual employees whose work will be "completed in not less than 10 days," and the total cost of labor is "not less than" $100. It doesn't matter how many men are employed to complete the work. The $100 labor-cost is for "personal services" only and does not include parts, materials, or supplies.

4.30 RESIDENCE EMPLOYEE – COVERAGE ISSUES

It is important to recognize the difference between the various Labor Code sections pertaining to residential employees, because an employer is exposed to civil damages where required coverage is not obtained. If coverage is compulsory under LC3715, the employer is required to purchase a standard policy of workers' compensation insurance. If this coverage is not obtained, the employer will be illegally uninsured, and the employee will have dual civil and workers' compensation remedies should the employee be injured before he has worked 52 hours or has earned $100. For residential employees who meet the criteria of LC3351-LC3352, coverage is mandatory, but it is provided under the comprehensive personal liability coverage of a homeowner's or renter's policy. Where this coverage was obtained, an employee's remedy for an injury is a claim for workers' compensation benefits under the Labor Code. However, if the employer did not purchase comprehensive personal liability coverage, the employee is restricted to seeking a civil remedy against the employer.

Some residential workers are exempt from workers' compensation coverage under both the old and new Labor Code sections (e.g. a babysitter who works one evening but is never again employed by the owner or tenant of a residential dwelling). These employees are not entitled to workers' compensation benefits under either a standard workers' compensation policy or a homeowner's policy. If injured, these excluded employees can sue the employer in civil court. They are not defined as "employees," so they cannot obtain an award of workers' compensation benefits.

4.31 ELECTION OF COVERAGE

Per LC4150, an employer may elect to secure the payment of compensation where coverage is not required by law. Coverage is voluntary for any person "an employer has in his employment" who is "not included within" the definition of "employeee" in the Labor Code, e.g. volunteers. Coverage is also voluntary for employees who, because they are excluded by the Labor Code, are otherwise "not entitled to compensation," e.g. residential employees who do not meet statutory threshold criteria (see 4.28).

Per LC4151, the employer makes an election by "insuring against liability for compensation" — the employer simply purchases a workers' compensation insurance policy. Alternatively, the employer can file a statement with the Division of Workers' Compensation reflecting that the employer "accepts the compensation provisions of this division." The employer cannot make an election to provide coverage unless the person who is being covered agrees and makes a "joint election" to come under the provisions of the Labor Code. Some persons may prefer to maintain civil actions against their employers for work-related injuries. Per LC4154, a worker who wants to reject the employer's offer to secure the payment of compensation must "give the employer notice in writing that he elects not to be subject to" the elective coverage that is being offered. The worker must provide this notice at the time of hire or "within five days after" the employer files the election.

4.32 WORKERS COVERED BY ELECTION

A number of Labor Code sections describe situations where coverage is elective but not required. If voluntary coverage is not obtained, the injured person is not entitled to compensation under the Labor Code. Some examples of common situations where coverage is elective include:

a. Self-Employed Vendors of Certain Publications (LC4157): "an independent contractor engaged in vending, selling, offering for sale, or delivering directly to the public any newspaper, magazine, or periodical" may be covered by election. Even if an employer provides elective coverage, the worker's status remains that of an "independent contractor for all other purposes," e.g. filing of income taxes. (Note: coverage is required for any such vendors who are not self-employed; if this fact is disputed after an injury occurs, the person's status will be determined according to the facts on a case-by-case basis.)

b. Officers and Directors (LC3351): when they are the sole shareholders of private corporations.

c. General Partners (LC3351): when they are working members of a partnership (except that if a private corporation is a general partner, (b) above applies).

d. Watchpersons (LC3358): when they are working for nonindustrial establishments and paid jointly by several persons.

Labor Code sections 3361.5-3364.6 allow for elective coverage of a variety of volunteers and excluded employees of governmental bodies. Workers' compensation coverage for such persons is provided upon the adoption of a resolution by the public entity. Per LC4155, the State, its political subdivisions, and every public agency is "conclusively presumed to have elected to come within the provisions of this division as to all employments otherwise excluded" from workers' compensation coverage.

4.33 EMPLOYEE BY PRESUMPTION

With all the various inclusions, exclusions and elective provisions, it can be difficult to readily identify all persons who are covered for workers' compensation benefits. Some assistance is provided by a statutory catchall provision. Per LC3357, "any person rendering service for another" is "presumed to be an employee" unless:

1. The person is an independent contractor, OR
2. The person is "expressly excluded" by a Labor Code provision.

This language somewhat simplifies coverage questions. These are the two items upon which an investigation should focus. Either item supports a denial of coverage for workers' compensation benefits under the provisions of the Labor Code. The only exception would occur where the employer has made an election of coverage under LC4150.

4.34 INDEPENDENT CONTRACTOR – DEFINED

An independent contractor is not an employee. He is a self-employed individual. When he works for other people he is, in effect, both an employer and his own employee. The person engaging an independent contractor is not an employer. He is a "principal." This distinction is important. An independent contractor is not an "employee" of an "employer." The Labor Code defines an independent contractor by listing factors that ordinarily distinguish employees from employers. Per LC3353, the term independent contractor "means any person who":

a. "Renders a service for a specified recompense for a specified result," AND
b. Is "under the control of his principal as to the result of his work only," AND
c. Is not under the control of his principal "as to the means by which such result is accomplished."

4.35 INDEPENDENT CONTRACTOR – PROVING STATUS

Proof of independent contractor status relieves the employer from any liability under the workers' compensation laws. Obviously, it is financially beneficial for an employer to prove that a worker is an independent contractor. Aside from being a self-employed individual, there is no simplistic definition of an independent contractor. The worker's status must be examined on a case-by-case basis.

Successful "proof of independent contractor status includes satisfactory proof" of specific factors listed in LC2750.5. Three factors that are necessary elements for proof of independent contractor status (except when a required contractor's license has not been obtained as explained in 4.37) are proof that:

1. "The individual has the right to control and discretion as to the manner of performance of the contract for services in that the result of the work and not the means by which it is accomplished is the primary factor bargained for," AND
2. "The individual is customarily engaged in an independently established business," AND
3. "The individual's independent contractor status is bona fide and not a subterfuge to avoid employee status."

In addition to specific required factors, LC2750.5 lists several cumulative factors that are indicative of an independent contractor relationship. Each of the required and cumulative factors are detailed separately in following sections (see 4.36-4.50).

4.36 CONTRACTOR – RIGHT OF CONTROL

The entity having control of the methods used to perform services is an employer. Per LC2750.5, an independent contractor "has the right to control" the "manner of performance of the contract for services." An independent contractor exercises control over himself and other employees he hires. When the right to control is not exercised overtly, it may be difficult to determine who possesses this right. However, "right to control" is the most important element of independent contractor status.

Control as a self-employed person is demonstrated when an independent contractor bargains for "the result of the work." There is a stated task to be accomplished. This is the "primary factor bargained for" and not how the job will get done. The principal designates what job he wants done, and the independent contractor determines the "means by which it is accomplished." The contract between the parties is a business contract for a specified recompense, not an employment contract.

4.37 CONTRACTOR – INDEPENDENT BUSINESS

Per LC2750.5, an independent contractor is "customarily engaged" in operating his own business that is an "independently established business." It exists separately from the business of the principal for whom the independent contractor performs services. To disprove an employment relationship, the principal must prove that two separate businesses are doing business with each other, and the owner of one of them (the injured worker) is self-employed.

There are certain aspects of every separately operated business that are unique and aid in distinguishing one business from another. These include:
1. Separate business address and business telephone number: necessary for potential clients to reach a business in order to obtain services that are offered; also the address used in filing state and federal tax forms; and the address where business records are maintained.
2. Business name: county records can be inspected in order to determine whether a Fictitious Business Name Statement has been filed, and, if so, the name of person(s) shown as the owner(s) of the business.
3. Licenses and permits: as required by cities and counties for the particular type of business conducted, usually public records available for inspection.
4. Printed stationery items: letterhead, invoices, and business cards containing the business name.
5. Tax identification number: this number is used when paying state and federal payroll taxes and also for a self-employed person's quarterly deposits of estimated income taxes.

Inquiries may reveal that the worker is a savvy business person in full compliance with all state and federal laws pertaining to the business. If not, further investigation should be made to determine the reasons for noncompliance with legal obligations. A savvy self-employed person may be conducting a business surreptitiously or under-the-table for the purpose of intentionally evading tax, insurance, and other payments. However, if noncompliance is due to ignorance of governmental requirements, this fact would raise doubts as to the worker's ability to be self-employed and own or operate a business.

4.38 CONTRACTOR – STATUS NOT A SUBTERFUGE

Per LC2750.5(c), the person's status as an independent contractor must be "bona fide." Employers are admonished not to rename their employees as "independent contractors." This would effectively be a "subterfuge to avoid employee status" and thereby to avoid legal requirements to secure the payment of compensation for employees.

It doesn't matter whether the parties sign a written contract calling the worker an "independent contractor." The actual facts will supersede any attempt to camouflage the true nature of the relationship. Per LC2804, any contract in which an "employee" waives his rights to benefits to which he is entitled "is null and void." Judges are interested in facts, not written documents that contain illegal agreements and/or false representations of the facts. The employer's presentation of a written contract is not the end of an investigation. The final step is to determine if the facts support the contractual provisions.

4.39 CONTRACTOR – CUMULATIVE FACTORS

Several cumulative factors are listed in LC2750.5 along with the three factors that are required for a WCAB determination of independent contractor status (see 4.35). Cumulative factors will not suffice as evidence in the absence of the required factors (see 4.36-4.38). They can however support the existence of an independent contractor relationship where it is disputed and the existence of required factors is not clear from the facts.

Cumulative factors are particularly useful in initially identifying an independent contractor through an investigation. The more cumulative factors that are determined to exist, the more convincing the argument in favor of independent contractor status. However, the general purpose of proving the existence of cumulative factors is to supplement, but not supplant, proof of the three essential facts that are required by LC2750.5 in order to prove the existence of an independent contractor relationship (see 4.35). Each of the cumulative factors that are indicative of independent contractor status are explained in detail in following sections.

4.40 CONTRACTOR – SUBSTANTIAL INVESTMENT

An independent contractor may make a substantial investment in the business of being self-employed. Per LC2750.5, there must be some investment "other than personal services in the business." This language refers to a financial investment. This could be tools, machinery, vehicles, or equipment. It is a type of investment that an employer would make, but its employees would not. The independent contractor may have existing business loan agreements wherein he states he is a self-employed person.

4.41 CONTRACTOR – ADVERTISES AS SELF-EMPLOYED

Per LC2750.5, an independent contractor must hold himself or herself out "to be in business for oneself." How did the principal learn of the services offered by the independent contractor? The independent contractor may advertise by word-of-mouth or by more formal means. Advertisements of a private business may be made in the classified section of the telephone directory, newspapers, fliers, or on radio or television.

Business cards are a form of advertisement for an employer. Employees may have business cards, but the company name being advertised is that of their employer. An independent contractor advertises his own business, not that of the principal. The independent contractor or his employees may have a uniform or a company vehicle that contains advertisements for the independent contractor's business. A dispute over independent contractor status need not be confined to assessing the credibility of the two parties to a contract. Supporting documentation or uninvolved witnesses may be available.

4.42 CONTRACTOR – PAID BY PROJECT

Per LC2750.5, an independent contractor might bargain for a contract "to complete a specific project for compensation." The end result is bargained for, not the time it will take the worker to accomplish the result. An independent contractor is paid by the job. He tells the principal how long it will take to complete the project requested. He is paid a set price for a specific result (although a fee may be based upon an hourly rate for an estimated number of hours). An independent contractor sets his own fees. The fee may be negotiated, but the independent contractor has the final say over the fee the principal will pay. The principal's control is limited to the selection of one independent contractor versus another with a lower fee.

An independent contractor does not ordinarily get paid by the hour, week, month, etc. Ordinarily, a flat fee is established as the contract fee. The contract terms may provide for payment in installments over a period of time, but this is different from payment of wages to employees.

Employers who set the rate of pay for their employees are legally required to deduct state and federal employment taxes prior to payment of wages. These deductions from pay are a strong indication of employee status, and it is unlikely an independent contractor defense will be successful if standard deductions were taken. However, a lack of pay deductions is not proof of independent contractor status. This fact may result from a subterfuge by the employer to evade payment of taxes for its employees.

4.43 CONTRACTOR – SETS OWN HOURS

An independent contractor ordinarily sets his own hours. The principal usually does not require an independent contractor to start and quit at set hours or to work a specific number of hours per day. The independent contractor may have to work the same hours as the principal's regular employees, because the principal locks the premises at set times of the day. If the work is in an open and accessible area, the independent contractor works when he pleases. A contractor's concern is to finish the work, since his fee is ordinarily contingent upon completion.

A contractor cannot be docked for coming to work late, nor can he be fired for absenteeism. (Note: a failure to perform under a contract that specifies payment at an hourly rate for only a set number of hours worked may give rise to an action for breach of contract.) At the work site, the independent contractor is in charge. No one supervises an independent contractor or tells him what to do, when to do it or how to do it. The independent contractor supervises the work being done and how it is done and is only responsible to his principal for the end result.

4.44 CONTRACTOR – SUPPLIES OWN TOOLS

Per LC2750.5, an independent contractor customarily supplies "the tools or instrumentalities used in the work." A plumber brings his own plumbing tools to the job, and a cement contractor brings his own cement mixer. Since the independent contractor is self-employed in his own independent business, which is ordinarily a different type of business from that of his principal, his principal is unlikely to have specialized tools or equipment on hand for his use. However, some tools and instrumentalities are "normally and customarily provided by employers." Items in this category can be provided by the principal without affecting the worker's status as an independent contractor. Such items could include a broom, pen, paper clips, writing tablet, chair, or a typewriter.

Allowing an independent contractor to utilize items that are readily available is simply a courtesy that may be extended by the principal. Any specialized tools other than those customarily located at a worksite must be supplied by the independent contractor, not a principal. The identity of the purchaser or the owner will assist in determining the worker's status.

4.45 CONTRACTOR – HIRES EMPLOYEES

Employers hire employees. An employee cannot create employment contracts to which the employer is not a party. An independent contractor can hire his own employees without knowledge of, or permission from, the principal. The independent contractor's right to hire his own employees is a basic right of any employer. The fact that an independent contractor has employees working under his direction and control supports his status as an independent contractor.

Employees of an independent contractor have no relationship at all with the principal. Their employment contract is between them and their employer who is self-employed (except that employees of certain unlicensed contractors may be held as a matter of law to be employees of the principal who contracted with the unlicensed subcontractor; see 4.48).

4.46 CONTRACTOR – WORK NOT SAME AS PRINCIPAL'S

This cumulative factor is similar to the required factor that the independent contractor have his own independently established business. Per LC2750.5, it is additional support of independent contractor status when the independent contractor performs "work that is not ordinarily in the course of the principal's work." An independent contractor relationship is more readily apparent when the independent contractor's business is different from the principal's business. One example of the presence of this factor would be a painter who contracts to paint the desks at an insurance company. Another would be an accountant who audits books at auto repair shops or shoe stores. Yet another would be an ambulance driver who transports injured employees to a hospital from a shoe store, a construction site, a physician's office, or anywhere else.

This factor will only support an independent contractor relationship when other factors are also present. This explains why it is referred to as a "cumulative" factor. This factor can be missing when an independent contractor relationship exists. A principal may require services of an independent contractor who is engaged in the same type of business. The employer may use an independent contractor to handle a short-term high volume of work instead of hiring additional employees. If an independent contractor and a principal have the same type of business, other elements must be examined to identify their relationship.

4.47 CONTRACTOR – SKILLS REQUIRED

Per LC2750.5, an independent contractor will ordinarily be "performing work that requires a particular skill." It is unlikely that an independent contractor could be successfully self-employed without having special skills. The level of skill, education, and training necessary to perform the work is relevant. Since he is selling his services, the independent contractor must have something of value to sell.

The right of control over the manner of doing the work is the most important requirement in proving independent contractor status. One explanation for the principal's lack of control is his ignorance of the skills necessary to do the work or supervise the work of the independent contractor. Usually, an independent contractor is more knowledgable and/or skilled in his line of work than the person for whom the work is performed. However, this is a cumulative factor. An attorney may be self-employed or an employee of a law firm. A doctor may be self-employed or an employee of a hospital.

4.48 CONTRACTOR – LICENSED FOR TYPE OF WORK

Possession of a State license for the type of work performed tends to support independent contractor status (as does possession of a business license or permit that cities and counties usually require self-employed individuals to obtain as a condition of conducting a business within their boundaries). However, the fact that the State requires a license to engage in a particular profession is not conclusive since many licensed individuals such as nurses, physicians, masseuses, or beauticians may choose to be employed rather than self-employed.

An important provision of LC2750.5 pertains exclusively to contractors who are engaged in activities for which a license is required under specific sections of the Business and Professions Code (commencing with Section 7000). Such contractors must possess "a valid contractor's license as a condition of having independent contractor status." If the worker possesses the required license, the employer can present other evidence to prove that the worker was an independent contractor. If the worker did not have the required license, the worker is deemed to be an employee despite any other evidence, no matter how overwhelming, to the contrary (except that employee status is not automatic for unlicensed residential workers because such workers are excluded from employee status by LC3352 if an injury occurs before they have satisfied time and money threshold criteria; see 4.28).

The general class of contractors referenced in LC2750.5 are those whose activities involve building construction, remodeling, and other improvements to real property. A determination of the licensing requirements that pertain to a specific type of contractor should be ascertained by direct reference to the Business and Professions Code and/or an opinion from legal counsel.

4.49 CONTRACTOR – INTENT OF PARTIES

Per LC2750.5, the parties must intend "that the work relationship is of an independent contractor status." The understanding of the parties is equally important in identifying independent contractors or employees. The parties' version of their intent is sometimes contradictory. When an independent contractor does not have any insurance, there appears to be a trend to claim employee status from the moment of injury. Likewise, where an employer has no insurance, there is a tendency to deem employees to be independent contractors. The presence of required and cumulative factors supporting an independent contractor status can help to resolve inconsistencies in the parties' statements of their intentions. It is possible that a self-employed individual may work intermittently as an independent contractor and an employee. The facts of the situation at hand are controlling, and previous work activities may be irrelevant.

4.50 CONTRACTOR – CAN BE SUED, NOT FIRED

This factor is related to the right of control. An employer has the right to control employees, including firing them. Per LC2750.5, an independent contractor "relationship is not severable or terminable at will by the principal." If the principal refuses to allow an independent contractor to complete a contractual agreement, the independent contractor has the right to file a civil action against the principal "for breach of contract." Likewise, if the independent contractor fails to perform under the contract, the principal may sue the independent contractor for breach of contract.

4.51 MULTIPLE EMPLOYMENT SITUATIONS

In the usual situation, one employee works for one employer. However, employment relationships can deviate from the norm in a variety of ways. The employee may work for two or any number of employers. There may or may not be a business relationship between the various employers. After an injury occurs, problems can develop with identification of the employer who is liable for benefits. There are situations where more than one employer will be liable for compensation to the same employee for the same injury. Special terms that refer to multiple employment situations include:

        1. Joint employment or dual employment,

        2. General-special employment, AND

        3. Concurrent employment

4.52 JOINT – DUAL EMPLOYMENT

Two or more employers will sometimes jointly enter into a contract of employment with an employee. The employee may perform separate services for each employer or services that are of mutual benefit to both employers. For instance, two self-employed individuals who lease separate portions of a large office in the same building may not be able to afford their own secretary, so they may jointly hire one secretary to work for both of them. The secretary does separate typing assignments for each of her employers but may do other tasks that are of benefit to both of them such as making tea or coffee, tidying the office areas, purchasing supplies or screening callers. Both employers contribute equally to her salary, although one employer may actually issue her paycheck. This is an example of a joint employment, or a dual employment, relationship. If an injury occurs, this employee may look to either one or both of her employers for workers' compensation benefits.

Similar situations are commonly found in offices where independent business persons share a common space. Business persons likely to engage in joint employments include physicians and attorneys. The watchpersons described in LC3358 who are paid by subscription agreements are engaged in a joint employment situation (see 4.28).

4.53 GENERAL-SPECIAL EMPLOYMENT

General-special employment is characterized by an employee being on the payroll of one employer while performing work for a different employer. The employer paying the wages is the general employer. The employer receiving the employee's services is the special employer.

In a general-special relationship, the intent of everyone is that the employee will return to employment with the general employer at a future time. The employment relationship with the general employer remains in effect during the temporary period of work for a different employer. Because this is the nature of a general-special employment, the employee is called a "loaned employee" while working for the special employer.

General-special employment situations are common in construction trades. Contractors sometimes loan employees to another contractor or subcontractor for a specific job or for a set period of time. An employer may require the short-term services of a skilled employee who is employed by someone else at the same work site. The employee's regular employer may be willing to loan the services of this employee on a temporary basis. The regular employer may wish to retain the employee in his employ but temporarily not have sufficient work for the employee to earn his keep. The employer would rather loan the employee to someone than pay him to be idle. The regular employer may be willing to loan an employee with specialized skills because of the potential need for a reciprocal arrangement in the future.

Usually the loaned employee remains on the payroll of the general employer who is his regular employer. However, this arrangement is a matter of convenience. The general employer may, instead, charge the special employer a fee equivalent to the salary of the "loaned employee." Whatever the arrangements, problems can arise if the employee is injured. The problem is in identifying which employer is liable for compensation. The employee has the right to seek benefits from one or both of his employers and may obtain an award that holds the employers to be both jointly and severally liable for the employee's compensation. Liability for payment of such an award between the employers is a topic addressed in the Insurance Code.

Per IC11663, the general employer is liable for the provision of workers' compensation benefits unless the special employer had the employee on his payroll. This section controls liability for payment of compensation between insurance carriers or self-insured employers. It pertains to the employers' rights against one another. The employee's general employer is liable for the "entire cost of compensation" if it continues to pay a loaned employee. The only exception to this liability occurs when the special employer puts the loaned employee on its payroll. In this case, "the insurer of the special employer is solely liable." This is a good example of the significance of payment of consideration despite the fact this term is not mentioned in the LC2750 definition of an employment contract. Liability for compensation adheres to the paycheck to a loaned employee.

4.54 CONCURRENT EMPLOYMENT

A concurrent employment situation is referred to in LC4453 as a situation where "the employee is working for two or more employers at or about the time of injury." This term applies to an employee who works more than one job. The employee could work a full-time and a part-time job, a day and a night job, or a weekday and a weekend job. One factor distinguishes concurrent employment from both joint and general-special employment: there is no connection between the employee's various employers. In fact, each employer may be totally unaware of the employee's other employments.

The word "concurrent" does not mean at exactly the same time. It means near the same time. The employee receives more than one paycheck each week, biweekly, or monthly. The regularity of the concurrent earnings entitles the employee to consideration of all earnings in establishing a compensation rate for benefit payments (that is why this employment situation is mentioned in LC4453 pertaining to compensation rates; see 8.36). However, the employer who employs the employee at the time of injury is the employer who is liable for the payment of benefits.

[5] INJURY

5.1 INJURY – IN GENERAL

The employee must sustain an injury as a prerequisite to entitlement to compensation. The term "injury" has a special meaning in the Labor Code. Some injuries will not be compensable because they do not meet all of the required elements of the Labor Code description of an injury. Other injuries will be noncompensable because the Labor Code relieves the employer from liability under specific circumstances. Isolated provisions of the Labor Code relating to compensability of injuries must be read in conjunction with all other provisions on the same topic.

5.2 INJURY – DEFINED

The term "injury," per LC3208, "includes any injury or disease arising out of the employment." This is not a dictionary-type definition, since the term itself is part of the "definition." Instead, the Labor Code describes a compensable injury as one that is work-related. The injury can result from trauma or disease (or under conditions specified in LC3208.05, from side effects of preventative health care after exposure to a bloodborne disease; see 5.4). An injury occurs when damage is sustained to "artificial members, dentures ... and medical braces of all types," regardless of whether there is any injury to the physical person of the employee. Compensation for injury includes costs necessary to repair or replace medical apparatus that was damaged in the injury (see 7.15 regarding the compensability of damaged eyeglasses or hearing aids).

Artificial limbs and dentures replace a normal body part. An employee whose foot is run over by a fork lift and injured has sustained a compensable injury. It does not matter if the injured foot was a normal body part that requires treatment or a prosthesis that requires repair and/or replacement. If the employee's teeth are broken by flying debris, it will not matter if the teeth are real. The employer is liable for injuries to all parts of the employee's body, whether natural or artificial. From the employer's perspective, expenses for repair and replacement of prostheses can be less costly than the compensation that would otherwise be owed if a natural body part was injured.

5.3 OCCUPATIONAL DISEASE OR ILLNESS

In LC3208, diseases arising out of the employment are defined as injuries. The term "occupational disease" is used in LC5500.5 and LC5412, and the term "occupational illness" is used in LC6409 to refer to diseases that are compensable. Some diseases are congenital, and many types of diseases or illnesses occur in the general population as well as the work population.

Examples of diseases include pneumonia, bronchitis, measles, tuberculosis, hepatitis, malaria, contact dermatitis, cancer, asbestosis (see LC4401-LC4411), and hemophilia. Use of the adjective "occupational" in the Labor Code makes it clear that all diseases are not, per se, injuries. A disease is only defined as an injury when the employment is the proximate cause of the disease (see 5.11).

A definition of "occupational illness" is found in LC6409 (a statute that requires examining physicians to file a report of every occupational injury or occupational illness; see 7.55). As used in LC6409, occupational illness "means any abnormal condition or disorder caused by exposure to environmental factors associated with employment, including acute and chronic illnesses or diseases that may be caused by inhalation, absorption, ingestion, or direct contact." (Note the absence of any reference to trauma, either specific or cumulative, as this is the essence of the distinction that is usually made between an occupational disease and these other types of injuries.) It is, however, possible for a minor trauma such as a needle-stick incident, that does not in itself constitute a compensable injury, to precipitate the onset of a disease (see 5.4).

5.4 HEALTH CARE WORKER – BLOODBORNE DISEASE

No distinction is made between health care professionals and anyone else as to compensability for diseases that are sustained in the course of employment. Regardless of occupation, all employees are entitled to compensation for work-related diseases. However, there is one special provision of California workers' compensation law that pertains exclusively to health care workers. Certain heath care workers (those referenced in LC3208.05) are entitled to compensation for certain preventative health care and certain adverse consequences of such care as a workers' compensation benefit. (The employer's payment for preventative health care for any other employees, such as gamma globulin shots after hepatitis exposure, does not constitute the provision of a workers' compensation benefit; see 7.3.)

Effective 1993, LC3208.05 defines "injury" to include the side effects of preventative health care that the employer provides to a "health care worker" for the purpose of preventing "the development or manifestation of any bloodborne disease, illness, syndrome, or condition recognized as occupationally incurred by" an appropriate governmental agency (e.g. Cal/OSHA or the Federal Centers for Disease Control). Only two diseases are mentioned by name in LC3208.05: "hepatitis, and the human immunodeficiency virus" (but included are any bloodborne diseases that may be identified as being occupationally related in the future). "Preventative health care" is defined to include care provided by a health care employer because the employee's job duties involve a "risk of occupational exposure," or because the employee has, in the course of employment, had "a documented exposure to blood or bodily fluid containing blood."

Examples of persons who may be entitled to preventative health care include nurses or dental hygienists who work in an AIDS ward at a hospital and therefore have a risk of exposure to a bloodborne disease. A documented exposure to a bloodborne disease means an incident that is properly reported, e.g. a needle-stick incident involving a hospital custodian or a laboratory technician. The employer is not required to provide preventative health care to all of its employees, only those whose duties involve the prerequisite type of exposure.

Labor Code Section 3208.05 specifically excludes liability for any workers' compensation benefits if a worker who "claims a work-related exposure ... tests positive within 48 hours of that exposure to a test to determine the presence of the human immunodeficiency virus." (However, this statute does not grant the employer any right to require an employee to undergo such testing.) The purpose of the test is to identify persons who already have the virus from those who do not. A positive test within 48 hours of exposure would indicate that the virus predated and therefore did not result from the recent work-related exposure. None of the provisions of LC3208.05 apply after an employee is diagnosed as having a bloodborne disease. Health care beyond this point in time would not be "preventative."

Disputes can arise when the preventative health care that is contemplated by LC3208.05 is provided by an entity other than the health care employer in whose employment a risk of exposure, or actual exposure, occurred. For instance, an employee who is receiving AZT anti-virus medication after a documented exposure to AIDS may obtain ongoing preventative health care during a one-month vacation out-of-state. The employer has no control, nor any opportunity to control, treatment provided by other entities. Thus, LC3208.05 does not obligate this employer to pay workers' compensation benefits if an adverse reaction to such treatment results in a need for treatment or disability (the employee may have other remedies available, e.g. a civil remedy based upon negligent acts of persons or entities who provided preventative health care).

Diagnostic procedures are not mentioned in LC3208.05, but diagnostic procedures are clearly compensable. Otherwise, it would not be possible for the employer to determine whether an employee who has been exposed to a bloodborne disease has a disease. Once an employee is diagnosed as having a bloodborne disease, necessary health care constitutes treatment for a disease rather than "preventative health care." The employer's liability for treatment for any type of disease (involving a health care worker or any other employee) is contingent upon a determination that the employee has sustained an injury that meets all of the required conditions for compensability (see 5.8).

5.5 AGGRAVATION OF DISEASE

The employee may have a disease that was not caused by the employment and therefore is not defined as an injury under LC3208. However, if the employment aggravates the preexisting disease, a compensable injury has occurred. Per LC4663, the employer's liability in such situations is limited to payment of compensation "only for the portion of the disability due to the aggravation ... which is reasonably attributed to the injury."

The employer is obligated to provide treatment to reduce the effects of the work aggravation, but it does not become obligated to effect a cure of the preexisting disease. The employer is obligated to provide medical treatment until the employee returns to his preinjury status, at which point treatment for the disease is no longer treatment for an industrial injury. The employer's liability for any other category of benefits that is owed is likewise restricted solely to compensation for the aggravative effects of the injury that was superimposed upon the preexisting disease (see 10.42).

Suppose a 40-year old computer programmer experiences back pain when lifting a heavy computer printout. The physician reports that the employee has sustained a back strain superimposed upon a preexisting degenerative arthritic condition. Per the physician, the injury has caused a temporary aggravation of the arthritic condition, and this minor injury will not result in any permanent disability. Prior to the injury, the employee was being examined by an orthopedist once a month, receiving physical therapy twice a month, and taking medication daily. As a result of the industrial injury, the employee is temporarily disabled for three weeks, needs physical therapy twice a week, will be examined weekly, and requires a new and different medication or an increased dosage of the prior medication. Facts such as these enable a determination of the point in time when the employer's liability ceases: when nothing is required except that which was already required before the back injury occurred.

5.6 SPECIFIC INJURY

Per LC3208.1, an injury can be "specific" or "cumulative." A specific injury occurs "as a result of one incident or exposure that causes disability or need for medical treatment." Examples of specific injuries include cuts, abrasions, fractured bones and ruptures. If the injury does not cause disability or require medical treatment, the injury may be a specific injury, but it is not a compensable injury. An injury is not compensable unless it gives rise to entitlement to workers' compensation benefits under the provisions of the Labor Code.

5.7 CUMULATIVE INJURY

Per LC3208.1, a cumulative injury occurs as a result of "repetitive mentally or physically traumatic activities extending over a period of time." Examples include a nervous breakdown by an employee exposed to repetitious work stress or a strained leg muscle in an employee who repeatedly carries heavy objects up flights of stairs. According to LC3208.1, it is the combined effect of "the repetitive traumatic activities extending over a period of time" that results in "disability or need for medical treatment." The common reference to cumulative injuries (CI) as cumulative trauma (CT) claims derives from this wording.

As is true of any type of injury, a cumulative injury may be a minor injury that requires medical treatment only, or the injury may be more serious and additionally entitle the employee to disability benefits. The repetitive trauma may occur over a short period of time, even one day. For instance, an employee who never felt specific pain may require medical treatment for generalized lower back pain at the end of a day when unusually heavy boxes or equipment were moved because a special project or a deadline necessitated extraordinary lifting duties. Sometimes the individual traumatic activity, or microtrauma, is repeated for many years before medical treatment becomes necessary or any disability results; e.g., a carpet layer whose job entails repetitious work in a kneeling position may work for twenty or thirty years before knee symptoms arise that necessitate medical attention or result in disability from cumulative trauma.

5.8 CONDITIONS FOR COMPENSABILITY

Per LC3600, the employer is liable for compensation to its employees "without regard to negligence." This wording serves as confirmation that the common law system has been abandoned (see 1.2). Per LC3600, the employer's liability for compensation is dependent upon a determination that three separate "conditions of compensation concur." Each of these will be covered separately in following sections, but all must be met. The absence of any one of these conditions relieves the employer from any obligation to provide compensation for an injury:

1. The parties are subject to the provisions of the Labor Code, AND
2. The employee is engaged in his employment at the time of injury, AND
3. The employment is the proximate cause of the injury.

5.9 PARTIES SUBJECT TO LABOR CODE PROVISIONS

Per LC3600, the employer and the employee must both be "subject to the compensation provisions" of the Labor Code when the injury occurs. There must be an "employer" as defined in the Labor Code and an "employee" as this term is defined. If the employee is excluded from compulsory coverage, the employee is not subject to the provisions of the Labor Code unless the employer made an election of coverage. Both parties must be subject to the jurisdiction of the WCAB. The claim must be filed before the expiration of any applicable statute of limitations or the WCAB may lack jurisdiction to award compensation for an injury.

5.10 EMPLOYEE IS PERFORMING A SERVICE

The activity that results in an injury must be related to the employee's performance of a service under his contract of employment. Per LC3600, the service must grow out of and be "incidental to" the employment. Also, the employee must be "acting within the course of" his employment. The fact that an injury occurs during working hours is not sufficient, nor is the fact that the employee is performing a service unless that service is work-related.

5.11 PROXIMATE CAUSE

Per LC3600, an injury must be "proximately caused by the employment, either with or without negligence." Negligence of the employer or employee is normally irrelevant. What is relevant is the existence of a cause and effect relationship between the employment and the injury sustained. The Labor Code requires this relationship to be one of proximate cause. The employment need not be the sole or exclusive cause of the injury, but there must be more than a remote connection to the employment. The term "proximate cause" has been interpreted judicially to mean that the employment must be one of the contributing causes without which the injury would not have occurred.

5.12 PRESUMPTION OF INJURY – PUBLIC EMPLOYER

Certain employees of public or governmental employers have duties that require them to risk their life and health in the performance of their duties. Some of these employees have a greater potential for developing certain medical conditions than is true of other persons who reside or work in the area where the duties are performed. For this reason, the Labor Code contains several rebuttable presumptions of injury. (Please note that the brief and summary information presented below is not sufficient for an understanding of the complexity of the legal issues entailed in claims involving these presumptions.)

Each presumption provides that if a particular type of employee is diagnosed with a particular medical condition, this condition is proximately caused by the employment and is therefore compensable unless the employer can present evidence that rebuts the presumption. The presumption is not conclusive, but absent proof to the contrary, the Labor Code dictates that a compensable injury has been sustained. The types of medical conditions for which a rebuttable presumption exists include:

1. Hernia
2. Pneumonia
3. Heart trouble
4. Tuberculosis
5. Cancer

The Labor Code specifies the categories of employees to which each presumption applies (LC3212-LC3213). The general category of employees to whom the presumptions apply is public safety employees, and more specifically, active law enforcement or active firefighting personnel. The presumptions do not apply to employees of a police or fire department whose principal duties are clerical in nature nor to telephone operators, dispatchers, machinists or mechanics. A further prerequisite for some public safety employees (e.g. some law enforcement employees under LC3212.5) is that the employee must have worked five years or more in the stated capacity or specified duties.

Each of the medical conditions that are rebuttably presumed to arise out of and in the course of employment must develop or manifest itself during a period when the employee is in active service (actually performing the duties specified in the Labor Code). However, this period can be extended beyond the date of termination of employment — for up to three calendar months for each full year of requisite service performed but in no event more than sixty (60) months from the last date actually worked (performing the specified duties).

5.13 PRESUMPTION OF INJURY – 90-DAY RULE

Effective 1990, LC5402 provides that "if liability is not rejected within 90 days after the date the claim form is filed under" LC5401(see 6.13), "the injury shall be presumed compensable." The presumption is not conclusive, so the employee is not automatically entitled to receive benefits every time that the employer fails to deny a claim within the allotted 90-day period. However, LC5402 provides that the presumption can be overcome "only by evidence discovered subsequent to the 90-day period." Per LC5402, all of the following conditions must exist before the presumption arises:

1. The employee filed a properly completed claim form with the employer (or else the employer refused to provide a claim form after notice of an alleged injury), AND
2. Ninety days have elapsed since the claim form was filed (or since the earlier date on which the employer's duty to provide a claim form arose if one was not provided), AND
3. The employer's claims administrator has not formally denied the employee's (or dependent's) claim.

Some employers are unaware of the legal obligation imposed upon them (by LC5401) or else intentionally refuse to provide a claim form after learning of an injury or a claim of an alleged work-related injury. It should be clear from the listing above that the employer's actions will not prevent any employee from receiving benefits that are due. The employee's claim will not be barred by any statutes of limitations periods that would otherwise limit the time in which the WCAB can award benefits (see 6.12-6.13); the employee may litigate a claim and be awarded benefits years after an injury occurred. Also, the employee can benefit from application of a rebuttable presumption that an injury is compensable (as explained below). The employer's refusal or its delay in providing a claim form may actually assist the employee in receiving benefits for a claim that the claims administrator might otherwise have successfully defended with evidence that was readily discoverable near the time of injury.

The provisions of LC5402 provide an incentive to promptly investigate and render a determination as to the compensability of a claim. Absent extenuating circumstances, the 90-day period can be thought of as the maximum time that is considered reasonable to deny a claim. In many cases, a reasonable time to conduct an investigation and notify the employee of a denial of benefits will be much shorter, e.g. where all relevant facts are easily discoverable and verifiable by telephone calls. No presumption arises under LC5402 if the employer denies a claim prior to expiration of the 90-day period allowed to investigate the compensability of a claim injury. When a valid basis for denying the claim exists, the employer will want to issue a denial within the 90-day period rather than trying to overcome a presumption of compensability thereafter.

Conceivably, an employee could ensure that a claim is presumed to be compensable by deliberately failing to cooperate in the employer's attempts to conduct an investigation. The employee may feign a willingness to cooperate that is defied by the employee's actions. For instance, the employee may describe witnesses but disclaim knowledge of names, or name witnesses and promise to provide telephone numbers or addresses that are never forthcoming, or agree to attend medical evaluations but always have a last minute excuse for a failure to attend.

Circumstances thus described warrant a denial of the claim within 90 days based upon the employee's lack of cooperation, but a denial notice may not be sent timely because the claimsperson fell for the con of "give me just one more chance." A defense of such a claim is still possible. The LC5402 presumption of compensability is surely not intended to encourage an employee to block an employer's investigative efforts nor to derive a benefit therefrom. It is possible that the employer might lose the right to use some evidence that was discoverable during the first 90 days, but the employee will have inadvertently ensured that other evidence remains undiscovered after 90 days. Furthermore, the employee's own testimony may be the only "evidence discovered subsequent to the 90-day period" that is necessary to rebut a presumption of compensability.

If information is needed to make a decision, the claims administrator is required to exercise due diligence by actively pursuing such information and acting upon it within a reasonable time after its receipt. Completion of investigations within 90 days of the filing of a claim form has been encouraged by appellate decisions that have precluded evidence that was reasonably available within the 90-day period (whether sought and not used or not sought) from being used to defend a claim thereafter. Per LC5402, once the 90-day period expires, the rebuttable presumption of injury can only be overcome by presenting evidence that could not reasonably have been discovered earlier.

In nonpresumption cases, the employee has the initial burden of proving the compensability of an injury by a preponderance of the evidence under LC3202.5. When compensability is rebuttably presumed under LC5402, it is the employer who has the burden of proving, by a preponderance of the evidence, that the employee's injury is not work-related. It is unlikely that the employer can meet this burden in borderline cases of compensability. The employer is more likely to be able to overcome the presumption in cases where evidence against compensability is clear and convincing, was diligently sought and was promptly acted upon after its receipt.

5.14 STATUTORY DEFENSES TO INJURY

Pursuant to LC3600, the employer is given seven specific defenses to an injury (and see 5.22 regarding psychiatric injuries). When the facts support the existence of one of these statutory defenses, no compensation is due the injured employee. These defenses (as explained in following sections) are referred to by the following terms that are descriptive of the subject matter of the defense:

1. Intoxication
2. Self-Inflicted Injury
3. Suicide
4. Initial Physical Aggressor
5. Off-duty Recreational Activity
6. Conviction of Felony
7. Post-termination Injury

5.15 INTOXICATION

The general term "intoxicant" would encompass any substance that is capable of altering the employee's physical or mental abilities. Such substances include narcotics, prescription medications, marijuana, and cocaine. Such substances may be used alone or used in combination with another substance. Effective 1991, LC3600 provides that an injury is not compensable if it "is caused by the intoxication, by alcohol or the unlawful use of a controlled substance" under Section 11007 of the Health & Safety Code. However, the employer may or may not owe benefits where an employee is alleged to be intoxicated at the time an injury is sustained.

Any intoxication defense requires a three-part burden of proof (plus proof of additional facts if a controlled substance is involved; see below). First, intoxication cannot cause an injury unless the employee has imbibed or ingested one or more intoxicants. Second, the employee must have been intoxicated at the time of the injury. Third, the employer must establish a cause and effect relationship between the employee's intoxication and a resulting injury. If the injury would have occurred regardless of the employee's intoxicated state, the intoxication cannot be said to have "caused" the injury. (See detailed discussion below regarding additional proof.)

Used an Intoxicant. A wide variety of intoxicants can be imbibed, ingested, injected, sniffed or smoked. The first stage of an investigation should determine all of the following:

a. Whether the employee used or consumed an intoxicant.
b. The name or identity of the substance used or consumed.
c. The quantity of the substance that was used or consumed.
d. The identity of any witnesses to the amount used or consumed.

Was Intoxicated. After establishing the precise identity of the intoxicant the employee used or consumed, the employer must next prove that the employee was intoxicated when the injury occurred. A blood test is ordinarily a key piece of evidence in an intoxication case. However, the absence of a blood test does not negate the employer's ability to defend a claim because intoxication can also be established by proof of the types of facts that are detailed below (likewise, the WCAB may rely upon extemporaneous facts to determine that the employee was not intoxicated even though the employee's blood alcohol level would constitute evidence of intoxication under Section 23153 of the Vehicle Code for purposes of driving a motor vehicle).

Numerous variables control the effect of different intoxicants on different individuals. Medical evidence is crucial to support any facts otherwise developed through an investigation. With this basic principle in mind, an investigation should focus on the following areas:

1. Determine the known physical effect of the intoxicant. Proof of extremely high blood levels of a substance can constitute prima facie evidence of impaired abilities regardless of variances in individual tolerances. (Note: a blood test is usually an important piece of evidence for purposes of documenting the presence of a particular intoxicant, but the absence of a blood test does not negate the employer's defense due to the availability of circumstantial types of evidence as detailed below.).

2. Determine the employee's known tolerance level. A low tolerance to small quantities can support intoxication in one individual where it would not in another; the weight and size of the individual may be determining factors.

3. Compare the employee's personal tolerance to his level of use or consumption on the date of injury. A quantity equal to or exceeding the amount known to produce intoxication is probative on the issue.

4. Identify every potential variable that controls the effects of the intoxicant such as quantity, quality, physical stature, concurrent use of other substances, general state of health or concurrent illness or disease. Some variables can support an intoxicated state with relatively low usage or a lower-than-usual intake, e.g. drinking alcohol on an empty stomach or concurrent with medications.

5. Determine the time elapsed between use or consumption of the intoxicant and the injury. The shorter the time, the less likely the employee could recover from the effects of the intoxicant.

6. Procure evidence documenting all behavior that was symptomatic of a reduced physical capacity or an intoxicated condition. Work records may reveal a reduced quantity or quality of work in the period between intoxication and injury.

7. Identify and statementize all witnesses. The most significant witnesses will be those who observed the employee closest to the time of injury.

The last and most difficult burden for the employer is to establish proximate cause between the employee's intoxication and the injury that the employee sustained. The employer must present evidence that demonstrates:

a. The actual mechanics of the injury and/or the manner of its occurrence. The employer may introduce photographs of the worksite into evidence or may even provide a reconstruction of the injury by expert testimony or video filming.

b. The employee's impaired state provides sufficient explanation for the mechanics of injury asserted by the employer, the occurrence of any injury at all, and/or the type of injury sustained. Reasonable inferences can be established from facts that are otherwise developed.

   c. The injury would not have occurred unless the employee was intoxicated at the time. Statements of all potential witnesses should be obtained, since medical evidence can be overcome by witnesses' observations of the employee's mental or physical behavior at or near the time of injury.

Cause of Injury. Intoxicated employees can sustain compensable injuries. When the ceiling collapses after a heavy rain, all employees standing beneath it are likely to be injured whether inebriated or sober. The most crucial and difficult part of the employer's defense will be establishing the fact that the injury would not have occurred in the absence of the employee's intoxication.

Controlled Substances

A "controlled substance" is defined in Section 11007 of the Health and Safety Code to mean "a drug, substance, or immediate precursor that is listed in any schedule" in Sections 11054-11058. For injury dates after 1990, the statutory intoxication defense in LC3600 would appear to bar compensability only in instances where the employer can prove that the specific intoxicant involved was alcohol or one of the controlled substances that are listed in Sections 11054-11058 of the Health and Safety Code.

The variety of substances listed in HSC11054-HSC11058 is voluminous. General categories of listed substances include hallucinogens, stimulants, depressants, and narcotics. Some specifically included substances are amphetamine, coca leaves, methadone, marijuana, Phenobarbital, morphine, and opium. Certain narcotics, such as codeine, are controlled in their pure form and when they comprise a specified percentage of another product. Substances controlled under HSC11007 are lawfully obtainable by medical prescription but only as specifically permitted under State laws that are intended to eliminate or avoid substance abuse in view of the known potential of some substances to form or sustain an addiction.

Besides establishing that intoxication resulted from the use of a specific controlled substance, the employer must prove that the employee's use of the specific substance was unlawful. An improper or negligent use is not necessarily an illegal use. The "unlawful use" criteria of LC3600 may involve a two-prong investigation to determine whether the controlled substance was obtained illegally and/or the controlled substance was obtained legally but used in an unlawful manner. For instance, proof of unlawful use may include evidence that the employee:

   a. Does not have a medical prescription for the substance, e.g. is using a substance that was properly prescribed but for a different individual.

   b. Does not have a valid medical prescription, e.g. a prior prescription has expired and/or has been materially altered.

Affiliated Issues & Defenses

The statutory intoxication defense does not pertain to 1991 or later injuries that are caused by the employee's lawful use of a controlled substance or use of any uncontrolled substance other than alcohol. A Labor Code 3600(a)(4) defense is not the proper basis for denial of a claim where the employee's intoxication results from the employee's use of nonprescription medicine while driving or operating machinery contrary to specific advice contained on package labeling or use of medically prescribed sleeping pills during working hours when such use was not intended by the prescribing physician. The employer can defend claims for compensation under such circumstances but must assert a defense other than an intoxication defense (see 5.8-5.11; compare to felony defense in 5.20).

Suppose an injury is sustained when an automobile mechanic falls into a seven-foot deep grease pit after intentionally inhaling carbon monoxide fumes. An intoxication defense is not a valid defense to the claim described here because carbon monoxide is neither alcohol nor a controlled substance (as explained above). However, a variety of other defenses are possible depending upon facts obtained by an investigation. Possible alternative defenses (there are many) include: the employment was not the proximate cause of the injury, the injury did not arise out of the employment or the injury resulted from a horseplay activity (and see 5.8 and 5.23-5.24).

5.16 SELF-INFLICTED INJURY

Per LC3600, "intentionally self-inflicted" injuries are not compensable. An injury is not intentional when it is caused by mere carelessness or negligence. Injuries resulting from negligent behavior are accidental, not intentional. An intentionally self-inflicted injury requires a deliberate action that is either intended to cause injury or is taken with deliberate disregard for the known potential for injury that would be apparent to any reasonable person.

The employer is not required to determine the employee's precise reasons for inflicting his injury. This burden would be inequitable, because it is illogical to expect any employee to cooperate in barring his right to benefits by providing such adverse information. For instance, if the employee intentionally injures himself for the purpose of fraudulently obtaining compensation, it is unrealistic to expect the employee to admit it. An employer can meet its burden of proof that the injury was intentionally self-inflicted by proof of the following facts:

1. The employee's actions were intentional, AND
2. The employee's behavior was not merely negligent, AND
3. The injury was caused by the employee's intentional act, AND
4. (a). An injury was the intentional result of the employee's intentional act, OR
   (b). The reasonably foreseeable or predictable result of the action taken by the employee is an injury, albeit a more minor injury than the one that was sustained.

Referring to the last item listed above, the courts have recognized that there is such a thing as an unintentional result of an intentional act. This judicial determination has provided employees with a potential means of overcoming the employer's self-infliction defense, even when the employee admits that his acts were intentional. For example, suppose the employee kicks a chair in anger and breaks his leg but denies any intent to injure himself. The employee may allege that his actions were rashly taken in a moment of anger without any thought of the potential consequences.

The employee's position may rely upon the fact that an injury is compensable when it results from behavior that is merely negligent. However, the employer can refute the employee's allegations by a reliance upon a common sense approach. Certain actions produce results that are common knowledge to any reasonable person. In kicking a chair hard enough to cause an injury, the employee may reasonably be considered to have intended a resultant injury. The employee could have taken some safer approach to venting his anger. Any reasonable person would expect an injury to result from such an intentional and forceful action. The reason most people do not vent their anger by such forceful actions is the common sense deterrent of potential bodily harm.

When a self-infliction defense is raised, an extensive investigation must be conducted to accumulate all available evidence that might cumulatively support the employer's position. The employee may have confided his intentions in advance of the injury. Hearsay evidence can be admitted in workers' compensation proceedings. Witnesses can testify regarding statements made directly to them or statements they overheard the employee make to third persons (hearsay evidence is not precluded). If the employee's motivation is suspected to be monetary gain, the employee's financial circumstances should be ascertained. If the employee alleges the injury was caused by mere negligence rather than intent, the employer can refute this allegation with evidence demonstrating the reasonable predictability of injury from specific intentional acts.

5.17 SUICIDE

Per LC3600, the employer does not owe any compensation if the employee "willfully and deliberately caused" his own death, meaning the employee committed suicide. There are several reasons why there are separate Labor Code provisions for fatal and nonfatal injuries that are intentionally self-inflicted. A suicide may occur long after a previous and admittedly compensable injury is sustained. Death claims give rise to a separate category of workers' compensation benefits thereby exposing an employer to a different liability. Also, it is the employee's financial dependents who are barred from compensation by a suicide defense.

The statutory suicide defense does not bar compensability in every case of death by suicide. The exact cause of death is a medical question and can be determined by examination or autopsy. The question of intentional versus unintentional death is not so easily determined.

A determination that the death was self-inflicted is merely the first stage of an employer investigation. The employer must also prove that the employee wanted to die and took deliberate steps to accomplish this result. If possible, the employer will present evidence that the employee had an entirely personal motivation or rationale for his decision to terminate his life. In all cases, the employer must refute any causal connection between a previous industrial injury and a later suicide. This is necessary because the law is well-established that all reasonable consequences or effects of a compensable injury are likewise compensable.

The problems with a suicide defense are best illustrated by example. Suppose the employee fell to his death from an upper story balcony at work or at home. From an investigation standpoint, the significant questions are: did he fall, did he jump or was he pushed?

An unintentional fall is not a suicide. Death is compensable when a fall is proximately caused by a prior compensable injury, e.g. poor vision or dizzy spells. A death is not compensable when it results from personal factors; e.g., the employee fell after losing his balance on a slippery surface. If the employee was pushed to his death for reasons unrelated to his employment, this is murder and not a compensable death (see 5.41). If the employee jumped out of the window, the employee committed suicide, but further evidence is required for the employer's defense. The deceased's dependents may allege that the employee jumped to his death to escape the intolerable pain from an injury or because of an inability to cope with the unsightly or debilitating effects of an injury. The employer can refute such allegations with evidence of compelling personal motivations for the suicide.

Dependents will frequently allege that the employee's depression over the effects of his injury resulted in an irresistible impulse to commit suicide. An irresistible action is not an intentional act. This allegation parallels the temporary insanity defense that has become popular and successful in criminal cases. The employer can refute this type of allegation with evidence that the employee was capable of taking a willful and deliberate action, that he did so, and that his reasons for doing so were entirely personal and independent of the occurrence of a prior industrial injury.

Consider another example. It may be undisputed that the cause of death was a drug overdose. If the drug was an illegal substance, the employer could argue that the death resulted from nonindustrial causes since the employer would not condone an illegal activity. The courts will not ordinarily sanction an illegal activity by awarding compensation. However, if the drug is a legal one, a great variety of possibilities exist. Some questions requiring answers are:
1. Was the drug provided for personal health problems or for an industrial injury?
2. Was the drug self-administered or was the dosage administered by someone else, e.g. a villain who wanted to murder the employee?
3. Did the employee intentionally or accidentally overdose; e.g., did the employee inadvertently self-administer the wrong dosage?

4. Was the employee cognizant of the effect of the medication that the employee administered voluntarily; e.g., did the employee take extra pain pills to alleviate severe pain without intending death?
5. Did the employee have a physical problem that would explain an accidental overdose, e.g. poor vision, poor memory or weak mathematical skills in counting pills?
6. Did the employee have a personal motivation for committing suicide; e.g., did the employee merely use conveniently accessible industrially prescribed medication to commit suicide for personal reasons?

All suicide cases require a thorough investigation of the employee's state of mind, state of health, and personal circumstances. The desire for monetary gain should not be discounted. Employees sometimes hope by their deaths to fraudulently obtain compensation for their dependents. Relatives and friends of the employee may possess information favorable to the employer's defense, but these persons are not likely to be impartial, particularly if they are the dependents or close friends of the dependents claiming benefits. Care should be exercised in avoiding undue reliance upon statements obtained from prejudiced witnesses.

5.18 INITIAL PHYSICAL AGGRESSOR

Per LC3600, the employee is not entitled to compensation for any injuries that result from "an altercation in which the injured employee is the initial physical aggressor." This statutory defense is yet another example of a denial of compensation for an intentional act. In this defense, the employee intentionally assaults another person who in turn retaliates and injures his aggressor. The initial physical aggressor is deemed to have caused his injury by his intentional act. The aggressor must intend to harm someone or there is no altercation. Where harm is intended, the initial physical aggressor is punished for his intentional act by being barred from compensation for injuries he sustains. Injuries to the innocent victim may or may not be compensable. In altercation cases, there are two questions to be answered by the investigation:

1. Who initiated the altercation or was the initial physical aggressor?
2. What was the subject matter of the dispute?

The word "physical" implies that the victim must actually be touched in some manner before a retaliatory injury to his aggressor is barred. An employee who is injured in retaliation for name calling has not physically assaulted another person no matter how offensive his choice of insults might have been. Employers have a right to expect a reasonable amount of self-control from their employees. Reasonable behavior does not cause injury to others. Judicially, it has been held that a person may be deemed to be an initial physical aggressor if he creates a reasonable belief in another individual that physical harm is intended and imminent, e.g. where an aggressor assumes a threatening posture and tone and rapidly approaches another person while wielding a weapon. It is unlikely that compensation would be denied to the intended victim of a serious injury who acts in self-defense to prevent a first blow by an assailant.

Both participants in an altercation can be barred from benefits. The victim's injury must be work-related before it will be compensable. This is where the subject matter of the dispute is important. If the dispute is totally personal in nature, injuries sustained in the altercation are not compensable for either participant. Two employees may engage in a fist fight as a result of comments regarding the appearance or physical attributes of one of their wives. Injuries sustained by either employee will not meet several basic requirements of LC3600. The injuries will not "arise out of the employment," nor can the employees be deemed to be "performing a service growing out of" the employment. The employer does not benefit from such acts.

An initial physical aggressor may strike a supervisor after receipt of an unsatisfactory performance appraisal. An argument with a coemployee may develop because one employee believes the other is not doing his share of the work. In such cases, the innocent victim is entitled to compensation for his injuries. The subject matter of the dispute establishes proximate cause between injury and employment for the injury to the innocent victim.

When the parties to the altercation are the sole witnesses, each will ordinarily place full blame on the other. The employer may have trouble identifying which employee is entitled to benefits and which one is barred from recovery. The employer can resolve this dilemma by requesting a consolidated hearing. An administrative rule, CR10590, allows for consolidation of proceedings in "two or more related cases" for "the purpose of receiving evidence." One judge can review both cases in one hearing and render separate decisions in each case. If the employees' claims were tried by two different judges, each might rely equally upon the credibility of the one employee whose testimony was heard. It is possible that both employees could be awarded benefits although one is statutorily barred from benefits. This result would be inequitable since the employer is entitled to be relieved of liability for injuries sustained by an initial physical aggressor. An opposite and equally inequitable result would occur if both employees were denied benefits although one is entitled to benefits.

5.19 OFF-DUTY RECREATIONAL ACTIVITIES

Per LC3600, injuries are not compensable when they arise out of "voluntary participation in any off-duty recreational, social, or athletic" activities that do not constitute "part of the employee's work-related duties." This defense is immediately followed by several exceptions. Compensability will be barred only if one of the exceptions does not apply. The employer may or may not owe compensation for injuries during activities such as company picnics, Christmas parties, or athletic games or events. Injuries from these activities are compensable if the activity is "a reasonable expectancy" or is "expressly or impliedly required by the employment."

When the employer orders an employee to participate, as is the employer's right to do, the activity is expressly required, e.g. where managers are required to attend company picnics. A "reasonable expectancy" of the employment is tantamount to an "implied requirement." Presence of the same elements will reveal that participation is not truly voluntary. Some criteria have been interpreted by the courts as being demonstrable evidence of a "reasonable expectancy" of the employment or an "expressly or impliedly" required participation. Ordinarily, injuries during participation will result in compensability if the employee can establish any of the following facts:

1. The activity takes place on the employer's premises during normal work hours.
2. The employee is paid for the time the activity is performed. Payment could be regular wages or compensating time off.
3. The employer rewards participants with special consideration in the workplace, e.g. assignment of choicest duties or work locations.
4. Nonparticipants are subject to repercussions for refusal to participate, e.g. termination or other disciplinary action.
5. The activity generates or maintains business clientele as opposed to having a mere side effect of improving employee morale; e.g., participants are both employees and clients, or the employer requires its name to appear on uniforms worn in public places for advertisement purposes.

Employees often develop personal friendships with their coworkers in the workplace and may arrange associations outside the work environment. Personal activities outside of the employment contract will not result in compensable injuries, even though the employer may know of the activity and not discourage it in any way. Absent the presence of some factor on the list above, the employer does not owe compensation where the following facts exist:

a. Participation is truly voluntary. Employees participate because they want to for their own personal reasons, e.g. exercise or socializing.
b. The activity is engaged in "off-duty" (not during regular working hours or times when the employee receives wages). Any planning that takes place at work is done solely for the employee's personal convenience.
c. The activity is "recreational, social, or athletic," and this type of activity is different from the employee's work duties.

A further aspect of the investigation amounts to proof of a negative: proving a lack of employer interest or involvement in the activity. Where this statutory defense applies, these two important elements of the employment contract will be missing: performance of a service that benefits the employer and control by the employer. The following factors can support the lack of an employment relationship during a recreational activity:

1. The employer is unaware that the activity takes place.
2. The employer is aware of the employee's participation but takes no active interest in the activity; e.g., the employer may be unaware of any specific details such as the identity of participants or the location of the activity.

3. The employer's interest in the activity is personal and not business oriented, e.g. where the employer donates personal monies for an activity or participates in it as an individual.
4. The employer is merely a sponsor or donor; e.g., money is donated for league fees, prizes or equipment out of generosity. Similar contributions may be made to comparable community activities.

5.20 FELONY CONVICTION – CRIMINAL ACTIVITIES

One of the employer's seven special statutory defenses applies to a specific type of criminal activity. For injuries on or after 7/16/93, LC3600 provides that the employer is not liable for payment of compensation where an injury is "caused by the commission of a felony, or a crime which is punishable as specified in" Section 17(b) of the Penal Code "for which he or she has been convicted."

Per PC17, a "felony" is defined as "a crime which is punishable with death or by imprisonment in the state prison." Penal Code Section 17(b) refers to circumstances where the court is allowed the discretion to punish a crime by imprisonment in state prison or in county jail or by a fine. For purposes of the Penal Code, a crime is deemed to be a misdemeanor if a sentence other than imprisonment in state prison is imposed. However, for workers' compensation purposes, the employer's statutory felony defense bars crimes that are punishable by imprisonment in state prison regardless of whether a lesser sentence is imposed for a felony (except that a plea bargain to a misdemeanor rather than a felony invalidates this provision of LC3600; see below).

The statutory felony conviction defense enables the employer to successfully refute compensability in any case where the employer can prove all of these essential facts:
1. The employee committed an act that constitutes a felony; e.g., the employee's actions satisfy all criteria for a specific crime under the Penal Code, AND
2. The employee was convicted for that specific felony, e.g. after a jury trial or a plea of guilty that negates the need for a jury to determine guilt or innocence, AND
3. Commission of that specific felony offense was the proximate cause of the injury sustained; e.g., the employee's commission of the felony was a contributing factor without which the injury would not have occurred.

The statutory felony defense is limited in scope. This defense does not pertain to cases where: the employee's crime is not defined as a felony under the Penal Code (e.g. where the employee is charged with a misdemeanor); the employee was admittedly guilty of a felony that caused the injury but was also charged with other crimes and, as a result of plea bargaining, convicted of a different crime; or, the employee was arrested for a felonious act that caused the injury but was granted immunity from prosecution in exchange for testimony against other criminals. However, injuries that result from any such criminal acts are definitely defendable. Nothing in the Labor Code can be reasonably construed to entitle any employee to the financial reward of compensation for injuries that arise out of and in the course of the performance of a criminal activity.

Criminal activities will not produce compensable injuries because the required LC3600 conditions for compensability will not be met (see 5.23-5.24). Performance of an illegal activity removes the employee from the course of his employment (in a legal sense) even though the employee is being paid, is on the employer's premises, or is commingling business and personal activities when injured. For instance, the employee may utilize a company car to transport illegal substances, or the employee may pocket money he receives as the employer's agent instead of putting it in the cash register or the bank. The fact that the employee somehow utilizes his employment to facilitate a personal criminal activity is irrelevant. Criminal acts are considered to be totally personal, not a service of benefit to the employer.

5.21 POST-TERMINATION INJURY

For injuries on or after 7/16/93, LC3600 provides the employer with a "post-termination" defense to a claim of injury. This statutory defense eliminates liability for compensation for certain claims that are presented subsequent to a termination or layoff or receipt of notice thereof. (Note: this defense excludes claims of psychiatric injury that are governed by the comparable provisions of LC3208.3; see 5.22.) The general rule is that an injury is not compensable if notice of a prior work injury is first presented after the employee's job ends or the employee is notified that the job will cease as of a definite date. However, LC3600 provides that the employee can overcome the employer's defense by demonstrating that at least one of the following conditions applies to the injury that is alleged:

1. The employer was aware of the claimed injury before the employee was notified of the termination, OR
2. Evidence of a claimed injury is contained in medical records that existed prior to notice of the termination of layoff, (but for psychiatric injury, actual "evidence of treatment" is required per LC3208.3), OR
3. The employee sustained a specific injury during the remaining period of continued employment subsequent to notification of the effective date of a termination or layoff, OR
4. The date of injury for an alleged occupational disease or cumulative injury "is subsequent to the date of notice of termination or layoff."

If within 60 days after notice, an anticipated termination or layoff does not occur, the employee's rights arise anew as if the prior notice had not been provided. Per LC3600, the "issuance of frequent notices of termination or layoff to an employee shall be considered a bad faith personnel action" (thereby vacating a potential defense to a psychiatric claim; see 5.22). In addition, the provision of frequent notices nullifies the applicability of the LC3600 post-termination defense to any claim of injury that may be filed by the employee.

5.22 PSYCHIATRIC INJURY

Psychiatric injuries are sometimes referred to as "stress claims" or "mental-mental" injuries, meaning no affiliated physical injury is claimed or present. The opposite of a "mental-mental" injury is a physical injury, e.g. a strained (or "stressed") muscle or a snake bite injury to a veterinarian. Distinguished from both of these is a "physical-mental" injury where a psychiatric injury is claimed to be a medically reasonable sequelae of a physical injury, e.g. where a slip and fall results in paraplegia that results in severe depression or anxiety. This latter type of injury may be thought of as two claims in one: a physical injury and a psychiatric injury (an example of a "multiple injury" claim).

All compensable injuries, psychiatric or otherwise, must meet the conditions for compensability set out in LC3600 (see 5.8). However, additional requirements for compensability apply to psychiatric injuries as set out in LC3208.3. Effective 7/16/93, the provisions of LC3208.3 apply to claims involving any of the types of psychiatric injuries that are described above; e.g. a psychiatric injury that is claimed as an effect of a severe ankle injury or a psychiatric injury without any accompanying physical injury.

Definition of Psychiatric Injury. Effective for injuries occurring on or after 7/16/93, a compensable psychiatric injury is defined by LC3208.3 to mean "a mental disorder which causes disability or need for medical treatment" and is "diagnosed pursuant to procedures promulgated under" LC139.2. These "Psychiatric Protocols," that were initially adopted by the Industrial Medical Council in 1993, establish the procedures for measuring, evaluating, and reporting psychiatric disability (and are available from the Industrial Medical Council upon request).

Medical Diagnosis. Per LC139.2, the Industrial Medical Council is required, following public hearings, to promulgate administrative regulations that "shall require that the diagnosis of a mental disorder be expressed using the terminology and criteria of the American Psychiatric Association's Diagnostic and Statistical Manual of Mental Disorders," (previously referred to as the "DSM IIIR," the 1994 revision of this manual is commonly known as the "DSM IV") or "other psychiatric diagnostic manuals generally approved and accepted nationally by practitioners in the field of psychiatric medicine." Absent awareness of other manuals, the DSM IV (or any later revision) may be presumed to be the only manual approved for the diagnosis of "mental disorders" since it is the only manual specifically referenced in LC3208.3.

Six-Month Rule

Since 7/16/91, aside from proving the necessary percentage of employment causation for a psychiatric injury (as explained below), the employee has the burden of proving one of two additional criteria. Per LC3208.3, "no compensation shall be paid pursuant to this division for a psychiatric injury related to a claim" that is made "against an employer" unless the employee can prove that the psychiatric injury:

1. Occurred after the employee "has been employed for at least six months" (that "need not be continuous") for the employer against whom the claim is filed, OR
2. Was "caused by a sudden and extraordinary employment condition" instead of a "regular and routine employment event," that is defined to include such things as "lawful, nondiscriminatory, good faith personnel" actions "such as discipline, work evaluation, transfer, demotion, layoff, or termination."

Although not specifically stated in the law, it appears that the contemplated waiting period before a compensable psychiatric claim can be presented runs six calendar months of active employment from the employee's date of hire. It is not necessarily relevant whether the employee works full time or part time. It may be reasonable to allege that the six-month period should be extended on a day-by-day basis for interruptions of employment, e.g. a personal leave of absence, jury duty, layoff or a one-week suspension as a disciplinary action. Changes in the employer's identity (e.g. by acquisition or divestiture) may or may not create a new six-month requirement.

Sudden & Extraordinary Condition

The employee need not be employed for six months in order to establish a compensable claim "if the psychiatric injury is caused by a sudden and extraordinary employment condition." This type of condition is contrasted with a "regular and routine event" but is not otherwise explained in LC3208.3. An employment condition that can be accurately categorized as "sudden and extraordinary" would appear to involve an event that is spontaneous, unexpected, unusual, and unlikely to recur. Such events may or may not involve a violent act.

A psychiatric claim presented the second week of employment may be attributable to an injury sustained when an employee is stuck in an elevator for four hours. A psychiatric reaction to a customer driving a car through the plate glass window in front of the desk where the employee was sitting at the time can no doubt be accurately described as a reaction to a "sudden and extraordinary" event. Likewise, the six-month rule would not appear to apply to an employee at a 24-hour gas station who is beaten and robbed after only four months of employment. Even at a work location in a high crime area with a history of robberies, an assault on an employee is still a sudden and unusual event in relation to most employee's assigned duties.

Injuries that result from extraordinary but personal events at the workplace will usually be noncompensable on other grounds. For instance, if the employee's spouse rather than a customer drove a car through the window at work, the injury may be a noncompensable result of a personally-motivated assault (see 5.40).

Burden of Proof

Predominant Cause. The employee has the burden of proving the compensability of a claimed injury. Per LC3208.3, in "order to establish that a psychiatric injury is compensable, an employee shall demonstrate by a preponderance of the evidence that actual events of employment were predominant as to all causes combined" (unless a violent act is involved; see below). The term "predominant cause" is not defined nor explained but is generally understood to mean not less than 51% of all contributory causes. Arguments may arise that this standard of proof equates to the LC3600 requirement that the employment must be the proximate cause of any compensable injury (see 5.11).

Violent Acts - Substantial Cause. In most cases, the employee must prove that the employment was the predominant cause of a psychiatric injury. However, an exception applies to cases where injuries result from "being a victim of a violent act or from direct exposure to a significant violent act." Under such circumstances, LC3208.3 provides that the employee must prove "that actual events of the employment were a substantial cause of the injury." In this regard, LC3208.3 defines "substantial cause" to mean at least 35% to 40% "of the causation from all sources combined." An evaluating physician will be asked to attribute the percentage of overall causation that is attributable to industrial factors, based upon an examination and a review of available medical and nonmedical records.

A violent act may be directed against the employee or a group to which the employee belongs. In a one-on-one physical assault, the employee is usually the only victim. Group violence could involve bombings, shootings, hostages or fires. An employee may be a witness to a violent act without sustaining any physical injury, e.g. where a coemployee is raped or beaten in the employee's presence. Where no physical injury is sustained, it may be disputed whether the employee is able to meet the employee's burden of proof, by a preponderance of the evidence, that such exposure is sufficient to constitute the substantial cause of a psychiatric injury.

Employer Defenses. Once the employee has alleged a claim of psychiatric injury, the employer will conduct an investigation to determine whether the employee has established the prerequisite amount of employment causation (predominant or substantial). Additionally, the employer's potential defenses to a psychiatric injury may be predicated upon evidence of any of the following:
1. The employee does not have a mental disorder.
2. The employee has been improperly diagnosed as having a mental disorder (e.g. using criteria other than required by LC139.2 or by a person not qualified to provide a diagnosis).
3. The employee has no medical disability nor any valid need for medical treatment (whether or not the employee has a properly diagnosed mental disorder).
4. The employee's disability or need for medical treatment is not caused by a properly diagnosed mental disorder (that will raise a question that the employer should be prepared to answer: what then is the cause?).
5. The events of employment that are alleged to have occurred did not in fact occur.

6. Only some, but not all, of the events that are alleged to have occurred did in fact occur.
7. Particular events that are alleged did occur, but significant details of events as alleged by the employee did not in fact occur.
8. The employee was not employed for six months prior to the date of an injury AND the injury did not result from any sudden or extraordinary employment event.
9. The employee is seeking compensation for a post-termination psychiatric injury that is barred by LC3208.3 (see below).

Psychiatric injuries are compensable when the employee meets the burden of proof required under LC3208.3, and a judicial determination of this fact is not necessary for every claim of psychiatric injury. Benefits should be promptly provided where compensability is clear from readily available facts such as knowledge of the details or the magnitude of an admittedly actual event of employment and nearly immediate disability or need for medical treatment. Under such circumstances, the employee may fully recover (or return to a preinjury status; see 7.8) after a short period of temporary disability or medical treatment.

Post-Termination Psychiatric Injury

Effective 7/16/93, special criteria must be met before the employee is entitled to compensation for a claim of psychiatric injury that "is filed after notice of termination or layoff ... for an injury occurring prior to the time of notice of termination or layoff." Per LC3208.3, the employee has the burden of demonstrating "by a preponderance of the evidence that actual events of employment were predominant as to all causes combined" and the existence of one or more following conditions:

1. The injury is caused by "sudden and extraordinary events of employment" (e.g. an injury results from a carjacking episode involving authorized use of a company vehicle), OR
2. The employer was aware of the claimed injury before the employee was notified of the termination, OR
3. Actual "evidence of treatment of the psychiatric injury" is contained in medical records that existed prior to notice of the termination of layoff (note that the requirement for *treatment* distinguishes this requirement from the LC3600 requirement that applies to other types of post-termination claims; see 5.21), OR
4. There is a finding "by any trier or fact, whether contractual, administrative, regulatory, or judicial" that the employee claiming a psychiatric injury was a victim of "sexual or racial harassment" (note that, effective 1994, investigations of prior sexual conduct in claims alleging sex-related injuries such as sexual harassment are subject to restrictions on discovery under LC3208.4.) OR
5. The employee sustained a psychiatric injury during the remaining period of continued employment subsequent to notification of the effective date of a termination or layoff (see 6.14 for distinctions in

determining the date of a psychiatric injury that is a cumulative injury rather than a specific injury).

5.23 AOE – ARISE OUT OF EMPLOYMENT

The term "AOE" refers to the LC3600 requirement that a compensable injury must arise out of the employment. An injury arises out of the employment when the nature of the activity resulting in the injury is work-related. All employment duties and some personal activities are considered to arise out of the employment relationship. An injury meets the AOE test when the activity performed at the time of injury is either specifically required or reasonably contemplated by the employment relationship. Employers have the right to control activities in which the employee does or does not engage. Therefore, unless expressly or impliedly prohibited, the employee's activities during the entire period of his employment are deemed to be AOE.

The injury arises out of the employment when a pilot cuts his hand while checking an airplane instrument panel. A sewing needle puncture wound will arise out of the employment where the employee is a seamstress. A question of AOE would arise if either of these employees sustained a dog-bite injury or was in an automobile accident. Dogs and automobiles have no immediately recognizable connection to their work duties.

Every compensable injury will arise out of the employment, but some injuries that have an employment connection will not be work-related. For example, injuries sustained at the workplace by an initial physical aggressor are not compensable even if the subject matter of the dispute is work-related.

Suppose heavily armed criminals make a random selection of a restaurant where they demand all the cash from the cash register and valuables from customers and employees who are present. Certain actions of an employee to protect and recover employer property are reasonable; e.g. where, with appropriate consideration for her own safety, a waitress attempts to view the license number on a getaway car. However, injuries sustained when the waitress engages the armed criminals in a high-speed automobile chase to recover her purse or other stolen property will arise from a personal activity that would not be required, condoned, nor contemplated by her employer (see 5.51, and compare to self-inflicted injury in 5.16).

5.24 COE – COURSE OF EMPLOYMENT

In addition to the requirement that an injury arise out of the employment, a compensable injury must also be COE or occur during the course of employment. An employee is considered to be in the course of his employment during the hours the employee is paid and/or required to be at the employer's premises and/or performing his duties. If a carpenter works from 8:00 to 5:00 p.m., an injury during these hours occurs in the course of his employment. If a supervisor is expected to work overtime without pay, injuries during the extra hours of work are COE. If a real estate agent shows a house to a potential buyer on a day the real estate office is normally closed, the agent is within the course of his employment while showing the property.

Some injuries that occur during the course of the regular workday will not occur in the course of employment. An employee can remove himself from the course of employment during normal working hours. For instance, an employee is not acting within the course of his employment when he attends the race track instead of making sales calls to clients or when he utilizes his business expense account to entertain his relatives without the employer's knowledge or permission. In situations such as these, the employee is deemed to have removed himself from the course of his employment by abandoning his employment to conduct his personal business.

As a general rule, any injury that arises out of the employment will normally also occur in the course of employment, because employees are in the course of their employment during any time that the activities they perform are encompassed under their employment contract. This rule applies regardless of receipt of wages, the location or the time of day.

The one critical test of compensability is the work-related nature of the employee's activity at the time of injury. The employee is deemed to be in the course of his employment any time he is actually engaged in his employment. Conversely, the employee is not within the course of employment when his activities have no employment connection. The "arise out of" and "in the course of" requirements are not always investigated separately. The absence of one or the other of these conditions will suffice to bar compensability, but in the majority of cases AOE and COE blend together. In fact, investigations of the issue of "injury" are commonly referred to as "AOE/COE investigations."

5.25 JUDICIAL RULES & DOCTRINES

The frequency of disputes regarding "arise out of" and "in the course of" requirements for compensability of injuries has resulted in the judicial development of various AOE/COE rules, doctrines, and exceptions. The employer's liability for an injury must be determined by a coordination of Labor Code provisions and the adjunct general principles established through case law, including WCAB decisions and decisions of the Court of Appeal and the Supreme Court.

The courts' decisions in past cases are predictive of the courts' interpretation of statutory language as it applies to particular factual situations in future cases. However, past rulings are subject to change by later decisions, and similar situations sometimes produce disparate judicial rulings. Case decisions that seem contradictory can be distinguished by a close reading of the variances in factual situations from one case to another. The general principles that have been established by case law will be detailed under their separate topics without any reference to specific actual cases. For application to a specific claim, the principles set out herein should be read in conjunction with recent appellate decisions on the same topics.

5.26 GOING & COMING RULE

The general rule is that injuries are not compensable during the course of a normal commute to or from a fixed place of business. A "normal commute" means the employee's regular route by a transportation mode of the employee's own choosing at fairly fixed or regular hours from day-to-day. A "fixed place of business" means the employee's customary work location where the employee performs the services for which he was hired. "To or from" means during the time the employee is traveling. This period ends when the employee arrives at work and commences when the employee departs from the fixed place of business. Generally, injuries are barred by the Going and Coming Rule when the following facts exist:

1. The employee has a fixed work location.
2. The employee has regularly scheduled hours of work.
3. The employee controls the time he must leave home in order to get to work by the hours established by the employer.
4. The employee selects the mode of transportation utilized.
5. The employee travels by a route of the employee's choosing.
6. The employer has no interest in nor exercises any control over the employee during the period of the commute.

Most employees are not employed twenty-four hours a day. The employment relationship is suspended during the hours the employee is at home or en route to or from the employment. During this period, the employer usually has no control over the employee's activities, and the employee does not perform any employment services. Traveling to work is not considered a service benefiting the employer. The commute is a direct benefit to the employee, since he will not get paid until he gets to work and performs a beneficial service for the employer. The employer does not derive a benefit until a service requested by it has been rendered.

Some injuries during a commute will not be barred by the Going and Coming Rule. There are numerous exceptions to the standard application of this rule. Any time the employer has some element of control over the employee, the employment relationship exists and any injury will occur in the course of employment regardless of the employee's physical location at the time. The facts of each case must be examined closely. Ordinarily, the employee is considered to be within the course of employment (at work) and the Going and Coming Rule does not bar injuries sustained when (as explained in following sections):

a. The employee has arrived at the employment.
b. The employee has not yet departed from the employment.
c. The employee is being paid at the time of injury.
d. The employer exercises control over the employee's route.
e. The employer exercises control over the employee's activities during the commute.
f. The employer controls the employee's mode of transportation.
g. The employee is injured close to the employment location both in time and space by a risk created by or connected to his employment.

5.27 WAGES PAID DURING TRAVEL TIME

Employers provide wages in exchange for services. From this fact, there is derived an inference that the employee is performing a beneficial service for his employer whenever wages are being paid. When the employer pays the employee for travel time, travel to and from the employment is considered to be a service rendered to the employer. The employment relationship exists during the commute, so injuries during travel are not barred by the Going and Coming Rule.

5.28 TRANSPORTATION CONTROLLED BY EMPLOYER

If the employer provides a company-owned vehicle or pays some or all of the employee's travel expenses to induce use of a personal vehicle, the employer is exercising control over the method of travel to and from work. The employer may require that the employee have a personal vehicle available for use in the employer's business but not pay any expenses incurred by the employee. In either instance, the employee's transportation is considered to be controlled by the employer and injuries involving the use of the vehicle are not barred by the Going and Coming Rule.

It does not matter how frequently the employee is called upon to use the vehicle for business errands nor does it matter that any business use of the vehicle occurs only during regularly scheduled hours of the work day. Whenever the employer restricts the employee's free choice of transportation, use of employer-designated transportation during a commute becomes a required condition of employment. The reasons for the employer's requirement need not be ascertained. The employee's compliance with an actual employment requirement during travel will usually suffice to bring the employee's commute within the course of his employment.

Carpools

Per LC3600.8, injuries that occur during an employee's voluntary participation in a government-sponsored alternative commute program are not compensable unless the employer provides wages or salary during travel periods. This statute was added to the Labor Code effective 1994 but with a statement of legislative intent that its provisions are declaratory in nature, intended "only to clarify, and not to explain, limit or otherwise alter the" rights of the employee or the employer. This language, in essence, makes the provisions of LC3600.8 retroactive (effective regardless of the date an injury is sustained).

Per LC3600.8, the "employer's reimbursement of employee expenses or subsidization of costs related to an alternative commute program shall not be considered payment of a wage or salary" during travel periods. Employers are permitted to provide workers' compensation benefits to employees who participate in a vanpool arrangement if the "vanpool vehicle is owned or registered to the employer" (the employer may wish to incur the costs of ownership of the vanpool vehicle in order to invoke the exclusive remedy provisions of the Labor Code rather than expose itself to civil liability in the event of injuries).

5.29 BOUNDARIES OF EMPLOYMENT PREMISES

The physical boundaries of the employment location have been determined by the courts and will not be found in the Labor Code. In identifying the exact moment of the employee's arrival or departure for purposes of the Going and Coming Rule, employer premises can generally be defined as: the work location and nearby areas where the employee's presence is required or the location is controlled by his employer. This definition can encompass areas that are physically distant from the exact address where the employee performs his work duties. Generally, the employee is considered to be at his place of employment when the employee:

1. Is physically located upon property owned by the employer.
2. Is on the premises where his work services are performed.
3. Is on property leased or rented by the employer.
4. Is at a location controlled by the employer; e.g., the employer does not own a parking lot but does pay parking costs when its employees use a designated lot.
5. Has entered a main building through which he must pass in order to reach his employment location.
6. Has reached premises that are owned or controlled by the employer even though a direct route to the worksite causes him to leave and then reenter the employer's premises to gain entry to his work location.
7. Is exposed to a hazard or risk of employment that extends beyond the physical boundaries of the employer's property.

Employment premises include every square inch of the worksite and adjacent property where title or ownership is traceable to the employer (see 5.30 regarding public sidewalks). This property is deemed to be employer premises while the employee is traversing such property for purposes of coming to or going from his worksite. All property owned by the employer is not employment premises, since the employee may not have any business reason for ever setting foot on every property his employer owns even when the property is in close proximity to the employee's worksite.

Injuries sustained on employer-owned property will not be work-related if the employee's presence is due to purely personal reasons. For example, the employer may be a county that owns extensive property covering hundreds of square miles. Injuries while county employees make personal use of county facilities on their personal time are not work-related, e.g. while visiting a county library, eating in a county cafeteria or using a county park. Injuries are not compensable merely because the employer owns the premises where they occur. Compensability requires the existence of an employment relationship at the time of injury.

5.30 PREMISES – UNDER EMPLOYER'S CONTROL

Some employers do not own any property. When an employer leases physical space such as an office or building and/or surrounding grounds or parking areas, the employer pays for the right to control this property under the terms of the lease or rental agreement. It would be ridiculous to assert that employees who are in the building where they are employed are not on their employer's premises because their employers do not own any property. For this reason, it is the employer's control over a particular area that determines the actual boundaries of the employment premises, and the employee is on his employment premises when he is physically present on property leased or rented by his employer. Additionally, for workers' compensation purposes, employment premises can include some adjacent areas outside the exact space specified in the employer's rental or lease agreement.

The worksite may be an internal space such as a suite on the upper floor of a tall building or a department store within a large shopping mall. The area under the employer's control is usually limited to the subspace it occupies. The owner of the property usually controls areas of access to inner locations such as entrances to the building, lobby areas, elevators, stairwells, etc. If the employer owned the building, the employee would clearly be on his employment premises as soon as he placed a foot on the employer's property.

The courts have commonly treated the perimeters of the employment premises equivalently whether or not a particular employer owns the building. The employee cannot realistically be expected to deliver himself directly to an upper floor office by ladder or helicopter. By its choice of location, the employer exerted control, within a limited space, over the route the employee must travel to reach the employment site. Therefore, the employee has arrived at the employment premises upon arrival at the building where the employee works or at immediately adjacent property through which the employee must pass to access the worksite.

Pursuant to LC3852, the employer has a right of recovery (a subrogation action) against the owners of the property as well as any other entities whose negligence and/or intentional acts cause injury to an employee, e.g. when an injury results from a defect in an elevator, a walkway, a carpet or any other hazard that the employee encounters en route to an internal work location in a building that is not owned by the employer. If the employer is held liable for workers' compensation benefits, it is entitled to seek reimbursement of its payments directly from any legally responsible parties.

5.31 EXTENSIONS OF EMPLOYMENT PREMISES

Complicated situations can occur where the employee's direct route to his work location causes him to arrive at, leave, then reenter employment premises. The employee has arrived at work when he first reaches property that is employer-owned or controlled. Suppose the employer owns a nonadjacent parking lot that is separated from the worksite by a public street or other property that lacks any connection to the employer. The employee's transit from the parking lot to his worksite and the reverse trip back to the lot is not barred by the Going and Coming Rule. Compensability bridges the gap between employment premises and nonemployment premises. The employee is in the course of his employment during his entire transit from the initial point of arrival to his designated worksite.

In applying the Going and Coming Rule, employment premises are not restricted solely to areas that are owned or controlled by the employer. This is the most difficult principle to understand, since it is based on liberal appellate extensions of otherwise apparent physical boundaries. The employee can be deemed to be at his employment even though the employee is not on his employer's premises. The employment premises (locations where injuries would be in the course of employment) extend outward a nonspecified distance that includes adjacent areas where the employee is exposed to special hazards or risks of the employment.

While walking to work on a public sidewalk, the employee may cross an alley near his employer's loading docks and a short distance from his worksite. Injuries along the employee's route to the worksite may ordinarily be barred by the Going and Coming Rule. However, the Going and Coming Rule will not necessarily bar an injury if the employee is struck by a company vehicle entering the public alley. The employment premises will include this location that is close to the worksite in terms of time, distance, and exposure to a work-related hazard. The employer's obligation to provide workers' compensation benefits for injuries such as this will be financially advantageous, since a nonindustrial injury could subject the employer to unlimited civil liability for the negligent acts of its employees.

5.32 PARKING LOT INJURIES

Parking lots that are owned, leased or controlled by the employer are considered to be part of the employment premises. Control over the employee's choice of parking lots can consist of paying all or part of the employee's parking costs. When the employee utilizes an employer-designated lot, he is partaking of a company benefit, and the Going and Coming Rule will not apply to injuries in the parking lot (or going to or from the lot and the worksite). However, this fact does not automatically equate to compensability for all injuries that may be sustained. All injuries occurring on employment premises are potentially compensable, but every compensable injury must also arise out of the employment regardless of whether it occurs on employment premises or elsewhere.

Some parking lot injuries will not meet the basic tests of compensability. An employee may arrange a clandestine meeting in the parking lot with a lover. Whatever the employee might be doing, it is unlikely that any resultant injuries could have an employment connection, since the employer is unaware of the employee's presence. An injury that occurs in an employer-owned or controlled parking lot will not ordinarily be compensable if:

a. A statutory defense to injury exists under LC3600, e.g. an off-duty recreational activity or initial physical aggressor.

b. The injury occurs beyond the period of time that could reasonably be contemplated to allow the employee to depart from the premises after working hours; e.g., the employee meets friends for dinner and is mugged when he returns to the lot for his car several hours later.

c. The injury arises from an entirely personal activity in which the employee simply chose to engage on the employment premises; for instance, the employee drove to work on a day off to meet a friend for lunch or to pick up a coemployee after work to go fishing.

d. The employee is making an unreasonable use of the premises; examples include drag racing and dope dealing.

e. The injury arises from reasons unrelated to the employment and/or the location of the parking lot; e.g., a criminal who observes the employee cashing her paycheck follows her for the purpose of robbing and assaulting her as soon as she parks and exits her car, and the lot was the employee's first stop.

5.33 WEARING UNIFORM – DURING TRAVEL

Employers sometimes require their employees to wear a uniform during working hours. The employer may not have suitable facilities for the employee to change from street clothes to work clothes at the employer's premises. If the employer requires the employee to wear a uniform to and from work, the employer has exercised some control over the employee during his commuting time. This is an extremely limited amount of control; it is limited to the type of clothing the employee wears, not his mode of transportation or the route traveled.

There may be a proximate cause between an injury and the uniform the employee is wearing. However, the mere fact that the employee is wearing a uniform at the time of injury is insufficient for compensability. Additional factors must be present (see also 5.34 regarding law enforcement officers). Factors leading to compensability could include the following:

1. The uniform requires a special mode of transportation; it is too bulky or heavy to be carried while walking or on a bus.

2. The uniform itself is a proximate cause of the injury; it is flammable or otherwise poorly designed for the safety of the wearer.

3. The uniform identifies the employee with his employer, and the injury is due to this connection; for example, where an irate customer wishes to harm an employee of a particular company.

4. The employee is performing a service of benefit to the employer at the employer's request; e.g., the employer requires the uniform to be worn because of potential advertisement benefits (if the employee is performing such a service, the employee is within the course of his employment regardless of how the employee is dressed).

Suppose the employee is a security guard who wears a uniform that includes a gun and holster. He may be assaulted by armed criminals while going home after a late night shift. The criminals may be apprehended and admit they assaulted the employee because they spotted his uniform and wanted to obtain his weapon. There is proximate cause between the injury and the uniform this employee was wearing. The injury arises out of the employment, because there is an employment connection between the requirement to wear the uniform and the injuries sustained.

There may be no connection whatsoever between an injury and the fact that the employee is wearing a uniform at the time. The employee may be broadsided in his car, hit someone else's car or just run his car off the road into a tree. The proximate cause of the injury may be mechanical difficulties with a vehicle, bad driving habits or any number of causes that have no relationship to the uniform or the employment. The reason for a fall at home might be the fact that a rug slipped, not the fact that the employee was wearing a uniform. In these situations, crucial elements of compensability are missing: the employee is not performing a service of benefit to the employer under the employer's direction and control and has not sustained an injury proximately caused by the employment.

The fact that a uniform is being worn does not prove the existence of the necessary elements that an injury arise out of and in the course of employment (be AOE/COE). In most instances, a uniform is only a tangential aspect of the employment. The employee's attire at the time of injury may be a supporting indication of either AOE, COE, or both, but it is unlikely to be conclusive by itself.

5.34 WEARING UNIFORM – SAFETY OFFICERS

Injuries to public safety officers have been held to be compensable while a uniform was worn en route to work. A common misconception is that compensability flows from the fact that a uniform is worn. If no service of benefit to the employer is being rendered, wearing a police uniform to work is no different from a compensability standpoint than a dentist or a flight attendant wearing a uniform while traveling to work. Compensability does not derive merely from the fact a uniform is worn; it derives from the usual tests of compensability.

A safety officer may be required to act in his official capacity if a potential crime is spotted en route to work. Should the officer spot a crime in progress and take official action, any injuries sustained will arise out of and in the course of employment. In this case, compensability will ensue regardless of whether the officer is wearing a uniform or street clothes at the time. If an injury is caused by the officer's intoxication, his injury is not compensable whether or not the officer was in uniform when injured. The proper focus of an investigation is to determine whether the elements of AOE and COE exist and whether there is proximate cause between the injury and the employment relationship (see 5.8 and 5.23-5.24).

5.35 SPECIAL MISSION – SPECIAL ERRAND

A special mission is interchangeably called a special errand. The employee is engaged in a special mission when he is performing a work-related service off the employment premises at his employer's request. A special mission represents an exception to the Going and Coming Rule. Injuries during travel to and from the worksite will occur within the course of employment when the employee is on a special mission for his employer. The following list describes the various ways in which the employee's activity could be considered to be a special mission:

a. The activity occurs off-premises, and the employee normally works at one fixed work location; e.g., the boss sends his secretary to a library.

b. The activity occurs at a location where the employee does not routinely perform his regular work duties; e.g., the employee is sent to a different office for two weeks to fill in for someone who is ill, or to a client's office, or to a formal class.

c. The activity is a work duty that cannot be performed on the premises, e.g. purchasing postage stamps or making bank deposits.

d. The activity occurs during hours the employee is not ordinarily required to work, e.g. before or after work or at lunch time.

e. The activity is not a normal duty, but it is a requirement of the employer and therefore part of the employment contract; e.g., the employer requests the employee to take an injured coemployee to a medical facility.

The special mission doctrine can encompass a broad variety of activities. The basis for extending compensability to off-premises injuries is the fact that the employment relationship exists at the time of injury, because the employee is performing a service for the benefit and at the specific request of his employer. The employee is not engaged in a special mission when he leaves the employment premises on his own volition to engage in personal activities of his own choice. Off-premises activities become services under the employment contract when the employer exercises a certain type of control over the employee's off-premises activities — the type of control ordinarily exercised by an employer over an employee.

Mixed Personal & Business Purposes. Injuries while engaged in special missions are usually compensable, but problems can arise when an employee also conducts personal and unrelated business of his own in conjunction with an employment errand. Suppose the employer requests the employee to make a bank deposit on his way back from lunch. If the employee is injured during a theft of the employer's money, the injury would arise out of the employment whether the employee was eating lunch or making the bank deposit. However, it is unlikely that there is any basis for compensability if the employee cuts his lip on a broken glass while eating lunch prior to undertaking the special trip to the bank. It appears the employer intended the special mission to begin after the employee concluded his lunch. The special mission has no connection to this injury or to any type of personal activities in which the employee chooses to engage during his regular lunch hour.

Personal Errand for Supervisor or Coworker. Employees sometimes perform personal missions for coemployees, that could include supervisors. An off-premises activity is not an employment mission just because it is undertaken at a supervisor's request or has some incidental relationship to the employment.

A supervisor may need a ride to a repair shop to pick up his car after work. If he asks a personal friend who is a subordinate to give him a ride, the nature of the request is personal. A collection may be taken to buy a birthday cake for a supervisor. The employee is not engaged in a special mission at the request of his employer when he uses his lunch time to pick up a cake at a bakery.

The voluntary activities mentioned above arise out of interpersonal relationships developed at the workplace, but they are not special missions, employment duties or services impliedly required under the employment contract. These activities are more appropriately labeled as off-premises social activities (see 5.19).

5.36 TRANSPORTING WORK TOOLS OR SUPPLIES

A phrase often repeated by claimspersons is "Always carry a file in your car because if you are ever in an automobile accident, your injuries will be work-related." Liberal appellate decisions have sometimes seemed to rely on this remote employment connection as a sufficient basis for finding off-premises injuries compensable. However, more modern trends in appellate decisions indicate that a remote connection will not suffice to meet the LC3600 requirement for proximate cause between the employment and resultant injuries. As a general rule, injuries during a commute taking work home for the employee's personal convenience are not work-related and therefore not compensable.

The fact that the employee was transporting a file folder or some other work material does not in and of itself establish the necessary elements for compensability. In fact, the employee's actions might be grounds for disciplinary action or criminal prosecution for theft of company property. It is possible that the employee may have appropriated work items for personal use, or items may have been removed from the workplace without employer knowledge, request, or express or implied permission.

There is no logical basis for extending compensability to circumstances where the sole employment connection is established by intentional and unilateral actions of employees. The LC3600 requirement that the employment relationship exist at the time of injury clearly requires the interaction of both an employer and an employee, not unilateral action by an employee.

From a compensability standpoint, the fact that an employee is transporting work materials is no more relevant than the fact that a uniform is worn while commuting to work. Transportation of work materials may have no causal connection with the occurrence of any injury. Suppose the employee took a work file home to perform some work in the evening. An injury while transporting the file back to work may result from causes that are entirely independent from this fact. There is no apparent employment connection if the employee is struck by a drunk driver while driving a car, gets stung by a bee while walking, falls off a bicycle when a tire blows out or is assaulted on a bus by a purse thief. The sole connection to the employment appears to be an entirely coincidental element: the employee had employer-owned property in his possession.

Considering all of the separate but cumulative requirements of LC3600, mere transportation of work materials at the time of an injury is a weak basis for extending compensability to an injury off the employment premises. If this is the only connection, it is a remote one, and satisfying the proximate cause test requires something more. Proximate cause could be established if the employee ordinarily walked to work or rode the bus, but he is injured in his personal car while transporting the employer's typewriter back to work. In this case, a special mode of transportation was necessary to transport the work materials and an injury resulted from use of the special transportation. The employee might drive his car to work daily. An accident may occur when the typewriter shifts position and he tries to keep it from falling off the front seat. In this case, resulting injuries would be proximately caused by the employment, because the work item itself played a causative role in the resultant injury.

The facts listed below tend to negate proximate causation between the employment and an injury while transporting work materials:

a. Transportation of work materials was voluntary and undertaken for the employee's own convenience.
b. The employer was unaware that any work materials were taken from or being brought to the premises.
c. The employer was aware of the employee's activity and did not prohibit it because he saw no harm in it, but he did not and would not require it.
d. The employee's use of his customary mode of transportation was unaffected by his transportation of work materials; in all other aspects the employee's commute did not differ from his commute on days when work materials were not transported.
e. The injury had no relationship to the transportation of work materials. The injury would have occurred regardless of whether the employee had work materials in his possession at the time, not because the materials were being transported.

5.37 WORK PERFORMED AT HOME

The single most important factor in determining compensability is the existence of the employment relationship at the time of injury, and this relationship can extend to the employee's home. Injuries are compensable when they arise out of the employee's performance under the terms of his contract of employment. The employer can limit the employment relationship to definite confines of time and location, or the employer can extend the usual limits by requiring performance of services for its benefit beyond the workplace. Special errands or special missions are one example of an off-premises extension. Work at home is another.

When the employer requires work performed in the employee's home, injuries during a commute to and from the regular work premises are not barred by the Going and Coming Rule. The employee's home becomes a second job site, and the employee is traveling between two worksites during his commute. This travel is the same as travel between two employer-owned premises at the employer's request. A defense to an injury may exist, but it will not be the application of the Going and Coming Rule.

The employer's requirements can be implied from the circumstances. For instance, a requirement appears to exist when an employer actively encourages work at home. In some workplaces, it is common knowledge that the employer expects to see employees depart with work materials in hand. Performance appraisals may document the employer's awareness and appreciation of work performed at home. Merit raises may be based upon the employee's extra efforts. Coemployees may have a common understanding of the employer's actual expectations and what it takes to do a "good job," get a good raise or get promoted. Under such circumstances, work at home would appear to be an implied requirement of the employment, since the employer is aware that work is performed at home, receives a benefit therefrom, and officially recognizes this practice in the workplace.

The employer's prior awareness or approval of work at home is not always a prerequisite for compensability of the employee's at-home injuries. An investigation should determine the type of work that was being performed and the reason it was performed in the home rather than at the workplace. A judge can find in favor of compensability when it appears reasonable that the employer would have requested work to be done at home if advance approval had been sought for the reasons provided. For instance, the reasons below could provide a basis for extending the course of employment into the employee's home without an employer's preknowledge:

   a. The work environment is not conducive to the completion of the assigned task, e.g. too noisy for the employee to concentrate.
   b. The employee must meet a deadline, and the designated task cannot be completed during regular work hours.
   c. The work requires extended hours and cannot be completed at the work location; e.g., a burglar alarm is automatically turned on at closing time.
   d. The work can only be performed in the home, e.g. where the employer requires documents to be translated, knowing the employee has a family member who can assist with this service.
   e. Work can be better performed at home; e.g., the employee is requested to do a detailed report that must be spread out in a large area, and no such facility is available at work.
   f. The employee has a special piece of equipment or a tool that is not available at the work location such as a home computer or calculator. The employer benefits by having the use of the item without having to purchase it.

At-home injuries are not compensable if the employee's activities are undertaken for his own convenience. The employee may be a slow worker who takes work home because he can't complete tasks in the same time as his peers or feels he is not working as hard as he should be during regular work hours. For example, the employee may spend a lot of time gossiping or making personal phone calls at work, and the purpose of working at home is to avoid the employer's discovery of his inadequate productivity. The employee may be a high achiever who voluntarily performs work at home so his productivity will exceed that of his peers. The employee may desire to impress superiors by making certain he is seen taking work home, but he may never do anything more than carry materials back and forth. The employment relationship does not extend to the employee's home when his off-premises activities are personally motivated and self-serving, because his employer does not derive any special benefit from the fact that work is taken home.

At-home injuries will require special scrutiny regarding the mechanics of the injury sustained. The employer is at a disadvantage in conducting an on-premises investigation to determine the employee's actual activities since the employee has complete control of the location where the injury occurred. The employee's assertions of his activities at the time of injury may be difficult to refute if work materials are admittedly present in the home. Information presented by any party having such advantage should receive the close examination it deserves in order to avoid undue emphasis on self-serving allegations (see 5.42 regarding a comparable situation in mysterious death cases). Home injuries require careful appraisal of any benefit to the employer, but such benefit will not establish compensability in the absence of an employer requirement that work be performed at home.

5.38 COMMERCIAL TRAVELER RULE

The Commercial Traveler Rule is an exception to the Going and Coming Rule that applies to employees who are required to travel out of town for business purposes. The special mission doctrine applies to local or one-day business trips. The Commercial Traveler Rule applies to situations where a special mission necessitates an overnight stay. The courts have provided many special considerations to commercial travelers in recognition of the fact that they are exposed to distinctly different hazards than those that may exist at the workplace or even while engaged in special employer missions of shorter duration.

A commercial traveler is within the course of his employment at all times during his travel. All business and many personal activities of the commercial traveler are considered to arise out of his employment. The following ordinarily personal activities are considered employment-related for commercial travelers:

    a. **Traveling:** The Going and Coming Rule does not apply. The employee is within the course of his employment portal-to-portal from his departure from his home until his arrival back home.

    b. **Obtaining food or drink:** These activities are reasonably contemplated by the employer's request, since they are reasonably necessary to accomplish the business purpose of the trip.

    c. **Obtaining or using lodging:** The principles that apply to the use of employer-provided housing under the Bunkhouse Rule apply equally to the use of lodging provided to a commercial traveler (see 5.48).

d. **Recreational activities:** The employee is reasonably expected to engage in some type of personal activities outside the times he is engaged in the business purpose of the trip. Basically, the principles that extend compensability to personal activities at the worksite under the Personal Comfort Doctrine will apply to the employee's off-premises activities (see 5.43).

The Going and Coming Rule does not apply during the trip, because the employee is not traveling to his usual place of business. The Going and Coming Rule will bar injuries prior to commencement and subsequent to termination of the trip. If the employee trips over a carpet in his home while packing a suitcase or cuts himself while shaving in preparation for the trip, the trip has not yet commenced. The business trip commences after the employee leaves his personal residence or premises to conduct his employer's business (or upon entering an employer owned or controlled vehicle that is used to and from the employee's residence for business travel; see 5.28).

In most cases, the business trip will end when the employee arrives back at his home, but the business trip can end sooner. The employee is no longer a commercial traveler when he decides to engage in a personal activity instead of going directly home. For example, the employee may reach his local neighborhood and decide to visit friends, stop at a bar, return library books or simply go for a drive rather than going home. Upon his decision to undertake a personal activity, the employee is no longer considered to be acting under the control of his employer as a commercial traveler.

The employer's prior knowledge or permission is not required for each personal activity in which a commercial traveler engages. The major factor leading to compensability will be a determination that the employee's activities were reasonable under the circumstances, considering the employee's distance from his home. Some activities will be reasonable in view of the environment where the employer's business is conducted. Examples include visiting tourist attractions, shopping for souvenirs or exploration of the local area. Additionally, almost any activity in which the employee regularly engages at home will be reasonable when he continues to engage in the activity during a trip, e.g. going to a movie, weight lifting, jogging or bowling.

The employer can establish valid defenses to liability for injuries sustained by a commercial traveler, but the employer's burden of proof is difficult. Basically, the employer must obtain evidence that is sufficient to establish that the employee's activity was blatantly unreasonable, not contemplated by the employer, one that the employer would have prohibited if permission were requested or illegal. Some examples of situations that could provide the basis for an employer defense include:

a. The activity was inherently dangerous; e.g., the employee attempted skydiving for the first time or paid $5.00 to wrestle a bear.
b. The site of the activity was remote from the location where the employer's business is conducted; e.g., the employee is injured in a

different city and his reasons for being there are unknown to the
employer.
c. The activity is criminal in nature; e.g., the employee was beaten and
   robbed while purchasing cocaine from a local dealer or engaged in
   illegal gambling.
d. The activity is intimate and too personal to involve any employer
   interest, e.g. a back injury or venereal disease from sexual relations.
e. The employee removed himself from the area of employer control
   and exposed himself to a personal risk of harm; e.g., the employee
   spends the night in the room of a prostitute, and the injury is one that
   would not have occurred if the employee had stayed in the hotel
   provided by the employer.
f. The employee abandons the business of the employer to conduct
   personal business, e.g., the employee skips a business meeting to go
   visit old college buddies.

5.39 SPECIAL RISK – ZONE OF DANGER

Some employees are susceptible to particular types of injuries by the nature of
their work duties or location. For example, employees who work with explosives
have a potential to be blown up. Liquor store employees are exposed to armed
robbers with a high enough frequency to consider their worksite to be a place of
danger. Lifeguards work in a zone of danger since dangers such as sunken logs,
carnivorous fish and panicking swimmers can result in injuries while performing
employment duties. Compensability is not usually disputed when an injury
results from a known hazard of the employment.

Compensability is commonly disputed when the hazard producing an injury is
out-of-the-ordinary and not overtly employment-related. In these cases,
employees may assert that the doctrine of "special risk" applies. Under this
doctrine, an injury is compensable if the employment placed the employee in a
zone of danger where the employee was exposed to a particular risk of harm by
virtue of the employment duties or location.

Suppose a female auto plant worker is robbed and beaten in a private parking
lot just after leaving work late at night. This after-hours injury appears to result
from a purely random criminal act without any employment connection. However, the injury would be proximately caused by the employment if the
employment placed her in a zone of danger wherein she was exposed to the
particular type of risk that resulted in her injury. To support compensability on
this basis, the employee would attempt to establish the following facts:
a. The hazard is related to the time of day the employee works; e.g., a
   similar hazard does not exist during a day shift when more employees
   would walk together to the parking lot.
b. The risk of harm to the employee was greater than to a member of
   the general public; e.g., the public is unlikely to use the parking lot
   at a late night hour, or the employee is exposed to a greater risk of a

traffic accident by having to make a left turn into cross traffic in order to enter or depart the employer's premises.

c. The risk of harm producing the injury is connected to her employment; e.g., the employee was exposed to the risk of a criminal assault in a fairly isolated area by her employer's requirement to work late at night.

d. The parking lot was a place of danger for employees; e.g., employees are the only persons in the vicinity at night, so only employees would be exposed to a criminal attack.

e. The hazard was a reasonably predictable risk for employees; e.g., the employer is aware that similar incidents have occurred in the past.

In the situations detailed above, the courts have found injuries to be compensable. However, other injuries that appear to have an even more overt employment connection may be found to be unrelated to the employment. Suppose the employee is shot and killed while acting within the course of his employment during a late night robbery at a liquor store. The initial impression would be that the employee was injured by a risk inherent in his employment. However, the employer could disprove any special risk arising out of the employment by a thorough examination of the facts. The employer could meet its burden of proof with evidence that the injury was a gangland-style murder precipitated by the employee's failure to pay large gambling debts.

5.40 ACTS OF GOD

Acts of God include such natural events as floods, landslides, lightning and earthquakes. As a general rule, Acts of God do not produce compensable injuries, because it is difficult for an employee to demonstrate how the employment was the proximate cause of such injuries. However, it is possible for injuries from such events to be compensable.

Lightning during thunder storms is not an entirely unpredictable occurrence. Few would argue that an employee who raises a flag on a metal flagpole is exposed to a greater risk of being struck by lightning than any member of the general public who may be in the vicinity when lightning strikes. If the employer requires the employee to take down the flag during a thunder storm, the employment would be the proximate cause of the injury even though the direct cause of injury was an Act of God. However, when a danger is apparent or commonly understood, the employee is given some responsibility to act reasonably by not exposing himself to it. The injury would not be compensable if the employee went out in a storm contrary to a directive of his employer or had adequate knowledge of an imminent danger but voluntarily chose to expose himself to the risk.

When natural disasters affect a large geographic area, some people may be at work at the time, some will be injured, and some will claim their injuries are work-related. An earthquake may be of sufficient magnitude to generate an immediate predilection of death and destruction in the minds of all who experience it. Some persons may suffer heart attacks or episodes of bleeding ulcers, or the stress of the event may result in a later need for treatment or counseling for a post-traumatic stress syndrome. The employment cannot be said to be the proximate cause of injuries that result entirely from a reaction to the natural event.

Some aspect of the employment may increase the risk of harm or create a special risk or danger resulting in an injury that would not have occurred if the employee had been located elsewhere. For instance, an employee who works in a windowless concrete building may be drowned in a flood after an earthquake that ruptures a dam at the worksite. If the only persons who drowned were those at this worksite, then the employment was the proximate cause of these deaths because the employment created a special risk of danger of death by drowning during the earthquake. If window glass is broken at all structures in the local area during an earthquake, it may be a matter of pure conjecture whether any employee would have sustained a more serious injury from broken glass at home than he did when glass broke at work or vice versa. An injury from broken glass that is due to the type of window glass at work or the employee's proximity to it may be compensable. However, if no special aspect of the employment was involved, the naturally occurring disaster would appear to be the proximate cause of injuries sustained at the worksite as well as those sustained by the general populace.

5.41 ASSAULTS BY NONEMPLOYEES

The employee may be assaulted at his place of employment or during a time when he is actively engaged in his employment duties. The employee's injuries are not compensable unless the injury arises out of the employment in addition to being within the course of employment. The assault may be personally motivated and have no connection to the employment. The assault may occur solely because of the employment, or the employment may be a contributory factor in the assault. In the latter two situations, the employee's injuries would be work-related; in the first, they would not.

An important aspect of the investigation is to determine whether the assailant was personally known to the employee. Proof of a personal relationship alone will not bar compensability because this fact does not negate proximate employment causation. It is also necessary to establish a personal motivation for the assault in order to refute any employment causation. The employer's investigation must be conducted on both a personal and employment level and must address potential facts that the employee may allege in support of compensability. The employee can establish a compensable injury by proving the following types of facts:

    a. The employee was exposed to a risk of harm because of his particular employment, e.g. an isolated work location or a place of danger.

    b. The employer was aware of the potential for harm; e.g., there were previous similar assaults, or the employer had advance knowledge that the employee was in potential danger.

   c. The employer increased the risk of harm to the employee, e.g. by knowingly directing an assailant where to find his intended victim.

   d. The employer failed to take adequate precautions for the safety of the employee; e.g., being aware of the potential for harm, the employer did not act and/or did not act reasonably in view of the situation.

   e. The employer failed to respond to the employee's reasonable requests for safety measures; e.g., the employee had repeatedly requested a lock installed on a public access door to an inner office or requested that a particular individual be denied access to the employee.

   f. The employee's duties motivated the assault; e.g., a landlord is assaulted while serving an eviction notice.

   g. The employee's duties assisted the assailant in making a personal assault; e.g., the assailant lures an outside sales representative to an isolated location by making a telephone request for the sales representative to perform his normal duties.

If a criminal shoots a bank teller during a holdup, the teller's injuries arise out of and in the course of employment. If the teller's husband shoots her because she is having an affair, the teller is acting within the course of her employment, but her injuries do not arise out of her employment. Problems arise when there is a mixture of business and personal factors that precipitate an injury at work, e.g. if the wife was dating a coemployee. An incidental employment aspect to a dispute will not establish proximate cause between the injury and the employment contract. Injuries resulting from a husband's sadistic response to his wife's infidelity are not the type of injuries over which any employer has control or could be presumed to have control, and there is no causal connection between such injuries and the employment.

The employer does not owe compensation for a totally personal assault and will not be liable for injuries if the employee's duties played no causative role in an assault, did not produce a risk of harm or did not increase the risk of harm to the employee. The nature of the employee's duties or employment may be inconsequential to the assailant. The assault may occur at work because this is where the employee happens to be when the assailant decides to seek him out. If the sole role of the employment is that it merely provides the place for the assault to occur, this role does not constitute proximate cause between injury and employment.

✳Workplace Violence Safety Act

An employee may suffer physical violence at work or suffer a credible threat of harm from an individual who poses a credible threat of future violence in the workplace. The prevalence of such acts led to enactment of the Workplace Violence Safety Act that is set out in CCP527.8, effective 1994. This Act provides the employer with certain remedies, but it was enacted with a statement of legislative intent that it does not obligate any employer to seek available optional remedies. (It remains to be seen whether this statement of legislative intent will suffice to eliminate liability for a serious and willful misconduct penalty under

LC4553 where an injury occurs after an employer chooses not to pursue an available remedy.)

Unlawful violence includes actual or threatened assault, battery or stalking (but not an employee's actions of self-defense or defense of others). To prevent unlawful violence in the workplace, CCP527.8 permits the employer to seek a temporary restraining order and an injunction on behalf of its employee. A restraining order is generally applicable for a 15-day period, but a civil court judge can issue an injunction for a duration of three years. (Note that, for purposes of CCP527.8 only, the term "employee" is defined to include volunteers or independent contractors who are performing services at the workplace.)

5.42 MYSTERIOUS DEATH

The employee may be found dead while in the course of his employment at his desk, in a company car, at his machine or at any location where his duties are customarily performed. When the cause of the employee's death is not readily apparent, the employee's death is referred to as a "mysterious death." The mystery relates to the compensability of the death, not anything more sinister. Compensability will depend upon whether there is proximate cause between the employment and the medical cause of death.

The investigation is very similar to a suicide claim with one major distinction. In a mysterious death case, it is undisputed that the employee was within the course of his employment at the time of death, since the employee was paid at the time and/or was located on the employer's premises. The investigation is directed exclusively to a determination of whether the death arose out of the employment. Medical evidence will establish the medical cause of death. The facts surrounding the death will determine whether proximate cause exists between the medical diagnosis and the employment.

The compensability issue can be decided solely upon a medical diagnosis. For example, the employee may be found dead in a room where the employee is exposed to toxic fumes. It may originally appear that the death resulted from fume inhalation. However, an autopsy might reveal that the cause of death was a stroke (see 12.29). The employee might originally be believed to be a victim of electrocution, showing the signs of such injury and working near electrical apparatus. The employer's investigation is concluded when it is determined that the reason for the death is nonindustrial; e.g. an allergic reaction to medications or a nonindustrial condition. Some medical conditions are known to have a lethal course independent of the employee's occupation, location or activities at the time of death. Examples would include cancer, an overdose of drugs or syphilis. It is thus possible for medical evidence to support a lack of proximate cause between death and the employment.

There are many reasons why medical evidence may be an insufficient basis for a denial of compensation. A precise cause of death may be unknown, even though a medical diagnosis is made. For example, death may result from a heart attack, but this medical diagnosis does not reveal whether the death is work-related or nonindustrial. Other examples of noncontrolling medical diagnoses are a stroke and collapsed lungs. Medical opinions may be divided as to an exact diagnosis, or medical experts may disagree as to the role the employment played in the death. There may be many equally valid opinions that could reasonably explain the employee's death.

A premises investigation is necessary whenever medical evidence is inconclusive regarding the proximate cause of a mysterious death. The facts surrounding the employee's death must be determined to the extent it is possible to do so. Additionally, the employer's defense can be based upon reasonable inferences that the facts suggest. The employer's investigation will focus on the following areas:

    a. The site of the death: does the location itself explain the death; e.g., the employee dies of heat prostration while working in the sun or near a blasting furnace?

    b. The potential for harm to the employee from the performance of his work duties: was the employee exposed to a risk of harm from his work, e.g. exposure to toxic fumes and death from a pulmonary function disorder? Was the employee located in a zone of danger?

    c. Indications that the employee was performing his work duties at the time of death, e.g. work materials in the immediate vicinity or articles the employee is holding or has on his person.

    d. Employee's statements to coworkers: did the employee have any physical complaints, and to what did he attribute such complaints?

    e. Observations of coworkers prior to death: what were the employee's activities on the day the injury occurred?

    f. Reconstruction of the employee's activities at the time of death: was the employee engaged in an employment activity, what type of work had been completed or was in progress, and was the completed work more or less than normal?

    g. Physical appearance of worksite at the time: what factors were ordinary and what elements were unusual?

In mysterious death cases, LC3202.5 requires the employee's dependents to prove industrial causation by a preponderance of the evidence, but they are at a disadvantage in proving employment causation by other than medical evidence. The employer controls the location where the death occurred, and the employer could have some reason to cover up the true facts of the situation, e.g. the existence of a safety hazard that could subject the employer to some kind of penalty. For this reason, the courts have consistently taken a skeptical view of employer investigations of their own premises and have developed a presumption that applies to mysterious death cases. Where the employee dies from indeterminable causes during the course of his employment, the death is presumed to be work-related. To overcome the presumption, the employer must produce every piece of evidence that will refute any reasonable inference that the death may be work-related.

5.43 PERSONAL COMFORT DOCTRINE

Under the personal comfort doctrine, it is possible for compensable injuries to occur while employees are engaged in personal activities that provide for their comfort in the workplace. The application of this doctrine is generally limited to personal activities that take place on the employer's premises during compensated work breaks. The activity must be one that has no inherent potential for injury. It must be one that the employer would not have prohibited if the employer had previous knowledge of the activity. Also, the activity must actually provide for the employee's own personal comfort.

At the workplace, employees daily engage in certain reasonably anticipated personal activities. In fact, the employer is legally required to provide for its employees' personal comfort to a limited extent. For instance, there are state laws requiring the provision of restroom facilities and drinking fountains. Injuries that occur while getting a drink or using the restroom are clearly within the course of employment. The significant missing link to compensability is the "arise out of employment" criteria (AOE) of LC3600. This hurdle has been overcome through appellate court interpretations of the meaning of "employment related."

Certain personal activities are a normal part of life for everyone, and it would be unreasonable for an employer to prohibit these personal acts or to demand that the employee leave the employer's premises. When a personal activity can be thus described, it is deemed to be employment related when it occurs on the employer's premises regardless of whether the employer has actual advance knowledge of a specific type of activity.

It is also possible for off-premises injuries to be compensable under the personal comfort doctrine. The employee's activities must be of the same nature as activities that would lead to compensable injuries on the employment premises. Additionally, the employer must be aware of the off-premises activity, and it must have the employer's express or implied approval. If all of these criteria are present, the personal comfort doctrine will apply to an off-premises activity. For instance, the personal comfort doctrine will apply to off-premises injuries during coffee breaks if the employer condones a routine practice of taking coffee breaks at a nearby restaurant.

The employee can have his employer's approval of an activity without making any specific request. It may be readily apparent from the activities of coemployees that the employer routinely grants similar requests, e.g. where some employees have obtained the employer's permission to make bank deposits during their coffee breaks, other employees also deposit their checks on payday, and no one has ever been reprimanded. An important factor in support of compensability is the employer's knowledge of the activity in advance of its occurrence and no prohibition of the activity.

Having granted approval for one occurrence of an activity, the employer is not presumed to condone all future repetitions of the activity. The employer must have knowledge that the activity is repeated before the employer can be found to sanction its continuance. However, the fact that the employer condoned an activity in the past supports the employee's allegation that the activity is not one the employer would prohibit. For this reason, the employer will have the burden of proving any restrictions on the approval previously extended.

The nature of the employee's activity is particularly relevant to the issue of compensability under the personal comfort doctrine. However, the types of activities that are encompassed under this doctrine are not specified anywhere, and a test of reasonableness must be applied to each case. There are some activities that no reasonable employer would condone. For instance, it is clear that this doctrine does not extend compensability to injuries arising out of unusual, bizarre, daring, risky or deviate activities, nor does it apply to activities with an inherent potential for injury to the employee or others.

Disputes commonly arise where the employer has extended approval based upon partial knowledge of the employee's activities. For instance, the employer may know that the employee is a karate expert and extend permission for the employee to do exercises during breaks. This permission does not imply approval of hand-chopping bricks or demonstrating killer moves on coemployees. Absent evidence to the contrary, the employer's condonation of the employee's activities is presumed to be restricted to approval of activities that a reasonable person would condone.

5.44 ACTS OF NECESSITY

This doctrine is really an alter ego of the personal comfort doctrine that extends compensability to a particular category of personal activities. An act of necessity can be defined as an activity that, if delayed, could result in harm to the employee's physical well-being. For workers' compensation purposes, this doctrine refers to acts necessary to maintain a state of health for performance of work duties during the course of working hours. Acts relating to personal or family emergencies outside of work are not encompassed.

The fact that the act is a necessary one supplants any requirement to obtain the employer's prior approval or to provide the employer with advance knowledge of the activity. Instead, compensability requires only a determination that the activity was reasonable to provide for the employee's health or safety at his worksite. Activities contemplated by this doctrine generally include such things as going to the bathroom or getting a drink of water. These particular acts may also be considered acts of convenience or personal comfort, but, if delayed, these acts eventually become acts of necessity.

Acts of necessity will ordinarily lead to compensable injuries any time during the course of employment. If an act of necessity takes place off-premises, the activity must be one that any employer could reasonably expect the employee to engage in on the employer's premises while the employee is being paid. For example, compensability will extend to the site of an off-premises restroom where the closest facility is not part of the employer's premises. The necessity of the act is more significant than the location where the activity is performed.

(Note: nonindustrial medical problems can also occur while engaged in an act of necessity; e.g., where an employee experiences the pain of an appendicitis attack, a ruptured aneurysm or a cyst on an ovary while en route to or from a restroom).

5.45 ACTS OF CONVENIENCE

Some personal activities will not lead to compensable injuries. When the employee alleges his activity was one of personal comfort or necessity, the employer could defend against compensability by showing that the personal activity was undertaken during the course of employment solely for the employee's personal convenience. Compensability can be refuted with evidence demonstrating that the activity was not one reasonably contemplated under the personal comfort doctrine nor could the activity be considered to be an act of necessity.

The employer's defense can be summarized as establishing, with evidence, that it was unreasonable for the employee to engage in the activity, the activity could not be reasonably contemplated, and the activity is one for which employer approval would not likely be sought or granted. A thorough investigation is necessary to determine the nature of the activity and the extent of the employer's knowledge of it. Specific aspects of the employer's defense include proof that:

a. The employer was unaware that the employee was performing the particular activity; e.g., the activity is performed surreptitiously or out of sight and sound of others.

b. The employer was not aware and would not have condoned the location where an activity was performed; e.g., an activity that would be compensable on the employer's premises under the personal comfort doctrine is performed off-premises without the employer's knowledge or consent.

c. The employer would not have condoned the activity if aware of its occurrence; e.g., the employer has never condoned similar activities and/or has prohibited similar activities.

d. The employer would have expressly prohibited the activity if permission had been requested; e.g., the activity would be objectionable to any reasonable employer.

e. The activity is a type that is not ordinarily engaged in by employees during the workday or at the workplace; e.g., the employee brings an antique gun to work and is injured when the gun accidentally misfires while he is cleaning it.

f. The activity is a unique type in which few persons engage at work or outside work.

g. The act or activity has an inherent potential for injury that would be known to the person performing the act.

h. The employer exerted no control over the employee at the time the activity was performed.

i. The activity was engaged in solely for the employee's own convenience, at his volition, and at a time and place he chose.

j. The employer received no benefit from the activity.

k. The employee's decision to engage in the activity was entirely personal without any consideration for the interests of his employer.

There are certain activities for which employees are unlikely to request permission. No employee will request advance approval where it is obvious that the employer would not permit the activity. Common sense is the best guide to activities in this category. For example, the employee might sustain an eye injury from light exposure while trying to make a copy of his face on the employer's copy machine. It is hard to imagine any employer giving permission to use business property in this way. Therefore, it is difficult to imagine the employee requesting his employer's advance permission to engage in this activity. It is illogical to assume that any employer would knowingly condone any activity that has the potential for harm to the employee, coemployees, customers or clients or the employer's property.

A potential defense to compensability will exist whenever the employee's activities take place off the employment premises even when the employer has granted permission to leave the premises. Compensability does not follow the employee when he leaves the employment premises for his personal convenience, because the employee is exposed to risks of harm that are not contemplated under the personal comfort doctrine. Examples would include a slip and fall injury on someone else's property, a physical assault or an automobile accident.

The employee may conduct his business during compensated breaktimes, or wages may be suspended during the employee's absence. In either case, the employer does not become liable for injuries that may occur during the performance of personal errands, e.g. donating blood or attending to medical, family or legal matters. Injuries will be compensable when the employee is engaged in a business errand at his employer's request or when the employee engages in acts of personal comfort on or off the premises. However, off-premises acts of personal convenience do not provide any special benefit to the employer, and the employer does not exert any control over the employee at the time. For these reasons, off-premises injuries while engaged in acts of convenience will not arise out of the employment.

The courts will generally try to achieve an equitable balance between compensating employees for injuries and penalizing employers for their courtesy in allowing employees to leave the premises to perform personal activities. Employers would not readily grant similar courtesies to other employees in the future if their actions would result in liability for injuries. While a particular employee may go uncompensated for a serious injury, all other employees at the workplace will benefit by the continuance of the employer's policy of permitting the use of work time for off-premises personal activities.

For on-premises activities, a potential defense to compensability will exist whenever a personal activity involves the use of special materials or equipment that must be brought from home. Injuries that are compensable under the personal comfort doctrine will not ordinarily require any items that are not already available at the workplace (with the exception of food, refreshments or small personal items such as combs that are usually carried by employees). However, acts of convenience may require special supplies or apparatus. For instance, the employee may decide to give herself a home permanent at work because it would be too messy to do at home. A chemical burn to the scalp or eyes would result from an act of personal convenience and would not be compensable. Likewise, if an employee decided to rebuild a carburetor during a coffee break and cut his hand on a wrench, the necessity for the use of personal tools indicates an act for personal convenience rather than one of personal comfort.

5.46 MEALTIME INJURIES

Mealtimes refer to periods of time set aside for eating a regular meal. It is not necessary that the employee actually eat food during a mealtime. It suffices that a particular time is designated for this purpose. Since many employees work round-the-clock shifts, the term "mealtime" is more appropriate for this topic than the term "lunch hour". The meal may be lunch, dinner or even breakfast. As a general rule, injuries during mealtimes will be compensable if the employee is paid at the time or remains on the employer's premises. Payment of wages is a basic factor in support of compensability no matter when or where an injury is sustained. The premises test is another strong factor in support of compensability for any injury. Both of these criteria denote a certain amount of employer control over the employee at the time of injury.

A common misconception is that all salaried employees have a paid lunch hour, because they don't have an hourly rate of pay. This is not true. Salaried employees have stated regular daily hours of work, and their pay can be stated as a daily or hourly rate of pay (as it is when salaried employees are paid sick leave or vacation pay; see 8.32). In nearly all cases, employees are not paid during mealtimes, but many employees are unaware of this fact. For instance, employees who work from eight to five are usually only paid for an eight-hour day. There are nine hours in this period that includes a one-hour unpaid lunch break.

A paid mealtime is very unusual but is sometimes provided. Payment of wages during a mealtime extends the personal comfort doctrine to this period. The employment relationship exists, the employee remains within the course of employment at any location where the employee might go, and any reasonable activities of the employee can lead to compensable injuries. If the employee does eat a meal, he remains in the course of his employment whether he eats on the employer's premises, at a restaurant or in his own home. Any injury that would be compensable during a breaktime under the personal comfort doctrine will be compensable during the mealtime.

Ordinarily, the personal comfort doctrine is not applicable when the employee is not paid wages, but on-premises mealtime injuries are an exception to this general rule. The employer exercises control over the employment premises and is therefore responsible for the risks of harm to which the employee may be exposed thereon. Mealtime injuries will be compensable when they result from a reasonable use of the employment premises and any items or facilities provided for the employee's use. For example, mealtime injuries will be compensable under the following circumstances:

a. The employee is obtaining food from a portable facility such as a commissary van that visits the employer's location each day at breaks or mealtimes; e.g., the employee falls in the street while going to purchase food to bring back to the employment premises.

b. Food is purchased from vending machines; e.g., the employee breaks a tooth on a piece of rock inside a candy bar.

c. Food is obtained in a cafeteria that is owned, controlled or provided by the employer; e.g., the employee gets food poisoning while eating.

d. Food is prepared in a lunchroom where refrigerators or cooking facilities are provided for employee use; e.g., the employee burns himself on a pan or gets dish soap in his eyes.

e. Food from home is eaten in an area provided for this purpose and an injury occurs that does not involve any personal food item; e.g., the employee is assaulted in the lunchroom or slips and falls.

f. Food is eaten at the employee's work station, because no other suitable location is available or provided or because the employee chooses to eat there; e.g., the employee sprains his back while trying to keep a beverage from spilling on his work materials.

g. The employee is using recreational facilities provided or allowed by the employer, such as a ping pong table, a swimming pool, an exercise room, or an atrium or patio; e.g., the employee is injured by a flying ping pong paddle or stung by bees that are attracted to his food.

h. The employee is making a reasonable use of the employer's premises; e.g., the employee chips his tooth while getting a drink from a drinking fountain, his foot is injured when it slips off the toilet flusher, or he is caught in a fast-closing elevator door.

i. The employee is engaged in a reasonable act of personal comfort; e.g., gazing out the window when a baseball flies in.

Mealtime injuries will not arise out of the employment if the connection between the injury and the employment is too remote to establish proximate causation even though the employee is paid and/or on the premises. The employment relationship would be a contributing cause of the injury if the employee got food poisoning from food provided by the employer in a company cafeteria. Food poisoning from food prepared at home but eaten at work is a different matter. If personal food becomes contaminated through some control of the employer, the employment would be the proximate cause of the injury. For example, the employer may provide a refrigerator that breaks down resulting in spoilage, but the employee has no reason to suspect any problem with his food until after he has eaten it, and the damage is done. However, no injury can be proximately caused by the employment absent some element of control by the employer. If the employee uses spoiled mayonnaise to prepare a sandwich to take to work, a resulting injury bears no relationship to his employment. Employers do not have any control over home food preparations nor could they have any possible opportunity to prevent such injuries.

In the case of uncompensated mealtimes, the Going and Coming rule bars compensability after the employee's departure and prior to his return to the employment premises. Additionally, every exception to the application of the Going and Coming rule applies equally to mealtimes and the start and finish of the workday. For instance, if a supervisor requests the employee to accompany him to a restaurant to discuss work matters, the employee will be engaged in a special mission during his mealtime. If the employee has an accident while driving a company car to a restaurant, the use of employer-provided transportation establishes proximate cause between the injury and the employment.

5.47 HORSEPLAY – SKYLARKING

The horseplay doctrine provides the employer with a defense to compensability for injuries that arise out of personal activities on the employer's premises or during times the employee is being paid. Employers are not deemed to impliedly permit or condone all employee activities that merely occur at work but are a result of the individual personality that each employee brings to the workplace. Horseplay and skylarking are interchangeable words that apply to the same factual circumstances. In either case, the employee's personal activities are acts of convenience that have an inherent potential for injury, and an injury does result, even though no injury was intended. This employer defense is often difficult to establish, since there is a fine line between compensable injuries that result from activities for the employee's personal comfort and noncompensable injuries that result from horseplay activities.

When the risk of harm from an activity is common knowledge to reasonable persons, it is not necessary for the employer to formulate express policies prohibiting employees from engaging in such activities. For example, a playful employee might fall to his death while walking the beams at a high-rise construction site for the amusement of coworkers and the amazement of pedestrians. This activity is clearly not contemplated under the personal comfort doctrine. Employees have a basic responsibility not to engage in any personal activity that may cause harm to themselves, other participants or even to innocent bystanders.

Horseplay can involve a tool or instrumentality that is related to the employee's duties or work location. Compensability will not ensue from this work connection. For instance, a farm employee is engaged in horseplay when he does a handstand on the driver's seat of a tractor while hauling a load of hay. Employers are not presumed to give carte blanche authority to their employees to make whatever use of work materials they prefer.

A horseplay activity may be a solitary endeavor or several employees may jointly engage in the activity. Innocent victims of a horseplay activity will be compensated for their injuries, but all active participants in the horseplay activity will be barred from compensation. Below are some examples of potentially harmful activities that would cause the employer to raise the defense of horseplay or skylarking:

    a. Recreational activities that utilize employer materials or property; e.g., shooting rubber bands, spitting paper wads, flying paper airplanes, doing a headstand on top of a ladder or sniffing glue.

    b. Activities performed on a dare, e.g. flirting with danger in any manner.

    c. Inherently dangerous activities, e.g. diving off a roof into an employer-owned swimming pool or intentionally smoking in restricted areas. (Note: dangerous activities can also provide the employer with grounds for the defense of serious and willful misconduct of the employee, but this defense only seeks a 50% reduction in the employee's compensation; a successful horseplay defense bars the employee from receipt of any compensation.)

    d. Activities intended to amuse oneself, e.g. spraying chemicals on the arm to see what the effect might be, arm wrestling, playful boxing matches or sick jokes like greasing toilet seats, setting fires in trash cans or setting off fire alarms.

    e. Activities that do not ordinarily occur in the workplace, e.g. demonstrations of tattooing techniques, practicing cooking of flambe foods for an evening cooking class, or eating or drinking contests.

The uniqueness of horseplay activities sets them apart from other activities that could be considered to be acts of personal comfort. It is unlikely that any employer would condone any of the above activities (but if so, the appellate courts have held that workers' compensation benefits are the exclusive remedy and the injured nonparticipants have no cause of action for damages against their coemployees). It appears improbable that any judge would extend such approval to employees under his or her supervision, and it would be equally rare to find employees engaging in such activities.

Employers can be held liable for injuries resulting from activities of which they have no advance knowledge. However, any activities in this category must be so eminently reasonable that the employer would probably not have prohibited the activity had the employer known about it.

5.48 BUNKHOUSE RULE

Some employees reside in housing that is owned, controlled or provided by their employers. Examples include apartment managers, farm laborers, motel managers, and live-in housekeepers. In such cases, the employee's personal residence is considered to be part of the employment premises. Under the bunkhouse rule, the employee is deemed to be within the course of his employment at all times he is on the employment premises, and injuries that arise out of a reasonable use of the premises will also arise out of the employment.

Bunkhouse employees can sustain compensable injuries while engaged in personal activities that would not ordinarily bear any connection to an employ-

ment relationship. Injuries resulting from the following types of activities would
be compensable under the bunkhouse rule:

  a. Sleeping; e.g., a rainstorm causes the ceiling or roof to collapse on
      the employee, or the employee dies in a fire.
  b. Eating; e.g., the employee chokes to death because assistance is not
      immediately available.
  c. Cleaning; e.g., the employee strains his back while vacuuming.
  d. Maintenance; e.g., a power lawn mower throws a small pebble into
      the employee's eye, or the employee cuts his hand while changing a
      broken light bulb.
  e. Repairs; e.g., the employee falls from a ladder while fixing a broken
      shutter.
  f. Use of the dwelling; e.g., the employee falls down the stairs or is
      attacked by a thief who chooses his victim because of the remoteness
      of the bunkhouse location.

Compensable injuries can also occur during a reasonable use of the premises
on which the bunkhouse is located. The employer has the right to restrict an
unlimited personal use of its premises by facility, by location or by activity.
Within the confines of the employer's designated limitation, a reasonable use of
the premises could include activities such as:

  a. Walking or hiking; e.g., the employee is bitten by a snake, has an
      allergic reaction from contact with poison ivy or trips over a log.
  b. Using vehicles provided by the employer; e.g., the employee is
      thrown out of a Jeep when it hits a rut, or he is injured while making
      repairs.
  c. Riding horses stabled on the premises; e.g., the employee is kicked
      or bitten.
  d. Using a pond; e.g., the employee gets an ear infection from swimming
      or injures his knee while launching a boat.

Some injuries sustained by bunkhouse employees will not be compensable.
Some activities are so personal in nature that they would never constitute part of
an employment relationship. Shaving, getting dressed, filling out income tax
forms, entertaining friends and sexual activities are in this category. These
activities defy any potential for employer control over the manner in which the
activity is performed or the fact that it is performed at all. Some factors that
negate proximate cause to the employment include:

  a. The injury results from a personally motivated assault, e.g. by persons
      to whom the employee owes money or persons who accuse the
      employee of cheating during a card game.
  b. The nature of the employment did not contribute to the employee's
      injury; e.g., the employee trips over materials lying on the floor
      because he is by nature a sloppy housekeeper, or the injury results
      from an intimately personal activity.

   c. The medical condition developed independently of any employment relationship; e.g., the employee has boils, gum disease, hemorrhoids, or pneumonia.

   d. The employee's use of the bunkhouse was not reasonable; e.g., the employee decided to barbecue indoors because it was raining and suffered smoke inhalation as a result, or the employee is injured when the tractor he is driving goes into a lake as he is attempting to drag the lake with a net to catch fish (fishing with a fishing pole would be a reasonable use of the lake).

5.49 DEVIATION FROM DUTIES

The employee is not entitled to compensation for injuries that occur during any period when the employee has materially deviated from the course or scope of his employment. With few exceptions, the deviation must be substantial in terms of the nature of the activity, the time it takes to perform the activity, and/or the distance from the work location. When the employer asserts this affirmative defense, the employer has the burden of proving that the employment was not the proximate cause of the injury. The employer can meet this burden by establishing that the employee abandoned the employer's business to engage in a personal activity that was unrelated to the employment, and an injury was sustained during the period of the deviation.

Disputes will most commonly arise when the employee's deviation is minor. For instance, an outside salesman may take his laundry to a cleaners that is on a direct route to his next business destination. This activity may take five minutes and take the employee only a short distance from his vehicle, but many injuries could occur in this short time. The employee could be shot by criminals who are robbing the cleaners, he could be hit by a car, or he could be mugged in front of the cleaners. No matter what happens to him at the cleaners, this employee is not performing a service of benefit to his employer.

Ordinarily, the fact that the employee is paid at the time of injury would mean that he was within the course of his employment. In the above example, payment of wages does not support this conclusion anymore than it would if the employee was at the cleaners on a paid holiday or vacation day. No doubt the reason this employee is being paid during his normal workday is due to his employer's belief that he is performing services under his employment contract instead of engaging in personal activities of his own choice.

Minor deviations are sometimes excused or may be forgiven through judicial decisions. This fact is usually a result of liberality rather than adherence to statutory requirements for compensability. Indeed, a judge may award workers' compensation benefits for injuries that occur under circumstances that constitute valid grounds for the termination of employment pursuant to the employer's established policies. This realistic comment regarding the judicial system should not deter the claimsperson from preparation of a defense in every case where the employee has removed himself from the course of his employment prior to the injury. A thorough investigation should be conducted to determine whether any of the following noncompensable elements can be supported by factual evidence:

   a. The employee's activity was personal and bore no connection to his employment; e.g., the activity was not a service of benefit to his employer, or at the direction of, or under the control of his employer.
   b. The employee was engaged in an illegal activity; e.g., the activity could not legally be required by an employer.
   c. The employer did not/would not condone such a personal activity; e.g., the employer may not care whether the employee takes his clothes to the cleaners or a laundromat, but the employer has a right to expect the employee will not do either while being paid to perform services for the employer.
   d. The employer does not derive any benefit from the employee's activity; e.g., the activity was personal in nature and the only person benefiting from it was the employee.
   e. Any connection to the employment is remote; e.g., the employer is not benefited by every personal activity in which the employee decides to engage while using a vehicle just because the vehicle is a company car.
   f. The employee abandoned his employment relationship by conducting personal business to the detriment of his employer's business; e.g., some business appointments were not kept or sales were not made while the employee was visiting friends or attending horse races.

5.50 MIXED BUSINESS & PERSONAL PURPOSES

The mixed purposes doctrine applies to situations where the employee has made a minor deviation from his employment to conduct personal business, but there is an intermingling of business and personal activities that makes it difficult to determine whose purposes were being served at the time of injury. Under this doctrine, injuries will be compensable if the employment alone provides a sufficient explanation for the employee's activities or location when injured or if the employee's activities are predominantly business rather than personal in nature. The employee remains within the course of his employment while conducting personal business as long as a sufficient nexus to the employment continues to exist. In most cases where mixed business and personal purposes are concurrently served, compensability will ordinarily prevail since the employment relationship continues to exist at the time of injury.

Personal business may be conducted at the same site and close to the same time that a business errand is performed. For instance, the employee may make a personal bank deposit immediately before or after he makes a deposit for his employer at the same bank. The employee's departure from the course of his employment is partial, not total. The predominant reason for the employee's presence in the bank is to perform the employer's business there. This deviation is not substantial, because the employee is at the precise location where the employer required the employee to be.

The employee's personal banking activity above is one that most employers would condone although this factor is not crucial to the compensability issue. More important is the fact that some injuries could just as easily occur if the employee did not have a separate personal purpose at the time. Injuries in this category will be compensable under the mixed purposes doctrine. Examples would include: being shot when the bank is robbed, getting caught in a revolving door while entering or exiting or slipping on a wet floor on a rainy day. It would be difficult for the employer to convince any judge that such injuries would not have occurred absent the employee's deviation from his employment to engage in personal business.

5.51 PERFORMANCE OF WORK – UNAUTHORIZED MANNER

When the employee performs work in an unauthorized fashion, he does not remove himself from the course of his employment. The word that may best describe his actions is "negligent," and LC3600 provides that negligence is not a defense to a work-related injury. The employee is not performing his job the way he should, but he is still performing his job. The employer is presumed to receive a benefit from the performance of work even though work is performed contrary to stated policies or standard procedures. For this reason, the performance of work in an unauthorized manner is not a defense to an injury. Injuries will be compensable if the facts reveal that the employee's goal was to perform his duties rather than some personal activity.

The employer may give precise instructions as to how to do the job. The employee may choose to do the job some other way. Failure to follow instructions may constitute grounds for disciplinary action including termination. However, none of the following reasons for the employee's actions provides a basis for a denial of liability for any injuries sustained:
  a. Confusion due to lack of understanding of the employer's instructions; e.g., the employee believes he is performing as directed.
  b. Obstinacy; e.g., the employee refuses to accept a new procedure and continues to use a previously authorized method.
  c. Outright insubordination; e.g., the employee refuses to accept or follow instructions from a particular supervisor.
  d. Personal preference to perform an activity in a variant manner; e.g., the employee believes he is better serving the employer's interests by the method of his choice, or he finds it easier to do the work the way he likes.

The reason for the employee's actions will determine the viability of any employer defense to an injury. Suppose the employee is a welder. All employees are well aware that welding work is not to be done unless a safety visor is worn, but the employee welds without one and sustains an eye injury. The employee may have a reasonable explanation for his actions; e.g., he welded in a tight area where the safety equipment impeded his access, or his visor was broken and another one was not available for his use. If true, these reasons would warrant an extension of compensability. However, the employee's allegations may be contrary to facts developed through other sources. The employer would have a defense to this injury if the facts reveal the injury was intentionally self-inflicted or resulted from a horseplay activity.

Suppose an employee is injured while en route to a business meeting in a company car. The car goes out of control when the employee increases his speed to evade a safety officer. A judge would take note of the existence of any employment aspects at the time: the employee is on a direct route to the meeting and has no destination other than the meeting, the employee is performing his employment duties (in an unauthorized manner), and his activities represent a mixture of business and personal purposes. Even so, the compensability of this injury is not clear.

The employer may take the position that the employee removed himself from the course of his employment by engaging in a dangerous activity of his personal choosing. The purpose of speed laws is to avoid injuries that are statistically probable at speeds in excess of posted limits. Therefore, the employee voluntarily chose to expose himself to the precise risk that produced his injury. Further, the employee's personal activity was an illegal act that could not be a condition of an employment contract, could not therefore arise out of the employment, and should not be rewarded by the payment of workers' compensation benefits. In practicality, the potential success of the employer's defense would likely depend upon how fast the employee was going. As the employee's speed increases over the speed limit, the unreasonableness of his action increases proportionately. If the employee's speed was a few miles over the speed limit, this minor infraction would probably be considered insignificant to a workers' compensation judge. However, any time the employee's speed exceeds that which could be considered reasonable to avoid an injury, the propriety of holding the employer liable for injuries resulting from this illegal activity would be questionable.

When an injury results from the performance of work in an unauthorized manner, the employer will have an additional issue to pursue. Per LC4551, the employee's compensation will be "reduced by one-half" when the injury "is caused by the serious and willful misconduct of the injured employee." This penalty against the employee will not apply when the employee is "under 16 years of age," or "the injury results in death," or the injury is severe enough to produce "a permanent disability of 70 percent or over." Two employees might sustain injuries in the same manner. The employee with minor injuries will be penalized by a 50% reduction in his compensation (including disability and medical payments; see and 1.9 and 7.71), but a more seriously injured employee will receive full compensation. There is one humanistic explanation for this apparent inequity. The more serious the injury, the greater the likelihood that the employee will be fired from his job because of his unauthorized activity and that workers' compensation benefits will be his sole source of income subsequent to the injury.

[6] STATUTES OF LIMITATIONS

6.1 STATUTES OF LIMITATIONS – IN GENERAL

A statute of limitations is a restriction on the period of time in which relief may be sought. The Labor Code provides specific rights and remedies to injured employees. There are legally defined time periods in which these rights may be pursued. Various Labor Code sections provide time limitations that apply to the legal remedies of employers as well as employees. This chapter will deal with employees' rights and the employer's defenses on the topic.

6.2 PURPOSE OF STATUTES OF LIMITATIONS

Time limits are set by law to encourage prompt pursuance of legal remedies. The purpose of set time limits is to ensure that evidence on the issues will be reasonably current, since it is difficult to reconstruct the mechanics of an injury long after its occurrence. With the passage of time, records may be lost or destroyed, and the memories of witnesses may fade. Further, witnesses may move or die, creating evidentiary problems for all parties involved as well as the judges who must render decisions. When evidence is old or can not be produced, additional court time is necessary to ascertain the facts that existed at some past point in time. This is an unfair burden on the judicial system, and it would also be unfair for an employee to use time as a weapon by pursuing a remedy long after the employer has the ability to produce otherwise relevant evidence.

6.3 EFFECT OF OPERATION OF TIME LIMITATION

When a statute of limitations bars a claim, it bars the employee's right to receive compensation. The statute of limitations does not bar the employee's right to file an Application for Adjudication of Claim. The employee has a right to file a claim for workers' compensation regardless of whether the claim is filed within the stated statutory period or beyond the stated time. Also, the employer has the option of asserting a statute of limitations defense or waiving this defense (see 6.29). Where the employer has properly raised a valid statute of limitations defense, the WCAB does not have authority to award compensation after the statute of limitations has expired. Thus, the effect of a successful statute of limitations defense is twofold: the judge cannot award benefits, and the employer is not liable for compensation.

6.4 DUTY OF EMPLOYER – NOTICES

Employees must have some notice or knowledge of a possible right to receive workers' compensation benefits in order for them to pursue such benefits. The employer has a variety of separately stated statutory duties to notify employees of their rights regarding entitlement to workers' compensation benefits. Notices regarding the employee's potential right to benefits, and how to claim such benefits if injured, are required in advance of any injury being claimed. Notices regarding the employee's current rights are required at specific intervals after the employer has received notification of a claimed injury. Notices regarding the employee's entitlement to separate categories of benefits are required during the provision and upon the termination of payment of such benefits. The employer's specific notice requirements are discussed individually in following sections.

6.5 TIME OF HIRE NOTICE

Per LC3551, the employer is required to "give every new employee, either at the time the employee is hired or by the end of the first pay period, written notice" of specific information that is contained in LC3550. This information includes "advice as to the injured employee's right to receive medical care, to select or change the treating physician ... and the right to receive temporary disability indemnity, permanent disability indemnity, vocational rehabilitation services, and death benefits, as appropriate." It is always appropriate to notify the employee of each of the benefits that are listed in LC3550 since it is not possible to predict which benefits may or may not be appropriate or meaningful to an employee (or the employee's dependents) at some future date when an injury is sustained.

The employer is required to notify each new employee of the fact that it is self-insured for workers' compensation benefits or else the name of its current insurance carrier. In either case, LC3550 requires that the employee be notified of "who is responsible for claims adjustment," e.g. the name, address, and telephone number of the insurance company or an adjusting agency that administers claims for a self-insured employer. This information is provided for the employee's protection and convenience. Any employee who chooses to do so can verify that the employer's workers' compensation coverage is current and valid, or an employee can contact a claimsperson directly regarding workers' compensation benefits.

The employer must specifically "identify to whom injuries should be reported." This notification enables employees to comply with an obligation of which they are informed at the time they are hired: per LC3550, the employer is required "to advise employees that all injuries should be reported to their employer." (Proof that this notice was provided can assist the employer in pursuing a statute of limitations defense at a later date, so it behooves the employer to be prepared to prove that the employee did in fact receive this notice at the time of hire, e.g. by requesting the employee to sign an acknowledgment.) Any time the employer is discussing workers' compensation benefits with an employee is a good time to explain the procedures whereby the employee can obtain and file a written claim form (see 6.12) as well as the penalties that would apply to a person who presents a fraudulent claim for workers' compensation benefits.

It is completely within the employer's discretion to require employees to report industrial injuries to a specifically named individual, to a person who is identified merely by title, or to any person within a particular department such as the "Personnel Department" or the "Safety Department." If the employer requires all injuries to be reported to a particular individual, employees cannot comply with their duty to report an injury unless the employer has notified them of the identity and location of this person, including a telephone number and address if this individual is not located at the employee's work location. For this reason, it is appropriate to provide such information to the employee at the time the employee is hired and advised that "all injuries should be reported."

The employer is also required under LC3550 to notify every new employee of the address and telephone number of the nearest Information and Assistance Officer. Most frequently, these individuals will be physically located at the district office of the WCAB that is nearest the employee's work location. If this is not the case, the employee must be notified of the nearest address where the employee could, if the employee chose to do so, visit an Information and Assistance Officer in person. The employer is not required to monitor staffing changes nor reprint any information pamphlets that it provides to new hires upon each staffing change within the Information and Assistance Unit. Providing employees with a correct telephone number and address will suffice to assist employees to exercise their right to the services of an Information and Assistance Officer (at no cost) should they desire.

Worker's Compensation Pamphlet

Employers customarily comply with the notice requirements of LC3551 by providing an employee with an information pamphlet. Per CR9882, the content of any such pamphlet must be "approved by the Administrative Director." The State publishes a pamphlet that can be utilized as is, or the employer or its insurance carrier can reprint the State's pamphlet verbatim and include their own logo or other identifying information.

Since 1994, LC139.6 requires the Division of Workers' Compensation to publish (and update as necessary) a "pamphlet advising injured workers of their basic rights under workers' compensation law, and informing them of rights under the American's with Disabilities Act, and the provisions of the Fair Employment and Housing Act relating to individuals with a disability." Specifically, a pamphlet shall include basic information concerning the compensability of work injuries, qualifying criteria for entitlement to various categories of benefits, "protections against discrimination because of an injury," and the procedures for resolving disputes. Per LC139.6 and CR9883, the State is required to publish pamphlets in English and Spanish.

Alternatively, an employer can devise its own pamphlet should it choose to do so, e.g. to include advice regarding the employee's right to receive supplemental company benefits such as a salary continuation benefit that is payable in addition to any temporary disability benefits that are required under the Labor Code. Any written notice that differs from the language of the State's pamphlet must be submitted to the State for approval in advance of its use and, if approved, must contain a clear statement that approval has been obtained (clarification of this requirement is available from the Information and Assistance Unit).

6.6 POSTING NOTICE

Per LC3550, the employer is required to post a notice that contains the same information employees are given at the time of hire (see 6.5). This notice must be posted "in a conspicuous location frequented by employees and where such notice may be easily read by employees during the course of the workday." A broom closet is not a conspicuous location, nor is the boss' private office. A lunch room bulletin board or a location near a time clock would be appropriate locations. A notice posted at a worksite in San Diego would not be "conspicuous" to employees who are employed at a worksite in Sacramento. If the employer has multiple worksites, it is apparent that the notice required by LC3550 must be posted at each of the separate worksites.

The required posting notice is usually printed and provided by the employer's insurance carrier free of charge. Insurance companies or self-insured employers can utilize a posting notice that is available from the State, or that they can reprint the State-published notice to include their own logos or other identifying information. Alternatively, they may devise a form that complies with the notice requirements of LC3550 that has been submitted to the Administrative Director of the Division of Workers' Compensation for approval prior to its use.

Information provided in an employee information pamphlet at the time of hire may no longer be accurate when the employee sustains an injury. For instance, an insured employer may become self-insured after an employee was hired. The employer's posting notice must be changed as necessary to ensure that the notice that is provided to its employees is accurate at all times. Whenever information in the employer's posting notice is changed to reflect a change in circumstances, although not required, it would inure to the employer's benefit to distribute updated employee information pamphlets to all employees. This action on the part of the employer can ensure that all of its employees are at all times aware of the current information that LC3550 intends the employer to make available to its employees.

Self-insured employers accept an obligation to comply with all of an employer's requirements under the Labor Code as a condition precedent to being permitted to obtain a Certificate of Consent to Self-Insure (see 2.14). However, insured employers are not held to this same standard of knowledge. For this reason, LC3550 provides in regard to the required posted notice that "insurers shall provide this notice to each of their policyholders, with advice concerning the requirements of this section and the penalties for failure to post this notice."

Per LC3550, the employer's failure to conspicuously post the required notice "shall constitute a misdemeanor, and shall be prima facie evidence of noninsurance" (see 2.19). Per LC3550(e), failure to provide the posted notice "shall automatically permit the employee to be treated by his or her personal physician with respect to an injury occurring during that failure" (but not any physician of the employee's choice; see 7.35). Although not stated in LC3550, an additional repercussion for the employer could be an adverse impact on a statute of limitations defense to a claim. For instance, the employee's failure to timely report an injury may be deemed reasonable and not a bar to a late-filed claim if the posted notice misadvises the employee as to the proper person or entity to whom claims should be reported.

6.7 POST-INJURY NOTICES – OVERVIEW

Notice of Potential Eligibility

The initial post-injury notice that the employer is required to provide to the employee (or dependents in the event of death) is a notice of potential eligibility for benefits. The required contents of this notice are detailed in LC5401. In essence, this notice will again advise the employee of the same information that the employee was previously provided at the time of hire as required by LC3551 and in the employer's posting notice as required by LC3550. In fact, the employer can use the information pamphlet that it provides to newly hired employees to comply with this notice requirement.

Depending upon how long ago the employee was hired, the contents of the information pamphlet that was provided then may have changed significantly. The requirement for provision of an additional information pamphlet when the employer receives knowledge of an injury ensures that the employee will receive an up-to-date notice of a potential right to benefits when these benefits are most relevant to the employee. (Note: the employee information pamphlet that is required to be made available to employees per LC138.4, LC139.6 and CR9883 "shall be available in English and Spanish.")

The employer's obligation is the same regardless of whether the employee properly reports an injury that is not disputed or the employer otherwise receives knowledge of a claimed injury that may later be denied. Per LC5401, the employer is required to provide a notice of potential rights "within one working day of receiving notice or knowledge" of any injury that "results in lost time beyond the date of injury or ... medical treatment beyond first aid." (As for the concurrent requirement to file an Employer's Report with the State, see 2.22.)

First Aid Exception

For 1994 or later injuries, LC5401 defines "first aid" to mean "any one-time treatment of minor scratches, cuts, burns, splinters, or other minor industrial injury" and makes no reference to the identity of the person providing such treatment. Since 1994, the employer's duty to provide the employee with a claim form and notice of potential rights to benefits (and concurrently file a report of injury with its insurer) is contingent upon the type of treatment that the employee receives, not the qualifications of the person providing treatment. (Note: per LC5401, first aid "shall not include serious exposure to a hazardous substance" as defined by LC6302 as "a degree or amount sufficient to create a substantial probability that death or serious physical harm in the future could result.")

For purposes of LC5401, "knowledge" of an injury has the meaning set out in LC5402. The employer clearly has knowledge upon receipt of written notice of an injury (required by LC5400 and LC5401; see 6.12). Per LC5402, the employer also has knowledge upon receipt of "knowledge of an injury, obtained from any source ... or knowledge of the assertion of a claim of injury sufficient to afford opportunity to the employer to make an investigation into the facts."

The employer is not required to provide a notice of potential eligibility for workers' compensation benefits to employees who require only first aid treatment. However, for the sake of consistency, it would appear in the employer's best interest to routinely provide a post-injury notice of potential rights within one working day of knowledge of every claim regardless of whether the injury results in lost time beyond the date of the injury, whether treatment beyond first aid is necessary, or whether the employer is also required to provide a claim form. This employer action encourages employees to seek, and enables employers to provide, timely benefits in the event of a worsening of the initial injury.

Since the initial post-injury notice should be provided within one working day of the employer's first knowledge of a claim, this notice will frequently be sent prior to the conclusion of an employer investigation. The notice encourages the employee to cooperate in an investigation so that the employer can make a prompt decision on the employee's entitlement to the receipt of the benefits that are described in the notice. The time of hire, posting, and initial post-injury notice of potential rights are collectively designed to enable an injured employee to pursue a claim for workers' compensation benefits before expiration of any statute of limitations. Therefore each notice provides information regarding available alternatives for pursuing a resolution of any disputes that may arise, including the employee's right to the services of an Information and Assistance Officer (free of charge), an attorney, and the WCAB.

Notice of Payment, Nonpayment or Delay

Following the initial post-injury notice that is required by LC5401, the next notice the employer is required to provide is determined by the employer's opinion regarding its liability. The employer may pay benefits, deny liability for any benefits or require more time to investigate. Separate notices are required for each of these situations. (Note: currently required notices, as specified in CR9810-CR9815, are covered in detail under applicable benefit topics.)

Per LC138.4, the Administrative Director has authority to prescribe separate notices for the "payment, nonpayment, or delay in payment" of the employee's benefits, "any change in the amount or type of benefits being provided, the termination of benefits, and an accounting of the benefits paid." Per LC138.4, such notices are required only "with respect to injuries involving loss of time" from work. However, effective 4/1/94, the employer's duty to provide post-injury notices to employees regarding payment, nonpayment or delay of benefits has been expanded to encompass more claims by altering the definition of the term "injury" in administrative regulations.

For purposes of the employer's duty to provide notices pursuant to LC138.4, CR9811 defines "injury" to mean any injury "which results in lost time beyond the date of injury, medical treatment beyond first aid, or death." The most significant effect of this change is the requirement for the provision of benefit information notices in medical-only cases (see 2.25) effective 4/1/94. Other major changes to regulations that, per CR9810, impact the provision of employee benefit information "notices required to be sent on or after April 1, 1994" (several of which enable significant cost savings to employers) are explained below.

Since 4/1/94, the claims administrator is no longer required to submit a copy of benefit information notices to the State. Instead, CR9810 requires the claims administrator to maintain copies of each notice that is sent "in paper or electronic form." The contents of required benefit notices continue to be specified in administrative regulations (CR9810-9815), but the previously utilized forms (Benefit Information Notice forms, or DWC 500 forms) have been abandoned. Per CR9810, benefit "notice letters may be produced on the claims administrator's letterhead," and a "single benefit notice may encompass multiple events." A single notice can include notice of the provision of other types of disability benefits that are offered by an employer; e.g. salary continuation benefits. A benefit information pamphlet must be included with the first benefit notice that is required (be it notice of payment, nonpayment or delay of benefits).

The claims administrator is required to concurrently serve copies of benefit notices on the employee's attorney, if any, along with all enclosures other than benefit notice pamphlets or benefit checks (e.g. a medical report or an explanation of benefits payable under a salary continuation plan). Regardless of whether the employee has an attorney, some notices will request a reply within a specified number of days from the date the notice was sent (postmarked); e.g. where the employee is asked to provide proof of self-employment earnings or the names of any witnesses to a claimed injury within 14 days. Per CR9810, deadlines for replies sent by mail are extended for 5, 10, or 20 days depending upon whether a reply is mailed from California, another state or another country, respectively.

6.8 DELAY LETTER

Per CR9812, a notice of delay is required for a delay in the provision of each type of indemnity benefit that is claimed or may be payable as well as a delayed decision as to liability for all benefits. All delay letters must specify an anticipated decision date. If more time is needed, another notice of delay is required within 5 days of the earlier decision date. For 1990 or later injuries, notice of a delayed decision regarding the compensability of a claim must include an explanation of the rebuttable 90-day presumption of compensability under LC5402 (see 6.13); per CR9812, this requirement applies to any notices that are required to be sent on or after 4/1/94.

Whenever the employer makes a final decision within fourteen days of its first knowledge that temporary disability benefits are being claimed, a delay notice is not required, because the employer is then required to send a notice of payment or else a notice of denial of workers' compensation benefits. Otherwise, the employer is required by LC4650 to notify the employee of a delay in the determination of the employee's entitlement to benefits. The 14-day period begins upon concurrence of knowledge of a claim of injury and disability resulting from the injury. This notice is commonly referred to as a "delay letter." Essentially identical requirements for the provision of a delay letter are found in the Labor Code and the Code of Regulations, as explained below:

   a. LC4650: requires a delay notice only when temporary disability benefits are claimed.
   b. LC138.4: requires a delay notice for claims involving any type of indemnity benefit, not just temporary disability (any claim except a "medical-only" claim; see 2.25).
   c. CR9812: requires a delay notice for claims involving any type of indemnity benefit, not just temporary disability (note that this regulation was adopted to implement the notice requirements of LC138.4).

The employer is not obligated to pay benefits if it does not possess necessary medical information, or available information indicates that there may be a valid medical or legal basis for denying liability for benefits. However, if the employer lacks sufficient information to establish its liability, it is obligated to conduct a prompt investigation to determine the facts and to notify the employee of the reason why a decision on the claim is being postponed. The employee should be notified of the specific nature of any additional information that is needed, the efforts that are being taken to obtain such information, and the anticipated date on which a decision can be made.

The purpose of the delay letter is to de-emphasize the litigation alternative to the resolution of disputes prior to the time that the employer has made a final decision on its liability. No action on the employer's part can better serve this goal than honest, timely, and continuous communication with the employee during the period that the employer is actively attempting to reach a decision on the claim. (Financial incentives for the conduct of prompt investigations abound in the Labor Code; for instance, the employer can avoid liability for medical-legal expenses under LC4620 by avoiding unreasonable delays in a determination as to the employee's entitlement.) In addition to the delay notice that the employer is required to provide, most employees are very appreciative of any additional communication that confirms that a real person (rather than a computer) is assigned to their claim and that this person shares the employee's interest in reaching a prompt decision.

6.9 DENIAL LETTER

Per LC138.4, the employer is required to notify the employee of its "rejection of any liability for compensation" but only "with respect to injuries involving loss of time" (cases where indemnity benefits are payable in additional to medical benefits). However, as of 4/1/94, CR9811 requires a notice of denial of liability for medical-only as well as indemnity claims (see 6.7). (Note: as of 1/28/94, CR10103 requires a claim log to contain an entry identifying each claim that is denied in its entirety.)

Pursuant to CR9812, notice that the claim is denied in its entirety must be provided within 14 days of the date this determination is made. In cases where the compensability of the injury is accepted, a denial notice is required within 14 days of a decision to deny liability for any particular category of indemnity benefits. Since 4/1/94, no particular form is required (although LC9812 mandates the inclusion of certain language). A denial notice is usually provided in a letter format and referred to simply as a "denial letter."

The employer's decision should be explained in language that will be readily understood by the employee. If the employer's reasons are explicit and written in terms the employee can understand, the employee may accept the employer's decision without complaint, thereby avoiding litigation of a noncompensable claim. The employee, of course, has the right to appeal the employer's denial. In fact, LC138.4 requires that a denial notice will concurrently provide notice of "the remedies available to the employee, and the employee's right to seek information and advice." The employer must inform the employee of the right to obtain information from an Information and Assistance Officer, free of charge, and the right to seek advice from an attorney. A denial letter implies that fees are involved in contacting an attorney but avoids detail, since any necessary explanation of attorney's fees will be provided by any attorney from whom the employee seeks advice (since 1990, LC4906 requires attorneys to advise potential clients of fees involved using a required Fee Disclosure Statement; see 1.20).

It serves the employer's best interests to carefully document the provision of a timely denial letter. The employee may disclaim receipt of a timely provided denial notice (possibly long after a claim file has been closed and sent to a storage facility or destroyed). In some past cases, the employer's statute of limitations defense was upheld or denied based upon a judge's assessment of who was the most credible witness: the employee who said no denial letter was received or the claimsperson who said a letter was sent.

Although not required, some employers choose to incur the expense of sending denial letters via "certified mail, return receipt requested, addressee only." This United States Post Office terminology means that a signed receipt will be returned to the employer that can aid in proving that a denial letter was received by a person at a particular address and on a particular date. However, absent satisfactory handwriting comparisons, a signed receipt does not constitute proof that a denial letter was received by the intended addressee (the employee or a dependent of a deceased employee). Some claimspersons provide a courtesy telephone notice of a denial of entitlement to compensation prior to sending a formal denial letter. Such calls should be carefully documented in the claim file.

Other persons or entities may have an interest in the status of the employee's claim for workers' compensation benefits. For instance, a medical provider may request a copy of the denial letter in order to comply with a provision of LC3751 that enables payment to be recovered directly from the employee after a claim for workers' compensation benefits has been formally rejected. A claimsperson can sometimes assist the employee in seeking other available benefits by directly confirming a formal denial of workers' compensation benefits (e.g. to Employment Development Department). An employee whose claim is denied is usually most appreciative of any suggested referrals to alternative sources of benefits or assistance in seeking such benefits. Claimspersons who speak with the employee prior to sending a denial letter may wish to inquire as to any further assistance that they may provide.

Per CR9812, the employer is required to provide a notice of denial within 14 days of its decision to deny liability for workers' compensation benefits. The generally understood maximum reasonable period of 90 days to make a decision to pay or deny compensation is derived from the provisions of LC5402. This statute provides that a claim is rebuttably presumed to be compensable if it is not denied within 90 days "after the date the claim form is filed under Section 5401." The starting date of the 90-day time period is the date that a claim form is filed by the employee or dependents. (Note: the employer's failure to provide a claim form to an employee will postpone the starting date of the 90-day period under LC5402.)

The most significant repercussion for an employer's failure to act within the 90-day period allowed by LC5402 is that the employee may become entitled to benefits by operation of a presumption of compensability. (There is also the possibility that the WCAB could order the employer to pay a 10% penalty under LC5814 upon a finding that "payment of compensation has been unreasonably delayed or refused.") Also, for 1994 or later injuries, LC5401 provides that the filing "of the claim form with the employer shall toll" the otherwise applicable one-year statute of limitations for filing an Application with the WCAB (see 6.19 and 12.31). The one-year statutes of limitations under LC5405 (or LC5406 for death benefits) is tolled (suspended) "until the claim is denied by the employer or else the injury becomes presumptively compensable" because no decision is made in the 90 days allowed by LC5402.

Knowledge of the existence of the presumption of compensability in LC5402 should encourage all employees to report claims timely and may operate to reward some employees with benefits for doing so (that is why the employer should question the reasons for any employee-controlled delays). However, there is no specific time period in which the employee is required to file a claim form (see 6.13). Conceivably, a claim form that provided the employer with its first knowledge of a claim of injury could be filed with the employer on the last day before a statute of limitations would otherwise have barred the claim, thus voiding a statute of limitations defense to the claim (but other valid defenses to the claim may exist).

In any case where the employer is not providing benefits, the employer must have a good reason for withholding compensation and be able to state precisely what this reason is. Hoping that information is out there somewhere that might support a denial is not a valid reason for a denial. Lacking information that is necessary to determine that the employee is entitled to compensation is a valid reason for a denial and can suffice as a basis for a denial of the claim prior to expiration of the 90-day period. However, it is never proper to deny a claim on this basis unless the employer can verify that reasonable attempts have been made to obtain necessary information.

For instance, a decision regarding the compensability of a claim may depend entirely upon a review of past medical or employment records that the employer has not reviewed because the employee has not yet complied with a reasonable request to sign an appropriate medical authorization form. Some may consider this to be an example of insufficient information to deny compensability. However, a valid denial may issue because the facts determined to date do not support the employee's entitlement to benefits and/or because the employee has failed to cooperate in the employer's investigation that is reasonably necessary to determine the employee's entitlement to benefits.

More than one denial notice may be issued on the same claim. Compensation may be provided subsequent to a denial notice, and, on rare occasions, a claim may be denied after some benefits have been provided. Nothing prevents the employer from conducting a further investigation of the facts or providing benefits upon knowledge of any facts that support the employee's entitlement to compensation after a claim has been formally denied. The employer's denial letter must provide the employee with an unequivocal denial, thereby also providing the employee with the right to appeal the employer's decision without further ado. However, when appropriate, the employer may wish to send a separate letter that informs the employee of the status of its ongoing investigation. Nothing precludes further forthright communication with the employee concerning the status of the employer's continued investigative efforts. Claims decisions are always based upon facts known at the time of the decision.

6.10 DENIAL – INSURED EMPLOYER'S RIGHTS

Since 1992, LC3761 requires insurers to notify employers within 15 days of receipt of any claim "filed against the employer directly with the insurer" before the insurer receives the Employer's Report that is required by LC3760 (see 2.22). Effective 1994, the employer is required "to notify its insurer in writing at any time during the pendency of a claim when the employer has actual knowledge of any facts that would tend to disprove any aspect of the employee's claim." (See CR10109 regarding good faith in investigations.) In such cases, if the insurer later decides to settle a claim rather than litigate its liability for payment, it may do so without permission from the employer. However, the employer has the right to make a written request to the WCAB to receive advance notice of any WCAB action or hearing concerning a settlement and may be entitled to a reimbursement of premium if the employer's position is ultimately upheld by the WCAB.

After a written request to the WCAB, the employer is entitled to 15 days advance notice if a hearing is scheduled. Effective 1995, LC3751 requires the insurer to notify the employer of "the time and place of the hearing at which the" settlement "is to be approved" and submit a proof of service to the WCAB. The WCAB is not required to conduct a hearing when the employer takes the position that a claim is not compensable contrary to the position of its insurance company. However, the insurer's failure to provide the required notice of any hearing that the WCAB may schedule will result in sanctions under LC5813 (see 1.18).

The WCAB has the authority to approve a settlement whether or not the notice that is required by LC3751 is provided. If the WCAB "determines that no compensation is payable" (which will only occur if a hearing is conducted), it can order the insurer to reimburse the employer "for any premium paid solely due to the inclusion of the successfully challenged payments in the calculation of the employer's experience modification" (see 2.12). The WCAB is precluded from ordering employees to refund any payments received.

6.11 DUTY OF EMPLOYEE – REPORT INJURY

The employer must have notice or knowledge of a claim before the employer can determine its liability and fulfill its obligation to provide compensation expeditiously. The person who suffers the injury is in the best position to know about it. Unless there are witnesses, no other persons will know about the injury until the employee tells them. The employee may not be sophisticated enough to know the difference between industrial and nonindustrial injuries. If the employee believes an injury or condition may be work-related, the employee is obligated to put the employer on notice of this fact. The employee has a basic obligation to notify the employer of an injury. The employer is entitled to notice and an opportunity to timely investigate the injury.

If the employer has complied with all preinjury notice requirements, the employee will have been advised at least twice in advance of any injury that the employee is required to report all injuries to the employer. The employee will have been advised of this duty once in the notice that was provided at the time of hire under LC3551 and again in the employer's posting notice under LC3550 and may also have received nonrequired notifications that the employer voluntarily provided, e.g. information disseminated at safety meetings.

6.12 CLAIM FORM – EMPLOYEE'S WRITTEN NOTICE

Per LC5400, "no claim to recover compensation ... shall be maintained" (meaning no WCAB proceedings will be held) unless the employer is served with written notice of the claim. This written notice need not be in any particular form but must be signed by either the employee or a dependent (in the event of death) or else an agent acting on either's behalf and provided to the employer "within thirty days after the occurrence of the injury." In actuality, the written notice required by LC5400 is seldom seen, since LC5402 provides that the employer's knowledge of an injury or a claim of injury from any source (whether oral or written, from an employee or a physician or from any other source) is equivalent to service of the written notice required by LC5400 (see 6.15-6.17). However, written notice of claims has become commonplace since 1990 due to the provisions of LC5401.

Employees (or their dependents) are required by LC5401 to provide the employer with written notice of a claim on a "claim form" (whether or not the separate written notice required by LC5400 is also provided). The required "claim form" has undergone several revisions. It is important that an employer provide its employees with the currently required version of the claim form, the Employee's Claim for Workers' Compensation Benefits (DWC Form 1) as set out in CR10118. For 1994 or later injuries, LC5401 requires a claim form to request the employee's "social security number, the time and address where the injury occurred," and the specific "part of the body affected by the injury." (Note: CR10396 requires all parties to a claim to promptly advise all other interested parties of their correct and current mailing address; if an Application for Adjudication has been filed, the parties must also notify the WCAB of any change of address.)

Per LC5401, a completed claim form "shall be filed with the employer by the employee, or, in the case of death, by a dependent" of the deceased employee, or by an agent, e.g. an attorney. Although the employee is required to file a completed claim form with the employer, a claim form filed directly with the employer's insurer or other claims administrator will be deemed to have been filed with the employer. (Note: the employer's failure to provide a claim form to an employee will not relieve the employer of its duty to timely provide any benefits that are due. Such failure can result in the injury being rebuttably presumed to be work-related, and the employer may also be assessed a penalty for a delay in the provision of compensation; see 2.27 and 5.13.)

Per LC5401, the employer (not its insurer or other claims administrator) is required to provide a claim form to an employee or dependent within one working day of knowledge of all injuries that result "in lost time beyond the date of injury or ... medical treatment beyond first aid" (see 6.7). The employer is required by CR10121 to, "within one working day of receipt of a claim form, ... date the claim form and provide a dated copy of the form to the employee and the employer's claims administrator." (Note: the date on which an insurer receives a completed claim form from an employer can affect certain reimbursement rights between the insurer and the employer; see 9.16.)

Per CR10101.1, the copy of the claim form that the employer forwards to its claims administrator shall show the date the employer received knowledge of the claim of injury, the date the form was provided to the employee, and the date a completed form was received from the employee. Where the employee does not return a completed claim form to the employer, the employer's documentation of the date the form was provided to the employee is an important piece of evidence should the employee later seek benefits after expiration of a statute of limitations.

When a claims administrator knows that a claim of injury is being presented but has not received a completed claim form (e.g. where a physician's report provides the first notice of a claim), a duty arises to determine if the employer has provided a claim form to the employee (or dependents). Per CR10119, the claims administrator has a duty to provide a claim form to the employee within 3 days of determining that one has not been provided by the employer or, if unable to ascertain this fact, within a maximum of 30 days of its first knowledge of the claim. The investigation required by CR10119 should involve minimal time or effort. A telephone call to the employer should suffice and, if it does not, a claim form should be sent to the employee immediately. The claims administrator should thereafter continue its investigation for the purpose of ensuring the employer's future compliance with its statutory duty to provide claim forms to its employees as required by LC5401.

6.13 CLAIM FORM – IMPACT ON RIGHTS

There is no logical reason for an employer to fail or refuse to provide a claim form upon knowledge of any injury or upon any request from an employee or dependents. The employer's failure to comply with its duty to provide a claim form within one working day of knowledge of a claim under LC5401 can result in assessment of an administrative penalty (see 2.27). The employer has a duty to make reasonable inquiries and pay compensation that is due whether or not a claim form is filed, and a completed claim form that is submitted by an employee may provide information that facilitates an investigation to determine the employer's liability for compensation. The employer's failure to timely pay compensation that is due can entitle the employee to penalty increases in compensation (automatically under LC4650 or upon a good cause finding by the WCAB under LC5814).

There is no specific period in which employees or dependents must comply with their statutory duty to file a completed claim form with the employer. There are certain inducements for filing and repercussions for failure to file a claim form (some but not all of which are mentioned herein). For instance, each right listed below is specifically contingent upon a claim form being filed and does not exist until a claim form is filed (pursuant to the referenced Labor Code Section).

1. **Late Payment Penalty:** right to an automatic increase of 10% of the amount of each temporary or permanent disability payment that the employer does not pay at the time it is due, commonly referred to as a "self-imposed penalty." (LC4650 and LC5401).

2. **Medical Evaluation:** the right to undergo an examination and obtain a written report from an Agreed Medical Evaluator or a Qualified Medical Evaluator at the employer's expense for a determination of any medical issue that is specified in LC4060, LC4061 or LC4062, e.g. the extent of any permanent disability or the need for continuing medical treatment (LC5401).

3. **Disability Rating:** the right to receive a summary rating of permanent disability that is prepared by the Disability Evaluation Unit based upon the evaluation of a Qualified Medical Evaluator (this right is derivative of #2 above; LC5401 and LC4061).

4. **WCAB Proceedings:** the right to file a Declaration of Readiness to request WCAB adjudication of disputed medical issues (this right is derivative of #2 above and arises only after an evaluation by an Agreed or Qualified Medical Evaluator; LC5401 and LC4061).

5. **Presumption of Compensability:** if the employer does not reject liability "within 90 days after the date the claim form is filed ... the injury shall be presumed compensable." The employer can overcome this presumption, but the "presumption is rebuttable only by evidence discovered after the 90-day period" (LC5402).

6. **Extension of Time:** for 1994 or later injuries, the one year statute of limitations under LC5405 and LC5406 for filing an Application with the WCAB (for regular or death benefits, respectively) is tolled from the date a claim form is filed until the claim is either denied or becomes compensable by operation of the 90-day presumption in LC5402 (LC5401).

Date Claim Form Filed. The above rights arise on the date a claim form is filed with the employer. A claim form is deemed filed on the date a completed form is personally delivered to the employer. If a claim form is mailed rather than personally served, the date the claim form is deemed filed depends upon the particular right that arises upon filing of the claim form.

For purposes of each right explained under #1-#4 and #6 above, a claim form is deemed filed on the date it is placed in the mail (evidence of filing includes the postmarked envelope in which the claim form was received and/or the return receipt provided by the United States Postal Service if mailed by certified mail). For purposes of other rights that are contingent upon filing a claim form such as the expiration date of the 90-day period explained in #5 above, a claim form is deemed filed on the date the employer actually receives the claim form (a "date received" stamp affixed to the claim form by the employer constitutes evidence of filing).

6.14 DATE OF INJURY – SPECIFIC vs. CUMULATIVE

Statutes of limitations are stated as a length of time following a specific act or event. In reference to the time to commence proceedings, the starting date is the date of injury (DOI). This date is different for specific injuries than for cumulative injuries (CI), that include stress and strain (S&S), occupational disease (OD), or continuing or cumulative trauma (CT) injuries (see 5.7).

There is only one date of injury for a specific injury. For a cumulative injury, the date of injury has a separate definition for different purposes. One date of injury is used for purposes of determining the benefit rates that apply, a different date of injury is used for determining the duration of the injury and the employers who are liable for benefits (see 2.10), and a third date of injury is used to determine whether the statute of limitations bars the filing of the claim. This section deals only with the date of injury for purposes of applying the statute of limitations.

Per LC5411, the date of injury for a specific injury is the date the "alleged incident or exposure" occurred. The employee could bump a knee on a desk or be overcome by noxious fumes. Regardless of the cause, by incident or exposure, the injury occurs on a specific date. The consequences of the injury can be traced to some specific event that occurred on a date certain. The statute of limitations period commences to run on this date.

A cumulative injury is the opposite of a specific injury. There is no one episode or event that produces an injury. Per LC3208.1, the injury occurs as a result of "repetitive mentally or physically traumatic activities extending over a period of time." Per LC5412, the date of injury for a cumulative injury is the date on which the employee first suffers disability, and the employee knew or should have known that the "disability was caused by his present or prior employment."

When the employee first suffers disability, the employee may not be aware that it is industrially caused. The employee may receive medical treatment for years before learning that the disability is work-related or could possibly be work-related. The statute of limitations period does not begin until the employee is aware of this connection; otherwise the employee's benefits could be barred before the employee had any need or reason to claim them. Once the employee files an application, it is clear that the employee has obtained the prerequisite knowledge. Notice can be received in many ways; e.g., the employee may obtain an opinion from legal counsel, or a doctor may advise the employee the condition is work-related. The employer has the burden of proving that notice was real advice, not a mere suspicion on the part of the employee.

It is possible for the employee to be aware that a condition is work-related before the employee suffers any disability from the condition. The employee may be diagnosed with early onset of black lung disease, asbestosis, or some other progressive condition. The employee will eventually suffer disability but may be able to continue working for years prior to becoming disabled. The employee must have a benefit to claim before it becomes reasonable to present a claim. Therefore, the employee must concurrently suffer disability and have reasonable a belief of employment causation before a cumulative injury "occurs." Both events could occur on the same date, in which case this date would be the date of injury. However, one event could occur days or years before the other. It does not matter which of the two events occurs first. The date of the second event will be the date of injury for a cumulative injury claim.

6.15 PREJUDICE DUE TO LACK OF NOTICE

Two Labor Code sections require an employee or a dependent to provide the employer with written notice of a claim. Timely filing of the claim form that is required by LC5401 (for 1990 or later injuries) satisfies the separate requirement of LC5400 for the provision of written notice of a claim. However, LC5400 does not require the use of any particular form, and the employer's prejudice for lack of notice defense is predicated upon the failure of the employee (or dependents) to provide the written notice that is required by LC5400.

The shortest statute of limitations is that contained in LC5400. The employee has 30 (thirty) days to present a written notice of a claim. There is no required form for this notice; all that is required is that the notice be in writing and provided to the employer in the time specified. Per LC5400, the employee's claim is barred if the employee does not provide the required written notice to the employer. This obviously harsh Labor Code provision must be read in conjunction with other sections on the same topic.

An exception to the 30-day statute of limitations is found in LC5403. The 30-day statute of limitations will not bar a claim unless certain facts are established. The employer must show that it was "misled or prejudiced" by the employee's failure to provide the required notice. If the employer can meet this burden of proof, the employee's claim will indeed be barred by operation of the 30-day statute of limitations. This is a difficult burden of proof but by no means impossible.

Misconceptions abound regarding the purpose and application of the 30-day statute of limitations. It cannot be used to deny every claim where notice is not received in thirty days or made in writing. However, it is not completely worthless or totally disregarded by judges. This statute of limitations can effectively bar or reduce the employee's compensation in the very few cases where the employer is able to prove prejudice (which can include cases where a claim form is filed more than 30 days after an injury). Where the statutory criteria for its application can be established, there is no reason for the employer to disregard this potentially valuable defense.

6.16 PREJUDICE – EMPLOYEE ALLEGATIONS

The employer's statute of limitations defense based upon prejudice for lack of notice within 30 days of an injury is subject to rebuttal evidence from the employee. A close reading of LC5400, 5402, and 5403 will reveal several exceptions to the operation of the 30-day statute of limitations in LC5400. The employee is not always required to give notice in writing, is not always required to give notice within thirty days, and sometimes is not required to give any notice at all.

Many allegations the employee may make will require little evidence. In fact, the employee's testimony may be all that is necessary to support the employee's position. Allegations commonly used to overcome the 30-day statute of limitations defense include the following:

a. Under LC5402, the employer or proper personnel had knowledge of the injury: an employer representative visited the injured employee at home after the injury, the employee's supervisor witnessed the accident, or the boss sent flowers while the employee was hospitalized.

b. The employee was at all times willing and available to provide information that the employer did not request; for instance, the employee was incapacitated at home and readily available for contact by telephone.

c. Per LC5402, the employer had sufficient knowledge to conduct an investigation of the facts; e.g., the employer knew the names of all witnesses, was provided with a copy of a police report or was provided with a detailed medical report.

d. The employer did not offer a medical exam that the employee would have agreed to attend.

e. The employer had knowledge of a claimed injury, but the employer did not provide the employee with any notice of potential rights regarding workers' compensation benefits as required by LC5401; e.g., that's why the employee sought medical attention from his private physician.

f. The employer provided a post-injury notice of potential rights to benefits (e.g. a pamphlet) that explained the procedures for requesting medical treatment, but the notice was not provided timely (see 6.7). The employee required immediate treatment, and the notice was received after treatment was obtained.

g. Per LC5403, the employee did not give any notice to the employer, but the employer wasn't misled in any way; e.g., the employee believed the injury was minor so did not report it until it became more consequential.

h. Per LC5403, the employer wasn't prejudiced by the employee's failure to give notice; e.g., the employee sought medical treatment from a properly qualified physician, the costs of treatment were reasonable, the treatment was effective, and the employer admits the injury was work-related.

i. Per LC5401, the employer had knowledge of a claimed injury but did not provide the employee with a claim form; the employee would have provided timely written notice using this form had it been provided.

6.17 PREJUDICE – EMPLOYER EVIDENCE

Prejudice means prejudice to a proper defense of the claim. The employer may assert that delayed notice precludes a determination of the extent of its liability. The employer may assert that its liability should be limited to that which would have existed had proper notice been given, because its liability would have been reduced by timely notice.

The employee's credible testimony can support an industrial injury absent any witnesses. Therefore, this defense is ordinarily used to limit the extent of the employer's liability for compensation that is payable rather than to attack the issue of injury. Prejudice for lack of notice can be established to limit the employer's liability for payment if the following facts are established:

a. The employee did not report the injury timely but had both the knowledge and ability to do so.

b. The delayed notice prevented the employer from properly determining the extent of its liability for medical treatment or disability.

c. The delayed notice increased the employer's liability; the employer's liability would be less if proper notice had been provided.

d. The employer would have taken specific action to determine its liability if timely notice had been provided.

e. The action taken by the employer would have fulfilled its legal obligations at lower costs.

f. The employer does not dispute the occurrence of the injury but only the extent of its liability therefor.

If the employer disputes any and all liability for an alleged injury (employer alleges the injury is noncompensable), obviously the employer would not have provided any treatment or benefits had timely notice been given. A different situation exists when the employer does not refute an injury but does contest the extent of the injury. The employee may have a surgery prior to giving notice of an injury. Subsequently developed facts may refute the necessity of the surgery in view of the nature of the injury, the appropriateness of the surgery in view of the medical diagnosis or the qualifications of the surgeon to perform surgery. The self-procured surgery may have been performed for a condition that was not a result of the industrial injury, or the surgery may have resulted in a worsening of the employee's condition.

An increased liability for benefits is evidence of prejudice. This could be an increased need for treatment or a longer period of disability. Monetary prejudice to the employer is measured by the difference between the extent of compensation that is claimed in the absence of timely notice and the lesser amount of compensation that the employer would be obligated to provide if notice had been received. The employer must show how it would have acted differently with earlier notice. The employer may produce medical evidence as proof that a different selection of physicians or earlier diagnosis or treatment would have reduced the extent of the employer's liability to pay compensation.

6.18 COMMENCEMENT OF PROCEEDINGS

WCAB proceedings include hearings (trials), conferences or arbitration. For 1994 or later injuries, filing of an Application for Adjudication of Claim (WCAB Form 1) is necessary to establish WCAB jurisdiction. Thereafter, a Declaration of Readiness to Proceed (WCAB Form 9) must be filed in order to request WCAB proceedings to be conducted (see 1.18).

Both LC4061 and LC4062 preclude the filing of a Declaration of Readiness to commence WCAB proceedings for adjudication of specified disputed medical issues until the employee has been examined by an Agreed or Qualified Medical Evaluator (see 7.75). Per LC5401, filing of a claim form is a prerequisite to the employee's right to obtain medical evaluations at the employer's expense under LC4060, LC4061 or LC4062. Therefore, although the filing of a claim form is not a statutorily required prerequisite to the filing of an Application for Adjudication, the employee is precluded from obtaining an adjudication of certain disputed medical issues unless and until a claim form is filed. (Note: filing of a claim form is not a prerequisite to employer-requested medical evaluations.)

Some statutory time limits apply exclusively to an initial request for commencement of proceedings, and other statutes of limitations apply to a request for the commencement of additional proceedings after a prior WCAB order, decision or award (reopening of a WCAB case; see 6.23-6.28 and 6.31). Separate statutes of limitations apply to a request for the initial commencement of proceedings for rehabilitation (11.34) and for death benefits (see 12.31) than apply for medical, temporary disability, and permanent disability benefits (see 6.19-6.25).

6.19 ONE YEAR FROM DATE OF INJURY

Per LC5405, where no benefits have been provided, the employee has a maximum period of one year from the date of injury to file an Application for Adjudication of Claim with the WCAB. For 1994 or later injuries, LC5401 provides that this one-year deadline is extended by the number of days from the date a claim form was filed with the employer until the date the claim was denied by the claims administrator. The extension of time that is allowed by LC5401 should not exceed 90 days. Per LC5402, a claim that has not been denied within 90 days after a claim form is filed is rebuttably presumed to be compensable. Unless the presumption is rebutted, benefits are owed and the employee can file a timely claim within one year from the last provision of benefits (see 6.22).

There are several reasons why an otherwise compensable claim would not be presented, paid or pursued within one year of its occurrence (or the 1-day to 90-day period of extension allowed by LC5401). For instance:

a. The employee believes the injury is minor at the time it is sustained.

b. The employee prefers to take care of his medical expenses himself rather than file a workers' compensation claim.

c. The injury is reported timely but does not require any treatment at the time it is sustained.

d. The employer offers benefits, but the employee rejects them.

e. The employee may prefer to see a doctor of his own choice during a period when the employer has medical control.

f. The employer may investigate the claim and formally deny liability for the employee's injury, and the employer's denial may be acceptable to the employee at the time it is received.

g. The employee is unaware that an injury or illness is work-related (e.g. an injury during a personal activity that may be compensable under the personal comfort doctrine; see 5.43).

The employee must know that a work-related injury has occurred, must be fully informed as to how to present or pursue a claim, and must voluntarily choose not to do so. Should the employee change his mind at a future date, the reason is irrelevant. The statute of limitations is clear — the employee must pursue his claim no later than one year after the date of injury. Generally, minor injuries don't get worse; they get better quickly. The greater the time elapsed between injury and symptoms, the less likely there is any medical connection between the two. One year is considered to be a fair and adequate period of time for the employee to discover previously unknown complications. This period is equally reasonable for the employee to appeal the employer's denial of liability or to simply change his mind. The employer is obligated to conduct timely investigations and render prompt decisions on its liability. The employee is obligated to pursue a claim no more than one year after the injury.

6.20 ONE-YEAR STATUTE – EMPLOYEE ALLEGATIONS

The employee's claim can still be "timely" (not barred by the statute of limitations) when no benefits have been provided and an application is filed with the WCAB more than one year from the date of injury. The employee may allege that an otherwise late claim is timely due to the tolling of the one-year statute of limitations that is permitted by LC5401; e.g. where a claim was denied twenty days after a claim form was filed and an application was filed with the WCAB less than one year and twenty days after the injury. The employee can also overcome the employer's one-year statute of limitations defense by showing that the reason for the late filing is the employer's (or claims administrator's) fault. For example:

a. The employer was aware of the injury but never advised the employee of a potential right to benefits or how to file a claim.

b. The employer had notice of the claim but did not accept or reject it.

    c. The employer misled the employee regarding the industrial causation of the employee's medical condition.

    d. The employer deceived the employee into believing there was no time period to pursue the claim.

    e. The employer delayed a denial of liability until more than 90 days after the employee timely filed a claim form, so the claim is rebuttably compensable under LC5402.

6.21 ONE-YEAR STATUTE – EMPLOYER EVIDENCE

The employer's defense does not rise and fall on the mere fact that an application was filed with the WCAB after the last day of a statute of limitations period (including any extension allowed by LC5401; see 6.18). The employer must overcome any employee allegations of improper employer action or inaction. Where the statute of limitations has run, the employer can support its defense by proof of facts such as the following:

    a. The employee was aware of the industrial nature of an injury or condition; e.g., the employee gave a history of a work-related injury to a physician, or the employee consulted a workers' compensation attorney within one year from the date of injury.

    b. The employee was informed how to report the injury: the employer has documentation that the employee received oral and/or written explanatory information.

    c. The employee was aware that notice of injury was required; for instance, the employee has a history of previous claims that were properly reported.

    d. The employee did not give timely notice to the employer; the first notice received by the employer was more than one year after the injury.

    e. The employer sent a formal denial letter well in advance of the expiration of the statute of limitations.

    f. The employee was advised of the applicable time limits (including the tolling provisions of LC5401) but filed a claim after expiration of the statute of limitations (or permitted period of extension under LC5401).

6.22 ONE YEAR FROM LAST PROVISION OF BENEFITS

Once the employer provides medical or disability benefits, the employee's time to commence proceedings with the WCAB is extended (different statute of limitations periods apply to rehabilitation and death benefits; see 11.34 and 12.31). Per LC5405, the statute of limitations is a one-year period, but the starting date is not the date of injury. The employee may file a timely claim within one year from either of the following:

    1. The "expiration of any period" of payment for temporary or permanent disability benefits, OR

    2. The "date of last furnishing of any" medical benefits.

The alternative one-year statute of limitations that are listed above can provide the employee with an indefinite period of time in which to timely file an initial WCAB claim for workers' compensation benefits. Each time the employee receives medical treatment or the employer issues a payment for disability benefits, the employee gets a new one-year period. In some cases, there will never be more than a year between the provision of medical benefits. In unlitigated cases where the employer is voluntarily providing payment of a permanent disability life pension, the employee can commence proceedings before the WCAB any time during his lifetime.

Most employees do not suffer severe injuries. There is usually a definite date on which medical treatment ends and a date that a final payment is issued for indemnity benefits. The one-year statute of limitations will begin to run on the date that the last workers' compensation benefit is provided and will expire when a year goes by without any further benefit being provided. Should a dispute arise, the employer must prove that benefits were not provided for more than one year because none were claimed nor known to be due.

Medical benefits are deemed to be provided as of the date the employee personally receives the benefit, not a later date on which the claims administrator pays a medical bill. For instance, medical benefits are provided on the date that the employee is examined by a physician, fitted for a prosthesis, or receives physical therapy. Indemnity benefits are provided on the date that the claims administrator issues a payment by placing it in the mail (usually the date that appears on the check, but the WCAB may rely upon a postmarked envelope as evidence that payment was made on a subsequent date). If disability checks are mailed late, the statute of limitations period can be extended.

The passage of time negates the assertion that further benefits are necessary as a result of the industrial injury. After a year without benefits, it is reasonable to assume some other explanation for the employee's symptoms; e.g., the employee may have suffered a new injury to the same part of the body, or a nonindustrial condition may develop. However, once the statute of limitations expires, the employee's claim is barred even in cases where claimed benefits are undisputably a result of the original injury. The employee must act timely to protect his rights. If any further claim is to be honored, it must be asserted within the one-year statute of limitations period.

Sometimes the employer makes what it believes to be a final payment. Then, after a fairly lengthy period of time, the employee presents a claim for additional treatment or disability. A claim must be presented prior to expiration of any applicable statute of limitations period that would bar further benefits (see 6.23-6.29). If so, the employer should arrange a medical appointment with specific instructions to the physician "for an exam only." If the consulting physician determines that further treatment is not necessitated by the industrial injury, payment for this exam does not constitute a provision of medical benefits for purposes of tolling the statute of limitations (payment would constitute a payment without an admission of liability under LC4909 and should be clearly denoted as such on the face of a check).

It is important to restrict a consulting physician to an exam only until the employer determines its liability for benefits. The employer has a right to determine its liability before it provides any benefits or payments. However, the employer may inadvertently eliminate a valid statute of limitations defense whenever a physician provides treatment under an assumed authorization to do so.

An insurance company may be deemed to have furnished medical benefits where it is not aware that the employee is receiving treatment at an employer health facility. The employer may be paying the employee's medical bills directly, or the employer may be submitting bills for industrial treatment to a group health care provider. The employer's actions bind its insurance company. If the employer has provided medical benefits directly, this should be determined by an investigation prior to pursuing a statute of limitations defense.

The actions of a treating physician who is authorized or paid by the employer can affect a statute of limitations defense. Once a physician has discharged a patient, the physician should be advised that no further treatment is authorized without prior permission from the claimsperson. This can be done by sending a standard form letter at the end of treatment. This simple task should be routine, but it is seldom done, and its omission can eliminate an otherwise successful statute of limitations defense. The claimsperson should provide the physician with written withdrawal of authorization with a copy being sent to the employee. Absent such notification, here are some potential problems that can extend the statute of limitations:

a. Although not included in a report, the physician told the employee to come back if the employee ever had further problems. The employee did return more than one year after the last provision of benefits. The doctor provided treatment but either did not request prior authorization or could not reach the claimsperson by telephone.

b. The employee called the treating physician and requested a refill of a previously prescribed medication. The physician called it in to a pharmacy. The employee paid for the medication, so the physician did not submit a billing, and the claimsperson was unaware of the event.

c. The employee calls and schedules an appointment with the previous treating physician, stating he is having further problems from the injury. The physician, assuming continued authorization, examines the employee and then sends a report to the claimsperson.

The problems listed above result from poor communication between the physician and the claimsperson. Whether the doctor should have known better or whether the claimsperson can refuse to pay his bill are irrelevant considerations, because the statute of limitations defense concerns the reasons for the employee's actions, not the physician's. The employee may allege a reasonable belief that the employer would provide additional benefits if any were needed from the effects of the industrial injury. This allegation is very helpful to the employee's position. It is even better for the employee if the doctor found something to treat. However, the employer can overcome such allegations if its defense is supported by evidence of the following:

   a. The employee was provided with all required notices, including notification of termination of benefits, AND/OR
   b. The employee was not misled regarding the employer's liability for further benefits.

6.23 FIVE-YEAR STATUTE – NEW & FURTHER DISABILITY

Once the employer provides benefits, a five-year statute of limitations is in effect. Per LC5410, the employee has five years from the date of injury "to institute proceedings for the collection of compensation." This statute of limitations does not apply to every case where benefits have been paid. It pertains only to the situation where the "original injury has caused new and further disability" and benefits have previously been paid either voluntarily or under the compulsion of a WCAB order, decision or award.

The manner in which the employee will "institute proceedings" is dependent upon whether the claim has been litigated. If the claim has not been litigated, the employee institutes WCAB proceedings by filing an Application for Adjudication of Claim. In workers' compensation cases, once an Application is filed, there is no required time period in which a decision must be rendered by the court. However, as soon as the WCAB has awarded compensation to the employee, the five-year limit in LC5410 applies to the claim. (If the award issued more than five years after the date of injury, the employee would not have the right to reopen the case under LC5410.)

After a court award has issued, a claim for new and further disability is a request for an alteration of the terms of the previous award. The employee does not file an Application, because one is already on file. The employee "institute(s) proceedings" for new and further disability by filing a Petition to Reopen his court case.

6.24 NEW & FURTHER DISABILITY – EMPLOYEE ALLEGATIONS

The five-year statute of limitations for seeking new and further disability does not apply unless certain events occur. The employee must have an injury. The employer must provide benefits for the injury. Thereafter, one of two things must occur. The employer terminates the provision of benefits and gives required notifications to the employee (see 6.10) or the employee goes longer than one year without needing medical treatment and/or being entitled to disability payments.

Labor Code 5405 permits an employee to commence WCAB proceedings for the collection of compensation any time within one year from the date of the last provision of benefits to the employee. The five-year statute of limitations in

LC5410 pertains to employees who seek additional benefits after the one-year statute of limitations in LC5405 has expired. The employee must meet the statutory criteria for application of the five-year statute of limitations. The employee must have a new disability or have additional disability, and the disability must be a direct result of the original injury.

A new disability is one of which the employee was not previously aware. A further disability is an additional need for the same category of benefits that was previously provided. The employee's allegations of new and further disability are commonly based upon such developments as:

a. Symptoms have arisen in a new part of the body; the original injury was to the left hip; disability has now arisen in the back as a result of a change in posturing due to the hip problem.

b. New symptoms have arisen in the same part of the body: the pain went away then returned; it has now reached the point where additional treatment is required to alleviate the symptoms.

c. The employee's injury has now resulted in disability: medical treatment enabled the employee to continue working after his injury, but now the doctor has put him on disability.

d. The employee now requires a new and further period of disability: the employee had returned to work but is no longer able to continue working.

e. The disability could not be discovered previously: the condition was misdiagnosed or had a subtle progression.

f. The employee's disability is more extensive than before: the condition may still be permanent, but the employee has become more physically limited than previously anticipated.

g. There is a significant change in the previous condition: the condition previously required physical therapy but now requires surgery.

6.25 NEW & FURTHER DISABILITY – EMPLOYER EVIDENCE

When the employer asserts that the five-year statute of limitations under LC5410 bars a claim, it rejects the employee's contention that the disability constitutes a "new and further" disability. The employee does not have five years from the date of injury to seek an award of additional benefits under LC5410 unless there is actually some change in the employee's previously known condition. Absent a new or further disability, the statute of limitations to commence proceedings is one year from the date of the last provision of benefits. To defend against a claim for new and further disability, the employer must prove that the disability is the same as it existed in the past. Successful proof of this one fact can produce two beneficial results:

1. If the claim is a reopening of a prior WCAB case, no additional compensation will be awarded, and the employer's liability will remain as it existed under the terms of the previous award.

2. If the claim was instituted by the initial filing of an Application for Adjudication of Claim, the employer can be successful in asserting

that the one-year statute of limitations bars the claim, and its liability will remain as it existed prior to the filing of the application.

The employee is not limited to one claim for new and further disability. The employee may present this claim on multiple occasions within five years from the date of injury. The employer may defeat the employee's claim on one occasion but become liable for additional compensation later on if a new and further disability does arise. In coordination with medical evidence, the employer will refute a claim for new and further disability by showing that:

a. The nature and extent of the employee's present disability was properly identified at some point in the past: the medical diagnosis and/or prognosis remains the same.

b. The employee's claim is for disability that accrued at a previous point in time: the employee is claiming a higher compensation rate for a previously awarded period of disability that occurred in the past.

c. The employee is claiming a new need for treatment that was recommended or known to the employee in the past: a doctor recommended that a ganglion be surgically removed, and the employee did not choose to have the recommended surgery until now.

d. The employee possessed sufficient knowledge to pursue his claim timely: the employee was aware of the nature and extent of his condition and was advised that the employer was willing to provide payment or was denying further liability.

e. The employee neglected to pursue his benefits in a timely fashion: the employee forgot how long he had to file or just didn't get around to it.

f. The employee chose not to pursue benefits until this time: the employee wanted to wait until he changed jobs or retired, or he had some other personal reason for his choice not to pursue his claim in a timely fashion.

g. The employee's petition is not supported by medical evidence: the petition was filed solely for purposes of preventing the expiration of the five-year statute of limitations that would otherwise bar reopening of the claim and not because of any change in the employee's condition (the WCAB may determine that good cause exists for allowing submission of a late-filed medical report, but this determination is unlikely absent unusual extenuating circumstances).

The employer would attempt to prove that the employee's presently-claimed disability is not new, no further or additional disability has developed, and the employee's disability is the same as it was prior to the expiration of the one-year statute of limitations. The reason the employee is categorizing his disability as "new and further" is because he now wants to receive benefits that he previously chose not to pursue. The employee is merely attempting a second chance to claim benefits that were previously claimed and denied or that he has not previously requested.

6.26 FIVE-YEAR STATUTE – REOPENING FOR GOOD CAUSE

Per LC5803, the WCAB has continuing jurisdiction over "all its orders, decisions, and awards," including Findings and Orders, Findings and Awards, and Orders Approving Compromise and Release settlements. The WCAB may "rescind, alter, or amend" its previous decisions whenever a party demonstrates there is "good cause" for doing so. Per LC5804, reopening is restricted to a period of five years from the date of injury. A Petition to Reopen must be filed before the expiration of the five-year period. Beyond this time, a previous award cannot be altered, and the prior decision will remain in effect.

Reopening under LC5803 is based upon a showing that a prior award was, and continues to be, inequitable. Information is known now that was not known at the time the award was issued. This information makes the award inequitable as it stands. Labor Code 5803 allows for reopening by either the employee or the employer. An award may be inequitable to either party, e.g. where the employer alleges that a prior award is inequitable because it was obtained by fraud or deceit. (Note: if the employer seeks reopening for the purpose of terminating a WCAB award "for continuing medical treatment and is unsuccessful," LC4607 permits the WCAB to order the employer to pay "attorney's fees reasonably incurred by the applicant in resisting the proceeding to terminate" the employee's previously awarded medical treatment.)

6.27 GOOD CAUSE TO REOPEN – EMPLOYEE ALLEGATIONS

Per LC5803, the employee can establish good cause to file a Petition to Reopen (WCAB Form 42) a previously closed WCAB file by showing that his disability has "recurred" or "increased." In other words, evidence of new and further disability under LC5410 also constitutes good cause to reopen under LC5803. The previous award is inequitable if it did not compensate the employee for the full effects of the injury. Both Labor Code sections provide the employee with a basis for reopening a WCAB file to claim new and further disability, but LC5803 provides additional grounds for reopening.

The employee need not have any new or further disability. The employee can still claim an inequity in the prior award. Good cause can be shown where some action or inaction of the employer prevented the employee from full knowledge of the extent of his condition, his right to benefits or his right to a hearing before the WCAB. There may be new evidence that has only recently come to the employee's attention. Some examples of the employee's allegations for good cause to reopen include:

a. The employer's failure to provide required notices (or timely notices) prevented the employee from awareness of his rights and an opportunity to pursue them.

b. The employer withheld relevant medical reports that would have made the previous award inequitable; e.g., a report indicated the employee's condition was work-related, but the employer denied any industrial causation.

c. The employee has discovered new evidence that could not have been discovered prior to the issuance of the award; e.g., the employee believed there were no witnesses to the injury but now discovers that there was a witness.

6.28 NOT GOOD CAUSE TO REOPEN – EMPLOYER EVIDENCE

If the employee's Petition to Reopen is based on the existence of new and further disability, the employer has its usual defenses to this ground for reopening (see 6.25). If other grounds for good cause are alleged, the employer must then refute each separate employee allegation. The employer must prove that no good cause exists to modify the terms of the previous award. The award may be equitable as it stands, or the employee's allegations may not constitute good cause to reopen. Depending on the employee's alleged grounds for reopening, the employer's evidence could attempt a showing that:

a. The employee is merely attempting to effect an untimely appeal of a previous award: the employee's allegations constitute grounds for a Petition for Reconsideration and the time for filing this petition has expired.

b. The employee's evidence is duplicative rather than new or different: the employee's complaints and disability remain the same as they were at the time the award issued.

c. The employee is really seeking a second opinion on evidence previously presented to support his claim: a "new" medical report varies little from a previous opinion presented by the same physician but not relied on by the judge.

d. The employee's allegation amounts to simply restating a previous disability; e.g., the employee has newly worded subjective complaints that are basically the same as those previously presented.

e. The employee has a new medical report, but the physician's opinions are the same as those contained in previously submitted medical evidence: there has been no change in the employee's subjective or objective factors of disability.

f. The employee's current condition is the same as it existed at the time of the prior award: present complaints are unchanged from the complaints the employee presented in a previous deposition, to a former doctor or via testimony at a past hearing.

g. The employee's current medical report does not present new disability; it merely disagrees with previous medical opinions: the employee is attempting to relitigate his claim.

h. The employee's allegedly "newly discovered" evidence was known to the employee prior to the award; e.g., the employee had stated there was a witness but failed to produce the witness previously.

i. The employee's "newly discovered" evidence was capable of discovery prior to issuance of the award; e.g., the employee had seen a physician of his choosing, but the employee did not procure a timely report from this doctor.

j.   The reason that the employee's present medical evidence is different is because the employee has given an improper history to the physician; e.g., the employee neglects to volunteer a history of nonindustrial accidents, conditions or treatment.

k.   The employee's medical evidence is different because the employee has suffered a new injury, or there is some similar reason for the employee's changed disability.

l.   The employee is dissatisfied with the original award, but the award is not inequitable: the employee has been awarded compensation appropriate to his disability.

6.29 WAIVER & ESTOPPEL

Waiver and estoppel are two factors that can negate an otherwise successful defense on a statute of limitations issue. By a waiver, the employer simply agrees to give up its right to raise this defense. The employer can effect a waiver by a direct or indirect action. By estoppel, the employer loses its right to pursue a statute of limitations defense. It loses this right by an action it took or failed to take in the past.

The employer can waive its statute of limitations defense by not timely placing this matter in issue. A statute of limitations issue is an affirmative defense. Per LC5705, this means that the "burden of proof rests upon the party or lien claimant holding the affirmative of the issue." Per LC5500, an Answer is required after an application has been filed. The Answer "shall be in writing" and shall delineate "all issues of disagreement." Per LC5505, "evidence on matters not pleaded by answer shall be allowed only upon the terms and conditions imposed by the appeals board or referee holding the hearing." This statutory provision is restated in WCAB Rules of Practice and Procedure. Per CR10484, additional matters can be pleaded after the Answer is filed, but "evidence on matters not pleaded by Answer" will be allowed only at the discretion of the WCAB.

If a statute of limitations defense is not raised in an Answer or an Answer is not filed, the employer may give the appearance of waiving this defense. The employer has an additional opportunity to raise the defense, but further success is dependent upon the judge's acquiescence at some later date. Per LC5409, a statute of limitations defense "may be waived," and the employer will be deemed to have exercised its right to waive this defense if it fails to "present such defense prior to the submission of the cause for decision." ("Submission" is defined in CR10301 to mean "the closing of the record to the receipt of further evidence or argument.")

The import of the various Labor Code sections and WCAB rules is clear. The statute of limitations defense is a "use it or lose it" defense. The employer should raise the issue in its Answer any time such defense appears appropriate. The employer is not in an optimum position when it untimely requests permission to raise a defense that asserts that the employee's claim is untimely. A successful defense will warrant a "Take Nothing" award, even in cases where industrial causation and disability are not disputed. The employer must present a reasonable explanation to the WCAB for its delayed assertion of this defense. A good reason could be some action of the employee that misled the employer such as placing the wrong date of injury on the application. A poor reason would be to claim an oversight or clerical error in the Answer the employer filed with the WCAB.

The employer may raise a statute of limitations defense timely and properly but still be precluded from presenting evidence in support of its defense. The employer will be "estopped" from use of this defense when the reason for the employee's late filing was the employer's fault. The employee may admit the claim is filed outside the statute of limitations period, but he can then establish mitigating circumstances that will excuse the delay. Some examples include:

a. The employer had knowledge of the injury or a claimed injury but failed to provide the employee with required notices.
b. A claimsperson misled the employee regarding the statute of limitations that applied to the claim.
c. The employer knew the employee's condition was industrially related but withheld this information from the employee.
d. The employer failed to advise the employee of his potential right to workers' compensation benefits.
e. The employer failed to advise the employee how to pursue a claim including his right to a hearing before the WCAB.
f. The employee filed a claim immediately upon discovery of his potential right to workers' compensation benefits.
g. The delayed filing was a direct result of the employer's actions, delayed actions or improper actions.
h. The employee could not reasonably have discovered his potential right to compensation benefits at an earlier date.

The claimsperson should be aware of acts that could estop the employer from use of a statute of limitations defense. All required notices should be provided within the required time periods. Where appropriate, any oral information to the employee should be confirmed with written documentation. Notices that are required upon termination of payments are sometimes included in the same envelope with a final check. If the employee cashes the check, the endorsed check is evidence that supports the employee's receipt of the required notice.

6.30 MINORS & INCOMPETENTS – EXTENSION OF TIME

Per LC5408, "no limitation of time ... shall run against any person under 18 years of age or any incompetent unless and until a guardian or conservator of the estate or trustee is appointed." For example, if a one year statute of limitations would otherwise apply, the one year begins from the date a minor has his eighteenth birthday or a guardian ad litem is appointed. The appeals board has the authority to "appoint a trustee or guardian ad litem to appear for and represent any minor or incompetent." This authority is granted by LC5307.5. The WCAB provides a form for this purpose entitled Petition for Appointment of Guardian ad litem and Trustee.

It is sometimes necessary to present evidence of the date on which a guardian was appointed, since the statute of limitations starts to run on that date. The Labor Code does not restrict the appointment of a guardian to the sole jurisdiction of the WCAB. An investigation should consider the fact that other courts such as the superior court also have authority to appoint guardians for purposes unrelated to workers' compensation matters.

6.31 GENERAL LISTING – STATUTES OF LIMITATIONS

There are a variety of statute of limitations periods that apply to claims for workers' compensation benefits and to claims for penalties arising out of an industrial injury claim. Listed below is a brief reference guide to the various statutes of limitations contained in the Labor Code:

a. LC5405: Commencement of proceedings for medical, temporary disability or permanent disability benefits.

b. LC5410: Instituting proceedings (usually by filing a Petition to Reopen, but sometimes by filing an Application for Adjudication of Claim) on grounds that the injury has resulted in new and further disability or a need for rehabilitation benefits.

c. LC5406: Commencement of proceedings for death benefits.

d. LC5406.5: Commencement of proceedings for death benefits in case of death from asbestosis.

e. LC5405.5: Commencement of proceedings for vocational rehabilitation benefits.

f. LC5408: Commencement of proceedings for incompetent or minor.

g. LC5803 and 5804: Request to reopen a previously closed WCAB case for good cause.

h. LC132a: Claim for penalty against the employer and/or its insurance company for discrimination after an injury.

i. LC5407: Commencement of proceedings to seek a penalty for serious and willful misconduct of employer.

j. LC5407.5: Commencement of proceedings to seek a penalty against employee for serious and willful misconduct.

[7] MEDICAL

7.1 MEDICAL BENEFITS – OVERVIEW

Per LC4600, the employer owes all medical expenses "reasonably required to cure or relieve from the effects of the injury." There must first be a compensable industrial injury as defined by the Labor Code, and there must be a direct relationship between the industrial injury and the medical expenses incurred. The expenses must be incurred as a result of a recommendation by a person who the Labor Code defines as a "physician"; the services must be provided by properly licensed medical personnel; and, the charges for all services must be reasonable. The employer is liable for payment of treatment-related expenses as well as medical examinations and reports that are required to determine the extent of the employer's liability for workers' compensation medical and disability benefits.

7.2 PRIVATE BENEFITS – COMPARED

Workers' compensation benefits have some features that are not ordinarily part of private medical plans. There is no deductible to be paid by the employee. There is no limit on the dollar amount of medical benefits that the employer will provide. There is no stated time limit for payment of benefits. The employee is entitled to reimbursement for mileage expense, and workers' compensation pays for all prescription medications.

The claimsperson must guard against attempts to obtain workers' compensation benefits because they are the preferred source of medical coverage. The employee may compare workers' compensation benefits to other sources of benefits, and it is unlikely that any other benefit plan will compare favorably to the extensive coverage provided under the Labor Code. The employee may prefer to receive workers' compensation benefits rather than more limited benefits under some other medical coverage, or the employee may not have any other source of payment for medical expense. Eligibility for workers' compensation benefits is not a matter of preference; it is a matter of meeting required criterion by having a compensable industrial injury.

24-Hour Coverage – Pilot Project

A pilot project was authorized by LC4612 in 1993. Employers participating in the pilot project are allowed to enter into contracts for health care services to coordinate all medical coverage, both industrial and nonindustrial. The general concept of one designated medical provider regardless of causation is referred to as "24-hour coverage." Employers who are most interested in this concept are ones who contribute large sums of money to provide health care benefits to their workers such as large employers and most health care employers, e.g. hospitals. These employers welcome the opportunity to have some control of overall medical costs for health care provided to their employees at their expense. Past efforts have been stymied because an employee has the right to choose to receive treatment from a medical provider outside of the employer's health care plan thirty days after an industrial injury is reported to the employer.

Employers who participate in the pilot project (that requires permission from the State) must allow their employees to choose "between the exclusive provider of care option and a traditional health benefits plan which allows employees to obtain workers' compensation treatment from" a physician of their choice (under certain conditions; see 7.39). An employee who selects the pilot project plan is merely agreeing to seek medical attention from the same place where he would go if he needed medical attention for any nonindustrial injury or condition.

The first pilot projects were implemented in 1995 in the larger counties in California. Pilot projects are initially approved for three years. Monitoring is provided by the State, and participants in the pilot project are assessed for their pro rata share of administrative costs incurred by the State. The Administrative Director of the Division of Workers' Compensation is required to provide a detailed report to the Legislature and the Governor that appraises the success of the pilot project in specific areas.

A preliminary report is due before the end of the second year of the project, and a final report to the Legislature is due within one year after the project ends. A detailed checklist of items for inclusion in these reports is set out in LC4612. The pilot project will be deemed to be a success if the program "compares favorably with that of employers and employees who are not in the program." Administrative regulations governing employers who choose to participate in the pilot project are found in CR10175-CR10181. (See IC1749.3 regarding the sale of such coverage.)

7.3 PREVENTATIVE MEDICINE

Preventative medicine is not covered under the Labor Code — except for a solitary situation that is found in LC3208.05 and applies exclusively to certain health care workers who are specified in this statute (see below). For all other employees, an industrial injury is a prerequisite to medical benefits. By definition, preventative medicine is provided to prevent an injury. It does not provide a cure or relief for an injury because no injury has occurred at the time it is provided.

An example of preventative medicine is a gamma globulin shot after exposure to hepatitis. If one worker is diagnosed to have hepatitis, the employer may direct all its employees to obtain this shot. The need for the shot arises out of the employment and during the course of employment. However, since the shot is given to persons who do not have hepatitis, coemployees who receive the shot have not sustained any injury. Group insurance may pay the costs of the shot. The employer may be willing to pay any deductible expense not covered under group insurance or to provide the shots at no cost to the employee. The employer is not required to pay for the shots but would certainly wish to avoid any outbreak of hepatitis in the workplace. Most employees would rather pay for the shot themselves than risk getting hepatitis. Regardless of who pays for the shot, this expense is not treatment for an industrial injury, and it is not covered under the Labor Code (unless the employee is one of the health care workers specified in LC3208.5, because the risk of exposure to hepatitis for such workers is recognized by law as exceeding that of workers in other employments).

Once there is a known case of hepatitis, there is also a very good chance that coemployees will contract the disease. Treatment for the condition itself would be work-related, assuming a doctor finds a reasonable connection between the workplace and exposure to the condition. Treatment required for an adverse reaction to the gamma globulin shot could also constitute a work-related injury.

This would be the case if the employer orders the employee to get the shot rather than making it voluntary on the employee's part or prohibits the employee from working until the employee has the shot.

Public Employers have a special liability for payment of preventative medical treatment under Section 1797.186 of the Health & Safety Code. When specified safety employees demonstrate that they were exposed to a contagious disease "while performing first aid or cardiopulmonary resuscitation services," they are "entitled to prophylactic medical treatment to prevent the onset of the disease." However, payment for such treatment is not a workers' compensation benefit for two reasons: this liability is not set forth in the Labor Code, and treatment is provided before any injury (disease) occurs.

Healthcare Employers have a special liability for the payment of preventative medical treatment under LC3208.05. Preventative treatment and treatment for an adverse reaction to such treatment are compensable if necessary due to a documented exposure to certain bloodborne diseases (see 5.4).

7.4 INITIAL DETERMINATION OF ELIGIBILITY

An employee may suffer pain or disability of unknown origin during working hours. There may be some reason to suspect possible industrial causation. If there isn't, the employee should simply be referred for private medical attention. If there is a possibility of a work relationship, a medical diagnosis is necessary. The employer should arrange for the employee to undergo an examination at a medical facility.

If the medical diagnosis reveals an industrial injury or condition, further workers' compensation benefits will be provided. This would be the case where the employee suffers spontaneous stomach cramps that the doctor diagnoses as an industrial hernia. If a nonindustrial problem is identified, the employee should be directed to obtain further medical attention on a private basis. This could occur where the employee lapses into unconsciousness, and the cause is medically determined to result from a failure to administer an insulin dosage for a diabetic condition.

By directing the employee to a particular doctor, the employer assumes liability for the expense of the diagnostic examination and any testing necessary to determine the cause of the disability. Per LC4909, payment of the initial examination fee does not obligate the employer to provide any additional benefits. Payment for this exam is not an admission of liability for any medical expenses subsequent to a nonindustrial diagnosis.

The employer will not always owe payment for an initial eligibility examination. If the employee sees a physician of his choosing, expenses for nonindustrial conditions are a private matter. It may be clear to the employee that the expense is due to a private problem. Regardless of who selects the examining physician, the employee may voluntarily pay for the exam himself. An objection to this expense usually arises when the employer sends the employee to a physician who charges more than the employee would otherwise have paid his own physician. The employer clearly owes the cost of the exam when the employer directs the employee to see a particular physician.

7.5 COVERED MEDICAL EXPENSES – IN GENERAL

The employer's liability for medical expenses is broadly stated in LC4600. Some items are specifically covered and mentioned by name. These include:

a. Medical treatment	e. Nursing care	i. Crutches
b. Surgical treatment	f. Medicines	j. Apparatus
c. Chiropractic treatment	g. Medical supplies	k. Orthotic devices
d. Hospital treatment	h. Surgical supplies	l. Prosthetic devices

The employer's liability for medical expenses is not restricted to those items that are named in LC4600. This section refers to the employer's liability as "including" these categories of medical expenses. Unspecified items that are comparable or analogous to named items are deemed to be covered; certain expenses are specifically covered by other Labor Code provisions; and the employer has the right to agree to provide payment for any type of treatment or expense that it is not obligated by law to provide. The crux of a determination of the employer's liability for any particular item is whether the item meets the three criteria (as explained in following sections) that LC4600 requires for every covered expense. The employer is not liable for any medical expense that was not:

1. "Reasonably required."
2. "To cure or relieve."
3. "From the effects of the injury."

7.6 TREATMENT – REASONABLY REQUIRED

Reasonably required expenses are those incurred in order to cure or relieve from the effects of an injury. Where a particular treatment results in an actual cure, it seems obvious, in retrospect, that the expense was reasonably required. However, other treatment might have achieved the same result at much less expense. In this case, the treatment obtained may be required but not reasonable in terms of its cost.

An expense is required when it is reasonably necessary. If the employee cannot be cured or cannot have relief from his injury without the expense, it is reasonably necessary. Medical attention for a full finger amputation is required, not optional. Without treatment, the employee's condition would deteriorate, a loss of blood could result in death, or an infection could set in which might necessitate a later amputation of the entire hand. However, there is a question as to what expenses are reasonably required.

A band aid and an aspirin would be unreasonable treatment for a finger amputation when compared with the accepted common method of treatment for this type of injury. Such treatment is unlikely to provide relief from the effects of the employee's injury. The employee may wish to fly to some other state to be treated by a doctor who he has heard is "the best in the world." The employee might stay in a motel near the doctor for the period of time he requires treatment. The expenses of such treatment would be unreasonable when adequate treatment is available in the employee's local area. The fact that the employee achieves a good result from self-procured treatment is not controlling. The employer is liable for expenses that are reasonably required but nothing more.

Optional Expenses are not required, so the employer is not liable for their payment. The doctor may prescribe crutches after an industrial injury to the employee's foot. The employee's preference to use a wheelchair instead of crutches is optional. The employer is only liable for the expense of providing the crutches. The doctor may opine that the employee should exercise his knee as much as possible following knee surgery. The doctor's nonspecific recommendation for exercises does not render the employer liable for any and all exercise equipment that the employee chooses to purchase. Where a particular type of apparatus is necessary and there are no viable alternatives, the employer is liable for this expense.

A physician may recommend swimming as an exercise. The employer is not necessarily obligated to provide swimming lessons, purchase a swimming pool or pay for a membership in a health club. A physician's recommendation for swimming will usually be based upon knowledge that the employee knows how to swim, likes to swim, and has a swimming pool or access to one. If the physician's recommendation is not based upon all of these essential facts, the physician should be asked to elaborate upon the type of exercise that is required and the range of choices for obtaining such exercise. This range of alternatives will reveal what is reasonably required at the employer's expense.

The employee may require an artificial leg. There is a broad range of prostheses available that vary in price and sophistication. The employee may insist upon having the most expensive model available. No one can prevent him from having what he wants; however, the employer's liability would be a portion of the cost, not the entire amount. It would be reasonable for the employer to contribute to the cost up to the amount that would be paid for a model that is reasonably required. The more serious the injury, the more likely that the employer will be generous in an assessment of what is reasonably required.

The term "medical treatment" does not encompass rare or experimental forms of treatment. The employer does not owe the cost of any treatment that has no proven or known medical value. Illegal treatment is not covered. An example would be a surgery or therapy performed by an individual lacking a required license. Unusual types of treatment are not ordinarily covered. Examples would include treatment provided by a hypnotist or an herb therapist. Treatment by Faith Healers or Christian Science Practitioners is not covered unless the employer voluntarily agrees to provide this treatment (see 7.30)

Exploratory Surgery performed without a specific diagnosis is not necessarily the employer's responsibility. The physician may not know what is wrong with the patient. If an industrial condition is not reasonably suspected to exist, the employer would not advance the costs for the surgery. The surgery may reveal the existence of an industrial condition. Upon such diagnosis, the employer will then be liable for the expenses of the exploratory surgery.

The employer is not liable for personal expenses the employee incurs while hospitalized for an industrial injury. The employer does not owe personal expenses such as the cost of special meals that the employee has delivered from outside vendors, sundry items purchased from the hospital gift shop, gifts for hospital staff or nurses or long distance telephone charges.

Generally, rare or experimental forms of treatment with no proven value are unreasonable where treatment with recognizable results is available. The cost of treatment is unreasonable when it exceeds the usual and customary cost for achieving the same result. Usual and customary care and the costs for the care are determined by the average standards existing in a particular locality. Reasonably required treatment is that treatment that is being provided to most of the people most of the time for the same type of injury or condition.

What is reasonable in a particular case? An answer could be obtained by polling physicians in the locality — a decision to deny liability for a particular type of recommended treatment must be based upon a decision of a physician. However, the need for polling is usually avoided since utilization review standards are available that provide information regarding treatment that is ordinarily provided for common types of injuries (see 7.10). Utilization review standards rely upon various types of available information regarding customary standards of care. (The employer may always agree to pay for a nonstandard type of treatment before it is provided; see 7.30.)

7.7 TREATMENT – CURE OR RELIEF

Some injuries or conditions cannot be cured. Examples include brain damage, asbestosis and an amputated leg. Medical treatment is successful when it provides optimum relief from the effects of such injuries. Some conditions require lifetime medical care to provide continuing relief. The employer owes the costs of either a cure or relief depending upon which can be achieved in view of the nature of the injury.

Experimental treatment is not covered because it is not known if a cure or relief results from the treatment. Some treatment is known not to provide a cure or relief. For instance, a chiropractor cannot perform surgery. Therefore, if the employee's condition requires surgery, treatment by a chiropractor will not cure the condition. Likewise, the highly developed skills of a brain surgeon could be inadequate to cure or relieve from third degree burns, an ulcer condition or an injury requiring a joint replacement. A cure or relief is an expected result of treatment that is rendered by a physician with appropriate qualifications and experience in successful treatment of similar conditions. The provision of such treatment at the employer's expense fulfills the employer's obligation for treatment. If a cure is not possible, the employer's liability is satisfied by payment of expenses necessary to achieve relief.

7.8 TREATMENT – FOR EFFECTS OF INJURY

The employer's liability is limited to expenses required to treat the industrial injury. Other medical problems may be diagnosed during the course of an examination or treatment for an industrial injury. These conditions may also require treatment. The coincidence of their discovery after the occurrence of an industrial injury does not obligate the employer to provide treatment.

Suppose the employee slips and falls and breaks a front tooth. During the exam, the dentist discovers a cavity in another tooth. Treatment for the uninjured tooth is not an expense owed by the employer. If the dentist discovers that the employee's teeth need cleaning, the employer does not owe this expense either. The dentist may discover gum disease. Treatment may be required for the employee's dental health. However, the employer does not owe any expense unless it is incurred for treatment necessary to cure or relieve from the effects of the injury to the broken tooth. In the above examples, there is merely a coincidence of discovery of a nonindustrial problem. The other problems are not an effect of the industrial injury.

The employee may be undergoing treatment for a nonindustrial problem at the time he sustains an industrial injury. The industrial injury may be treated by the same physician. The employer's liability is limited to the expenses required for treatment of the industrial injury. Suppose the employee is under active care for a degenerative arthritic condition. Thereafter, the employee sustains a back strain while lifting. All treatment necessary to cure or relieve from the effects of the back strain is the employer's responsibility. The employer is not liable for routine medical care that the employee previously required. The employee may continue to require such treatment regardless of the injury to his back. Likewise, the employee may be under treatment for diabetes and then suffer an industrial ulcer injury. The employer is obligated to treat the effects of the industrial injury. The employer is not responsible for treatment of all the medical problems that a particular employee may have at the same time he is suffering from the effects of an industrial injury.

7.9 TREATMENT GUIDELINES

Per LC139, the Industrial Medical Council is required to "adopt guidelines for the treatment of common industrial injuries." These guidelines are intended to improve the overall quality, while at the same time controlling the costs to provide, medical care for industrial injuries. The Industrial Medical Council coordinates its activities with the Administrative Director of the Division of Workers' Compensation to "monitor and measure changes in the cost and frequency of the most common medical services." The guidelines adopted by the Industrial Medical Council based upon such data "shall reflect practices as generally accepted by the health care community." The goal is to assist in recognition of professionally recognized standards. Encompassed within these standards are "appropriate and inappropriate diagnostic techniques, treatment" and "adjustive modalities, length of treatment, and appropriate specialty referrals."

The Industrial Medical Council has adopted protocols and guidelines for evaluation and treatment of a variety of commonly occurring injuries. The Administrative Director utilizes this information to comply with the LC139 duty to "adopt model utilization protocols in order to provide" statewide "utilization review standards."

7.10 UTILIZATION REVIEW STANDARDS — official med. fee schedule

Effective 7/1/96, CR9792.6 requires each insurer that "implements or maintains a utilization review system" to comply with "model utilization protocols" that have been adopted by the Administrative Director pursuant to LC139. Requirements for "utilization review standards" (UR standards) are detailed in CR9792.6. "Utilization review" is defined as a "system used to manage costs and improve patient care and decision making through cases by case assessments of the frequency, duration, level, and appropriateness of medical care and services to determine whether medical treatment is or was reasonably required to cure or relieve the effects of the injury." Utilization review procedures can be applied prospectively to requests for authorization to provide health care services or retrospectively to determine the reasonableness of fees requested for services that were provided.

Utilization review standards are applied when a health care provider makes a written request for authorization for payment "for a specific course of proposed medical treatment" (including treatment described in an initial treatment plan or other reports required by CR9785; see 7.80). Per CR9792.6, a "written" request includes a request submitted by mail, in person, by FAX or E-mail.

Employers are permitted to develop a utilization review system without State approval. However, as of 7/1/96, the employer must make a written summary of the utilization review system available upon a request from the Administrative Director (that will probably be made when a medical provider protests a denial of recommended services or fees). The employer's system will integrate treatment and evaluation guidelines and protocols adopted by the Industrial Medical Council. However, it is likely that the employer will also incorporate other available information that has broad-base support within the medical community.

Per CR9792.6, a written response is required within seven days of receipt of a health care provider's written request. Regardless of the details by which an employer implements its personalized system, every utilization review system must meet these "minimum standards" as set out in CR9792.6:

1. A written response must be provided "no later than seven working days after ... receipt of the request and any necessary supporting documentation" (e.g. a response must be mailed no later than the 10th if a request is received on the 1st day of the month and the insurer is closed on weekends).

2. The written response must include:
   a. A specific "authorization, denial, or notice of delay" in decision on the request. (Lack of information is not a sufficient reason for a denial absent "documentation of a bona fide attempt to obtain the necessary information.")
   b. A means of identifying the request (e.g. an internally-designated code number assigned to this specific request).
   c. The "name and phone number of a *responsible* (emphasis added) contact person" (a person capable of explaining the decision, but not necessarily the person who made the decision).
3. A notice of delay "shall state what additional information is required to make a decision and when a decision regarding the request is expected to be made."
4. A decision to deny a physician's request must be made by "a physician with an unrestricted license by his or her licensing board who has education, training, expertise, and experience that is pertinent for evaluating the specific clinical issues or services under review." (Note: this physician may perform utilization review services under a contractual fee arrangement rather than as an employee of the employer or claims administrator.)
5. "Only medically-based criteria shall be used in the ... decision-making process," and the "criteria applied in a particular case shall be made available to the affected health care provider." This criteria must be provided to an injured employee only after a written request from the employee. In all cases, such criteria must be:
   a. Based on professionally-recognized standards (e.g. protocols and treatment guidelines adopted by the Industrial Medical Council under LC139).
   b. Developed "with involvement of actively-practicing health care providers."
   c. Be "peer-reviewed."
   d. Be evaluated and updated "at least annually."
   e. Be "signed and dated by the physicians responsible for development."
6. A "written explanation of the basis for the denial" (or reduced charges) – but only if the health care provider disagrees with a denial of requested authorization (or a reduction of charges) for services.

Health care providers who are dissatisfied with the employer's utilization review decision may lodge a complaint with the Administrative Director of the Division of Workers' Compensation. If the Administrative Director determines that a utilization review system fails to comply with the requirements of CR9792.6, the employer will be provided with written notice and allowed up to 90 days "to correct the noted deficiency." A failure to timely correct such deficiencies can result in assessment of administrative penalties under LC129.5.

(Note: no right of appeal of the Administrative Director's decision is specifically set out in CR9792.6, but the employer would have a right to appeal any resultant assessment of an administrative penalty; see 2.27.)

Medicine is not a precise science. There is more awareness and acceptance of new types of treatment as time passes. Any treatment owed by the employer must meet the basic criteria of LC4600. The purpose of the treatment must be to provide a cure or relief from the effects of an injury. The employer has potential liability for treatment expenses whenever the treatment received has an actual beneficial effect on the employee's recovery.

7.11 CONCURRENT NONINDUSTRIAL CONDITIONS

Treatment for concurrent nonindustrial conditions can become an obligation of the employer in some, but not all, cases. The employer will owe expenses for treatment of nonindustrial conditions when one of the following relationships exists:

a. The industrial injury causes the need for treatment for the nonindustrial condition.
b. The industrial injury results in an increased need for treatment of the nonindustrial condition that would not have been required absent the industrial injury.
c. The industrial injury cannot be treated effectively without also treating the nonindustrial condition.
d. Treatment for the industrial injury and the nonindustrial condition are inseparable.
e. The nonindustrial condition is interfering with the employee's treatment or recovery from the industrial injury.
f. Treatment for the nonindustrial condition would not be necessary at this time if the industrial injury had not occurred.

Elective surgery for a nonindustrial condition is not covered even if the surgery is performed at the same time as surgery for an industrial injury. An employee may elect to have a vasectomy at the same time he undergoes surgery for an industrial hernia. The employer owes all costs related to the hernia surgery. The employer does not owe any additional expenses related solely to the vasectomy. The surgeon should detail all expenses and deduct those incurred for the vasectomy. The ultimate effect is that the employer's liability remains exactly the same as if only the hernia surgery had been performed.

The employer does not owe the costs of hospitalization where an employee is admitted for a nonindustrial condition and concurrently receives treatment for an industrial injury. For example, a pregnant employee may have an industrial injury to her back. When the employee gives birth, the employer is not liable for the costs of hospitalization or delivery of the baby. It may be necessary to have an orthopedic physician continue treatment while the employee is hospitalized. The employer owes the cost of hospital treatment for the industrial injury, not the entire cost of the private hospitalization.

The injured employee may have a nonindustrial high blood pressure condition, and a physician may refuse to perform surgery for an industrial injury until the employee's blood pressure is brought under control. In this case, treatment for high blood pressure is necessary in order to properly treat the industrial injury. The nonindustrial condition is interfering with the doctor's ability to effectively treat the industrial injury, and the industrial problem cannot be treated without also treating the other condition.

The employer is not obligated to cure the employee's high blood pressure, but the employer is obligated to provide treatments that will reduce the employee's blood pressure to a level that makes him an acceptable surgical risk. Regarding the method and expense to control the employee's high blood pressure, the usual test for reasonableness applies. One fact is clear: the employer is not responsible for the costs of controlling high blood pressure in every case where the injured employee suffers from this condition.

The employee may have diabetes. The employee may be under active medical care for this nonindustrial condition, or the employee may be unaware of its existence until after an industrial injury. Suppose the employee sustains a fracture to his tibia requiring surgery. The diabetic condition may flare up and cause complications. Multiple surgeries may be required where one surgery would have sufficed for an employee without diabetes. An internist may be called in to treat the diabetes in conjunction with orthopedic treatment for the fracture. Circulatory problems may develop that result in a leg amputation and increased disability from the injury.

The employer is liable for full medical expenses in all of the above situations. In each instance, the treatment for the diabetes cannot be separated from the treatment for the industrial injury, and the need for treatment for the diabetic condition is actually an effect of the industrial injury.

If treatment for a nonindustrial condition is not necessary to provide proper treatment for the industrial injury, the employer does not have any liability for treatment for the nonindustrial condition. When the employer is responsible for treatment of a nonindustrial condition, the employer's liability ceases when:

1. The employee has returned to his pre-injury status, OR
2. Any further treatment for the nonindustrial condition is required independently of any continued treatment for the industrial injury, OR
3. Further treatment is required solely for the nonindustrial condition.

Refer to the diabetes example above. At some point, the employee may recover from the leg fracture but may still require treatment for his underlying diabetic condition. At this point, the employer's liability terminates for any expenses related to the diabetes. Such treatment would no longer meet the statutory criterion that it be required to cure or relieve from the effects of an industrial injury.

7.12 SUBSEQUENT INJURIES

The employee may sustain a further injury to the same part of the body that was injured in an industrial injury. The employer can be liable for treatment for subsequent injuries. The employer is not responsible for anything and everything that may happen to the employee after an industrial injury is sustained, but there are situations where a later injury occurs as a direct result of the industrial injury. There may be a cause and effect relationship between the industrial injury and the subsequent injury. If the industrial injury is the proximate cause of a subsequent injury, the employer is obligated to provide treatment for both injuries.

Suppose the employee sustained a crushing injury to his foot and is using crutches. One of the crutches slips out from under him, and he falls and fractures his arm. It appears that the employee would not have sustained the second injury to his arm if he had not been using crutches for his industrial injury. Therefore, the industrial injury may be considered to be the proximate cause of the subsequent injury. The employer owes the costs of medical treatment for both injuries (as well as any temporary or permanent disability that may result). The second injury, in effect, was caused by the first injury.

Suppose the employee is driving his car to a doctor's office to receive treatment for an industrial finger injury. The employee's car is struck by a vehicle that runs a red light. The employee sustains multiple injuries in the automobile accident. Whatever the nature of the employee's additional injuries, appellate courts have ruled that the cost of treatment will be borne by the employer. The employee's subsequent injuries would not have occurred if the employee had not had an industrial injury. An employee's injuries during travel necessary to receive treatment for an industrial injury are considered to be an effect of the industrial injury.

The employee may sustain an industrial injury when hot coffee is spilled at work burning his arm. His physician then prescribes pain medication that the employee takes. He has an allergic reaction to the medication that causes a respiratory failure. The employee is rushed to the hospital and requires extensive treatment. The adverse reaction is clearly the result of treatment provided for the industrial injury. The employer is liable for all of the employee's additional medical expenses.

The employer is not liable for subsequent injuries that have no connection to the industrial injury. If an employee who requires crutches after an industrial injury to his foot is riding in a car when he drops a cup of coffee and burns his arm, there is no cause and effect relationship between the first injury and the later one. If the neighbor's dog bites the leg of an employee who is recovering from work-related burns to his arm, a proximate cause between the two injuries does not exist. A later injury must actually result from the industrial injury or from treatment provided for that injury before the employer owes any additional expenses. The employer is only liable for treatment of subsequent injuries if the subsequent injury is an "effect" of an industrial injury.

7.13 TREATMENT – NURSING CARE

Nursing services are covered when these services are recommended by a physician. There is no Labor Code requirement that nursing services be provided by a registered nurse. Rather, the provider must be qualified and competent to perform the services that the doctor recommends. The doctor must specify the exact nature of the services being recommended. The services must be reasonably required as part of a treatment program for the industrial injury. Nursing services may be provided in a hospital, a physician's office or in the employee's home.

Nursing services are medical in nature; their purpose is to aid in the care or treatment of the injured employee. Services such as housecleaning or babysitting may personally benefit the employee but are not medical services. The fact that the employee is physically unable to perform such tasks does not obligate the employer to pay for them. Costs for dry cleaning the employee's clothes or mowing his lawn are living expenses, not medical expenses. These services could be arranged for and rendered without the provider ever meeting the employee or having any direct contact with the employee. Nursing services are rendered directly to the employee and assist in the employee's medical progress.

Nursing services can include incidental services that are not medical in nature. A nurse may prepare a meal or a special diet in the employee's kitchen. Nursing services would reasonably include washing the dishes and cleaning up thereafter. The basic service is still nursing, and the non-nursing chores would constitute a small component of the nursing services.

Gratuitous care provided by family members does not ordinarily warrant any employer liability for charges for these services. Nursing services must be recommended by a physician before the employer is liable for their expense. If the doctor recommends nursing services and a relative is competent and willing to provide the service, the employer may authorize the relative to do so. Alternatively, the employer may arrange for the necessary services to be provided by someone else. Where compensability of an injury or just the provision of custodial nursing services is disputed, the WCAB may order the employer to provide reimbursement for self-procured custodial nursing services on a retroactive basis, e.g. where an injury was initially denied and a spouse quit a job in order to provide such services to the employee.

One consideration regarding the provider of services is the potential for creation of an employer-employee relationship. The employee can employ and pay a provider of his choosing. The employee can be paid an advance for medical expense and then use the money to arrange for his own nursing services. If the employer pays a relative of the employee directly, such individual may claim an employment contract should an injury occur while providing nursing services. The employer would have defenses to such a claim but would incur the costs of defending the claim. It is wise to avoid such expenses by providing nursing services in a manner that eliminates any potential for such claims. When an employer pays a nursing service company or a self-employed individual, no employment relationship is created with the employer.

7.14 TREATMENT – MEDICINES

The term "medicines" is not defined in the Labor Code. Medicine in general refers to substances that have a known medical benefit when used in the treatment of illness, injury or disease. Medications or drugs are covered when they are recommended or prescribed by a properly licensed physician and are reasonably necessary to cure or relieve from the effects of the injury. Some medicines are available over-the-counter (without a doctor's prescription). A physician's recommendation of a nonprescription medicine can suffice to impose liability on the employer.

Herbs, teas, homemade remedies, secret potions, food additives, dietary sup-plements, and vitamins are not medicines. The therapeutic value of these and any other items that can be prescribed or dispensed by any person without any type of license whatsoever is questionable, and the fact that a licensed medical or health professional recommends the use of the item does not, ergo, elevate its status to a "medicine." For instance, the ordinary purpose of vitamins is to maintain a general state of health by supplementing a person's choice of diet, not to cure or relieve from the effects of an injury. There are many gray areas, but generally the employer is not liable for payment for any item whose purpose is to improve a general state of health nor for any so-called "medicinal" remedies that have little or no proven benefit in the treatment of industrial injuries.

The treating physician may be aware of the employee's use of self-prescribed vitamins or other items and may report that he has no objection to their continued use. The physician's acquiescence may equate to an opinion that the item will not harm the employee. This is not an actual medical recommendation for the item. This type of statement does not sanction the employee's use of a substance as part of a medical treatment program, nor does it obligate the employer to pay for the item. If the physician's meaning is unclear, the physician should be requested to provide a medical opinion on the necessity for use of the item or its beneficial effect, if any (e.g. an effect capable of measurement, observation or detection).

7.15 TREATMENT – MEDICAL SUPPLIES

"Medical supplies" is a broad category that includes crutches and all other supplies that are dispensed, prescribed or recommended by a physician. Medical supplies include items such as bandages, eye patches, anesthetics, casts, splints, bedpans, ace bandages, stump stockings and heel lifts. Also included are medical supplies that are provided by a physical therapist (per LC3209.5) or a hospital. The provision of medical supplies is not contingent upon receipt of concurrent medical treatment. Medical supplies can still be reasonably required after the termination of active medical treatment, e.g. a lifetime need for the use of a knee brace or an artificial eye.

Medical supplies have a common feature. Such supplies are not ordinarily necessary or used by a person unless he or she is suffering from the effects of an injury or illness. These items are predominantly purchased at medical supply companies rather than general department stores. If an item could be regularly used by all members of the employee's family, the categorization of the item as "medical" is questionable.

Medical Apparatus

Medical supplies include medical equipment or devices that have been specifically adapted or designed to assist in the performance of physical activities. The apparatus allows an employee to perform an activity that would otherwise be precluded or impaired. For instance, a wheelchair provides mobility for a person who cannot walk without assistance. An in-home hospital bed with an exercise trapeze can reduce hospitalization costs and assist with medical rehabilitation after a surgery. Portable oxygen tanks can increase the employee's mobility, including travel to medical appointments. As to the reasonableness of costs, apparatus may be required on a temporary or permanent basis. The duration of use depends upon the likelihood of the employee's recovery to the point where the employee no longer needs the apparatus. Where the need is temporary, the employer should evaluate the costs of rental versus purchase. The employer must make this cost comparison to determine what expense is reasonably required to fulfill its liability.

Orthotic & Prosthetic Devices

Effective 1995, the term "artificial members" was replaced with "orthotics and prosthetic devices and services" in the list of covered medical expenses in LC4600. This change in wording clarifies but does not expand the employer's existing liability for artificial members, orthotics and prosthetics. Prosthetic devices are covered. A prosthesis is a man-made replacement for a normal part of the body. The prosthesis can be internal or external. Included are such things as artificial limbs, artificial eyes, joint replacements and dentures. A wig may be reasonably required where a head injury results in a permanent loss of hair. The employer is liable for the initial cost of prosthetic devices and any necessary repair or replacement costs. An "orthotic" is a man-made support for a body part. Common orthotics include a cervical collar or an arch support. A back brace or cervical collar may restrain motion within a pain-free range. An orthotic device for the employee's work shoes may maintain stability of an injured ankle joint during ambulation or climbing ladders.

Eyeglasses & Hearing Aids

Where an industrial injury results in an initial medical need for eyeglasses or hearing aids, such items are clearly compensable. However, the employer's liability must be investigated when the employee's eyeglasses or hearing aids are alleged to have been damaged during the course of employment.

Per LC3208, the employer is not liable for repair or replacement costs for eyeglasses or hearing aids "unless injury to them is incidental to an injury causing disability." This language contains two requirements. First, in addition to injury to the item itself, there must also be a concurrent injury to the employee's person. Any part of the employee's body will do: an eye, an arm, or a leg. Second, the concomitant injury must cause "disability," a term used in the Labor Code to mean inability to work. If all that is injured or damaged is glasses (that reasonably includes contact lenses) or a hearing aid, the employee has not sustained a compensable injury, and no workers' compensation benefits are owed.

The employee might drop his glasses and step on them, or the employee might damage the wiring in his hearing aid while attempting to replace a battery. Employees may argue that they are medically disabled from their employment until the apparatus is repaired; e.g., where a farsighted bookkeeper, who does not have a spare pair of glasses readily available, cannot perform normal duties until the glasses are replaced. It is usually undisputed that a person who wears corrective optical lenses or a hearing aid is disabled to some degree without the use of this item; otherwise there would have been no reason for a medical prescription for the item. However, absent a concurrent injury "causing disability" in addition to any disability that is due to the loss of use of the damaged item, the employer is not liable for repair or replacement of glasses or hearing aids.

The legislative history of LC3208 provides clarification of the requirement for "disability." In 1949, LC3208 stated that the incidental injury must cause "disability in excess of seven days" before the employer was liable for damage to eyeglasses or hearing aids. In 1951 this period was reduced from seven days to three days. In 1953 this section was again amended to delete the words "in excess of three days." The term "disability" clearly means a medical inability to perform employment duties for a period of time, and any period of disability will suffice since there is no longer a stated minimum period of lost time from work.

Many employers pay for eyeglasses and hearing aids whenever the employee sustains a concurrent injury to their physical body that requires medical treatment beyond first aid. The reason some employers pay these claims even when liability for such payment is not imposed by law is because it is usually less expensive and more expedient to pay the expense than to litigate the dispute. (Besides, LC2802 requires the employer to indemnify employees for all losses they sustain "in direct consequence of the discharge of" their duties; e.g. where eyeglasses are in a company truck that is stolen.)

7.16 TRANSPORTATION EXPENSES – GENERALLY

Per LC4600 and LC4621, the employer is liable for "all reasonable expenses of transportation" when an employee submits to a physician's exam "at the request of the employer," the Administrative Director, or the WCAB. This language implies that the employer only owes mileage expense if the employee is requested to attend an examination. In actuality, mileage expense is routinely paid for travel necessitated for treatment, testing, hospitalization or medical examinations. Transportation expenses specifically include mileage reimbursement, bridge tolls, meals, lodging and wage replacement payments (subject to a test of reasonableness). Other expenses can be covered when they are reasonably required even though they are not specifically listed in the Labor Code, e.g. parking costs for a medical examination or mileage to a pharmacy to pick up a prescription on a separate trip from that to visit a physician.

7.17 MILEAGE EXPENSE

Per LC4600, all employees will receive the same rate of payment for mileage expense regardless of the date of injury (an exception to the general rule that benefits are payable under the terms of the law in effect on the date of the injury per LC4453.5). This rate is not specified in LC4600. Instead, LC4600 requires payment to be made at the "mileage rate adopted by the Director of the Department of Personnel Administration pursuant to" GC19820 (but not less than 21 cents per mile). The current mileage rate, that is commonly referred to as the "State rate," is the rate at which mileage expense is payable to State employees who travel for business. Effective 7/1/97, this mileage rate was increased to 31 cents per mile (mileage accrued for travel during the period 1/1/90-6/30/97 is owed at 24 cents per mile). The current mileage rate can be verified by any State employee.

Per LC4600, the employer owes "mileage fees from the employee's home to the place of the examination and back." However, if the employee goes to the exam from work rather from home, mileage expenses must reflect the actual miles traveled. The law intends, and the employer wishes to ensure, that the employee does not receive a financial profit by being paid for an expense that was not incurred (see 1.9).

The Labor Code states that mileage expense and bridge tolls must be paid in advance when an examination is scheduled at the employer's request. These are the only two transportation expenses that are payable in advance of the expense being incurred, and the employee is not required to attend the scheduled examination unless these expenses are paid in advance.

A transportation expense check is ordinarily enclosed in the same envelope with the notice of appointment letter for employer-scheduled examinations (but will be provided when copies of medical and nonmedical records are served for employee-scheduled appointments with a panel-QME; see 7.79). Otherwise, it is customary for the employee to record mileage expenses for regular ongoing treatment and request reimbursement at intervals. This avoids the frequent issuance of checks for small amounts. It also saves time as the claimsperson can review several expense claims at once (but an administrative penalty can be assessed if transportation expense that is owed is not paid within 60 days of the employee's request; see CR10111.1).

To ascertain if the expenses are "reasonable," it is appropriate to measure the claimed distance by reference to a map. To ascertain whether the expenses are related to the industrial injury, the dates submitted by the employee should be compared to billing statements submitted by the physician. By this review, the employer can determine any unreasonableness of the claimed expenses and decline payment for same. For example, the employer is not responsible for mileage expense that is claimed for attending a scheduled medical examination that the employee failed to attend. The physician's reports or bills would be the source of this information. Receipts are the proper documentation for such things as bridge tolls or parking expense.

7.18 PARKING COSTS

Parking costs are not mentioned in the Labor Code. However, parking costs are commonly incurred and may constitute a reasonable expense of transportation. Parking fees are reasonable when free parking is not readily available, but optionally incurred parking costs are not a reasonable expense. The nature of the employee's injury may be a pertinent consideration; for example, the employee may have difficulty ambulating. Until the employee incurs a parking expense, the necessity or the reasonableness of the expense is often incapable of determination. Therefore, parking expenses are usually reimbursed only after they are incurred and proper documentation is available.

7.19 TRANSPORTATION BY FRIEND OR RELATIVE

The employee may arrange for a friend, neighbor or relative to transport him. The employee may or may not choose to provide payment to this person. The employer is not obligated to pay chauffeur's wages to the driver. The employer's obligation does not change; it is obligated to pay mileage reimbursement at the rate specified in LC4600 regardless of who does the driving.

7.20 CAB OR BUS FARE

Public transportation is appropriate where it is the employee's preferred mode of transportation. If the employee regularly uses bus transportation, the employee is entitled to the actual cost of this transportation to and from physician's exams. This expense would be in place of mileage reimbursement. The employer cannot require the employee to utilize public transportation in circumstances such as these:

a. The employee has personal objections to this form of transportation.
b. The employee's medical condition makes such transportation difficult or inappropriate.
c. Public transportation is not readily accessible or available.
d. The use of such transportation would require an inordinate amount of time or inconvenience for the employee.

Cab fare is not ordinarily a reasonable expense, but there are exceptions. This expense is unreasonable when it is the employee's preference but is not required. This expense is reasonable when the employee's physical condition warrants it, there is some urgency for a physical exam, and/or other transportation is not available. It is unlikely that a taxi would be the only mode of transportation available, and an actual necessity for such expensive transportation should only arise on an infrequent or emergency basis.

7.21 AMBULANCE TRANSPORTATION

The employer is liable for ambulance transportation to a hospital immediately following a serious injury (see 2.22 regarding Cal/OSHA notice requirements that may apply). This is expense also owed when ambulance transportation between medical facilities is necessary. The employee's physical condition may necessitate ambulance transportation from his home to medical examinations or treatment. This could occur where the employee's condition requires constant medical monitoring or immediate access to medical equipment or paraphernalia.

The employee may be unable to leave his home without physical assistance yet not require medical monitoring; e.g., the employee has two full leg casts. An alternative to ambulance transportation is provided by private companies with specially equipped and chauffeured vehicles available on a fare basis. Such companies provide transportation services for individuals with disabilities within a community. The use of private services may be more reasonable than ambulance transportation depending upon the employee's medical condition and the availability of such services.

7.22 TRAVEL ADVANCES

Travel expense may be paid as a lump sum advance against anticipated expenses. Lump sum travel advances are usually considered only in cases where:
   a. A frequency of transportation expenses is anticipated.
   b. The employee might otherwise fail to attend exams due to financial inability to incur transportation expenses.
   c. The integrity of the employee is known to the claimsperson.
   d. The money can be expected to be used as intended.
   e. The employee agrees to keep detailed records and to submit these at reasonable intervals.
   f. The employee agrees to return any money that is advanced but not needed for transportation expenses.

The employee uses the advance to pay for expenses as they are incurred and later submits a log showing how the money was spent. The claims administrator reviews the records after the fact. When the travel advance is used up, a decision is made whether to provide another lump sum advance. Advance payments are a control mechanism that can be very useful. They can avoid the need to review frequent expense claims. They can prevent failure to undergo examinations or treatment because an employee does not have the financial ability to pay for this expense without prepayment. Lump sum transportation advances are not appropriate where the employee is likely to use the money for other purposes or has abused the privilege of a previous lump sum advance.

7.23 MEALS & LODGING

Both LC4600 and LC4621 contain a provision for the expenses of meals and lodging in attending an exam requested by the employer, the Administrative Director or the WCAB. These expenses are a combined benefit; meals are ordinarily payable only when lodging is owed. This statutory provision does not obligate the employer to provide a lunch with every exam. It provides for the rare occasion where an employer will request the employee to travel an extraordinary distance to attend an exam.

The employee may move out of the State. If the employer wishes the employee to attend an exam in California, the employer must assume the expenses necessarily incurred by the employee in traveling to the exam. The employee is obligated to attend exams scheduled by the employer in order to maintain a claim. The employee cannot bribe the employer by refusing to attend an exam unless arbitrary and excessive transportation expenses are provided in advance. The test of reasonableness is applied to determine what amounts the employer owes. First class air fare, hotels or restaurants are not reasonable where other alternatives are both reasonable and available. The employer's liability is not limited to the most economical means, nor is it extended to the most expensive means.

It is up to the claims administrator to decide how involved it wishes to become in the employee's travel arrangements and accommodations. Usually, an estimate of the employee's total expenses is paid in advance. Any claims for additional expenses are later reviewed along with receipts for incurred expenses. It is important to clearly specify in advance any limits on the expenses the employer is willing to pay. This is the best way to avoid incurring unnecessary or exorbitant expenses and later disputes regarding what was authorized in advance.

Some employers fulfill their obligation by providing payment for meals and lodging at the "State rate," referring to the daily travel allowance that State of California employees (including WCAB judges) receive when travel is required by their jobs. The Rules and Regulations of the State Board of Control regulate this expense that is specified in a daily amount including both food and lodging. This amount is increased from time to time. Any State employee could supply the current amounts. It appears reasonable that an injured employee can obtain meals and lodging for the same cost that a judge can obtain these items. Employees who claim reimbursement for a higher amount will be entitled to have their claims reviewed by a WCAB judge who is limited to a lesser amount for travel expenses.

7.24 LOST WAGES – EXAMINATIONS

Per LC4600, an employee is entitled to "one day of temporary disability indemnity for each day of wages lost" when the employee submits to an exam at the employer's request. This benefit only applies in special circumstances, since it is unusual for a medical exam to cause the employee to lose an entire day from work. For instance, a physician may plan to do extensive and time-consuming testing; an employee who has moved may have to travel here from another state if the employer wishes the employee to be examined locally; or, an employee who lives in a remote area may have to travel a great distance to a physician's office.

The Labor Code requires as a prerequisite for this benefit that the employee incur a "day of wages lost," restricting this benefit to situations where the employee is working and loses a full day's wages because he attends an exam instead of working. The employee may be receiving temporary total disability benefits, in which case a duplicate payment of temporary disability is not required for the date of the exam. Likewise, there are no lost wages to replace when the employee is able to work but does not have a job. The employee may allege he is disabled from working, but he may not be receiving any temporary disability because the employer disputes his entitlement to this benefit. In this case, the employee's allegation that he is unable to work negates any claim that wages were lost while attending an exam.

Mileage and bridge tolls are required to be paid in advance "at the time" the employee "is given notification of the time and place of the examination." However, LC4600 does not require an advance payment of temporary disability indemnity as replacement for wages lost in attending an exam. Until the employee attends the exam, it may not be possible to determine whether a day's wages will be lost, and an advance payment could result in an overpayment that the employer cannot recover from the employee.

There may occasionally be a valid basis for voluntarily providing payment in advance for each anticipated day of lost wages necessitated by the exam. An advance payment could be appropriate where an out-of-state employee must travel to California for an examination and a wage loss is certain to occur or where an advance payment would eliminate the possibility that the employee might refuse to attend the scheduled exam. The problem with advance payments is that the employer may have difficulty in receiving reimbursement if no wage loss occurs.

7.25 LOST WAGES – TREATMENT

Sometimes the employee is able to work without disability during a period of active treatment; for example, the employee may lose wages when he leaves work to receive physical therapy three times a week for two hours each time. Most employers do not pay wages for hours when the employee is not at work regardless of the reason for the employee's absence (some employers will pay the lost wages, or sick leave or vacation pay may be utilized to provide a wage payment, but these cases do not involve the problem discussed here).

An employee who sustains a wage loss may believe he is entitled to be paid, and because the reason for the wage loss was treatment for an industrial injury, he may demand payment from the claimsperson. This situation presents a problem, since the claimsperson must explain why benefits will not be provided for a monetary loss that is admittedly a result of an industrial injury.

Temporary disability benefits, both total and partial, are ordinarily owed only in cases where the employee is medically disabled from working. The only exception to this statement is found in LC4600: the employer owes "one day of temporary disability for each day of wages lost" in submitting to an examination "at the request of the employer." It is questionable whether any reasonable interpretation of LC4600 would create a liability in the circumstances described above: the employee loses a partial day of wages, not a full day; the lost time is for treatment, not for an examination; and the lost time is for appointments arranged for by the employee, not scheduled by the employer. This situation is distinctly different from that described by LC4600, and it is doubtful that the legislature intended this section to be interpreted to provide employees with wage-replacement benefits on an hour-by-hour basis for routine employee-scheduled medical appointments.

7.26 MEDICAL PROVIDERS – DEFINED AS PHYSICIANS

For workers' compensation purposes, the term "physician" as defined in LC3209.3 "includes physicians and surgeons holding an M.D. or D.O. degree, psychologists, acupuncturists, optometrists, dentists, podiatrists and chiropractic practitioners licensed by California state law and within the scope of their practice as defined by California state law." Unless otherwise specified, all Labor Code references to a "physician" refer to any of the persons listed in LC3209.3. However, the fact that these persons are all defined as physicians under the Labor Code does not alter nor supersede their individual licensing requirements nor extend the scope of services each can legally provide as specified under the provisions of the Business and Professions Code that pertain to each of these persons.

Physicians who conduct examinations or provide treatment to employees who are claiming workers' compensation benefits must comply with all applicable laws, rules, and regulations. Physicians must familiarize themselves with required forms and procedures for billing and reporting purposes. Great assistance in this regard is provided by the *Physician's Guide to Medical Practice in the California Workers' Compensation System.* This publication is of particular benefit to physicians who are seeking appointment as Qualified Medical Evaluators (see 7.75), but it is also an excellent reference for all physicians involved in the workers' compensation field. This guide is available from the Industrial Medical Council, P.O. Box 8888, San Francisco, CA 94128.

Physician & Surgeon

The phrase "physician and surgeon" refers to doctors who are licensed under the Business and Professions Code to do these two things that a nonphysician medical practitioner is not licensed to do: perform surgery and prescribe medication. A doctor of osteopathy who holds a D.O. degree may or may not also have an M.D. degree. These designations are alternative, so an osteopath will utilize one or the other but not both. Osteopaths are considered to be physicians and surgeons under the Business and Professions Code as well as the Labor Code. An osteopath can prescribe medications and perform surgery.

A doctor of dental science specializes in treatment of the teeth, gums and related structures. Dentists can perform surgery and prescribe medications. A podiatrist, or podiatric surgeon, is a licensed physician and surgeon whose practice is devoted entirely to the foot and ankle. Identified by the designation D.P.M., a podiatrist specializes in treatment of acquired deformities, congenital disorders and trauma of the foot and ankle. The scope of practice of a dentist or podiatrist is restricted to a particular part of the body, but both of these physicians are licensed to perform surgery and prescribe medication.

Medical Practitioner

Special provisions of the Labor Code address certain nonsurgical medical practitioners by title. For instance, LC3209.4 specifically states that an optometrist may not "represent, advertise, or hold himself out as a physician." (The doctor of medicine who specializes in treatment of the eye is an ophthalmologist.) The LC3209.3 definition of a chiropractor as a "physician" is specifically restricted in LC3209.6 and "does not imply any right or entitle any chiropractor to represent, advertise, or hold himself out as a physician." The Labor Code authorizes chiropractors to provide treatment to injured workers but does not allow a chiropractor to use the designation of M.D. or otherwise advertise as a "physician." Notwithstanding the inclusion of chiropractic practitioners in the Labor Code definition of a "physician," chiropractors are not licensed as physicians under the Business and Professions Code and cannot prescribe medications nor perform surgery.

Services and supplies provided by physical therapists are specifically covered under LC3209.5. Unlike optometrists and chiropractors, physical therapists are not defined as physicians under LC3209.3. Services of physical therapists are ordinarily provided at the request of someone who is defined as a physician under the Business and Professions Code (and, only a properly qualified physician can render opinions that entitle an employee to disability benefits).

Defined as QME vs. Defined as Physician

Being defined or "qualified" as a physician for purposes of providing treatment or services to injured workers is not the same thing as being a Qualified Medical Evaluator (QME). A Qualified Medical Evaluator who performs the medical evaluations that are required by LC4060, LC4061 or LC4062 and is appointed by the Industrial Medical Council must possess the qualifications specified in LC139.2 in addition to being defined as a physician under LC3209.3 (see 7.75).

The employee's treating physician may possess Qualified Medical Evaluator status. However, a physician is precluded from providing treatment to an employee while acting in the capacity of a Qualified Medical Evaluator. Otherwise, the possibility would exist that a Qualified Medical Evaluator might recommend treatment in order to derive an income from providing such treatment. Occasionally, an employee who has the right to receive treatment and to change treating physicians will obtain treatment from a physician who has evaluated the employee as a Qualified Medical Evaluator. However, the provision of treatment voids this physician's Qualified Medical Evaluator status for this employee's claim.

7.27 PSYCHOLOGISTS

Psychologists use the designation Ph.D., that indicates possession of a Doctorate of Philosophy degree. Some, but not all, psychologists are authorized to provide treatment for industrial injuries. Per LC3209.3, a psychologist who is qualified must possess "a doctorate degree in psychology" and be "a licensed psychologist" under "California state law." Additionally, LC3209.3 requires that a licensed psychologist must have a minimum of "two years of clinical experience in a recognized health setting" or meet the standards established by the "National Register of Health Service Providers in Psychology" (to be included in the National Register, a psychologist must have two years of experience). A psychologist who meets all of the above criteria is defined as a "physician" in the Labor Code.

A psychologist is not a doctor of medicine and therefore is limited in the scope of services that can be provided for industrial injuries; e.g., a psychologist cannot prescribe medication. This distinction is further emphasized by LC3209.3(c) that provides that "when treatment or evaluation for an injury is provided by" a properly qualified "psychologist, provision shall be made for appropriate medical collaboration when requested by the employer." This means the employer may have a genuine medical doubt as to its liability when the sole medical opinion in the case is from a psychologist, and the employer has a statutory right to confirm or rebut opinions provided by psychologists with medical opinions. To determine its liability for benefits, the employer is entitled to obtain an opinion from a psychiatrist or some other doctor of medicine.

7.28 MARRIAGE COUNSELORS & SOCIAL WORKERS

Since 1986, LC3209.8 provides that payment for services rendered to injured workers by "marriage, family, and child counselors and clinical social workers" is contingent upon "the approval of the employer" (with one exception, as explained below). Furthermore, the employer cannot opt to provide counseling services by an MFCC or LCSW (Licensed Clinical Social Worker) unless these services meet four precise criteria. However, it is unlikely that any employer would deny liability for payment when counseling services meet all four statutory criteria in that such services are:

1. Recommended by "a licensed physician and surgeon" (as opposed to a psychologist or a chiropractor), AND
2. Provided "for treatment of a condition arising out of the injury" (as opposed to treatment for unrelated, concurrent personal problems), AND
3. Provided by an individual who is properly "licensed by California state law."
4. Within the scope of practice of the counselor or social worker "as defined by California state law" (in the Business and Professions Code).

The practitioners listed in LC3209.8 are not authorized to "determine disability," but counselors are not relieved from their responsibility to submit written reports covering all other aspects of their treatment. Any counselor who treats an injured worker is expected to submit reports and a treatment plan that includes the nature and scope of any services that are recommended, the purpose and intended result of such services, how and when a determination can be made as to whether the services are accomplishing a beneficial result, and the anticipated duration of any further services. However, the counselor's opinion of disability status, if given, will not entitle the employee to receive any disability benefits. Note above that a counselor's involvement requires a recommendation by a "physician and surgeon," and an opinion of a physician can support a claim for temporary or permanent disability benefits.

Effective 1992, there is one instance where LC3209.8 eliminates the requirement that liability for payment of counseling services is contingent upon the employer's optional advance approval. The employer can be ordered to pay for such services after the fact in any case where it "refused to authorize any treatment for the condition" that was treated by the counselor, e.g. any case where the employer denies the claim in its entirety. This provision would apply to an accepted claim where the employer authorizes treatment only for physical injuries (but would not apply if the employer refused to authorize counseling services from an MFCC but did authorize treatment by a psychologist or psychiatrist). The employer will not be ordered to pay for self-procured counseling services unless a judge first determines that the claim is compensable and such treatment was reasonable "pursuant to this division" (note the criteria listed above; see also 7.64 regarding self-procured expenses).

7.29 ACUPUNCTURISTS

Acupuncturists are included in the listing of persons encompassed within the general definition of physician since 1989 (initially for a four-year trial period that was thereafter extended through 12/31/98). Per LC3209.3, an acupuncturist is defined as "a person who holds an acupuncturist's certificate issued pursuant to" specific sections of the "Business and Professions Code." Acupuncture is a form of healing practice that utilizes the insertion and gentle manipulation of thin needles to stimulate certain points or positions on or near the skin and other nonsurgical techniques such as oriental massage. Acupuncturists are not physicians and surgeons and cannot perform surgery or prescribe medication.

A recommendation by a physician and surgeon is not a prerequisite to treatment by an acupuncturist. However, it is clear that a properly licensed physician must be concurrently involved in any case where the employee is claiming entitlement to temporary or permanent disability benefits because, per LC3209.3, acupuncturists are not authorized to "determine disability." This restriction is exactly the same as that which applies to MFCC's (and would likewise apply to other nonphysician practitioners such as physical therapists) and does not relieve acupuncturists from their responsibility to submit reports. It does however mean that an acupuncturist cannot be a Qualified Medical Evaluator for purposes of preparing the reports of permanent disability that are required by LC4061 (see 7.75). An acupuncturist can render an opinion on a solitary disputed issue: need for acupuncture treatment.

7.30 MEDICAL PROVIDERS – BY AGREEMENT

Per LC3209.7, the employer can be liable for the costs of any type of nonspecified "therapy, treatment, or healing practice" only if the employer voluntarily agrees in writing to accept liability for these expenses. No specific practitioners are mentioned by name in LC3209.7, but the employer's voluntary acceptance of liability would appear to apply only to persons whose services are not covered under any other Labor Code section; e.g., Faith Healers or Christian Science Practitioners.

The employee may desire or demand a type of therapy or treatment that is not specifically mentioned in the Labor Code. The employee may wish to be treated by a person engaged in a "healing practice" that is not a recognized form of the practice of medicine. Unusual modes of treatment may be sought as an alternative to medical, surgical or hospital services, or the employee may supplement regular medical care with some other form of treatment or healing practice. When the employer agrees to this type of treatment, the employer's liability continues to be restricted to services that "cure or relieve from the effects of an industrial injury."

An agreement for treatment expense under LC3209.7 must be in writing. The employer and the employee both have a right to terminate the written agreement by providing seven days advance written notice. There is always the possibility that an employer representative may enter into a written agreement with an employee that is disagreeable to, but binding upon, its claims administrator. Fortunately, LC3209.7 describes the procedure to enter into such an agreement and the procedure to terminate the agreement. The claimsperson may terminate the employer's agreement by giving written notification to the employee.

7.31 MEDICAL PROVIDERS – QUESTIONABLE LIABILITY

The Labor Code definition of "physician" states who is included but does not state who is excluded. The employer can voluntarily assume liability for payment of any type of treatment or service, but there are gray areas where the employer's actual obligations under the Labor Code are not clearly delineated. The employer cannot base a refusal to pay medical expenses on the fact that a particular type of practitioner is not specifically mentioned in the Labor Code. The listing of specific practitioners as "physicians" in LC3209.3 is prefaced by the broad term "includes." By inference, other practitioners are included who are not listed.

A claims judgment problem arises when treatment is provided by a hypnotist, herbologist, reflexologist, healing masseuse, nutritionist or some other person who is not specified in LC3209.3. For example, treatment by a physical therapist may or may not be disputed depending upon a particular case, even though the services of physical therapists are covered under LC3209.5. When physical therapy is provided by prescription from a doctor of medicine who at all times remains the treating physician, the employer will usually not object. However, the employer may disclaim any liability if the only form of treatment being provided is physical therapy, or all treatment is being provided by any person who is not defined as a physician in LC3209.3.

The employer's basic liability for medical benefits is contained in LC4600. The employer does not owe the cost of any treatment unless the treatment is reasonable in view of the nature and extent of the industrial injury and provides either a cure or relief from the effects of the injury. If the treatment rendered meets these criteria, this fact can overcome an objection that treatment was not provided by a medical provider listed by name in the Labor Code.

7.32 MEDICAL CONTROL – SELECTION OF PHYSICIANS

Medical control refers to whether the employee or the employer has the right to select the treating physician. Generally, the employer exercises medical control initially upon notice of an injury. The employee has the right to be treated by an employee-selected physician 30 (thirty) days after the date the injury was reported to the employer. This waiting period is waived or reduced for employees who have predesignated a "personal physician" (see 7.35) or "personal chiropractor" (see 7.36). Employees have the right to request a change of physician at any time. The employer has the right to regain medical control after the employee receives treatment from an employee-selected physician, but only under specific circumstances (see 7.44).

The employee also has the unrestricted right under LC4605 to obtain medical opinions from any physician of his choice "at his own expense" at any time. However, it is more likely that the employee will exercise the right to a consultation with a Qualified Medical Evaluator should the employee dispute a medical determination of the primary treating physician (see 7.75). The employer owes the expense of this type of consultation under LC4061 or LC4062.

7.33 PRIMARY TREATING PHYSICIAN

Primary Role - Explained

For 1994 or later injuries, CR9785.5 provides that there "shall be no more than one primary treating physician at a time" (PTP). When multiple injuries or conditions necessitate concurrent treatment by multiple health care providers, one physician is required to assume the role of the primary treating physician. Per CR9785.5, the physician who assumes this role is required to identify himself or herself as such in writing to the employer and the employee (in a medical report or a required treatment plan; see 7.47 and 7.56). If the employee has only one treating physician, this physician is, by default, the employee's "primary treating physician."

Ordinarily, the physician who is most actively involved in the employee's medical care will assume a lead role. However, CR9785.5 refers to the primary treating physician as one who is "primarily responsible for managing the care of an injured employee who has examined the employee at least once for the purpose of rendering or prescribing treatment and has monitored the effect of the treatment thereafter." For instance, the primary treater may be an orthopedic surgeon who is monitoring the employee's progress from treatment that is actually being provided by a physical therapist or an acupuncturist.

The initial primary treating physician may pass this responsibility to another physician upon discharging the employee from further care. The employee may have initially required active treatment from an orthopedist, an internist, and a burn specialist with the orthopedist being the primary treater. When orthopedic treatment is no longer required, good sense may dictate that the most actively involved of the other two specialists thereafter assume the role of the primary treater. Should a change occur, it is imperative that both the employee and the employer are informed of the identity of the new primary treating physician.

Special Reporting Requirements

A primary treating physician is also a primary reporting physician and is required to incorporate concurrent findings of other treating physicians into a single report. Per LC4061.5, the primary treating physician or "the physician designated by that treating physician ... shall render opinions on all medical issues necessary to determine eligibility for compensation. In the event that the employee is under active care from more than one treating physician, a single report shall be prepared by the physician primarily responsible for managing the worker's care that incorporates the findings of the various treating physicians."

The parties can avoid the costs and delays of an otherwise mandatory referral to an Agreed or Qualified Medical Evaluator by agreeing to resolve any medical issue based upon the findings of the employee's treating physician. Failing such agreement, any party can rely upon the findings of the treating physician as evidence before the WCAB (see 7.75) Under certain circumstances, a presumption of correctness will apply to the disputed findings of the treating physician to which an opposing party objects (whether or not this treating physician is deemed to be a "primary treating physician"; see 7.79).

A referral for a comprehensive medical-legal evaluation by an Agreed or Qualified Medical Evaluator is not required when a party disputes a determination of a consulting, rather than a treating, physician. However, the treating physician's opinion may be asked to comment on the findings of a consultant who did not report in the capacity of an Agreed or Qualified Medical Evaluator. If a party disputes the treating physician's opinions concerning the findings of such a consultant, this dispute requires a referral to an Agreed or Qualified Medical Evaluator.

Discharge From Treatment – Contested

Per CR9785.5, if "the primary treating physician discharges the employee from further treatment and there is a dispute concerning the need for continuing treatment, no other primary treating physician shall be identified unless and until the dispute is resolved." This dispute requires an opinion from an Agreed or Qualified Medical Evaluator. If the WCAB determines that "there is no further need for continuing treatment, then the physician who discharged the employee shall remain the primary treating physician." In this event, the employer does not owe bills for treatment by any other physician(s). If it is determined that further treatment is necessary, a new primary treating physician can be selected by whoever has medical control (see 7.39). This will nearly always be the employee since the resolution of this dispute will usually take longer than the employer's maximum 30-day period of medical control (see 7.40).

Presumption of Correctness – Sanctions

In limited situations, the determinations of a treating physician are rebuttably presumed to be correct. When a presumption applies, it establishes the findings that the Qualified Medical Evaluator must rebut, pursuant to LC4062.9, "by a preponderance of medical opinion indicating a different level of impairment" (see 7.80). The statutory the presumption of correctness of the findings of the treating physician in LC4062.9 has been judicially held to apply to all opinions of the treating physician, not opinions on permanent disability only.

Whether or not a presumption applies, opinions of the treating physician will either precipitate the prompt provision of benefits to the employee or else provide the basis for a referral to an Agreed or Qualified Medical Evaluator, depending upon whether the employee is represented by an attorney. It is because of the importance of the opinions of the treating physician that, in any litigated case, sanctions can result if the WCAB determines that a treating physician has submitted a deficient report (see 7.80).

7.34 INITIAL TREATMENT – EMPLOYEE'S CHOICE

Per CR9780.1, nothing "shall prohibit an employer from permitting an injured employee to be treated by a physician of the employee's choice." However, the employee has only one statutory right to select the physician who provides initial treatment (and cannot select a chiropractor; see 7.40). Per LC4600, employees have the right to predesignate a qualified "personal physician" at any time before an injury occurs. To exercise this right, the employee must notify the employer in writing of the name and address of the personal physician. After this notification is made, the employee may seek treatment from the personal physician immediately after an industrial injury is reported to the employer.

7.35 PERSONAL PHYSICIAN

Qualifications

The employee's choice of a personal physician is restricted, because LC4600 sets out four requirements that a physician must meet before qualifying as a personal physician. If the employee does not have a physician who meets the four statutory requirements, the employee cannot predesignate a personal physician. Per LC4600, a personal physician must meet all of the following requirements:

1. The physician must be a "physician and surgeon" who is "licensed pursuant to" specific sections of the Business and Professions Code (see 7.26). A doctor of medicine and a doctor of osteopathy are properly licensed. A chiropractor, a psychologist or an acupuncturist are not qualified to be selected as a "personal physician" because they are not licensed under the necessary sections of the Business and Professions Code.

2. The physician must have previously directed the medical treatment of the employee and be the employee's "regular" physician and surgeon. It doesn't matter what treatment the employee received, but the employee must have been treated rather than just evaluated or examined. The employee cannot select a physician in some random fashion because the employee must have an established physician-patient relationship with the physician.

3. The physician must possess the employee's past medical records. These records will contain information regarding past treatment, consultations, surgeries or hospitalizations including the names of other physicians or medical facilities.
4. The physician must possess the employee's medical history. The history will contain information such as previously diagnosed conditions or injuries, known allergies and types of medications the employee has taken. This information can alert the physician to possible complications that might develop after an industrial injury.

Required Employee Notice

Per LC4600, the employee is required to provide the employer with written preinjury notice of the selection of a personal physician, and LC4601 requires the same preinjury notice when the employee selects a personal chiropractor. (See 7.36 for important distinctions between a personal physician and a personal chiropractor.) There is no required format, but LC3552 requires the employer, upon request, to "provide the employee with an appropriate form" for the purpose of indicating the name of the employee's personal physician.

An employer-devised notice form could request information such as the signature of the physician or chiropractor, an acknowledgment of the application of a medical fee schedule, and confirmation of the physician's awareness of reporting requirements for industrial patients. At a minimum, the physician should be asked to verify that he or she meets the four statutory requirements to qualify as a personal physician under LC4600 or as a personal chiropractor under LC4601. Employers should avoid routine acceptance of employee notices without any review of their contents. Lack of a preinjury objection constitutes an acceptance of liability for treatment by the physician designated in the employee's written notice. This indirect acceptance can be avoided by verifying the physician's qualifications when the notice is received or at least before an injury occurs.

There is one instance where the employee will not be required to provide preinjury written notice of the selection of a personal physician. Per LC3550, the employer is required to post a notice that advises all employees of their preinjury right to select the initial treating physician (see 6.6). Failure to post this notice automatically permits the employee to be treated by a personal physician immediately after an injury is reported. However, LC3550 does not permit initial treatment from any physician of the employee's choice at the employer's expense. The physician who is selected by default is still required to meet the statutory requirements for a personal physician (e.g. cannot be a psychologist or an acupuncturist.

Personal Physician Not Available

The legislature anticipated that some problems might arise where an employee predesignates a personal physician. The employee may be injured at a time when the personal physician is unavailable to provide treatment. In most instances, the personal physician cannot be reached during evening or night shifts. The personal physician may be on vacation, his office may be closed on the date of injury, or the doctor may be located a great distance from the employee's work location. Under CR9780.2, the employer is given a continuing duty to provide emergency and first aid treatment. If the employee requires further treatment, the employee may obtain such treatment from his personal physician at the employer's expense.

The personal physician's specialty area may be inappropriate for the type of injury sustained. For example, an orthopedic personal physician would not be the appropriate medical specialist for treatment of a serious burn injury or a knife wound to the lungs or abdomen. If the personal physician is not qualified to treat the injury or declines to provide treatment, the employer has the right to designate a physician to treat the injury. When this situation occurs, the employer regains initial medical control.

The employee's right to designate a personal physician must be exercised prior to the occurrence of an injury. Once an injury occurs, the employee does not have any statutory right to either select the initial treating physician or to change a selection that was previously made. Sometimes an employee will change his mind and decide he does not want to be treated by his designated personal physician. The employee's rejection of a predesignated physician provides the employer with the right to select the initial physician. The employee's next right to choose his own treating physician arises thirty days after the injury is reported.

7.36 PERSONAL CHIROPRACTOR

Pursuant to LC4601(b), the employee has the option of predesignating a "personal chiropractor" instead of a personal physician. A personal chiropractor must meet four statutory requirements. These requirements are not shown separately here as the only way they differ from the qualifications for a personal physician is the use of the word "chiropractor" and the adjective "chiropractic" in reference to licensing requirements, prior treatment, records, and history (see 7.35). To exercise this right, the employee must provide the employer with preinjury written notice of the name and address of the personal chiropractor. The manner in which an employee exercises the right to select a personal physician or a personal chiropractor is essentially the same, but distinctions do exist .

The major distinction between a personal physician and a personal chiropractor involves the right of initial medical control. Per LC4600, the employee has the right to receive initial treatment from a personal physician. However, LC4601(b) requires employees who predesignate a personal chiropractor to exercise their right to "one change of physician" under LC4601(a) as a prerequisite to any employer liability for payment of treatment from that chiropractor (see 7.43). The employer therefore retains the right to select the initial treating physician, since there cannot be a change of physician until the employee has seen a physician. The employer's initial period of medical control may be very brief since the employee has the right to request a change of physician at any time and may do so immediately after an initial examination by an employer-selected physician.

7.37 FIRST AID

The definition of "first aid" found in LC5401 is used for most workers' compensation purposes. This definition applies to the duty to provide a claim form to an injured employee who requires treatment beyond first aid (see 6.12), the duty to provide first aid treatment to an injured employee per CR9780.2, and the duty to file an Employer's First Report of Work Injury (see 2.22).

Effective 1994, LC5401 defines "first aid" to mean "any one-time treatment of minor scratches, cuts, burns, splinters, or other minor industrial injury." This statute makes no reference to the identity of the person providing such treatment (for the brief period of 1991-1993, treatment provided by or in consultation with a physician was deemed to be medical treatment, not first aid.) A distinction between first aid and medical treatment is contingent solely upon the type of treatment that the employee receives, not the qualifications of the person providing treatment.

Injuries that can be effectively treated with first aid "do not ordinarily require medical care." Per CR9780, a licensed physician can render first aid, but it is still considered first aid and not medical treatment. First aid treatment is usually the only treatment provided for very minor injuries such as small cuts, splinters, first degree burns, minor abrasions or scratches. Any nonmedical person can render first aid. In fact, the employee may administer first aid to himself.

Regardless of the date of the employee's injury, certain treatment must be performed by properly licensed medical personnel. Such treatment is not first aid; it is medical treatment. An unlicensed coemployee cannot suture a deep laceration even if the injured employee acquiesces. This procedure is medical treatment and not first aid. Since 1991, LC5401 likewise provides that first aid "shall not include serious exposure to a hazardous substance" as defined by LC6302 (as "a degree or amount sufficient to create a substantial probability that death or serious physical harm in the future could result").

7.38 EMERGENCY TREATMENT

Per CR9780, the term "emergency treatment" is defined as treatment that is required "immediately following an industrial injury" where, if the treatment is not received immediately, the "likelihood of the employee's maximum recovery" could be decreased. This term refers to medical treatment, not first aid. If "a state, county, or local fire or police agency is called to the site of an accident involving" a serious injury or death of an employee, LC6409.2 requires the responding agency to notify the nearest office of Cal/OSHA "by telephone immediately." For instance, a report is required if paramedics transport an employee with serious head or spine injuries to a hospital by ambulance. Per LC6409.1, the employer also has a duty to report a serious injury or death to Cal/OSHA immediately by "telephone or telegraph."

Injuries resulting in compound fractures, extensive blood loss, and/or loss of consciousness require immediate medical attention. A delay in treatment could adversely affect the employee's recovery, possibly even resulting in death. An immediate diagnosis is required so that these conditions can receive proper treatment. The employer is obligated to provide necessary emergency treatment in all cases, including cases where the employer does not have the right to select the treating physician at the time the emergency arises. For instance, an employee who predesignated a personal physician in writing prior to an injury retains the right to be treated by that personal physician subsequent to the emergency (see 7.34).

A need for emergency treatment can occur at any time during the employee's recovery. The employee may experience a symptom that the treating physician had cautioned would constitute an emergency. However, certain symptoms would be recognized as a medical emergency by most nonmedical people, e.g. unusual bleeding or sudden blindness. The employee's next scheduled medical appointment may be days or weeks away, but treatment is needed now. In some cases, the employee may require ambulance transportation to an appropriate facility where emergency medical attention can be provided.

The employer has a continuing duty to pay for emergency treatment including transportation expenses that are reasonably necessitated by a medical emergency. An emergency may arise during a period where the employer has the right to select the treating physician (see 7.41). If the situation is an "emergency," the employee may make arrangements for treatment at the employer's expense. However, the employer regains medical control following the emergency treatment.

A dispute may arise as to what is, or is not, an emergency need for treatment. The employee's description of an "emergency" may be a misnomer, possibly an attempt to seek employer payment for a physician of the employee's choice during a period of employer medical control. There is no emergency if a delay in treatment would have no effect or only a minimal effect on the employee's recovery. The employee may merely require prompt medical attention within a reasonable period of time but not on any immediate or urgent basis. A physician is the person best qualified to resolve a dispute regarding whether a need for medical attention constitutes an emergency need for treatment.

7.39 AFTER 30 DAYS – EMPLOYEE'S CHOICE

Per LC4600, any employee who has not previously received treatment from an employee-selected physician or chiropractor gains the right to select one 30 (thirty) days after the injury was reported to the employer (provided that the employee still needs treatment). This right can be exercised immediately upon expiration of the 30-day period or at any future time when treatment is required for the injury. When the employee exercises this right by requesting a change of physician under LC4601 the new physician is called an "employee-selected physician."

An employee who received initial treatment from a personal physician received treatment from an employee-selected physician. This fact is recognized by CR9780 that defines the term "employee-selected physician" to mean the employee's "personal physician" as well as a "physician or facility selected by the employee more than 30 days from the date the injury is reported." Some employees who give preinjury written notice of a selection do not receive treatment from a personal physician or personal chiropractor after an injury (e.g. where a different medical specialty is required). Any employee who has been treated solely by employer-selected physicians gains the right to select an employee-selected physician after the 30-day waiting period.

7.40 INITIAL TREATMENT – EMPLOYER'S CHOICE

The employer has the right to select the initial treating physician in two instances. If the employee did not give preinjury written notice of a selection of a personal physician or a personal chiropractor, the employer then has the right to select the initial treating physician and any other treating physicians for a period of 30 days from the date the injury was reported. If the employee did predesignate a personal chiropractor, the employer has the right to select the initial treating physician (because LC4601 requires the employee to exercise the right to one change of physician before the employer is required to authorize treatment by the personal chiropractor; see 7.36).

Even if the employee properly selected a personal physician or personal chiropractor, the employer regains the right of selection of the treating physician, or medical control, for the initial 30 days after an injury was reported in any case where:

    a. That physician or chiropractor is not available or refuses to provide treatment.

    b. That physician or chiropractor is not qualified to treat the particular injury sustained; e.g., a different medical specialty is needed.

    c. The employee does not wish to receive treatment from that physician or chiropractor.

Nothing in the Labor Code prevents an employee from refusing to be treated by an employer-selected physician. In fact, LC4605 guarantees the "right of the employee to provide, at his own expense, a consulting physician or any attending physicians whom he desires." When the employer has the right to select the treating physician, the employee has the right to arrange his own treatment as long as he is willing to incur the expense of the treatment himself. LC4605 does not distinguish between the physician's fee and other medical expenses such as medications or therapy. The employer may have a valid basis for not paying the physician's professional fee. However, the employer may still be obligated for other treatment expenses, e.g. expenses that would be incurred no matter who selected the treating physician.

7.41 AFTER 30 DAYS – EMPLOYER-SELECTED PHYSICIAN

In cases where the employee does not have the right to treatment by a personal physician or personal chiropractor, the employer's right of control over selection of treating physicians is confined to the first thirty days after reporting (except see 7.2 for the exclusive provider option and 7.42 regarding treatment by a health care organization). On the thirty-first day, the employee has the right to receive treatment from an employee-selected physician. The employee may choose not to exercise this right at all or may not exercise it immediately. If so, the employer can continue to select the treating physicians, but the employer's continued medical control is subject to the employee's agreement. Should the employer desire to retain medical control, the employer must provide a treating physician who is so acceptable to the employee that the employee has no desire to be treated by a different physician.

Where adequate treatment is initially provided by the employer, the employee may not wish to transfer treatment to some other physician. The employee may develop rapport with the treating doctor and confidence in the physician's abilities. If the employee has undergone surgery, a new physician may be reluctant to assume follow-up care, or it may make little sense to transfer treatment to a new physician when only a short period of additional treatment is needed. These are some of the reasons why an employee may prefer to have the employer retain medical control. The employee's consent need not be in writing. It is sufficient that the employee is aware of his right to select a physician but prefers not to do so.

The employee's various statutory rights to select the treating physician are intended to allow the employee to arrange for adequate medical care with a physician in whom the employee has confidence. These rights are not intended to encourage repeated changes or doctor-shopping. If the employee remains dissatisfied and in need of treatment after selecting more than one treating physician, the employee can change treating physicians again. In actuality, the employee has a continuous right to a change of treating physicians whenever there is a reasonable basis for a change (an issue that may be disputed by the employer). Likewise, the employer has a continuous right to regain medical control after it has previously reverted to the employee but only upon a showing of good cause by filing a petition (see 7.44).

7.42 AFTER 30 DAYS – HEALTH CARE ORGANIZATION

Period of Employer's Medical Control

Ordinarily, the employer is limited to 30 days of medical control pursuant to LC4600 (see 7.44). For 1994 or later injuries, it is possible for the employer to control medical treatment for a period of 90, 180 or 365 days from the date an injury is reported. Extended periods of medical control are available only to employers who choose to enter into contracts with Health Care Organizations (HCO's) pursuant to LC4600.3 and LC4600.5.

Qualifying criteria for certification as an HCO by the Administrative Director of the Division of Workers' Compensation are set out in LC4600.5 as is the application process. The essential distinctions that determine the employer's period of medical control when it contracts with certified HCO's per LC4600.3 are listed below (note: "employer-paid" means payable at least 50% by the employer or pursuant to a collective bargaining agreement):

a. **90 Days.** The employee is not eligible for employer-paid nonoccupational health care coverage.

b. **180 Days.** The employee did not predesignate a personal physician or personal chiropractor and the employee is eligible for employer-paid nonoccupational health care.

c. **365 Days.** The employee predesignated a personal physician or personal chiropractor who is affiliated with one of the HCO options provided by the employer (presumably the same one selected to provide occupational health care although not specifically required), and the employee is eligible for employer-paid nonoccupational health care.

The periods shown above start from the date an injury is reported to the employer. Per LC4600.3, in no event is the employee allowed to obtain treatment outside a designated HCO "until 90 days from the date the injury was reported." However, other variables can affect the period of employer medical control. The employee has the right to obtain emergency treatment from a medical provider or facility that "is not a member of the" employee's HCO (care beyond the emergency need would resume with the employee's HCO). Changes in the provisions of a collective bargaining agreement can give rise to the right to choose a different HCO or may eliminate prerequisite criteria for the use of a previously selected HCO.

Per LC4600.3, employees who choose to receive care from an HCO "must receive treatment for all occupational injuries and illnesses" from their selected HCO. However, the employee's right to be treated by a predesignated personal physician or a personal chiropractor is coordinated with, but not replaced by, statutory provisions regarding the use of HCO's (see 7.35-7.36). Employees have the right to predesignate a personal physician (LC4600) or a personal chiropractor (LC4601) at any time prior to an injury, including the right to change an earlier selection. In fact, LC4600.3 requires the employer to provide its employees with an opportunity to select a personal physician or personal chiropractor at least once each year.

The employee is initially entitled to select from HCO options offered by the employer at the time of hire and also has the right to select a different HCO annually thereafter. The employee has the right to reselect from HCO options during any specified open enrollment period. The employee also has the right to change to another HCO option on the date of renewal or termination of the employer's contract with an HCO that was previously chosen to provide occupational health care to the employee (and may be providing on-going care for a work-related injury). Per LC4600.3, a copy of the employee's selection of a medical provider, that must be in writing, must be "maintained in the employee's personnel records."

Right to Change of Physician – Consultation

Certain prior rights of the employee are incorporated into an HCO program. Per LC4600.3, the employee has the right to a consultation from a participating physician for a second opinion, but this right is restricted to an opinion "on a matter pertaining to a diagnosis from a participating physician." Also, employees who are enrolled in an HCO have a right to "no less than one change of physician." Upon a request for a change of physician, the HCO is required to provide the employee with a list of participating physicians within 5 days so that the employee may make a selection. If, for whatever reason, the employee's HCO no longer contracts with the employer, the employee is allowed to opt to continue on-going treatment with the HCO. If the employee opts not to continue treatment with the HCO, "the employer may control the employee's treatment for 30 days from the date the injury was reported." If this 30-day period has already expired, the employee has the right to select the alternative medical provider.

Certification as a Health Care Organization

Certification as a Health Care Organization is possible for such entities as: health care service plans that are licensed under the Knox-Keene Health Care Service Plan Act (HSC1353), licensed disability insurers, or any entity that is authorized as a Workers' Compensation Health Care Provider Organization (a WCHCPO or HCPO) by the Commissioner of the Department of Corporations. Entities that can apply for authorization as a WCHCPO include workers' compensation insurers and third-party administrators (see 2.15). Qualifying criteria for authorization as a WCHCPO by the Department of Corporations are set out in LC5100-LC5210 (as are requirements regarding such areas as advertisements, operation exclusively on a fee-for-service basis, financial and other disclosures, employee grievances, and procedures for reviewing costs, quality of care, and utilization of proffered services and facilities).

Any entity that seeks certification as an HCO by the Administrative Director of the Division of Worker's Compensation must meet all requirements that are set out in LC4600.5 (in addition to licensing requirements pursuant to other State laws). These requirements involve such areas as: extensive record keeping, financial solvency, cooperative programs for promoting employee safety and early return to work after an injury, a written patient grievance policy, and maintenance of records sufficient to determine the cost effectiveness of the plan. An HCO is specifically required to make chiropractic treatment available to employees who desire such treatment, and disputes as to the need for chiropractic care are to be resolved by a utilization review process established by the HCO. Administrative regulations regarding certification standards for HCO's are set out in CR9770-CR9779.2.

Selection of HCO to Treat Employee

The employer is not required to offer occupational health care by HCO's. If the employer wishes to provide occupational health care through HCO's, LC4600.3 controls the options that an employer must make available to its employees (employer options are also affected by requirements for collective bargaining under State and federal laws). The basic limitations that determine the number and type of HCO's that may be available to an employee are explained in the list that follows.

1. The employer must contract with at least two HCO's.
2. At least one of the HCO options "must be compensated on a fee-for-service basis" (as opposed to a capitated fee basis where fees are developed on a per capita basis: per employee, per month).
3. If the employer wishes to offer services of an HCO that is "the workers' compensation insurer that covers the employee or is an entity that controls or is controlled by that insurer" (as defined by IC1212), the employer must offer at least one other HCO option to which this description does not apply.

Prior to selecting an HCO, the employee is entitled to receive notice of available options. Notices are required to provide sufficient detail to enable an employee to exercise a right of choice between all options. A combination notice/enrollment form that is required by CR9779.3 is printed in CR9779.4. This form (a DWC 1194 form) is entitled "Choosing Medical Care For Work-Related Injuries and Illnesses" (front side) and "Making Your Choice" (back side). The form provides general information about HCOs and serves as an enrollment form. Alternatively, the form allows an employee to formally document a decision not to enroll in an HCO. The employer has the right to select an HCO for the employee if the employee, for whatever reason, fails to choose an HCO after being properly notified of available choices.

While requirements for certification as an HCO may appear overly cumbersome to an employer, the burden of compliance with statutory requirements is on the HCO, not the employer. A decision to utilize the permitted HCO option is ordinarily cost driven considering historical costs to provide workers' compensation benefits. However, employers must also give consideration to any additional time and expense that such programs may ultimately entail (e.g. the use of employer staff and facilities relative to the provision of notices, record keeping requirements, and resolution of disputes).

7.43 CHANGE OF PHYSICIAN – BY EMPLOYEE

Per LC4601, the employee has the right to request "one change of physician." This request can be made any time after an injury. During the first thirty days from the date the employer receives the notice of the injury, the employer has the right to select the new treating physician or chiropractor; the solitary exception to this statement occurs in the situation where the employee has selected a personal chiropractor (see 7.36). When the employee exercises the right to a change of physician after the expiration of the 30-day period, the employee then has the right to select the new treating physician.

A frequently asked question is: how many times does an employee have the right to change treatment from one physician to another? The Labor Code is not ambiguous on this issue. Per LC4601, as amended effective 1/1/91, "if the employee so requests, the employer shall tender the employee one change of physician" (note use of singular word "physician"), and the "employee at any time may request that the employer tender this one-time change of physician" (note repeated use of the word "one"). However, despite the clear wording of LC4601, this statute has been judicially determined to restrict the employee to a one-time change of physician only during the initial 30 days after an injury is reported. During this period, the employer has the right to select any new treating physician or chiropractor (see 7.40).

The employee's right to request a change of physician more than 30 days after the injury is reported is a continuous right that is subject only to a test of reasonableness. The employee does not and never has had any right to change treating physicians repeatedly in a search for the perfect physician, the ultimate cure or more favorable medical opinions. However, there are many situations where the employee is reasonably entitled to more than one change of physician.

Where the employee requires treatment from treating physicians in different medical specialties, the employee would appear to have a right to a change of physician for each separate medical specialty. A change of treating physician would appear to be reasonable if the treating physician retires, the employee moves a great distance away, the physician's license to practice is revoked, the employee loses confidence in the physician's ability to provide effective treatment, or the employee's benefits are delayed because the physician does not submit timely reports as required. Any grounds that would constitute good cause for termination of a consultation with a Qualified Medical Evaluator would likely be deemed by the WCAB to constitute a reasonable basis for a transfer of treatment from the offending physician (see 7.79).

Employer's Response

The employee may change his mind and decide he does not want to be treated by a personal physician. The employee may be dissatisfied with the physician selected by the employer. The employee may prefer treatment by a chiropractor. The employee does not have to provide any reason; the employee need only request a change of physician. The request can be oral or written. Per LC4601, "the employee at any time may request that the employer tender this one-time change of physician," and the employer has five working days to respond (the response need not be in writing, but written confirmation of an oral response is usually appropriate).

If the employee's request is received during the first thirty days after an injury is reported, it is important for the employer to respond timely. Otherwise, the consequence for the employer's delay is that the employer loses its right to select the new treating physician during this brief period that the employer has medical control (see 7.40).

If the employee waits thirty days before exercising the right to request a change of physician, the employer is required to authorize treatment by a physician of the employee's choosing, who can be a chiropractor or any other person who is defined as a physician in LC3209.3. Occasionally, the employer is willing to relinquish its rights. For instance, the employer is unlikely to insist on exercising its right of selection where the employee wishes to be treated by a physician who is unobjectionable to the employer, and/or the employee requests a change of physician near the end of the 30-day waiting period (see 7.40).

It is wise to ask an employee his reason for requesting a change of physician. If the employee really wants a second opinion on a recommended surgical procedure or treatment plan but is otherwise content with the treating physician, a consultation would be more appropriate. The employee may have unrealistic expectations and wish to change physicians because the current physician makes him sit in the waiting room for an hour before an exam or will not spend a lot of time listening to him. These complaints are likely to be repeated regardless of any change of physician. Therefore, the employee may benefit from the counseling of the claimsperson in making effective use of the right to a change of physician without disrupting the continuity of necessary treatment.

7.44 CHANGE OF PHYSICIAN – BY EMPLOYER

Petition To Regain Medical Control

The employer also has the right to request a change of treating physician or chiropractor. Per LC4603, the employer may exercise its right at any time. The procedure for the employer's request is more complicated than the procedure for employees. Per CR9786, the employer makes its request directly to the Administrative Director of the Division of Workers' Compensation.

The employee does not have to provide any reason at all when he requests a change of physician. The employer must give a specific reason along with an explanation or medical evidence supporting its request. The reason must be acceptable to the Administrative Director or the employer's request will not be granted. The Labor Code gives the employee the right to be treated by an employee-selected physician. Since the employer is requesting that this right be taken away from the employee, the employer's request will not be granted routinely.

The employer's request for a change of treating physician is made by filing a petition entitled "Petition for Order Directing the Employee to Select Employer's Designated Physician" (Form DWC 280). The employer's petition must be based upon good cause. The petition is filed with the Administrative Director of the Division of Workers' Compensation. Per CR9786, the employer's petition must be "verified" (it must be signed under penalty of perjury). It must include a "verified statement of facts and/or supportive documentary evidence." It must include proof of service of the petition and any attachments on the employee or else his attorney and on the "employee-selected and currently treating physician or chiropractor." (The petition is not necessary to transfer treatment between employer-selected physicians.)

Good Cause for Petition

The grounds that constitute good cause for granting the employer's petition are limited to those currently specified in CR9786. Good cause can be established by proof including medical evidence in support of any one, or a combination of, these grounds (as fully explained in 7.45-7.49):

1. The initial report that is required within five days of the physician's initial examination was not submitted timely or is inadequate.
2. Progress reports were not submitted timely or were inadequate on two or more occasions.
3. The treatment that is currently being provided is inappropriate in view of the nature and extent of the employee's injury.
4. Current treatment is inconsistent with the written treatment plan that was submitted by the physician as required by CR9785.
5. The treating physician is not located within a reasonable geographic area.

Submission & Review Procedures

The petition form requires the employer to designate the names, addresses and specialties of a panel of five physicians who can provide appropriate treatment if the petition is granted. In cases where the employee is receiving chiropractic treatment, the employer is required to include the name of one chiropractor on the panel. Per CR9786, the petition "shall be filed and verified under penalty of perjury" and "be accompanied by any supportive documentary evidence ... and proof of service on the employee ... or the employee's authorized attorney or representative." The employee has a right to file a response, including "any supportive evidentiary documents" within "20 days after service of the employer's petition." The employee's response must likewise be "verified under penalty of perjury."

The Administrative Director may grant or dismiss the petition, set it for hearing or refer the matter to the WCAB for a factual determination (e.g. a judge, whose identity is not disclosed to the parties, may actually render the opinion that the Administrative Director provides to the petitioner). Additionally, CR9786 provides that the Administrative Director "may elect to attempt informal adjustment of the employer-employee dispute."

The time allowed for action before a petition is deemed denied by virtue of nonaction upon it is specified in CR9786. This regulation has undergone numerous amendments in past years. Changes in time periods for filing and for action by the Administrative Director generally apply to all petitions filed after the change. However, the grounds that establish good cause, as explained in this text, apply solely to cases where "the initial examination" " (presumably an examination by the offending physician) occurred after 9/30/93.

Petition Granted

When an employer's petition is granted, the employee will receive an "Order Requiring Employee to Select an Employer-Designated Physician." The employee must then select one physician from the panel of five that the employer submitted in its petition. The employee may investigate the panel before making a selection. The employee may review the new physicians with his own physician or make other inquiries. Once the Order issues, the employer regains medical control over the employee's treatment. The employer is liable for the payment of services provided by the previous employee-selected physician only until the date of the Order. Thereafter, the employer does not owe any further treatment costs or any further charges that are submitted by the employee's previous physician.

7.45 GOOD CAUSE – REPORTS LATE OR INADEQUATE

A physician's opinion of the nature and extent of disability is a necessary prerequisite to the provision of benefits to an injured worker because the employer cannot monitor the appropriateness or effectiveness of medical treatment without medical reports. Per CR9786, the employer has good cause to file a petition to regain medical control if the physician fails to submit an initial report within five days of an initial examination (see 7.55). Good cause also exists if a timely report "is inadequate due to material omissions or deficiencies." However, before filing its petition, the employer should attempt to ascertain the reason for noncompliance and whether it is likely that less formal methods of communication with the physician are all that is necessary to produce full compliance with reporting requirements.

Good cause for filing a petition also exists where the employer has fulfilled all of its duties, but the physician has failed to submit the progress reports that are required by CR9785 (see 7.56). However, in the case of on-going progress reports, CR9786 provides that good cause for filing a petition does not exist unless the physician fails "to submit timely and complete reports on two or more occasions." The multiple failures need not be consecutive; the physician may submit one report on time, the next one late, the next on time, and so forth. The employer's petition may be predicated upon a lack of reports, deficiencies in reports, untimely submission of reports or any combination of these grounds that arise on separate dates.

One late, missing or inadequate report is not sufficient to establish good cause for a petition to regain medical control (it is not likely that an employer would transfer treatment from any employer-selected physician on this basis). Furthermore, the employer has a duty under CR9784 to notify the physician of the reporting requirements of CR9785. If the employer fails in its duty, the physician's failure to report is excused, and the employer does not have good cause to complain. Thereafter, CR9786 provides that the physician is entitled to a second chance to submit required progress reports, but no more.

7.46 GOOD CAUSE – TREATMENT INAPPROPRIATE

Good cause exists for the employer to request a change of treating physician under LC4603 when the treatment being received by the employee is inappropriate. The employer can demonstrate good cause by showing that present treatment is:
   a. Not resulting in a cure or relief from the effects of the injury.
   b. Not capable of resulting in a cure or relief.
   c. Causing a deterioration of the employee's condition.

   d. Being provided by a practitioner who is not properly qualified to treat
      the particular injury.
   e Delaying the employee's recovery.
   f. Unreasonably protracted for the type of injury sustained.

Medical evidence is required to show why the present treatment is inappropriate, how the treatment is inappropriate, and what treatment would be more appropriate. The employer's petition must be supplemented with medical reports substantiating each portion of the employer's position including the fact that the employer "is prepared to offer more effective treatment."

It is not enough to criticize the treatment being provided. The employer must show how it can overcome any problems with the current treatment. Any of the five physicians (or four plus one chiropractor) designated on the panel within the employer's petition must be capable of providing appropriate treatment if the employer's petition is granted.

An opinion that current treatment is inappropriate may initially be rendered by medical resource staff. For instance, the claimsperson may be informed of this opinion by a staff physician who routinely reviews medical reports as part of a utilization review program (see 7.10). This opinion may also be provided by a consulting physician; e.g. where the treating physician requests a referral to a consultant and then disagrees with the findings of the consulting physician. Regardless of the medical source for an assertion that current treatment is inappropriate, LC4062 requires that an opinion be obtained from an Agreed or Qualified Medical Evaluator when a party disputes "the extent and scope of medical treatment" (see 7.75). For 1994 or later injuries, the evaluation required by LC4062 must be obtained prior to petitioning for a change of treating physician (and may in fact resolve the dispute, that is the intended purpose of LC4062 evaluations).

Per CR9786, additional procedures apply to cases where treatment that is alleged to be inappropriate is "consistent with the treatment plan submitted pursuant to" CR9785 (see 7.47). Within 15 calendar days of receipt of a treatment plan, the employer must notify the physician of the medical basis for its objections or else the fact that it is "scheduling a consultation with another physician" (an Agreed or Qualified Medical Evaluator) for the purpose of "assessing the treatment plan." For 1994 or later injuries, both notifications will be provided simultaneously. This notice requirement should be construed in a positive light as an opportunity to reduce costs. The provision of supportive details to the treating physician may result in modifications to the treatment plan that annul the basis for the employer's objections.

The fact that the plan is not submitted using the form required by CR9785 does not constitute good cause to file a petition. The employer is allowed 15 days from receipt of the prerequisite consultant's report to notify the treating physician of the medical basis for its objection(s) to a proposed treatment plan. Good cause for filing a petition exists upon providing such notice (and meeting the criteria explained above).

7.47 GOOD CAUSE – TREATMENT PLAN ISSUES

Per CR9786, the employer can establish good cause for filing a petition to regain medical control when it can show that "current treatment is not consistent with the treatment plan submitted pursuant to" CR9785 (see 7.56). There are many reasons for the employer's position. Treatment may be continued after the estimated completion date in a written treatment plan. The physician may commence a new type of treatment or increase the frequency of a form of treatment that is consistent with the treatment plan. The employer is not disputing the provisions of a written treatment plan. Rather, it is the employer's contention that there is no treatment plan that encompasses current treatment. As a practical matter, the employer is not likely to complain when treatment that is effective is not consistent with a written plan (so establishing good cause will usually also require a showing that current treatment is inappropriate).

7.48 GOOD CAUSE – NOT REASONABLE GEOGRAPHIC AREA

The employer's LC4063 petition to regain medical control will be granted where it makes "a clear showing that the employee-selected physician or facility is not within a "reasonable geographic area." This term is defined in CR9780. The definition does not address itself to any specific distances from the employee's residence, job site or treatment facility. Instead, consideration is given to several factors that may necessitate receipt of treatment outside the employee's immediate geographical area. The employer's petition must examine all pertinent factors, and the employer must show that appropriate and equivalent treatment is available at a specific and closer location.

The employee is not required to seek treatment at the closest available facility. The employee might have a significant medical history that warrants treatment by a physician who has the employee's past medical records available for review. The employee may require extensive concurrent treatment for a nonindustrial condition. The employee-selected physician may be qualified and competent to render treatment for both the injury and the nonindustrial problem. The employee may not speak English and may therefore travel outside the local area to receive treatment from a physician who can communicate with the employee. The employee's medical condition may require treatment in a particular medical specialty, but such specialists may not be available in the employee's locality. These are some of the factors that are considered in determining the boundaries of a "reasonable geographic area."

If the employee lives in a rural area, the employer may have no objection to a treatment facility one hundred miles from the employee's home. However, when an employee resides in a metropolitan area, traveling fifty miles or even thirty miles may be unreasonable. When the employer contests the reasonableness of the distance, the employer must be prepared to overcome any explanations the employee may provide to justify his extended travel.

7.49 NOT GOOD CAUSE – TREATMENT UNNECESSARY

The employer may take the position that the employee is not in need of any further treatment contrary to the opinion of the treating physician. A disputed issue of need for treatment requires referral to an Agreed or Qualified Medical Evaluator for a determination (per LC4062 if the employee's condition is not yet permanent and stationary, otherwise per LC4061; see 7.75). Per CR9786, this type of dispute does not constitute good cause for filing a petition to regain medical control. This dispute involves a legal issue that should be brought before a judge in litigation proceedings. If the employer completely denies responsibility for any treatment, there is obviously no purpose to be served by filing a petition for a change of treating physicians. The question in such cases is whether to provide treatment at all, not which physician should be selected to provide treatment.

7.50 CONSULTATIONS – OVERVIEW

The term "consultation" means a one-time examination for the purpose of obtaining a medical opinion. A consultation encompasses an examination and report only. The evaluation may include reasonably required diagnostic tests. No treatment is provided by a consulting physician. If treatment for the injury is necessary, the employee returns to the care of the treating physician subsequent to the examination. If the employee is represented by an attorney, necessary consultations can be provided by mutually agreed upon physicians. For 1994 or later injuries, whether or not the employee has an attorney, various Labor Code sections provide both the employer and the employee with equivalent rights to consulting physicians of their choice as summarized below.

   a. **Initial Evaluation:** at employer's request to determine compensability of injury prior to a decision to pay or deny a claim (LC4060 and LC4620). Although not required, this consultant will ordinarily be a Qualified Medical Evaluator.
   b. **Compensable Claim - No Dispute:** a consultation at request of the employee (LC4601) or the employer (LC4050) for a second opinion to clarify medical information; e.g. the need for a surgery recommended by the treating physician.
   c. **Compensable Claim - Medical Dispute:** consultation by a Qualified Medical Evaluator of the employee's choice or the employer's choice for the purpose of determining any disputed medical issue (LC4060, LC4061, LC4062).

For 1994 or later injuries, the admissibility of LC4050 consultant's reports is limited due to statutory restrictions on the use of consultants other than Agreed or Qualified Medical Evaluators. However, the parties continue to have the right to obtain "second opinions" where necessary clarification is sought for the purpose of determining whether a dispute exists. For instance, an employee may exercise the right to a consultation under LC4601 to obtain a second opinion regarding the need for a surgery or type of treatment that is recommended by the treating physician. The employer may exercise its LC4050 right to a consultation for comparable reasons. For instance, the employer may desire an opinion from a physician with a different medical specialty or may seek an opinion on an issue that has not yet been addressed by the treating physician. (Note: formal medical evaluations by Agreed or Qualified Medical Evaluators are not allowed for any injury or body part for which the employee has not yet filed a claim form.)

Frequently, a treating physician will recommend that a consultation be obtained. The treating physician will specify the reason for this request and identify the type of specialty that is appropriate. The employer, as the provider and payor of benefits, is entitled to advance notice of the need for such referral per LC9785. This notice also allows the claimsperson to provide appropriate administration of the claim. Depending upon the facts of a particular case, it may be the claimsperson or the treating physician who makes necessary arrangements for a consultation. Arrangements would include: selecting a consultant, scheduling an appointment, notifying the employee of the examination, arranging for movement of medical and nonmedical information between the treater and the consultant, and designating where the consultant's opinion should be sent. If the treating physician makes a direct referral, savvy consultants will usually contact the claims administrator in advance of their involvement to ensure that they have preauthorization for payment of services.

7.51 CONSULTATION – AT EMPLOYEE'S REQUEST

Per LC4601, the employee has a right to have a consultation with a physician or chiropractor of the employee's choice "in any serious case," and the employer is obligated to pay for the expense of this examination. The employee can request a consultation at any time. This includes the first thirty days after an injury is reported.

It appears that only employees with "serious" injuries are entitled to a consultation, but LC4601 does not further explain what constitutes a "serious" injury. Some assistance is provided in LC6302 which defines a "serious injury" for purposes of the employer's duty under LC6409.1 to report such injuries immediately to the Division of Occupational Safety and Health (Cal/OSHA). Per LC6302, a "serious injury" means one "which requires inpatient" (overnight) hospital treatment or results in an amputation of "any member of the body" or a "serious degree of permanent disfigurement. "

Few would argue that a case is "serious" when a doctor has recommended surgery, and the employee desires a second opinion. Likewise, most would agree that a paper cut or a first degree burn were minor injuries. However, it is questionable whether a back strain, a fractured toe, or a nonperforated ulcer are "serious." Any injury is serious to the person who is suffering from its effects, and thus it becomes a claims decision whether or not to provide a consultation in a particular case. Consideration should be given to the nature of the injury and the progress or lack of progress of a recovery from the injury. Also considered would be supplemental factors such as the cost to the employer and the need to receive additional medical information.

It is necessary to identify the employee's reason for requesting a consultation because the employee's freedom to choose any physician is affected by such variables as the medical issue involved and whether the employee is represented by an attorney. For 1994 or later injuries, the provisions of LC4061-LC4062 appear to collectively require that all disputes regarding determinations of a treating physician must be referred to an Agreed or Qualified Medical Evaluator (including disputed compensability of a claimed injury per LC4060; see 7.75).

7.52 CONSULTATION – AT EMPLOYER'S REQUEST

Per LC4050, the employer has the right to require the employee to undergo examinations by consulting physicians of the employer's choice at the employer's expense. This right exists "whenever the right to compensation exists," that means in any compensable case. If the employer is obligated to provide benefits, the employer is entitled to determine the extent of compensation that it is obligated to provide.

Per LC4050, the employer has the right to require the employee to "submit to examination at reasonable intervals." The employer's need for medical information will control the frequency of consultations. The employer must have accurate and detailed medical information in order to fulfill its legal obligations. Without such information, the employer cannot timely furnish all benefits the employee is entitled to receive. For instance, monthly orthopedic consultations may be necessary to verify disability benefits if treatment is provided by an employee-selected acupuncturist who is authorized under LC3209.3 to report on treatment but not disability (see 7.29).

As of 1994, a referral to an Agreed or Qualified Medical Evaluator is required if the employer disputes a determination of the treating physician and the employee has filed a claim form for an injury to the body part involved in the dispute (see 7.75).Where an evaluation by an Agreed or Qualified Medical Evaluator is not required, employers continue to have the right to LC4050 consultations. There are many reasons why the employer would request a consultation. Any of the reasons shown below will warrant a consultation regardless of whether the treating physician was selected by the employer or the employee:

a. Concern over an extensive period of disability for the type of injury sustained.
b. Concern that inadequate medical attention is being provided: e.g. the employee's condition is not improving or is deteriorating.
c. Lack of knowledge of the employee's diagnosis or a current prognosis due to delinquent or skimpy medical reports.
d. Lack of knowledge of the employee's condition because the treating physician lacks knowledge of workers' compensation terms and how to properly report on disability status.

Treatment by Consulting Physician. Any consulting physician (e.g. one selected by the employee under LC4601 or the employer under LC4050) is usually instructed that an appointment is scheduled for an "examination only" and that "no treatment is authorized." However, the consultant is often asked to provide an opinion as to the nature and extent of treatment, if any, that is recommended. The employer may authorize the consulting physician to provide any recommended treatment, but the employer is not legally required to extend its authorization beyond the cost for an exam and report. Therefore, the appointment letter to the physician must specify whether or not treatment is authorized in the event the consulting physician finds the employee to be in need of treatment.(Note: treatment should not be provided by a medical-legal consultant who performs an evaluation as a Qualified Medical Evaluator; see 7.75).

A consultant will usually be authorized to provide treatment when the employer is liable for the provision of medical treatment and the employer has no objection to the provision of treatment by this particular physician. The purpose of the consultation may have been to obtain a second opinion regarding the need for a surgery. If the employee prefers to have the surgery performed by the physician seen in consultation, this change of treating physician would most likely be authorized by the employer. Suppose a chiropractor requests an orthopedic consult, and a consulting orthopedic specialist recommends surgery. The employee now needs to be receive treatment from an orthopedic specialist, not a chiropractor. If the consulting orthopedist is willing to perform the surgery, approval of treatment by this physician may be preferable to a transfer of treatment to another orthopedic physician.

Most consultations will be at the request of the treating physician. The employer should have the opportunity to instruct the consultant as to authorization for treatment, because CR9785 requires the treating physician to inform the employer at the time that the "employee is referred to another physician for consultation."

Scheduling Consultations. The employer usually requests a LC4050 consultation for the purpose of soliciting very specific information from the physician. The desired information can be condensed into a series of questions that the physician is requested to answer (see also 7.79 regarding scheduling of consultations with Agreed or Qualified Medical Evaluators).

It is the responsibility of the claimsperson to direct the physician's attention to the precise matters on which a medical opinion is requested. A thorough appointment letter can avoid the necessity to later request clarification from a physician. Clarification of reported opinions usually necessitates a supplemental report, possibly a re-exam, and most certainly an additional bill. No physician wants to be told how to conduct an exam or what medical findings the physician is to make and include in a report. However, most physicians are busy enough to appreciate careful directions in an appointment letter since these assist physicians in making the best use of their time and avoiding any problems with prompt receipt of payment for their efforts.

The employer may have a valid legal basis for declining liability for treatment even if a physician indicates that treatment is necessary. The purpose of the exam may be merely to evaluate the extent of disability so that a settlement can be negotiated on a claim where the compensability of the injury is contested in its entirety. There may be a potential defense to the entire claim such as a statute of limitations defense. The purpose of the evaluation may be to determine the employer's potential liability in the event the employer is unsuccessful in proving its defense before the WCAB (because if the employer does not obtain a medical opinion from a doctor of its choosing before a WCAB hearing, the judge can issue an award based solely on the employee's medical reports).

It is expensive and embarrassing for an employer to incur liability for benefits as the direct result of a poorly worded letter to the consulting physician. Where the appointment letter is unclear, the consultant may provide treatment under an implied authorization from the employer. It might appear that the employer had determined its defenses were weak and therefore decided to assume liability for treatment. This is a situation to be avoided before it happens by the use of a specific letter of instruction to the consulting physician. The words "consult only" and "no treatment is authorized" are clear enough to avoid any misunderstanding regarding which services are authorized. The consulting physician prefers clear instructions to a later dispute over payment for unrequested services that were performed.

It is common practice to notify the physician whether or not authorization is extended to bill for testing and diagnostic procedures in addition to an examination fee. Such procedures are often necessary in order for the physician to formulate a proper medical opinion. These procedures are costly and should not be authorized unless they are actually necessary. Often such work-ups will have been done by previous physicians involved in the case.

All available information should be forwarded to a consulting physician. Neglecting to forward information already obtained and paid for could cause the employer to incur expenses for duplicate and/or unnecessary services. The consulting physician may wish to take repeat X-rays or repeat other testing done in the past. There are many reasons that warrant authorization for duplicate services. Among these are:

    a. A long time has expired since previous tests were done.
    b. Additional X-rays from a different view are necessary.
    c. Past records are definitely unavailable.
    d. A report is needed with some urgency and there is insufficient time to forward past records, e.g. before an upcoming hearing date or before the date of a scheduled self-procured surgery.
    e. Previous tests are inconclusive; e.g., an electromyogram was performed too soon after an injury.

The claimsperson must obtain necessary medical information and at the same time resist incurring unnecessary medical expense. It is important to reach an understanding with the physician regarding what is truly necessary in the way of repeat or additional procedures and what will or will not be authorized. The goal of a consultation is to obtain specific information and to pay whatever is necessary but to avoid payment for services that are irrelevant to the provision of benefits to the employee.

Notice of Scheduled Examination. The employer must provide the employee with a "written request" to submit to a scheduled consultation pursuant to LC4050 (see 7.79 regarding scheduling of medical-legal consultations with Agreed or Qualified Medical Evaluators). The appointment letter must contain the time and place of the exam. At the time notice is given, the employer must also provide advance payment of mileage expense and bridge tolls under LC4600 (see 7.17).

Per LC4051, the employer's request must be reasonable in view of the employee's physical condition and must consider the employee's ability to attend the scheduled exam. The employee cannot be expected to attend an exam if the employee is hospitalized or does not receive sufficient advance notice that an exam is scheduled.

In litigated cases, CR10418 additionally requires the party who schedules a consultation to "notify all parties ... of any medical appointment scheduled for the purposes of a medical-legal evaluation" (see 7.79). If the employee has an attorney, the employer sends an appointment letter to the employee and a copy to the attorney or agent. Regardless of who schedules the consultation, CR10418 requires that notice be provided to the opposing party or its attorney "at the same time" that the employee "is advised of the appointment."

Employee's Rights

Some employees are inordinately suspicious of employer-selected physicians, suspecting that such doctors lack empathy and are paid to downgrade the employees' disabilities in their reports. It is a fact that benefits are provided to the employee based upon information that is contained in medical reports. Thus, it is understandable that employees are concerned about the contents of physician's reports on their conditions. However, various Labor Code sections give employees certain protections against possible inaccuracies in medical reports.

Certification of Consultant. Per LC4602, the employee may request the employer to obtain certification of the competency of any LC4050 employer-selected consulting physician. The procedure for doing this is explained in CR9796, and CR9799 explains the criterion for competency. The sole criterion for certification is that the physician's "field of practice is related to the injury or problem." The Administrative Director notifies the employee whether or not the employer's consultant is certified.

Certification might assuage the employee's qualms about attending the consultation. Additionally, this procedure could be useful from the employee's point of view by creating a delay in attending an exam. From the employer's standpoint, obtaining certification may be beneficial in later reviewing a consultant's opinion with the employee. The employee will receive a letter from the

Administrative Director that the employee might interpret as a stamp of approval of the physician by the State of California.

Employee's Physician Present. Employees have the right to have a physician of their choice accompany them during any employer-scheduled examination. Per LC4052, the employee exercises this right "at his own expense." An evaluation under LC4061 or LC4062 by a Qualified Medical Evaluator who was selected from a panel is not an employer-scheduled evaluation. However, the provisions of LC4052 appear to apply to a Qualified Medical Evaluator who is selected directly by the employer under LC4060 or LC4061 (see 7.78 and 7.81). Per LC4052, the employee exercises this right "at his own expense."

Rebuttal Consultations. Per LC4065, the employee has the unrestricted right to obtain medical opinions from any physician of his choice "at his own expense" at any time. However, it is more likely that the employee will only undergo consultations that are paid for by the employer. If the employer's reason for a consultation is actually an objection to a finding of the treating physician, the employee is then entitled to a consultation at the employer's expense. However, in this case, the employee would not possess an unrestricted right of selection since the consultant would have to be an Agreed or Qualified Medical Evaluator (depending upon which is required by LC4061 or LC4062; see 7.75).

7.53 CONSULTATION – FAILURE TO ATTEND

The employee's failure or refusal to attend any employer-scheduled consultation can *Not* adversely effect the employee's right to benefits. A "refusal" ordinarily refers to an outright oral or written refusal to attend an examination. It happens, but rarely. Ordinarily, the employee simply fails to attend.

Some employees will fail every scheduled examination and may provide seemingly valid reasons for each failure. Good reasons for failure to attend do occur, and the claimsperson may agree to reschedule an examination — once. However, it may concurrently be appropriate to advise the employee of the repercussions for an additional failed examination — regardless of the reason for an additional failure to attend. Repercussions for failure to attend a consultation are found in LC4053-LC4054, as explained below.

Failed Examination – Proceedings Suspended

Per LC4050, the employer has the right to request the employee to attend medical examinations, and an employee who is claiming compensation is required "to submit to examination at reasonable intervals." Per LC4053, "so long as the employee, after written request of the employer, fails or refuses to submit to such examination or in any way obstructs it, his right to begin or maintain any proceeding for the collection of compensation shall be suspended." Proceedings are likewise suspended if the employee fails to attend an examination by an Agreed or Qualified Medical Evaluator. Both LC4061 and LC4062 prohibit the filing of a Declaration of Readiness to Proceed with the WCAB until any evaluation that is required pursuant to these statutes has occurred.

During the period of the employee's failure to attend an examination, the employee cannot receive a WCAB award of benefits because the employee is not entitled to request any WCAB proceeding. Although not required, prudent practice warrants that the employer formalize the status of the employee's rights by requesting the WCAB to issue an Order Suspending Proceedings (that is usually done in conjunction with a request that benefits be barred pursuant to LC4054 as explained below).

It is the employee's right to WCAB proceedings that is suspended under LC4053, not the employee's right to workers' compensation benefits. The employee's failure to attend a consultation does not justify an automatic cessation of benefits. Benefits known to be due must be continued. As to disputed benefits, once the employee submits to an examination, the employee may be entitled to receive any retroactive benefits that have accumulated. It is possible for the employee to be barred from the receipt of benefits for failure to attend a LC4050 medical examination. However, this result will not occur unless the employer pursues its available recourse under LC4054 as explained below.

Failed Examination – Benefits Barred

Per LC4054, if the employee "fails or refuses to submit to examination after direction by" the WCAB or "in any way obstructs the examination, the employee's right to the disability payments that accrue during the period of such failure, refusal or obstruction, shall be barred." (Note that a disputed medical issue involving entitlement to disability benefits must be evaluated by an Agreed or Qualified Medical Evaluator per LC4061 or LC4062.) If the employee fails to attend an employer-scheduled consultation under LC4050, the employer has the right under LC4054 to request the WCAB to order the employee to "attend an examination." When the employer petitions the WCAB for this relief, its petition will concurrently request the WCAB to:

1. Issue an order suspending proceedings, AND
2. Issue an order directing the employee to attend a medical exam, AND
3. Issue an order that bars the employee's right to compensation under LC4054 for any period that the employee fails to submit to such exam.

The employer may request the WCAB to exercise its authority under LC5701 and direct the employee to attend a LC4050 examination by a particular physician, and a judge may allow this request if that physician is known by reputation to be competent and unbiased. Otherwise, the provisions of LC5703.5 will apply. A judge can refer an unrepresented employee to a Qualified Medical Evaluator "selected by the appeals board," subject to the employer's acquiescence to pay for the costs of an examination by such physician (see 7.77). If the employee fails to attend a LC4061 or LC4062 examination, the employer will request the WCAB to order the employee to attend the required examination with an Agreed or Qualified Medical Evaluator.

Disability benefits will not be barred unless a repeat failure occurs after the WCAB orders the employee to attend an evaluation. Suppose the employee thereafter fails an examination that the employer requests the employee to attend on January 1st but does attend an examination by the same physician on July 1st. If the physician reports that the employee is and has been continuously temporarily totally disabled, the employer is liable for temporary disability payments that accrue on or after July 1st, but it is not liable for any temporary disability payments from January through June (subject to the terms of the prior order of the WCAB barring benefits). If the physician reports that the employee's condition has been permanent and stationary since at least January 1st, the employee is entitled to receive the number of weeks of disability payments that are payable for his percentage of disability minus the number of weeks and days of permanent disability payments that have accrued during the period of January 1st through July 1st (see 10.18).

Failure to Attend – Excused

The employee can avoid a LC4050 employer-scheduled consultation but still be entitled to all benefits. The employee's failure to submit to an exam is excused if the employer does not provide proper notice or fails to provide advance mileage expense (but advance payment of one day of temporary disability for wages lost in attending the exam is not required; see 7.29). If the exam must be rescheduled, the employer may have continued liability for medical and disability benefits depending upon the contents of previously received medical reports.

7.54 MEDICAL REPORTS - GENERALLY

Physicians who undertake the treatment of injured employees have thereby subjected themselves to the reporting requirements of the workers' compensation laws. Claimspersons cannot practice medicine without a license. They are not qualified to determine the employee's medical and disability status. The only person so qualified is a physician. No matter how competent the physician is in treatment areas, the physician must also be willing and able to write and submit reports. Otherwise, the physician should simply refuse to undertake an exam or treatment.

Employers provide temporary disability, permanent disability and rehabilitation benefits to an employee based upon information contained in medical reports. A lack of reports impedes the employee's prompt receipt of any other benefits except medical treatment. Failure to submit reports can also result in a lack of rapport between the claimsperson and the employee. The physician may provide information to the employee that is not forwarded to the claimsperson. When the employee does not receive workers' compensation benefits timely, the employee may view the claimsperson as the problem rather than the physician. This, in turn, can result in the employee's desire to litigate a claim in the absence of any real disputes.

Common Contents of Medical Reports

All physicians who provide examination or treatment for a work-related injury are required to submit written reports of their findings. Mandatory forms are used to comply with some, but not all, reporting requirements. However, the need for consistency in the contents of reports from examining physicians is of the utmost importance. Guidance in this regard is found by coordinating the provisions of CR9785 entitled "Duties of the Employee-Selected Physician," CR10978 that is entitled "Physicians' Reports as Evidence," and LC4628 pertaining to medical-legal reports. Regardless of the date of injury or whether or not litigation is pending, a coordination of all of these sections reveals the type of information that is expected from every reporting physician as detailed below. (Note: LC4064 restricts the report of an Agreed or Qualified Medical Evaluator to a determination of "contested medical issues" only.)

1. **Date of examination:** regardless of when opinions are reported, this date controls changes in the employee's entitlement to benefits as well as the fee schedule that applies to the physician's charges.
2. **Date of report:** reports are referred to by this date in correspondence, and if supplemental reports are submitted without a re-exam, this date assists in identifying the chronology of reported opinions.
3. **Name of employee:** use of nicknames or multiple variations of names creates problems in communication and matching reports to files at the physician's office, the claim department, and the WCAB.
4. **Address of employee:** verification of a current address will always be appropriate, and notice of any change is beneficial so that correspondence or checks to the employee will not be mailed to an incorrect address.
5. **Employee's history of injury:** the physician is expected to ask appropriate questions to obtain a history that is complete in essential details (such as the date and mechanics of how the injury occurred) and to comment on the reason for any omission of such details.
6. **Employee's medical history:** a physician is expected to comment on any areas of omission, inaccuracies or conflicts between any information provided by the employee and that obtained from other sources, e.g. prior medical records, court records and/or an investigator's report that have been provided for the physician's review. Also, CR9785 specifically directs a treating physician to inquire as to "any significant prior injuries or disabilities."
7. **Employee's medical complaints:** a physician is expected to provide a professional opinion on the validity of the employee's self-reporting of areas such as the extent to which initial post-injury complaints vary from current complaints, the benefit derived from treatment that has been provided, the need for further treatment, and complaints that are either temporarily or permanently disabling.
8. **Medical treatment:** a medical diagnosis and prognosis; the nature, scope, frequency, and anticipated duration of treatment that is recommended; dates and results of any tests, studies or surgical procedures that have been performed; and names of all medicines that have been prescribed.

9. **Temporary disability:** starting and ending dates of periods of temporary total or partial disability; the date the employee was released to return to work; and, the physician's opinion as to work activities that can and cannot be performed or any temporary restrictions under which the employee could return to work while partially disabled.

10. **Rehabilitation:** an opinion as to the employee's medical eligibility for rehabilitation benefits based upon the extent of permanent disability, if any, that is expected to result after the employee has received the maximum benefit of medical treatment (see 11.15-11.17).

11. **Permanent and stationary status:** the date the employee's condition became or is expected to become permanent and stationary.

12. **Subjective disability:** a description of those factors of permanent disability that are entirely self-stated by the employee, and a physician's opinion as to the validity of each (see 10.29).

13. **Objective disability:** a description of all factors of disability that are determined by the physician, e.g. by measurements (see 10.28).

14. **Apportionment:** a clear identification of all factors of disability that resulted from the industrial injury and any other factors of disability that are present but have a different cause (see 10.39).

15. **Conclusions:** opinions formulated through application of the physician's expertise to the information derived from the evaluation process including reasons therefor and the source of all information reported as fact.

16. **Signature of the physician:** an original signature is required, not the physician's initials, not the physician's name signed and initialed by another person, not a faxed signature and not a rubber-stamped signature. These alternatives to an original signature do not comply with the statutory requirement that the reporting physician make a written declaration of the veracity of information included in a comprehensive medical-legal evaluation under penalty of perjury.

17. **Identity of participants:** the names and roles of anyone other than the physician signing a report who participated in the examination (which in most cases will include someone other than the physician but should not necessarily include everyone on the physician's staff) or participated in the nonclerical preparation of the report (that includes most everyone who did anything except type or spell-check the report).

If a physician requires instruction on the topic of report writing, the claims administrator can and should provide assistance. The physician may be provided with a copy of applicable administrative regulations (e.g. CR9785, CR10606, CR10978) or Labor Code Sections 4628 and 139.3 (pertaining to medical-legal examinations and to disclosure of significant beneficial ownership interests of Agreed and Qualified Medical Evaluators; see 7.73 and 7.80.) Alternatively, these multiple requirements may be consolidated into a form letter for distribution to all physicians.

7.55 DOCTOR'S FIRST REPORT

Per LC6409, every physician "who attends an injured employee shall file a complete report" to the employer's insurer. The sole situation where the physician is required to submit the report directly to an employer rather than an insurer is when the employer is self-insured (in this situation, the employer is the insurer). The form required for the physician's report is entitled "Doctor's First Report of Occupational Injury or Illness" (Form 5021). The insurer or self-insured employer is required to file a copy of the physician's report with the State within five days of receipt.

Regardless of who files a copy with the State, the original of the Doctors First Report form must be maintained in the claim file by the administrator of the employer's claims. (A correctly filled out form complies with the physician's CR9785 duty to submit an initial report; see 7.45.) An original signed medical report constitutes medical evidence, and the employer may be required to file the original of this report with the WCAB if the claim is later litigated.

The State compiles statistics from Doctor's First Report forms that classify injuries by nature, severity, and occupation and can provide a basis for implementation of safety measures designed to reduce the frequency or severity of industrial injuries. However, some data collected from physicians serves affiliated purposes. For instance, the requirement for physicians to provide an "ICD-9 Code" along with a diagnosis in item #20 on the form enables diagnoses to be reviewed using a common standard. An ICD-9 Code refers to use of the structure contained in the *International Classification of Diseases, 9th Revision,* developed by the U.S. Department of Health and Human Services. The ICD-9 codes have relevance for certain fee structures under federally funded programs that are not (at least not yet) pertinent to workers' compensation purposes.

Blank copies of currently required report forms are available from the State Division of Labor Statistics and Research (P.O. Box 420603, San Francisco, CA 94142), but employers and doctors can reproduce the form at their option. Per CR14005, persons reproducing the form "may rearrange the header block to permit imprinting" of certain individualized information such as their names, addresses or codings for internal purposes. The physician is permitted by CR14003 to submit reports to the insurer or self-insured employer by facsimile transmission, modem or other computer media (and it is anticipated that the physician's report, as well as the Employer's Report of Occupational Injury or Illness (Form 5020), will eventually be transmitted to the State in the same manner; see 2.22).

Since 1988, the employee has been required to complete a portion of the Doctor's Report form "describing how the injury or illness occurred." However, LC6409 provides that the employee's failure to do so "shall not excuse any delay in filing the form" by the physician, e.g. where the employee is in a coma. Per

LC6409, the physician is required to provide the required report "on forms prescribed for that purpose" to the insurer or self-insured employer "within five days of the initial examination." The insurer or self-insured employer is required to file such reports with the State "within five days of receipt." Per LC6413.5, a "physician who fails to comply" with any reporting requirements under LC6409 can be assessed a civil penalty of $50 to $200.

Per LC6412, "no physician's report" (as required by LC6409) "shall be admissible as evidence to bar proceedings for the collection of compensation, and the portion of any physician's report that is completed by an employee shall not be admissible as evidence in any proceeding before" the WCAB. All physicians' first reports are admissible as evidence in WCAB proceedings (and the court requires originals of medical reports to be filed). However, the employer is prevented from relying upon information from the employee in the physician's report as evidence to support a statute of limitations defense or to defeat the employee's entitlement to benefits (this restriction does not apply to civil or criminal proceedings; e.g. as evidence of fraud).

The restriction on the admissibility of the employee's written statement operates to protect an employee from being penalized by any honest but carelessly phrased statements that are made prior to obtaining advice from an attorney. This restriction does not however prevent the employer from otherwise proving the existence of any facts that may be derived from the employee's written statement; e.g. where the employee admits that an injury resulted from an altercation in which the employee was the initial physical aggressor (see 5.18). Nothing prevents the employer from presenting evidence that is admissible to prove necessary facts that would bar compensability, including testimony of witnesses, the employee's deposition, or other documents such as applications for other benefits wherein the employee repeated statements contained in the physician's initial report form.

Pesticide Poisoning

Ordinarily, LC6409 requires a physician to submit a Doctor's First Report of Occupational Injury or Illness (Form 5021) only to the employer's insurer (or the employer if self-insured). However, if treatment is provided for pesticide poisoning "or a condition suspected to be pesticide poisoning," the physician and the insurer (or self-insuring employer) are each required to submit a copy of the Doctor's First Report to the Division of Labor Statistics and Research.

Effective 1995, the physician is additionally required to "file a complete report within 24 hours of an initial examination with the local health officer by facsimile transmission or other means." An affidavit certifying that the required report was provided to the local health officer must accompany the report that is filed with the insurer/self-insurer. Per LC6409, the physician shall not be compensated for an initial diagnosis or treatment unless the insurer (or self-insurer) receives a report with the required affidavit attached. The employer is relieved of liability for payment for services rendered in conjunction with the report if a physician fails to report to the local health officer as required.

Review of Doctor's First Report

The Doctor's First Report (Form 5021) should be the first piece of medical information received by the claimsperson after an injury occurs. Information in this report should be compared to information contained in the Employer's Report (Form 5020; see 2.22). Potential issues to compensability may be apparent, and an investigation may be necessary. The physician's diagnosis may raise a question regarding industrial causation. Unfamiliar diagnoses or terms should be researched with appropriate medical personnel. If the only condition diagnosed was nonindustrial, the claim would be promptly denied.

Assuming no compensability issues exist, the claimsperson utilizes this report in several ways. The physician's prognosis indicates the severity of the injury. Referral to a medical specialist may be warranted and/or referral to a rehabilitation counselor (see 11.18). The physician's opinion of disability status provides the basis for commencing benefit payments to the employee. Initial reserves can be evaluated and posted to the claim, and the claimsperson can establish a diary date for the next claim file review (see 2.25).

Treatment Plan. The physician's recommendations for treatment should be reviewed carefully and in conjunction with the diagnosis and prognosis since the physician's initial findings and recommendations serve as a benchmark for monitoring an employee's recovery from the effects of an injury (see 7.47 and 7.56). Identification of deficiencies in an initial report should precipitate prompt communication with the physician; e.g., notification of reporting requirements is appropriate where a physician recommends treatment on an indefinite basis rather than for a finite period or reports disability without assessing the employee's current physical capabilities (see 11.17).

The Industrial Medical Council has promulgated a form (as required by LC139) for optional use by a treating physician. Per CR37, a primary treating physician "or the physician designated by that physician" can opt to use the Treating Physician's Determination of Medical Issues Form (IMC Form 81556) to render "opinions on all medical issues necessary to determine eligibility for compensation" pursuant to LC4061.5. Per CR37, this report form (that is available from the Industrial Medical Council) is referred to by its abbreviated title as the Treating Physician's Form. Any reporting format that provides necessary information is acceptable, and a final report from a treating physician will almost always be submitted in a narrative format.

7.56 PROGRESS REPORTS

Per LC4603.2, physicians who undertake treatment for work-related injuries or illnesses are required to submit periodic reports at intervals designated by administrative regulations. Per CR9785, a progress report is required "no less frequently than every 45 days or 12 visits with the physician or a provider prescribed by the physician, whichever occurs first, in the form and manner prescribed by the Administrative Director." (The physician is required to report, not to examine; e.g., the physician may report on the employee's progress as reviewed with a physical therapist).

As part of each progress report, a treating physician is required to explain any need for continuing treatment. The initial report that was required of the physician under CR9785 should have included the physician's opinion as to "the planned course, scope, frequency and duration of treatment, including an estimated date of completion of treatment." Any subsequent recommendation for new or continued treatment should be provided in conjunction with an appraisal of the progress of the employee's recovery from the effects of an injury or illness in view of treatment already received. One of three results is possible: the employee's condition improved, stayed the same or got worse. Physicians should bear in mind that they are preparing opinions for review by nonmedical personnel. Any improvement in the employee's condition is best expressed by comparison of the employee's separate physical capabilities before and after treatment was provided.

Per CR9785, there are specific circumstances and changes in the employee's condition that warrant a prompt reporting of such change. These include:
1. A change in temporary disability status.
2. A need for and/or hospitalization and/or surgery.
3. The disability has become permanent and stationary.
4. Any unexpected and/or significant change in the employee's condition.
5. Any significant change in a previously reported treatment plan.
6. A recommendation for a medical consultation.
7. A determination that the employee is medically eligible for vocational rehabilitation.

Additionally, the employer is entitled to receive a report whenever "the employer reasonably requests additional information." A physician is expected to present estimates of the duration of temporary disability, the extent of permanent disability, and the nature of anticipated future treatment. Updated information should be requested prior to the expiration of the disability period encompassed in the physician's previous estimate. The claimsperson must at all times have a medical report in file that pertains to the employee's present medical status. Time gaps in medical information cause gaps in the employee's receipt of benefits and may subject the employer to penalties for an unreasonable delay in the provision of benefits.

7.57 FINAL MEDICAL REPORTS

A final report means the treating physician's last report following the end of active treatment. This report should contain factors of permanent disability that enable the claimsperson to compute a permanent disability rating. The employee may be fully recovered without any permanent disability and without any need for further treatment; the employee may have permanent disability but be discharged from further medical care; or the employee's condition may be permanent and stationary and also require further medical treatment. The physician's opinions are the basis for the employer's assessment of its liability for further medical benefits or for lifetime medical benefits (and precipitate a review of the adequacy of claim file reserves; see 2.25). The doctor's report may be final only on the issues of temporary and permanent disability in which case supplemental reports will still be required on continued medical care.

A final medical report from a treating physician, regardless of how well written, will not necessarily be the final medical report that provides the basis for a determination of the employer's liability for the provision of further benefits. For 1994 or later injury dates, the treating physician's opinions on certain issues (such as the extent of permanent disability, the need for lifetime medical treatment or other issues that are specified in LC4061 and LC4062) may be rebutted by opinions of a Qualified Medical Evaluator (or an Agreed Medical Evaluator if the employee is represented; see 7.75).

7.58 FAILURE TO SUBMIT REPORTS

The offending treating physician may be one selected by either the employee or the employer. The employer can petition the Administrative Director to regain medical control if an employee-selected physician does not submit required reports (see 7.60). If the employer does not wish to change the treating physician but only requires a report, there are alternative measures in lieu of filing a petition for medical control. At some point it may be necessary to schedule an exam with another physician.

The first physician should be notified that any charges will be disputed if the expense of another physician must be incurred in order to obtain a report. The employer is simply telling the physician that it does not intend to pay twice for obtaining one report. The employer wants to know what benefits it owes, and the employer is perfectly justified in taking action that is necessary to enable it to provide benefits owed to the employee. It makes no difference who selected the delinquent physician. The employer should enforce the same reporting requirements on each and every attending physician.

7.59 MEDICAL RECORDS – ACCESS TO

Laws that protect employees from unlimited access to their medical records include the Freedom of Information Act, the Privacy Act and the Confidentiality of Medical Information Act (see CC56-CC56.37). Once an employee files a workers' compensation claim, the employer is entitled to full medical information regarding the industrial condition. Medical facilities will not release past medical records without a signed authorization from the patient or a subpoena. These facilities are concerned about lawsuits against them for improperly disclosing personal information relating to their patients. The claimsperson should be equally concerned in this regard. Information obtained for purposes of handling a workers' compensation claim should not be used or disseminated for any other purpose. Special privacy precautions that are required for claims involving HIV (human immunodeficiency virus) or AIDS (auto-immunodeficiency syndrome) are legally complex; clarification of laws impacting the handling of claims that involve these conditions should be obtained from legal counsel.

Physicians are not required to retain records indefinitely. The American Medical Association (AMA) can provide advice on the time requirements for maintenance of medical records. Records are sometimes retained beyond legally required periods. Further retention depends upon the policies of a medical facility and the space available for storing past records. The age of medical records is often directly related to their usefulness — the most beneficial records are usually the most current records available before an industrial injury.

The employee's right to receive copies of medical reports that are obtained as part of the processing of a workers' compensation claim is dealt with in CR9810. This administrative regulation requires the claims administrator to make copies of medical reports "available to the employee upon request," with the exception of "psychiatric reports which the physician has recommended not be provided to the employee." However, this CR9810 language does not necessarily preclude employees from access to their own psychiatric records.

The employee has the right to file an Application for Adjudication of Claim and request a WCAB resolution of this dispute. The WCAB has jurisdiction to determine if good cause exists to preclude the employee's access to medical records. Since recourse exists, the employer should evaluate the overall potential success of litigating the matter versus simply providing the employee with psychiatric records. A refusal to provide records should not be based solely upon a recommendation in a psychiatrist's report that lacks supporting rationale considering the facts of the case. The employee cannot object or agree to the findings of the treating physician if the employee is not provided with the opportunity to review the physician's findings. Thus, preventing the employee's access to medical records jeopardizes the potential for the prompt resolution of disputes utilizing the Qualified Medical Evaluator process (see 7.75).

7.60 MEDICAL RECORDS – OBTAINING

The employee is obligated to provide any information that pertains to the claim for workers' compensation benefits upon a request from the claimsperson. This includes signing a medical release where necessary to ascertain the nature and extent of the employee's alleged industrial injury. Per CR9783, the employee is required to sign a release if an employee-selected physician requires one as a prerequisite to the submission of information to the employer. The employee is not required to sign blanket authorizations or to release information that is not relevant to the claimed injury.

Medical releases can be hand-delivered by the employee, sent through the mail or personally delivered to the medical facility by a copy service. The employee may be willing to deliver a release and/or request a medical facility to act promptly in forwarding its records to the claimsperson. The employee's assistance can facilitate the handling of the claim where a decision on the payment of benefits to the employee is being withheld pending receipt of medical information. When a release is mailed to a facility and there is any urgency for receipt of the records, an accompanying letter should request telephone contact if records cannot be provided immediately. For instance, some facilities do not have copy machines, in which case it may be necessary to utilize a professional copy service.

Copy services deliver the medical authorization (or subpoena) and take a portable copy machine with them. The medical facility can require a fee for location, production or copying of the records. When a copy service is used, the service advances the charges and includes these in its bill. Copy services handle rush requests and may be the most expedient method for obtaining necessary records, but this method of procuring records is more expensive than a mail request.

If records are sought through use of a subpoena, LC4055.2 requires the "party who subpoenas medical records ... concurrent with service of the subpoena" to "send a copy of the subpoena to all parties of record in the proceeding." If a copy service obtains records using a subpoena, the copy service will serve a copy of the subpoena as required by LC4055.2. It is for this purpose that copy services routinely request names and addresses of parties to a claim. However, LC4055.2 does not require a copy service to serve copies of medical records obtained by subpoena on opposing parties. The use of a copy service to make extra copies and serve such records on other parties is entirely optional on the part of the requester of records. It is rare that this task cannot be performed in-house at less expense, but sometimes the extra expense is warranted due to time restraints.

7.61 MEDICAL RECORDS – PURPOSE OF REVIEW

Past medical records are relevant when an employee previously has had similar symptoms or has received treatment for the same condition or part of the body prior to claiming a work injury. From a claims standpoint, medical records serve three purposes:

1. To assist in a medical determination of whether or not an industrial injury has been sustained (a threshold issue for a compensability determination).
2. To enable a distinction between treatment provided for industrial versus nonindustrial conditions (a cost issue and particularly necessary in cases where the employee receives concurrent industrial and nonindustrial treatment for the same body part).
3. To document any preexisting disability that could provide a basis for an apportionment of permanent disability (a legal issue that needs to be addressed before a claim is concluded by settlement or trial).
4. To identify conditions that may complicate treatment (a medical control issue and a cost issue).

Past medical records are forwarded to physicians to assist them in formulating medical opinions based upon an accurate medical history. Sometimes a physician may learn of the existence of prior records during the course of an examination.

Whenever the physician comments on prior treatment or complaints, the claimsperson should follow up by arranging to procure any and all available medical records so the doctor can review these records.

After any party has filed an Application For Adjudication of Claim form with the WCAB, the employer has the right to subpoena the employee's medical records. (Nothing prevents the use of signed medical authorization forms to obtain medical records regardless of the date of injury.) Records of treating physicians could include the patient's chart, appointment sign-in sheets or any other office records pertaining to the patient. Hospital records could include the names of consulting physicians (whose records could also be subpoenaed) or prior X-rays of the same body parts to which a current injury is claimed.

A full review of available records may reveal relevant information that is not contained in any report submitted by the treating physician. This information may be of benefit in resolving disputes regarding the employer's liability for benefits and/or payment of medical bills. Not to be overlooked in terms of the records of treating physicians are the records of a personal physician or personal chiropractor who was designated in writing by the employee prior to an injury (see 7.46-7.49). Even when the employee's personal physician or personal chiropractor does not provide treatment for the current injury, prior treatment records should exist and may be relevant to a determination of issues involved in the current claim.

7.62 INTERPRETERS

During Treatment

Interpreter fees must meet the basic test of "reasonably required" before the employer has any responsibility for payment. It is improbable that an employee would first require the services of an interpreter after an industrial injury. The claimsperson can inquire about the employee's language abilities in the preinjury employment.

The employee and the treating physician may not speak the same language. The employee can not make known his complaints. The physician cannot explain the treatment program or give instructions on the use of medications. An interpreter would be a "reasonably required" solution to such a dilemma. However, there may be viable options that could avoid the need to incur professional interpreter fees. A physician who is bilingual is are the ultimate solution in the situation where the injured employee does not speak English. Alternatively, a physician may have bilingual employees on staff. Sometimes, the employee will prefer a friend or relative to serve as an interpreter. School age children sometimes have a better command of the English language than their parents and can serve quite adequately as interpreters should the employee so desire.

At Medical Examinations

Since 1994, LC4600 requires the employer to pay for interpreter services at medical examinations that the employee "submits to" at the request of the employer or the WCAB. (This language would appear to exempt the employer from liability for charges for a "no-show" evaluation since no services are rendered if the employee does not "submit to" a requested examination, but see CR9795.3.) The employer is liable for interpreter services only if "the employee does not proficiently speak or understand the English language." When owed, services must be provided by a "qualified interpreter," subject to specified sections of the Government Code. Per GC11435.05, "language assistance" is defined to mean "interpretation or written translation ... for a party or witness who cannot speak or understand English or who can do so only with difficulty."

The employer has a duty to notify the employee of the right to interpreter services and to make appropriate inquiries to determine the need for such services before the medical examination. (Per CR9795.5, the party who is designated to serve a notice of a WCAB hearing, deposition or other type of setting where interpreting services are recoverable under CR9795.3, is required to include a statement with such notice that explains the right to have an interpreter present.) The employer also has the burden of proof if it alleges that interpreter services that are requested by an employee are not reasonable. As a general rule, the employer will provide and pay for services of a qualified interpreter whenever an employee requests. It is usually deemed more cost effective to pay for requested interpreter services than to later litigate the issue should the employee complain of a lack of understanding of information that was communicated in English.

At Nonmedical Events

Per CR10564, a party who produces a witness in WCAB proceedings who requires interpreting services is responsible for arranging "for the presence of a *qualified* interpreter" (emphasis added; see above). For 1994 or later injuries, interpreter services for depositions and deposition-related events such as reviewing a transcript for accuracy are a covered expense under LC5710. Interpreter services at WCAB hearings and nonspecified "settings" (such as Rehabilitation Unit conferences) as required by the Administrative Director are covered under LC5811. (See CR9795.1-CR9795.4.)

Fees For Interpreting Services

Per LC4600, fees for services and expenses (e.g. travel time and mileage) of qualified interpreters are payable in accordance with a "fee schedule prescribed by the administrative director." This fee schedule is set out in CR9795.3, that also allows the employer to voluntarily utilize interpreters who are not certified as required by LC4600 and to enter into payment agreements for fees that are higher or lower than fee-scheduled amounts. Per CR9795.4, all bills for interpreter services are payable "within 60 days after receipt ... of the bill." The employer is required to pay uncontested amounts and to make a written objection to contested amounts (that includes specified details) within this period.

The reasonableness of charges for interpreting services is addressed in administrative regulations CR9795.1 - CR9795.4 and CR10564. For 1994 or later injuries where services are rendered in conjunction with a medical-legal evaluation, CR9795.3 sets out a schedule of reasonable fees for services of interpreters." Amendments to this fee schedule took effect 4/1/97 that apply to services rendered on or after this date. For instance, no distinction is currently made between interpreters of the Spanish language versus any other non-English language. Also, interpreters are currently entitled to be paid the greater of the rates set out in the Superior Court fee schedule in the county where services are rendered or "the market rate." This term is defined by CR9795.1 to mean an amount that " has actually been paid for recent interpreting services" (that the interpreter has the burden of establishing through submission of relevant documentation per CR9795.3).

Interpreter Certification – Qualifications

Per LC4600, the employer's liability is limited to services provided by a "qualfied interpreter," a term that is defined to mean one who is "certified, or deemed certified, pursuant to" GC11435.05-GC11435.65 or GC68566. Government Code Section 11435.30 requires the State Personnel Board to "publish annually an updated list of certified administrative hearing interpreters." Interpreters appearing on this list have "met minimum standards in interpreting skills and linguistic abilities," but do not necessarily have proficiency or even general knowledge of terminology or procedures germane to the field of workers' compensation law. This fact may give rise to objections to charges for services of even certified interpreters; e.g. where a party alleges it was adversely affected because an interpreter lacked understanding and thereby misconstrued and misinterpreted relevant terminology in a particular case.

Alternative certification criteria are found in GC68566. This statute defines a "certified court interpreter" as a person who "holds a valid certificate ... issued by a certification entity approved by the Judicial Council." Per GC68562, the Judicial Council approves entities such as a school, testing agency, or public agency (like the Division of Workers' Compensation) to certify language interpreters. However, per GC68562, the Judicial Council adopts "requirements for interpreting proficiency, continuing education, certification renewal... discipline ... standards of professional conduct," and guidelines for fees charged.

Per LC4600, "qualified interpreter" includes one who is "deemed certified" under the Government Code. Clarification is provided in CR9795.1 that enables use of noncertified interpreters for good cause where it is otherwise determined that "a qualified interpreter cannot be present." For medical examinations, the parties can agree to use an uncertified interpreter. Per CR9795.1, such interpreters are referred to as being "provisionally certified," a term with more positive connotations. Use of provisionally certified interpreters at WCAB proceedings or Rehabilitation Unit conferences is subject to approval of the person presiding at the proceeding.

7.63 TERMINATION OF MEDICAL BENEFITS

Medical benefits usually terminate when the employee is fully recovered from the effects of an injury, but the employee's right to benefits can terminate earlier.

Employees can settle their right to future medical benefits at the employer's expense (but only with the approval of the WCAB); this right is one of many that are customarily released as part of a Compromise and Release type of settlement. A statute of limitations may bar the employee's right to continued medical benefits regardless of the fact that continued treatment is unquestionably necessary for an industrial injury (see Chapter 6), e.g. after the period of time allowed to alter a WCAB award as discussed below. Some employees never fully recover from their injuries, and it is possible for an employee to be awarded lifetime medical (LTM) benefits.

A judge can award lifetime medical benefits when medical evidence supports a continuous need for future benefits. The WCAB award may be general and provide for "future medical treatment," or the terms of the award may be specific and limited to stated medical expenses, conditions or body parts. For instance, in drafting a stipulated settlement document for a single injury that involved treatment to the back and right eye, the claimsperson may include a stipulation (but only if supported by medical evidence) that the employer is liable for the provision of further treatment for the back only and not for the eye. A "lifetime medical" award is not always an award of lifetime medical treatment. Sometimes an award will limit the employer's liability to payment for repair or replacement of medical apparatus instead of treatment.

An award will be based upon medical evidence, but, once an award issues, the terms of the award will determine the extent of the employee's future benefits. The terms of a newly-issued award should be carefully reviewed upon receipt as a party may wish to seek reconsideration of the award (for one of the grounds specified in LC5903 "within 20 days after service of any final order, decision or award"). The terms of the award can also be changed if a case is reopened for good cause during a period of five years from the date of injury (that requires filing of a Petition to Reopen; see 6.26). After this time expires, the award remains unaltered for the employee's lifetime (although the WCAB retains jurisdiction to enforce the terms of the award should the existing terms be disputed).

7.64 MEDICAL EXPENSE – SELF-PROCURED

An expense is "self-procured" when it is incurred without prior authorization from the employer. The employee may claim reimbursement for treatment that was obtained and paid for. A physician may submit a billing where the employer has no prior awareness of the physician's involvement in the case. The employer may or may not be liable for the payment of self-procured expenses. A lack of advance authorization is not a sufficient basis for denying payment. The employer must review its liability for the expense after the fact. If the expense was "reasonably required to cure or relieve from the effects" of a compensable injury, the employer is obligated to pay for the expense under LC4600. The employer may dispute the amount of the charges incurred rather than its liability for the particular expense. A partial or reduced payment may be warranted.

The employer may have a valid defense to a self-procured medical expense in its entirety. Examples of situations that may relieve the employer from liability for self-procured expenses are:

a. The expense was not "reasonably required": the employer offered to provide all that was reasonably required, but the employee chose to incur an optional expense.

b. The treatment did not result in a cure or relief: the employee's condition deteriorated as a result of self-procured treatment, there was a lack of improvement or there was no noticeable effect whatsoever, and medical evidence existing before such treatment was procured recommended against such treatment.

c. The expense was not related to the effects of an industrial injury: the expense was incurred for a nonindustrial condition, a nonindustrial injury, or totally for the personal benefit of the employee.

d. The employee did not sustain an industrial injury: the occurrence of an injury or its compensability is disputed (when the employer takes this position, all of the employee's medical expenses will be self-procured unless and until the claim is determined to be compensable).

e. The industrial injury is not compensable: the employer admits an industrial injury occurred but has a defense to the claim in its entirety. Jurisdiction and statute of limitations are examples of such defenses.

f. The expense was not medical in nature: the employer has no statutory obligation to pay for nonmedical expenses such as grocery shopping, dog walking, laundry costs or lawn mowing. These expenses are a liability of the employee who incurs the expense. (See 1.9 and 10.3 regarding compensation versus damages.)

g. The expense involves fraud or deceit on the part of the employee; e.g., the employee asked the physician for pain medication, but the prescription was actually intended for and used by another person (see 5.14).

h. The treatment is provided by a physician or practitioner who is not properly licensed or qualified.

i. The treatment involves an illegality: it may be illegal for the treatment to be provided at all or for a particular individual to provide the treatment.

The employer may admit that the expense was reasonably incurred for an industrial injury. However, the employer may still deny any liability for payment of the expense. The Labor Code provides for situations where the employee will owe his own medical expenses. For instance, the employer would assert that the employee was personally liable to pay any incurred medical expenses in the following situations:

1. The employee did not have a right to select a treating physician of choice at the time the employee incurred treatment-related expenses.

2. The employee exercised the right under LC4605 to obtain treatment at the employee's own expense.

3. The employee exercised the right under LC4052 to have a physician of choice present "at his own expense" at an employer-scheduled exam.

4. The employee incurred a medical expense after a statute of limitations barred his right to benefits (see 6.3).

5. The employee obtained further treatment after a Compromise and Release settlement was approved that released the employer from liability for further medical benefits.

6. The employee incurred expenses that are not owed by the employer under the terms of a Findings and Award; e.g., the medical evidence upon which an award was based obligates the employer to pay for the repair and replacement of a knee brace, but the employee self-procured physical therapy to his shoulder.

7.65 MEDICAL EXPENSE – TREATMENT

Medical billings are reviewed to determine whether the medical provider should receive payment in full or in part. Any fees for nonindustrial treatment are deducted. Questionable items are identified, and clarification is requested from the provider. Billings from medical providers are usually compared to the *Official Medical Fee Schedule,* and the physician's bill may be reduced to scheduled charges for services (see 7.68).

Billing disputes with physician's offices can create animosity. Billing disputes can also result in the physician's refusal to continue to examine or treat the employee. Nevertheless, the claimsperson must resist payment for unnecessary or unreasonable medical expenses. When disputes arise, they must be resolved. If at all possible, billing disputes should be handled in a manner that will not cause any disruption in the employee's treatment program. Communication regarding billings should not involve the injured employee. Disputes should involve only the medical provider and the claimsperson.

Labor Code 3751 provides that after "an employee has filed a claim form" (see 6.12), "a provider of medical services shall not, with actual knowledge that a claim is pending, collect money directly from the employee." However, a physician (hospital or other medical provider) can seek payment directly from the employee if "the medical provider has received written notice that liability for the injury has been rejected by the employer" (a copy of a denial letter), and "the medical provider has provided a copy of this notice to the employee." Medical providers who violate LC3751 "shall be liable for three times the amount unlawfully collected, plus reasonable attorney's fees and costs." Although not set out in LC3751, the employee would presumably be the person entitled to recover all amounts improperly collected, the monetary penalty, and any fees and costs paid to an attorney.

Pursuant to LC4603.2, the employer's liability for "payment for medical treatment provided or authorized by the treating physician" does not arise until the employer receives a "separate, itemized billing together with any required reports" (see 7.54-7.58). The employer is obligated to pay any uncontested portion of each bill within 60 days after receipt of prerequisite information. Per CR9792.5, if a report and bill are received separately, the 60-day period commences on the date of receipt of "whichever is received later." As to contested amounts, the employer is required to advise the medical provider within the 60-day period of "the items being contested, the reasons for contesting these items, and the remedies available to the physician if he or she disagrees," except that the employer need only provide written advice that " a request has been made for an audit of the bill" when the "bill includes charges from a hospital, outpatient surgery center, or independent diagnostic facility."

If the employer fails to pay uncontested amounts and/or provide the required written notice about contested amounts within 60 days of receipt of prerequisite information, the employer owes the amount unpaid plus 10% of this amount as penalty plus interest computed at a daily rate retroactive to the date of receipt of prerequisite information. The rate of interest is the same as that owed on payments of WCAB awards (that was last increased to 10% in 1981). Should the WCAB later determine that the employer owes an unpaid amount that was timely contested, the employer owes the contested amount plus a 10% penalty plus interest at a daily rate "from the date the amount was due until it is paid." In this case, interest is owed from the 61st day after receipt of prerequisite information, not the date of receipt.

NOTE – Any interest or penalty that an insurer is obligated to pay under LC4603.2 will not affect the amount of the employer's premium. Such payments are not considered payment of a medical or indemnity expense, so they will not be included in the reserves posted to a claim file (see 2.25).

7.66 MEDICAL EXPENSE - PROHIBITED REFERRALS

Effective 1994, LC139.3 provides that it is unlawful for a medical provider to refer the employee to a person or facility in which "the physician or his or her immediate family has a financial interest" (a self-referral). For this purpose, "immediate family" is defined as including the physician's parents, spouse, children, and children's spouses (not included are such relatives as sisters, uncles, grandparents). A "financial interest" is defined in expansive terms and encompasses situations where any type of subterfuge is used to avoid detection of a prohibited financial arrangement.

General types of behavior that are prohibited by LC139.3 include self-referrals to owned facilities, schemes such as cross-referral arrangements (referrals in exchange for referrals from others) or almost any other type of profit-driven reciprocal arrangement. Physicians are precluded from offering or receiving payment "whether in the form or money or otherwise, as compensation or inducement for a referred evaluation or consultation." The intent of prohibiting certain referrals and financial arrangements is to ensure that a physician's decisions regarding the provision of medical examinations, treatment, and related services are need-oriented rather than profit-motivated.

It is important to note that LC139.3 does not prohibit every imaginable type of referral or arrangement that inures to the physician's financial interest. This statute does require a physician to disclose a financial interest (as defined) "to the patient ... in writing at the time of the referral," thus enabling inquiries to be directed to determine whether such interest is a prohibited financial interest. For example, referrals to sisters or brothers are not prohibited under LC139.3 unless such referrals involve a prohibited action such as a cross-referral arrangement or other financial benefit to the entities involved. Also, LC139.31 sets out many exceptions to activities that otherwise appear to be expressly prohibited under LC139.3; e.g. certain activities are not prohibited if the employer provides advance authorization.

Physicians are barred from claiming payment "for a good or service furnished pursuant to a referral prohibited under" LC139.3 (subject to exceptions set out in LC139.31). However, a burden of investigation is placed upon payors who are an insured employer, an insurer, or a self-insured employer. Per LC139.3, such payors are prohibited from paying "a charge or lien for any good or service resulting from a referral in violation" of this statute.

A payor has a vested interest in determining if a violation has occurred prior to payment, since there is also a penalty against a payor who pays a bill in violation of LC139.3. Although not specifically stated, it appears that a penalty would not apply unless the payor knowingly violated the statute. For instance, payors could violate LC139.3 by paying a physician who refuses to respond to reasonable inquiries regarding ownership of a clinical laboratory that tested blood urine or tissue at the physician's request. Payors can also violate the statute independently of any action of a physician; e.g. by offering a prohibited rebate or discount (the offer itself is prohibited, whether or not it is accepted by the physician).

The penalties for improper action on a physician's part are quite severe and are intended to operate as sufficient deterrents to prohibited acts. The lowest penalty for a violation of LC139.3 is a civil penalty of up to $5,000 that applies to a physician who engages in the misdemeanor offense of making self-referrals. Any other type of violation of this statute "is a public offense and is punishable upon conviction by a fine not exceeding" $15,000. An appropriate licensing board may also implement disciplinary action for a physician's violation of LC139.3.

As of 1994, LC5703 places restrictions on certain information that the WCAB can "receive as evidence ... and use as proof of any fact in dispute." With regard to disputed fees for reports of treating or examining physicians, statements "concerning any bill for services are admissible ... only if made under penalty of perjury that they are true and correct to the best knowledge of the physician." This provision applies regardless of whether a bill for services is actually prepared and submitted for payment by the physician's employee or other billing agent. A physician's "reports are admissible as evidence ... only if the physician has further stated in the body of the report that there has not been a violation of" LC139.3 (that prohibits certain referrals as discussed above) "and that the contents of the report are true and correct to the best knowledge of the physician." This statement must also be made "under penalty of perjury."

If a physician fails or refuses to provide the statements required by LC5703, the physician's report and/or bill are inadmissible as evidence. This statutory provision prevents a physician from seeking adjudication of a disputed billing during any period when the employer is precluded from utilizing the physician's report as evidence at any WCAB proceeding. Note that the physician's actions can also have an adverse impact upon other entities who seek payment for examination-related services such as X-rays or electrocardiograms. Until the physician will attest to the veracity of reported findings and billings, a shadow of doubt exists concerning the employer's liability for payment of any treatment or examination-related service in violation of LC139.3 (as discussed above).

7.67 REPORTS – PREREQUISITE TO PAYMENT

A report is required by LC6409 from every physician who renders treatment for an industrial injury or condition. Per LC4603.2, the employee-selected physician is required to submit a report as a prerequisite to payment, and the employer is not obligated to pay any physician's bills until required reports are received (meaning each separate report that is required by CR9785; see 7.54-7.57). Benefits cannot be provided to the employee unless the claimsperson has a medical report with up-to-date information on the employee's disability and treatment status. Payment of the physician's bills is secondary in priority to the provision of benefits to injured workers. Physicians are required to submit reports so that employers can promptly determine and provide full benefits to injured employees. Delays in reporting or inadequacies in medical reports adversely affect the employer's ability to fulfill its legal obligations to injured employees who are entitled to receive workers' compensation benefits.

The employer cannot determine its liability for medical expenses without a medical report because a report is necessary in order to make an intelligent review of the reasonableness of the charges included in a billing statement. Payment of medical billings prior to receipt of reports could encourage delays in medical reporting and therefore is not required. Payment is customarily withheld pending receipt of a medical report describing all services that appear on the billing statement. This policy creates some leverage in requesting and obtaining a medical report and inures to the benefit of the injured employee. It becomes economically advantageous for the physician to submit a report as soon as possible so his or her bill will be paid. Also, the employer is assured of prompt receipt of reports that enable it in turn to promptly provide benefits to injured workers.

7.68 OFFICIAL MEDICAL FEE SCHEDULE

The authority for an *Official Medical Fee Schedule* for workers' compensation billings is established by LC5307.1. This statute requires the Administrative Director of the Division of Workers' Compensation to "adopt and revise" this fee schedule "no less frequently then biennially." Per CR9791.1, persons wishing to purchase a copy of the latest revision of the *Official Medical Fee Schedule* or to obtain the separate Instructions for Payment of Inpatient Hospital Bills (see below) can request ordering information by writing to the Division of Workers' Compensation, (Attention: OMFS Order), P.O. Box 420603, San Francisco, CA 94142.

The *Official Medical Fee Schedule* was completely revised during 1993 (and has undergone subsequent revisions) and now encompasses many types of services that were previously omitted (e.g. the services of nonphysician practitioners such a acupuncturists, MFCC's, and physical therapists). However, the most significant distinction from the prior fee schedule is the current use of so called "CPT" codes from the *Physician's Current Procedural Terminology,* as published by the American Medical Association.

This CPT coding system lists services or procedures by descriptive phrases that are associated with a five-digit code number. This system represents a national standard in that many physicians already use CPT codes and descriptors for billings submitted to third-party payors of nonworkers' compensation patients (e.g. Medicare). However, for workers' compensation purposes, it is the Administrative Director who establishes the level of reimbursement that is deemed reasonable for each procedure that is encompassed within the fee schedule.

Unit values are assigned the various procedures that are listed and coded in the *Official Medical Fee Schedule.* The Administrative Director then adopts conversion factors (stated as dollar values) that are multiplied by the allowable unit value to determine the fee allowable for any particular procedure. The use of conversion factors allows the Administrative Director to revise the amount of fees that are deemed reasonable on a biennial basis (as required under LC5307.1) by changing only conversion factors without the necessity to change all descriptors code numbers or unit values. Current unit values are set out in CR9792.

The monetary value of any service or item that is listed in the fee schedule can be computed by simple arithmetic. Some companies have programmed fee schedule information into computers, and some provide billing review services for a fee. If a service is not used, then the responsibility for applying the schedule may be given directly to the claimsperson. The schedule itself contains necessary instructions for its use. A bill will not be paid promptly or in full if a physician inadvertently uses the wrong code number for the service provided, or code numbers are omitted from the billing statement. The physician's office is usually happy to correct such problems in order to be paid.

The *Official Medical Fee Schedule* no longer constitutes "prima facie evidence of the reasonableness of fees charged." Effective 1994, LC5307.1 provides that the Official Medical Fee Schedule "shall establish reasonable maximum fees" payable for medical services that are covered by the schedule (although exceptions continue to be permitted; see 7.69). From time to time, fees for additional types of services are included in the fee schedule. For instance, LC5307.1 was amended effective 1/1/94 to require that the *Official Medical Fee Schedule* include the maximum reasonable fees for services "for health care facilities licensed pursuant to" HSC1250 "and drugs and pharmacy services" that are provided on or after 1/1/95.

The Health Facility Fee Schedule, which is more commonly known as the Inpatient Hospital Fee Schedule, is compromised of definitions, billing codes, and instructions that are set out in CR9790.1 and CR9792.1. These administrative regulations were adopted effective 12/31/96 with a proviso that this fee schedule is effective only for "services on or after April 1, 1997" (but litigation regarding this fee schedule delayed the intended implementation date). For purposes of this fee schedule, CR9790.1 defines an "inpatient" as a person who is formally admitted "with the expectation that he or she will remain at least overnight and occupy a bed, even" though the employee is thereafter discharged or transferred to another facility prior to an overnight stay, e.g. due to an unexpected change in the employee's medical condition. Instructions for the application of the inpatient fee schedule are available from the address shown above.

7.69 MEDICAL FEE SCHEDULE – EXCEPTIONS

Per LC5307.1, medical providers are prohibited from charging higher fees for workers' compensation patients than for private patients. Subject to this limitation, nothing prohibits a medical provider from being paid reasonable fees that are accompanied "by itemization and justified by an explanation of extraordinary circumstances related to the unusual nature of the medical services rendered." Per LC5304, the employer can agree to pay charges in excess of fee schedule amounts. Also, LC5307.1 specifically exempts a physician's fee for services related to an initial comprehensive industrial medical-legal evaluation from application of the fee schedule that applies to nonmedical-legal examinations.

Fees exceeding fee-scheduled amounts are permissible. However, two key provisions of LC5307.1 act in concert to discourage requests for fees exceeding fee-scheduled amounts. For services rendered on or after 1/1/94, the *Official Medical Fee Schedule* specifies "reasonable maximum fees" and, as a general rule, higher fees are not deemed reasonable in the absence of "extraordinary circumstances" (that usually refers to complexity factors such as the types of issues involved rather than merely the length of time entailed in performing an evaluation. (See also CR9795 for a listing of complexity factors that affect fees allowed for medical-legal evaluations.)

Many factors will affect the employer's opinion of the reasonableness of fees charged on a particular case. Billing disputes create alienation and destroy rapport. In some areas, limited numbers of physicians are willing to provide examinations or treatment of workers' compensation patients. There is little reason to eliminate such physicians from future cases if they provide satisfactory treatment and write thorough reports. However, in any metropolitan area, there is no reason for the employer to authorize treatment by any physician whose fees are known to be exorbitant or unreasonable in comparison to fees of other physicians in the vicinity.

7.70 PROVIDER OBJECTS TO AMOUNT PAID

A physician who objects to a reduction of a bill will usually direct an inquiry to the claimsperson. The physician may have used the wrong fee schedule code number to describe the services performed, or the physician may have billed for services under the mistaken impression that he had authorization to perform such services. A reasonable explanation from the physician may convince a claimsperson to authorize payment in full, or the employer may be willing to compromise the disputed amount if the physician is willing to accept a partial payment as payment in full.

When services are provided for a compensable industrial injury, the physician cannot collect payment directly from the employee (see 7.65 regarding denied claims). The WCAB has exclusive jurisdiction to adjudicate such disputes per LC5300, and LC4903 provides a lien right to any medical provider. Occasionally, the physician or a collection agency may threaten the employee with the filing of a civil action for unpaid medical bills because they are unaware that the WCAB is the court of proper jurisdiction. The employee should not become an active participant in any billing disputes between a medical provider and the employer. The claimsperson can assist the employee by notifying the medical provider of the proper recourse for billing disputes.

7.71 MEDICAL-LEGAL EXPENSE – OVERVIEW

Per LC4620, "a medical-legal expense means any costs and expenses incurred by or on behalf of any party ... for the purpose of proving or disproving a contested claim." It would not be fair for the employer to succeed in a contested claim merely because the employee could not afford to obtain medical evidence that would otherwise result in a favorable WCAB decision for the employee. For this reason, the employer is obligated to reimburse an employee for specific medical expenses that an employee incurs "to prove a contested claim." The specific medical-legal expenses that the employer is obligated to pay, as listed in LC4620, are:

a. X-rays for diagnostic, not treatment, purposes.
b. Laboratory fees and fees for other diagnostic tests.
c. Medical reports: this expense includes a fee for a physician's professional services including an examination, history, review of records, necessary research and report preparation.
d. Medical testimony, e.g. a fee for the physician's time when the physician is requested to provide clarification of reported findings at a deposition.
e. Interpreter fees but only when needed.
f. Medical records, e.g. the costs to procure past medical records from physicians or hospitals when relevant to a current claim.

Treatment-related expenses are not medical-legal expenses. When the employee's right to receive medical treatment is disputed, the employee has a right to obtain a medical-legal report on this issue. However, the employee's right to reimbursement of medical-legal expenses does not include any expenses on the list above that were incurred for treatment rather than an examination.

For 1994 or later injuries, restrictions apply to the procurement of medical-legal evaluations ("by other than the treating physician" per LC4060) where compensability of an injury in its entirety is disputed on a medical, rather than a legal, basis (see 7.81). The employee does not have a right to obtain a medical-legal evaluation at the employer's expense until the employer has denied the claim or else the claim is presumed compensable under LC5402 (because the employer did not pay or deny the claim within 90 days; see 5.13). Once either of these threshold criteria have been satisfied and a claim form has been filed with the employer, LC4060 then restricts an employee's selection of a medical-legal consultant to a physician who is a Qualified Medical Evaluator or, if the employee is represented by an attorney, an Agreed Medical Evaluator (see 7.78). (Prior to the time that these threshold criteria are satisfied, LC4060 would appear to limit the employee's medical evidence to the of reports of treating physicians.)

A "contested claim" cannot exist before the employer "knows or reasonably should know that the employee is claiming entitlement" to some benefit arising from a "claimed industrial injury." Thus, regardless of the date of injury, a medical expense will not be incurred for the purpose of proving a contested claim unless and until the employer knows a claim is being made. However, LC4620 additionally requires that "one of the following conditions exists" before a "contested" claim exists:

1. The employer denies the claim in its entirety or "rejects liability for a claimed benefit." For instance, the employer may accept a back injury as compensable but deny liability for concurrent treatment of an underlying condition of obesity, high blood pressure or arthritis (This is a dispute as to the nature and extent of a benefits that are owed for an accepted claim, not a dispute as to compensability of the entire injury, so any medical-legal reports will be subject to LC4061-LC4062, not LC4060.)

2. The employer "fails to respond to a demand for the payment of benefits after the expiration of any time period fixed by statute for the payment of indemnity." For instance, an initial payment of temporary disability benefits is payable within fourteen days from knowledge of an injury and disability, but LC4650 also permits extensions of this time period.

3. The employer "fails to accept liability for benefits after the expiration of a reasonable period of time within which to decide if it will contest the claim." Debates on this topic abound, and time periods are found in a variety of Labor Code sections; e.g., for 1990 or later injuries LC5402 provides that 90 days from the filing of a claim form is deemed reasonable for this purpose. However, a shorter or longer period may be reasonable depending on the facts of a given case (and see the time limits that are set out in CR9793).

Per LC4621, the employee is precluded from obtaining a medical-legal evaluation at the employer's expense "during the first 60 days after" a claim form "has been filed." However, this waiting period does not apply where LC4061 or LC4062 require an earlier referral to a Qualified Medical Evaluator (to evaluate a contested finding of the treating physician in a compensable case). For 1994 or later injuries, if any injured body parts are accepted as compensable, a claim is considered a compensable injury, and requirements for evaluations to resolve disputed medical issues are controlled by LC4061 and LC4062 (see 7.75). The 60-day waiting period could apply when a referral to an Agreed or Qualified Medical Evaluator is required by LC4060 (subject to conditions explained above; e.g. where a claim is denied within the 60-day period). Also note that LC4061 and LC4062 do not require referrals to Agreed or Qualified Medical Evaluators if the medical determination that is being disputed was not made by a consulting, not a treating, physician.

There is a basic distinction between medical-legal consultations under LC4620 and consultations at the request of an employee under LC4601 or an employer under LC4050 (see 7.51 and 7.52). All consultations have the purpose of determining medical facts, and nonmedical-legal evaluations may involve an initial determination of whether a particular disability, condition or illness is work-related. However, only a medical-legal evaluation involves a "contested" medical issue. A medical-legal consultant is immediately placed in a forensic role which usually equates to higher fees being reasonable due to a greater expenditure of a physician's time. (See 7.71 regarding application of the medical-legal fee schedule to certain reports of treating physicians.)

The LC4620 definition of "medical-legal expense" includes costs that are incurred by the employee, the employer, the WCAB, and the administrative staff of the Division of Workers' Compensation (e.g. an Information and Assistance Officer who has authority under LC5703.5, "upon agreement of a party to pay the cost," to refer an unrepresented employee to a Qualified Medical Evaluator "selected by the medical director"). All medical-legal reports have been included within the LC4620 definition of "medical legal expense" so that one medical-legal fee schedule can apply regardless of the identity of the requester.

The meaning of a "party" who is entitled to reimbursement of medical-legal expenses as defined by LC4620 is explained in LC4621 that provides that "the employee, or the dependents of a deceased employee, shall be reimbursed for his or her medical-legal expenses reasonably, actually, and necessarily incurred." A lien claimant is not an employee or dependent. For this reason, a medical provider whose bill has been denied is not entitled to be reimbursed for the costs of a consultation by another medical provider for the purpose of obtaining an opinion that supports the lien claimant's right to payment.

Per LC3207, the word "compensation" means "every benefit or payment conferred by Division 4 upon an injured employee." Medical-legal expense is a benefit provided under Division 4 of the Labor Code, and an award of medical-legal expense is therefore an award of compensation. Per LC3600, the employer is not liable for payment of compensation unless specific "conditions of compensation concur" (see 5.8). One of these conditions is that "both the employer and the employee are subject to the compensation provisions" of the Labor Code. Some workers are not entitled to receive compensation because they are not defined as employees, and others who are defined as employees are specifically excluded from entitlement to compensation (see 4.24). Coordination of these statutory provisions reveals that an employee who is not entitled to compensation under LC3600 would not therefore be entitled to medical-legal expenses.

7.72 MEDICAL-LEGAL – PAYMENTS & PENALTIES

Per LC4622, the employer must pay bills for bona fide medical-legal expenses after receipt "of all reports and documents required by the administrative director incident to the services." The specific documents that are required are set out in CR9793. For services rendered on or after 8/31/93, a bill for a medical-legal expense is deemed "received" upon receipt of "an itemized billing, a copy of the medical-legal evaluation report, and any verification required" by CR9795 (that contains the medical-legal fee schedule and billing requirements). The Administrative Director of the Division of Workers' Compensation has also directed physicians to submit billings using an "HCFA 1500 (12-90)" form. The form itself is available from the American Medical Association, but physicians are required to complete the form according to special instructions that are available from the Administrative Director.

Per LC4622, payment (or an objection to payment) is due "within 60 days after receipt" of a written medical-legal billing and supporting documentation with one exception. The entire bill or a portion of the bill may be withheld if, within the 60-day period, the employer makes a valid written objection to the expense. The employer can become liable for the payment of interest and a penalty on any balance "for which the employer was liable" that remains unpaid after 60 days from receipt if:

1. The employer fails to provide payment and does not make an objection to an expense, OR
2. The employer does not make a timely objection (e.g. before expiration of the 60-day period), OR
3. The employer makes a timely objection that is later determined to be invalid by the WCAB.

The amount of the penalty and the rate of interest are specified in LC4622. Interest accumulates at "the rate of 7% per annum" from the date of receipt of the bill until the date of payment. (Note: the rate of interest that applies to compensation payable under a WCAB award pursuant to LC5800 and to late payments for medical treatment expense pursuant to LC4603.2 are controlled by the Code of Civil Procedure; since 1981 and until the next change, this interest rate is 10% pursuant to CCP685.010 and CCP685.020.)

The late payment penalty is a straight 10% of the unpaid balance of the bill. The interest and penalty are not cumulative: the employer does not owe a penalty on the interest it pays, nor does it owe interest on the amount of the penalty. The interest and penalty are computed separately, and each is added to the amount of the unpaid bill. The longer that the employer waits to provide payment, the greater the interest that will accrue. However, the penalty remains the same regardless of the time that transpires between receipt of the bill and payment.

SAMPLE (a). A medical-legal expense of $600 is paid one year after receipt.

Penalty: 10% = .10 × $600.00	$ 60.00
Interest: 7% = .07 × $600.00	+ 42.00
Total of penalty and interest	$102.00
Amount of unpaid bill	+600.00
Total Payment Due	$702.00

SAMPLE (b). The employer voluntarily paid $200 of a $500 bill within 60 days but neglected to object to the balance. The employer decides to make a voluntary payment of the remaining $300 on the 100th day after the bill and report were received.

Interest for one year: 7% = .07 × $300.00 = 21.00
Daily rate of interest: $21.00 ÷ 365 days/yr = $00.05753

Amount of Unpaid Bill	$300.00
Penalty (10% × $300.00)	30.00
Interest (100 days × .05753/day)	+ 5.75
Total Payment Due	$335.75

The employer has historically had a basic obligation to provide prompt payment of bills that are owed. Since 1991, LC4625 has specifically required prompt payment according to the terms of LC4622 for all medical-legal charges that do not exceed amounts deemed reasonable under the applicable medical-legal fee schedule (see 7.74). Per LC4622, if the employer is liable for the payment of a medical-legal expense and does not dispute the reasonableness of the full amount billed, the employer is required to provide payment of the uncontested charges within 60 days of receipt of required documentation. Otherwise, the employer will owe a penalty and interest on the unpaid charges. (None of the statutes that require payment of medical-legal expenses require payment of bills that are inappropriately labeled as a "medical-legal" billing.)

LC4622 also addresses the situation where the employer paid charges that were believed to be reasonable and did not exceed fee-scheduled amounts before the employer received information that constituted a valid basis for an objection. For instance, a delayed response to an inquiry to a licensing agency revealed that the physician was not properly licensed, or based upon information obtained from the employee in a deposition, fees were paid for a medical-legal evaluation conducted with the participation of prohibited participants under LC4628 (7.73). Conceivably, the employer could protect itself against this eventuality by providing a general written objection with payment of any currently undisputed amounts, e.g. a notice of the employer's intent to seek reimbursement at any future time when it becomes aware of facts that reveal that the employer was not liable for an amount that was paid. (Nothing prevents the employer from making a valid objection to payment of medical-legal expenses under such circumstances at any time during or after the 60-day period in LC4622.)

Per LC4622, if the employer makes an objection within the 60-day period to an amount billed at or below an applicable fee-scheduled amount and the WCAB sustains the employer's objection, the WCAB "shall order the physician to reimburse the employer for the amount of the paid charges found to be unreasonable." The manner in which the employer seeks this reimbursement is specified in LC4625: "if the employer contests the reasonableness of the charges" that it has paid, "the employer may file a petition with the appeals board to obtain reimbursement of the charges from the physician that are considered to be unreasonable."

Confusion is likely whenever multiple statutes specify requirements on a solitary topic. Some people think that as long as the amount a physician charges does not exceed the amount that is presumed reasonable under the medical-legal fee schedule, the employer has no right to object to payment and owes a penalty and interest if the full amount billed is not paid within the 60-day period in LC4622. However, there is no statutory provision that requires the employer to pay a physician's charges as submitted simply because they do not exceed fee-scheduled amounts. The employer is never required to pay charges that are unreasonable (e.g. charges for services that were not rendered; see 7.73). Whenever the employer can prove that charges billed are unreasonable, the WCAB will not order the employer to pay such charges, and the employer will therefore not be ordered to pay a penalty or interest on such charges.

7.73 MEDICAL-LEGAL – OBJECTION TO PAYMENT

The employer's liability for medical-legal expense is limited to specific items that are listed in LC4620, and LC4621 requires that the expense of such items must be "reasonably, actually, and necessarily incurred." Furthermore, LC4621 provides that reasonableness and necessity issues "shall be determined with respect to the time when the expenses were actually incurred." In combination, these two Labor Code sections provide the basis for valid objections to medical-legal billings (see also 7.80 and CR9793-CR9795). Some, but not all, of the objections the employer may raise are:

a. The charges are for treatment, not an exam: the costs of self-procured treatment are not an expense necessary to prove a contested claim.
b. The charges are for services that were not actually provided, e.g., the employee did not undergo laboratory tests or X-rays.
c. The expense was not necessary "to prove a contested claim" because benefits were not disputed at the time the expense was incurred; e.g., the bill is for an evaluation of temporary disability status, but the employer was providing temporary disability benefits at the time of the evaluation.

d. The expense was not necessary at the time it was incurred; e.g., a "medical-legal examination," was performed before the employer was informed that any medical issue was contested, or a previously performed diagnostic test was repeated without good cause.

e. The expense was not reasonably incurred: the expense is for an unreasonable duplication of a previously performed examination or service; or the medical expenses appear to be procured without any purpose other than to increase the financial obligations of the employer.

f. The amount of the charges are unreasonable; e.g., the billing represents an inordinately high charge for services compared to industry standards, and no reasonable explanation has been provided to support the deviation (see 7.74).

g. Required documentation was not submitted: a bill was received for a medical-legal examination, but the physician did not submit a medical report or any currently required billing form (see 7.72).

h. The person claiming reimbursement of medical-legal expenses is not an employee or dependent who is entitled to compensation; e.g., the person is an independent contractor, an employee who is excluded from coverage under the workers' compensation laws or a lien claimant.

i. The person who provided a medical service was not properly licensed or qualified, e.g. an orthopedist conducts psychological testing as part of an evaluation for a knee injury, or a psychiatrist did not possess a valid license to practice medicine in California at the time of a medical-legal evaluation.

j. The physician utilized the services of prohibited participants or failed to make the written disclosures that are required by LC4628 (as explained below).

Evidentiary Value of Report. Per LC4620, the employer is not liable for any related costs of a medical report "unless the report is capable of proving or disproving a disputed medical fact, the determination of which is essential to an adjudication of the employee's claim for benefits." (The legislation that amended this language in LC4620 effective 4/3/93 contained a statement that the amended language was declaratory of existing law, not new law.) A physician's failure to use a required reporting format is not determinative on the issue, since LC4620 requires that the WCAB "give full consideration to the substance as well as the form of the report, as required by applicable statutes and regulations." Greater emphasis is placed upon substantive defects such as the physician's omission of key issues or failure to adequately support opinions.

If a so-called "medical-legal report" does not meet required criteria, the employer is not liable for any medical-legal expense incurred "incidental to the production of a medical report." By successfully disproving the evidentiary value of the medical report, the employer can eliminate liability for such affiliated expenses as diagnostic tests and interpreter fees. The provisions of LC4620 eliminate the need for the employer to separately litigate its liability for such incidental expenses.

Diagnostic Tests. Since 8/31/93, CR9794 specifically restricts an employer's liability for payment for diagnostic testing performed in conjunction with a medical-legal evaluation. The employer is not liable for any cost for diagnostic testing unless the physician's report includes "the subjective complaints and physical findings that warrant the necessity for the tests." Also, charges for diagnostic tests will not be recoverable as medical-legal expense "if adequate medical information is already in the medical record provided to the physician" (unless the employer preauthorizes such tests). (See also 7.66.)

Prohibited Participants. Effective 1990, LC4628 prohibits persons other than the "physician who signs a medical-legal report" from any involvement in the examination or the "nonclerical preparation of the report" with two exceptions: the physician is permitted to delegate "the initial outline of a patient's history or excerpting of prior medical records," and a nurse may perform "functions routinely performed by a nurse, such as taking blood pressure." The physician retains full responsibility for ensuring the accuracy and completeness of information contained in a report. Repercussions for a physician's use of prohibited participants and/or failure to disclose permissible participants include: the report is inadmissible as evidence; the employer does not owe payment of any "expense incurred in connection with the report"; and, a WCAB judge can assess the physician with a civil penalty of up to $1,000 for each separate violation.

Overhead and Clerical Expense. Permissible charges are restricted by LC4628 to "direct charges for the physician's professional services." Such charges are defined to include "reasonable costs of clerical expense necessary" to produce the report and "reasonable overhead expense." A valid objection may be made where the employer can establish that the amount billed for the physician's services includes excessive clerical expense or overhead expenses of any person or entity other than the examining physician.

Independent Contractor Physician. Since 9/30/92, LC4628 requires certain entities who submit bills for services performed by another to disclose amounts paid to independent contractors who performed services relative to the evaluation. The required disclosures enable the employer to investigate its liability for the payment of medical-legal expenses related to the physician's services. For instance, the employer would raise an objection to the reasonableness of a medical-legal billing if a physician performed a medical-legal evaluation for a flat fee of $500, but a biller seeks payment for $1400.

Declaration Under Penalty of Perjury. Since 1990, a physician's failure to comply with any provision of LC4628 eliminates the liability of the employer for any expense involved and makes a report inadmissible as evidence. Since 9/30/92, the physician who signs a medical-legal report is required to include a declaration "under penalty of perjury" attesting to the veracity of each required disclosure. This declaration "shall be dated and signed by the reporting physician and indicate the county wherein it was signed." In addition, the signing physician is specifically required to attest or disclose:

1. The "date when and location where the evaluation was performed."
2. That the "physician or physicians signing the report actually performed the evaluation."
3. Whether there was full compliance with the "guidelines established by the Industrial Medical Council" (or the Administrative Director of the Division of Workers' Compensation pursuant to LC139.2), and if not, a detailed explanation for any variance.
4. The "name and qualifications" and nature of involvement of any person(s) "who performed any services in connection with the report" that were not clerical in nature.

Curriculum Vitae. As of 1994, LC4628 entitles the employer to certain information from "the physician who signs the medical-legal report." If the employer so requests, LC4628 requires the physician to "provide a curriculum vitae ... and include a statement concerning the percent of the physician's total practice time that is annually devoted to medical treatment." (A "curriculum vitae" is a document that describes the physician's qualifications; it usually includes information on such topics as licensing or certifications held, professional background, and any special areas of training, achievement or expertise.)

The curriculum vitae information that is provided by the physician pursuant to LC4628 may indicate one or more valid defenses to medical-legal expenses; e.g. if the physician does consultations only, the physician lacks the necessary qualifications to perform an evaluation as a Qualified Medical Evaluator (see 7.75). No time period is specified in LC4628 for the employer to make its request. However, it is appropriate to seek such critical information at the earliest possible opportunity and in advance of any services being rendered by the physician. For instance, a request may be initiated immediately upon receiving notice that an appointment has been scheduled with a Qualified Medical Evaluator who was selected by the employee's attorney.

Dispute Resolved Before Examination. Occasionally, a dispute will be resolved by the parties to a claim after a medical-legal evaluation has been scheduled. If there is no longer any reason for an evaluation to be performed, CR9793 requires the employer to notify the physician of this fact in order to avoid liability for payment. A physician is not entitled to payment for a medical-legal examination that is performed after the required notification is received. However, a physician who acts as an Agreed or Qualified Medical Evaluator is entitled to payment if a report for an examination that was performed prior to the employer's notification is timely served on the parties as required pursuant to LC139.2 (within 30 days; see 7.80). These limitations on the employer's liability under CR9793 apply to all costs relative to a medical-legal evaluation; e.g. diagnostic testing, laboratory services and x-rays. For this reason, the employer will want to provide the required notice to all involved medical providers, not just the examining physician.

Valid Written Objection. The employer makes a valid objection to a medical-legal expense by providing written notice of the amount of the expense that is objectionable and the precise reason for its objection. Objections to only a portion of an amount billed must be identified as such (see CR9794). For instance, if the employer objects to a medical provider's use of a particular procedure code in a billing, the employer's objection should include a reference to the procedure code that the employer believes is reasonable under the applicable fee schedule. Per LC4622, the objection must be served on the provider of services and the injured employee, or, when represented, the employee's attorney.

The employer's failure to provide a written objection does not invalidate certain defenses that the employer may raise pursuant to LC4620(b) and (c). For instance, the employer is not obligated to provide a written objection to a "medical-legal" billing where no contested claim existed at the time the expense was incurred or where a medical report is not capable of proving or disproving any disputed medical fact.

As of 1994, LC5703 restricts the use of an examining physician's report or billing statement as evidence unless required statements and disclosures are provided under penalty of perjury (see 7.66). If a physician fails or refuses to provide the required attestations, the WCAB is precluded from receiving the physician's report or bill as evidence: that, in turn, relieves the employer from liability for payment for a medical-legal evaluation. Per LC4620, the employer is not liable for the costs of medical evaluations nor any adjunct costs (e.g. for testing or interpreter fees) "unless the medical report is capable of proving or disproving a disputed medical fact ... " A report that is inadmissible as evidence cannot constitute proof of any fact(s).

Many objections that apply to medical treatment-related expenses also apply to medical-legal expenses. For a discussion of objections to payment for medical treatment and examination-related expenses, see 7.64.

7.74 MEDICAL-LEGAL – FEE SCHEDULES

Per LC5307.6, the Administrative Director is required to "adopt and revise a fee schedule for medical-legal expenses as defined by" LC4620. This fee schedule is separate from the fee schedule created under LC5307.1 that pertains to treatment related expenses (see 7.68). The medical-legal fee schedule that is required by LC5703.6 is set forth in CR9795 (effective 8/3/93). The medical-legal fee schedule in CR9795 applies only to cases where a medical-legal examination is performed on or after 8/3/93, the operative date of this regulation. (Effective 1/28/94, a separate fee schedule in CR9795.3 applies to fees and expenses of interpreters who provide services in connection with a medical-legal evaluation.)

The medical-legal fee schedule applies to all (not just "initial") "comprehensive medical-legal" evaluations and includes fees for follow-up examinations and supplemental reports by the same physician. Per CR9795, "complexity of the evaluation is the dominant factor determining the appropriate" fee allowable under the current fee schedule (not just the time involved).

Pursuant to LC5307.6, the medical-legal fee schedule shall consist of "a series of procedure codes, relative values, and a conversion factor." The relative values for various procedures are based on "the relative complexity of various types of medical-legal evaluations, the amount of time spent by the physician in direct contact with the patient, and the need to prepare a written report."

The fee schedule itself, that appears in CR9795, provides that the "fee for each procedure is calculated by multiplying the" designated "relative value by" a specific dollar amount (originally established at $10) and "adding any amount applicable because of" permissible modifiers. For instance, the procedure code ML102 that refers to a basic evaluation is assigned a relative value of 50, and $10 × 50 = $500, using a conversion factor of $10 for the date of the evaluation. The use of permissible modifiers enables fees for an evaluation to be increased by a set percentage based upon factors that ordinarily warrant a greater expenditure of the physician's time. For instance, the $500 fee in the example would be increased by 10% if an interpreter was necessary and an additional 25% if the physician was also an Agreed Medical Evaluator (see 7.78) for a total of $675 ($500 + $50 + $125).

The "procedures" referred to by CR9795 are actually types of evaluations. Different relative values are established for evaluations that are basic, complex, involve "extraordinary circumstances," are follow-up examinations, or involve a supplemental report (as defined in CR9793 and CR9795). Each type of evaluation is described by its distinguishing complexity factors. Physicians who bill for a procedure (evaluation) that has a higher relative value than a "basic medical-legal evaluation" are required to specify the complexity factors that warrant a higher fee.

For "evaluations involving extraordinary circumstances," the physician is additionally required to provide a "verification under penalty of perjury of the total time spent by the physician" in performing each of the separate activities that comprise the total hours billed. In this situation, unlike any other medical-legal evaluation, the physician's services are billable at a specified hourly rate, that is also the reason why it can be said that the current fee schedule does not actually set a "maximum" fee.

The Labor Code does not prohibit medical providers from charging usual and customary fees that exceed fee-scheduled amounts (except medical providers are prohibited from charging higher fees for workers' compensation patients than for other patients). However, the provisions of LC5307.6 make it difficult for medical-legal providers to recover fees in excess of fee-scheduled amounts. Requests for higher fees always require itemization and explanation of the circumstances that justify a higher fee. The medical-legal provider is additionally required to show that "extraordinary circumstances justify a higher fee." If this issue is contested, the provider can recover a fee for testimony before the WCAB if: the medical provider testifies pursuant to the employer's subpoena; the WCAB determines the dispute in favor of the provider; and, the WCAB determines that a fee exceeding the fee schedule is justified by extraordinary circumstances. Otherwise, the physician might recover higher fees but will not be paid for the time spent testifying.

Providers of medical-legal services are specifically prohibited from requesting or accepting fees in addition to those authorized pursuant to LC5307. A lengthy listing of techniques by which a provider might attempt to recover prohibited fees is contained in LC5307 (e.g. by "a discount, rebate, refund ... whether in money or otherwise, from any source"). The prohibition applies regardless of whether higher fees are sought directly or through some type of intermediary person or process. Physicians who attempt to collect higher than allowable fees are "subject to disciplinary action by the appropriate licensing board" and, if the provider is a Qualified Medical Evaluator, by the Industrial Medical Council as well. Note that, since 8/3/94, CR9794 requires physicians to "keep and make available to the administrative director upon request" for a period of three years "copies of all billings for medical-legal expense" filed "by date of examination."

Multiple fee schedules can apply to services that are rendered in conjunction with a medical-legal evaluation. The professional fees of an evaluating physician are subject to the medical-legal fee schedule. Fees for interpreter services necessitated by a medical-legal examination are subject to the fee schedule set out in CR9795.3. Since 7/1/84, LC4626 specifically provides that "all charges for X-rays, laboratory services, and other diagnostic tests provided in connection with an industrial medical-legal evaluation shall be billed in accordance with the official medical fee schedule" (see 7.68-7.70). The reasonable value of such services does not increase when a claim is contested, so it is not reasonable for a provider to charge higher fees merely because services were rendered in conjunction with a medical-legal type of examination. If expenses are incurred on multiple dates, the applicable fee schedule is the one in effect on the date when each expense was incurred.

For 1994 or later injuries, all evaluations by an Agreed or Qualified Medical Evaluator that are required by LC4061 or LC4062 will be medical-legal evaluations because such evaluations are not required absent a need for medical evidence to resolve a contested medical issue. A treating physician's fees can also be payable pursuant to the medical-legal fee schedule. However, the medical-legal fee schedule will not apply unless the fees are incurred for an evaluation that is not treatment-related, and the expenses meet the LC4620 definition of a "medical-legal expense" and satisfy criteria specified in CR9793. For instance, the report must address a "disputed medical fact or facts specified by" a party, or the report must be "capable of providing or disproving a disputed medical fact essential to the resolution of a contested claim." Per CR9795, any fees of a treating physician that are payable pursuant to the medical-legal fee schedule are payable at 80% of the value that would otherwise be payable for a scheduled procedure.

7.75 QUALIFIED MEDICAL EVALUATOR – OVERVIEW

————Filing of Claim Form with the Employer is a Prerequisite to an Evaluation
By an Agreed or Qualified Medical Evaluator at the Employer's Expense ————

Creation and Goals

Since 1991, LC139.2 has required the Industrial Medical Council to establish criteria for appointment, reappointment, and termination of appointment of Qualified Medical Evaluators (QMEs). The function of these evaluators is the provision of expert opinions, not treatment, for 1991 or later injuries where a claim form has been filed. Use of especially qualified medical evaluators is intended to accomplish several goals: to reduce the number of, and thereby the employer's costs for, medical evaluations; to expedite the evaluation of medical issues thereby enabling the expeditious provision of benefits that are due; and, to reduce unnecessary or premature litigation of medical issues. Additionally, the State's monitoring of the reports of Qualified Medical Evaluators is ultimately intended to result in the establishment of standardized procedures for improving the general quality of the medical reports of all physicians.

Qualifications & Appointment

A physician seeking appointment as a Qualified Medical Evaluator must complete a detailed application form. This form (and/or a list of evaluators who have been appointed) is available from the Industrial Medical Council, P.O. Box 8888, San Francisco, CA 94128.

Besides specific experience and credentials (that differ for physicians, chiropractors, and psychologists), the qualifications for appointment of Qualified Medical Evaluators as set forth in LC139.2 include a requirement that a physician devote at least one-third of "total practice time to providing medical treatment." Physicians who are otherwise exceptionally well qualified (including physicians who are retired) may also be appointed, but "in no event shall a physician whose full-time practice is limited to the forensic evaluation of disability be appointed."

A physician is also required to pass a written examination that is "administered by the Industrial Medical Council for the purpose of demonstrating competence in evaluating medical issues in the workers' compensation system" (except that a limited number of physicians who were involved in drafting the exam are not required to take the exam). Details regarding appointment and reappointment are set out in CR10-CR20. (See 7.26 regarding a physician's guide that is available from the Industrial Medical Council.)

Pursuant to Business and Professions Code 730, when QME status is required to perform an evaluation, a physician's failure to be properly appointed as a Qualified Medical Evaluator constitutes unprofessional conduct and is grounds for disciplinary action. However, performing an evaluation for which QME status is required without having such status does not constitute unprofessional conduct under BPC730 if the physician possessed QME status at the time of assignment to a QME panel or, for represented employees only, was certified as a QME at the time of a referral. Advertisements regarding services of Qualified Medical Evaluators must comply with restrictions specified in LC139.43-LC139.45 and CR150-CR159.

Qualified Medical Evaluators are appointed for two-year terms, and they may be reappointed upon request for subsequent two-year terms, subject to payment of a required fee. (Per LC139.2 fees for appointment or reappointment are "deposited into the Industrial Medicine Fund to be used for administration of the Industrial Medical Council"). Per LC139.2, physicians seeking reappointment must continue to meet the qualifications required for initial appointment as a Qualified Medical Evaluator and must satisfy requirements for continuing education as approved by the Industrial Medical Council (CR50). Also, the physician must avoid submission of reports that fail to meet the IMC's minimum reporting standards (LC139.2 specifies procedures whereby the WCAB will notify the Industrial Medical Council of defective reports; see 7.80). The Industrial Medical Council has authority to suspend or terminate an appointment or place an evaluator on a probationary status. Effective 8/31/94, procedures that govern disciplinary actions involving Qualified Medical Evaluators are set out in CR51-CR53.

Per LC139.2, the Industrial Medical Council is required to cite a Qualified Medical Evaluator for certain violations of rules and regulations promulgated by the Council (including a failure to conduct an examination or submit a report within required time periods) but only after five or more repetitions of a particular violation within a two-year period. The Council's authority to terminate the appointment of a Qualified Medical Evaluator after a hearing is discretionary, with the solitary exception that a current term of appointment shall be terminated if the physician loses the license required to practice in California.

When & Why Use is Required – Brief Summary

The mandatory evaluation process is designed to expedite a determination of certain disputed findings of treating physicians. The two most commonly disputed medical issues involve the extent of permanent disability benefits that are payable and a determination of the employee's entitlement to lifetime medical benefits. A formal medical evaluation by an Agreed or Qualified Medical Evaluator is required if a party disputes the treating physician's determination of these two medical issues, and the State will serve the parties with permanent disability ratings that are calculated from these evaluations.

A formal evaluation is also mandatory when a party disputes treating physician's findings on any other medical issue. Notices are required under various circumstances to inform all employees of their rights and the procedures for obtaining a formal medical evaluation. Intended compliance with the requirements regarding resolution of disputed medical issues is not left to chance: no WCAB proceedings will be conducted to resolve disputed medical issues for which the required determination by an Agreed or Qualified Medical Evaluator has not been obtained (see 6.13).

Treating Physician – In Lieu of QME.

For injuries between 1991-1993, the parties are prohibited by LC4061 from utilizing the opinions of treating physicians for a final determination of certain medical issues even where such issues are not disputed. Unfortunately, this prohibition causes unnecessary delays for employees and increases costs for employers in cases that could otherwise be resolved without any necessity for an additional medical evaluation. (Note: as a practical matter, the WCAB will not usually require an additional medical evaluation to which an employee objects before issuing an award of benefits that are undisputably due the employee based upon the existing medical evidence.)

Effective 1994, but applicable only to 1994 or later injuries that are indisputably compensable, a referral to an Agreed or Qualified Medical Evaluator (depending upon whether the employee is represented) is not required unless the employer or employee are dissatisfied with a medical determination of the treating physician. The parties now have the right to utilize solely the opinions of the treating physician to resolve all claims. However, referral to an Agreed or Qualified Medical Evaluator is required by LC4061 and LC4062 when a party disputes virtually any opinion reported by a treating physician.

Treating Physician – Sanctions for Deficient Report.

Every physician who examines or treats an employee for a work-related injury is expected to provide a written report. A basic, essential requirement of written reports is that all appropriate issues be addressed and that adequate support be provided for all opinions rendered (see CR10606). For 1994 or later injuries, it is particularly imperative for a treating physician to submit well-supported opinions. The findings of a treating physician may be relied upon as evidence to rebut the findings of a Qualified Medical Evaluator.

A party who is satisfied with the determinations of the treating physician usually has no reason to obtain additional medical evidence. Except where both parties seek an opinion from a Qualified Medical evaluator of their choice to rebut the determinations of a treating physician, a presumption of correctness attaches to the findings of this treating physician (see 7.79). In some cases, a party may rely upon these findings to submit a proposed permanent disability rating to a judge (see 10.37). However, insufficiencies in a treating physician's report can negate its evidentiary value, thereby causing the party who relied upon this report to be left without any adequate evidence to refute the opinions of a Qualified Medical Evaluator procured by an opponent.

For the reasons explained above, certain sanctions apply if the WCAB determines that a "treating physician's report contains opinions that are the result of conjecture, are not supported by adequate evidence, or that indicate bias." Per LC4068, the WCAB is required to provide written notice of this determination to the Administrative Director of the Division of Workers' Compensation. The Administrative Director will maintain records that enable compliance with a statutory duty under LC4068. Written notice is required to be given to the "physician's applicable licensing body" if the Administrative Director believes "that any treating physician's reports show a pattern of unsupported evidence." If the physician is a Qualified Medical Evaluator, notice is also required to be given to the Industrial Medical Council.

Mandatory Referral – Admitted Injury.

Prior to 1994, LC4062 required a referral to an Agreed Medical Evaluator or a Qualified Medical Evaluator (an A/QME) only if a dispute involved one of four specified medical issues and then only if the employee was represented by an attorney. Referrals were required by LC4061 for an evaluation of three specified issues (see listing below) regardless of whether any dispute existed. The requirements of LC4061 and LC4062 applied regardless of whether a dispute involved a medical determination of a treating or a consulting physician.

For 1994 or later injuries, a referral to an Agreed or Qualified Medical Evaluator is mandatory only if a medical determination of the treating physician is contested (for purposes of LC4061 issues, a dispute is deemed to exist whenever the parties do not agree to resolve such issues based upon the findings of the treating physician). Where a dispute exists, a referral to an Agreed or Qualified Medical Evaluator is mandatory regardless of the nature of the contested issue or whether or not the employee has an attorney. (Note: continued distinctions that affect the rights of represented and unrepresented employees are explained in 7.76-7.81).

Mandatory Referral – Disputed Injury.

Prior to 1994, evaluations by an Agreed or Qualified Medical Evaluator were not required if the compensability of the injury was in issue. Previously, opposing parties obtained comprehensive medical-legal evaluations from medical consultants that each selected. For 1994 or later injuries a referral to an Agreed Medical Evaluator (for represented employees) or to a Qualified Medical Evaluator is required by LC4060 if compensability of the injury in its entirety is disputed on a medical, rather than a legal, basis (see 7.81), and the employee has filed a completed claim form (see 6.13).

Issues Requiring Referral – Listing.

As of 1994, three Labor Code sections require referral of disputed medical issues to an Agreed or Qualified Medical Evaluator (but only after a claim form is filed). Each of these sections mandates referral for distinctly different contested medical issues as noted below:

a. LC4060: Compensability of the injury in its entirety.
b. LC4061:
1. Whether the injury has resulted in any permanent disability;
2. The extent of permanent disability resulting from the injury.
3. Whether the injury has resulted in a need for further medical care after the employee's condition is permanent and stationary (see 10.8).
c. LC4062: Any medical issue not covered by LC4060 or LC4061.

7.76 QME PRELIMINARY NOTICES – ALL EMPLOYEES

Per LC4061, the employer is required to provide certain preliminary written notices regarding the mandatory use of Qualified Medical Evaluators to determine certain medical issues. A notice is required in all cases where temporary disability benefits were paid (for even one day) and regardless of whether the employee is represented by an attorney (see 7.76). Each notice will be based upon medical information in the employer's possession, which may be information provided by treating physicians and/or consulting physicians of the employer's choice.

Concurrently with the final payment of temporary disability benefits, LC4061 requires the employer to provide the employee with one of the three notices and the supplemental notifications that are explained below.

1. **Notice of Delay.** Permanent disability benefits are or may be payable but the employee's condition is not yet permanent and stationary, so a determination of the employee's entitlement to permanent disability benefits is premature at this time. No rights arise with the provision of this delay notice, but the employee must also be notified of the future right to receive notice of one of the two decisions explained below which the employee will have the right to contest.

2. **Notice of Denial.** Permanent disability benefits are or may be payable and the employee's condition is now permanent and stationary. The employee must also be notified of the procedures for obtaining the formal medical evaluation that is required for a determination of the extent of permanent disability and the need for any further medical care (see 10.13). The employer's decision may be made subsequent to the last payment of temporary disability benefits or in cases where the employee was not entitled to temporary disability benefits. If so, the employer is required by LC4061(d), within 5 working days of knowledge of permanent and stationary status, to notify the employee of its decision and the procedures for obtaining a formal medical evaluation.

3. **Notice of Decision.** No permanent disability benefits are payable. The employee must also be notified of a right to contest the employer's denial of liability for permanent disability benefits by obtaining a formal medical evaluation and the procedures for doing so. If this decision is made after the provision of the delay notice in #1 above, written notice to the employee is then required within 14 days of the employer's decision.

The initial notices that LC4061 requires upon the last payment of temporary disability benefits are required for all employees, whether represented by an attorney or not. As of 4/1/94, such notices will advise the employee of the rights and procedures regarding the mandatory use of Agreed or Qualified Medical Evaluators in cases where a party disputes a medical determination of the treating physician and a claim form has been filed (see CR9810-CR9812).

If the employee's condition is permanent and stationary, an initial notice will include notification of the employer's position that: (1) permanent disability benefits are payable, the amount that is payable, and whether or not further medical benefits will be provided (and the employer will concurrently provide an unrepresented employee with the form used to request "assignment of a panel of three" Qualified Medical Evaluators; see 7.77); or, (2) no permanent disability has resulted from the injury. If the employee's condition is not yet permanent and stationary, a subsequent notice is required within 14 days of the employer's decision regarding these issues. (For 1991-1993 injuries, a subsequent notice that permanent disability benefits were payable was required in 5 days, not 14 days, of the employer's decision.)

Notices that are required by LC4061 are limited to the issues of entitlement to permanent disability benefits or continued medical care after the employee's condition has become permanent and stationary. For all other medical issues, LC4062 requires the party who disputes a medical determination of a treating physician to provide written notice of its objection to the opposing party. A notice of objection is required "within 20 days of receipt of the" treating physician's report if the employee has an attorney or "within 30 days ... if the employee is not represented by an attorney."

Employer notices required by LC4061 will encourage employees to act promptly, but LC4061 does not specifically require a notice from an employee who disputes a medical issue. The 20/30-day periods specified by LC4062 may be construed as a reasonable period for the provision of employee notice of any dispute, except LC4062 also provides that these "time limits may be extended for good cause or by mutual agreement." In all cases, it will behoove the employer to assume the responsibility for inquiring whether the employee disputes a determination of the treating physician. This assertive action on the employer's part (and within the time limits specified by LC4062) will enable timely initiation of the dispute resolution process by which disputed medical issues may be resolved.

7.77 QME SELECTION – UNREPRESENTED EMPLOYEES

Where an employee is unrepresented, LC4062.1 prohibits the employer from seeking the employee's agreement to use a particular evaluator. (The term Agreed Medical Evaluator pertains solely to cases where the employee is represented at the time a medical-legal evaluation is required.) The nature of the issue(s) in dispute determine whether the employee will be entitled to an evaluation by any Qualified Medical Evaluator of the employee's choice or one selected from a panel of three provided by the Industrial Medical Council.

If the injury is disputed in its entirety, LC4060 permits the employee to select any Qualified Medical Evaluator from the list of currently appointed physicians, subject to general threshold requirements (e.g. proper qualifications in view of the disputed medical issues and located within a reasonable geographic area). Employees can obtain names of evaluators in the appropriate specialty from an

Information and Assistance Officer at the nearest WCAB district office. In all other cases (all compensable cases), LC139.2 requires the Medical Director of the Industrial Medical Council to assign a panel of three Qualified Medical Evaluators from which the employee must select one, who is called a "panel-QME." If the primary treating physician's determination of any medical issue is disputed, LC4061 and/or LC4062 require the employer to "provide the employee with a form prescribed by the medical director with which to request" a panel.

An unrepresented employee is generally limited to one evaluation by a Qualified Medical Evaluator selected from a panel of three provided by the Industrial Medical Council, but exceptions exist. The various statutes pertaining to the employee's right to an evaluation by a Qualified Medical Evaluator include:

a. An evaluation by a QME of the employee's choice per LC139.3 if the Industrial Medical Council does not provide a panel within 15 working days after a request.
b. An additional QME evaluation at the employer's expense when a panel-QME evaluation is terminated for good cause per LC4061.
c. An additional QME evaluation at the employer's expense where the employer engages in an ex parte communication with the panel-QME that is prohibited by LC4062.2.
d. An evaluation by a QME selected by the WCAB " upon the agreement of a party to pay the cost," per LC5703.5.
e. An evaluation by a QME selected by the Medical Director or the WCAB " upon the agreement of a party to pay the cost", with the employee's consent, after a dispute has been submitted to an Information and Assistance Officer, per LC5703.5.
f. The employee is entitled to an evaluation with a different QME at the employer's expense when a panel-QME fails to provide a timely report per LC4062.5 and LC139.2 (within 30 days for a 1994 or later injury).

For 1994 or later injuries, both LC4061 and LC4062 mandate a referral to a panel-QME if either an unrepresented employee or the employer dispute a medical determination of the treating physician. Although LC4061 and LC4062 address different issues, the process for selection of a panel-QME is the same regardless of the medical issue involved or the identity of the party who disputes the issue. Upon knowledge of a dispute, both statutes require the employer to "immediately provide the employee" with a notice of pertinent rights and the form required "to request assignment of a panel" Effective 8/31/94, regulations that apply to the process of obtaining a panel of Qualified Medical Evaluators are set out in CR30-CR35.

The Medical Director is required to assign a panel "within five working days after receiving a request." However, because this brief deadline may not be met, LC139.2 also provides that if "a panel is not assigned within 15 working days, the employee shall have the right to" select "any qualified medical evaluator of his or her choice" within a reasonable geographic area and selected directly from the list of Qualified Medical Evaluators maintained by the Medical Director.

Hopefully, it will be rare for the Medical Director to be unable to provide a panel within the maximum 15-day period allowed because the Medical Director's failure to do so has an adverse impact upon the employee's rights. For instance, the form used to notify the employee of a panel is required to inform the employee of each physician's "specialty, number of years in practice, and a brief description of his or her education and training." This information is intended to assist the employee in selecting an evaluator. However, if the Medical Director does not assign a panel, the employee might not otherwise receive this information.

The Medical Director's inability to provide a panel within 15 days will also cause the employee to lose another right that otherwise exists: the right to an evaluation by a Qualified Medical Evaluator of the employee's choice at the employer's expense to rebut the determination of a panel-QME. This right, that is provided under LC4064, does not exist when the employee is dissatisfied with an evaluation from a Qualified Medical Evaluator who is chosen directly by the employee instead of from a State-selected panel. (The reports of treating physicians are admissible in WCAB proceedings and may therefore be used to rebut the findings of a nonpanel-QME.)

The employee also has the right to obtain an attorney but may exhaust some right prior to obtaining an attorney. For instance, upon representation by an attorney, the employee would not have the right under LC4061 to select a new Qualified Medical Evaluator at the employer's expense for any previously contested medical issue(s) for which the employee had already obtained a determination from a Qualified Medical Evaluator of the employee's choice who was not selected from a panel. For instance, if the solitary issue referred to a Qualified Medical Evaluator was the nature and extent of the employee's permanent disability, the employee is not entitled to a reevaluation of this issue upon obtaining legal counsel. (An attorney may raise new issues, or another evaluation may become reasonable due to the passage of time or a change in the employee's medical status, or the parties may mutually agree upon a referral to a different physician for the purpose of resolving disputed issues).

An evaluator selected from a panel might not be able to conduct an examination within required time frames (60 days from the employee's request under CR33). A panel-QME might not submit a report within 30 days as required by LC139.2 (although the employee has the right to waive enforcement of this requirement for a limited period under LC4062.5). In either instance, the employee has a right to request the name of a replacement Qualified Medical Evaluator for the previous panel of three (from the Industrial Medical Council), and the employee remains entitled to a formal medical evaluation.

Per LC4061, the employee has the right to terminate an examination with a panel-QME for "good cause," e.g. the physician makes racial or sexist remarks that cause the employee to be personally concerned about receiving a fair evaluation (see 7.79). If the employee exercises this right, the employee is entitled to another evaluation by a physician selected from a new panel of Qualified Medical Evaluators (except that the new physician can be any Qualified Medical Evaluator of the employee's choice if the new panel is not provided timely after a request to the Medical Director).

Additional evaluations are also possible for employees who are unrepresented. Per LC5703.5, a judge has authority to refer an unrepresented employee to a Qualified Medical Evaluator."selected by the appeals board," and an Information and Assistance Officer has authority to refer an unrepresented employee to a Qualified Medical Evaluator "selected by the medical director." However, these referrals can only be made "upon the agreement of a party" (almost always the employer) "to pay the cost." If the employer refused to pay for an evaluation after a request from a judge or an Information Officer, it is likely the employee would obtain the services of an attorney, in which case the procedures described in Section 7.78 would apply.

For 1994 or later injuries, the number of medical reports that are admissible in WCAB proceedings is restricted by LC4061 and LC4062. Both of these statutes provide that the "report of the" QME "and the reports of the treating" physician(s) "shall be the only admissible reports and shall be the only reports obtained by the employee or the employer on the issues subject to" these statutes.

Unrepresented employees no longer have the right to a second evaluation by a QME of the employee's own selection at the employer's expense for the purpose of rebutting a determination of a panel-QME (nor the 1991-1993 right to employer-paid attorney fees under LC4064 if they do not obtain a rebuttal evaluation after the employer contests the findings of a panel-QME). Effective 1994, this former right is replaced with the employee's right to a panel-QME evaluation for the purpose of rebutting a finding of the treating physician. Regardless of the date of injury, neither LC4061 nor LC4062 specifically require the employer to pay for a second evaluation of the same disputed medical issue merely because the employee subsequently obtains the services of an attorney (although payment may be provided as a term of a settlement agreement or upon an order of the WCAB).

7.78 AME/QME SELECTION – REPRESENTED EMPLOYEES

For 1994 or later injuries where an employee is represented by an attorney, both LC4061 and LC4062 mandate a referral to an Agreed or Qualified Medical Evaluator (A/QME) only in cases where the employee or the employer dispute a medical determination of the treating physician (see 7.75 for listing of disputed issues for which a referral is required). The distinction between the two statutes involves the event that must occur before a referral is required. For LC4061 issues, the parties must have knowledge of the existence of a dispute. For LC4062 issues, "the objecting party shall notify the other party in writing of the objection within 20 days of receipt of the report."

Timely objections are essential since a party may otherwise be deemed not to have any objections to the opinions that were submitted by a treating physician. A party may be deemed to have waived its right to an evaluation pursuant to LC4062 unless, for each particular determination of the treating physician that is disputed, the party:

1. Notifies the opposing party of its objection, AND
2. Makes its objection within 20 days of its receipt of the treating physician's report, AND
3. Makes its objection in writing.

When a medical referral is required by LC4062, the procedure for selecting a physician to evaluate the disputed issue is the same for 1991 or later injuries. The parties have a duty to attempt to select an Agreed Medical Evaluator within 10 days of written notice of a dispute. The parties have the right to agree to extend this period for up to 20 additional days. Except for reports of a treating physician, any medical evaluations of a disputed medical issue that are obtained during the period allowed for selection of an Agreed Medical Evaluator are not admissible in WCAB proceedings. An Agreed Medical Evaluator (AME) can be any physician who is mutually agreeable to the parties and need not be a Qualified Medical Evaluator.

The parties may not be able to mutually agree to any particular physician. If not, then after expiration of the 10-day period (or any agreed upon period not to exceed 30 days total), the parties have the right to obtain an evaluation from a Qualified Medical Evaluator of their choosing to resolve any disputed medical issue.

The expense of a comprehensive medical-legal evaluation by a Qualified Medical Evaluator would not appear to be reasonable or necessary if requested by a party who has no objection to any findings of the treating physician. However, LC4062 provides that a "nonobjecting party may continue to rely on the treating physician's report or may select a qualified medical evaluator to conduct an additional evaluation." Per LC4062, "neither party may obtain more than one comprehensive medical-legal report" except "at their own expense."

If the employee retains an attorney after a medical issue has been evaluated by a Qualified Medical Evaluator, the employee does not gain any right to a repeat evaluation of the same medical issue at the employer's expense. Likewise, changing attorneys does not generate a right to repeat evaluations of the same issues by a different Agreed or Qualified Medical Evaluator.

A represented employee is generally limited to one such evaluation at the employer's expense. However, if a dispute arises regarding a determination of the treating physician that has not yet been evaluated, the employee is entitled to an examination by an Agreed or Qualified Medical Evaluator for a determination of the newly disputed issue. (and will usually return to same evaluator who previously reported on the claim).

A restriction on the use of an Agreed Medical Evaluator in compensable cases is set out in both LC4061 and LC4062. If the parties cannot reach an agreement to utilize an AME within the time allowed (10 days maximum unless both parties agree to a 20-day extension), the parties are precluded from using an Agreed Medical Evaluator at any later time. This restriction is intended to encourage the parties to utilize one evaluator, because the employee can avoid the delays and the inconvenience of submitting to multiple examinations, and it is cost-efficient for the employer to pay for one evaluation instead of two. (Note: in common practice, the WCAB encourages the parties to agree to use a single evaluator where the employee is represented by an attorney even if an agreement was made outside the limited time period specified in LC4061 and LC4062).

The parties are not restricted in the use of an Agreed Medical Evaluator where the compensability of the injury in its entirety is disputed. In this instance, LC4060 permits the parties to agree to refer disputed issues to a single evaluator "at any time." The exception provided by LC4060 usually inures to the benefit of the WCAB as well as the parties, since it is not necessary for the WCAB to adjudicate disputes that the parties are able to resolve by their own efforts.

The employer may choose to utilize an Agreed Medical Evaluator in cases where it does not contest any finding of the treating physician. This action may be preferable to adopting a wait-and-see attitude and waiting for receipt of an evaluation from a Qualified Medical Evaluator of the employee's choice who may be objectionable to the employer (for whatever reason, based upon current or prior evaluations from this physician).

Use of an Agreed Medical Evaluator provides the employer with some, albeit limited, control as to the selection of a particular physician. The parties' mutual agreement to information that is presented to an Agreed Medical Evaluator in advance of an evaluation can enhance the potential that the physician's formal medical evaluation will enable the parties to resolve disputed issues without further ado. True, the employer will pay more for an evaluation from an Agreed Medical Evaluator than a Qualified Medical Evaluator (CR9795). However, it may be preferable to pay a little more in exchange for the right to participate in the selection of, and the right to joint communication with, an Agreed Medical Evaluator.

7.79 AME/QME EVALUATION PROCESS
Scheduling of Appointment

Appointments with Qualified Medical Evaluators who are selected directly by a party (not from a panel provided by the Medical Director) will be scheduled by the party who selected the evaluator. An unrepresented employee is responsible for scheduling an appointment after a panel-QME has been scheduled. A employee who is represented by an attorney is responsible for scheduling an appointment with an Agreed Medical Evaluator, but this duty is commonly deferred to the claims administrator (who will schedule an appointment and provide the employee with written notice of the examination date).

It behooves the physician to communicate with the employer immediately whenever a request for an appointment is received from an unrepresented employee rather than presume that the employer will have no objection to its liability for payment for services rendered. Also, it is imperative for all parties to know the date of any scheduled examination with an Agreed Medical Evaluator or a panel-QME as far in advance as possible because certain preliminary actions that do not involve the evaluator require the parties' advance knowledge of the date of the evaluation.

If the evaluator is a panel-QME, LC4062.2 requires each party to serve the opposing party with copies of all information that it proposes to provide to the evaluator at least 20 days before such information is provided to the evaluator. Such information includes an "issues letter" that informs the evaluator of the parts of the body involved and specifies the disputed medical issues for which an evaluation is being requested, records of treating physicians, other relevant medical records, and nonmedical records such as personnel records or investigation reports. A party has a right to object to nonmedical records only. If a party objects to specific nonmedical records, those records "shall not be provided to the evaluator."

For all employees, represented or not, LC4600 and LC4061 require the employer to provide estimated mileage expense (and bridge tolls when appropriate) in advance of an examination. The employer will ordinarily include payment for transportation expense with written notice of an examination that it scheduled with a Qualified Medical Evaluator of its choice. However, a panel-QME or an Agreed Medical Evaluator needs to inform the employer of the date and time of any appointment that is scheduled directly by an employee. (If a party schedules an evaluation with a Qualified Medical Evaluator of its choice after an Application for Adjudication has been filed, CR10418 requires each party to provide notice of an appointment to its opponent). The employer's failure to provide advance payment of required transportation expense due to the physician's failure to provide notice of an appointment (or to any other reason) can excuse the employee's failure to attend a scheduled examination.

Required Forms - Provision to Physician

When the issue of extent of permanent disability (a LC4061 issue) is to be evaluated, two forms that were previously submitted directly to the Disability Evaluation Unit are routed through the evaluating physician as of 4/1/94. After the employer receives notice of a scheduled appointment with a panel-QME for an unrepresented employee (CR31.2-CR34.1), the employer is required to provide the employee with the Employee's Permanent Disability Questionnaire form (DEU Form 100). Per CR10160, the employee is required to complete the form and provide it to the physician at the examination.

For all employees, represented or not, the employer is also required to provide a completed Request for Summary Rating Determination (DEU Form 101) to the physician prior to the date of the scheduled examination (CR10160-CR10160.5). The employer's form will assist the physician by providing the address of the correct office of the Disability Evaluation Unit to which the physician is required to submit a report (according to a venue list provided by this Unit). Depending upon whether the employee is unrepresented or represented, either one or both of the completed DEU rating forms are required attachments to the physician's report. These requirements ensure that the Disability Evaluation Unit will concurrently receive all of the documents it requires before performing a summary rating.

The employer may wish to review a copy of the employee's questionnaire form prior to a panel-QME evaluation. Information contained in a completed questionnaire form may raise new or auxiliary issues that can be dealt with prior to the panel-QME evaluation. For instance, new details regarding the employee's actual job duties may warrant further investigation for the purpose of identifying medical eligibility for rehabilitation benefits or the correct occupational group to be used for rating purposes. One solution to such concerns is to use a write-through multicopy form (like the employee's claim form) and include a postage-paid return envelope with a questionnaire form. Of course, nothing prevents the employer from actively seeking the same information at an earlier opportunity; e.g. by requesting the treating physician to make the same type of inquiries or discussing such topics with the employee.

The Employee's Permanent Disability Questionnaire form may arguably constitute a part of the medical record after a Qualified Medical Evaluator has reviewed and commented upon information contained therein. However, prior to a scheduled appointment, a completed questionnaire form is a nonmedical record. As such, it appears that LC4062.2 gives the employee the duty to serve the completed form on the employer, and the employer has the right to "use discovery to establish the accuracy or authenticity of" this nonmedical record "prior to the evaluation" (see also CR35). The claimperson's advance review can assist the employee in avoiding prohibited ex parte communications with a panel-QME, that would lead to all costs and certain expenses of a panel-QME evaluation being payable by the employee (as explained below).

Communication With Parties

Parties who directly select a Qualified Medical Evaluator of their choice are not restricted in their oral or written communications with the evaluator. Ex parte communications are prohibited if the evaluator is an Agreed Medical Evaluator or a panel-QME. (Note: an evaluation by a panel-QME will only be performed if the employee is not represented by an attorney.)

The parties are required as part of their agreement to use an Agreed Medical Evaluator to agree to any information that will be provided to the evaluator. If the evaluator is either an agreed upon or panel-QME, LC4062.2 requires that all communications with the evaluator "shall be in writing and shall be served on the opposing party 20 days in advance of the evaluation." Subsequent communications are permitted but are also required to be written and "shall be served on the opposing party when sent" to the evaluator.

If the employer engages in a prohibited ex parte communication with a panel-QME, LC4062.2 provides that the employee "may elect to terminate the" evaluation and obtain an "evaluation from another qualified medical evaluator, or proceed with the initial evaluation." Any party who engages in ex parte communications with an Agreed Medical Evaluator or a panel-QME may be "charged with contempt before the appeals board and shall be liable for the costs incurred by the aggrieved party as a result of the prohibited communication, including the costs of the formal medical evaluation, additional discovery costs, and attorney's fees for related discovery."

The employee's communication with the evaluator may or may not constitute a prohibited ex parte communication. An agreed upon or panel-QME must communicate with the employee in order to conduct an evaluation. The employee's provision of oral or written information at the physician's request during an evaluation is not an ex parte communication. However, the employee would be engaging in an ex parte communication if the employee presented previously undisclosed and unsolicited nonmedical records to the evaluator during an evaluation. Both the employer and the employee are entitled under LC4062.2 to the service of records and an opportunity "to use discovery to establish the accuracy or authenticity of nonmedical records prior to the evaluation."

Termination for Good Cause

Upon commencement of an examination with an Agreed Medical Evaluator or a panel-QME, LC4061 requires the evaluator to provide the employee with "a brief opportunity to ask questions concerning the evaluation process and the evaluator's background." The employee is thereafter required to participate in the evaluation, with one exception. An unrepresented employee has the right to terminate a panel-QME evaluation for "good cause," such as the physician's demonstrable prejudice toward the employee or the physician's request that the employee "submit to an unnecessary medical examination or procedure" (e.g. repeat x-rays).

If an unrepresented employee exercises the right to terminate an evaluation for good cause, the employee is entitled to an evaluation by a different Qualified Medical Evaluator selected from a new panel (the employer will request the Industrial Medical Council to issue a new panel upon notice of the terminated evaluation). This right exists regardless of whether the employee actually had good cause to terminate the evaluation, and the employer will owe the costs of the alternative evaluation.

The initial evaluator may or may not be entitled to payment for services related to the terminated evaluation. Per LC4061, if the WCAB later determines "that the employee did not have good cause to terminate the evaluation, the cost of the evaluation shall be deducted from any award the employee obtains." If a judge determines that the employee had good cause to terminate the examination, the employer will rely upon this determination to defend any claim for charges incurred on the basis that such charges are neither reasonable nor necessary.

The right to terminate an evaluation for good cause under LC4061 does not specifically apply to an evaluation of an unrepresented employee by any Qualified Medical Evaluator who was directly selected by the employee nor to any evaluations where the employee is represented by an attorney. However, both LC4061 and LC4062 provide that specified limitations on the number of evaluations allowed to each party do not apply if the WCAB "determines there is good cause to permit a party to obtain an evaluation from another physician." Surely the grounds that constitute good cause for an unrepresented employee to terminate a panel-QME evaluation constitute equally good cause for a represented employee to terminate an evaluation. The significant distinction is that, when the employee is represented by an attorney, there is no specific statutory provision pertaining to payment of a physician's fees for an evaluation terminated on this basis.

Scope of Evaluation

For 1994 or later injuries, LC4061 requires an Agreed or Qualified Medical Evaluator to "address all contested medical issues arising from all injuries reported on one or more claim forms prior to the date of the employee's initial appointment with the medical evaluator." This language restricts the scope of the evaluation as to the parts of the body that the physician is authorized to evaluate as well as the specific issues that are to be included in a report (and LC4061 only applies to three specific issues; see 7.75). This language does not extend carte blanche authority to a physician to evaluate every conceivable medical issue.

An evaluation is deemed to be a "comprehensive medical evaluation" (as that term is used in LC4061) when the physician has completely addressed those medical issues that are being contested. Comparable language in LC4062 reemphasizes the fact that the purpose of any work performed by an Agreed or Qualified Medical Evaluator is to "prepare a report resolving the disputed issue"; i.e. any issue subject to LC4062 to which a party has made a written objection. Billing disputes that would surely result from needless evaluation of uncontested issues can be avoided by a careful review of the treating physician's findings and cover letters that inform the Agreed or Qualified Medical Evaluator of the specific issues that are contested. For the sake of thoroughness and caution, a cover letter may additionally designate the medical issues that are not contested.

Consultations & Testing

Consultations are deemed appropriate when they are reasonably required in order for the evaluator to provide a report that is complete and accurate. For 1994 or later injuries, only LC4061 specifically permits an Agreed or Qualified Medical Evaluator to consult with other physicians, so consultations are limited to cases involving issues specified by LC4061 (not LC4062; see 7.79). In such cases, LC4061 permits an Agreed or Qualified Medical Evaluator to obtain consultations only "from any other physicians who have treated the employee."

A consultation usually includes an examination, but the cost and delays involved can sometimes be avoided. In lieu of referring the employee for an examination, it may be appropriate instead for an Agreed or Qualified Medical

Evaluator to make a written inquiry to a treating physician and request a written response to specific questions. (In actual practice, an Agreed or Qualified Evaluator will review all existing medical records but will rarely, if ever, consult with a treating physician.)

An Agreed or Qualified Medical Evaluator is not prohibited from referring the employee to an organization in which the evaluator has an ownership interest for a necessary consultation or for testing. However, LC139.3 requires the evaluator to disclose a "significant beneficial interest," as that phrase is defined in Business and Professions Code Section 654.2 (basically either 5% or $5,000 or more of total ownership). A disclosure is required at the time the referral is made and again in the evaluator's report. (Note: the provisions of LC139.3 apply to treating physicians and medical-legal evaluators.)

Additional restrictions apply to referrals for diagnostic tests. Per CR9794, the employer shall not be "liable for the cost of any diagnostic test provided in connection with a comprehensive medical-legal evaluation report unless the subjective complaints and physical findings that warrant the necessity for the test are included in the" evaluator's report.

Prohibited Participants

The evaluator is required to personally conduct an examination and compose a report. Limited aspects of the evaluation process that may be delegated to another person are specified in LC4628. The penalties for using any prohibited participants or failing to disclose permissible participants are severe (see 7.73).

Evaluation Protocols & Guidelines

Evaluation protocols and guidelines for the evaluation of various types of disabilities were first adopted by the Industrial Medical Council effective 8/31/94 pursuant to the mandate of LC139.2. These include Psychiatric Protocols, Guidelines for Evaluation of Pulmonary Disability, Cardiac Disability, and Immunologic Testing, as well as Ethical Guidelines for Qualified Medical Evaluators (copies of each are available from the Industrial Medical Council per CR43-CR48). Additionally, Qualified Medical Evaluators must comply with minimum time guidelines for face-to-face contact between physician and patient that vary according to medical specialty area and complexity factors involved (CR49-CR49.9).

Multiple Issues – Multiple Evaluations

The dispute regarding a treating physician's evaluation (for which LC4061 or LC4062 require referral to an A/QME) may involve a determination by one or more treating physicians of different medical specialties. In cases involving a single treating physician, more than one finding of this physician may be disputed. If multiple issues are disputed by the parties, it is also possible that some disputed issues may be subject to the procedural requirements of LC4061 and others to LC4062. Per LC4064, the employer is "liable for the cost of each reasonable and necessary comprehensive medical-legal evaluation obtained" pursuant to LC4060, LC4061, or LC4062. However, LC4064 requires each physician who evaluates employees as an Agreed or Qualified Medical Evaluator to "address all contested medical issues arising from all injuries reported on one or more claim forms."

Treating Physician – Presumption of Correctness

For a 1994 or later injury, a presumption of correctness attaches to the findings of the treating physician when either the employer or the employee chooses to rely upon these findings instead of exercising the right to select a Qualified Medical Evaluator. Per LC4062.9, the "presumption shall not apply where both parties select" a Qualified Medical Evaluator. The treating physician's findings are not presumed to be correct if both the employer and the employee contest such findings, that is why the presumption would not apply if the parties used an AME to resolve disputed medical issues. The presumption applies only if one additional evaluation is obtained, and it is obtained from a Qualified Medical Evaluator.

The treating physician's findings will not always be presumed correct (as explained above). Pursuant to LC4062.9, "the findings of the treating physician are presumed to be correct" in limited circumstances. When the presumption applies, it applies to any issue that a Qualified Medical Evaluator may be called upon to evaluate in a compensable case (issues under LC4061 or LC4062 but not LC4060; see 7.75). However, LC4062.9 provides that this rebuttable presumption "may be controverted" only "by a preponderance of medical opinion" on one issue only: the "level of impairment" (see 10.37 regarding proposed ratings of permanent disability). The term "impairment" is generally used to refer to permanent disability, but for purposes of the presumption in LC4062.5 will probably be construed as encompassing any type of disability (e.g. temporary disability or impairment for purposes of medical eligibility for rehabilitation).

For 1994 or later injuries, a Qualified Medical Evaluator needs to ensure that any opinions that differ from the determinations of the treating physician are carefully explained. Where conflicting opinions exist, medical opinions of the Qualified Medical Evaluator will have little evidentiary value unless set out in sufficient detail to be capable of overcoming a presumption of correctness that may apply to the findings of the treating physician. (See also 7.45 regarding inadequacies of treating physician's opinions.)

Subsequent Evaluations

An employee may receive full benefits after evaluation by only one Agreed or Qualified Medical Evaluator, or multiple evaluations may be necessary (see 7.77-7.80). An underlying goal of an Agreed or Qualified Evaluator should be the provision of a formal medical evaluation that will provide the basis for an expeditious resolution of a disputed medical issue. To be avoided are any actions or inactions of the evaluator that might result in a need for additional evaluations to resolve the same medical issues. For instance, the evaluator wishes to ensure that no employee will have good cause to terminate an evaluation. Also to be avoided is a need for an additional evaluation due to deficiencies in an evaluator's report or a failure to provide a formal medical evaluation within required time periods (see 7.80).

Both LC4061 and LC4062 provide that the employer or the employee "may obtain additional reports at their own expense" in addition to obtaining reports that are required pursuant to these statutes. These provisions give the employer an advantage in that the employer is usually better able to absorb the cost involved in exercising this right. However, a caveat is necessary since both LC4061 and LC4062 also restrict the number of reports that are admissible as evidence in cases where the employee is not represented to the reports of treating physicians and the report of a Qualified Medical Evaluator. Any disputes involving this apparent discrepancy will be resolved by the WCAB.

7.80 AME/Q ME REPORTS– OVERVIEW

Terms

The final product of the evaluation process is, of course, a report. The written report of an Agreed or Qualified Medical Evaluator is referred to interchangeably in the Labor Code as a "formal medical evaluation," or "comprehensive medical evaluation," or a "comprehensive medical-legal evaluation" (CMLE). In common practice, the report of an Agreed Medical Evaluator or a Qualified Medical Evaluator is referred to as a "medical-legal report," since the purpose of such evaluations is to resolve contested medical issues (see 7.71).

Submission of Report – Time Limit

Absent good reason such as the delayed receipt of test results or necessary information from a consulting physician, evaluators are required by LC139.2 to submit their formal medical evaluations within 30 days of an evaluation (rather than 45 days as required for 1991-1993 injuries). If the evaluator is a panel-QME, the employee has the right under LC4062.5 to agree to an extension of time using a required form (see CR38-CR38.4 for regulations governing extensions of time). Unless the employee exercises this right, the employer is not liable for payment of the report of a panel-QME that is not provided timely. The Medical Director is required by LC139.2 to review the quality and timeliness of formal medical evaluations on a continuous basis and to submit an annual report to the Administrative Director that includes recommendations for improvements to the evaluation system.

Submission of Report – Summary Form

Regardless of the disputed issue involved, both LC4061 and LC4062 require Agreed or Qualified Medical Evaluators to serve their "formal medical evaluation on the employee, employer, and the administrative director." In addition to a written narrative report, LC4061 and LC4062 require the physician to file a form entitled "Qualified or Agreed Medical Evaluator's Findings Summary" (IMC Form 1002). The "summary form" is predominantly utilized to assist the Disability Evaluation Unit in preparation of a permanent disability rating (see 10.36).

When the employee is represented and evaluations are obtained from Qualified Medical Evaluators selected by opposing parties, the formal medical evaluation is provided to the party who requested the evaluation. The evaluator's report will be utilized by the parties to resolve disputed issues. If the nature and extent of permanent disability benefits is in dispute, it is common for the parties to request the Disability Evaluation Unit to assist in negotiation efforts by issuing consultative ratings (under the authority of CR10154 and as described in CR9758). Alternatively, the evaluator's medical-legal report will be used as evidence in support of a party's contentions at a WCAB proceeding.

For LC4062 issues, the parties will utilize the evaluator's report to resolve disputed issues informally or as evidence before the WCAB (see 10.38 regarding submission of proposed permanent disability ratings). In cases where the nature and extent of permanent disability is not contested, the copies of evaluator's reports that are submitted to the State are used for general purposes such as accumulating statistics on the types of issues for which evaluations are performed.

Evaluation Contested - Pay or Litigate

Per LC4061, if the evaluation from a treating physician or an Agreed or Qualified Medical Evaluator resolves any issue regarding the extent of permanent disability or need for continuing medical care so as to require payment of compensation, the employer shall commence payment or "promptly commence proceedings" (this duty arises with the receipt of a summary rating based upon the evaluation). For 1991-1993 injuries, LC4061 specified that the employer was required to file an Application for Adjudication, since filing of this form was necessary to commence WCAB proceedings. For 1994 or later injuries, a Declaration of Readiness must be filed to commence WCAB proceedings, together with an Application for Adjudication if this form has not previously been filed.

Evaluation Contested – Attorney Fees

For 1991 or later injuries and regardless of the issue involved, the employer is liable for attorney fees (see 1.17) in addition to the employee's compensation when the employer commences WCAB proceedings to contest the evaluation of an Agreed Medical Evaluator. Per LC4066, the employer is liable for attorney fees "regardless of the outcome," even if every issue disputed by the employer is resolved in the employer's favor! (Presumably the employer only owes fees for services performed by an attorney after the date on which the employer commences WCAB proceedings). For 1994 or later injuries, LC4064 additionally provides that the employer is liable for attorney fees incurred when the employee is unrepresented at the time that the employer files an Application for Adjudication with the WCAB to contest the findings of a Qualified Medical Evaluator (see 7.77). For 1991-1993 injuries, this right is issue-dependent (as explained below). As of 1994, this right exists regardless of the particular issues that are disputed by the employer (LC4060, LC4061, or LC4062 issues).

For unrepresented employees with a 1991-1993 date of injury, the employer owes attorney fees in addition to the employee's compensation in one situation only. Attorney fees are owed if the employer objects to an evaluation of a panel-QME by filing an Application for Adjudication and the unrepresented employee does not obtain a rebuttal evaluation from a Qualified Medical Evaluator of the employee's choice. The employee's LC4064 right to rebut the findings of a panel-QME continues to apply to 1991-1993 injuries but only for LC4061 issues.

For unrepresented employees with 1994 or later injuries, the employer's liability for attorney fees under LC4064 appears to apply to any case where the employer is required to commence WCAB proceedings by filing a Declaration of Readiness rather than an Application for Adjudication as specified in LC4064. An apparent intent of LC4064 is to penalize an employer who continues to contest an employee's entitlement to benefits after receipt of all medical evidence in the case. For unrepresented employees with 1994 or later injuries, both LC4061 and LC4062 limit admissible medical reports to those of the treating physician(s) and a panel-QME. An actual effect of LC4064 is to penalize an employer by assessing it with liability for attorney fees in addition to compensation due the employee in situations where the employer's position is upheld by the WCAB.

The major distinction between LC4061 and LC4062 is that LC4062 does not require the employer to commence WCAB proceedings if it disputes the findings of the Agreed or Qualified Medical Evaluator. To the contrary, LC4062 precludes either party from filing a Declaration of Readiness until receipt of allowable evaluations from Agreed or Qualified Medical Evaluators (for 1991-1993 injuries, LC4062 precluded the filing of an Application for Adjudication).

If evaluations from Agreed or Qualified Medical Evaluators do not enable the parties to resolve disputed issues, the next logical step is to request WCAB proceedings. Thus, the net effect of both LC4061 and LC4062 is to require the employer to pay benefits or commence WCAB proceedings after receipt of permissible evaluations from Agreed or Qualified Medical Evaluators. The employer appears to be relieved from this requirement only if it does not dispute the findings of an Agreed or Qualified Medical Evaluator. In this event, the employee has the right to commence WCAB proceedings. (An administrative penalty may be assessed under LC129.5 if the employer acts in a manner that is intended to force an employee to commence proceedings so that the employer can circumvent liability for attorney fees that would be owed if the employer commenced proceedings.)

Evaluation Rejected – Minimum Standards Not Met

If the parties are unable to resolve disputed medical issues utilizing the evaluation of a Qualified Medical Evaluator, the Qualified Medical Evaluator's report may be considered at a WCAB hearing. Per LC139.2, the WCAB may reject the evaluation of a Qualified Medical Evaluator on the basis that the Qualified Medical Evaluator 's report "fails to meet minimum standards established by the Industrial Medical Council or the" WCAB. If the Qualified Medical Evaluator 's report is rejected by the WCAB (either a "judge or the appeals board" after a judge's decision is appealed; see 1.16), LC139.2 requires the

WCAB to "make a specific finding to that effect" and give notice to the Qualified Medical Evaluator and to the Industrial Medical Council. The rejection is deemed to have "become final" when "the time for appeal has expired."

Ordinarily, the finding of rejection by the WCAB will be included in the terms of an award, and the party who wishes to contest the rejection must do so by filing a timely appeal of the award (see 1.19). Per LC139.2, a request for reappointment as a Qualified Medical Evaluator can be denied if six or more of the Qualified Medical Evaluator's reports that were considered at a WCAB hearing were specifically rejected (by a judge or by the WCAB after an appeal) in the Qualified Medical Evaluator's "most recent two-year period" of service as a Qualified Medical Evaluator. (Reappointment of physicians with more than five rejected reports is discretionary by the Industrial Medical Council.)

7.81 AME/QME – DISPUTED INJURY

New as of 1994 is the LC4060 requirement for use of an Agreed or Qualified Medical Evaluator (A/QME) where the compensability of the injury in its entirety is in dispute (but, per LC5401, only if a claim form has been filed with the employer, and an "agreed" evaluator is only permissible when the employee is represented). In the past, opposing parties usually obtained medical-legal evaluations from physicians of their own choice or agreed to utilize one physician to resolve such disputes. No restrictions applied to the number of medical-legal evaluations that a party could obtain except that the employer's liability was restricted to medical-legal expenses that were both reasonable and necessary when incurred. The impact of LC4060 is two-fold. This statute creates a waiting period before the employee can obtain a medical-legal evaluation at the employer's expense "by other than the treating physician," and it limits the number of evaluations the employee is entitled to receive at the employer's expense.

For 1994 or later injuries, LC4060 requires the use of an Agreed or Qualified Medical Evaluator in any case where "a medical evaluation is required to determine compensability" of an injury. For example, it may not be disputed that the employee has bilateral tendonitis, a hearing loss and high blood pressure. However, medical records may reveal extensive treatment for each of these conditions on a nonindustrial basis prior to filing of a claim of industrial injury. If an injury to "any part or parts of the body is accepted as compensable," LC4060 does not apply. Evaluations of contested medical issues in compensable cases are, instead, subject to the provisions of LC4061 and LC4062 (e.g. an evaluation to determine disputed medical causation is required by LC4062 if the employer accepts a claimed back injury but disputes liability for leg, hip and psychiatric conditions that are alleged as sequelae of the initial back injury).

A referral to an Agreed or Qualified Medical Evaluator is not required unless the employer denies the claim or the claim "becomes presumptively compensable" (that would occur pursuant to LC5402 if "liability is not rejected within 90 days after the date a claim form is filed"). When a referral is required and the employee is represented, LC4060 permits the parties to utilize an Agreed Medical Evaluator "at any time" (unlike LC4061 and LC4062 that prohibit the use of an Agreed Medical Evaluator after expiration of the time allowed to reach an agreement).

Conceivably, LC4060 permits the use of an Agreed Medical Evaluator if an issue continues to be disputed after either party has exercised the right to use a Qualified Medical Evaluator. If the employee is not represented by an attorney, the employee and the employer each have the right under LC4060 to select a Qualified Medical Evaluator of their choice (unlike LC4061 and LC4062 that require the use of a panel-QME). Per LC4060, "the division" (meaning Information and Assistance Officers within the Division of Workers' Compensation) "shall make available" to unrepresented employees "the list of medical evaluators compiled" by the Industrial Medical Council. Represented or not, employees will be notified of their rights regarding the A/QME process pursuant to LC4060 as part of the denial notice that is required by LC138.4 (see 6.9).

Certain provisions of LC4060 are unique to the A/QME system. For instance, LC4060 is the only statute that allows the parties to utilize an Agreed Medical Evaluator (for a represented employee only) outside of the limited time period that applies to LC4061 and LC4062 issues (minimum of 20 and maximum of 30 days). Unlike LC4061 and LC4062, LC4060 does not require that a dispute arise from a determination of a treating physician. A medical dispute must exist, but the dispute for which LC4060 requires the use of an Agreed or Qualified Medical Evaluator may arise from the report of a consulting physician, hospital records, or a physician who previously provided treatment for a different injury or type of claim.

(THIS PAGE LEFT BLANK INTENTIONALLY}

[8] COMPENSATION RATE

8.1 AVERAGE EARNINGS – OVERVIEW

For workers' compensation purposes, "earnings" refer to the value of the consideration that an employer provides to an employee in return for the performance of work. Earnings can be paid as wages, by a transfer of something that has a cash value or by some combination of both. Earnings mean the employee's gross, not net, earnings. "Average weekly earnings" generally refers to a weekly earnings amount that, when multiplied by fifty-two weeks, does not exceed actual gross earnings within the same period. Averaging weekly earnings for worker's compensation purposes involves application of legal concepts to mathematical computations.

8.2 WAGES vs. NONMONETARY EARNINGS

Wages are stated as a dollar and cents amount payable for a specific period of time worked or per unit of work, e.g. by the week or per units sold (commissions). Nonmonetary earnings can be alternative to or supplemental to the provision of wages. Some employees receive specific goods or services in return for services they perform rather than receiving wages that would otherwise be used to purchase these items. Nonmonetary items provided by the employer will only constitute earnings to the employee when the item has a specific cash value and is provided in lieu of an equivalent payment of wages.

8.3 EARNINGS – FOOD, LODGING, FUEL

Per LC4454, "earnings" are defined to include "the market value of board, lodging, fuel ... which can be estimated in money." The value of an item constitutes earnings only when the employee accepts employment partly or totally because the item is provided. Market value means the price that persons in the open market would be likely to pay if the item was offered or available for sale, and this value represents a dollar and cents amount of earnings paid to the employee.

The word "board" refers to meals. Free meals in restaurants may provide a major incentive in accepting the employment; e.g., seasonal employees in resort areas may prefer to receive meals rather than receive higher cash wages. Some employees work in an isolated location or in employer-provided housing where they have little or no options as to their meals. Other employees may accept a live-in job where meals with a family are expected as part of the job, or the employee may bargain for free meals in exchange for his services. When an employee is merely allowed an employee discount, this employer benefit does not necessarily constitute board. It may be a matter of preference whether the employee eats employer-provided food or brings food from home, and food may not be provided in lieu of otherwise higher wages.

"Lodging" refers to the employer's provision of living facilities throughout the period of employment. Lodging may be provided at no cost to the employee or at a lower cost than offered to the general public. If an apartment manager pays less rent than other tenants, the amount of the reduction in rent is earnings. Where the employee pays nothing for the lodging, its customary rental value is included in the employee's earnings. It is not relevant how much other people pay for rent in the same area. The market value of the lodging where the employee resides is all that is considered as earnings.

The word "fuel" could be interpreted to mean a company car, payments designated as reimbursement of operating expenses for required use of a personal car on a continuous basis, or a fairly regular payment for the expense of other forms of transportation (e.g. in lieu of a company car). Earnings are measured on an incurred cost basis for amounts expended by the employee that are then reimbursed by the employer. Otherwise, earnings are ordinarily equivalent to the direct cost to the employer.

8.4 EXPENSE PAYMENTS vs. EARNINGS

Employers sometimes reimburse their employees for minor work-related, out-of-pocket expenses. When an expense is predominantly nonrecurring or infrequent, the employer's payment is not considered to be earnings. For instance, the employer may send the employee on a work errand in the employee's car and reimburse the employee for a tank of gas, or the employee may be reimbursed for expenditures of a business luncheon meeting or tuition for a class or seminar. The employer's willingness to provide reimbursement for small expenses does not ordinarily influence an employee's decision to accept offered employment at the offered amount of wages. Employees are not likely to demand payment of a higher wage in lieu of these reimbursements, because the employer retains the option of providing payment for these expenses or declining to incur the expense. For these reasons, amounts provided as reimbursement for the actual costs of isolated expense items are not earnings.

The employer's willingness to provide payment for certain expenses that are admittedly work-related and frequently incurred does not convert the value of the expense to earnings after an injury is sustained. Per LC4454, earnings "shall not include any sum which the employer pays to or for the injured employee to cover any special expenses entailed on the employee by the nature of his employment." Special expenses of employment could include the expense of such things as:

1. Special footwear: steel-toed shoes, soft-soled shoes, or boots (including shoe-repair costs.
2. Special clothing: heavy duty pants, uniforms or costumes (including dry cleaning costs).
3. Special transportation: use of personal vehicle, toll bridges or public transit systems to travel between worksites.

The employee may be paid a set amount per week as payment for special expenses necessitated by virtue of a particular employment. Over time, the employee may lose sight of the fact that some small amount, such as $10/wk, is specifically designated as "car allowance" or "uniform allowance." Many employees automatically include expense payments whenever they are asked how much they earn, e.g. when applying for a charge card. Some employees will not utilize expense payments for an intended purpose; e.g., the employee may carpool with a coworker so each incurs only half of the transportation costs anticipated by the employer, or a relative of the employee may dry clean the employee's clothes for free.

If the employee sustains a work injury, the employer should exclude the amount of special expense payments from earnings that are reported to the claimsperson (e.g. in a wage statement; see 8.45). If the employee alleges such amount represents payment of earnings, an investigation of the facts is warranted. The primary fact to determine is: did (or would) the employee receive payment of the disputed amount during any week when the employee was paid vacation pay or sick pay? Special expenses of employment will not be incurred during periods when the employee is not at work; e.g., a car allowance is not necessary to pay the employee for the use of a personal car for business and uniforms need not be cleaned to wear to work on days when the employee is not working. If vacation pay or sick leave payments exclude the disputed amount, this amount is a special expense of employment, not earnings.

8.5 COMPANY BENEFITS vs. EARNINGS

A variety of employer-paid benefits have no earnings value to the employee. These benefits come under a category that is commonly referred to as "fringe benefits," and each shares a common element because the employee cannot choose to receive higher wages instead of receiving the benefit. Per LC4454, "earnings" do not include such things as the employer's payments of premiums for medical, dental or disability plans and contributions to supplemental savings and/or stock acquisition programs. The employer's payments for these particular benefits are usually made to a third party such as a bank or insurance company. However, many nonwage benefits can be provided directly to the employee.

An employee may not receive any immediate financial benefit from the employer's provision of the item. For example, the employee does not receive any benefit from the employer's payment of health insurance premiums unless and until the employee has a need to incur medical expense. In some cases, any benefit to the employee may be indirect; e.g., the employee's dependents may be the actual beneficiaries of an employer-provided medical insurance policy or a life insurance policy.

Benefits are provided directly to the employee when an item is provided for the employee's personal use or consumption. For instance, the employer may provide free coffee for all employees or free use of a company swimming pool, boat, exercise room, ping pong table, mountain lodge or recreational vehicle. The provision of these items may provide an incentive to work for one employer rather than some other employer, and the employee may mentally equate a benefit to a higher level of wages than he receives. However, it would be absurd for an employee to demand higher wages if he declined receipt of a benefit such as a demand for increased wages because the employee does not drink coffee. One reason why fringe benefits are not considered to be earnings is that the cash value of a benefit is incapable of assessment on an individual basis when it is a matter of personal preference whether or not any employee receives the benefit at all or to what extent.

8.6 VERIFICATION OF CLAIMED EARNINGS

The employee has the burden of proving the amount of earnings received, but earnings are presumed to be correct as claimed in the absence of any evidence to the contrary. Therefore, the level of earnings claimed by the employee should be verified by another source and documented to the extent it is possible to do so.

The employer is the primary source of earnings verification but not always the best or only source. Occasionally, earnings the employer reports to its claims administrator are inaccurate, the employer may deny providing any earnings at all and/or, records may have been lost, destroyed or never maintained. Information may be available from some third party source, or a dispute may involve only the employer's word against the employee's.

In the event of a dispute, the employer should be requested to provide all documentation that supports its position. Likewise, the employee should be asked to recommend the manner in which the claimsperson can obtain verification and/or documentation of claimed earnings, e.g. information from third party sources such as coemployees or customers of the employer. The employee's earnings may be accepted as claimed when the employer's credibility is suspect and not supported by documentation. The claimsperson may agree to a compromised earnings amount when the employer and the employee appear equally credible in their disparate positions.

8.7 EARNINGS DOCUMENTATION – FROM EMPLOYEE

In most cases, any documentation of earnings the employee possesses will have been provided by an employer. For instance, the employee may possess pay stubs, copies of an employment contract that states earnings, correspondence from an employer or copies of receipts for cash payments. The employee's W2 form is sufficient documentation of earnings actually received from an employer. When there are multiple employers, the employee's income tax return form will list all earnings that were reported to the IRS. If the employee objects to a review of his complete tax return, any personal and irrelevant information can be blocked out before the form is presented to the claimsperson for a review of the earnings information it contains.

An employee who holds multiple jobs should be asked to provide the names and addresses of all employers so that earnings information can be solicited directly from each of these employers. If required, the employee should sign any authorization form that is necessary for release of this information. The employee may be willing to deliver forms to an employer for completion, and this assistance can avoid delays in the receipt of this information. However, it is usually best to require completed documents such as wage statements to be forwarded directly to the claimsperson rather than the employee to avoid the potential for alterations.

8.8 SELF-EMPLOYMENT INCOME vs. EARNINGS

A self-employed person is both an employer and an employee, so earnings records are self-maintained. The injured employee has full control of his business records and is expected to present adequate documentary evidence to support all claimed earnings. The employee's reluctance or refusal to voluntarily produce whatever earnings information is requested creates an inference that claimed earnings are exaggerated.

It is possible to deduce a maximum potential amount of annual earnings from annual business receipts and expenditures. Detailed records of cash receipts and expenditures are basic records maintained by any business. The annual cash receipts of a self-employed person are business income, not personal earnings. All normal operating costs of the business such as rent and supplies are paid from cash receipts. After deducting all business expenses, the remaining portion of business income or profit represents the maximum amount of money that the business had available for the owner's personal use. Claimed earnings are feasible if they do not exceed this upper limit, but actual earnings can be a lesser amount.

Business income does not become earnings until money is transferred from the business to the personal possession of the owner for his personal disposal. In some cases, the owner may receive minimal earnings or none at all from his business. Even when his business is profitable, the owner's self-support may be entirely dependent upon earnings or income from another source. Profits may be retained in business bank accounts for future purchases or invested on behalf of the business. If the business did not make a profit, the business will not have sufficient income to provide any earnings to its owner. For instance, if the business spent $40,000 for operating expenses but only received $20,000 in annual receipts, the owner must have used some other income such as personal savings or loans to support his unprofitable business as well as himself.

Self-employed individuals are required to pay taxes on personal income received from their business. Income tax filings are the most accurate documentation of self-employment earnings and should be requested whenever the veracity of other business records is questioned. Other types of evidence would not be considered reliable unless capable of verification by a third source. For example, some self-maintained records can be verified by comparison to bank records. A business will ordinarily maintain a written record of the payee, purpose, and amount of all cash disbursements, e.g. a check register or copies of canceled checks. Records of deposits to personal checking accounts can provide additional confirmation of the amount of business income that was transferred to the owner personally.

8.9 PRESUMPTION OF EARNINGS – PARTNERS

Per LC4457, in those cases where workers associate "themselves under a partnership agreement, the principal purpose of which is the performance of labor on a particular piece of work," a partner's earnings "shall be deemed to be" $40.00/wk whenever his actual earnings "are not otherwise ascertainable." A partner is automatically entitled to a compensation rate of two-thirds of these earnings, or $26.67, for worker's compensation benefits. Partners will benefit by proving the amount of their actual earnings at any amount above $40, because evidence of actual earnings will void the application of LC4457. A partner who is able to produce proof of actual earnings will surely do so.

8.10 EARNINGS DOCUMENTATION – FROM EMPLOYERS

Employers are legally required to keep separate earnings records for each of their employees. All earnings must be recorded, because the employer pays state and federal payroll taxes from these records. The employer's records should include the date of hire, the rate of pay, the hours worked per week and the effective date of any raises. Additionally, the employer should have copies of its canceled checks, or, if the employer pays cash, the employer may have signed receipts from the employee.

From its records, any employer should be able to complete a wage statement for each of its employees upon request. A wage statement is a form that lists the employee's earnings separately week by week for a one-year period (see also 8.45). Some employers refuse to complete wage statements, because the form is tedious and time-consuming to complete. However, when weekly earnings fluctuate, a weekly earnings history must be obtained in order to compute an average weekly earnings amount.

As a general rule, it is best to request a formal wage statement when it is needed but not as a routine request. If all that is really needed is the total amount of earnings for each quarter or some other period, the employer can usually provide this information with a phone call or a quick note (except that the claims administrator has a duty to obtain a sufficiently detailed wage statement whenever reported earnings are less than the statutory maximum average weekly earnings amount, because the claim file must contain evidence that the employee earned a lesser amount (see CR10109).

The claimsperson should be alert to the fact that occasionally an employer may not be an unbiased source of earnings information. The employer may be known to be a friend or relative of the employee or to have demonstrated animosity towards the employee. The formality of a wage statement should not deter the claimsperson from taking steps to ascertain the accuracy of reported information when there is any reason to suspect its validity, e.g. by comparison to time cards or check stubs. In litigated cases, copies of the actual records from which a wage statement was prepared can be subpoenaed.

8.11 UNDOCUMENTED EARNINGS – IN GENERAL

Some or all earnings may be paid in cash and not documented in any fashion, e.g. cash wages or gratuities. Knowing that the employer will be unable to produce contrary documentation, an injured employee might claim higher earnings than were actually received. The claimsperson must evaluate the probable reasonableness of claimed earnings and apply good judgment to establish an estimated average weekly earnings amount that represents the employee's probable earnings.

The best evidence of undocumented earnings is the employee's own reporting of his income to the Internal Revenue Service or a copy of his income tax return. If the employee alleges that his full earnings were not reported in his tax return, he raises questions as to his veracity – was he correct in his prior statements of earnings or his present allegations? The employee's insistence that his tax return was incorrect subjects him to an anonymous report to the IRS by any private citizen for underpayment of taxes on the amount of claimed higher earnings. The reporting individual remains nameless and thus has little fear of any type of repercussion. These reports are not routinely made by claimspersons, although there is really nothing to prevent them.

It is not the claimsperson's job to discover cases of income tax evasion. The goal is to establish a compensation rate that is based upon earnings actually received by the employee. When earnings are undocumented, average weekly earnings are nearly always a compromised earnings amount and the employee's credibility is a major consideration in determining this amount. When the employee refuses to produce an income tax return or any other information within the employee's control, such information is usually presumed to contain facts that contradict the level of earnings alleged. The earnings amount to which the claimsperson will agree will reflect the extent to which the employee's allegations appear to be reasonable versus self-serving and whether such allegations are otherwise verifiable.

8.12 UNDOCUMENTED EARNINGS – CASH WAGES

Some employers pay their employees in cash rather than by check. Their reasons for doing this may or may not be legitimate. Construction trades with day to day employees commonly pay workers in cash. Some employers pay employees in cash, keep no records whatsoever and then deny a person worked for them at all. When neither party has any documentation of earnings, it is necessary to determine which individual is more credible.

Coemployees are a prime source of supplemental information, since they can provide verification of the injured employee's earnings based upon what they themselves are earning. If there are no coemployees, the employee's probable earnings can be established by a comparison method. It is reasonable to presume that the employee would receive wages at or near the same amount that is being paid to similarly qualified employees who perform comparable work for other employers in the same locale.

8.13 UNDOCUMENTED EARNINGS – TIPS & GRATUITIES

Certain jobs provide a base wage, but it is anticipated that the employee will have additional earnings in the form of tips paid in cash by customers. Federal laws require gratuitous earnings to be reported to the IRS as income. However, this is an area of law where many are guilty of not adhering to strict legal requirements.

It is not uncommon for employees to earn high tips and report only a portion of these on their income tax returns in order to reduce their tax liabilities Then, after an injury, the employee wishes to have his "real income" used to compute average weekly earnings so that his compensation rate will be higher. Usually, the person most knowledgeable of the actual amount of tips received is the employee who wishes to have his weekly compensation rate established at the highest possible amount. When an employee has claimed different amounts for different purposes, it is obvious that the accuracy of claimed earnings is questionable and an investigation of claimed earnings is therefore necessary.

Coemployees are often aware of the approximate amount of tips received by other employees. If not, they can at least verify the amount of tips they receive and this information can provide a basis for determining the reasonable range of tips in a particular establishment. The employer should be asked to provide an opinion as to the reasonableness of claimed tips as well as the overall credibility of the employee. In some businesses, such as restaurants, the employer can provide further assistance by reporting the weekly sales based upon receipts. Assuming that a percentage of total receipts would be paid in tips, these records enable a realistic assessment of actual tips.

Cash earnings in many businesses can be appraised in the same manner, e.g. determining the number of cars parked per day in a valet parking lot. When the injured employee is the solitary employee at a particular establishment, it may be prudent to locate employees at similar establishments in the same locality for verification of the level of their usual and customary tips.

8.14 SOCIAL SECURITY RECORDS

The Social Security Administration keeps records by employee name and social security number that document quarterly earnings. This information is compiled from payroll information submitted by employers and the records will show earnings from all employers for whom the employee worked during a year. These records are useful in cases where the employer(s) is now out of business or won't cooperate by supplying earnings information. Social Security records are extremely helpful in cumulative injury or occupational disease cases where earnings information is needed from past years, because these records include the names and addresses of the employers as well as the total wages paid by each. The Social Security Administration won't release information without the employee's written consent submitted on a special authorization form that is provided by this federal agency.

8.15 AVERAGE WEEKLY EARNINGS – EARNING CAPACITY

Earning capacity refers to an employee's ability to earn. Some limits on earnings are controlled by the employee and some limits are controlled by his employers. Other limits exist due to the employee's competitiveness with other job applicants in the open labor market. The earnings actually received by an employee are factual evidence of the employee's ability to earn as well as his desire to earn. Thus, the employee's actual earnings are used to measure his earning capacity. The employee's earning capacity is stated as a weekly earnings amount called average weekly earnings (AWE).

"Average" is a mathematical term. To find an average for any group of numbers, you add them together for a total, then divide the total by the number of separate numbers in the group. The employee's weekly earnings are averaged in this way. The averaging balances out fluctuations over a period of time and enables the employee's earning capacity to be stated as one weekly amount. An average is usually computed from earnings received during a one-year period but shorter periods may be used (see 8.45-8.50). Per LC4451, "average annual earnings shall be taken at fifty-two times the average weekly earnings" of the employee. Put another way, earnings are verified to be "average" weekly earnings when 52 times this amount equals (or nearly equals) annual earnings actually received by the employee in the one-year period of earnings reviewed.

The employee's average weekly earnings amount should accurately represent the employee's present, continued or future weekly earning capacity. The amount used for an average weekly earnings figure should be an accurate prediction of continued earnings that were interrupted at the time an injury occurred. Earnings used to compute an average are those that are most likely to be predictive of continued earnings if the employee had not been injured. Per LC4455, such earnings are determined by facts in existence "at the time of the injury." However, depending upon the circumstances, the employee's average weekly earnings, or earning capacity, can be computed from present, past or future, but not yet realized, earnings. A combination of these can also be used.

8.16 EARNING CAPACITY – USE OF PAST EARNINGS

Weekly earnings can fluctuate regularly. Earnings in the week when an injury occurs may merely form a small part of a continuing and changing cycle. Earnings are not expected to continue at this weekly level; the employee's cyclical earnings are expected to continue. Therefore, past earnings (preinjury earnings) are used to compute the employee's average weekly earnings. An average of past earnings will represent the employee's reasonably anticipated continued earnings on a weekly basis.

In general, past earnings will be used to compute average weekly earnings in these situations:

    a. The employee is a seasonal or temporary employee with an established pattern of periods of earnings followed by periods of no earnings.

    b. The employee has permanent employment, but the employee's weekly earnings frequently go up or down.

There are two basic reasons for weekly fluctuations in pay for employees who are steadily employed by one employer:

    1. The employee's rate of pay is constant, but the hours worked vary from week to week, e.g. overtime work or an on-call employee.

    2. The employee works a constant number of hours weekly but receives variable earnings, e.g. tips or commissions.

8.17 EARNING CAPACITY – USE OF PRESENT EARNINGS

Present earnings means earnings during the seven days immediately preceding an injury. Current weekly earnings may be all that are necessary to measure the employee's earning capacity. Past earnings are irrelevant after there has been a permanent change from past earnings levels. Past earnings can be the same as the employee's present earnings. Future earnings may be unknown, except that present earnings are reasonably anticipated to continue at the current level. In such cases, the employee's present earnings are an accurate reflection of the employee's present, as well as continued, earning capacity. Irrelevant past earnings and unknown future earnings are not considered. The employee's date-of-injury earnings, or present earnings, are the proper basis for computing average weekly earnings.

Present earnings means the earnings the employee would have made the week he was injured if he had worked the entire week as scheduled. In general, present earnings accurately measure earning capacity when:

    1. A permanent full time employee has changed jobs in the last year and the new job is also a permanent full time job.

    2. A permanent part time employee has accepted a permanent full time employment or vice versa. The employee's current earnings represent a permanent change from prior earnings.

    3. A permanent employee had a recent raise. Future earnings would continue at the current level, not a previously lower level.

8.18 EARNING CAPACITY – USE OF FUTURE EARNINGS

Post-injury earnings refer to earnings the employee would have received if the injury had not precluded continued employment. These earnings are used when the employee is in the process of changing earning capacity at the time of the injury. At the point where the employee's earning capacity would have increased or decreased, future unrealized earnings can be approximated and used to compute an average weekly earnings amount that applies thereafter. Post-injury earnings do not affect the amount of the employee's average weekly earnings until the known effective date of an imminent change.

There is a critical distinction between provable facts of future earnings and hopes, dreams or plans that may be temporary in nature and are not capable of proof by any reasonable methods. For instance, the employee may tell everyone he does not plan to work after retiring in two weeks, but a future change in family finances could cause the employee to go to work for a different employer. The employee may intend to do consulting work after retirement and may have taken steps such as purchasing business licenses but there may never be any clients willing to pay for such services. Present earnings or past earnings would more accurately reflect the earning capacity of these employees post-injury. The fact that is provable is that each of these employees will retire, not that they will stay retired or that they will obtain earnings if they seek work (that explains the historical reluctance of appellate courts to sanction reductions in the employee's average weekly earnings based upon anticipated post-injury reductions in earnings.).

There is a danger in using future earnings amounts that the employee has not received. Forecasting future events usually amounts to pure guesswork. Until the event takes place, it is usually just as reasonable to anticipate that it will not occur. Any employee could allege that his near-future earnings will be different from present and past earnings. Any person to whom this statement was made would most likely inquire as to the basis for this allegation. The employee may be aware of an imminent event such as the starting date of a new job or the effective date of a raise, or the employee may have advance knowledge from reliable sources of a cost of living increase.

Anything is possible when speaking of future events. However, some things are more probable than others. The probability of future earnings can be assessed. Average weekly earnings at the time of an injury are presumed to continue into the future unless evidence exists that a change in earnings is expected to occur at a specific future date. When such evidence is convincing, the employee's average weekly earnings should be based upon reasonably anticipated future earnings. It is not necessary that the employee actually receive the future earnings but only that it can be ascertained that a disability prevents the employee from receiving these earnings at a specific time. Per LC4453, this determination is controlled by facts existing "at the time of injury."

Future earnings will be used to compute average weekly earnings when evidence of future events exists at the time of injury, as illustrated in the following situations:

1. The employee has already quit his current job and another employer has hired him, set his wages and provided a definite starting date.

2. The employee recently completed an apprenticeship program and has been notified of the effective date of a promotion and pay increase.
3. The employee has taken a written examination, successful completion of which will automatically qualify the employee for a 5% pay increase retroactive to the date of the test, but test results are not yet available.

8.19 EARNING CAPACITY – NEED TO REASSESS

It may be necessary to compute the amount of the employee's average weekly earnings more than once. The average weekly earnings amount initially established on a claim may represent a temporary appraisal of the employee's earnings pending receipt of additional earnings information. Present earnings, or date of injury earnings, may be used for the known duration of their continued receipt. Occasionally, these earnings are a temporary deviation from an established pattern. On the date that a prior average weekly earnings amount fails to reflect the employee's earning capacity, a new average weekly earnings amount will be computed. A revised average weekly earnings amount may be based upon past earnings or future unrealized, whichever is appropriate for assessing continued earning capacity. If it is known at the time of injury that the employee's current earning capacity will undergo a permanent change on the date of a known future event, then the employee's average weekly earnings will ordinarily be assessed as of the date of injury and again as of the date of the future event (see 9.5).

Earnings selected to compute an initial average weekly earnings amount are based upon facts in existence at the time of injury. These facts determine whether present, past or future earnings will be used immediately to compute average weekly earnings and/or at some time in the future to recompute average weekly earnings. In the following examples, average weekly earnings will be recomputed after the injury using information that is known on the date of injury:

1. The employee works frequent overtime and a pay increase was scheduled to take effect on a future date. On this date, earnings will be recomputed using the new hourly rate, but the average hours worked per week will be taken from the past. Future earnings information will be combined with past earnings information to compute average weekly earnings.
2. The date of injury job is a temporary assignment and the employee has a starting date for a different job. As of such date, future unrealized earnings will be used to compute a new average weekly earnings amount that will be used from that date forward.
3. The date of injury job is a temporary assignment and the employee has not made any future plans. On the date the present job would end, average weekly earnings will be recomputed using past earnings.

8.20 REFERENCE GUIDE – RECOMPUTE EARNINGS

There are a great number of possible earnings situations. The employee's average weekly earnings may be computed once using either present, past or future earnings. This situation is the most common and does not require further clarification. However, an initially established average weekly earnings amount will be changed as of the date when this amount ceases to represent the employee's probable continued earnings if not disabled (as determined from earnings information that is known at the time of injury).

Any earnings situation that necessitates the use of different amounts of average weekly earnings for different periods of disability payments will usually fall under one of the major categories listed below. The list is provided only as a guide. Its purpose is to facilitate the recognition of factors that affect the selection of past or future earnings to compute a replacement average weekly earnings amount that will be used as of the date of a known future event.

Increase in Earnings is Anticipated

If anticipated earnings can be verified as to amount and have some definite effective date, future earnings will be used to compute a new average weekly earnings amount from that date forward. A recomputation might be necessary where:

a. An employee who belongs to a union is injured a week before the effective date of a cost of living increase, and the collective bargaining agreement also provides for an hourly pay increase effective in three months with the amount being linked to the employer's year-to-date profits at that time.

b. A part time employee was promised a full time position upon graduation from college and graduates from college after an injury, or a law clerk was promised a raise upon passing the State Bar examination and this event has occurred.

c. The employee is awaiting a decision on a grievance that the employee filed alleging he had been performing work out-of-classification and paid less than the appropriate hourly rate of pay for the last nine months.

Decrease in Earnings is Anticipated

Depending upon the reason for the decrease, average weekly earnings may be computed only once or recomputed as of the date of the change based upon probable future earnings. If earnings at the time of injury were a temporary deviation from a past cycle, past earnings must be used to compute average weekly earnings. However, future unrealized earnings will be used as of the date when there is a verifiable new and permanent change in earnings (see also 8.18 and 9.5). In the following examples, there is a reasonable certainty that the employee's earnings will decrease on a specific date:

a. The employee was paid as a supervisor when injured during a supervisor's three-week leave but would thereafter receive regular, and lower, wages.

b. The employee was injured at a temporary job that had a definite termination date; previous employment was only on an intermittent basis.

   c. The employee's payroll classification was being downgraded, he had been advised that advance notice of the effective date of an anticipated decrease in pay would be provided within sixty days.

Earnings Increased – Post-Injury

As of the date of the change, average weekly earnings will be recomputed utilizing the new earnings information if there is specific demonstrable evidence of an increase in the employee's earning capacity. For example:

   a. The employer verifies home-office approval of an employee's preinjury request for a transfer to a higher paying job with a definite starting date.

   b. The employer verifies completion of a job restructuring program, that was in progress at the time of injury, and that an affiliated increase in pay applies to the employee as of a specific date.

   c. The employee returned to work and had a performance appraisal that was scheduled but not yet conducted when an injury occurred, and the employee receives a retroactive pay increase based upon such appraisal.

Earnings Decreased – Post-Injury

The mere fact that the employee's earnings would have decreased anyway if an injury had not occurred is not necessarily sufficient proof of a post-injury reduction in the earning capacity (see 8.18 and 9.5). An increase in post-injury earnings is generally accepted as proof of an increase in the employee's earning capacity, but the reverse is not true.

Average weekly earnings will not be recomputed as of the date of a post-injury decrease in weekly earnings absent evidence to support an actual change in the employee's earning capacity. There must be proof that lower earnings are truly representational, not merely an aberration. If so, average weekly earnings will be recomputed as of the effective date of the change using reasonably continued earnings beyond this point in time. Bearing in mind that employees usually resist any reduction in the amount established as their average weekly earnings, earnings will undeniably decrease on the date of any of the specific post-injury events described below.

   a. All persons in the employee's job classification are notified that overtime work will no longer be necessary, or they are notified of an across-the-board permanent reduction in pay.

   b. The employee was scheduled to commence a different and lower paying job (an important fact to determine might be whether this change was at the employee's request and for the employee's benefit, e.g. where the employee wanted a job with no overtime work or the employee requested a demotion out of a supervisory position).

   c. The employee is incarcerated in a penal institution for a specific period of time that could be months, years or for life (see 9.19 and 10.16).

8.21 AVERAGE WEEKLY EARNINGS – BASICS

If the employee earns the same amount each week, no mathematical averaging is necessary. No matter how many weeks are used, the average weekly earnings figure will not change. The earnings for any week are the employee's average weekly earnings.

Where weekly earnings vary, averaging balances out ups and downs in earnings to produce a weekly earnings amount that is representative of the earnings the employee actually receives on a continuing basis. An average weekly earnings amount will always lie between the highest number and the lowest number in the grouping.

SAMPLE (A). Average Earnings – Not Highest Or Lowest Earnings

$ 800	$ 600	$ 850
900	900	900
800	700	800
+ 900	+ 800	+ 950
$3400 ÷ 4 = $850/wk	$3000 ÷ 4 = $750/wk	$3500 ÷ 4 = $875/wk

The accuracy of the average weekly earnings amount increases as the number of weeks of earnings used to compute the average increases. In most cases, an average will be considered accurate when it is based upon all weeks of earnings in a one-year period preceding the injury (per LC4453(c-3)).

Averaging too few weeks of earnings will produce a distorted average weekly earnings figure. Isolated weeks with inordinately high or low earnings will "weight" the average so that it is not truly representative of the employee's average weekly earnings.

Note the difference in average weekly earnings amounts obtained using two separate isolated periods of four weeks as opposed to an eight-week period of earnings as shown below.

SAMPLE (B1). Averaging Distorted By Too Few Weeks of Earnings.

$ 600	$ 600
900	900
700	700
+ 800	800
$3000 ÷ 4 = $750.00	850
	900
$ 850	800
900	+ 950
800	$6500 ÷ 8 = $812.50
+ 950	
$3500 ÷ 4 = $875.00	

SAMPLE (B1). Averaging Distorted by Too Few Weeks of Earnings.

$ 732 $ 732
  800   800
  900   900
+ 800   800
$3232 ÷ 4 = $808.00   700
                                     650
$ 700   675
  650   + 600
  675                              $5857 ÷ 8 = $732.13
+ 600
$2625 ÷ 4 = $656.25

8.22 COMPENSATION RATE – TWO-THIRDS OF AWE

The employee's compensation rate for all workers' compensation indemnity benefits is computed by taking two-thirds of the employee's average weekly earnings, subject to separate minimum and maximum limits that apply to each category of benefit that the employee is paid (refer to text sections for each benefit category). The basic two-thirds formula is specified by LC4653 for temporary disability benefits and by LC4658 for permanent disability benefits. Per LC4702, the death indemnity benefit is payable "in the same manner ... as temporary total disability indemnity," and LC139.5 contains comparable wording regarding the compensation rate for rehabilitation indemnity benefits.

Mathematically there are several ways to find the amount that equals two-thirds of average weekly earnings. Two-thirds of average weekly earnings (AWE) will result from use of any of the formulas shown in the chart below. The choice of a particular method is usually a matter of personal preference (although use of any decimal variation of .66667 is strongly discouraged for reasons explained in 8.23 below).

TWO-THIRDS OF AVERAGE WEEKLY EARNINGS	
1. AWE × ⅔ (fraction)	~~4. AWE × .66667~~
2. AWE × 2 ÷ 3 (calculator)	5. Monthly Earnings ÷ 6.5
3. AWE ÷ 1.5	6. Annual Earnings ÷ 78

8.23 COMPENSATION RATE – FROM WEEKLY EARNINGS

Once an average weekly earnings (AWE) amount has been identified, there are three commonly used methods for computing two-thirds of this amount. Regardless of the method that is used, decimal numbers must be rounded off to two decimal places so that the compensation rate (CR) can be stated as a dollar and cents amount. The rounding off process can produce inaccurate results if computations are not carried out a sufficient number of decimal positions before rounding off. To double-check the accuracy of the compensation rate, the results obtained with one method can be compared to the results obtained when an alternate method is used. Each of the three methods described below should produce the same weekly compensation rate to the penny.

1. Calculator Computations With Fraction Two-Thirds

When the fraction ⅔ is used, computations of the compensation rate require two steps. Average weekly earnings will be multiplied by two and the result of this step is divided by three.

$$\text{AWE } \$609.00 \times 2 = 1218 \div 3 = \$406.00/\text{wk CR}$$
$$\text{AWE } \$672.00 \times 2 = 1344 \div 3 = \$448.00/\text{wk CR}$$
$$\text{AWE } \$735.00 \times 2 = 1470 \div 3 = \$490.00/\text{wk CR}$$

2. Shortcut Method – Division By 1.5

Mathematically, the reciprocal of the fraction ⅔ is 1.5 (3 ÷ 2 = 1.5). Therefore, dividing earnings by 1.5 will produce the same result as multiplying by ⅔.

$$\text{AWE } \$609.00 \div 1.5 = \$406.00/\text{wk CR}$$
$$\text{AWE } \$672.00 \div 1.5 = \$448.00/\text{wk CR}$$
$$\text{AWE } \$735.00 \div 1.5 = \$490.00/\text{wk CR}$$

3. Use of Decimal Equivalents Such as .667 – Discouraged

A word of caution is necessary when using abbreviated decimal equivalents of the fraction ⅔. The compensation rate will be inaccurate and too low if average weekly earnings are multiplied by .66, .666, or .6666 and rounded off. The compensation rate will be inaccurate and too high if .667 or .6667 is used and the result is rounded off. The following chart demonstrates the inconsistencies that can occur when various decimal equivalents are used.

$$\text{AWE } \$735 \text{ wk} \times .667 = \$490.245 = \$490.25/\text{wk CR (incorrect)}$$
$$\text{AWE } \$735 \text{ wk} \times .6667 = \$490.024 = \$490.02/\text{wk CR (incorrect)}$$
$$\text{AWE } \$735 \text{ wk} \times .6666 = \$489.951 = \$489.95/\text{wk CR (incorrect)}$$
$$\text{AWE } \$735 \text{ wk} \times .66666 = \$489.995 = \$490.00/\text{wk CR (correct)}$$
$$\text{AWE } \$735 \text{ wk} \times .66667 = \$490.002 = \$490.00/\text{wk CR (correct)}$$

The decimal equivalent of the fraction ⅔ that is necessary to produce the correct compensation rate is .66667 (2 ÷ 3 = .666666).

$$\text{AWE } \$609.00 \times .66667 = 406.002 = \$406.00/\text{wk CR}$$
$$\text{AWE } \$672.00 \times .66667 = 448.002 = \$448.00/\text{wk CR}$$
$$\text{AWE } \$735.00 \times .66667 = 490.002 = \$490.00/\text{wk CR}$$

8.24 COMPENSATION RATE – FROM MONTHLY EARNINGS

There are two basic methods for computing a compensation rate when earnings are stated as a monthly amount. The compensation rate can be computed from a monthly earnings amount in one step. The drawback to this method is that it will not reveal the amount of the employee's average weekly earnings. In the second method, monthly earnings are first converted to a weekly amount before the weekly compensation rate is computed.

1. Two Steps – Convert Monthly Earnings To Compensation Rate

There are $4\frac{1}{3}$ weeks in a month: 52 wks/yr ÷ 12 mos/yr = 4.3333 wks/mo. To convert monthly earnings into average weekly earnings, divide monthly earnings by 4.3333. To ensure accuracy in the average weekly earnings amount, carry this division out to three places and round up from the third decimal position whenever that number is 5 or greater. Next, multiply average weekly earnings by two-thirds to obtain the weekly compensation rate.

$2639/mo ÷ 4.3333 = 609.004 = AWE 609.00 × $\frac{2}{3}$ = $406.00/wk CR
$2912/mo ÷ 4.3333 = 672.005 = AWE 672.00 × $\frac{2}{3}$ = $448.00/wk CR
$3185/mo ÷ 4.3333 = 735.005 = AWE 735.00 × $\frac{2}{3}$ = $490.00/wk CR

Always use the four-place decimal 4.3333. The use of 4.3, 4.33, or 4.333 will produce an average weekly earnings amount that is pennies off and will also cause the weekly compensation rate to be inaccurate.

$3185/mo ÷ 4.3   = 740.697 = AWE 740.70 × $\frac{2}{3}$ = $493.80 CR (incorrect)
$3185/mo ÷ 4.33   = 735.565 = AWE 735.57 × $\frac{2}{3}$ = $490.38 CR (incorrect)
$3185/mo ÷ 4.333   = 735.056 = AWE 735.06 × $\frac{2}{3}$ = $490.04 CR (incorrect)
$3185/mo ÷ 4.3333 = 735.005 = AWE 735.01 × $\frac{2}{3}$ = $490.00 CR (correct)

2. Short Cut – Convert Monthly Earnings Into Compensation Rate

A one-step computation can produce a weekly compensation rate without first computing an average weekly earnings amount. This procedure is useful for a quick computation of the compensation rate from earnings reported as a monthly amount and/or double-checking the compensation rate computed by another method. Simply divide the monthly earnings amount by 6.5, and the result will be the employee's weekly compensation rate (two-thirds of average weekly earnings).

Monthly Earnings $2639.00 ÷ 6.5 = $406/wk CR
Monthly Earnings $2912.00 ÷ 6.5 = $448/wk CR
Monthly Earnings $3185.00 ÷ 6.5 = $490/wk CR

8.25 COMPENSATION RATE – SEMIMONTHLY EARNINGS

Do not confuse semimonthly earnings with being paid every two weeks (26 paychecks a year). An employee who is paid semimonthly gets paid twice a month (24 paychecks a year). There is not an even number of weeks in a month, so semimonthly earnings cannot be divided in half for a weekly earnings amount. Rather, semimonthly earnings are multiplied by two to produce monthly earnings, and the compensation rate is then computed from monthly earnings.

Semimonthly earnings $1319.50 × 2 = $2639/mo

$2639/mo ÷ 4.3333 = AWE $609.00 × $\frac{2}{3}$ = $406/wk CR
$2639/mo ÷ 6.5   = $406/wk CR

Semimonthly earnings $1456.00 × 2 = $2912/mo

$2912/mo ÷ 4.3333 = AWE $672.00 × 2⁄3 = $448/wk CR
$2912/mo ÷ 6.5　　　　　　　　　　　　　= $448/wk CR

8.26 COMPENSATION RATE – FROM ANNUAL EARNINGS

There are two methods for computing a weekly compensation rate from annual earnings. One method computes average weekly earnings before the compensation rate is computed. A second method produces a compensation rate in one step without identifying average weekly earnings.

1. Two Steps – Convert Annual Earnings To Compensation Rate

There are 52 weeks in a year. Dividing annual earnings by 52 will produce an average weekly earnings amount that is then multiplied by two-thirds to produce the weekly compensation rate.

$34,944/yr ÷ 52 = AWE $672.00 × 2⁄3 = $448/wk CR
$38,220/yr ÷ 52 = AWE $735.00 × 2⁄3 = $490/wk CR

2. Short Cut – Convert Annual Earnings Into Compensation Rate

The short cut method converts annual earnings directly into a weekly compensation rate. This is accomplished by dividing annual earnings by the number 78.

$31,668.00/yr ÷ 78 = $406.00/wk CR
$34,944.00/yr ÷ 78 = $448.00/wk CR
$38,220.00/yr ÷ 78 = $490.00/wk CR

8.27 REVERSE COMPUTATIONS – RATE INTO EARNINGS

Some one-step methods produce a compensation rate without revealing an average weekly earnings figure. A weekly compensation rate can easily be converted into the employee's average weekly earnings by applying a reversal of the formula used to compute the compensation rate from an average weekly earnings amount.

1. Convert Compensation Rate Into Average Weekly Earnings

The weekly compensation rate converts into an average weekly earnings amount when the compensation rate is multiplied by either the fraction 3⁄2 or 1.5.

CR $406/wk × 1.5 = $609 AWE or $406/wk × 3 = 1218 ÷ 2 = $609 AWE
CR $448/wk × 1.5 = $672 AWE or $448/wk × 3 = 1344 ÷ 2 = $672 AWE
CR $490/wk × 1.5 = $735 AWE or $490/wk × 3 = 1470 ÷ 2 = $735 AWE

2. Convert Compensation Rate Into Monthly/Annual Earnings

Reverse computations can also be used to double-check the accuracy of the compensation rate computed from monthly or annual earnings.

Earnings $2639/mo ÷ 6.5 = CR $406/wk × 6.5 = $2639/mo
Earnings $2912/mo ÷ 6.5 = CR $448/wk × 6.5 = $2912/mo

$31,668yr ÷ 78 = CR $406/wk × 78 = $31,668/yr
$38,220/yr ÷ 78 = CR $490/wk × 78 = $38,220/yr

8.28 ASSESSING AVERAGE EARNINGS – PRELIMINARY STEPS

Assessment of average weekly earnings is an individualized process. Before any earnings are averaged, it is necessary to know certain relevant facts regarding the employee's earning circumstances. According to LC4453, relevant facts are facts existing and capable of proof "at the time of injury." In particular, the following information should be ascertained by a preliminary investigation:

    a. Source of all earnings, e.g. one or more jobs or employments versus self-employments.

    b. Category of employment, e.g. temporary or permanent, full time or part time.

    c. Rate of pay and frequency, e.g. hourly pay or commissions, paid weekly or monthly.

    d. Continuity of date of injury earnings, e.g. whether long-term continued earnings should be based on past, present, future unrealized earnings or some combination of these.

8.29 REFERENCE GUIDE – FOUR EARNINGS SITUATIONS

All earnings situations will be described by one (or some combination) of the four subsections of LC4453(c). Before average weekly earnings can be computed, it is necessary to identify the subsection that most accurately describes the employee's earnings situation, because this subsection will also set forth the method to be used in computing the employee's average weekly earnings. Where the employee's situation is accurately described under more than one subsection, computations will require a coordination of each of the separately described methods for determining an average weekly earnings amount.

The method for computing average weekly earnings in a variety of specific situations will be covered in text sections that follow. However, the list below summarizes the basic provisions of each subsection of LC4453 to aid in identifying the subsection(s) to be applied to a particular employee. Each situation below is identified by the number of the subsection of LC4453 that pertains to this particular earnings situation.

    (c-1) **Regular Full Time Employment.** The employee works 30 hours or more per week for one employer on a regular basis.
                  AND/OR

    (c-2) **Multiple Employments.** The employee is employed by "two or more employers at or about the time of injury."
                  AND/OR

    (c-3) **Irregular Weekly Earnings.** The employee's earnings are paid on a piecework or commission basis (not hourly), and/or earnings regularly vary in amount from week-to-week, OR

    (c-3) **Set Pay For Irregular Hours.** The employee's earnings are "specified to be by the week, month, or other period." The employee is paid a set amount regardless of hours worked.
                  AND/OR

    (c-4) **Part Time Employment.** The "employment is for less than 30 hours per week" on a regular basis with one employer.

(c-4) **Intermittent Employment** (as opposed to irregular earnings in permanent employment); for instance, the employee is a temporary or seasonal employee who is not employed on a regular ongoing basis by any particular employer.

(c-4) **Multiple Methods Apply.** The employee's customary earnings situation is described by a combination of the above methods; e.g., the employee is a part time employee who has regular weekly earnings.

(c-4) **Other Methods Do Not apply.** None of the above descriptions accurately describe the employee's customary earnings situation and/or his probable continued earnings.

8.30 REFERENCE GUIDE – METHOD TO COMPUTE AWE

The four separate approaches to computing average weekly earnings that are described under one of the four subsections of LC4453(c) are set out below. Additional details are provided in subsequent sections under topics that identify specific earnings situations. The four different approaches or methods are:

LC4453(c-1)

The employee's average weekly earnings are found by multiplying the number of working days a week times the daily earnings at the time of injury or the number of hours worked per week times the employee's hourly rate of pay.

LC4453(c-2)

This section contains two alternative methods for computing average weekly earnings. The correct method depends upon whether or not the job in which the employee was working at the time of injury pays the highest hourly rate of pay. Referring to the job where the employee was injured, the methods are:

a. Highest hourly rate: add together weekly earnings from all jobs.

b. Not highest hourly rate: the hourly rate of pay for the job where the injury occurred is multiplied times total hours worked per week in all employments.

LC4453(c-3)

The employee's actual weekly earnings are added together and then averaged for one year preceding the date of injury. If the employee did not work for his date of injury employer for an entire year or was not employed the full preceding year, earnings are averaged for such shorter periods of time as may be presumed to produce an accurate average weekly earnings amount (good judgment controls sufficiency of earning period).

LC4453(c-4)

This subsection does not set out any particular method. Rather, this subsection requires an independent review of each situation and application of one, or some combination, of the above methods or any other reasonable approach that is likely to result in an average weekly earnings amount that represents the employee's continued earning capacity at the time of injury.

NOTE – In the following sections, notice the reference to the appropriate subsection of LC4453 in the topic heading. Sample problems do not necessarily contain a date of injury. For actual cases, amounts referred to as average weekly earnings (AWE) in sample computations must fall within the range of the statutory minimum and maximum earnings limits specified in LC4453 on the date the injury occurred (and for the particular category of indemnity benefits that is payable).

8.31 (c-1) FULL TIME JOB – EXPLAINED

Per LC4453(c-1), a full time job is defined as one in which the employee works 30 hours or more per week and five or more days per week for one employer. The language of this section does not recognize the advent of the four-day workweek, but any employee who is employed for 30 hours a week or more in one job is considered to be employed full time.

Labor Code 4453(c-1) applies to permanent full time employees whose earnings are a set amount per week regardless of whether earnings are stated as an hourly, monthly or other rate of pay. The rate of pay is constant, the number of hours worked per week is constant, and the employee's earnings are consistently the same from one week to another over long periods of time.

A full time employee may receive occasional increases in pay, usually on an annual basis, but changes in weekly earnings are infrequent and are usually based upon such things as seniority, merit or cost of living adjustments. The employee's earnings at any given time are anticipated to continue at the same level in this particular job.

The employment may be the first full time position ever held by the employee, and the employee may be injured the first hour on the job. Labor Code 4453(c-1) still applies if, but for an injury, the employee's status would continue to be that of a full time employee. In fact, this section could apply to a temporary full time employment. However, in the case of a temporary job, average earnings computed under this section must also be recomputed to reflect the employee's probable continued average weekly earnings as of the termination date of this employment.

8.32 (c-1) FULL TIME JOB – DAILY RATE OF PAY

If the employer reports earnings as a daily rate of pay, it is necessary to know how many days a week the employee works. Average weekly earnings (AWE) are found by multiplying the daily rate times the days worked per week.

SAMPLE (a). Ron earns $125/day and works 5 days a week.

$$5 \text{ days} \times \$125/\text{day} = \$625 \text{ AWE}$$

SAMPLE (b). Lynda earns $147/day and works 4 days a week.

$$4 \text{ days} \times \$147/\text{day} = \$588 \text{ AWE}$$

8.33 (c-1) FULL TIME JOB – HOURLY PAY & SET HOURS

If the employer reports earnings as an hourly rate of pay, it is necessary to know the total hours worked per week. Average weekly earnings are found by multiplying the hourly rate by the hours worked in one week.

SAMPLE (a). Oscar earns $15.00/hr for 40 hrs/wk.

$$\$15.00 \text{ hour} \times 40 \text{ hrs/wk} = \$600.00 \text{ AWE}$$

SAMPLE (b). Barbara earns $10.00/hr for 35 hrs/wk.

$$\$10.00/\text{hr} \times 35 \text{ hrs/wk} = \$350.00 \text{ AWE}$$

8.34 (c-1) FULL TIME JOB – REGULAR OVERTIME PAY

The LC4453(c-1) method for computing average weekly earnings will still apply when the employee works overtime as long as the employee works the same number of hours of overtime each week. In this event, the employee's earnings will be the same amount from week to week despite the receipt of overtime earnings. The employer should simply be asked to state the amount of the employee's weekly earnings.

If the employer reports earnings as an hourly rate of pay, it is necessary to determine the total number of hours worked per week. Since overtime pay is usually paid at either time and a half or double-time, it is additionally necessary to know how many hours were worked at each hourly rate in order to compute an average weekly earnings amount.

SAMPLE (a). Marilyn's regular earnings are $120/day for 8 hrs/day, 5 days/wk. She also earns consistent overtime pay for 5 hrs/wk at time and a half.

$$\$120.00/\text{day} \div 8 \text{ hrs/day} = \$15.00/\text{hr} \times 1.5 = \$22.50/\text{hr}$$

Regular wages	$15.00/hr × 40 hrs/wk =	$600.00
Overtime pay	$22.50/hr × 5 hrs/wk =	+112.50
		$712.50 AWE

SAMPLE (b). George earns $12/hr for 40 hrs/wk. George also earns $18/hr for 5 hrs/wk on a continuous basis.

Regular wages	$12.00/hr × 40 hrs/wk =	$480.00
Overtime pay	$18.00/hr × 5 hrs/wk =	+ 90.00
		$570.00 AWE

8.35 (c-1) FULL TIME JOB – SHORT TIME ON NEW JOB

An injury that occurs during the first week or first hour on a new full time job may prevent the employee from receiving promised earnings. If the employee's earnings would reasonably have continued at a constant weekly rate of pay with steady hours, method (c-1) is still used. The employer can state the weekly earnings the employee would have been paid if he had not been injured or the rate of pay and the routine number of hours or days of work each week.

SAMPLE (a). Vicki is injured the first hour on a new full time job. Per the employer, Vicki's earnings were set at $16.80/hr for 40 hrs/wk.

$$\$16.80/hr \times 40/hrs/wk = \$672.00 \text{ AWE}$$

SAMPLE (b). Ken is injured his fourth day on a new full time job. Per the employer, earnings were set at $14/hr for 40 hrs/wk. Also, Barry was to work 8 hours every Saturday at $20/hr.

$$
\begin{array}{lll}
\$14.00/hr \times 40 \text{ hrs/wk} = & \$560.00 & \text{Anticipated regular earnings} \\
\$20.00/hr \times 8 \text{ hrs/wk} = & \underline{+160.00} & \text{Anticipated overtime earnings} \\
& \$720.00 & \text{AWE}
\end{array}
$$

8.36 (c-2) MULTIPLE EMPLOYERS – EXPLAINED

Average weekly earnings will be computed under LC4453(c-2) whenever the employee regularly receives earnings from multiple employers, although not necessarily for the same days or same weeks. The most common situation is one where the employee works two jobs. However, any combination of employments is possible, and any number of employers is possible. The employee may perform one job, but more than one employer may pay his weekly wages, e.g. dual or joint employment situations. The employee may have separate jobs and receive wages from different employers in the same weeks, e.g. concurrent employments. The employee may work a weekday and a weekend job, a day and a night job, a full time and a part time job or any other combination of jobs.

(c-2) Method For Computing AWE – Explained

Labor Code 453(c-2) contains two separate methods or formulas. The correct method that applies to a particular claim cannot be identified until the employee's earnings from each employment are stated as an hourly rate of pay. In all cases, it is necessary to know whether or not the employee received his highest hourly rate of pay on the job where the injury occurred. Additionally, computations cannot be performed under one of the two formulas until the number of hours worked per week in each employment are known. In all cases, the hourly rate of pay that is used in computations under the (c-2) method will be the employee's average hourly rate of pay for each employment. Likewise, the hours worked each week will always be the average number of hours worked per week in each job (see 8.53).

It is sometimes necessary to compute average weekly earnings for some of the employee's jobs under one or more of the other subsections of LC4453 before earnings from all employments can be combined under subsection (c-2). Separate and preliminary computations are necessary for each employment where the employee's earnings are not specified as an hourly rate and/or the employee does not work a specific number (the same number) of hours each week. In these cases, average weekly earnings as well as the average weekly hours of work must be computed independently by another method (usually (c-3). Once this information is obtained, the hourly rate of pay in any job can be determined by dividing average weekly earnings by the average number of hours worked each week.

(c-2) Financial Impact on Employer & Employee

Using either method in LC4453(c-2), the employee's average weekly earnings will always be greater than actual earnings from the job where the injury occurred. If other jobs pay the same or a lower hourly rate, every penny the employee earns raises his average weekly earnings amount. A portion of earnings from jobs with a higher hourly rate will be discounted, but the employee's average weekly earnings will still be higher than if they were computed solely from the job where the injury occurred.

An employee who does not receive full credit for all actual weekly earnings from all jobs is likely to be upset. However, the employee will always receive a financial benefit under the (c-2) method while the employer who pays benefits will always be adversely affected because the employee's average weekly earnings will include earnings that this employer did not pay.

Under any subsection of LC4453, the employer who is liable for payment of benefits is the employer for whom the employee was working at the time the injury occurred. This employer will pay two-thirds of the employee's average weekly earnings as a weekly compensation rate, and, under the (c-2) method, the employee's weekly benefit will exceed the amount of the weekly wages this employer paid (refer to examples in 8.37-8.39).

The employer who pays benefits has no way to recover any contribution from the employee's other employers, nor does its insurance carrier have any right to collect premiums from those employers. Additionally, even though premiums are based upon an employer's annual payroll, the insurer who becomes obligated to provide benefits cannot collect premium from its policyholder based on the earnings that an employee receives from some other employment.

The (c-2) method recognizes the fact that after an injury with one employer, earnings will also be lost from any other employment from which the employee is also disabled. The injury that prevented the employee from receiving these additional earnings occurred in the employ of one employer. For this reason, this employer has been made financially responsible for payment of a benefit rate that considers the employee's additional loss of earnings from other employments. Even so, there is an obvious inequity in requiring an employer to provide benefits based on two-thirds of higher average weekly earnings than it actually paid. This inequity is recognized by the legislature to the extent that the employer who is liable for the provision of benefits is allowed to discount all earnings paid by other employers at higher hourly rates of pay.

8.37 (c-2) JOB WHERE INJURED – HIGHEST HOURLY RATE

Per LC4453(c-2), when the employee is injured on the job that pays the highest hourly rate of pay, the employee's average weekly earnings are computed by taking 100% of the aggregate of the employee's "earnings from all employments computed in terms of one week." The employee's hourly rate on the job where the injury occurred must be compared to the hourly rate of pay on his other jobs in order to know that this job paid the highest hourly rate. Therefore, it is necessary to know the hourly rate of pay in each job. However, the hourly rates of pay in each job are not used to compute the employee's average weekly earnings after this initial determination, nor are the number of hours worked per week in each job. The employee's earnings from all employments are simply added together for an overall weekly earnings amount.

SAMPLE (a). Diane works a full time job where she earns $600/wk, and her rate of pay is $15/hr. She also works a part time job where she earns $84/wk at $12/hr. Diane is injured on the full time job (highest hourly rate).

$$\$600/wk + \$84/wk = \$684 \text{ AWE}$$

SAMPLE (b). Phyllis is injured on a full time (FT) job where she earns $18/hr and works 30 hrs/wk and also has a part time (PT) job for 10 hrs/wk that pay $14/hr.

FT job pays $18.00/hr × 30 hrs/wk	$540.00
PT job pays $14.00/hr × 10 hrs/wk	+140.00
	$680.00 AWE

SAMPLE (c). Theresa works three part time jobs each week. She is injured on the job paying $18/hr. Both of the other jobs have a lower hourly rate of pay.

Job A $18.00/hr × 10 hrs/wk	$180.00
Job B $14.00/hr × 20 hrs/wk	280.00
Job C $12.00/hr × 10 hrs/wk	+120.00
	$580.00 AWE

8.38 (c-2) JOB WHERE INJURED – NOT HIGHEST RATE

The employee may be injured on a job that does not pay his highest hourly rate. He may work more hours a week for this employer than for any other, the job may be his only full time job and he may receive the highest weekly earnings from this employer. However, the hours worked per week are not controlling — the hourly rate of pay in the employment where the injury occurred controls the method that is used to compute an average weekly earnings amount.

Per LC4453(c-2), "the earnings from employments other than the employment in which the injury occurred shall not be taken at a higher rate than the hourly rate paid at the time of the injury." The employee's average weekly earnings are computed by multiplying the hourly rate in the job where the injury occurred times the total hours worked each week in all employments.

SAMPLE (A). Cheryl works a full time job where she earns $480/wk at an hourly rate of $12/hr. Cheryl is injured on a part time job where she earns $200/wk at $10/hr.

PT job @ $10.00/hr (lower rate, must use)	20 hrs/wk
FT job @ $12.00/hr (higher rate, cannot use)	+40 hrs/wk
$10/hr × 60 hrs/wk =	$600.00 AWE

SAMPLE (B). Joanie has a full time job for one employer where she works for 30 hrs/wk. She earns $16/hr on her full time job. Joanie is injured on a part time job where she earns $12/hr for 10 hrs/wk.

(B1). Joanie's actual earnings prior to injury.

PT job	$12.00/hr × 10 hrs/wk	$120.00/wk
FT job	$16.00/hr × 30 hrs/wk	+480.00/wk
		$600.00/wk Actual Earnings

(B2). Joanie's average weekly earnings at time of injury.

$$40 \text{ hrs/wk} \times \$12.00/\text{hr} = \$480.00 \text{ AWE}$$

(B3). Alternative procedure for computing Joanie's average earnings.

PT job	10 hrs/wk × $12.00/hr	$120.00/wk
FT job	30 hrs/wk × $12.00/hr	+360.00/wk
		$480.00 AWE

8.39 (c-2) MORE THAN TWO JOBS & HOURLY RATES

The employee may have more than two jobs. One job may have a higher hourly rate than the job where the injury occurred and another job may have a lower rate of pay than this job. The hourly rate in all other jobs is compared to the hourly rate of pay in the job where the injury occurred. The employee's average weekly earnings will be the sum of the following:

1. The employee's average weekly earnings on the job where injured, AND
2. The sum of the employee's average weekly earnings in all other jobs that pay a lower hourly rate, AND
3. The hourly rate on the job where injured multiplied times the total hours worked per week in any other jobs that pay a higher hourly rate of pay.

SAMPLE (A). Rhonda earns a different hourly rate in each of her three jobs. She is injured on Job A that pays $8/hr. Job B and Job C pay $6/hr and $10/hr respectively.

(A1). First, tally Rhonda's actual earnings from all jobs. The average weekly earnings amount that is computed in the formula must be less than Rhonda's actual weekly earnings from all employments because Rhonda was injured on Job A, but Job C paid the highest hourly rate of pay.

Job A	$ 8.00/hr × 20 hrs/wk	$160.00/wk
Job B	$ 6.00/hr × 10 hrs/wk	60.00/wk
Job C	$10.00/hr × 20 hrs/wk	+200.00/wk
		$420.00/wk Actual Earnings

(A2). For the first step of the formula, add together the average weekly earnings from Job A where the injury occurred and weekly earnings from all jobs that pay the same or a lower hourly rate of pay.

Job A $8.00/hr × 20 hrs/wk $160.00/wk
Job B $6.00/hr × 10 hrs/wk   + 60.00/wk
                                 $220.00/wk AWE for Jobs A and B

(A3). Second, for any jobs that paid with a higher rate of pay than Job A where the injury occurred, multiply the total hours worked in those jobs times the hourly rate of pay in the job where Rhonda was injured.

Job C 20 hrs/wk × $8.00/hr = $160.00 AWE for Job C

(A4). Combine average earnings from lower and higher paying jobs.

Job A + B $220.00/wk
Job C   +160.00/wk
            $380.00 AWE (not $420/wk – see (a1))

SAMPLE (B). Jack has four jobs with different rates of pay. He is injured on Job A that pays $12.00/hr.

(B1). Add actual weekly earnings from all of Jack's employments.

Job A $12.00/hr × 10 hrs/wk $120.00/wk
Job B $15.00/hr × 20 hrs/wk   300.00/wk
Job C $14.00/hr × 5 hrs/wk   70.00/wk
Job D $10.00/hr × 15 hrs/wk   +150.00/wk
                                  $640.00/wk Actual Earnings

(B2). Combine average weekly earnings from all of Jack's employments.

Job A $12.00/hr × 10 hrs/wk $120.00/wk
Job B $12.00/hr × 20 hrs/wk   240.00/wk
Job C $12.00/hr × 5 hrs/wk   60.00/wk
Job D $10.00/hr × 15 hrs/wk   +150.00/wk
                                  $570.00/wk AWE

SAMPLE (C). Paul works four jobs every week. He is injured on Job A that pays a higher rate than two jobs and a lower rate than one job.

(C1). Add actual weekly earnings from all of Paul's employments.

Job A $20.00/hr × 16 hrs/wk $320.00/wk
Job B $12.00/hr × 8 hrs/wk   96.00/wk
Job C $15.00/hr × 10 hrs/wk   150.00/wk
Job D $30.00/hr × 4 hrs/wk   +120.00/wk
                                  $686.00/wk Actual Earnings

(C2). For jobs with same or lower hourly rate, Paul gets full credit for average weekly earnings in each.

Job B	$12.00/hr × 8 hrs/wk	$ 96.00/wk
Job C	$15.00/hr × 10 hrs/wk	+150.00/wk
		$246.00/wk

(C3). For jobs at higher rates, Paul only gets credit up to the hourly rate of pay in the job where he was injured:

$$\text{Job D} \quad \$20.00/hr \times 4\,hrs/wk \;=\; \$80.00/wk$$

(C4). Combine average weekly earnings from all employments. Paul will get full credit for his weekly earnings in Job A because he was injured on the job that paid his highest hourly rate.

Job A	$20.00/hr × 16 hrs/wk	$320.00/wk
Job B + Job C		246.00/wk
Job D		+ 80.00/wk
Average Weekly Earnings		$646.00/wk

(C5). Check your computations. Paul's average weekly earnings should be less than his actual earnings from all jobs on the date of injury:

$646 AWE is less than actual earnings of $686/wk.

8.40 (c-3) IRREGULAR EARNINGS – EXPLAINED

In most instances, the employee is paid an hourly rate; he works the same number of hours each week; and his earnings are the same amount from week to week on a fairly steady basis. However, earnings don't always fall into this normal pattern. When they don't, the employee's earnings are deemed to be irregular. The term "irregular" addresses itself only to the employee's earnings and has nothing to do with the category of employment, e.g. permanent or temporary. The method set out in subsection (c-3) will be used to compute average weekly earnings whenever the employee's earnings are irregular in either of the following ways:

1. Earnings are not consistently the same amount each week the employee works, OR
2. Earnings are not stated at a fixed hourly rate for a set number of hours each week.

8.41 (c-3) WAGE STATEMENTS - OVERVIEW

When earnings are irregular, a wage statement (WS) must be obtained from the employer. Per LC4453(c-3), past weeks of earnings must be averaged for such "period of time, not exceeding one year, as may conveniently be taken to determine an average weekly rate of pay." No minimum number of weeks is specified, but common sense should determine whether sufficient weeks of earnings are available from which to compute an average in cases where the employee was employed less than an entire year. If the period of reported earnings is too short, average weekly earnings should be computed under method (c-4) rather than (c-3).

The purpose of averaging earnings is to identify a representative average weekly earnings figure, one that is not arbitrary or based upon isolated short periods of uncharacteristically high or low earnings. The employee should not be penalized by a low average weekly earnings amount just because the injury happened to occur during a week with unusually low earnings. Likewise, the employer should not be penalized by paying compensation rates that are based upon higher than average earnings during the week when an injury occurred. An average weekly earnings amount is accurate and fair for both the employee and the employer when it realistically reflects the employee's average level of weekly earnings on a continuous and long-term basis.

8.42 (c-3) WS – QUARTERLY TOTALS FOR EARNINGS

The employer may report earnings as quarterly totals rather than separately by week. A quarter is 13 weeks (52 wks/yr ÷ 4 quarters). It is perfectly acceptable to compute average weekly earnings from quarterly earnings amounts as long as the employee has a full 52 weeks of earnings. The earnings from all quarters are totaled then divided by 52, the total weeks in a one year period, to produce the amount of the employee's average weekly earnings.

1st	Q. Earnings	$ 6,250.00
2nd	Q. Earnings	6,805.50
3rd	Q. Earnings	5,750.00
4th	Q. Earnings	+ 8,194.50

$27,000.00 Annual Earnings ÷ 52 wks = $519.23 AWE

8.43 (c-3) WS – ABERRANT HIGH/LOW EARNINGS

A wage statement may reveal isolated weeks with exceptionally high or inordinately low earnings. These weeks may represent a fluke in the employee's usual level of earnings, merely a short period when earnings were different from all other weeks. An example of increased earnings would be extra hours worked on a special one-time project, such as gathering records to prepare for an income tax audit. An example of reduced earnings would be one week without overtime work due to the breakdown of a company vehicle used for making deliveries. An employee without paid sick leave may have an aberrant period of two weeks without earnings while recovering from an automobile accident.

The period of the variance doesn't matter; the significance of identifying these short-term variances is that they are nonrecurrent. There is nothing "average" about such isolated deviations, and these weeks of earnings do not comprise part of the employee's regular earnings pattern.

In situations of unrepresentatively high or low earnings, all transient weeks of earnings should be eliminated from consideration in computing average weekly earnings. The number of weeks of aberrant earnings as well as the amount of earnings in each of these weeks should be subtracted from the totals reported on a wage statement. The number of weeks remaining is then divided into the total amount of earnings reported to compute the amount of the employee's average weekly earnings.

8.44 (c-3) WS – CYCLICAL HIGH OR LOW EARNINGS

A wage statement may reveal intermittent periods of high and low earnings. The employee cannot request that consideration be given only to his highest weeks of earnings or his "best" weeks. Likewise, the employer cannot ignore particular weeks where earnings greatly exceed earnings in most other weeks. The average weekly earnings amount should be computed using every week of earnings that forms part of the employee's continuous, although varying, earnings pattern.

HELPFUL HINT – In cases of repetitious fluctuations in weekly earnings, the employee's highest and lowest week of earnings should be identified on the wage statement. After an average weekly earnings amount is obtained, it should be compared to earnings in these two weeks. If the average weekly earnings amount is truly a representative average, it should be higher than the lowest week's earnings and lower than the highest week's earnings. If it isn't, there is probably a mathematical error in the computations, or the correct number of weeks or total earnings amount was not used in the computations.

8.45 (c-3) WS – SOME WEEKS WITHOUT EARNINGS

If a wage statement reveals weeks of earnings interspersed with weeks where no earnings were paid, a reason should be sought for all week(s) without earnings. The purpose is to identify nonrecurrent lapses in earnings as opposed to normal earnings patterns. A wage statement will not reveal recurrent annual fluctuations in earnings, since this document only reports one year of earnings information. If an annual pattern is suspected (e.g. a one-month unpaid leave of absence each year), it will be necessary to ask the employer to review its earnings records from previous years for verification.

A temporary lapse in earnings may be due to circumstances beyond the employee's control. For example, the employee may lose three weeks of earnings due to a broken leg, a personal emergency such as a death in the family or a plant closing while a chemical spill is cleaned up. Under such circumstances, the temporary lapse in earnings should be ignored because of the unlikelihood of its recurrence. All weeks in which earnings are representative should be deducted from the total weeks reported on the wage statement. The employee's average weekly earnings are computed by dividing this adjusted number of weeks into the total earnings reported.

SAMPLE (a). Assuming that the earnings pattern shown in the six-week period below was repeated throughout the wage statement, the employee's average weekly earnings would be correctly computed by dividing total earnings by the total number of weeks in the earnings period. Compare the inaccurate result that

is obtained when weeks without any earnings are ignored. The correct average
weekly earnings amount is $350/wk.

Week 1	$ 700.00	$ 700.00
Week 2	–0–	–0–
Week 3	–0–	–0–
Week 4	$ 700.00	$ 700.00
Week 5	–0–	–0–
Week 6	+ 700.00	+ 700.00
	$2100.00 ÷ 6 wks = $350 AWE	$2100.00 ÷ 3 = $700 AWE

SAMPLE (b). Mary earns $400/wk and regularly works every other week. Per a
wage statement, earnings during an entire year preceding the injury total $10,400.
Mary had 26 weeks with earnings of $400/wk and 26 weeks without any earnings.

Correct $10,400/yr ÷ 52 wks = $200.00 AWE

Incorrect $10,400/yr ÷ 26 wks (weeks with earnings) = $400/wk

HELPFUL HINT – To double-check the accuracy of any AWE amount, multiply
it by 52 wks/yr. If the result is greater than the employee's actual annual earnings,
the AWE amount is not correct. The above employee's "average" weekly
earnings must be less than $400/wk, because the employee's annual income was
less than $20,800.

8.46 (c-3) WS – EARNINGS NOT A FULL YEAR

Where the employee has not worked an entire year in an employment, averaging any shorter period of earnings may or may not produce an accurate average
weekly earnings amount. Generally, an earnings history of approximately six
months will produce an accurate average weekly earnings amount using the (c-3)
method. Averaging earnings for any period less than six months may or may not
be accurate.

Regardless of the number of weeks that are averaged, there is a simple method
for determining whether or not the average weekly earnings amount obtained is
truly average for the period reviewed. Compare the average weekly earnings
amount obtained to the employee's actual weekly earnings for each week shown
on the wage statement. Find the total number of weeks in which earnings
exceeded the average weekly earnings amount and the total number of weeks
with lower earnings. If actual earnings equaled or exceeded the average weekly
earnings amount for at least half of the weeks reported, then the average weekly
earnings amount is probably accurate. If the employee earned less than the
average weekly earnings amount for more than half of the total weeks, good
judgment should dictate whether it is necessary to use a different method to
compute the employee's average weekly earnings.

SAMPLE: A wage statement reports earnings for a period of seventeen weeks,
the duration of Norina's employment with this employer prior to an injury.
Norina's total earnings in this period were $9775.00.

$$\$9775.00 \div 17 \text{ wks} = \$575.00 \text{ AWE}$$

Wk 1	$500 (−)	Wk 7	$550 (−)	Wk 13	$550 (−)
Wk 2	$600 (+)	Wk 8	$600 (+)	Wk 14	$550 (−)
Wk 3	$550 (−)	Wk 9	$575 (+)	Wk 15	$625 (+)
Wk 4	$600 (+)	Wk 10	$550 (−)	Wk 16	$575 (+)
Wk 5	$625 (+)	Wk 11	$600 (+)	Wk 17	$600 (+)
Wk 6	$600 (+)	Wk 12	$525 (−)		

Weeks paid at $575 or more = 10; number of weeks paid at less than $575 = 7.
AWE appears to be fairly represented by $575.

8.47 (c-3) PIECEWORK PAY – EXPLAINED

The employee may be paid by "piecework" and not by time. Piecework pay is a set amount for a unit of work completed. On piecework pay, earnings commonly fluctuate from week to week. Swings in earnings may reflect the employee's level of productivity or might reflect the amount of work available from the employer. The garment manufacturing industry commonly provides piecework pay as do several other types of manufacturing concerns. It is not necessary to determine the number of units of work completed per week in order to establish an average weekly earnings amount for employees who are paid on a piecework basis. It is only necessary to average the employee's actual weekly earnings for a reasonable period of time prior to an injury using a wage statement that should report the employee's earnings as weekly totals.

8.48 (c-3) COMMISSION PAY – EXPLAINED

Commission pay refers to a system of payment whereby the employee's earnings are based upon the cost of a product or service that is sold. The employee may earn a percentage of the cost of the product, or he might be paid a set dollar amount per unit sold. There are several standard procedures for providing payment to commissioned employees. The employee may be paid a salary plus commissions, just straight commissions or a salary draw against future commissions.

In straight commission work, the employee doesn't have any earnings at all unless and until a commission is paid, so the employee's earnings equal the amount of commissions actually received. Salary plus commissions means the employee earns a regular amount of salary independent of any commission income. When commissions are payable in addition to a base level salary, earnings will include the full amount of salary plus any commissions actually paid to the employee.

If the employee is paid a "draw" or a "draw against commissions," the employee receives regular earnings in a set amount, but this amount is later deducted from earned commissions before they are paid. The draw represents an advance payment of future unearned commissions and is really a loan that the employee owes the employer when commissions are payable. When computing average weekly earnings, the employee does not get credit for the full amount of his draw and the full amount of earned commissions. Commissions are only paid to the employee in amounts exceeding the balance of his draw account. The employee's weekly earnings equal the amount of his draw plus the dollar amount of commissions that are paid to him.

In any type of commission work, there is usually a time lag between the date of a sale and the receipt of a commission. For example, a real estate agent may earn a commission when a deposit is accepted towards a sale, but the agent may not be paid any commission until after the close of escrow. This event could take place months after signing a purchase agreement. When reviewing earnings of commissioned employees, average weekly earnings must be based on amounts that were actually paid to the employee as documented by a wage statement or other evidence. Estimated potential commissions that have not been paid are not considered.

SAMPLE: Chris is a part time salesperson who is paid straight commissions only. The employer submits a wage statement that lists all earnings for one year prior to the injury and shows quarterly totals. In his best week, Chris received $2000. Chris never received less than $1,000 in any week, but there were many weeks where he had no earnings.

$15,000.00	1st Q. Employee had earnings in	13 of 13 wks
8,000.00	2nd Q. Employee had earnings in	6 of 13 wks
2,000.00	3rd Q. Employee had earnings in	2 of 13 wks
+ 6,000.00	4th Q. Employee had earnings in	+4 of 13 wks
$31,000.00 ÷ 52 wks/yr = $596.15 AWE		25 of 52 wks

8.49 (c-3) VARIED EARNINGS – AVERAGE HOURLY RATE

The LC4453 (c-3) method for computing average weekly earnings can also be utilized to compute an average number of hours worked per week and/or an average hourly rate of pay for any employment. Sometimes, it is necessary to obtain this information before average weekly earnings for multiple employments can be computed using the (c-2) method. For each employment, the number of hours worked each week can be obtained from a wage statement or determined by some other means. Hours per week are averaged by dividing the total hours worked in a given number of weeks by the number of weeks in the same period (ordinarily a one-year period unless the employee was employed a shorter time). When the employee's average weekly earnings are divided by the average number of hours worked per week, the result is an average rate of pay per hour in this employment.

SAMPLE (a). Julio works a regular 40-hour week and earns $12/hr. Julio also receives overtime pay at $18/hr on a continuous basis for a different number of hours from week to week. The information below is taken from a wage statement submitted by the employer.

Earnings in one-year period: $37,440 ÷ 52 wks/yr = $720 AWE
Hours worked in same period: 2600 ÷ 52 wks/yr = 50 hrs/wk average
AWE $720.00 ÷ 50 hrs/wk = $14.40/hr average

SAMPLE (b). Helen is paid straight commissions and works a regular 40-hour workweek. Based upon a wage statement that was submitted by Helen's employer, Helen's earnings for one year prior to the injury total $24,960. There were some weeks where Helen had no earnings at all and one week where she earned $4000.

$$\$24,960/yr \div 52\,wks/yr = \$480.00\,AWE$$
$$AWE\ \$480.00 \div 40\,hrs/wk = \$12.00\ average\ hourly\ pay$$

SAMPLE (c). Earl, a waiter, earns $5.25/hr for 40 hrs/wk and also earns tips in irregular weekly amounts. Per Earl's income tax return, total earnings for the previous year were $18,200. Per a wage statement, Earl's wages for the same period were $10,920. Either method below should produce the same hourly rate of pay.

$$Total\ earnings\ \$18,200 \div 52\,wks/yr = \$350.00\,AWE$$
$$AWE\ \$350 \div 40\,hrs/wk = \$8.75\ average\ hourly\ earnings$$

Paid by employer	$10,920 ÷ 52 wks	= $210 AWE ÷ 40 hrs/wk	$5.25/hr
Paid in tips	$ 7,280 ÷ 52 wks	= $140 AWE ÷ 40 hrs/wk	+3.50/hr
		Average hourly pay =	$8.75/hr.

8.50 (c-3) VARIED HOURS – AVERAGE HOURLY RATE

Some employees work a varying number of hours from week to week without any effect on their level of earnings. For instance, a salaried employee may receive the same amount of earnings regardless of hours worked, and a salesman who is paid straight commissions receives the same commission per sale regardless of the number of hours he works. Under these circumstances, the employer may not maintain any accurate record that documents actual hours of work. Even so, it is still possible to identify an average number of hours worked per week for any employee.

Any employer should be able to state an employee's base hours, meaning the minimum number of hours that the employer expects a particular employee to work each week (this number of hours is usually discussed at the time that the employee is hired). When coemployees are paid an hourly rate of pay, the regular workweek for these employees will usually reveal the base hours for other employees at the same place of employment. For instance, if hourly employees work a 40-hour week, then any of the employer's full time employees would be expected to work this number of hours.

Once the weekly base hours of work are identified, this number is divided into the employee's average weekly earnings to compute an average hourly rate of pay. The average weekly earnings amount is a mathematical constant; it will not be altered during computations of an average hourly rate. However, the employee's hourly rate of pay will decrease as his hours worked per week in the formula are increased. Conversely, the use of an inaccurately low base number of hours will produce a falsely inflated average hourly rate of pay.

SAMPLE (a). Bob sells carpets. Bob is paid straight commissions, and his average weekly earnings have been computed to be $500 per week. Observe the difference in hourly pay when different base hours are used to compute an average.

AWE $500 ÷ 20 hrs/wk = $25.00 average hourly pay
AWE $500 ÷ 30 hrs/wk = $16.67 average hourly pay
AWE $500 ÷ 35 hrs/wk = $14.29 average hourly pay
AWE $500 ÷ 40 hrs/wk = $12.50 average hourly pay
AWE $500 ÷ 60 hrs/wk = $ 8.33 average hourly pay
AWE $500 ÷ 80 hrs/wk = $ 6.25 average hourly pay

In this example, the more hours Bob works, the less he earns on an hourly basis. In fact, if Bob were even more industrious (but did not earn any more commissions), use of actual hours worked above a base number could result in an hourly rate of pay that would be less than the State minimum hourly wage.

To avoid such a harsh and inaccurate result, any hours worked per week over the base hours are not used to compute an average hourly rate of pay. Likewise, should an employee claim that he can do his job in half the time that others can, base hours would still be used (rather than a reduced number of hours that would result in computation of a higher hourly rate).

SAMPLE (b). Frank is on salary and earns $1200 semimonthly. Frank does not have a set hourly rate of pay and is not paid for overtime. Per Frank, he usually works 30 to 50 hrs/wk. Per Frank's employer, Frank is expected to work an average of 40 hrs/wk.

$1200 semimonthly earnings × 2 = $2400 mo.
$2400/mo ÷ 4.3333 wks/mo = $553.85 AWE
AWE $553.85 ÷ 40 hrs/wk = $13.85 average hourly pay

SAMPLE (c). Jerry is an insurance claim examiner. who is paid a salary of $712/wk. Jerry claims that he works an average of 70 hrs/wk. Per the employer, Jerry is expected to work a minimum of 40 hrs/wk, as are all other commissioned, salaried, and hourly coemployees. No additional pay incentive is provided for any hours worked in excess of 40 hrs/wk.

Correct: AWE $712/wk ÷ 40 hrs/wk = $17.80 average hourly rate
Incorrect: AWE $712/wk ÷ 70 hrs/wk = $10.17 average hourly rate

The correct rate is $17.80/hr. because Jerry earns a minimum hourly rate of $17.80/hr if he works the minimum base hours per week that are required by the employer.

8.51 (c-4) NONSPECIFIC METHOD – EXPLAINED

Other LC4453 Methods Don't Apply

Subsection (c-4) is a catchall provision that applies to any case where the other methods set forth in LC4453 "cannot reasonably and fairly be applied" to compute the employee's average weekly earnings. The other subsections apply solely to earnings from jobs that are steady, consistent, long-term, established or permanent. No subsection except (c-4) can be "fairly applied" to:

   a. Temporary earnings situations that are subject to change, OR
   b. Situations where there has been a recent and permanent change in weekly earnings, OR
   c. Mixed earnings situations where two or more subsections of LC4453(c) jointly apply to the employee's earnings, OR
   d. Situations characterized by erratic patterns in either the level of weekly earnings or frequency of receipt, OR
   e. Situations where earnings are received from a part time employment, defined to mean any job in which the employee is employed "for less than 30 hours per week."

Combining Methods & Applying Judgment

Unlike other subsections of LC4453, (c-4) does not set out any particular formula for computing average weekly earnings. Rather, this subsection requires that the employee's average weekly earnings "shall be taken at 100% of the sum which reasonably represents the average weekly earning capacity of the employee at the time of his or her injury, due consideration being given to his or her actual earnings from all sources." Basically, this subsection requires the average weekly earnings amount to be computed in a manner that will produce an accurate result. By implication, this result will be accomplished when all pertinent earnings information is utilized to assess the employee's earning capacity.

Subsection (c-4) does not prevent the application of methods (c-1), (c-2) or (c-3) just because the employee's earning situation does not meet the precise criteria contained in these sections. In fact, (c-4) actually requires the use of any method that can be "reasonably and fairly applied." For instance, no other section describes part time employment, but average weekly earnings from a part time job with set hours and a set rate of pay would be computed using method (c-1). If the employee was paid commissions in a part time job, then method (c-3) would be appropriate. Likewise, if the employee had more than one employment, earnings from each would be averaged utilizing the appropriate subsection and then combined using method (c-2).

An average weekly earnings amount must reflect the employee's earning capacity. However, an employee's earning capacity cannot always be identified by merely computing an average level of actual weekly earnings using a different subsection. Good judgment may require the isolated selection of past, present, future unrealized earnings or some combination of these as the correct basis for computing an average weekly earnings amount. It may also be necessary to compute more than one average weekly earnings amount to apply to different periods of time. In effect, the method required by (c-4) can be considered to be the application of good judgment rather than the use of standard formulas to assess the probable level of continued weekly earnings after an injury.

8.52 (c-4) SEASONAL EARNINGS – EXPLAINED

When an employee is engaged in seasonal employment, the employee's earnings at any point in time during a calendar year form part of a repetitious annual pattern that is characterized by periods of earnings followed regularly by periods of reduced earnings or no earnings at all. The employee has a regular occupation that is only engaged in during its "season," meaning that portion of the year when this type of work is offered by employers. For example, climate controls the availability of work for fruit pickers or ski lift operators, and economic cycles control the length of employment for income tax preparers. In the off-season, the employee may seek different employment or he may remain unemployed. The employee returns to his seasonal occupation once this type of work is again available, so any employment(s) in the off-season are only accepted on a temporary or interim basis.

Seasonal Earnings - Method For Computing AWE

For seasonal employees, earnings in the employment where an injury occurs comprise part of an ongoing earnings cycle, but these earnings do not represent the employee's long-term continued earnings. These earnings only reflect the employee's earning capacity for the duration of that job and not beyond.

In common practice, the employee's average weekly earnings are computed solely by using earnings from the employment at the time of injury. These earnings are used for the known duration of this employment, because it is reasonably predictable that the employee would have continued to receive these earnings during this period but for the injury. However, average weekly earnings are thereafter recomputed for any periods of disability after the termination date of the temporary employment. Since the employee's earnings are cyclical, and a full cycle is one year, average weekly earnings are computed by averaging earnings in the 52-week period preceding the injury.

The procedures described above are those in standard use. Arguably, an employee could assert that his average weekly earnings after termination of the temporary employment should be based upon a 52-week earnings period going backward from the anticipated termination date of this job, thereby giving the employee full credit for all weeks of earnings in this employment. The employee is not likely to make this assertion unless earnings in his most recent employment are higher than past levels of earnings, e.g. due to increases in general wage levels from one year to the next or because the employee fortuitously found an exceptionally high-paying temporary job.

However, some other employee would most likely object if the employer wished to include all weeks of earnings from the recent job when these earnings are exceptionally low and/or when use of these weeks of earnings would exclude a period of higher past earnings from the averaging (more than 52 weeks prior to the termination date of temporary employment). Equity to both the employer and the employee thus require the standard application of the methods described in the above paragraph (but only in cases where the employer does not adhere strictly to LC4453 by establishing average weekly earnings by averaging past earnings "at the time of the injury").

8.53 (c-4) SEASONAL EARNINGS – COMPUTATIONS

A seasonal employee is accustomed to continual changes in weekly earnings. Such fluctuations are acceptable to the employee based upon the factual record of past earnings and employments. Therefore, when the employee's earning capacity changes after an injury, average weekly earnings will be recomputed to reflect the change. In this way, the average weekly earnings amount will continue to reflect the employee's earning capacity throughout the period of disability. The samples below demonstrate how judgment is applied to earnings information that is relevant to the employee's earning capacity subsequent to an injury. Each sample refers to the same employee.

SAMPLE - Situation (a). Don is injured on 11/25/96 while temporarily employed as a ski lift operator that is his seasonal occupation. Per the employer, Don was hired to work from 11/25/96 - 4/15/97 only. Don earns $10/hr for 40 hrs/wk. If Don is disabled a short period of time, these earnings alone may be used to establish an average weekly earnings amount (as long as the disability does not extend beyond the end of this employment).

$10.00/hr $\times$ 40 hrs/wk = $400.00 AWE for 11/25/96 - 4/15/97

SAMPLE - Situation (b). The disability extends beyond 4/15/97. To determine Don's continued earning capacity, average weekly earnings will be computed from a base period of 52 weeks preceding the date of injury. In the off-season, Don works as a waiter and makes more money than he does in his preferred occupation as a ski lift operator. Per a wage statement, Don's earnings from the ski resort for 11/23/95 - 11/24/96 were $8000 in 20 weeks. In the previous year, the resort closed before 4/16 due to warm weather and lack of snow. Per Don's pay stubs and tips reported on his income tax return, earnings from waiter jobs total $14,960 for 11/23/95- 11/24/96 (32 weeks).

Ski job	$ 8,000	20 wks	
Waiter job	+14,960	+32 wks	
	$22,960 ÷	52 wks	= $441.54 AWE after 4/15/97

SAMPLE - Situation (c). Later events can affect the employee's earning capacity. For example, the claimsperson hears on the radio that the ski season will be extended this year due to an abundance of snow. The ski lift employer verifies that this employment would have been extended an additional 11 weeks, through 6/11/97. Per Don, he would have stayed at this job as long as it was available. The average weekly earnings that are computed solely from this employment will apply through 6/11/97. The average weekly earnings computed from 52 weeks of preinjury earnings apply to any periods of disability after 6/11/97.

$400.00 AWE for 11/25/96 - 6/11/97   (see Sample (a))
$441.54 AWE after 6/11/97   (see Sample (b))

8.54 (c-4) TEMPORARY EARNINGS – EXPLAINED

Employment is temporary when it has a known termination date. Either the job itself will not be available in the future or the employee does not intend to continue in the employment. The employer may set a time limit on the job; for example, where a department store hires part time help to work only during a holiday season or busy period. The employee may set the time limit; for example, where a school teacher works a temporary summer job between school terms. These situations are contrasted to permanent employment where continued future employment is reasonably contemplated until the employee retires.

Temporary employments are an established pattern for some employees. Past employment records may document the fact that the employee willingly accepts intermittent periods of low earnings or no earnings. Some employees self-limit their earnings to set levels or for set weeks in a year. The reasons for this may be within the control of the employer or the employee. The employee may be so well qualified that, although he would prefer permanent employment, permanent employment is not readily available in the employee's occupation or at the salary level the employee seeks. The employee may lack the education, skills, ability, enthusiasm or personality to obtain continuous employment. The employee may be financially situated so that he does not need to work at all unless he desires to be employed, or employers may find something disagreeable about the employee that makes them unwilling to hire or retain the employee on a permanent basis.

In the case of a seasonal employee, repetitious temporary employment results from the fact that the employee's choice of occupation restricts his employment in this occupation to certain weeks of the year. A pattern of temporary employment can also result from the high degree of competitiveness within particular occupations. For instance, glamour occupations such as acting, singing, modeling, radio announcing and newscasting offer permanent employment to very few people. An employee may command high wages when temporarily employed in his chosen career, he may have supplemental income from one or any number of other employments and/or he may remain unemployed when work is not available in his chosen field.

Earnings, as well as jobs, are deemed to be temporary whenever it is known that a change will occur after an injury. The level of the employee's weekly earnings can be temporary when his employment is permanent. For instance, present earnings are temporary when the employee continues to receive his customary weekly earnings prior to the effective date of a merit pay increase or after the date the employee has made definite plans to leave a permanent employment. Earnings under such circumstances are comparable to earnings from a temporary employment since the level of weekly earnings at the time of injury is not expected to continue beyond a specific date.

Temporary Earnings – Method for Computing AWE

When the level of weekly earnings at the time of injury is temporary but the employee's previous earnings pattern has not been one of intermittent or erratic earnings, average weekly earnings must be computed using only those earnings that continue to reflect the employee's weekly earning capacity after his injury. The reason for a temporary level of earnings will determine whether average weekly earnings should be computed using past, present or future unrealized earnings and whether average weekly earnings will be computed once or require recomputations on future dates (refer to 8.15-8.19).

The method for computing average weekly earnings for employees whose current earnings pattern is one of temporary or seasonal jobs will be the same. The only real distinction between such employees is that a "temporary" employee need not have any particular occupation. In all other aspects, the earnings history of a temporary employee can mimic the earnings history of a seasonal employee. Therefore, intermittent periods of past earnings will be averaged for one year prior to the injury to reflect the employee's long-term continued future average weekly earnings after the termination date of the temporary employment. Prior to this date, probable earnings from the temporary job are ordinarily used to compute an average weekly earnings amount that will apply for the duration of this employment.

It is sometimes appropriate to exclude all earnings from the most recent employment when computing average weekly earnings. When the employee has a history of fairly continuous temporary employments at approximately the same level of weekly earnings, an average of past earnings will produce an average weekly earnings amount that accurately reflects the employee's weekly earning capacity both during and after his most recent employment. Also, past earnings alone will be used to compute an average weekly earnings amount when earnings from the most recent employment are unusually high or low but the duration of this employment would have been very brief, e.g. one or two days.

8.55 (c-4) TEMPORARY EARNINGS – COMPUTATIONS

Temporary periods of earnings will never constitute the sole basis for assessing the employee's earning capacity. The employee may or may not have any reasonable expectancy of additional earnings after termination of a temporary employment. The length of the temporary employment can also be an aberration; the employee may have never been previously employed for so long or so short a period of time. The level of earnings at the time of injury may be inordinately higher or lower than any previously received or realistically probable future earnings. This level of earnings may represent the initiation of a new earnings pattern or the repetition of a prior pattern. The sample problems below will demonstrate how the facts of individual cases affect the manner in which average weekly earnings are computed.

SAMPLE (A1). Average weekly earnings (AWE) for duration of job.

Matt is an unskilled laborer. He desires permanent employment but has not been able to find a permanent position. Matt's previous history is nearly con-tinuous employment for a number of employers in each year. Matt was hired as a full time temporary employee from 3/1 - 4/11 only (six weeks). He was paid $6/hr for 40 hrs/wk.

$6.00/hr × 40 hrs/wk = $240.00 AWE for 3/1 to 4/11 only

(A2). Average weekly earnings after termination of job.

Per Matt, he would be out there looking for a job again. Per wage statements from Matt's employers, Matt's total earnings were $12,738.38 in the 52 weeks preceding 3/1.

$12,738.38 ÷ 52 weeks = $244.97 AWE after 4/11

SAMPLE (B). Earnings from temporary position not utilized.

Ruth works for a temporary employment agency where all work assignments are temporary. The agency pays Ruth $9/hr. Hours worked per day vary from 4 to 8 hours and Ruth customarily accepts assignments from one day to six weeks in duration. Ruth is injured the first day of a two day secretarial assignment in which she would have worked 7½ hours each day. Earnings from this temporary assignment are representative of Ruth an earnings pattern but are too brief to reflect an average amount of weekly earnings. Per a wage statement from the employer, total earnings in the previous year were $16,920.00.

$16,920.00 ÷ 52 wks/yr = $325.38 AWE

SAMPLE (C). Average weekly earnings require recomputation.

Shirley, an employee of a temporary employment agency, is injured the first day of an eight week assignment. Per the agency, Shirley's wages for this assignment were set at $9/hr for 40 hrs/wk, but Shirley usually works less than 5 days/wk and worked 50 separate assignments in the previous year. Shirley's earnings at the time of injury are higher than any normal eight week period for Shirley. Therefore, these earnings should be used independently of past earnings for the anticipated duration of their receipt. Per a wage statement, Shirley's earnings for 52 weeks preceding the injury were $11,130.00.

$9.00/hr × 40 hrs/wk = $360.00 AWE for 8 weeks post-injury
$11,130.00 ÷ 52 wks/yr = $214.04 AWE after end of temporary job

SAMPLE (D). Kathy was hired to work 10/1 - 12/31 only as a sales clerk during the holiday season. Kathy's wages were set at $8/hr for 40 hrs/wk. Per the employer, no further employment would be offered. Per Kathy, the last time she was employed was over ten years ago, she only took this job to earn money for a special vacation, and she did not intend to seek any further jobs after the end of this temporary position.

$8.00/hr × 40 hrs/wk = $320/wk for 10/1 - 12/31
Actual weekly earnings are $ -0- for 1/1 - 9/30
$320/yr ÷ 52 wks/yr = $6.15 AWE as of 1/1 and thereafter

SAMPLE (E). Hank is an engineering consultant who was hired for a temporary position to work on a special project from 1/3 - 2/28 only. The employer verifies earnings at $16/hr for 40 hrs/wk. Previously Hank worked as a short-term consultant for several employers. The present employer offered a permanent position that Hank refused. Hank plans to continue consulting work but does not want a permanent job, because he states he likes to be able to take time off whenever he wants. In the year preceding this job, Hank earned $15,231.04 from a variety of jobs.

$16.00/hr × 40 hrs/wk = $640.00 AWE for 1/3-2/28 only
$15,231.04 ÷ 52 wks = $292.90 AWE after 2/28

SAMPLE (F1). Average weekly earnings for duration of job.

Michelle is seeking a movie career and has an agent. An injury occurs during a three day temporary acting job while Michelle is on a one week vacation from her usual job. Michelle has a permanent full time job as a manager in a grocery store and has had this job for several years. Michelle had a flat contract fee of $2000 for the acting assignment during the week she was injured, 9/6-9/12.

Earnings in week of injury = $2000 (exceed statutory maximum)
AWE for 9/6 - 9/12 = statutory maximum earnings stated in LC4453

(F2). Average weekly earnings after temporary job ends.

Michelle states she would quit her job at the market if she could ever land a big part in a major film. In the year prior to this injury, Michelle earned $2000 from one acting job. Per a wage statement, Michelle's earnings at the market during this same period were $28,000. There are two ways in which average weekly earnings can be computed. The correct method would depend upon whether or not the unusually high earnings from the acting job were considered to be truly representative of Michelle's weekly earnings capacity.

(F3.1). One year average – Including income from acting jobs

$ 2,000   (÷ 52 wks = $ 38.46 AWE from acting)
+28,000   (÷ 52 wks = $538.46. AWE from market)
$30,000 ÷ 52 wks = $576.92 AWE after 9/12

This method in (F3.1) would be correct only if there was a reasonable factual basis for anticipating that Michelle would earn a minimum of $2,000 from acting jobs from year to year on a routine basis. For instance, at the time of injury, Michelle may have already accepted another acting job with a definite starting date, or past annual patterns document the regularity of at least $2000/yr from acting jobs. However, without this type of factual evidence, there is usually no way to predict the receipt of any future earnings from temporary jobs in highly competitive occupations of this nature.

(F3.2). One year average – Excluding income from acting jobs
$28,000 ÷ 52 wks = $538.46 AWE after 9/12

The method shown in (F3.2) would be correct if earnings from an acting job represent a temporary and drastic deviation from an established earnings pattern, and this level of weekly earnings is not likely to be received with any type of regularity. Despite her stated desire, Michelle may or may not ever obtain another acting job and future earnings from acting jobs may best be described as "iffy." However, Michelle is regularly employed as a grocery store manager, and the facts support her continued receipt of $538.46/wk from this employment. Therefore, after 9/12, an average of these earnings alone will comply with the language of LC4453(c-4) that requires an average weekly earnings amount to be computed in a manner that "reasonably represents the average weekly earning capacity of the employee" and the anticipated weekly loss in earnings in future weeks after an injury. The facts do not support Michelle's continued receipt of earnings from acting jobs on any average or continuous basis in the future.

SAMPLE (G1). Injury after short time on new job.

John was an assembly line worker at an auto plant. The plant shut down with much speculation as to whether the shut down is temporary or permanent. John takes a new job working full time for a different manufacturing company. Per John, he would quit the new job if he could return to his job at the auto plant. Per the new employer, the job is permanent unless John decides to quit. The new job began on 4/26/96 and the date of injury was 5/15. John was hired to work 40 hrs/wk for $11.60/hr. On the date of injury John was a permanent full time employee.

$$\$11.60/hr \times 40 \text{ hrs/wk} = \$464.00 \text{ AWE as of } 4/26$$

(G2). Preferred job becomes available.

Per the auto company, John's union was called back to work on 12/13. John has a job when he is physically able to return to work. Per this employer, John is paid union scale and earns $16.00/hr for 40 hrs/wk. Absent an injury, John would be a permanent full time employee at the auto plant.

$$\$16.00/hr \times 40 \text{ hrs/wk} = \$640.00 \text{ AWE on } 12/13 \text{ and thereafter}$$

(G3). Later change in probable earnings.

Per the auto plant, John has been notified of a termination of employment effective 6/15/97, the date that this employer went out of business. As of 6/15, factual evidence of continued earnings is limited to earnings from the job at the manufacturing plant (per g-1 above). Even so, the earnings from the auto plant may continue to more closely approximate the employee's preinjury earning capacity pursuant to LC4453.

SAMPLE (H). Injury shortly before new permanent job.

Tracy was originally hired for a permanent part time job. The employer liked Tracy's work and later offered her a permanent full time position. Tracy was injured on the part time job on 7/1, two weeks before the full time position was scheduled to begin. On the part time (PT) job, Tracy made $11/hr for 20 hrs/wk. The full time job (FT) pays $12/hr for 40 hrs/wk.

PT job $11.00/hr $\times$ 20 hrs/wk = $220.00 AWE for 7/1 - 7/14
FT job $12.00/hr $\times$ 40 hrs/wk = $480.00 AWE as of 7/15

SAMPLE (I). Injury shortly before termination of job.

Cindy is a nurse at a hospital where she has worked for three years. Cindy requested, and the employer has granted, a one year leave of absence without pay to begin on 11/4. Cindy plans to stay home with her family for a year. She is injured her last day on the job and will be disabled for six weeks. Cindy was earning a regular salary of $90/day for 5 days/wk. The date of injury was 11/3 and this was the last day worked in this employment.

$90/day $\times$ 5 days/wk = $450.00 AWE

It might seem that Cindy's average weekly earnings should be computed as zero to reflect her projected actual earnings after 11/3. However, note that it is only Cindy's earnings that are voluntarily reduced, not her earning capacity. Cindy's ability to earn continues at the level of $450/wk.

AWE as of 11/4 = applicable statutory minimum in LC4453

SAMPLE (J). Employee laid off after injury.

Steve is an engineer for an aerospace company who sustained an injury on 3/20. While disabled, Steve is notified of a layoff that affects all employees in his job classification who have equal or less seniority. Steve's regular earnings are $730/wk. Per the employer, the layoff is effective on 5/16, and it is anticipated that Steve will be called back from the layoff by 7/15.

AWE from 3/20 - 5/16 = $730.00
AWE from 5/16 - 7/15 = $730.00

A layoff is an economic adversity that Steve would have been subjected to regardless of any injury. Despite the specific demonstrable evidence that Steve's earnings from this particular employer would have decreased post-injury, there is no evidence of a change in Steve's earning capacity at the time of injury. It is simply not humanly possible to predict whether Steve would have sought or obtained alternative employment during the layoff period. The provisions of LC4453 are intended to avoid conjecture as to future events by requiring an assessment of earnings only at or near the time of injury rather than engaging in speculation as to whether the employee would have been employed, would have been employed with a particular employer, or would have been employed for more or less money absent the injury.

SAMPLE (K1). Injury shortly before change in earnings.

Joy is a high school math teacher who sustains an injury on 6/2, two weeks before the end of the school year on 6/15. Joy has already tendered her resignation and accepted a permanent full time position as a computer programmer. The starting date of the new job is 7/8, three weeks after the end of the school year. Joy plans to take a three week vacation before commencing the new employment. Joy receives an annual salary of $30,000 that is paid over the ten month school year.

$$\$30,000 \div 52 \text{ hrs/wk} = \$576.92 \text{ AWE through } 6/15$$

(K2). Earnings during interim period before new job begins.

Joy did not plan to work at all during the weeks of 6/16 - 7/6. Although she was removing herself from the labor market for these three weeks, Joy's average weekly earnings for this period are not the statutory minimum average weekly earnings amount.

Joy did not effect a permanent change in her earning capacity for these three weeks. In the case of teachers, earnings are usually stated as an annual amount that is paid within a ten month period. Teachers can be considered to have a two month paid vacation. This pay is included in their salary paid during the ten months they teach. (Note: some teachers are paid their annual salary over a 12-month period.)

$$\text{AWE} = \$576.92 \text{ until } 7/8 \text{ (starting date of new job)}$$

(K3). Earnings after commencement date of new job.

Per the new employer, Joy was hired as a permanent full time computer programmer at a rate of pay of $700/wk, or $36,400 annually.

$$\text{AWE} = \$700.00 \text{ on or after } 7/8$$

SAMPLE (L1). Injury shortly before change in earning capacity.

Greg has been employed in a permanent full time job for the same employer for two years. Greg has recently enrolled in a four year college and plans to go to school full time beginning 9/19. The employer has agreed to allow Greg to work as a permanent part time employee commencing on 9/19. As far as the employer is concerned, Greg has a job there as long as he wants one and can work full time again whenever he wants. Greg is injured on 8/29 while working full time.

In the full time job, Greg earns $540/wk. In the part time job, the earnings will be $13.50/hr for 20 hrs/wk. (It may be argued that the injury prevented Greg from changing his mind about returning to work full time, but evidence may exist to refute this allegation; e.g., school tuition is fully paid, class schedules have issued, or dormitory fees have been paid.) Based upon the facts presented here (all of which are subject to proof at the time of the injury), average weekly earnings would be as follows:

$$\text{Full time job} = \$540.00 \text{ AWE through } 9/19$$
$$\text{Part time job} = \$13.50/\text{hr} \times 20 \text{ hrs/wk} = \$270.00 \text{ AWE after } 9/19$$

(L2). Earnings during weeks between jobs.

Greg will take a two week vacation before 9/19, the date he will begin to go to college and start working part time. Some judgment is required to determine the average weekly earnings amount that represents Greg's earning capacity for 9/5 - 9/18. Using the facts given, arguments may be presented for any of the following positions:

  a. AWE = zero, because no earnings will be received during this two week period. This alternative is not reasonable since it would result in cessation of benefits during a period of undisputed medical disability.
  b. AWE = $540, because Greg's previous earning capacity still exists up to the date of the new earnings pattern on 9/19. This alternative is reasonable in view of how the concept of earning capacity is applied to computations of average weekly earnings.
  c. AWE = $270, because the effective date of the change in earning capacity is 9/5, and any earnings paid after this date will be paid at this level. However, note that wages of $270 will not be paid before 9/19.

[9] TEMPORARY DISABILITY

9.1 TEMPORARY DISABILITY – DEFINED

The term "disability" is generally accepted to mean a medical impairment from a preinjury level of physical ability. A temporary disability is a physical incapacity that is expected to be completely cured or improved with proper medical attention. A physician measures physical disability. A claimsperson assesses the amount of the reduction in weekly earnings that results from a physical impairment and the weekly compensation rate at which benefits are payable.

A temporary disability (TD) is distinguished in the Labor Code from a permanent disability (PD). The distinction is one of time or the duration of the adverse physical effects of an injury upon the employee's ability to earn wages. Temporary disability benefits provide a wage replacement benefit during the weeks in which the employee actually sustains a wage loss. Permanent disability benefits compensate the employee for a future loss of weekly earnings that is anticipated to result from the permanently disabling effects of a particular injury (but need not actually occur as a prerequisite to receipt of this category of wage replacement benefits).

9.2 TEMPORARY TOTAL DISABILITY

A temporary total disability produces a total loss of weekly earnings. During the time the employee is temporarily totally disabled, the employee cannot earn any wages because the employee is physically unable to perform any work. Subject to statutory minimum and maximum average weekly earnings amounts, the full amount of the employee's weekly loss of earnings is used to compute the weekly rate at which temporary total disability benefits will be paid (see 9.4).

The concept of total disability is generally thought to refer to disability for any type of work. This is opposed to incapacity to perform the job the employee had when an injury was sustained. Under this general premise, the employee would not have a total disability unless the employee was physically restricted from any and every type of work in the open labor market.

In actuality, the term "temporary total disability" (TTD) has a more restricted application. A disability is considered to be total if the employee is physically unable to return to work in his usual and customary employment. Most employees have one job and if they are disabled from performing that job, their disability is considered to be total disability. An employee who has multiple jobs at or near the time of injury will be totally disabled if the injury prevents a return to work for all employers (e.g. where the employee is disabled from a day job and a night job).

9.3 TEMPORARY PARTIAL DISABILITY

A temporary partial disability (TPD) produces a partial, rather than a total, loss of weekly earnings. The disability is partial when the employee has recovered to the extent that the employee is physically capable of performing some work but not full normal duties. Partial earnings that are available from an employer who is willing to provide employment while the employee is partially disabled, are deducted from the employee's normal earnings (but not more than statutory maximum earnings under LC4453) to determine the amount of the employee's partial weekly loss of earnings. This amount is then used to compute the weekly rate at which temporary partial disability benefits will be paid (see 9.6).

A physician may release the employee to return to "modified duty" or "light duty," and an employer may be willing to provide reduced earnings in exchange for the performance of such duty. Modified work could involve being temporarily relieved from performing specific duties required in the employee's usual and customary occupation. Light work could involve a temporary assignment to a position with less physically demanding duties or possibly a return to work in the employee's usual occupation for less hours than a full work day. The employee may be able to perform regular duties but only for half days, or the physician might release the employee for work on a trial basis attempting four hours the first week, six the second week, etc.

Like temporary total disability, temporary partial disability refers to physical incapacity in the occupation in which the employee would reasonably return to work if physically able to do so. In most instances, the employee returns to work in the same job where the injury occurred. When this employment is no longer available (for whatever reason) it is necessary to determine the post-injury reduction in weekly earnings that is reasonably a result of the employee's partial physical incapacity.

An employer may or may not afford the employee the opportunity to return to light or modified work while the employee is partially disabled. Where the employee is willing and able to return to work but the employer restricts employability, the employee's disability continues to be compensable as temporary total disability (see 9.20).

9.4 COMPENSATION RATE – TOTAL DISABILITY

Per LC4653 and LC4654, the weekly compensation rate for temporary disability benefits is two-thirds of the employee's "average weekly earnings." The method for computing an average weekly earnings amount from the employee's actual average weekly earnings is controlled by LC4453 (see 8.15-8.21). This statute also specifies the situations where a statutory average weekly earnings amount is required to be used instead of the amount computed as the employee's actual average weekly earnings. A statutory maximum limits the amount of actual earnings that will affect the compensation rate of employees with fairly high earnings, and for 1991 or later injuries, a fluctuating limit applies to the use of actual earnings on the low end of the scale as explained below.

Maximum Compensation Rate

The highest level of weekly earnings that can affect the employee's compensation rate for temporary disability is the maximum average weekly earnings amount stated in LC4453. Any earnings over and above the statutory maximum average weekly earnings amount are ignored. The net effect of limiting the average weekly earnings level is to reduce the percentage of actual earnings that high wage earners will receive for a weekly temporary disability benefit. A person who earns $200/wk will receive ⅔ of his average weekly earnings. A person who earns $900/wk will not receive ⅔ of his average weekly earnings; this person will only receive ⅔ of the maximum average weekly earnings set by law in LC4453. It is possible for an employee with uncommonly high earnings to have a correctly computed compensation rate that pays only 20 to 30% of actual average earnings rather than 66 ⅔%.

Highly paid employees usually have more disposable income (after payment for life necessities such as food, clothing and shelter) than do low wage earners. These employees have earnings they save or use to purchase insurance to assist them during an interruption in earnings. Such persons may be upset that there is a maximum limit on temporary disability benefits, but they may be able to maintain their same standards of living while disabled through wise advance planning for emergencies. Additional financial assistance is sometimes available. It is helpful for a claimsperson to know of possible eligibility for state or federal benefits or company benefit programs so that an appropriate referral can be made. Also, in cases of severe injuries and emergency financial needs, the claimsperson is sometimes willing to provide a voluntary advance payment of permanent disability benefits.

There are national trends towards establishment of temporary disability rates that closely approximate the employee's actual weekly loss in wages. However, there is also some resistance to full reimbursement, since it is believed to be a disincentive to return to work when equivalent income is received without working (unless earnings are unusually low; see minimum rates below.). The higher the employee's earnings, the greater this disincentive would be. This premise underlies the existence of a maximum compensation rate.

Automatic Maximum Rate – Some Public Employees

Per LC4458-4458.2, certain volunteer police officers and firefighters are entitled to the maximum temporary disability compensation rate "irrespective of... remuneration" from their employment. The maximum rate is automatic and not based upon the employee's actual earnings. Per LC4458.6, these employees will receive a maximum weekly benefit rate even if the employee is retired when he first "suffers 'an injury'." Disaster service workers are also entitled to the maximum rate under LC4453.

Minimum Compensation Rates

Effective 1991, there are two alternative minimum compensation rates for temporary total disability (and a third alternative, a presumption of earnings, that only applies if the employee is a partner; see 8.9). One minimum rate is $126/wk. This rate is computed as ⅔ of the statutory average weekly earnings amount of $189/wk that, per LC4453, applies to any employee who earns between $126/wk and $189/wk. However, the minimum compensation rate can be much less. Alternatively, for any employee who earns $126 or less, the employee's actual earnings are payable as the employee's compensation rate. (Note: payment of full earnings as a compensation rate will actually provide an employee with more money than payment of weekly wages, because state and federal income taxes would be deducted from wages paid if the employee continued working.)

Labor Code 4453 requires that the employee's actual average weekly earnings be compared to $189/wk. If the employee earned less than $189/wk, then the employee's weekly earnings are multiplied by 1.5, and this result is compared to $189/wk. If this result is more than $189/wk, the employee's average weekly earnings are deemed to be $189/wk. If this result is $189/wk or less, then 1.5 times the employee's actual earnings are deemed to be the employee's average weekly earnings, and $2/3$ of this amount produces the compensation rate for temporary total disability benefits.

The examples below illustrate how the statutory alternative minimum earnings limits in LC4453 are applied to different amounts of weekly earnings. First the amount of the employee's "average weekly earnings" is computed from actual earnings pursuant to LC4453 (see Chapter 8). Next, in every case, the employee's average weekly earnings are compared to $189. Earnings are deemed to be $189 whenever the employee's average weekly earnings equal or exceed $189. Lastly, two-thirds of the employee's average weekly earnings (AWE) produces the employee's compensation rate (CR) for temporary total disability benefits.

Earnings $180/wk × 1.5 = $270　so use $189 AWE × $2/3$ = $126 CR
Earnings $150/wk × 1.5 = $225　so use $189 AWE × $2/3$ = $126 CR
Earnings $126/wk × 1.5 = $189　so use $189 AWE × $2/3$ = $126 CR
Earnings $100/wk × 1.5 = $150　so use $150 AWE × $2/3$ = $100 CR
Earnings $ 26/wk × 1.5 = $ 39　so use $ 39 AWE × $2/3$ = $ 26 CR

NOTE: Mathematically, 1.5 times the employee's earnings will be less than $189/wk whenever the employee's actual earnings are less than $126/wk, and $2/3$ of this amount will equal the employee's actual earnings. Therefore, the compensation rate for any employee who earns $126/wk or less will be the same amount as the employee's average weekly earnings.

Employees with fairly low earnings will be paid at a compensation rate equivalent to 100% of their wage loss (e.g. $120/wk earnings = $120/wk rate). However, employees with weekly earnings between $126-$189/wk will all be paid $126/wk as a compensation rate. An employee who earns $180/wk may question the reason for payment of $126/wk as a compensation rate based on knowledge that this rate is also being paid to a coworker who earned $130/wk (almost one-third less money per week!). This result is simply required by law, and it operates to provide a greater financial incentive to return to work for employees with higher earnings.

9.5 CHANGE IN LAW – CHANGE IN RATE

General Rule – Law Effective on Date of Injury

Per LC4453.5, benefits payable to an employee "shall not be affected by a subsequent statutory change in amounts of indemnity payable," and if the law changes after an injury, the employee's benefits "shall be continued" under "the law in effect at the time of injury." This language reaffirms a basic principle of workers' compensation: laws in effect on the date of the injury control the employee's benefits. This language mandates that any recomputations of a compensation rate that are necessitated by a post-injury change in the employee's earning capacity (see 8.20) are subject to the minimum and maximum average weekly earnings amounts that were in effect pursuant to LC4453 on the date of the employee's injury. Even if legislation increases the maximum average weekly earnings amount in LC4453 during the same year that the employee's injury occurred, the employee's compensation rate will not be affected by a change that becomes effective subsequent to the date of the injury.

As a general rule, any legislation that increases benefits subsequent to the date of an injury will not have any effect on the employee's compensation rate. It is necessary to refer to the wording of the law on the date the employee was injured to determine the average weekly earnings limits that apply. One exception to this general rule is set out in LC4461.5 and pertains exclusively to payments of "temporary total disability" that are made more than two years after an injury, as explained below.

Two-Year Rule – Law Effective on Date of Payment

Effective 1990, LC4453 provides that average weekly earnings are determined from facts known at the time of injury and "calculated according to the limits in this section in effect on the date of injury." Thereafter, LC4453 mandates that average weekly earnings amounts thus established (different limits apply to different categories of indemnity benefits) "shall remain in effect for the duration of any disability resulting from the injury" with one, and only one, exception, as provided in LC4661.5.

Per LC4661.5, when temporary total disability payments are "made two or more years from the date of injury," the employee's compensation rate "shall be computed in accordance with the temporary disability indemnity average weekly earnings amount specified in Section 4453 in effect on the date" each payment is made. The formula for computing the compensation rate does not change. The compensation rate for temporary disability is always computed by taking two-thirds of the employee's average weekly earnings at the time each payment is due. However, the amount of the employee's actual average weekly earnings (as determined at the time of injury) is now compared to the maximum earnings limit specified in LC4453 on the date of each payment, not the (possibly lower) earnings limit in effect on the date of injury.

Computing a Rate Increase

Employees who were eligible to receive the maximum compensation rate payable for temporary total disability on their date of injury can receive one or more increases in their compensation rate under LC4661.5. The employee's compensation rate will not increase unless the employee's average weekly earnings exceeded the statutory maximum average weekly earnings amount in effect on the date of injury and the statutory maximum average weekly earnings amount was increased after the injury.

Two years after the date of the injury (DOI), the employee's compensation rate must be reevaluated each time the statutory maximum earnings amount is increased. (Note: all changes prior to 1994 took effect on 1/1; all increases in the statutory maximum earnings amount in 1994, 1995, and 1996 have 7/1 effective dates.) The employee's rate is not automatically increased to a current maximum compensation rate (CR). The employee's compensation rate will not increase unless the employee's actual weekly earnings equal or exceed the current maximum average weekly earnings (AWE) amount in LC4453.

SAMPLE (a). Jackie's earnings are $600/wk. When she was injured on 3/3/94, statutory maximum average weekly earnings of $504 produced a maximum compensation rate of $336/wk. On 3/3/96, Jackie continues to be temporarily totally disabled. On this date, Jackie's earnings are less than statutory maximum AWE of $672.

> 3/3/94   Earnings $600.00 = $504.00 AWE × ⅔ = $336.00/wk CR
> 3/3/96   Earnings $600.00 = $600.00 AWE × ⅔ = $400.00/wk CR

SAMPLE (b). Marsha's actual average weekly earnings were $702 when injured on 8/2/94. She received the maximum rate of $406 based on statutory maximum earnings of $609. Temporary total disability benefits were owed from 8/2/94 until 6/12/97. The statutory maximum AWE amount was increased to $672 on 7/1/95 and $735 effective 7/1/96.

> 08/02/94 - 08/01/96   Earnings $702/wk = $609.00 AWE × ⅔ = $406/wk CR
> 08/02/96 - 06/12/97   Earnings $702/wk = $702.00 AWE × ⅔ = $468/wk CR

SAMPLE (c). Ben's average weekly earnings (AWE) are $860. Temporary total disability benefits are owed from the DOI on 1/1/94 until 6/15/97. In January 1994, statutory maximum average weekly earnings (AWE) of $504 produced a maximum compensation rate of $336/wk. The maximum statutory AWE amount was increased to $609 effective 7/1/94, $672 effective 7/1/95, and $735/wk as of 7/1/96.

> 01/01/94 - 12/31/95 Earnings $860/wk = $504 AWE × ⅔ = $336/wk CR
> 01/01/96 - 06/30/96 Earnings $860/wk = $672 AWE × ⅔ = $448/wk CR
> 07/01/96 - 06/15/97 Earnings $860/wk = $735 AWE × ⅔ = $490/wk CR

After Two Years – No Decrease in Rate

A truism about LC4661.5 is that when it affects an employee, it operates to increase the employee's compensation rate. The statutory minimum average weekly earnings amount in LC4453 was decreased in 1990 (from $168 to $147), and in 1991 it was essentially eliminated (except that a minimum average weekly earnings amount of $189 continues to apply to employees with actual earnings in the range of $126-$189). For this reason, LC4661.5 was amended effective 1990 to make it clear that the use of the current minimum average weekly earnings amount in LC4453 on the date temporary total disability benefits are paid is prohibited whenever two-thirds of this amount would produce a "lower payment because of a reduction in the minimum average weekly earnings applicable" under LC4453.

Take the case of an employee who earned $50/wk when injured on 6/14/88 and was paid at the minimum compensation rate of $112/wk ($\frac{2}{3}$ of $168 statutory minimum average weekly earnings). The compensation rate for temporary disability benefits would have been $98 ($\frac{2}{3}$ of $147 statutory minimum average weekly earnings) if this employee was injured in 1990 and $50/wk (1.5 × this employee's actual earnings) for a 1991 or later date of injury. Any temporary disability benefits paid to this employee more than two years after the date of injury (and until the employee's return to work) will continue to be payable at $112/wk.

06/14/88 - 06/13/90 Earnings $50/wk = $168 AWE × $\frac{2}{3}$ = $112 CR
06/14/90 - 12/31/90 Earnings $50/wk = $168 AWE × $\frac{2}{3}$ = $112 CR (not $98)
01/01/91 - 05/07/91 Earnings $70/wk = $168 AWE × $\frac{2}{3}$ = $112 CR (not $50)

Change in Earnings – Effect on Rate

Post-Injury Increase in Earnings. The employee's temporary disability rate can be increased based on increased earnings after an injury (unless and until the employee's earnings equal or exceed the applicable maximum average weekly earnings amount in LC4453). Per LC4453, the employee's average weekly earnings are computed using earnings information that is known "at the time of his or her injury," that may include knowledge of post-injury increases in earnings on specific dates (see 8.18).

Some persons rely upon the wording of LC4653 as requiring an employer to appraise an employee's actual wage loss continuously throughout the period of temporary total disability. Per LC4653, "if the injury causes temporary total disability, the disability payment is two-thirds of the average weekly earnings during the period of such disability, consideration being given to the ability of the injured employee to compete in an open labor market."

The purpose of LC4653 is to establish the amount of the compensation rate for temporary total disability benefits as two-thirds of the employee's average weekly earnings. However, the wording of this section appears to require a continuing appraisal of average weekly earnings during the period of temporary disability payments and, by past appellate interpretation, has been held to require a recomputation of the employee's compensation rate whenever an injury prevents the employee from receipt of an increase in earnings after the injury.

The courts have categorized the required proof of increased earnings as "specific demonstrable evidence." Actual receipt of higher earnings would be demonstrable evidence of increased earnings, but an employee's allegation of higher earnings would not constitute evidence (specific, demonstrable or otherwise). If an employer cannot verify an alleged post-injury increase in earnings and no other documentary evidence exists, the potential for receipt of such earnings is a matter of conjecture, not fact.

Sometimes an employee returns to work after an injury, receives a pay increase, and then becomes disabled from the initial injury. The employee may have been back at work a brief period or many months (e.g. where the employee needs foot surgery but wishes to schedule surgery after a temporary replacement has been trained). If the date and amount of the pay increase were capable of determination at the time of the injury, then the employee's average weekly earnings should be changed as of the date of this post-injury pay increase (see 8.17 - 8.19) without any specific request from the employee. However, a demand for an increased compensation rate based upon a post-injury pay increase about which no one knew and therefore could not appraise at the time of injury may equate to a claim for damages. Many employees expect to be compensated for every financial consequence of a work injury.

The employee's earning capacity can increase without actual receipt of any increased earnings. For example, a raise can take effect post-injury, but the employee's disability may prevent receipt of higher earnings. Traditionally, the courts will not interpret the law in a way that penalizes an employee for sustaining an injury. Therefore, the employee need not actually receive higher earnings in order to have a compensation rate based on the increased earnings. The employee can return to work and receive a wage increase, or the employee can present evidence that increased post-injury earnings would be received if he was not disabled. Facts such as these should be considered in appraising the employee's average weekly earnings whenever such facts are capable of assessment at the time of the injury as required by the express provisions of LC4453.

As a result of amendments to LC4453 that took effect 1/1/90, LC4453 now provides that benefits "calculated according to the" minimum and maximum average weekly earnings limits in 4453 "in effect on the date of injury ... shall remain in effect for the duration of any disability." This language appears to require the employer to determine the amount of an employee's average weekly earnings for all indemnity benefits as of the date of injury, based upon facts known about the employee's earnings at the time of the injury (that can include evidence of post-injury changes in earnings). Per LC4453, the employee's compensation rate can subsequently be increased if LC4661.5 applies, which allows some employees to receive a higher compensation rate because of an increase in the maximum weekly earnings limit in LC4453 (not a post-injury increase in the employee's earnings; see 8.18).

Post-Injury Decrease in Earnings. Just as the employee's compensation rate can be increased, it can also be decreased after an injury. The statutory authority for either change would be found in LC4453 and LC4653. Events that lower the employee's average weekly earnings as of a specific post-injury date are not ignored, and it is not necessary that the employee actually receive reduced levels of earnings (or no earnings). What is necessary is evidence sufficient to prove that a disability is all that prevents the employee from receipt of a reduced level of earnings. In the words of the courts, evidence must be "specific demonstrable evidence." Even so, the courts have usually shown reluctance to reduce an employee's compensation rate (and see 9.19 regarding post-injury incarceration.)

9.6 PARTIAL DISABILITY – WAGE LOSS FORMULA

The employee can sustain a partial wage loss when he returns to work while still disabled and receives reduced earnings. Per LC4654, the employee's compensation rate is "two-thirds of the weekly loss in wages" during the period of temporary partial disability. According to LC4657, a "weekly loss in wages" means "the difference between the average weekly earnings of the injured employee and the weekly amount that the injured employee will probably be able to earn during the disability."

No earnings limits are stated in LC4654, so earnings used to compute temporary partial disability benefits are therefore subject to the statutory maximum and minimum average weekly earnings limits specified in LC4453 (that would apply if temporary total disability benefits were payable to the employee). Coordination of these Labor Code sections yields the following formula for computing an employee's wage loss (WL) and temporary partial disability compensation rate (CR).

WAGE-LOSS FORMULA

AWE   Average Weekly Earnings for temporary disability benefits

−WE   Weekly Earnings, or wages earned, while disabled

WL   Wage Loss per week × ⅔ = compensation rate for TPD

NOTE: Earnings amounts used in the wage-loss formula will always be the lesser of the employee's actual average weekly earnings or else the applicable statutory maximum average weekly earnings amount in LC4453.

Some people are under the mistaken impression that the employee's compensation rate is computed differently for temporary partial disability than it is for temporary total disability benefits. However, the formula set out above is used to compute all temporary disability benefits. The reason for the misconception regarding two formulas is demonstrated by the samples that follow: the subtraction step in the formula is performed mentally when the disability is total; whereas, all the steps of the formula are written out when the disability is partial.

SAMPLE (a). Kathleen earned $660/wk when she was injured at work on 4/3/97. Kathleen was temporarily totally disabled for several weeks before returning to work on a light duty basis earning $330/wk while partially disabled.

	Temporary Total Disability:	Temporary Partial Disability:
AWE	$660.00	$660.00
−WE	− 00.00	−330.00
WL	$660.00 × ⅔ = $440/wk CR	$330.00 × ⅔ = $220/wk CR

SAMPLE (b). Bruce earned $564/wk when he was injured on 11/27/96. He was temporarily totally disabled for several weeks and then returned to work on a light duty basis earning $282/wk while partially disabled.

	Temporary Total Disability:	Temporary Partial Disability:
AWE	$564.00	$564.00
−WE	− 00.00	−282.00
WL	$564.00 × ⅔ = $376/wk CR	$282.00 × ⅔ = $188/wk CR

Additional computations can be performed to double-check the validity of the results that are obtained from using a wage loss formula. The employee's compensation rate for temporary partial disability has to be less than his temporary total disability rate since it is always two-thirds of a smaller wage loss. When partial wages and partial disability payments are added, their sum can never equal or exceed the amount of earnings the employee would receive if he was not disabled at all.

In Sample (b) above, compare the following amounts:
1. When paid full wages, the employee receives $564/wk.
2. When totally disabled, the employee receives $376/wk.
3. When partially disabled, the employee will receive $470/wk ($282 in wages plus $188 as a temporary partial disability benefit).

9.7 PARTIAL DISABILITY – HIGH/LOW EARNINGS

Maximum Earnings

Part or all of the employee's actual wage loss while partially disabled may be a noncompensable wage loss. Earnings in excess of the statutory maximum average weekly earnings amount that applies to a particular employee are not used in any step of a wage loss formula.

If the employee's earnings when not disabled exceed the statutory maximum earnings amount, a portion of the employee's actual wage loss while totally disabled will be noncompensable. If the employee's actual earnings while partially disabled exceed the statutory maximum earnings amount, the entire wage loss is noncompensable. The following samples compare the correctly computed compensation rate with the incorrect result that would be obtained if actual earnings were used in error (instead of "average weekly earnings" computed pursuant to LC4453).

In samples (a) and (b) below, incorrect use of actual earnings produces a higher compensation rate for partial disability benefits than the rate that would be payable if the employee were temporarily totally disabled (⅔ of maximum AWE). In samples (c) and (d) which follow, note how use of actual earnings instead of the statutory maximum earnings amount produces a compensation rate for temporary partial disability benefits in cases where the employee is not entitled to receive this benefit.

SAMPLE (a). Hattie was earning $700/wk when injured on 1/17/96. Hattie returns to work on 3/21/96 at reduced wages of $300/wk. Statutory maximum AWE are $672. The correct temporary partial disability (TPD) rate is $248/wk.

AWE	$672.00		$700.00	Actual earnings
−WE	−300.00		−300.00	Actual earnings
WL	$372.00 × ⅔ = $248.00 CR		$400.00 × ⅔ = $266.67	

SAMPLE (b). Howie was earning $800/wk when injured on 2/28/97. Howie returns to work on 3/19/97 at reduced wages of $455/wk. Statutory maximum AWE are $735. The correct TPD rate is $186.67/wk.

AWE	$735.00		$800.00	Actual earnings
−WE	−455.00		−455.00	Actual earnings
WL	$280.00 × ⅔ = $186.67 CR		$345.00 × ⅔ = $230.00	

SAMPLE (c). Terry is injured on 6/1/94 while earning $1200/wk. Statutory maximum AWE were $504 on the DOI but are $735 when Terry returns to work on 2/13/97. While partially disabled, Terry earns reduced wages in the amount of $800/wk (an actual wage loss of $400/wk). However, no temporary partial disability payments are payable to Terry.

AWE	$735.00		$1200.00	Actual earnings
−WE	−735.00		− 800.00	Actual earnings
WL	$ 00.00 No benefit payable		$ 400.00 × ⅔ = $266.67	

SAMPLE (d). Darlene is injured on 6/15/94 while earning $578/wk. She returns to work on 11/13/94 while partially disabled and receives reduced wages in the amount of $524/wk. Statutory maximum AWE are $504. Cynthia is not entitled to any temporary partial disability payments.

AWE	$504.00		$578.00	Actual earnings
−WE	−504.00		−524.00	Actual earnings
WL	$ 00.00 No benefit payable		$ 54.00 × ⅔ = $ 36.00	

Low Earnings

For 1991 or later injuries, caution is necessary when computing a temporary partial disability compensation rate for employees whose average weekly earnings amount is established by law at a higher amount than the employees' actual average weekly earnings. This category includes employees with earnings in the range of $126 - $189, whose average weekly earnings are collectively set by law at $189. This category also includes all employees with earnings less than $126/wk, since LC4453 establishes average weekly earnings for such employees as 1.5 times the employees' actual average weekly earnings.

For the employees referenced above, LC4453 requires the use of a statutory average weekly earnings amount when computing a compensation rate for temporary total disability benefits (the lessor of 1.5 × actual average weekly earnings or $189). However, the statutory minimum earnings amount cannot be used in computations of a temporary partial disability compensation rate without producing illogical results, as demonstrated in the examples that follow. For such employees it will be necessary to use actual average weekly earnings to compute a compensation rate for temporary partial disability benefits, (not $189/wk or 1.5 times actual average weekly earnings).

SAMPLE (e). When she was injured on 5/9/96, Ginger was earning $150/wk as a part-time dental hygienist. Per LC4453, her average weekly earnings are the statutory minimum, $189. Ginger is totally disabled until 5/16/97 and receives a temporary total disability compensation rate of $126/wk. On 5/16/97, Ginger returns to work while partially disabled, and the employer pays reduced wages of $125/wk.

    1. Illogical Computation: Notice that no number used in the formula matches any actual earnings amount involved in this example. Ginger has a wage loss of $25/wk, not $1.50/wk.

AWE	$189.00	Statutory minimum AWE for $150/wk
−WE	−187.50	Statutory minimum AWE for $125/wk
WL	$ 1.50	

    2. Illogical Computation: the amount of a computed wage loss cannot exceed the amount of the known actual lost wages for an employee. Ginger's actual wage loss is $25/wk.

AWE	$189.00	Statutory minimum AWE
−WE	−125.00	Actual weekly earnings received
WL	$ 64.00	Exceeds actual wage loss

    3. Logical Computation: this is the only method that can produce a result for Ginger that is equivalent to that for any high wage earner.

AWE	$150.00	Actual average weekly earnings
−WE	−125.00	Actual weekly earnings received
WL	$ 25.00	× ⅔ = $16.67 CR (+ $125 wages = $141.67/wk)

SAMPLE (f). When he was injured on 10/7/96, Ryan's actual earnings were $40/wk. Therefore, Ryan's average weekly earnings are 1.5 times this amount or $60/wk per LC4453. Ryan received temporary total disability benefits at a compensation rate of $40/wk. On 3/3/97, Ryan returns to work while partially disabled, and the employer pays reduced wages of $35/wk.

    1. Illogical Computation: Ryan has a wage loss of $5/wk.

AWE	$60.00	Statutory AWE (1.5 × $40 Earnings)
−WE	−52.50	Statutory AWE (1.5 × $35 Earnings)
WL	$ 7.50	Exceeds actual wage loss ($40 − $35 = $5)

2. Illogical Computation: a partial wage loss cannot result in Ryan receiving more money than if he received full wages. Note that the total payments Ryan would receive based upon the calculation below would be $51.67/wk — which exceeds Ryan's wages of $40 when not disabled.

AWE	$60.00	Statutory AWE (1.5 × $40 Earnings)
−WE	−35.00	Actual weekly earnings received
WL	$25.00 × ⅔ = $16.67 CR (+ $35 wages = $51.67/wk)	

3. Logical Computation: this method will produce a result that is equivalent to that for any high wage earner and does not provide Ryan with more money than he would earn if not disabled.

AWE	$40.00	Actual average weekly earnings
−WE	−35.00	Actual weekly earnings received
WL	$ 5.00 × ⅔ = $3.33 CR (+ $35 wages = $38.33/wk)	

9.8 PARTIAL DISABILITY – NO EARNINGS

Temporary disability benefits can be paid on a wage loss basis in cases where the employee is medically capable of receiving partial earnings but does not do so. Per LC4657, the amount of the employee's weekly loss in wages can be determined by comparing his average weekly earnings to "the weekly amount that the employee will probably be able to earn during the disability." The employee's temporary partial disability compensation rate is two-thirds of the employee's estimated loss in weekly earnings instead of the employee's actual loss in earnings. For instance, if the employee declined his employer's offer to return to work on light duty at reduced wages, the employer would be asked to state the amount of weekly earnings the employee would have received if he had returned to work (see also 9.24).

9.9 DAILY DISABILITY – DAILY RATES

Per LC4655, when the employee has a "temporary disability that is at times total and at times partial" during the same week, "the weekly disability payment during the period of each total or partial disability" must be computed separately. The weekly compensation rate is computed once as if the employee's wage loss was total the whole week and again as if the employee's wage loss was partial for the entire week. Weekly compensation rates are based upon a seven day calendar workweek regardless of the number of hours or days actually worked (see 9.11). Dividing the weekly compensation rate by seven produces a daily compensation rate that is then multiplied times the number of days of temporary total or partial disability.

In the following samples, note that earnings which the employee receives for any days after the employee is no longer disabled are not considered when computing the employee's weekly rate (are not used in the wage loss formula). Such earnings have no effect whatsoever on the employee's compensation rate for either temporary total or temporary partial disability benefits. The weekly earnings amount that is used in the wage loss formula (as required by LC4653, LC4654, and LC4655) will always be comprised exclusively of earnings received for those days during a calendar week when the employee was temporarily partially disabled.

SAMPLE (a). Justin earned $650/wk when injured on 6/8/96 and was entitled to be paid temporary total disability (TTD) benefits until Tuesday 11/19/96 when he returned to full duty at full wages. The final check for TTD benefits for Sunday and Monday would be computed as shown below.

        AWE $650.00
       −WE   − 00.00
        WL $650.00 × ⅔ = $433.33/wk CR ÷ 7 = $ 61.90/day CR
                                                    ×   2
                                                   $123.80 TTD owed

SAMPLE (b). Mark earned $650/wk when injured on 6/8/96 and is entitled to be paid temporary partial (TPD) benefits until Wednesday 11/20/96 when he returned to full duty at full wages. While partially disabled, Mark received $350/wk in wages for performing light duties. The final check for TPD benefits for Sunday through Tuesday would be computed as shown below.

        AWE $650.00
       −WE   −350.00
        WL $300.00 × ⅔ = $ $200.00/wk CR ÷ 7 = $28.57/day CR
                                                      ×   3
                                                     $85.71 TTD owed

SAMPLE (c). Michael earned $650/wk when injured on 6/8/96. Temporary total disability benefits were owed through Monday 11/18/96. Michael returned to work on Tuesday 11/19/96 performing light duties for which the employer agreed to pay partial wages of $450/wk. Michael's condition improved, and he returned to full duties for full pay on Friday 11/22/96. Using the daily compensation rates computed in Samples (a) and (b), Michael's final check for temporary disability (TD) benefits would be computed as shown below.

        $61.90/day TTD × 2 days = $123.80
        $28.57/day TPD × 3 days = + 85.71
                                  $209.51 TD due for week

9.10 QUALIFYING CRITERIA FOR BENEFITS

The employer does not owe temporary disability benefits unless the employee is qualified to receive such benefits. Simply put, an employee is entitled to receive temporary disability benefits if the employee sustains a temporary wage loss as a result of a compensable disability. There are actually five separate qualifying criteria. If any of the criteria that are listed below are not met, the employee is not qualified to receive temporary (neither total nor partial) disability benefits.

1. The employee must have a medical disability that precludes him or her from working, AND
2. The disability must be temporary, rather than permanent in nature, AND
3. The disability must be a result of a compensable industrial injury, AND
4. The employee must sustain a wage loss, AND
5. The wage loss must result from the work-related disability.

By definition, the employee must be "disabled" before being entitled to temporary "disability" benefits, and the disability must be "temporary." Pursuant to LC3600, the employee is not entitled to any workers' compensation benefits unless the employee first sustains an industrial injury. Therefore, the disability must be the result of a compensable industrial injury.

Per LC4650, the employer does not owe temporary disability payments if "the employer continues the employee's wages under a salary continuation plan" (see 9.33). Pursuant to LC4653 and LC4654, the weekly benefit level is computed as a portion of the employee's weekly loss in wages (see 9.4 and 9.6). These facts make it clear that temporary disability benefits are not owed unless the employee sustains a temporary wage loss as a result of a compensable industrial injury. This is the only possible conclusion to be derived from a coordination of all the statute sections that pertain to temporary disability benefits.

The employee's medical eligibility for temporary disability benefits can only be established by a person who is defined as a "physician" pursuant to LC3209.3 (as well as the Business and Professions Code; see 7.26). Both acupuncturists and MFCC's are statutorily precluded from determining an injured worker's entitlement to temporary (or permanent) disability (see 7.28-7.29). Per LC3209.8, "marriage, family, and child counselors and clinical social workers" are not authorized to "determine disability." This language does not relieve counselors from their responsibility to submit written reports covering all other aspects of their services. However, a counselor's opinion of disability status, if given, will not entitle the employee to receive any disability benefits. Likewise, LC3209.3 provides that acupuncturists are not authorized "to determine disability."

9.11 INITIATION OF PAYMENTS – FIRST PAYMENT

Since 1990, LC4650 requires that "the first payment of temporary disability indemnity shall be made not later than 14 days after knowledge of the injury and disability, on which date all indemnity then due shall be paid, unless liability for the injury is earlier denied." In actuality, the starting date of the 14-day period is the day on which the employer first learns that the employee is temporarily disabled as a result of a work-related injury, which will not necessarily be the same day that the employer first knew of an injury.

The 14-day period for an initial payment is a maximum period, but since temporary disability benefits are a wage replacement benefit, an employee will appreciate a payment as soon as possible. The first payment that is made after a determination of the employee's entitlement usually will not include payment for a full two week period (e.g. payment may be made only for days of disability that have already gone by).

Before making an initial payment, it is necessary to certify the period of disability with a physician. The treating physician is the appropriate source of an opinion on the anticipated duration of disability, and the employer can verify whether the employee has returned to work (possibly with modified duties). Payment is required by the 14th day of lost time, and written medical opinions are not a prerequisite to payment. Telephone inquiries are usually the fastest method of obtaining necessary information regarding disability status. Some physicians can provide this information by facsimile transmission, but oral information gathering also provides the claimsperson with an opportunity to make other inquiries relative to medical management of the claim.

The Labor Code does not distinguish between calendar days and scheduled work days. Disability benefits are always paid on the basis of a seven-day workweek regardless of the employee's actual scheduled days of work. If the doctor says the employee is disabled for a certain number of days, it is not necessary to determine if the period of disability includes a scheduled vacation day, a holiday, or Saturday or Sunday. In fact, it does not matter if the employee has a job to return to. Days of disability can be determined solely from medical information without any reference to a calendar. Once this information is known, the claimsperson need then determine if payment is owed for the three-day waiting period (see 9.12).

The employer is not required to pay in advance for days of disability that have not yet occurred. If additional payments of temporary disability benefits are anticipated, then at the time an initial payment is made, LC4650 requires (unless payments are made under a salary continuation plan; see 9.33) the employer to notify the employee of the day of the week on which the next payment will be made. This day will be the same day of the week that a first payment is issued since LC4650 requires subsequent payments to be provided every 14 days.

A claims administrator may choose to issue all temporary disability checks on a particular day of the week. Many holidays are celebrated on Mondays or Fridays, but the claims administrator can structure itself so that temporary disability payments owing on all claim files are issued only on Tuesdays or only on Wednesdays and Thursdays. Initial payments to employees can be staggered to achieve this result. For instance, the employee may initially be paid for a period of 1 to 6 days of accrued disability to ensure that the next payment will become due 14 days later on the same day of the week as the initial check was issued.

The language of LC4650(a) implies that the employer is required to pay temporary disability benefits within the specified 14-day period unless compensability of the injury is "denied" within this time. Except, LC4650(c) refers to another alternative that would relieve the employer from making a payment when liability for payment of temporary disability benefits is disputed: the employer can send a delay letter within the 14-day period that advises the employee "why payments cannot be made ... and when the employer expects to have the information required to make" a decision (see 9.15). For purposes of the word "denied" in LC4650(a), a delay letter will suffice to notify the employee that liability for temporary disability benefits is "denied" at this time or "denied" until notified to the contrary.

The precise wording of LC4650(a) appears to require a payment of temporary disability benefits where the employer has valid grounds for denying the compensability of the injury but has not done do so within the 14-day period. This harsh result appears negated by LC5402 which provides that a claim is not presumed to be compensable unless "liability is not rejected within 90 days" after the date the employer receives a completed claim form (6.13). The employer has a basic duty to act assertively to determine its liability for benefits and to provide prompt payment of all benefits that are due. However, the employer is not obligated to provide benefits to an employee who is not entitled to receive benefits based upon relevant medical and legal facts that are known to the employer but not yet relayed to the employee (see also 6.9).

9.12 WAITING PERIOD

California requires a three-day waiting period (WP) before temporary disability benefits commence unless one of three possible exceptions applies. The first three days of disability could also be called the first three days of lost time, lost wages, or wage loss. Per LC4650.5, no waiting period applies to civil service employees who are victims of violent crimes. In all other instances, LC4652 provides that the employee is entitled to payment for each day of temporary disability only if:

1. The employee is disabled more than 14 days, OR
2. The employee is "hospitalized as an inpatient."

Per LC4652, the date of injury is counted as day one of the waiting period "unless the employee was paid full wages for that day. Therefore, it is necessary to determine whether the employee was paid in full for the date of injury, a fact that the claimsperson will need to ascertain through contact with the employer (unless a particular employer has set policies on this matter that are known to the claimsperson). Conflicts between information obtained from the employer and the employee should be resolved by reviewing available documentation such as an employee's pay check stubs. Credibility issues may require application of good judgment, e.g. where a day worker is paid cash but the employer and employee disagree whether payment was provided/received for the date of injury.

For purposes of computing the waiting period, a "day" means a calendar day, not a 24-hour period from the moment of injury. The waiting period accumulates as whole days, not on an hour-by-hour basis. The solitary exception to this general rule is the date of injury: the date of injury counts as a full day of disability for purposes of the waiting period regardless of how small the actual amount of lost wages for this day may be. An injury may not produce immediate disability, or the disability may be intermittent. The employee might accumulate three days of disability over an extended period of time, and the days need not be consecutive.

Per LC4652, an employee who is "hospitalized as an inpatient for treatment required by the injury" is eligible for temporary disability payments commencing on the date of hospitalization or the first day of disability, whichever occurs first. An employee who is hospitalized at some later date is entitled to a retroactive payment for the first three days that the employee was disabled. If hospitalization occurs on the date of injury, there is no waiting period. Temporary disability benefits would then be owed for each day of temporary disability.

The number of hours spent at a hospital or the fact that treatment is provided at a hospital is not controlling, although the type of treatment received may be relevant as explained below. The term "inpatient" in LC4652 refers to a formal admission to a hospital and generally contemplates an overnight stay. However, a morning admission and afternoon discharge for a surgical or testing procedure would appear to qualify as hospitalization for purposes of waiving the three-day waiting period for temporary disability benefits. Spending an entire night in the emergency room of a hospital without being admitted as an inpatient would not constitute hospitalization for a minor injury (but could if a hospital visit extended into an admission for a serious injury).

A modern medical trend is the utilization of outpatient facilities for many medical procedures that have historically been performed only on an inpatient basis. Where an outpatient facility is utilized in lieu of formal hospital admission, some employers will waive the three-day waiting period for temporary disability benefits. This waiver encourages the use of outpatient facilities that provide the same services that would otherwise be provided in a traditional hospital setting at a higher cost. A refusal to pay the waiting period when outpatient facilities are utilized (a refusal that is permitted by the clear wording of LC4652), would create a disincentive for employees to use more cost-effective facilities.

The employee will also be paid for all days of disability when "temporary disability continues for more than 14 days." Unless the employee was hospitalized during the first 14 days, the first three days of lost time would remain unpaid on the 14th day of disability. (In this event, the initial payment of temporary disability benefits on the 14th day of disability would pay the employee for 10 days of disability.) No temporary disability will be paid for the first three days if the employee is disabled for exactly 14 days. The employee must be disabled a total of 15 days before the waiting period is owed. The claim file should contain a cumulative log of the number of days of temporary disability that have been paid to date. Once the employee accumulates 15 days of disability, the employee is entitled to retroactive payment for the first three days of disability. (Unless the employee was hospitalized on an earlier date, payment for the waiting period should be included in the check that provides payment for the 15th day of disability).

The employee's disability may last a total of one, two or three days. If this is the extent of the period of disability, the employee is not entitled to payment of temporary disability benefits (except per LC4650.5, no waiting period applies to civil service employees who are victims of violent crimes). The employee may sustain a loss in wages, but the employer has no liability under the Labor Code to compensate the employee for the lost earnings. This circumstance is an example of a wage loss that is noncompensable under the Labor Code (and also an example of a financial loss that constitutes damages, not compensation, and is not owed by the employer under LC3209).

The waiting period created by LC4652 applies to "temporary disability indemnity." This term encompasses disability that is either total or partial in nature, and there is only one waiting period per employee per injury. Ordinarily, the waiting period accumulates only during periods of total disability because LC4652 describes the waiting period as "days after the employee leaves work." An employee who is partially disabled is working and receiving wages, although the employee may return to work for reduced hours per day or days per week.

Full days of lost earnings while partially disabled could be deemed to count towards the three-day waiting period under LC4652 (e.g. where the employee is working two days per week on a trial basis, those days that the employee is not at work could count towards the waiting period), but this is not common practice. Since the purpose of the waiting period is to encourage employees to return to work, the waiting period is not usually applied to days encompassed within the employee's weekly work schedule. Rather, the waiting period is applied only to periods of total disability.

9.13 PAYMENTS – NOT AN ADMISSION OF LIABILITY

The employer can make a prompt payment of temporary disability benefits without accepting any liability for benefits. Per LC4909, the employer may make a voluntary payment "when there is any dispute or question concerning the right to compensation." The claim may be one that requires an investigation that cannot be completed immediately. Benefits are sometimes delayed in cases where the employer ultimately determines that benefits are owed. The investigation that reveals benefits are owed may itself cause a delay in the prompt provision of benefits. If it appears probable that the claim will be found to be compensable, a short period of payments without any admission of liability may be in order. This payment can assist in establishing rapport with the injured employee.

If the employer later accepts liability, in retrospect, the advance payment was the right thing to do. However, there is always the possibility that an advance payment may turn out to be one that the employer does not owe, and LC4909 does not provide the employer with any right of collection to recover the money from the employee. Since the advance payment can be any amount of the employer's choosing, the employer should never suffer too seriously from this adverse consequence.

The employer's denial of liability may not be sustained if the employee pursues a claim at the WCAB. Should the employer be ordered to provide benefits, the employer can claim full credit for any previous payments that were made in accordance with LC4909. It is helpful to have documentation of the employer's reliance on this section, e.g. a specific reference to this statute on a check payable to the employee or in an accompanying piece of correspondence. Per LC4909, previous employer payments "may be taken into account by the appeals board in fixing the amount of the compensation to be paid." When a Judge is required to do something, the Labor Code uses the word "shall." The use of the word "may" makes some employers a little hesitant about their potential receipt of a full credit. Therefore, some caution should be exercised when making payments prior to accepting liability for payment.

9.14 PAYMENTS – MANNER & FREQUENCY

Immediately Negotiable Instrument

Per LC4651, the employer is required to make disability indemnity payments "by any written instrument" that "is immediately negotiable and payable in cash, on demand, without discount at some established place of business in the state." The "business" referred to here means a bank. The employer is not obligated to provide a payment that is immediately negotiable at any place of business the employee may choose such as the employee's local grocery store. The Labor Code prohibits payments by sight drafts; this means of payment was formerly a common practice although drafts could not be converted immediately to cash even at the bank against which they were drawn. Payment by check is permissible and the customary form of payment at present. (See also 9.17.)

The employee should not have to travel great distances to convert a disability check into cash. This would create an unnecessary hardship on the employee. Ordinarily, checks are issued on banks that have local branch offices where the checks can be cashed. Occasionally, an employee will move out of the state and still receive temporary disability payments. The employer is not required to open a bank account in the other state. The workers' compensation laws provide for payment that is immediately negotiable in this "state," not any state.

Frequency of Payments

The provisions of LC4650 control the frequency of temporary disability indemnity payments after the first payment is made. Per LC4650, subsequent payments "shall be made as due every two weeks on the day designated with the first payment." The only permissible exception applies when "the employer continues the employee's wages under a salary continuation plan" (see 9.33). In such cases, a payment is considered to be on time if it is provided on the employee's regular payday (that might be weekly or monthly). In all other cases, a timely payment means one issued on the correct day of the week and no later than 14 days after the preceding payment was issued.

Since 1990, all categories of disability benefits (meaning all indemnity or wage loss benefits) are payable on a retroactive basis. Payment is only required for days of temporary disability that have occurred after the last date for which payment was provided and before the date the current payment is made (per LC4650, the employer is required to pay only days that are "due"). Overpayments should be rare since each time a payment issues, the claimsperson will have had a full 14 days to determine if another payment is owed.

Retroactive payments of workers' compensation indemnity benefits provide the employer with a financial benefit. The employer has the right to earn interest on anticipated payments of temporary disability benefits (that may amount to a negligible amount on a single retroactive payment on a single claim but can mean large sums when multiplied by many retroactive payments on many claims). However, the extra costs involved in any late payments of temporary disability benefits can negate any potential interest savings the employer might otherwise have experienced (see 9.16).

9.15 BENEFIT PAYMENT NOTICES

Per LC138.4 and CR9812, a variety of notices are required when the employer provides payment of temporary disability (permanent disability, rehabilitation, or death — any indemnity) benefits. These notices will inform the employee that benefits are being paid, the category of benefit that is being paid, the first date for which benefits are being paid, the day of the week on which continuing benefits will be paid, the rate of payment and how this amount was calculated, the date and reason for any change in the rate of payment and/or the category of benefit being provided, the last date for which benefits were provided, the reason for termination of payments, and a summary or accounting of the benefits that were provided.

Benefit payment notices are intended to provide an employee with sufficient information to enable the employee to ascertain whether or not the employer is providing the proper amount of benefits that the employee is entitled to receive. The notices are not intended to educate employees on every nuance of the workers' compensation laws but merely to provide enough information so that a person who is not knowledgeable in workers' compensation matters might have some manner of identifying blatant or obvious errors. For instance, contrary to information provided in a benefit notice letter, the employee might know for a fact and be able to prove that his average weekly earnings were a higher amount, that there is a mathematical error in the claimsperson's calculation of the weekly rate of payment, and/or that he did not return to work on the date specified in the notice.

Per CR9810, required benefit "notice letters may be produced on the claims administrator's letterhead." A "single benefit notice may encompass multiple events." For instance, a notice of termination of temporary total disability benefits may include a summary of benefits provided, a notice of commencement of temporary partial or permanent disability benefits, an explanation of how a new reduced weekly rate of payment was determined, and an explanation of how the amount of the employee's permanent disability benefits will be determined (see 7.76). If no further temporary disability benefits are owed, this notice may also include, an explanation of how the amount of the employee's permanent disability benefits will be determined; e.g. a single notice can also include a notice of the provision of other types of disability benefits that are offered by an employer; e.g. salary continuation benefits. A benefit information pamphlet must be included with the first benefit notice that is required (be it notice of payment, nonpayment or delay of benefits).

Continuing notices enable the employee to promptly request a judicial determination of disputed benefits that were not previously placed in issue. For instance, a dispute regarding the employee's entitlement to temporary disability benefits may first arise after the employer notifies the employee that the rate of payment is being reduced or that such benefits are being terminated. Careful wording of the employer's explanation of a reason for every change in payments can help to avoid unnecessary disputes where the employer is fully complying with its obligation to provide benefits.

All notices require a referral to the claimsperson as well as notice of the employee's right to seek information from another source such as an Information and Assistance Officer or an attorney of the employee's choosing. Commencement of litigation does not relieve the employer of its obligation to provide benefit payment notices. When an employee is represented by an attorney, the employer should also send copies of benefit notices to the employee's attorney. However, benefit notice copies should only be sent to the employee's attorney after the attorney has provided the employer with a properly completed Fee Disclosure Statement (DWC Form 3) as required by LC4906.

The claims administrator is not required to submit a copy of benefit notice letters to the State. Instead, CR9810 requires the claims administrator to maintain copies of each notice that is sent; copies may be maintained "in paper or electronic form." The contents of currently required benefit notices are specified in administrative regulations CR9810-9815 (previously utilized Benefit Information Notice forms or DWC 500 forms have been abandoned).

The claims administrator is required to concurrently serve copies of benefit notices on the employee's attorney, if any, together with all enclosures other than benefit notice pamphlets. Regardless of whether the employee has an attorney, some notices will request a reply within a specified number of days from the date the notice was sent (postmarked); e.g. where the employee is asked to provide proof of self-employment earnings or the names of any witnesses to a claimed injury within 14 days. Deadlines for replies sent by mail are extended for 5, 10 or 20 days depending upon whether the employee mails a reply from California, another state or another country, respectively.

Antifraud Notice. Effective 1997, IC1871.8 permits an insurer (including a self-insuring employer) to provide a special notice regarding fraudulent receipt of temporary disability benefits. The notice is optional, but when a notice is provided, this wording is mandated by law:

"Warning: Acceptance of employment with a different employer that requires the performance of activities that you have stated that you cannot perform because of the injury for which you are receiving temporary disability benefits could constitute fraud and could result in criminal imprisonment for up to five years and a fine of up to fifty thousand dollars ($50,000) or double the amount of the fraud, whichever is greater."

Per IC1871.8, the antifraud notice can be provided on a check itself or on another document that is provided concurrently with a check for temporary disability benefits. The latter option avoids the need to print separate checks to be used solely for payments of temporary disability benefits. A check with a tear-off section containing the notice would comply with IC1871.8 and make it unlikely that any employee would ever deny receipt of the notice.

9.16 LATE PAYMENTS – PENALTIES

Failure to pay any payment of temporary disability benefits at the time such payment is due (meaning within the 14-day period allotted by LC4650) may result in increased costs for the employer. Under certain circumstances, LC4650 requires the employer to increase the amount of temporary disability that was delayed by 10%.

Some people refer to the 10% increase required by LC4650 as a "self-imposed penalty," based upon the belief that it is within the employer's control to avoid late payments. The 10% self-imposed penalty under LC4650 applies to two categories of benefits only: temporary disability and permanent disability. When a self-imposed penalty is owed, it is paid to the employee concurrently with the late disability payment.

Per LC5401, "a claim form must be filed with the employer prior to the injured employee's entitlement to late payment supplements" under LC4650. If the employer does not provide any temporary disability payment at the time it is due, employees who have filed a claim form are entitled to receive the amount of compensation that was due plus a self-imposed penalty that is computed as 10% of the amount of the late payment, with certain exceptions.

A self-imposed penalty can apply when the employer continues "wages under a salary continuation plan, as defined in" LC4650 (see 9.33). If the employee is ordinarily paid twice each month, an employer who continues wages will not owe a self-imposed penalty because wages are not paid every 14 days as would otherwise be required by LC4650. Likewise, the employer is not required to issue each wage payment on the same day of the week (e.g. always on a Wednesday) in order to avoid a self-imposed penalty. However, paying salary benefits late (after the employee's regular payday) or paying a lesser amount than the employee's compensation rate for temporary disability benefits would give rise to a penalty. When a late payment penalty is owed, it is computed as 10% of the temporary disability benefit (or permanent disability benefit) that was owed, not the amount of a salary continuation check that gave rise to the penalty.

Per LC4650, a self-imposed penalty does not attach to a "payment due prior to or within 14 days after the date the claim form was submitted to the employer" (see 6.13). This language has been strictly construed by the Audit Unit as negating the application of a self-imposed penalty to the first payment owed after a claim form is filed. For instance, if the employee filed a claim form immediately upon suffering a disabling injury, a first payment would be "due ... within 14 days after" the date of injury. Therefore, should this payment be made untimely, no automatic increase applies. A self-imposed penalty would thus first apply to the employee's second payment that is payable on the 28th day after the injury (as LC4650 requires temporary disability to be paid every 14 days).

Whether or not the employee has filed a claim form, the employer's failure to pay compensation in a timely fashion can result in a WCAB order to pay a 10% penalty for unreasonable delay under LC5814 (and assessment of an administrative penalty if the late payment is discovered during a State audit; see 2.26). However, the fact that the employer owes a 10% self-imposed penalty under LC4650 is insufficient in and of itself to support an order to pay a LC5814 penalty because:

1. The 10% increase that is owed pursuant to LC4650 is payable regardless of the reason for the delay, whether reasonable (e.g. the claims operation was closed due to a fire or a bomb scare on the date the payment was due) or unreasonable (the claimsperson was on vacation). The 10% increase under LC5814 applies only to delays that are unreasonable.

2. The 10% increase under LC4650 is an automatic penalty that applies to all late payments of temporary disability benefits in cases where a claim form has been filed, including many cases that may never involve any action by the WCAB. A LC5814 penalty is not payable unless a party who desires to be paid this penalty commences WCAB proceedings, proves to the satisfaction of the WCAB that the delay in payment was unreasonable, and is awarded a penalty (except that the employer may voluntarily agree to provide payment of a full penalty or a compromised value rather than defend a weak position in court, e.g. as a term of a settlement that is submitted for WCAB approval).

A 1991 amendment to LC4650 applies exclusively to insured employers. Per LC4650, the 10% self-imposed penalty for any temporary or permanent disability payment that is "due less than seven days after the insurer receives the completed claim form from the employer" is not an indemnity payment (and can be later collected from the employer). Self-imposed penalties thus described do not affect claim file reserves (see 2.24) nor the amount of premium owed by the employer. Per IC11661.5, such self-imposed penalties are not an insurable risk (e.g. a 10% self-imposed penalty that is owed because the first payment of temporary disability was due on 2/22 but the insurer made a late payment on 8/17 after a claim form was received from the employer on 8/12 and the insurer took five days to complete an investigation of the claim).

Per LC4650, the insurer is required to "notify the employer in writing, within 30 days of the payment, that the employer is obligated to reimburse the insurer." This notice is merely an advance notice of potential future liability, because the employer is not obligated to reimburse its insurer unless the aggregate total of the self-imposed penalties exceeds $100 in a policy year. In this event, the insurer will bill the employer at the end of the policy year, and the employer will have 60 days to reimburse its insurer for the amount billed or else file an appeal with the Department of Insurance. If the aggregate total of self-imposed penalties attributable to the employer's delay in forwarding a claim form to its insurer does not exceed $100 in a policy year, the employer is not required to reimburse its insurer. (Note: comparable provisions regarding reimbursement for late payment supplements under LC4650, or so-called "self-imposed penalties," that are attributable to an employer error are commonly included in contracts between self-insured employers and third-party administrators).

9.17 PAYEE – EMPLOYEE ONLY

Per LC4902, "no compensation, whether awarded or voluntarily paid, shall be paid to any attorney at law or in fact or other agent, but shall be paid directly to the claimant." This section prohibits payment of compensation to anyone except the injured employee without specific statutory authority or else a WCAB order. Per LC4902, payments made "in violation of this section" will not "be credited to the employer." If a payment is made improperly to someone else, the employer still owes the payment to the employee, so the employer will have to pay twice. (Exceptions apply if the employee is a minor, the employee is incarcerated in a state penal institution, or the injured worker owes court-ordered support payments; see 9.18-9.20).

It seems logical that disability payments should be paid directly to the injured employee, but occasions arise where some other person requests the employee's checks to be made payable to them. Relatives, former spouses, friends, attorneys, landlords, or other entities may request that the employee's compensation be paid directly to them. For instance, an insured employer may seek partial reimbursement for salary continuation benefits (see 9.33) that it mistakenly paid concurrent with the payment of temporary disability benefits. Whatever reasons are given, the prospective payee may have no intention of giving the money to the injured employee. If checks are not made payable in the employee's name, it is quite possible that the employee will not receive benefits to which the employee is entitled.

The employee may request that temporary disability checks be mailed to someone else's address such as an attorney or employer (e.g. where an employer will provide a check for full salary in exchange for the employee signing over a temporary disability check for a much lower amount). This is an entirely different situation. First, the check is still payable only to the employee. Second, the employee is making the request. The employee has a right to designate the address where he wishes to receive his mail (and, when litigation is pending with the WCAB, a duty under CR10396, , to promptly furnish the employer with a "current mailing address" after any change). It is wise to require written confirmation of such requests to make certain it is the employee who is making the request. This documentation can be useful if the employee later denies making such a request and/or receipt of disability payments.

Per LC4651, the employer can deposit an employee's compensation payments directly into "an account in any bank, savings and loan association or credit union of the employee's choice in this state." This can only be done where "the employee has voluntarily authorized such deposit." Insurance carriers do not usually do this, since special arrangements would be necessary. Self-insured employers may utilize this procedure, especially where the employee's paycheck is usually deposited directly into a designated account (but separate authorization must be obtained for direct deposit of compensation payments).

9.18 PAYEE – EMPLOYEE IS MINOR CHILD

Per LC3605, compensation payments "due an injured minor may be paid to him." Benefit checks should be payable to the minor with one exception. Payments must be made to a "parent or guardian" if these persons give "the employer or ... insurance carrier written notice that" they are claiming "such compensation." Upon receipt of written notice, the compensation check would be made payable directly to the parent or guardian. The check can contain information that makes it clear that the payment is provided for the minor child, e.g. "Edith Turner, as parent of Jimmy Turner, a minor." Confirmation should be obtained that the person claiming compensation is the legal parent or guardian.

Payments in the name of the minor prior to the written notice are "a full release of the employer and insurance carrier for the amount so paid." When an employee later has a guardian appointed or turns 18, the employee "cannot disaffirm" previous payments made directly to him. The payee can change, but LC3605 does not change the amount of compensation owed by the employer. The employer can increase its liability voluntarily by continuing to pay the minor after written notice from a parent or guardian. In this case, the employer does not get credit for any payments improperly paid to the minor.

9.19 PAYEE – EMPLOYEE INCARCERATED

The employee may become incarcerated after a compensable injury was sustained. Since 1989, the provisions of LC3370 control the payment of temporary disability indemnity benefits to any employee who was injured prior to imprisonment in a state (but not a federal or a county) penal or correctional institution.

Per LC3370, an employee who becomes incarcerated after an injury "shall not be entitled to any temporary disability indemnity benefits while incarcerated in a state prison." The employee is barred from receipt of benefits, but the employer is not relieved of its obligation to make temporary disability payments. The employer is required to pay temporary disability benefits, that would otherwise be payable to the employee, to the employee's dependents, if there are any.

Dependents are defined in LC3370 to mean only "the inmate's spouse or children, including an inmate's former spouse due to divorce and the inmate's children from that marriage." Dependency for workers' compensation purposes is generally understood to mean financial dependency (under LC4701). Therefore, persons who are qualify as dependents under LC3370 would appear to be persons to whom the employee has a legal obligation for financial support, e.g. not all former spouses, only a former spouse to whom the employee owed alimony payments under a court order. (Note: for injuries on or after 9/22/92 where an incarcerated employee owes payment of court-ordered support payments, the provisions of LC3370 must be coordinated with other applicable laws in order to determine the appropriate payee(s); see 9.20). Properly qualified dependents can be identified by soliciting information from the employee, interviews with persons who previously worked with the employee, a review of personnel records, and a review of public records of marriages and divorces.

If there are no proper dependents, LC3370 requires the employer to pay temporary disability benefits "to the State Treasury to the credit of the Uninsured Employer's Fund" for any periods of disability during which the employee is incarcerated. This money is not held in trust for the employee. The employee has no right upon release from incarceration to payment for any periods of temporary disability during the incarceration. Temporary disability payments will only become payable directly to the employee if the employee is temporarily disabled subsequent to being released from incarceration.

9.20 PAYEE – CHILD & SPOUSAL SUPPORT ORDERS

Since 9/26/84, the Division of Workers' Compensation has been involved in the Workers' Compensation Notification Project. The Administrative Director of this Division has been required by LC138.5 to cooperate with the Director of the State Department of Social Services "in the enforcement of child support obligations" by assisting with the provision of "information concerning persons who are receiving permanent disability benefits or have filed an application" with the WCAB. Additional legislation took effect 9/22/92 as urgency legislation that affects payments of workers' compensation temporary disability benefits (but not any other category of indemnity benefits) to injured workers who owe court-ordered support payments to their children, spouse, or family.

In reviewing the following information, keep in mind that multiple persons may have rights that can be exercised independently; e.g., the employee may owe support payments to children from different marriages who reside in different states. Note that amendments to CC4720 provide that "it is the intention of the Legislature to ensure that the State of California remains in compliance with federal regulation for child support guidelines." Also, CC1699 provides that a "foreign support order" (one valid in another state) can be registered and enforced in California.

Definitions pertinent to this topic are found in Section 4390 of the Civil Code and Section 704.160 of the Code of Civil Procedure. Per CC4390, "earnings" include "workers' compensation temporary disability benefits," so a "wage assignment" includes an assignment of such benefits. (Since 1990, when a person is ordered to pay support, CC4390.3 provides that the court will "include a wage assignment order.") Per CCP704.160, "support" includes obligations "owing on behalf of a child, spouse, or family ... and includes past due support or arrearage when it exists" as well as "a judgment for reimbursement of public assistance" (if provided to the employee's financial dependents). A "support judgment creditor" (SJC) is a "person to whom support has been ordered to be paid" by the Superior Court. The employee is a "support judgment debtor" (SJD) who owes "a duty of support."

"During the payment of temporary disability benefits," CCP704.160 provides that a support judgment creditor may "directly or through the appropriate district attorney, seek to apply the temporary disability benefit payments to satisfy the support judgment by an assignment of earnings for support or any other applicable enforcement procedure." (A district attorney's office will be involved when a support judgment creditor is a public agency seeking reimbursement for public assistance, e.g. payments provided as Aid to Families with Dependent Children (AFDC) under the Welfare and Institutions Code). A claimsperson need not respond to oral requests for payment but is required to comply with a wage assignment order from the Superior Court that assigns temporary disability payments to a support judgment creditor.

Per CCP704.160, the amount of temporary disability benefits to be withheld pursuant to the assignment of earnings or other enforcement procedure "shall be 25 percent of the amount of each periodic payment or any lower amount specified in writing by the judgment creditor or court order, rounded down to the nearest dollar" (e.g. $26.26 and $26.96 would both be rounded downward to $26). The employer is permitted to deduct "an amount reflecting the actual cost of administration of" the wage assignment up to a maximum of $2 per payment. The employer's cost to process any check usually exceeds two dollars (e.g. the cost of the check, envelope, postage, use of equipment and labor). Thus, $2 will probably be routinely deducted from the amount otherwise payable to a support judgment creditor or the District Attorney.

9.21 TIME LIMIT ON PAYMENTS

Temporary Partial Disability

For all injuries "occurring on or after January 1, 1979," there is a time limit on payments that applies only to payments of temporary partial disability payments. Per LC4656, aggregate temporary partial disability payments "shall not extend for more than 240 compensable weeks within a period of five years from the date of the injury." The number of temporary partial disability payments will depend on the date the employee first became partially disabled and whether the temporary partial disability payments were consecutive or intermittent. The 240 week limit means cumulative weeks of payments, not calendar weeks. If temporary partial disability is first paid close to the end of the five-year period, payments cease at five years. The employee is not entitled to any temporary partial disability payments after five years regardless of the number of weeks of payments that were made within the five year period.

Temporary Total Disability

The only Labor Code section that contains a time limit for payments of temporary disability benefits is LC4656. There is a time limit for payments of temporary partial disability benefits. However, there is no time limit on payments of temporary total disability benefits for any injury that occurred on or after 1/1/79, the effective date of this change in the law.

A time limit does apply where the WCAB has issued a final award of benefits to the employee — the employee has five years from the date of injury to reopen a WCAB file to seek an award of additional temporary disability benefits. If a Petition to Reopen is not filed within the five year period allowed, the WCAB lacks jurisdiction to award further temporary disability benefits. For instance, suppose the WCAB awards the employee lifetime medical benefits based upon a physician's recommendation that a future surgery may be necessary. If the employee has the surgery more than five years after the date of injury, the employee will be entitled to medical benefits but no temporary disability benefits. If the employee has the surgery within the five year period and the WCAB grants a Petition to Reopen, no further time limit applies to payment of temporary disability benefits until the WCAB again issues a final order, decision, or award regarding temporary disability benefits (e.g. the WCAB approves a Stipulations With Request For Award or a Compromise and Release settlement document).

9.22 TERMINATION OF LIABILITY FOR PAYMENTS

There are a variety of reasons why the employer's liability for temporary disability benefits could end. Such reasons include:
   a. The employee does not have a loss of earnings.
   b. The employee refuses available employment and earnings.
   c. The employee is not medically disabled.
   d. The disability is not a result of the industrial injury.
   e. The employee unreasonably refuses medical treatment or evaluations.
   f. The disability is permanent and stationary.
   g. A Petition to Reopen a prior WCAB award was not timely filed (within five years of the date of injury), so the WCAB lacks jurisdiction to award additional periods of temporary disability benefits.
   h. The employee dies.

Concurrent with the last payment of temporary disability benefits, LC138.4 requires the employer to provide a notice of termination of benefits along with an accounting of benefits paid (see 9.15). For 1991 or later injuries, LC4061 requires concurrent notification of applicable rights pertaining to the evaluation of permanent disability by an Agreed Medical Evaluator (for represented employees) or a Qualified Medical Evaluator (see 7.76). Regardless of the date of injury, additional procedures apply if benefits were being provided under the compulsion of a continuing award of temporary disability benefits (because a judge determined disputed entitlement to such benefits in the employee's favor).

Liability for payments is continuous pursuant to the terms of the WCAB award until the employer files a Petition to Terminate Liability for Temporary Disability Indemnity (DWC/WCAB Form 46). Per CR10462, this petition "shall be filed within 10 days of the termination of such payments." Per LC4651.1, there is a "rebuttable presumption that such temporary disability continues for at least one week following the filing of such petition."

Labor Code 4651.1 has been construed to require the employer to pay one more week of temporary disability benefits concurrently with the filing of the petition. An additional week need not be paid if the employer is able to state with certainty (by naming the date and place) that the employee has returned to work. In all other cases, if a judge grants the employer's petition, the employer will then seek credit for the one week overpayment of temporary disability against any permanent disability benefits that may be owed. (Per LC4651.2, "no petitions filed under" LC4651.1 "shall be granted while the injured worker is pursuing a rehabilitation plan.")

9.23 STOP PAYMENTS – NO LOSS OF EARNINGS

Temporary disability benefits are not owed when the employee returns to work and receives normal earnings and/or when the employee is temporarily disabled but receives normal earnings under a qualified salary continuation plan (see 9.33). In either case, there is no wage loss to replace. Per LC4653 and LC4654, the weekly rate of payment for temporary disability benefits is two-thirds of the employee's weekly loss in wages. An employee who has no loss of earnings is therefore entitled to be paid $0.00/wk.

The principles above apply to payments of monetary earnings as well as nonmonetary earnings (see 8.2-8.3). For instance, an apartment manager who receives free rent is receiving nonmonetary earnings equal to the dollar amount it would cost to rent the apartment. If the employer requires the employee to move out of the apartment or to pay rent while disabled, the employee will sustain a wage loss. If the employee continues to receive free rent while temporarily disabled, the employee has no loss of earnings to replace. The employee may reside at the same apartment throughout a period of disability, initially paying rent while totally disabled, then later receiving free rent when once again medically able to perform normal duties.

9.24 STOP PAYMENTS – REFUSAL OF EARNINGS

A physician may release the employee to return to work with temporary medical restrictions, or the employer may offer modified work at reduced earnings that the employee may refuse to accept because the employee believes the modified employment is too difficult, boring, demeaning or otherwise objectionable. The employee cannot be forced to work. However, disability payments will reflect any voluntary reduction in earnings due to restrictions on earnings that are self-imposed. Available earnings will be treated as if they were received. For the duration of the temporary partial disability, the employee will be entitled to receive temporary partial, not temporary total, disability benefits.

Only a physician can determine disability. This fact benefits the employee because it is not proper for a claimsperson to cease disability payments based upon the claimsperson's personal disagreement with a physician's opinion that the employee is disabled. In fact, failure to provide benefits upon this basis could subject the employer to a ten percent penalty under LC5814 for an unreasonable refusal to provide compensation due the employee. Likewise, the employee's nonmedical belief that he continues to be disabled contrary to a physician's opinion is equally improper as a basis for the provision of disability benefits (but can entitle the employee to an opinion from an Agreed or Qualified Medical Evaluator at the employer's expense).

When the employee refuses to return to work after being medically released, a continued total or partial wage loss is not a result of a medical disability and is therefore not compensable (with certain exceptions as explained below). The employee's interests are usually best served by making a sincere attempt to return to work. Upon reevaluation, a physician is much more likely to revise a previous opinion of disability status if the employee actually attempted work and can credibly explain any difficulties that were experienced.

It is wise for a claimsperson to ascertain an employee's reasons for disagreeing with a physician. If there is any reason to believe that the employee may still be disabled despite the physician's opinion to the contrary, payment for a consultation with another physician may be appropriate (see 7.50).

An evaluation by an Agreed or Qualified Medical Evaluator will be required if the employee provides a written objection to the treating physician's opinion of disability status. However, the objectionable opinion may have been provided by a consulting physician, or the employee may wish to resolve the dispute without a formal objection or medical evaluation, or it may be the opinion of an Agreed or Qualified Medical Evaluator to which the employee objects. Life is not always simple. Under such circumstances, an agreement to obtain a second opinion may lead to further rapport by allowing an unrepresented employee the benefit of the doubt and, whether the employee has an attorney or not, forestall the need to incur the costs of otherwise certain litigation proceedings.

Labor Code 4657 provides that the employee's probable loss in weekly earnings while partially disabled "may be computed from the proportionate loss of physical ability or earnings power caused by the injury." Occasionally it is known that the employee will not return to work in the job where the injury occurred. For instance, the employee may have been fired, or he may have retired after his injury. Some employees simply choose not to return to work for the same employer or any other employer. In assessing the weekly level of voluntarily reduced earnings, LC4657 provides that "due regard shall be given to the ability of the employee to compete in an open labor market." An appraisal must be made if at all possible of the viability of the employee's return to work in any available job and the reasonable level of earnings that are available to the employee while partially disabled.

Where a preinjury job is no longer available to the employee, employers have historically had difficulty in proving that the employee's nonemployability was voluntary. Despite the provisions of LC4657, payments of temporary total disability benefits are commonly continued if an employee is released for modified or light duties in a preinjury job that is no longer available. For instance, temporary total disability benefits continue where the employer on the date of injury offers a return to work for half-days at half pay in accord with the physician's temporary restrictions, but the employee has previously retired, been fired or resigned from this job.

The employee may allege that the employer has not made a bona fide offer of temporary employment because the offer is unreasonable as to the particular work site, duties, or location. The employer may offer a return to work on the evening or night shift to a day shift worker who, both now and prior to the injury, has no child care services available outside of normal working hours or who attends evening college classes. Offered employment may involve a distinctly greater commute such as thirty more miles one-way and/or at a location that precludes use of the employee's customary mode of transportation by bus or a carpooling arrangement. The employee may agree to return to any offered work or worksite because the employee will receive more money in wages than would be paid as compensation benefits. However, a refusal to accept employment under circumstances such as those described above would not appear to provide a reasonable basis for termination of temporary total disability benefits (compare to the types of offers of modified duties that terminate the employer's liability for rehabilitation benefits; see 11.26).

9.25 STOP PAYMENTS – NOT DISABLED

The employee is not entitled to temporary disability indemnity benefits after the employee has been medically determined to be physically capable of returning to full regular duties. At this point, any loss in earnings would not be the result of a medical disability and therefore would not be compensable. (If the employee disagrees with the treating physician's determination that the employee is not disabled, the employee has the right to obtain an evaluation by an Agreed or Qualified Medical Evaluator; see 7.75.) Some examples of situations that can produce noncompensable earnings losses after the employee is released to return to work are:

    a. The employer's business is not open on the day the employee is released to return to work, e.g. a weekend or holiday.

    b. The employee is not scheduled to work; e.g., the employee must be scheduled a week ahead of time for work in the following week, or the employee is an on-call employee.

c. The employee does not have a job; e.g., the job where an injury occurred was temporary, the employee was fired, or the employer closed down or moved out of state.

d. The employment is not available for a period of time; e.g., the employee has been laid off, or his union is out on strike.

9.26 STOP PAYMENTS – DISABILITY NONINDUSTRIAL

The employee can be fully recovered from the effects of the industrial injury but still be disabled from work. The medical disability could result from a condition that has no connection to the industrial injury. If so, the employee's continued disability is nonindustrial and therefore noncompensable. For example, the employee may be ill with a cold, in the late stages of pregnancy, disabled from a nonindustrial automobile accident, suffering from a nonindustrial disease, or hospitalized for a nonindustrial surgery.

9.27 STOP PAYMENTS – REFUSAL OF TREATMENT

Per LC4056, "no compensation is payable" when the employee's "disability is caused, continued, or aggravated by an unreasonable refusal to submit to medical treatment." Where the employer takes this position, it appears the claim will be litigated. The employer cannot be absolved of liability unless "risk of treatment is, in the opinion of the appeals board ... inconsiderable in view of the seriousness of the injury." This language makes it clear that the case must be brought before the WCAB where the employer's opinion on this issue must be supported by evidence. The injury need not be categorized as a "serious" one. Rather, the unreasonableness of the employee's refusal must be proportionate to the "seriousness of the injury."

The employer would certainly object to any expansion of its liability for temporary disability payments that is controlled by the employee. This would be true regardless of the type of injury or its severity. There is a distinction between the period of disability caused by an injury and a disability that is caused by an injury but voluntarily prolonged. The disputed period of disability would be the period where the employee exercises control over the employer's liability for payment.

There are many reasons why an employee would refuse treatment or exams, thus prolonging the period of temporary disability. Some grounds that would cause the employer to raise an objection to payment of temporary disability benefits after this refusal include the following:

a. Dishonesty or fraud; e.g., the employee's intent is to receive more compensation than he would otherwise be entitled to receive.

b. Extraordinary fear of treatment; e.g., the employee fears a type of treatment, testing or surgery that represents the only known method of treatment or the common standard of medical practice.

c. Religious grounds; e.g., the employee's religion prohibits surgery without which the employee's condition may deteriorate to a life-threatening state.

d. Disability status cannot be verified; e.g., the employee will not attend an exam with a Qualified Medical Evaluator, and the employee's physician will not provide information.

Where an additional medical opinion would be of benefit in resolving the disputed opinions of a treating physician, an evaluation by an Agreed or Qualified Medical Evaluator is required by LC4062. The party raising the dispute initiates the evaluation process by serving the opposing party with a written objection specifying the details of their position.

9.28 STOP PAYMENTS – PERMANENT & STATIONARY

Per LC4650, the employee's disability can be either temporary or permanent, but not both at the same time. When the employee's condition "becomes permanent," the employee is no longer entitled to continued temporary disability payments. As a general rule, the employee's condition becomes permanent and the employee's entitlement to temporary disability payments ceases as of the date a physician declares the disability to be "permanent and stationary"(see 10.8). An evaluation by an Agreed or Qualified Medical Evaluator may be required to resolve a dispute as to the treating physician's opinion of whether the employee's disability is temporary or permanent in nature (see 7.75).

9.29 STOP PAYMENTS – DEATH

Per LC4700, temporary disability payments shall not be made "for any period of time subsequent to the death of the employee." At the time of death, there may be accrued days of temporary disability payments that have not yet been paid. Any temporary disability due the employee up to the date of death "shall be paid to the dependents, or if there are no dependents, to the personal representative of the deceased employee or heirs or other persons entitled thereto, without administration." (If there are no such persons, LC4706.5 requires payment to the State; see 12.25)

Assuming all temporary disability payments have been paid timely, the amount unpaid should be a small sum. If someone described in LC4700, such as a wife or child, requests the unpaid temporary disability, it should be paid to this person. There is no requirement to notify the WCAB of this payment or the identity of the person to whom payment is made. This is the meaning of the phrase "without administration." Payment of accrued compensation is usually a "pay and close" situation for the claimsperson. The file is closed when this final payment is made. However, the employer will want the WCAB to issue an order directing payment in cases where multiple individuals are claiming the accrued benefits or in cases where payments of temporary disability were being made under compulsion of an award (see 9.22).

9.30 OVERPAYMENTS – CREDIT & RESTITUTION

The employee may be paid an excess amount of temporary disability compensation for a multitude of reasons. The overpayment may be for more days than were due, or the overpayment may result from payment at an improper rate.

Overpayments usually result from the claimsperson's conscientious efforts to provide regular timely payments. They may also result from computer errors, or fraud may be involved. The employer may owe future compensation, either later periods of temporary disability or future permanent disability payments. If so, the employer will claim a credit for its overpayment against its future liability for compensation. If no future compensation will be due, the employer must attempt recovery directly from the employee.

The first action is always to make a request that the employee return the money that the employee received but was not entitled to be paid. If the error was the claimsperson's, the request should admit this fact and be phrased in a tactful fashion. Some employees will immediately return the overpaid amount. Occasionally the employee will not be able to return the money immediately; the overpayment may be a large sum of money that the employee has already spent. The claimsperson can reach an agreement with the employee for repayment in installments at set intervals that are convenient for the employee.

The employee may refuse to refund the overpayment, and the employer may not have any unpaid benefits against which to take a credit. The employer must decide if sufficient money is involved to warrant formal pursuit of a collection. If the employee obtained benefits or excess benefits through some form of deceit, the employer should seek restitution through the WCAB (and refer the matter to the Fraud Division of the Department of Insurance; see 2.30).

If the case is not litigated, the employer can initiate litigation to seek a WCAB determination on the matter. The WCAB can issue an Order Directing Restitution that orders the employee to repay the employer. If the employee does not repay the money within a reasonable period of time after being ordered to do so, the employer could file a certified copy of the order with the "clerk of the superior court" under LC5806. The employer could then obtain an immediate judgment to enable it to effectuate a recovery under the terms of the WCAB order.

9.31 SUPPLEMENTAL & ALTERNATIVE BENEFITS

When an employee is temporarily disabled, the employer is legally obligated to provide temporary disability payments under LC4650. This is generally true regardless of the employee's concurrent entitlement to any other type of benefit. Other benefits are usually supplemental, and their receipt will not affect the employer's liability for temporary disability payments. However, some other benefits may be alternative and become a credit against amounts owed as temporary disability. The sections that follow will discuss some common benefits that an injured worker may be eligible to receive in addition to or in lieu of workers' compensation benefits.

9.32 ONE YEAR SALARY – PUBLIC EMPLOYEES

The Labor Code provides a special disability benefit to certain public safety and fire personnel who are listed in LC4800, 4800.05, 4804.1, 4806, 4850, 4850.5, and 4850.7. With limited exceptions (as found in LC4850.5-LC4850.7), employees who are eligible for this special benefit must be a "member of the Public Employees' Retirement System" (PERS) or are "subject to the County Employees Retirement Law of 1937" (CERL). If so, they are entitled to receive their usual "salary in lieu of temporary disability or rehabilitation maintenance allowance payments," if any, that would be payable "for the period of the disability, but not exceeding one year." The Internal Revenue Service has ruled that the required salary continuation benefit is a workers' compensation benefit rather than wages, so salary paid in lieu of temporary disability or maintenance allowance benefits is nontaxable income to the employee.

The salary continuation benefit for some employees will not be payable for an entire year. Under LC4850, this benefit ceases on "such earlier date as he or she is retired on permanent disability pension." Effective 1995, a special provision applies to sworn members of the California Highway Patrol when "disability is solely the result of cumulative trauma or injury." In such cases, the salary payments to the employee "shall be limited to the actual period of temporary disability or entitlement to" rehabilitation "maintenance allowance, or for one year, whichever is less." If the disability lasts more than one year, LC4853 provides that payments for continued disability are subject to the Labor Code provisions for regular "disability indemnity" payments.

Public employers pay salaries out of monies collected as taxes. Taxpayers, who benefit from services provided, pay salaries of public employees. The special salary benefit is provided to a class of employees who serve the public and risk their lives and safety while doing so. When these employees are injured in the performance of their duties, the public they serve actually pays the special salary continuation benefit. If the public employer purchased a workers' compensation insurance policy, the taxpayers contributed to this expense as well.

The provision of statutorily required salary payments (e.g. under LC4850) constitutes payments under a "salary continuation plan" as defined in LC4650 (see 9.33). The manner in which the employer's provision of such payments will affect the cost of its workers' compensation insurance premiums is subject to negotiation with its insurer.

When the employer is required to continue salary, its insurance company is not required to pay temporary disability benefits. However, insurance premiums are ordinarily based on anticipated payments of all benefits owed to an employee. Legislators did not intend to provide a windfall benefit to insurance companies or to make employers pay twice for the same thing. If the employer pays salary, LC4850 permits an insured public employer to request its insurance company to pay it directly any amounts that "the insurer would be obligated to make as disability indemnity to the injured." By this provision, the insurer is liable for equal benefit payouts for all of its insureds. If the employer requests reimbursement, the insurer must pay the employer an amount equivalent to the amount the employee would otherwise be paid as temporary disability benefits. This payment can be paid "to the insured" in its own name.

9.33 OTHER PAYMENTS – SALARY CONTINUATION PLAN

Effective 1990, LC4650 provides that neither temporary nor permanent disability benefits are payable when "the employer continues the employee's wages under a salary continuation plan." Since temporary and permanent disability indemnity benefits are both wage replacement benefits (see 9.1), the employer is not required to provide these benefits if the employer continues payments of full wages to an employee as a company benefit. (Note: the provision of salary continuation benefits to an employee who is disabled from working constitutes the provision of an employee benefit, not payment of wages earned.) Effective 1991, the term "salary continuation plan" is specifically defined in LC4650. A plan that will relieve the employer from its liability to provide either temporary or permanent disability benefits must meet these three requirements:

1. "The plan is paid for by the employer pursuant to statute, collective bargaining agreement, memorandum of understanding, or established employer policy," AND
2. Salary is provided on the employee's regular payday (or else the payment would be late and subject to imposition of a 10% late payment supplement per LC4650; see 9.16), AND
3. Salary cannot provide a lesser amount than the employee's compensation rate for temporary or permanent disability benefits (the benefit that would otherwise be payable to the employee at the time).

The employer's plan might provide full salary for a few months and half salary for an additional period. If a check for full salary would provide a net payment that is less than the employee's compensation rate for temporary disability benefits (that could be the same as gross pay for a 1990 or later injury; see 9.4), then temporary disability benefits are payable. If the amount of a check for half salary would be less than the rate at which temporary disability benefits would be paid, the employer is obligated to pay temporary disability benefits whether or not salary benefits are continued.

When the employee is temporarily or permanently disabled, the employer cannot avoid its obligation for disability benefit payments at the employee's compensation rate by paying some lesser amount as wages. As a rule, payment of full wages relieves the employer from liability for the payment of temporary or permanent disability benefits, but payments of partial wages while an employee is temporarily totally disabled can only supplement, but not replace, temporary total disability benefits.

Many employees receive their usual wages during the period of disability. The employer may continue to pay full wages under the compulsion of a union contract, because it likes the employee, or because it does not know that the employee is entitled to receive temporary disability benefits. Many small employers have no idea what benefits are provided under the workers' compensation laws; informational materials on workers' compensation may be filed away unread or misunderstood. Communication between the employer and its claims administrator regarding wage continuation benefits is usually optimum if the employer is self-insured and/or a large employer and poorest when an employer is a small company whose claims are administered by an insurance company or other third party administrator.

Occasionally the employee is concurrently paid temporary disability benefits and full wages. The employer has the right to make a gratuitous payment to the employee, but it is difficult to imagine an employer this magnanimous. It is more likely that the employer was unaware that its insurance company was paying concurrent temporary disability payments to the employee. When this situation occurs, it is usually the result of poor communication. The insurance company has a legal obligation to provide temporary disability payments unless it is notified that the employer will continue to pay full wages under a salary continuation plan (as defined above). The insurance company does not have any legal right to the reimbursement of temporary disability payments from the employee, nor is it obligated to reimburse the employer.

There will not be any duplication of payments if the employer notifies its carrier that it will provide wages. If duplication occurs, it is the employer who must request the employee to reimburse it for wages in an amount equaling concurrent temporary disability benefit payments.

Duplicate payments can be avoided. The employer may intend for an employee to receive overall payments equivalent to full salary. The claimsperson can notify the employer of the amount that will be payable as a workers' compensation benefit. The employer can then provide the difference between the temporary disability payments and the employee's normal pay. If an employer who does not have a qualified salary continuation plan insists on providing full salary, the employer may be deemed to be making a gratuitous payment to the employee rather than a payment in lieu of temporary disability benefits.

Per LC3754, "payment in whole or in part of compensation by either the employer or the insurer shall ... be a bar to recovery against each of them of the amount so paid." However, an employer without a qualified salary continuation plan may not succeed in alleging that continuation of wages satisfies the carrier's obligation for temporary disability benefits since the employee is not sustaining a wage loss. The insurer can be relieved from liability for payment of temporary disability indemnity benefits for each week of salary that is paid by the employer under a qualified plan. However, the insurer must provide the employee with a benefit notice letter that explains why temporary or permanent disability benefits are not being paid (see 9.15).

Effective 1990, LC4650 relieves employers who continue wages from any liability for payment of a 10% increase in temporary disability benefits for a failure to pay wages every 14 days and on a day of the week specified with the first payment. Effective 1991, LC4650 provides this relief only to employers who continue "the employee's wages under a salary continuation plan." However, since 1991, LC4650 provides equivalent financial repercussions for the delayed provision of wage payments or workers' compensation indemnity payments. If the employee does not receive payments of salary continuation benefits on the employee's regular payday, the employer will owe a 10% self-imposed increase of the amount of the temporary disability benefit that would be owed if wages were not continued.

9.34 OTHER PAYMENTS – SICK LEAVE

The employee may be eligible for benefits under the employer's sick leave program (many small employers do not provide paid sick leave). The employee cannot be required to utilize accrued sick leave during periods when temporary disability is owed. Per LC3752, "liability for compensation shall not be reduced or affected by any ... other benefit whatsoever due to or received by" the employee. The employee can agree to use accrued sick leave benefits in order to receive a higher total amount per week than the compensation rate for temporary disability alone (as is true for vacation benefits; see 9.35). However, the payment of sick leave benefits can not reduce the rate of payment for temporary disability benefits.

The claimsperson is not expected to understand the sick leave programs of every employer for whom claims are administered nor to explain the employer's sick leave policies to its employees. Questions the employee may have that are related entirely to sick leave benefits are appropriately deferred to the employer. The claimsperson is expected to determine that accrued sick leave benefits will not be used to replace or reduce the employer's liability for payment of temporary disability benefits. Necessary inquiries should be made prior to the first payment of temporary disability so the accompanying benefit information notice can advise the employee exactly who is paying what and for what reason (when available, an appropriate attachment would be an employer-devised pamphlet that explains the employer's sick leave policies).

An insured employer may pay sick leave benefits directly to an injured employee without the claimsperson's knowledge. In that case, it is unlikely that the employee could misconstrue the payments of sick leave benefits as payments of workers' compensation benefits. When separate checks from separate entities provide payment for each benefit, it should be clear to the employee which entity paid what and where questions regarding each benefit should be directed. Sometimes (especially when the employer is a large one or is self-insured) temporary disability payments are supplemented by sick leave benefits within the same check. If so, the benefit information notice the employee receives upon payment of the workers' compensation benefits must explicitly identify how the single-check payment breaks down into each benefit and where questions should be addressed (see 9.15).

Sick leave benefit programs vary from one employer to the next. In most cases, the employer's plan will provide for an offset of temporary disability payments against sick leave salary continuation benefits on a dollar to dollar basis as opposed to a day for day basis. The employee's daily compensation rate for temporary disability benefits is deducted from the daily rate for sick leave benefits. The remainder is paid as a supplemental sick leave benefit, and the employee's accrued sick leave is debited by this amount (as opposed to deducting a full day of sick leave for each day when any sick leave, even a small amount, is paid to supplement disability benefits).

9.35 OTHER PAYMENTS – VACATION PAY

The employee is entitled to receive vacation pay concurrently with payments of temporary disability. Vacation pay is not the same as the payment of regular wages. Paid vacation time is provided at the employee's regular rate of pay, but the employee is not required to work during the time it is paid. Vacation pay is an accrued company benefit that accumulates during periods when the employee is working. In most cases, the employee is entitled to the payment of accrued vacation pay if the employee's employment terminates. Vacation pay is an employer-provided benefit that just happens to be provided in the same amount as regular wages. As such, LC3752 prohibits any offset of vacation pay against temporary disability payments.

The employer can grant or disallow vacation time at its option. The employee may request vacation while disabled in order to receive more income than just temporary disability payments. The employer may grant vacation, since the employee is off work anyway. Otherwise, the employee could return to work after a disability, then go off again on vacation. An employer who grants vacation leave might supplement temporary disability payments with full vacation pay (the employee receives full payment for both benefits for the same days/weeks) or just the number of hours of vacation pay that are needed to provide a combined weekly total that is equivalent to normal weekly wages (the sum of both payments is the employee's regular earnings).

The employer cannot reduce the employee's accrued vacation benefits by the amount of any temporary disability benefits that are owed. The employer is prohibited from withholding the payment of temporary disability benefits until the employee first uses up any accrued vacation pay or from debiting the amount of temporary disability payments from accrued or future vacation benefits. Any such reduction of vacation benefits would penalize the employee for having an injury. This result is prohibited by LC3752 (and explains why some benefit payment notices require advice regarding the coordination of payments of vacation benefits and temporary disability benefits to be provided in the same notice; see 9.15).

9.36 OTHER PAYMENTS – PRIVATE INSURANCE

The employee can receive concurrent temporary disability and payments under any number of private insurance plans. Disability insurance may make house payments for the employee, monthly payments for a charge card balance, or loan payments on a car. The claimsperson need not inquire as to the employee's supplemental benefits under private insurance plans. Per LC3752, temporary disability payments do not consider receipt of other insurance payments: the employer's "liability for compensation shall not be reduced or affected by any insurance ... whatsoever due to or received" by the employee.

The employee may have private long-term disability (LTD) insurance, also called group disability insurance. The purpose of this insurance is to protect against loss of income during a period of medical disability. This type of policy usually provides payment equivalent to full or partial wages. Most long-term disability policies contain a clause that states coverage is not provided for any disability that is payable under the workers' compensation laws. The employee's entitlement to workers' compensation benefits may be disputed. In this case, the group disability carrier must provide benefits under its contract. If it is later determined that the disability was work-related, the group disability carrier can file a lien in the workers' compensation court case.

A lien would be filed under LC4903(c) for "reasonable value of the living expenses of an injured employee or his or her dependents." The terms of the disability policy will determine the validity of a lien under the express language of LC4903. The WCAB may determine that the employer was liable for temporary disability payments. If so, the WCAB can order the employer to reimburse the disability carrier for payments made while liability was disputed. The employer's liability for temporary disability payments is unaffected by the existence of a long-term disability policy. The amount of the temporary disability obligation does not change. However, the WCAB may order payments made in the name of a payee other than the employee, such as a long-term disability insurance company.

9.37 OTHER PAYMENTS – EDD – STATE DISABILITY

California has a disability insurance program to which employees contribute by payroll deductions. Some employers have established voluntary disability plans that they administer (subject to State approval). In all other cases, benefits are disbursed by a state agency called the Employment Development Department (EDD). Per authority provided under the Unemployment Insurance Code, this State agency administers and provides unemployment compensation disability (UCD) benefits. Such benefits are also known as state disability insurance (SDI) benefits.

Many people confuse workers' compensation with state disability insurance. There are important distinctions. Employees contribute to the cost of their state disability benefits, and these benefits provide compensation for their nonindustrial disabilities. Employees do not contribute toward the costs of workers' compensation benefits, and workers' compensation benefits compensate employees for industrial disabilities. To qualify for either benefit, the employee must be disabled from working. If the employee broke a leg skiing, disability payments would be provided under the state disability plan. If the employee broke a leg while working, temporary disability payments would be provided as a workers' compensation benefit. The cause of the disability determines the benefit the employee is entitled to receive.

Questions may arise as to the correct benefit to which the employee is entitled. As of 1990, whenever an employee files a claim for state disability benefits, the Employment Development Department is required by Unemployment Insurance Code Section 2629.1 to "make an initial determination as to the claimant's entitlement to other benefits."

Upon a determination that an employee is eligible for workers' compensation benefits, the Employment Development Department will notify the employer of this decision and provide the employee with the same information pamphlet regarding workers' compensation benefits that employers are required to provide to employees (see 6.5). Per UIC2629.1, an employer's receipt of the Employment Development Department's notice constitutes "knowledge of an injury" pursuant to LC5402 ("from any source"), and such knowledge gives rise to the employer's duty to promptly investigate and timely pay or deny liability for temporary disability benefits. The Employment Development Department will commence payments of state disability benefits within 14 days after the provision of its notice to the employer unless the employer or its insurer has already paid or has agreed to commence payment of workers' compensation benefits.

The employer may dispute liability within the first 14 days after the Employment Development Department's notice of a claim but later either accept liability for temporary disability benefits or else be found liable for such benefits by a final decision of the WCAB. Within 60 days of either occurrence, the employer is required by UIC2629.1 to reimburse the Employment Development Department for unemployment compensation disability benefits that were provided in error plus interest on this amount "at the annual rate provided in Section 19521 of the Revenue and Taxation Code." Per UIC2629.1, the "employer shall also pay a penalty" of 10% of the amount reimbursed to the Employment Development Department if the WCAB "finds that the failure of the employer to pay other benefits upon notice" by the Employment Development Department "was unreasonable and a penalty has not been awarded for the delay under" LC5814 (see 2.27).

Submission of a settlement for WCAB approval cannot absolve the employer from any obligation that is described above. The Employment Development Department has certain rights if the employer submits a settlement that requests the WCAB to disallow reimbursement for the lien of the Employment Development Department in whole or in part. Per LC4904, the WCAB "shall not be prohibited from approving a compromise and release agreement on all other issues and deferring to subsequent proceedings the determination of a lien claimant's entitlement to reimbursement if the defendant in any of these proceedings agrees to pay the amount subsequently determined to be due." Absent such agreement, if the Employment Development Department objects to a proposed payment of less than the full amount of benefits it has paid, the WCAB is required to "determine the extent of" the Employment Development Department's "entitlement to reimbursement on its lien and make and file findings on all facts involved in the controversy over this issue."

Additional requirements of LC4904 apply only to a 1991 or later injury. After the employer has been served with an Employment Development Department lien, LC4904 requires the employer to provide two separate written notices to the Employment Development Department. The employer is required to notify the Employment Development Department "in writing, as soon as possible, but in no event later than 15 working days after commencing disability indemnity payments" to the employee. The employer is additionally required to notify the Employment Development Department "in writing, within 10 working days of filing an Application for Adjudication of claim, a stipulated award, or a compromise and release with the appeals board."

Upon a decision that the employee's disability is work-related, the employer's obligation for temporary disability payments is not disputed. The claimsperson will want to notify the Employment Development Department to terminate state disability payments and immediately commence temporary disability payments. Notification to the Employment Development Department is important. The employer will not receive credit for any temporary disability payments made concurrently with Employment Development Department payments where the employer is on notice the Employment Development Department payments are being made. In this case, the WCAB could order the employer to pay the Employment Development Department lien without any right to recover the duplicated temporary disability payments that were provided to the employee.

9.38 OTHER PAYMENTS – EDD – UNEMPLOYMENT

Unemployment Compensation Insurance (UCI) is a state benefit under the provisions of the Unemployment Insurance Code. Employers are assessed for the full costs of this program without any employee contributions. The benefits are administered by the Employment Development Department to persons who are involuntarily unemployed, and an employee must be actively seeking employment to be eligible for weekly unemployment benefits.

The employee may claim temporary disability and unemployment benefits for the same periods of time. An employee who is totally disabled is not eligible for unemployment payments. Per LC4903, the Employment Development Department may file a lien for reimbursement of unemployment payments that were provided during periods of total disability. An employee who is partially disabled may be eligible for concurrent payments of temporary partial disability and unemployment benefits. However, LC4654 requires the amount of the weekly temporary disability payment to be reduced by the weekly amount of unemployment benefits.

9.39 PARTIAL DISABILITY – UNEMPLOYMENT BENEFITS

An employee can receive unemployment benefits while temporarily partially disabled. In fact, eligibility for unemployment compensation is evidence that the employee is only partially disabled, since an employee can only qualify for this benefit when willing and physically able to work. Per LC4654, the employee's temporary "disability payment shall be reduced by the sum of unemployment compensation benefits." The amount of the weekly payment received from unemployment is deducted from the employee's temporary total disability compensation rate, not the employee's average weekly earnings. The employee is entitled to payment of the remainder as a temporary partial disability benefit.

In effect, unemployment benefits are treated as an alternate workers' compensation payment rather than as wages. The employee is entitled to receive both benefits but only up to a maximum total amount equal to the employee's compensation rate for temporary total disability benefits. There is a rationale for this offset of benefits. Under California laws, the employer is required to contribute to the cost of both benefits, and the employee's entitlement to both benefits arises from the same injury. (Note: effective 1991, UIC2629 provides that disability benefits are not payable by the Employment Development Department for any days when the employee receives "or is eligible to receive" workers' compensation temporary disability benefits; see 9.37.)

9.40 TAX STATUS OF DISABILITY PAYMENTS

Per Section 6334 of the U.S. Code, "There shall be exempt from levy ... any amount payable to an individual as workmen's compensation ... under a workmen's compensation law of the United States (or) any State." This language means that California workers' compensation benefits are not taxable income to the employee. The employer should not deduct taxes from any workers' compensation indemnity payments provided to the employee, and the employer does not owe any employer payroll taxes on payments of temporary disability or any other workers' compensation benefit. For those public employees who are entitled to receive up to one year of salary "in lieu of" temporary disability payments, the continued salary is not taxable income (see 9.32). This payment is a payment of compensation under California's workers' compensation law.

Sometimes the employee thinks taxes are being deducted from workers' compensation payments when they are not. The employer may provide full or partial wages during the disability. Wages are taxed as income. One check may include a payment for temporary disability benefits and a payment of partial wages. Employees become confused when they see any deductions were taken for taxes, but the employer is required to withhold taxes for all wages paid over and above the amount of workers' compensation benefits that were provided in the same check.

9.41 NO APPORTIONMENT OF DISABILITY

The employer's liability for temporary disability benefits is unaffected by concurrent disability that is not caused by the industrial injury. This concept is best explained by example. The employee fractures an arm at work and is disabled for six weeks. The employee is also disabled due to a nonindustrial bunion surgery and complications therefrom for four of these six weeks. The employee would have been disabled for four weeks with the foot surgery absent the industrial arm injury. The employer owes all six weeks of temporary disability payments, not just the two weeks where the disability was solely due to the industrial injury, because the employer cannot apportion any of its liability for temporary disability benefits between concurrent industrial and nonindustrial causation.

The existence of concurrent disability due to other causes does not lessen or increase the employer's liability for payment of temporary disability benefits. The employer cannot benefit financially from the employee's misfortune of being concurrently disabled for nonindustrial conditions. At all times, the employer is liable for the entire period of disability that is reasonably a result of the industrial injury. Occasionally it is necessary to have a physician estimate the period of disability that would reasonably result from the industrial injury. While disabled after an industrial back injury, the employee may be hospitalized for several weeks for a subsequent nonindustrial automobile accident. The physician must tell the claimsperson the date when the disability from the industrial injury would reasonably have ended assuming no subsequent injury had occurred. After this date, continued disability would be solely nonindustrial, and the employer would not owe further temporary disability payments.

The employer does not owe any temporary disability payments for disability that is not due to the effects of the industrial injury. In the fractured arm example above, the employee may become disabled with the flu after the first six weeks of industrial disability. The employer does not owe further temporary disability payments just because the employee continues to be disabled (unless continued disability is a reasonable consequence of the industrial injury; e.g. where an additional week of disability is necessary to stabilize a nonindustrial heart condition after a complication arose during surgical fixation of fractured bones in the arm). If the injury caused six weeks of industrial disability only, this is exactly the period the employer owes. The employer's liability will never be shorter than the full period of industrial disability.

9.42 APPORTIONMENT OF LIABILITY FOR PAYMENTS

There is an important distinction between apportioning liability for payment and apportioning causation of disability. It is permissible to apportion liability for payment of disability that is admittedly owed. This type of apportionment is called "contribution," because multiple liable employers will contribute to the overall cost of compensation that is owed to an employee. Where there is concurrent industrial and nonindustrial causation for the same day of disability, this day is considered to be a full day of industrial disability (see 9.41). It is not permissible to request the employee to contribute any percentage of the temporary disability benefit payment that is owed for any day of industrial disability. In order to apportion liability for payment, two or more employers must be jointly liable for the payment of temporary disability benefits.

Apportionment of liability is common in cases involving a cumulative injury or an occupational disease. There is no specific moment of injury. The employee alleges that a period of employment trauma or exposure was responsible for a resultant overall disability. Several employers or insurance companies may be liable for benefits, each for different periods of employment. The employee will not receive several temporary disability checks that jointly produce full payment for temporary disability benefits. One company will provide temporary disability benefits.

Per LC5500.5, after the WCAB issues an award, the employer providing payments can "institute proceedings before the appeals board for the purpose of determining an apportionment of liability or right of contribution." The other liable employer(s) can be ordered to reimburse the employer who provided benefits. The employers share liability for benefits which means they share the total costs of the employee's benefits. Their contribution is based upon their proportionate share of the period of employment that contributed to the overall disability. Since 1990, arbitration proceedings are mandatory under LC5275 for disputes regarding contribution (and voluntary since 1991 for any issue if all parties agree). Therefore, the proceedings referred to in LC5500.5 are instituted by submitting the matter to arbitration, except that LC5270 precludes arbitration unless the employee is represented by an attorney.

(THIS PAGE LEFT BLANK INTENTIONALLY)

[10] PERMANENT DISABILITY

10.1 PERMANENT DISABILITY – IN GENERAL

The Labor Code does not contain a definition of permanent disability per se. Rather, the Labor Code lists the factors that constitute a compensable permanent disability (see 10.2). However, permanent disability has been defined by case law as a medical disability that permanently impairs earning capacity, impairs the normal use of a body part or adversely affects the employee's ability to work at and/or compete for any employment of the employee's choice. A disability is compensable when it is a result of an industrial injury.

Disability is "rated" by a process that enables medical factors of disability to be stated as a percent. The employee's disability is compared to a total loss of ability to seek and obtain employment. The employee's percentage of disability may be as low as 0% or as high as 100%. A zero rating means the injury had little or no affect at all on the employee's ability to work. A 100% rating means the employee is effectively noncompetitive when the employee's physical abilities are compared to those of nondisabled individuals. Each percent of disability is equivalent to a dollar amount of permanent disability benefits (see 10.18).

10.2 FACTORS AFFECTING PERCENT OF DISABILITY

Four factors are considered "in determining the percentages of permanent disability" (PD) resulting from an injury. Per LC4660, "account shall be taken of" each of the following factors:
1. The "nature of the physical injury or disfigurement."
2. The "occupation of the injured employee."
3. The employee's "age at the time of such injury."
4. The employee's diminished ability "to compete in an open labor market."

Physicians identify the nature of an injury by rendering a diagnosis. A layperson can determine whether an injury is to a foot or an arm, but a physician determines whether the injury is a fracture or nerve damage. Physicians generally describe permanent disabilities in terms of any limitation of motion, pain, weakness or reduced endurance in the performance of work duties. Additional factors that must be addressed by a physician include the need for use of a medical brace or other medical apparatus or the presence of any labor disabling cosmetic disfigurement.

The employee's occupation is determined by an inquiry to the employer. If the employee had more than one employer, the correct occupation is the one in the job where the injury occurred. Age on the date of injury is determinative.

A closed labor market would be one where abilities are not the sole basis for employment, e.g. where employment is additionally contingent upon residency in a specific locale or blood relationship to the employer. Such situations are rare and have no relevance to permanent disability. In workers' compensation, an underlying concept is the belief that nondisabled employees have freedom of choice among all employments available in the "open labor market." This term refers to all types of employment that any employer might offer, not just those types of jobs that the employee has previously performed.

— "Diminished ability" refers to a post-injury reduction in the employee's ability to perform work tasks that may be required by any employer in the open labor market. The disability need not be apparent in the particular job in which the employee chooses to engage. In fact, there is no requirement that the effect of the disability ever be observable in a work setting. The disability is compensable when it exists and it would affect the employee's ability to do some type of work.

10.3 DAMAGES – NOT COMPENSABLE DISABILITY

Employees often confuse permanent disability benefits with civil damages. Some employees erroneously believe that permanent disability benefits provide payment for their pain and suffering, the full amount of their lost wages, any personal expenses they incur as a result of an injury and any type of permanent disability, even one that is not labor disabling. None of these items are compensable under the workers' compensation laws.

Per LC3209, "damages" are "contrasted with compensation." The word damages "means the recovery allowed in an action at law," or items the employee could recover if the employee had the right to sue someone in civil court for his or her negligence. Per LC3207, "compensation" includes all benefits that the employer becomes obligated to pay under the terms of the Labor Code, and the employer's obligation for payment of permanent disability benefits does not include any payment for items of damages.

10.4 DISABILITY – NONCOMPENSABLE

A disability is not compensable if the employee is impaired in the performance of some activity that is personal in nature, but the disability will not affect the performance of any employment activity. The injury may cause a loss of sex drive or impotence. A male employee may feel the injury has ruined his life if he can no longer father a child. After the injury, an employee who is an exercise enthusiast may have occasional pain in his neck that restricts him from standing on his head for more than ten minutes. The sole effect of this disability may be that he can no longer engage in a customary form of exercise such as yoga. Neither of the above disabilities affect these employees in the performance of any work tasks ordinarily required by employers.

The employee may have an unsightly scar at the site of a surgical incision. The location of the scar, its appearance, and its potential impact in the open labor market all determine whether there is any compensable disability. If the scar is on the face, some employers may reject the employee for employment or promotion based on an aversion to this cosmetic disfigurement. (The likelihood of such discriminatory behavior has traditionally been assumed for workers' compensation purposes whether or not it in fact occurs, although discrimination upon the basis of a cosmetic disfigurement is currently prohibited under a variety of state and federal laws, e.g. the federal Americans With Disabilities Act; see 11.36). If the employee is a belly dancer, a scar on the abdomen could be considered labor disabling for workers' compensation purposes. In most cases, the mere presence of a scar on the abdomen or in some other location that is not ordinarily subject to observation in the workplace will not provide any basis for entitlement to permanent disability benefits.

The employee's disability may be so minimal that it would not be likely to have any noticeable effect in the open labor market. Some disabilities will not entitle the employee to even 1% of permanent disability. For example, if the employee loses 10% of the preinjury ability to grip, this grip loss is not a rateable disability (according to the rating schedule; see 10.31)). This disability is considered so minor that its effect in the labor market would be negligible. In this same category are such disabilities as a dull ache in the neck with changes in the weather, a psychiatric disability that manifests itself only when working for one particular supervisor (versus in the open labor market), or a pain that only occurs if a finger is physically manipulated into a certain position.

Rateable factors of permanent disability can only be established by a physician who is properly qualified under the provisions of the Labor Code (see 7.26). Per LC3209.8, "marriage, family, and child counselors and clinical social workers" are not authorized "to determine disability." Acupuncturists are included in the general definition of "physician" in LC3209.3, but LC3209.3(e) provides that "nothing in this section shall be construed to authorize acupuncturists to determine disability." Therefore, any factors of permanent disability reported by an MFCC, social worker or acupuncturist that are not also reported by a properly qualified physician constitute nonrateable factors of disability.

10.5 PERMANENT TOTAL DISABILITY – DEFINED

Per LC4452.5, the employee is permanently totally disabled (PTD) when the employee's disability produces a rating of 100%. The employee's physical condition may actually deteriorate or even result in death at a future date. A 100% disability does not mean the employee cannot get any worse; it just means the employee is legally as disabled as you have to be to receive the maximum workers' compensation benefit. There are four specific disabilities that are statutorily presumed to rate 100% (see 10.6). Any other disabilities that have an equivalent effect upon an employee's ability to compete in the open labor market will also receive a 100% rating.

The employee may still be able to do some type of work despite the fact the employee has effectively lost the ability to compete with nondisabled job applicants for almost all employments. However, there is little likelihood that the employee will ever be able to overcome a 100% disability or rehabilitate himself to any significant degree. (Note: an actual wage loss is not a prerequisite for entitlement to permanent disability benefits so receipt of wages does not reduce the employee's entitlement to this category of benefits; see 9.1.)

10.6 PERMANENT TOTAL DISABILITY – PRESUMED

Four disabilities are conclusively presumed to result in a virtual removal of the employee from the labor market. Per LC4662, these are:

1. "Loss of both eyes," or sight.
2. "Loss of both hands," or use.
3. Total paralysis or "practically total paralysis."
4. Incurable imbecility or insanity resulting from "an injury to the brain."

The above disabilities automatically receive a 100% permanent disability rating. The presumption is conclusive; no evidence will be admissible to convince a judge to award some lower percentage. Many other disabilities can result in a 100% rating, but none are presumed to do so. For any other disabilities, the employer may dispute the extent of permanent disability and present evidence to show that the employee's disability is less than total.

10.7 PERMANENT PARTIAL DISABILITY

According to LC4452.5, any disability that rates 99¾% or less is a permanent partial disability (PPD). Prior to 4/1/97, permanent partial disability included any disability that rated ¼% - 99¾%. As a result of the 1997 amendments to the *Schedule for Rating Permanent Disabilities*, disabilities are now stated as whole numbers. For employees with injuries on or after the effective date of these 1997 amendments, permanent partial disability means disability that rates 1% - 99%.

As long as the employee can compete in even 1% of the labor market, the employee is partially, not totally, disabled. The employee retains sufficient skills to enable the employee to compete for available employments. The employee's competitiveness is reduced but still exists. The higher the rating, the greater the portion of the labor market where the disability is likely to affect the employee's ability to compete for jobs. As the rating decreases, so does the potential impact of the employee's disability on the ability to obtain employment and the level of earnings of the employee's choice.

10.8 PERMANENT & STATIONARY

The employee's disability cannot be rated (converted to a percentage figure) until the employee's medical condition becomes "permanent" as opposed to temporary (but permanent disability benefits may be owed to the employee before this determination is made; see 10.11). Per the 4/1/97 *Schedule For Rating Permanent Disabilities* (and CR10152), a "disability is considered permanent after the employee has reached maximum improvement or the employee's condition has been stationary for a reasonable period of time". A physician determines the date on which a medical condition becomes permanent in nature. The term used to refer to the employee's condition as of the date of this medical determination is "permanent and stationary" (P&S).

The employee may dispute a physician's determination since temporary disability indemnity benefits are not payable after the employee's condition is permanent and stationary, and the compensation rate for permanent partial disability benefits is in most cases substantially lower than the rate at which temporary disability benefits would be paid to the employee. The employer may be the objecting party, since a premature determination of the permanency of the employee's disability would result in payment of an inflated value for permanent disability. Should a dispute arise, LC4062 requires that written notice of the objection be provided to the opposing party. In this event, an examination by an Agreed or Qualified Medical Evaluator is required to address the disputed medical issue (see 7.75).

Maximum improvement need not occur before a medical determination of permanent and stationary status. Per CR10152, a disability can become permanent based upon a physician's opinion that the employee's "condition has been stationary for a reasonable period of time." The employee may be improving all the time, but the degree of improvement may be so minimal that no change of any significance is ever expected. If the employee's condition remains at essentially the same level for some lengthy period of time such as three to six months, the disability is deemed stationary and ready for rating, e.g. where an employee remains undecided for months as to whether to undergo a surgery that is recommended to improve the employee's condition but without which the condition will not deteriorate.

When the disability is permanent and stationary, a rating should accurately reflect the employee's present and future disability. The disability should be unlikely to change for the better or worse at any future time. This is the meaning of permanent as opposed to temporary disability. In the example of the surgery above, the physician would be asked to describe the existing permanent disability as well as the improved disability anticipated if surgery were performed. The employer is obligated to pay for either: (1) existing permanent disability but no costs of future surgery, or (2) anticipated disability if the employee undergoes surgery and the costs of such surgery. The employer is not obligated to pay for both current disability and the costs of future surgery (since the purpose of the recommended surgery is to reduce the level of permanent disability).

10.9 COMPENSATION RATE – OVERVIEW

There are three subcategories of permanent disability benefits. The method for computing the compensation rate and the statutory minimum and maximum average weekly earnings amounts that apply depend upon the extent or percentage of the employee's permanent disability. Separate minimum and maximum earnings limits apply within each category. It is possible for an employee to have a different compensation rate for each category of benefits below that the employee becomes entitled to receive (refer to *Workers' Compensation Benefit Rate Chart* at back of text):

    a. -0- to 99¾%   Permanent partial disability compensation rate.
    b. 70 to 99¾%   Permanent partial disability life pension rate.
    c. 100%   Permanent total disability life pension rate.

10.10 COMPENSATION RATE – PARTIAL DISABILITY

Per LC4658, compensation rate for permanent partial disability is two-thirds of the employee's actual average weekly earnings subject to the minimum and maximum average weekly earnings amounts specified in LC4453 on the date of injury. Since 1991, LC4453 specifies progressively higher maximum earnings amounts for higher percentages of disability. As a result, multiple maximum compensation rates are in effect on any given date of injury. The correct rate for a particular employee will depend upon the employee's earnings and the percentage of disability sustained.

The compensation rate for both temporary disability and permanent partial disability benefits is computed as two-thirds of the employee's average weekly earnings. However, a very significant difference exists. Per LC4453, the amount of the employee's average weekly earnings for permanent partial disability benefits is not adjusted upwards by multiplying by 1.5 in cases of low earnings (less than $126/wk; see 9.4) as is required for total disability benefits (both temporary total and permanent total disability). In cases involving low earnings, it is the employee's actual average weekly earnings amount that is compared to the statutory minimum average weekly earnings limits in LC4453. The permanent partial disability compensation rate for all employees, regardless of level of earnings, is computed as two-thirds of their average weekly earnings but not more nor less than the average weekly earnings amounts specified in LC4453 on their date of injury.

For high wage earners, the statutory maximum average weekly earnings limit that applies to computations of a permanent partial disability compensation rate will be lower than that which applies to the employee's temporary disability benefits. It is possible for an employee to have the same compensation rate for temporary disability and permanent partial disability benefits since the range between the statutory minimum and maximum average weekly earnings amounts for each type of benefit have historically overlapped to some extent. However, the great majority of employees will receive a lower compensation rate for permanent partial disability benefits because the use of a lower maximum average weekly earnings limit means that less of their earnings can be used to compute their compensation rate for this indemnity benefit.

NOTE: Whenever the employee has low earnings and actual average weekly earnings were multiplied by 1.5 to compute an average weekly earnings amount for purposes of temporary benefits, the employee's lower actual average weekly earnings amount will be used instead to compute a compensation rate for permanent partial disability benefits.

1/1/91 - 6/30/94 – Two Maximum Rates

For 1991-6/30/94 injury dates, there are two maximum compensation rates for permanent partial disability benefits. Effective 1991 (for the first time in workers' compensation's history in California), LC4453 specified two maximum average weekly earnings limits for a single category of benefits. The earnings limit that applies to a particular employee is determined by two variables: the percentage of the employee's "final adjusted" permanent disability rating (after adjustment for age and occupation; see 10.25) and the employee's earnings.

If a permanent disability rates 24.75% or less, the lower maximum earnings amount in LC4453 applies, and the maximum compensation rate for any employee with earnings of $210/wk or more would be $140/wk. For employees whose disability rates 25% or more, a higher maximum average weekly earnings amount of $222/wk applies. The maximum compensation rate for permanent partial disability for any employee with a rating of 25% or more and earnings of $222/wk or more will be $148/wk. However, the permanent partial disability compensation rate for an employee with much higher earnings, say $600/wk, would be $140/wk if the employee's disability rated 18% (or any other percentage less than 25%).

As of 7/1/94 – Four Maximum Rates

For 7/1/94 or later injuries, LC4453 contains five separate average weekly earnings limits for permanent partial disability indemnity benefits. There is only one minimum earnings limit, but there are four maximum earnings limits. The minimum average weekly earnings limit is not affected by the percentage of the employee's permanent disability. All employees who are determined to have minimum average weekly earnings will receive the same compensation rate for permanent partial disability benefits regardless of their percentage of disability (any percentage than 100%).

Date of Injury 7/1/94 - 3/31/97: Multiple maximum average weekly earnings limits can apply to computations of an individual employee's permanent partial disability compensation rate. Per LC4453, a progressively higher maximum earnings amount applies when the final adjusted rating is less than 15%, 15%-24.75%, 25%-69.75%, or 70% to "less than " 99.75%. Note that the top range in LC4453 does not include a rating of exactly 99.75%. Despite this legislative oversight, it would appear reasonable in practice to treat a 99.75% disability as being within the top range. The continued use of previously applicable and lower average weekly earnings limits for cases with a 99.75% rating would result in the payment of a lower compensation rate to an employee who was determined to have a 99.75% disability than to an employee with the same earnings who had a 99.50% disability.

Date of Injury 4/1/97 or Later: There was no legislative change in the incremental ranges of rating percentages that appear in LC4453 and are listed above. However, percentages of disability that are determined by using the 4/1/97 edition of the *Schedule For Rating Permanent Disabilities* are stated as whole numbers only. Therefore, for 4/1/97 or later injuries, LC4453 permits the use of progressively higher maximum earnings in computing a permanent disability compensation rate when the final adjusted rating is 1%-14%, 15%-24%, 25%-69%, or 70%-99% rather than at the break-off percentages shown above (e.g. a disability that mathematically rates 24.50% or 24.75% would be increased to a 25% rating according to instructions set out in the 4/1/97 schedule that require rounding up of percentages to the next whole number).

Exceptions to Minimum Rate

The statutory maximum and minimum average weekly earnings amounts that apply to computations of a permanent partial disability compensation rate are stated in LC4453 alongside those that apply to temporary disability payments. As is true of temporary disability benefits, there are exceptions to the standard application of the stated maximum and minimum average weekly earnings amounts in computations of the employee's permanent partial disability rate (as explained below).

Partners

When the employing entity is a partnership, LC4457 provides that the average weekly earnings of a partner "shall be deemed to be forty dollars" when his average weekly earnings "are not otherwise ascertainable." This statute does not mention either temporary or permanent disability. Therefore, it appears that this statute will establish the employee's compensation rate at $26.67/wk for both permanent partial and permanent total disability benefits in those cases to which it applies (see 8.9 for further explanation).

Minors

"If the injured employee is under 18 years of age, and his incapacity is permanent," the average weekly earnings from which his compensation rate is computed will be determined by the provisions of LC4455. Per LC4455, the employee's average weekly earnings will be the "weekly sum" that the employee "would probably be able to earn at the age of 18 years, in the occupation in which he was employed at the time of injury or in any occupation to which he would reasonably have been promoted if he had not been injured."

An assessment of future earnings must ignore the employee's reduced capacities resulting from the injury and predict the future earnings "under ordinary circumstances," assuming no injury had occurred. Relevant information would include facts regarding past employments, educational endeavors, existing skills, and the efforts and ability to improve competitiveness in the open labor market. If the employee's probable earnings can be determined, the permanent disability compensation rate will be two-thirds of the employee's projected average weekly earnings as of age 18 subject to the statutory minimum and maximum earnings limits in LC4453 that were in effect on the date of injury. However, if probable earnings at age 18 "cannot reasonably be determined," the employee's "average weekly earnings shall be taken at ... $105" (that provides the employee with a compensation rate of $70/wk).

Rate For Optional PD – With VRMA Benefits

An employee who is being paid vocational rehabilitation maintenance allowance benefits may also be entitled to optional supplemental payments of permanent disability benefits (see 11.7). If so, the compensation rate for optional permanent disability payments is computed by subtracting the employee's compensation rate for a vocational rehabilitation maintenance allowance from the employee's compensation rate for temporary total disability benefits.

The employee may be receiving payments of permanent disability pursuant to a WCAB award when entitlement to rehabilitation benefits arises. Preaward and post-award cases must be treated differently in order to avoid penalties for improper withholding of benefits due the employee. When permanent disability supplements are owed prior to an award, the sum of the employee's compensation rate for a vocational rehabilitation maintenance allowance and optional permanent disability supplements cannot exceed the amount of the employee's compensation rate for temporary total disability benefits. However, this limitation does not necessarily apply to post-award cases.

In the examples below, compare the employee's temporary disability rate with the sum of the rate payable for rehabilitation benefits and the rate owed for optional permanent disability benefits that are payable concurrently pursuant to LC139.5. Notice that the compensation rate for optional permanent disability payments that are owed under LC139.5 exceeds the rate at which permanent disability was awarded to the employee.

SAMPLE (A). Date of Injury:	01/01/97	02/01/97	06/01/96
Percentage of Permanent Disability	91%	11%	14%
Temporary Disability Rate	$490	$490	$ 448
Rehabilitation, VRMA Rate	−246	−246	−246
Rate for Optional PD Supplements	244	244	202
PD Rate Payable Under Award	−230	−140	−140
	+ 14	+104	+ 62

In the above examples, the employee has a choice and may opt to receive more permanent disability per week than the rate that was awarded. If so, the employee can file a petition with the WCAB to request an order directing the employer to pay permanent disability at a higher rate during the period of the employee's entitlement to vocational rehabilitation maintenance allowance benefits. It is unlikely that the WCAB would disallow the petition since the employee is merely claiming benefits that are owed pursuant to the terms of LC139.5. Therefore, it may prove cost effective for the employer to opt to provide payments of permanent disability at a rate in excess of that awarded rather than incur the expense of resisting the employee's petition. (If such a petition were filed and granted, the employer would not be entitled to claim any interest credit under LC5101 because this situation does not involve an advance payment of benefits owed; see 10.20.)

SAMPLE (B). Date of Injury:	02/01/97	03/01/97	05/01/95
Percentage of Permanent Disability	88%	12%	77%
Temporary Disability Rate	$375	$375	$ 406
Rehabilitation, VRMA Rate	−246	−246	−246
Rate for Optional PD Supplements	129	129	160
PD Rate Payable Under Award	−230	−140	−168
	−101	−11	−8

In the above examples, the compensation rate for permanent disability pursuant to a WCAB award is higher than the rate at which optional permanent disability benefits would be owed pursuant to LC139.5 in the absence of an award (as explained above). Under these circumstances, the employer may believe that it is entitled to a reduction in the rate at which permanent disability benefits are payable. The employer may petition the WCAB for an order directing payment at a lower weekly rate for any permanent disability payments that are owed concurrently with payments of vocational rehabilitation maintenance allowance benefits. However, the employee would have the right to object to the employer's petition, and it is unlikely that the WCAB would order a reduction in previously awarded benefits (for the same reasons referenced in Sample (A) above). Therefore, the employer may prefer to continue payments in accordance with the WCAB award (even though the rate awarded exceeds the rate at which optional permanent disability payments would be owed in the absence of an award) rather than litigate this issue.

10.11 LIFE PENSION RATE – PARTIAL DISABILITY

The formula for computing the compensation rate for a permanent partial disability life pension is set out in LC4659(a). This section also contains a statutory maximum average weekly earnings amount that applies solely to computations of permanent partial disability life pension benefits. The compensation rate is computed by taking "1.5 percent of the average weekly earnings for each 1 percent of disability in excess of 60%." For purposes of a permanent partial disability life pension, the employee's average weekly earnings "shall not be taken at more than" the maximum earnings limit specified in LC4659 for the date of the employee's injury.

No minimum earnings amount is specified in LC4659(a). Therefore, the minimum average weekly earnings amount that can be used to compute a life pension is the statutory minimum average weekly earnings amount that applies to the particular employee's permanent partial disability benefits. Ordinarily, this will be the minimum average weekly earnings amount that is specified in LC4453 for permanent partial disability benefits for the employee's date of injury (unless some exception applies; see 10.9). Do not confuse the employee's average weekly earnings with the compensation rate for temporary disability or permanent disability. An average weekly earnings amount is used in the computation of a life pension rate, not a compensation rate amount. Also, note that the actual average weekly earnings of low wage earners are used, not the adjusted average weekly earnings amount (1.5 times earnings) that may be used to compute a compensation rate for payments of temporary disability benefits to the same employee.

The formula for computing the compensation rate for a permanent partial disability life pension involves the steps shown below. As a preliminary step, the correct amount of earnings to be used in the formula is determined. Thereafter, the remaining three steps can be performed in any order:

1. Compare the amount of the employee's average weekly earnings to the maximum average weekly earnings limit in LC4659(a) and the minimum average weekly earnings amount for permanent partial disability benefits contained in LC4453 on the date of the employee's injury.
    a. Use the maximum weekly earnings amount in LC4659(a) if the employee's average weekly earnings exceed this amount, OR
    b. Use the minimum average weekly earnings amount that is specified in LC4453 if the employee's earnings are less than this amount (in this case, the same earnings amount will be used to compute the life pension rate and the employee's compensation rate for permanent partial disability benefits), OR
    c. Use the employee's average weekly earnings when this amount is less than the maximum earnings amount in LC4659(a) and equal or greater than the statutory minimum average weekly earnings amount in LC4453.
2. Multiply the employee's average weekly earnings amount by 1.5% (use the decimal .015).
3. Subtract 60% from the employee's percentage of disability (answer will be a whole number, not a percentage).
4. Multiply the result of step #2 by the result of step #3, or vice versa, to obtain the compensation rate for the life pension (LP).

SAMPLE (a). The date of injury (DOI) was 6/30/94, earnings are $800/wk, and permanent disability (PD) rates 80%. (Note: AWE = Average Weekly Earnings and LP = Life Pension.)

Earnings $800/wk = $107.69 AWE (statutory maximum for life pension)
AWE $107.69 × .015 = $1.6153
80% PD − 60% PD = 20 (this number is 20 not 20%)
20 × $1.6153 = 32.3060 = $32.31/wk Life Pension rate

SAMPLE (b). DOI 5/11/95. AWE $300. PD rating is 95%.

AWE = statutory maximum for life pension = $157.69
AWE $157.69 × .015 = $2.3653
95% PD − 60% PD = 35 (35 not 35%)
35 × $2.3653 = 82.7825 = $82.78 LP rate

SAMPLE (c). DOI 4/4/96. Earnings are $670/wk. PD rating is 83¼%.

$$AWE = \text{statutory maximum in LC4453} = \$207.69$$

$$AWE \;\$207.69 \times .015 = \$3.1153$$
$$83.25\% \text{ PD} - 60\% \text{ PD} = 23.25 \;(\text{not } 23¼ \%)$$
$$23.25 \times \$3.1153 = 72.4307 = \$72.43/\text{wk LP rate}$$

SAMPLE (d). DOI 2/6/97. AWE are $90. PD rating is 78¾%.

Earnings $90/wk = $105.00 AWE (statutory minimum for life pension)

$$AWE \;\$105.00 \times .015 = \$1.5750$$
$$78¾\% \text{ PD} - 60\% \text{ PD} = 18.75 \;(\text{not } 18.75\%)$$
$$18.75 \times \$1.5750 = 29.5312 = \$29.53/\text{wk LP rate}$$

SAMPLE (e). DOI 3/3/97. AWE $780. PD rating is 75%. Note that the steps in the formula can be performed in a different order without affecting the result.

$$AWE = \text{statutory maximum in LC4453} = \$257.69$$

$$AWE \;\$257.69 \times .015 = \$3.8653$$
$$75\% \text{ PD} - 60\% \text{ PD} = 15 \;(\text{not } 15\%)$$
$$15 \times \$3.8653 = 57.9802 = \$57.98/\text{wk LP rate}$$
OR
$$75\% \text{ PD} - 60\% \text{ PD} = 15 \;(\text{not } 15\%)$$
$$15 \times .015 = .2250$$
$$.2250 \times \$257.69 = 57.9802 = \$57.98/\text{wk LP rate}$$

10.12 LIFE PENSION RATE – TOTAL DISABILITY

Per LC4659(b), "if the disability is total, the indemnity based on the average weekly earnings determined under Section 4453 shall be paid during the remainder of life." The compensation rate for permanent total disability is two-thirds of the employee's average weekly earnings but not more than the maximum nor less than the minimum earnings limit specified in LC4453 on the date of the employee's injury (except lower minimums apply when the employee is a partner or a minor; see 10.9, that also explains how minimum average weekly earnings are computed).

Historically, the minimum and maximum average weekly earnings limits that applied to temporary total disability benefits under LC4453 applied interchangeably to permanent total disability benefits. Since 1990, one maximum average weekly earnings amount in LC4453 applies to both temporary disability and permanent total disability benefits, but the minimum average weekly earnings amount for permanent total disability is higher.

It is currently possible for employees with low earnings to receive a higher compensation rate for permanent total than for temporary total disability benefits. For instance, for a 1996 injury, the minimum compensation rate for permanent total disability benefits is $112/wk (two-thirds of minimum average weekly earnings of $168/wk). The average weekly earnings of an employee with actual average weekly earnings of $80/wk is $120 (1.5 × actual earnings). This employee's compensation rate would be $80/wk for temporary total but $112/wk for permanent total disability benefits.

Computations of the permanent total disability rate will be as easy, or possibly as complicated, as the computation of the employee's temporary total disability rate. In the majority of cases, the employee's compensation rate will be the same for both benefits. However, there are four exceptions to the general rule that the employee's compensation rate for permanent total disability will be the same amount as his compensation rate for temporary total disability. An exception applies to employees with low earnings as explained above. One exception pertains solely to minor employees (see 10.9), another applies to partners (see 10.9), and the other exception relates to the application of LC4661.5.

Post-injury increases in statutory average weekly earnings amounts in LC4453 will not affect the employee's compensation rate for permanent total disability, because LC4661.5 does not apply to permanent disability benefits (use of current statutory earnings limits two years after the date of injury; see 9.5). Therefore, if the employee had one or more increases in his temporary disability compensation rate under LC4661.5, his compensation rate for permanent total disability will be lower than the weekly rate at which his temporary disability benefits were paid. Per LC4453.5, the statutory maximum average weekly earnings amounts that are used for computations of permanent disability benefits will be those in effect in LC4453 on the date the injury was sustained.

10.13 INITIATION OF PAYMENTS – FIRST PAYMENT

Since 1990, LC4650 requires that the first payment of permanent disability "shall be made within 14 days after the date of the last payment of temporary disability indemnity." If it is known on the date of the last payment of temporary disability benefits that permanent disability benefits will be owed (because a physician has reported this opinion or it is obvious from knowing the nature of the injury sustained), then the first payment of permanent disability benefits is required to be paid no later than the 14th day thereafter. The initial check will usually provide payment for 14 days of accrued permanent disability benefits (because even if the employee is determined to have only 1% permanent disability, more than two weeks of benefits would be payable; see 10.20).

For 1991 or later injuries, if it is known that permanent disability benefits may or will become due, then the employer is also required to provide a written notice to the employee concurrently with the last payment of temporary disability benefits. The notice will advise the employee of applicable rights regarding an evaluation of permanent disability by an agreed upon or Qualified Medical Evaluator (see 7.76).

The employer is required to commence payments of permanent disability based upon knowledge of a medical determination of the extent of permanent disability that is now present or is expected to result from the injury in the future. The employer's liability is not contingent upon a medical determination that the employee's condition is currently permanent and stationary or knowledge of the full extent of the employee's permanent disability. The employer's liability is contingent upon knowledge of reasonable evidence that an injury will result in permanent disability (evidence that would cause the claimsperson to establish a claim file reserve for permanent disability benefits on an admittedly compensable claim when the employee is admittedly entitled to permanent disability benefits; see 2.25).

First Payment – No Temporary Disability Paid

It is possible for the employee to sustain a permanent disability but continue working and never receive any temporary disability benefits. The Labor Code does not specifically address the employer's liability to commence permanent disability benefits in this situation. However, entitlement to permanent disability benefits is not contingent upon sustaining an actual wage loss (see 9.1), and LC4650 makes it clear that the employer is expected to commence permanent disability payments before the full extent of the employee's permanent disability is capable of a medical determination. In view of these considerations, it would appear that an initial payment of permanent disability benefits is appropriate based upon a preliminary determination that permanent disability will result from the employee's injury and that the employee is not temporarily disabled, with the one exception explained below.

The employee may continue to be paid wages under a salary continuation plan beyond the point in time when the disability changes from temporary to permanent in nature (becomes permanent and stationary see 10.8). In this event, LC4650 may relieve the employer from liability for the provision of permanent disability benefits concurrent with the provision of full or partial wages (see 9.33).

Labor Code 4650 recognizes the fact that permanent disability benefits are a wage replacement benefit (as are all other workers' compensation indemnity benefits; see 2.25). However, the weekly amount of the salary continuation benefit cannot be less than the weekly rate that the employer would otherwise be obligated to pay as the employee's permanent disability compensation rate (this restriction likewise applies to wages continued during periods of temporary disability). A first payment of permanent disability is due within 14 days of a determination that the employee's disability is no longer temporary in nature if the weekly amount of salary continuation benefits available from the employer is less than the weekly compensation rate for permanent disability benefits (either partial or total, whichever type of permanent disability exists).

If wages are continued by the employer, it is necessary to compute the employee's compensation rate for permanent as well as temporary disability benefits and have both rates documented in the claim file (especially since it is possible for the employee to have a different compensation rate for nearly every indemnity benefit that may be owed). These rates can then be compared to the amount of any partial wages continued by the employer. The Labor Code does not distinguish between gross wages and net wages. However, all compensation rates are computed from gross wages, so absent a specific statutory provision setting out an exception, it is gross wages (full or partial) continued by the employer that must be compared to the weekly rate of payment for permanent disability benefits.

No consideration is required for the fact that permanent disability benefits are not taxable income (meaning the full amount is available for the employee's use); whereas, income taxes are payable out of gross wages paid to the employee. In fact, a decision to pay permanent disability because the rate is higher than fully paid but net wages would be tantamount to a payment of damages (in the amount of the dollar difference between the employee's net wages and a higher compensation benefit rate; see 10.3).

Multiple Disabilities – Different P&S Dates

One injury can cause multiple disabilities. Each injury may become permanent on a different date. In such cases, the employee's disability is not permanent until the entire disability is permanent (not as soon as any part of the injury becomes permanent). Prior to this time, the permanent disability that resulted from the injury cannot be rated, because its full extent is not known. For instance, an employee with serious leg and wrist injuries may receive treatment from an orthopedist for the leg injury and an orthopedic hand specialist for the wrist injury. The leg disability may become permanent and stationary days, months or years prior to the wrist injury.

A party may dispute the treating physician's finding that part, but not all, of the employee's condition is permanent and stationary (this finding may actually be based upon a finding of another treating physician that is incorporated into the report of a primary treating physician). A dispute may arise as to the extent of disability for only one body part or condition (e.g. just the leg but not the wrist in the example given above). In such cases, LC4061-LC4062 appear to require "piecemeal" referrals to an Agreed or Qualified Medical Evaluator for opinions at the time a dispute arises (see 7.75 et seq). No statutory provision specifically permits deferral of these issues until the treating physician determines that an employee's entire disability has become permanent and stationary.

10.14 PAYMENTS – METHOD & FREQUENCY

The method of payment is the same for temporary and permanent disability benefits regardless of the date of the employee's injury (see 9.14). Per LC4651, all disability indemnity payments must be made with a written instrument that "is immediately negotiable and payable in cash" (meaning a check but not a draft).

Requirements for the frequency of payments and potential penalties for late payments are the same for temporary and permanent disability benefits. Effective 1990, LC4650 provides that payment of "temporary or permanent disability indemnity payments subsequent to the first payment shall be made as due every two weeks on the day designated with the first payment." However, payments are timely if provided on the employee's regular payday if the employer "continues the employee's wages under a salary continuation plan" (see 9.33).

Payments are owed on a retroactive basis. Each check makes payment only for the number of days of permanent disability benefits that have accrued (are known to be owed) since the last date for which a payment was provided and the date that the current payment of permanent disability benefits is made. Accrued days means days of permanent disability that are known to be due and a number of days that, when subtracted from total days anticipated to be payable, does not result in a negative number (or else the payment would result in an overpayment of permanent disability benefits). If the employer does not provide any payment when it is due, the employer may also be liable for a 10% self-imposed penalty pursuant to LC4650 (the same as for temporary disability payments; see 9.16).

Benefit Information Notices

Both LC138.4 and CR9812 require a series of benefit information notices to be provided to employees for every type of indemnity benefit including permanent disability. As a general rule, a notice letter (no specified format) is required with a first and last payment as well as any change in rate or type of permanent disability (or any other indemnity) benefit being provided (see 9.15). Many notices will include information regarding a required referral to an Agreed Medical Evaluator or a Qualified Medical Evaluator when a party disputes a finding of the treating physician (see 7.76).

Penalty for Late Payments

If any payment of permanent disability benefits is not paid within the required 14-day period, the employer can be ordered to pay a 10% penalty under LC5814, but only if a judge determines that compensation was unreasonably delayed (see 9.16). In cases where the employee has submitted a claim form, the employer will automatically owe a 10% self-imposed penalty that is computed as a 10% increase in the amount that was not paid at the time it became due. However, LC4650 provides that "no increase shall apply to any payment due prior to or within 14 days after the date the claim form was submitted to the employer," nor when "the employer continues the employee's wages under a salary continuation plan, as defined" (see 9.33).

10.15 PAYMENTS – DURATION

Permanent Total Disability

For a 100% disability rating, installment payments are payable for the remainder of the employee's lifetime at the employee's compensation rate for permanent total disability benefits. (This rate may or may not be the same as the rate at which temporary total disability benefits were paid; 10.9). Payments cease only upon the employee's death.

Life Pensions

Life pension payments for permanent total or permanent partial disability are premised upon the belief that an employee will require lifetime assistance to adapt to the effects of any disability that is extensive enough to qualify the employee for this benefit. The employee's ability to compete in the open labor market is so seriously reduced that it is presumed that the disability will have a significant adverse affect on the employee's competitiveness for employment during the remainder of life. Therefore, a limited number of weeks of benefit payments is considered inadequate to fully compensate the employee for the impact of his disability.

An employee may desire to work and actively seek employment. However, where a disability is 70% or greater, the employee has only 30% or less of the skills considered necessary for obtaining and holding employment. Employability may be completely dependent upon the sympathy of employers rather than the employee's physical abilities. For this reason, the fact that an employee obtains employment does not necessarily contradict the continued existence of a disability at a 70% or greater level of severity.

When the employee retires from the labor market, the employee may still be affected by the disability. The employee may lose substantial earnings in the years following the injury due to an inability to obtain high-paying jobs or to hold long-term employment. A reduction in earning capacity may also limit the employee's ability to save money from earnings in order to provide for post-retirement financial needs. Because of these lifetime effects of the disability, life pension payments continue past the employee's normal working years and terminate only upon the employee's death.

Permanent Partial Disability – Generally

The employee's overall disability will be stated as a percentage out of 100%. For permanent disabilities of 99¾% or less, the employee will receive permanent partial disability payments for a specific number of weeks at the employee's permanent partial disability compensation rate. For disabilities between 70 and 99¾%, the employee is additionally entitled to receive a life pension that is payable at the employee's permanent partial disability life pension rate and commences as of the next benefit payment date period following payment of the last weekly installment of permanent partial disability. Regardless of the percentage of disability, permanent disability payments cease when the employer has paid the number of weeks of benefits that are payable for a particular percentage of disability or the employee dies, whichever occurs first.

Pay Up to Reasonable Estimate of Amount Due

Per LC4650, "where the extent of permanent disability cannot be determined at the time of the last payment of temporary disability indemnity," the employer "shall continue to make" permanent disability payments "until the employer's reasonable estimate of permanent disability due has been paid." Usually, anticipatory payments are based on the treating physician's projection of permanent disability. This same information is used to establish claim file reserves (see 2.25), but additional considerations apply. Payments are usually based upon the employer's conservative estimate of the full amount due to the employee in situations such as those listed below.

1. The employee's condition is not yet permanent and stationary.
2. The employee's condition is permanent and stationary but a required evaluation by an Agreed or Qualified Medical Evaluator has not yet been obtained.
3. The Disability Evaluation Unit has not yet issued a rating of a medical report.
4. A party is appealing a rating that has been issued by the Disability Evaluation Unit.
5. An appeal is pending after the WCAB has awarded benefits paid after a trial.
6. Valid liens that the WCAB can order to be paid out of the employee's permanent disability benefits (as listed in LC4903) are known to exist, but the final amount of one or more lien claims is not yet known (e.g. liens for child support obligations, landlord's liens, attorney fees or liens for self-procured medical treatment).

One factor that affects the amount payable to the employee is the reasonable potential for attorney fees or other liens against compensation to be deducted from the employee's disability benefits. Also, there is always the possibility that the employee's condition will improve rather than deteriorate with further treatment. Sometimes the employer's assessment of disability turns out, in retrospect, to have been too high. The Disability Evaluation Unit might determine that a particular medical report rates lower than the employer's preliminary rating of the same report.

For the above reasons, estimates of the amount of permanent disability that may ultimately be due are made conservatively. The intent in all cases is to pay the greatest amount of permanent disability that can be paid without resulting in an overpayment (especially where there are no other benefits or only medical benefits remaining to be paid against which the employer would seek a credit for the overpaid amount; see 9.30).

Liens Against Compensation. A lien may be formally filed using a WCAB lien form, or the employer may simply have reasonable knowledge of the existence of a lien claim against the employee's permanent disability benefits. It is sufficient that the employer is aware that someone is or will be requesting the WCAB to order some of the employee's permanent disability benefits paid to him or her instead of the employee. Where such liens exist, it is then reasonable for the employer to withhold the dollar amount of the employee's permanent disability benefits that it believes the WCAB might ultimately order it to pay directly to a lien claimant.

Attorney Fees

Whenever the employee has been represented by an attorney, it is always reasonable to withhold some percentage of the total amount of permanent disability benefits that are believed to be owed unless a current or former attorney specifically waives a fee. As a general rule, attorney fees are deducted from benefits the employee is otherwise entitled to receive, but there are a few exceptions where attorney fees are payable in additional to permanent disability benefits (see 2.27 and 7.80). As a general rule, if the employee is represented by an attorney, or was represented at any time after a claim was filed, the employer knows that the attorney will ordinarily request a fee. The employer also knows that the normal range of fees is 9% to 12% because this range is stated on the Fee Disclosure Statement required by LC4906 (a copy of which is printed in CR10134).

The employer could ask the employee's attorney to state the exact percentage or dollar amount of the employee's permanent disability benefits that the attorney plans to request as a fee (the employer does not pay any money to the attorney until the WCAB approves the amount of the fee). However, this is not usually done. Absent the attorney taking the initiative to notify the claimsperson of the percentage of the employee's benefits that should be withheld, an anticipated fee of 12% to 15% is customarily withheld (because a sufficient number of attorneys have been known to be awarded fees in the 15% range).

Knowledge that an attorney is representing the employee is equivalent to knowledge that the attorney will expect to be paid for such representation (except no fee will be payable to an attorney who chooses to represent an employee who has already received full payment of all benefits owed). Should the employer fail to withhold sufficient funds to cover attorney fees that the WCAB awards or orders to be paid, the employer can be ordered to pay the shortage, not the employee. Since 1990, the employer receives knowledge of legal representation when it receives the Fee Disclosure Statement (DWC Form 3) that is required by LC4906 and must be signed by both the attorney and the employee. Effective 1992, LC4903 precludes the WCAB from awarding a fee to any agent or representative of an employee who is not an attorney (the employee can be represented by a nonattorney, but the WCAB cannot award any fee to such layperson).

Pay Until Full Amount Paid

Since 1990, LC4650 specifies that "if the amount of permanent disability due has been determined," the employer is required to continue payments "until that amount has been paid." The amount of permanent disability that the employer has determined to be due will, in all cases, be reviewed by a judge (usually upon submission of settlement documents, but possibly after a trial if benefits are disputed). However, it is not likely that a Judge would ever determine the employee to be entitled to a lesser amount of permanent disability than the amount that the employer agrees to or admits it owes.

The full amount due can be deemed "determined" when the employer receives a summary rating based on the report of a Qualified Medical Evaluator and the parties agree to enter into a settlement based upon the rating that has been determined by the Disability Evaluation Unit. If the employee has not been represented by an attorney and there are no other lien claimants seeking payment of part of the employee's permanent disability benefits, payment should continue without interruption until the employee has been fully paid.

In some cases, the full amount of permanent disability due will be determined by the WCAB after litigation proceedings and perhaps after an appeal of the Judge's determination has been ruled on by the court of appeal or the Supreme Court. In most cases, the full amount due is determined by the parties and thereafter presented, via settlement documents, for WCAB approval.

It is not uncommon for the WCAB to determine that the employee is entitled to a higher amount of permanent disability than that agreed upon by the parties. However, it is rare for the WCAB to determine that a lesser amount is owed in the absence of special circumstances; e.g., fraud or deceit by a party or a physician. When the employer agrees to a settlement of permanent disability benefits (based upon the findings of a treating physician or of an Agreed or Qualified Medical Evaluator when required), the full amount due under LC4650 is the full amount that is undisputedly owed to the employee. The only exception applies to cases where the employer is aware of liens against compensation (as explained above).

The employee is not required to sign settlement documents or await WCAB approval in order to receive full payment of permanent disability benefits that are undisputedly owed. If there are no known liens and no dispute as to the amount of permanent disability owed, LC4650 requires continued payments until that undisputed "amount has been paid." A statutory requirement for payment in full of undisputed amounts is intended to reduce unnecessary litigation.

A dispute may arise after all permanent disability has been paid. If so, no fee against permanent disability benefits would be payable to an attorney who chooses to represent an employee who has already received full payment of permanent disability benefits. An attorney could seek a fee for efforts in resolving disputed permanent disability benefits only from any "new money" – meaning any additional compensation that the WCAB may award as a result of the attorney's efforts on the employee's behalf. (An attorney would be entitled to fees for efforts expended relative to future issues that arise, e.g. a fee from vocational rehabilitation maintenance allowance benefits for representation in pursuing this category of benefits.)

10.16 PAYMENTS – EMPLOYEE INCARCERATED

The employee may become incarcerated after sustaining a compensable injury. For 1989 or later injuries, the provisions of LC3370 control the payment of permanent disability benefits to any employee who was not a prisoner when an injury occurred but is thereafter incarcerated in a state (as opposed to a county or federal) penal or correctional institution.

Per LC3370, "no benefits shall be paid to an inmate while he or she is incarcerated." If permanent disability benefits were being paid, payments to the employee cease as of the date of incarceration. If permanent disability benefits were accrued but not yet paid and/or entitlement to permanent benefits first arises during incarceration, the employer owes payments, but the employee is not the recipient of the payment (see 9.19 regarding temporary disability benefits).

Any permanent disability benefits that would otherwise be paid to the employee while incarcerated in a state penal institution "shall be paid to the dependents of the inmate." Dependents, for this purpose, are specifically defined by LC3370 to mean "the inmate's spouse or children, including an inmate's former spouse due to divorce and the inmate's children from that marriage." Since dependency for workers' compensation purposes is generally understood to mean financial dependency, this definition would appear to limit dependents to those whom the employee has a legal obligation to support, e.g. not all former spouses, only a former spouse to whom the employee owes either alimony payments or arrearage of spousal support payments pursuant to a court order (see 9.20).

The employee is available to be asked to identify his dependents. However, the employee's full cooperation cannot be assumed. The identity of qualified dependents can also be obtained by an investigation, including interviews with persons who previously worked with the employee, a review of personnel records and a review of public records of marriages and divorces.

If the employee does not have any properly qualified dependents, benefits due the employee "shall be held in trust for the inmate by the Department of Corrections during the period of incarceration" (information as to how the payee's name should appear on the check and where the payment is to be mailed would be obtained from this State agency). Benefits that are held in trust are payable to the employee upon release from incarceration. Also, any benefits that become due for periods of time subsequent to the employee's release are payable to the employee.

10.17 PAYMENTS – ACCRUED AT DEATH

Per LC4700, no "permanent disability payments shall be made for any period of time subsequent to the death of the employee." However, the employer is required to pay the employee's dependents or personal representative "any accrued and unpaid compensation" on the date of death. Per LC4706.5, if there are no such designated persons, the State of California is entitled to receive the accrued compensation. In either case, the accrued benefits are payable "without administration." The employer determines the proper payee and provides payments. There is no requirement for prior WCAB approval (except that if benefits were being paid under compulsion of an award or if multiple persons claim available benefits, the employer will seek an order from the WCAB directing how benefits are to be paid).

The employee's daily compensation rate for permanent disability (as well as all other indemnity benefits) is $1/7$ of the weekly rate. To determine the amount of compensation that accrued prior to the employee's death, the employer will multiply the daily benefit rate times the number of days between the date of death and the last day for which benefits were paid. Regardless of the exact time of death, the date of death will not constitute a day (a 24-hour period) of disability. No permanent disability benefits accrue or are payable for the date of death.

10.18 CONVERTING PERCENTAGES TO DOLLARS

Each percentage of disability below 100% is equivalent to a specific number of weeks of benefit payments. When this number of weeks is multiplied by the employee's weekly compensation rate, the product is the total dollar value of the employee's permanent disability benefits. For 1992 or later dates of injury, the graduated scale that determines the number of weeks that are owed is set out in LC4658(b). As the percentage of disability goes up, the number of weeks payable at the employee's compensation rate also increases. The break off points are listed in LC4658 in a somewhat confusing manner. For purposes of clarity, the break-off points are shown below in a slightly different format than shown in the statute.

From	00.00 through 09.75%	=	3 wks/percent
Over	09.75 through 19.75%	=	4 wks/percent
Over	19.75 through 24.75%	=	5 wks/percent
Over	24.75 through 29.75%	=	6 wks/percent
Over	29.75 through 49.75%	=	7 wks/percent
Over	49.75 through 69.75%	=	8 wks/percent
Over	69.75 through 99.75%	=	9 wks/percent

The number of weeks that are payable for different ranges of percentages are "cumulative." This means the weeks payable for a 35% rating will not be 7 weeks times 35%. Instead, the number of weeks is computed by adding the "cumulative" values for each component percentage of disability on the graduated scale as demonstrated in the examples that follow.

SAMPLE (a). The employee's disability rating is 35%; earnings were $246/wk at the time of injury on 2/17/97; and, the employee's weekly compensation rate is $164/wk.

$$
\begin{array}{rcrcll}
(\text{Under } 10.00\%) & & 09.75\% & \times\ 3\ \text{wks} = & 29.25\ \text{wks} \\
19.75\% - 09.75\% = & 10.00\% & \times\ 4\ \text{wks} = & 40.00\ \text{wks} \\
24.75\% - 19.75\% = & 5.00\% & \times\ 5\ \text{wks} = & 25.00\ \text{wks} \\
29.75\% - 24.75\% = & 5.00\% & \times\ 6\ \text{wks} = & 30.00\ \text{wks} \\
35.00\% - 29.75\% = & +5.25\% & \times\ 7\ \text{wks} = & +36.75\ \text{wks} \\
& 35.00\% & & 161.00\ \text{wks}
\end{array}
$$

161.00 wks × $164/wk = $26,404.00

SAMPLE (b). The disability rating is 23%; the date of injury is 4/4/97;; earnings are $600/wk; and, the employee's compensation rate is $160/wk.

$$
\begin{array}{rcrcll}
23.00\% - 19.75\% = & 3.25\% & \times\ 5\ \text{wks} = & 16.25\ \text{wks} \\
19.75\% - 09.75\% = & 10.00\% & \times\ 4\ \text{wks} = & 40.00\ \text{wks} \\
(\text{Under } 10.00\%) & +9.75\% & \times\ 3\ \text{wks} = & +29.25\ \text{wks} \\
& 23.00\% & & 85.50\ \text{wks}
\end{array}
$$

85.50 wks × $120/wk = $10,260.00

It is not usually necessary to compute the number of weeks payable for the employee's percentage of disability since charts are readily available that list the weeks payable for every percentage of disability through 99.75%. Once the number of weeks is known, it is a simple enough matter to multiply this number times the employee's compensation rate. Note that as a result of 4/1/97 amendments to the *Schedule for Rating Permanent Disabilities*, all ratings for injuries occurring on or after the effective date of the amendments will be stated as whole numbers. Quarter percentage point incremental increases in the employee's percentage of disability now apply only to pre-4/1/97 dates of injury.

10.19 PAYMENTS – INSTALLMENTS

Installment Payments – Required

The employer is required to provide installment payments of permanent disability benefits pursuant to LC4650. Permanent disability payments are intended to provide financial assistance during a period of rehabilitation from the permanent effects of an injury ("rehabilitation" in this context refers to economic rather than physical or vocational rehabilitation). The number of weeks of benefits that are payable for the employee's percentage of disability reflect an anticipated period of adjustment to the income-impairing effects of the employee's particular disability in the open labor market. If benefits were paid in a lump sum, the money could be used in some manner that is unrelated to the intended function of incremental permanent disability indemnity payments. For instance, relatives or creditors may become the actual recipients of benefit payments that are intended for the employee.

For 1990 or later injuries, the intended purpose of installment payments permanent disability benefits defies appraisal by historical standards. Many employees who sustain minor injuries will return to work at full wages during active medical treatment before their condition becomes permanent and stationary (see 10.8). Per LC4650, the employer is required to commence payments of permanent disability benefits to such employees no later than 14 days after the last day for which the employee was paid temporary disability benefits and regardless of whether the employee's condition has yet stabilized (see 10.14).

Anticipatory payments are required based upon a physician's opinion that an injury will ultimately result in permanent disability, and LC4650 requires payments to continue until the full amount of estimated disability has been paid (except that it is reasonable for the employer to hold back the full amount of reasonably anticipated liens; e.g. estimated attorney fees when the employee is represented by an attorney.) Since 1990, it is therefore possible for employees to be fully paid for the effects of a permanent disability before the disability itself is permanent in nature.

Employer's Right to Earn Interest

At any given time the employer knows exactly how many weeks it will take to pay the employee the total dollar value of any particular percentage of permanent disability benefits. The employer can invest the unpaid balance of benefits and earn high interest on this money right up to the date each installment payment is due. The employer has a right to earn interest on this money, because the law requires installment payments, not lump sum payments. The employee does not have any right to claim the interest that the employer earns or that the employee could otherwise earn on the unpaid balance of the employee's disability benefits, nor does the employee have the right to receive the unpaid balance of benefits in a lump sum upon demand. Indeed, if the employee dies before all installments have accrued, the employer is only liable for accrued and unpaid days of benefits on the date of death (see 10.17).

Lump Sum Payments – Permissible

Per LC5100, the WCAB can order payment of all or part of the employee's future compensation in a lump sum. Payment of installment benefits in a lump sum pursuant to a WCAB order to do so is commonly referred to as a "commutation" of benefits. The employee requests a lump sum payment by filing a Petition for Commutation of Future Payments (DIA-WCAB Form 49) with the WCAB. On the form or by attachments the employee must provide a reason for this request.

The WCAB is not required to order a lump sum payment upon request, and, due to the subversion of the statutory purpose of installment payments, does not routinely grant requests for lump sum payments. The employee's request will not be granted unless a judge determines that a lump sum payment is permissible under the authority of LC5100. This section lists several valid grounds for granting a commutation. It is not necessary to review each of these reasons in detail, since one of these is a catchall provision that appears to provide ample room for the use of judicial discretion in any case that may arise: a judge can order the employer to pay benefits in a lump sum in any case where a commutation "is for the best interest of the applicant."

In all cases, it is the judge, not the employee, who determines if a lump sum payment is truly in the best interest of the employee. In making this determination, a judge will attempt to strike a balance between the employee's desire for a lump sum and statutory requirements for installment payments of all indemnity benefits.

A judge may award a lump sum payment when it is likely to foster the employee's medical recovery or rehabilitation from an injury. For instance, the purpose of a lump sum may be to obtain vocational rehabilitation services that the employer would not otherwise be obligated to provide due to dollar caps on rehabilitation benefits (see 11.28). A lump sum payment might also be deemed appropriate where an employee seeks to self-procure treatment of a type (e.g. rare or experimental) or by a provider (e.g. services from a vitamin therapist or from a relative) that would otherwise be contested by the employer.

10.20 COMMUTATION – CREDIT FOR LOST INTEREST

Per LC5101, the employer is entitled to receive a credit for its loss of investment income when it is ordered to pay future installment payments of the employee's weekly benefits in a lump sum. The employer's credit is set by law at 3% per annum. The amount of the interest credit will reduce the employer's liability for benefits by this same amount. As a result, when benefits are paid in a lump sum, the employee will receive the actual dollar value of his unpaid payments minus the amount of the interest the employer is losing. The reduced value of the employee's benefits is referred to as the "present value" of the employee's disability benefits or the "commuted value" of future and as yet unaccrued benefits.

At first glance, commutations sound advantageous for the employer. The amount the employer will be ordered to pay as a lump sum will be less than the sum of the installment payments it would otherwise owe. However, the employer can only receive credit for lost interest at the rate of 3% per annum on the amount paid in advance, because this is the interest rate allowed under LC5101. It would be rare to find an employer whose actual loss of interest income did not exceed the minimal rate of return permitted by LC5101 (this interest rate was last changed effective 1946 when it was reduced from 6% to 3% per annum). Thus commutations are usually not in the best financial interests of any employer, and commutations are rarely requested by an employer.

10.21 COMMUTATION – VARIATIONS

The mathematical procedure for computing the amount of the employer's interest credit on a lump sum payment of permanent disability benefits differs for full and partial commutations. One procedure is used when all permanent disability that remains unpaid at the time of a WCAB award is to be paid in a lump sum. A different procedure is used when only a portion of the unpaid balance is ordered paid in a lump sum. (The mathematical method for computing the employer's interest credit is not set out herein.)

The most commonly allowed partial commutation is a lump sum payment for the employee's attorney's fees. The attorney receives the full amount of attorney fees after an award issues. The remaining balance of the employee's permanent disability benefits is thereafter reduced by the amount of the lump sum payment to the attorney and the amount of the employer's interest credit on this lump sum payment. There are several ways that the employee's remaining benefits can be affected by any partial commutation of permanent disability benefits. The WCAB determines how the employee's payments will be affected at the same time it orders a commutation. Below is a list of possible alternatives and the effect each one will have on the employee's remaining installment payments:

1. **Commutation Off Far End of Award.** The employee receives installment payments for fewer weeks than the actual number of weeks payable for the percent of disability. Payments cease at the time when the number of future weeks of payments equals the amount of the employer's interest credit on a previous lump sum payment.

2. **Commutation From Near End of Award.** The employee does not get a first payment until the number of weeks representing the employer's interest credit have passed. The employee's payments

cease on the same date they would end if there had not been any commutation.

3. **Commutation Spread Over Entire Award.** The employee will receive weekly payments for the same number of weeks that would be paid without any commutation, but the amount of the weekly payment is less than the employee's compensation rate. Each payment is reduced by a small amount. When all weekly payments are added together, their sum is the commuted value of the employer's lump sum payment.

4. **Commutation Spread Over Portion of Award.** This is a variation of #3 above. The employee's payments are reduced for a specific period of time rather than the entire duration of payments, and the number of weeks of payments is not affected.

10.22 COMMUTATION – LIFE PENSION CASE

Per LC5101, for purposes of determining the present value of future benefits, the "probability of the beneficiary's death" is disregarded except for commutations of life pension payments. This language refers to the fact that the number of weeks of benefits the employer owes in life pension cases is contingent upon the employee's estimated life expectancy. Individual life expectancies will differ, and therefore the weeks of life pension payments can vary from one employee to another even when their percentage of disability is the same.

"In estimating the present value of a life pension," CR9885 requires that the weeks of the employee's remaining anticipated life expectancy be taken from the "most recent 'U.S. Life Tables.'" There are separate tables for males and females, because statistics have revealed that sex is a determinative factor in a person's longevity. The tables are compiled by the U.S. Dept. of Health & Human Services from information obtained in the decennial census.

In order to compute the present value of future payments in a permanent partial disability life pension case (rating 70% to 99¾%), it may be necessary to perform a two-step calculation. There are two major distinctions between payments of the employee's permanent partial disability benefits and permanent partial disability life pension benefits: the manner in which the number of future weeks of payments are found and the weekly benefit rate. Therefore, the commuted value of lump sum payments of each category of benefit must always be computed separately whenever the amount to be commuted involves both categories of benefits.

10.23 RATING SCHEDULE

Pursuant to LC4660, the State has adopted a "schedule for the determination of the percentage of permanent disabilities" that "shall be prima facie evidence of the percentage of permanent disability to be attributable to each injury covered in the schedule." The official title is *Schedule for Rating Permanent Disabilities,* but the schedule is commonly referred to as the "rating manual" or the "schedule." The schedule is a product of extensive effort and voluminous research to determine the comparative effects of various types of disabilities on an employee's ability to compete in the open labor market.

The schedule sets out a six-part formula for converting medical factors of disability into percentages of disability. Once a physician describes the factors of disability, an attorney, a judge, or any mathematically inclined layperson can "rate" any medical report. The steps involved in finding the percentage of disability consider all the factors of disability that are listed in LC4660 (see 10.2 and 10.24-10.27).

Whenever the schedule is modified, LC4660 provides that any amendment "or revision thereof shall apply prospectively ... only to injuries on and after" their effective date. Historically, revisions to the schedule were incorporated into the existing schedule. However, in 1996 the Administrative Director of the Division of Workers' Compensation adopted a significantly revised schedule that, per CR10151, applies to injuries on or after 4/1/97. The prior schedule continues to apply to pre-4/1/97 dates of injury. The separate schedules can be ordered through private sources or from the State of California's Publication Unit, Material Management Warehouse, P.O. Box 1015, North Highlands, CA 95660 (as commodity #7540-937-1031-4 for the April 1997 edition or as commodity #7540-937-1030-2 for the prior edition as last published in July 1978).

The current rating schedule was developed in response to 1994 amendments to LC4660 that mandated the Administrative Director of the Division of Workers' Compensation to revise the schedule before 1995. The amendments specified that the revision was to "include, but is not limited to an updating of the standard ratings and occupations to reflect the current labor market." Per LC4660, the Administrative Director cannot adopt proposed changes "in standard disability ratings" until they are approved by the Commission of Health and Safety and Workers' Compensation (see LC75-LC78 for further details regarding this Commission).

4/1/97 Rating Schedule - Overview of Changes

The current schedule is more compact in size than its predecessor as it is printed lengthwise on letter size paper instead of legal size paper. The schedule now includes definitions of a variety of commonly used terms as well as explanations of concepts and rating principles that are derived from case law. Also included are fairly comprehensive general instructions and examples. Additional types of disabilities have been assigned a standard rating, and some scheduled disability numbers from the prior schedule no longer correspond to the same disability/body part in the revised schedule. Another improvement for the user's convenience is the inclusion of a percent to fraction conversion chart in the Tables section of the schedule.

The occupation section of the schedule reflects modern day occupations and uses a three-digit numbering scheme that enables greater precision in determining the appropriate occupational group number for a particular employee (the prior schedule assigned listed occupations a two-digit group number that held no special significance). Three-digit group numbers now categorize occupations according to a general strength level on an ascending scale of arduousness from 1 to 5 (first digit), one of eight general occupational categories or else a ninth miscellaneous category (second digit) and distinguishable subcategories within a particular strength or occupational category (third digit). For instance, group number 490 is assigned to a vice investigator, 251 to an inside or outside insurance investigator, and 111 to an investigator of credit fraud.

Disabilities are rated according to one of two major "indexes of disability." Another index could be the need for a brace or for the use of an appliance. One major index refers to a rating based upon objective and subjective factors of disability as described by a physician. A second major index refers to the use of work capacity guidelines to describe a disability. (Both indexes can apply to the same claim, in which case the schedule requires the use of the index that results in a higher percentage of disability.) Work capacity guidelines for lower extremity disabilities are now set out separately from those that apply to torso disabilities (e.g. pulmonary or back disabilities).

The adjustment of a standard rating for the employee's age uses five-year increments rather than two as before. The adjustment for occupation uses a smaller number of occupational variants than before. (See also 10.24-10.26 for specific details regarding rating of disabilities using the 4/1/97 schedule.)

10.24 STANDARD RATING

The rating schedule lists different types of disabilities separately by a body part or function (e.g. amputation of arm, impairment of function of wrist or loss of vision). Each listed disability is designated by a "disability number." There is a pattern to the way disabilities are listed. The schedule is set up head to toe, e.g. 1-Brain, 7-Arms, and progressively higher disability numbers for fingers, spine, legs, and toes. Every conceivable type of disability that might result from an injury is not listed nor assigned a standard rating in the schedule. This fact has produced the terms "scheduled disabilities" and "nonscheduled disabilities." Each listed disability is assigned a "standard rating" between 1% to 100%. The standard rating to be used for any nonscheduled disability is determined by applying judgment to select the most analogous scheduled disability and its assigned standard rating. The term "judgment rating" refers to the determination of a standard rating for disabilities in such cases.

The standard rating compares the employee's disability to all other possible disabilities. A 2% standard indicates that the employee is unaffected in his ability to compete in 98% of the labor market. Out of all conceivable work activities, the employee's disability would restrict only 2% of such activities. The employee is 2% more disabled than a person without any disability. The employee is 98% less disabled than a person who is completely noncompetitive in the labor market.

10.25 RATING FORMULA

The ease with which the rating formula can be explained should not mislead anyone into thinking that the process is simple. Rating of permanent disabilities is probably the most complicated aspect of compensation claims. Knowledge of basic mathematical principles is essential. The person who performs a rating must be able to read and understand medical reports without being a physician. The rater must know the statutory and case law relating to ratings without necessarily being an attorney. The basic principles of permanent disability rating are straightforward. However, there are many complicated areas that require a course of instruction for a complete understanding. A formal class is greatly beneficial, if not absolutely necessary, to achieve proficiency in this area. No attempt will be made here to explain the intricacies of the rating process.

The basic formula is the same for all ratings from the simplest disabilities to the most complex. A rating formula is written down in six separate parts that are separated by dashes as shown below. It is customary to omit the dash between steps (3) and (4) in the formula, but there are six separate steps to the formula, not five.

SAMPLE (a). A 35 year old general construction carpenter has an amputation at the distal joint of the big toe on the left foot. The date of injury is 6/18/97 (after revisions to the schedule took effect on 4/1/97).

$$\begin{array}{cccccc} (1) & (2) & (3)\ (4) & (5) & (6) \\ 14.231 & -\ 5\ - & 380\mathrm{I} & -\ 8\ - & 7\% \end{array}$$

Step (1) shows the disability number for this injury as listed in Section 2 of the *Schedule for Rating Permanent Disabilities,* Step (2) shows the standard rating of 5% for this disability that is listed in the schedule next to the disability number. (It is a matter of personal preference whether the percent sign is shown next to the standard rating in this part of the formula, e.g. 5% instead of 5.) Step (3) shows the "group number" designated for the employee's occupation. This number is obtained from a general listing of occupations in Section 3 of the schedule. In step (4), the employee's occupational group number is compared with the disability number in Section 4 of the schedule where these two items intersect on a chart at the letter "I" that is called the "occupational variant."

The standard rating is then modified to reflect the effect of this injury on a carpenter. In Section 5 of the schedule (5), 8% represents the point where the occupational variant "I" intersects with the disability number 14.231. In Section 6 of the rating schedule (6), this modified standard rating is further modified by the employee's age. On a chart, an 8% rating intersects with age 35 at 7.

SAMPLE (b). A 35 year old general construction carpenter has an amputation at the distal joint of the big toe on the left foot. The date of injury is 3/31/97 (before the schedule was revised).

$$\begin{array}{cccccc} (1) & (2) & (3)\ (4) & (5) & (6) \\ 20.731 & -\ 5\ - & 31\,\mathrm{G} & -\ 6\ - & 5{:}3 \end{array}$$

NOTE: For injuries occurring prior to 4/1/97, disability percentages are shown in the rating schedule by quarter percents as 0:1, 0:2, or 0:3. In the above example, the loss of a great toe entitles a 35 year old carpenter to a rating of 5:3. This rating can be referred to interchangeably as a rating of 5:3 ("5 colon 3"), 5:3%, 5¾%, or most commonly as 5.75%. As of 4/1/97, all final rating percentages are stated as the nearest whole number (e.g. any decimal number exceeding .49 that results from calculating the employee's fractional loss of a scheduled disability is rounded upward).

10.26 OCCUPATION – AFFECT ON STANDARD RATING

In the *Schedule for Rating Permanent Disabilities,* the standard rating is not based on any particular occupation. The standard rating considers the relative importance of a particular disability in the overall labor market. Depending on the employee's occupation, this standard may or may not fully reflect the labor disabling effect of the disability on this particular employee. The occupational variants in the rating schedule allow for an adjustment of the standard rating to reflect the varying significance of the same disability in different types of occupations. For example, an amputated finger will cause greater disability for a typist than for a salesperson, and a hearing loss will be less labor disabling for a gardener than for a teacher.

For 4/1/97 or later injuries, occupational variants in the rating schedule range from "C-J" (for earlier injuries, occupational variants range from "A-L"). If the use of the schedule produces an "F" variant for the employee's occupation, the standard rating will remain the same after modification for occupation using either the old or the new schedule. An "F" variant reflects the fact that the employee's injury does not cause any greater or lesser disability in the employee's particular occupation than is already contemplated in the standard rating. The standard rating will decrease for variants less than "F" and increase for variants exceeding "F" in alphabetical order.

The employee's job title may be too vague to associate with a specific occupation. Examples are "supervisor," "technician," and "repairman." When the job title is one commonly used in a variety of totally different occupations, a job description is often necessary to identify the true nature of the occupation. The expense of a formal job analysis is usually not necessary, but sometimes one has previously been performed for the employee's position (e.g. where one was previously obtained in order to determine this employee's or a coemployee's vocational feasibility for rehabilitation benefits; see 11.16). Since 1992, it is fairly routine for most employers who come under the provisions of the federal Americans With Disabilities Act to have accumulated detailed written information concerning the essential functions of various jobs (see 11.36).

The employee's occupation may not be listed in the schedule, because the schedule does not list every occupation by name. Also, some occupations did not exist when the schedule was written or when it was last updated occupationally in 1997. Like nonscheduled disabilities, the employee's occupation is compared to listed occupations (according to physical requirements, not job titles; see 10.23). One of these will have comparable physical demands to the employee's occupation. The group number for the listed occupation is then used in the formula. The *Dictionary of Occupational Titles* is an excellent reference book that describes the actual duties of hundreds of different jobs and enables the employee's duties to be analogized to an occupation that is listed in the schedule.

10.27 AGE – AFFECT ON STANDARD RATING

The *Schedule for Rating Permanent Disabilities* assumes that employees who are older will be more severely affected by a particular disability than younger employees. Older employees have two hurdles to overcome. One is the nature of their particular disability. The other is the fact that they must compete for employment with younger and more able-bodied individuals. The rating schedule was compiled prior to many State and Federal laws that currently prohibit employment discrimination based on age. However, the fact that age prejudice can affect employability was recognized and incorporated into the rating schedule.

For 4/1/97 or later injuries, the schedule lists ages in five-year increments, and the median age group is age "37-41" (the pre-1997 schedule uses two-year increments, and the age at which a standard rating does not change is age "38-39"). A standard rating using either schedule will increase proportionately as the employee's age exceeds the median age, and the standard rating will decrease for ages below the median age. If the employee is the median age, the rating formula will produce the final percent of disability after modification for occupation. There is no modification for this age group, so the rating will not be altered in the last step of the formula (see 10.24).

The employee's age is ordinarily computed by subtracting the employee's date of birth from the date of injury. The disability may not be rated until years after the injury, so this computation ensures the use of the employee's age on the date of injury. In rare cases, the employee's correct age may be disputed. For example, the employee may allege that he lied and understated his age in an employment application. When the employee learns that his rating would increase for his correct age, the employee is usually willing to provide necessary documentation that verifies his correct date of birth.

10.28 MEASUREMENT OF OBJECTIVE DISABILITY

Objective disabilities are capable of measurement or direct medical substantiation. A fused ankle is one example. Another would be a loss of vision that requires corrective lenses. The disability itself is unlikely to change from one physician to the next. A possible area of variance is the method of measurement that is used by different examining physicians. To eliminate variances on this basis, CR9725 requires physicians to use standard methods for measuring work related disabilities. These standards are contained in the 1960 edition of *Evaluation of Industrial Disability*, edited by Packard Thurber. This book contains photographs showing the placement of measurement devices, simplistic explanations of techniques for obtaining measurements, and information concerning the complete range of measurements required from the physician in industrial injury cases.

Since 1990, LC139.2 charges the Industrial Medical Council with the task of promulgating (through the public hearing process; see 1.7) regulations that will establish "procedures to be followed by all physicians in evaluating the existence and extent of permanent impairment and limitations resulting from an injury." Such procedures are deemed necessary "in order to produce complete, accurate, uniform, and replicable evaluations." Further, "the procedures shall require that an evaluation of anatomic loss, functional loss, and the presence of physical complaints be supported, to the extent feasible, by medical findings based on standardized examinations and testing techniques generally accepted by the medical community."

Treatment and evaluation guidelines that have been adopted in response to the legislative mandate in LC139.2 are available upon request from the Industrial Medical Council. For instance, protocols and guidelines have been developed that establish detailed procedures for evaluating psychiatric, pulmonary, cardiac, and immunologic disability (CR49.2-49.8).

10.29 MEASUREMENT OF SUBJECTIVE DISABILITY

A subjective disability is one that is stated or described by the employee but cannot be accurately measured by any physician. An example would be "inability to concentrate in stressful situations." Another example is "slight pain when lifting any object weighing over ten pounds." Per the 4/1/97 rating schedule, subjective factors of disability "may include pain, numbness, weakness, tenderness, paresthesia, and sensitivity." Subjective factors of disability can be as equally labor disabling as objective factors. There is no requirement that a disability be objective or visible, and the employee is entitled to permanent disability benefits if his disability is entirely subjective in nature. However, the employee's assertions of disability do not replace medical opinions as to the existence and extent of the disability.

The physician's job does not end with a mere recital of the employee's complaints. The role of the physician is to render a medical opinion as to the validity of the disability described by the employee. The physician should consider the nature of the injury, the credibility of the employee, and the medical feasibility of the employee's self-described disability. The physician's evaluation of disability should be an objective medical opinion of subjective factors of disability.

In order to determine the percentage of disability, subjective disabilities must be described in terms of their effect on the performance of work. Excellent guidelines are provided in CR9727, and additional explanation is provided in Packard Thurber's book, *Evaluation of Industrial Disability* and various guidelines that have been adopted by the Industrial Medical Council (see 10.28). It is insufficient for a physician to merely restate the employee's self-described disability. The reporting physician is also expected to comment upon the validity of any self-described factors of disability. When reporting subjective factors of disability, the physician must:

1. Describe the activity that produces the disability; e.g., the employee experiences pain (or weakness, aching, or numbness) in his knee when he climbs ladders or stairs.
2. Tell how long the disability lasts once it occurs; e.g., there is pain on lifting that ceases when the employee is not lifting, or the employee has excruciating headaches that begin in late morning and last from two to four hours.
3. Explain the activities that are precluded by the disability and what the employee can do with the disability; e.g., the employee can raise his arms overhead but cannot perform overhead lifting, or the employee can work in a dust free environment but has wheezing attacks when exposed to chemical fumes.
4. Give an opinion of the means necessary to provide relief and the time period before the employee can resume an activity. For instance, the employee must stop performing a particular activity; or an aspirin gives satisfactory and fairly immediate relief; or, the employee must take a ten minute break after heavy lifting for an hour.

Historically, evaluations of temporary as well as permanent disability have focused upon determining only that an employee was disabled. The modern trend is a positive focus with physicians being expected to identify existing physical capabilities at the time of each evaluation. An early example of this changed emphasis was a 10/1/89 change in CR9785 that continues to require physicians to fully explain any recommendations for continued treatment at least every 45 days during active treatment (e.g. what beneficial effect has occurred as a result of the treatment that the employee has received in the preceding 45 days?).

Labor Code 4636 requires a treating physician to render an "opinion concerning the physical capabilities of the employee at the time of each report" that is required at least every 60 days during the pendency of a determination of medical eligibility for rehabilitation benefits. Additionally, a review of the provisions of the federal Americans With Disabilities Act (that applies to many California employers; see 11.36) will reveal a major emphasis upon identification of physical abilities: determining what work an employee with a disability is capable of performing rather than determining that the employee is disabled.

10.30 MEASUREMENT OF PAIN – SEVERITY

The physician will ask the employee to describe the pain that the employee is experiencing. Having heard the employee's description, the physician must then render a medical opinion on the severity (degree or level) of pain. It is important for physicians to use terms that have commonly accepted meanings so that employees with similar disabilities will be compensated equally (see 10.36 regarding efforts of the Industrial Medical Council in this regard). To achieve uniformity in reporting subjective disabilities, CR9727 lists four terms that should be used to categorize the level or severity of pain. Use of these standard terms enables the pain to be rated or converted to a percentage of disability. These terms and their meanings are:

1. **Minimal Pain:** the pain constitutes an annoyance but does not impair the performance of any work activity. Pain in this category is not rateable and does not entitle the employee to any benefits; e.g., the employee's wrist aches when the weather changes.
2. **Slight Pain:** the employee can stand the pain but there is some handicap in performing an activity that brings on the pain; e.g., the employee's knee hurts when he bends so he bends more slowly than before the injury.
3. **Moderate Pain:** the employee is able to tolerate the pain, but there is a noticeable handicap in performing an activity that causes the pain to occur; e.g., the employee's finger hurts when he types and the pain causes him to make errors.
4. **Severe Pain:** the employee cannot tolerate an activity that causes the pain to occur; e.g., the employee gets such excruciating headaches when he tries to read that he is simply unable to read at all.

Use of only one of the four terms described above may be inaccurate for describing a particular disability. Physicians are encouraged to describe the level of pain as accurately as possible by using any combination of the terms that is more definitive of the employee's degree of pain. For instance, the severity of pain may be described as minimal to slight, slight to moderate, or moderate to severe.

10.31 MEASUREMENT OF PAIN – FREQUENCY

The employee's disability may vary in severity from time to time depending upon the activities performed and the employee's tolerance for pain. For this reason, a description of the severity of pain may be insufficient to quantify the extent of a disability. Unless a pain is present all of the time, it is also necessary to know how often the pain impairs the employee's ability to perform any affected activities In a report, the physician must render an opinion on the frequency of occurrence as well as the duration of the pain in addition to correlating the pain to specific work activities and evaluating the severity of the pain. Four standard terms are used to describe the frequency of pain. The physician should be thoroughly familiar with each of the following terms and their meanings:

1. **Constant:** the employee has the disability all or almost all of the time.
2. **Frequent:** the employee has the disability approximately 75% of the time.
3. **Intermittent:** the disability is only present approximately 50% of the time.
4. **Occasional:** the disability manifests itself approximately 25% of the time (there is no noticeable effect of the disability for approximately 75% of the time).

The above terms can be combined to more accurately describe the actual frequency of the pain. For example, the frequency of the pain may be described as: occasional, becoming intermittent at times; intermittent, becoming constant upon performance of specific activities; or occasional upon awaking, frequent by late morning, and constant by late afternoon.

With the exception of constant pain involving neck, back, pelvis, and abdominal disabilities, all ratings of permanent disability that are based on frequency of pain are nonscheduled disabilities for which a standard rating must be derived. The standard rating for any scheduled disability assumes that the disability exists all or nearly all of the time. Likewise, when the employee's pain is categorized as "constant," the employee's pain is deemed to be present all of the time. However, if the pain is not always present, a standard rating must reflect the frequency of occurrence. The full value of a standard rating for constant pain is reduced by up to approximately one-fourth for a frequent pain and one-half for pain that is intermittently disabling. If the pain is occasional, approximately one-fourth of the value for constant pain will be used in the rating formula instead of the scheduled standard rating for the most analogous scheduled disability.

10.32 WORK RESTRICTIONS – PROPHYLACTIC

Disabilities can be stated in terms of restrictions or preclusions from the performance of designated activities, and a restriction can be based on objective and/or subjective factors of permanent disability. One employee may be objectively restricted from climbing ladders due to a fused knee joint. The same restriction could be based on pain factors. The percentage of disability would be the same for a different employee who is precluded from climbing ladders based on the physician's opinion that this activity causes pain that is categorized as severe. It does not matter whether a restriction is based on objective or subjective factors of disability. These employees have the same degree of disability, since they are both equally restricted from climbing ladders. Another employee would also be equally disabled if the physician stated the employee was prophylactically restricted from climbing ladders. This type of restriction is the most difficult to grasp. The percentage of disability will be the same in all three cases, but the last employee is physically able to climb ladders.

A prophylactic restriction is a precautionary or preventive restriction. This type of restriction can be based upon either objective or subjective factors of disability. The physician is not saying the employee cannot climb ladders: the physician is saying the employee should not do this activity. A physician gives a work restriction on a prophylactic basis when the physician believes that the employee's condition would deteriorate and result in increased disability if the employee performed the particular activity. For example, the employee may have instability of the knee joint after a knee surgery. The physician may believe that climbing ladders would cause the joint to give way and cause further damage to the knee joint. If so, the physician would restrict this activity on a prophylactic basis.

The use of the word "prophylactic" reflects the physician's belief that the employee is physically capable of performing the restricted activity. The employee may not have any problem if the employee climbs ladders once or even several times, but the physician believes the employee would be taking a health gamble by engaging in this activity. The employee is encouraged not to take this gamble by receiving the same disability benefits as another employee who cannot climb ladders. Both employees are deemed to be equally affected in their competitiveness in the labor market, because there is little difference between the employee who cannot climb ladders and the employee who has a high probability of further disability upon performing this activity.

The compensability of disability that is prophylactic in nature results from appellate decisions. For workers' compensation purposes, a prophylactic disability enjoys equal status to any other permanent disability. However, it remains to be seen how or if liability for payment for this type of disability under state workers' compensation laws may affect the obligations of an employer under the federal Americans With Disabilities Act (see 11.36).

10.33 WORK CAPACITY GUIDELINES

The 4/1/97 rating schedule contains a chart called "Spine and Torso Guidelines" and another called "Lower Extremity Guidelines" (or "Guidelines for Work Capacity" in the prior schedule). These charts enable certain disabilities to be described as a reduced capacity for performing specific work activities. Each of the guidelines contemplates that the employee has lost a different percentage of his preinjury capacity to perform such activities as lifting, bending, stooping, pushing, pulling, climbing, standing, and/or walking. The guidelines apply to disabilities to the neck, back, pelvis, rib cage, pulmonary system, abdominal area, lower extremities and from heart disease.

The types of disabilities to which the work capacity guidelines apply can all produce comparable disability for the same work activities. Standard ratings are listed next to specific descriptions of work activities. These standard ratings are used in the rating formula in place of the standard rating that appears in the schedule next to the appropriate disability number, e.g. 12.1-back or 11-3-heart (18.1-back or 6.3-heart in the prior schedule). A physician can describe the employee's disability by reference to one of the possible categories of work capacity described in the guidelines or by any appropriate combination of the categories.

The use of the work capacity guidelines to describe a permanent disability requires the physician to compare the employee's preinjury capacity with his post-injury capacity. A statement that the employee is restricted from lifting weights in excess of fifty pounds is meaningless in assessing disability because the employee may not have been able to lift this weight prior to the injury. It is preferable for the physician to state the amount of weight the employee was previously able to lift versus the weight the employee can now lift. The reduction in lifting capacity can then be stated as a loss of a specific percentage of an employee's preinjury capacity for lifting. Likewise, the physician must compare every restriction, limitation or preclusion that is reported with the employee's preinjury capacity to perform the activity. In all cases, the validity of the physician's opinion will be dependent upon the physician's ability to explain the factual basis upon which the physician was able to determine the employee's preinjury capacity.

10.34 MULTIPLE DISABILITIES – PYRAMIDING & OVERLAP

Pyramiding & Duplication – Single Injury

When the employee sustains multiple disabilities as a result of a single injury, disabilities to separate parts of the body are rated separately, but the separate percentages are not necessarily added together. The term "pyramiding" refers to the fact that simple addition of separately-rated disabilities can produce a combined percentage of disability that distorts the true overall effect of an injury on the employee's ability to compete in the labor market. A variety of procedures are used to ensure against pyramiding of disabilities from a single injury.

No matter how many separate disabilities the employee may have, the maximum overall rating for any single injury cannot exceed 100%. Further, if the employee is not 100% disabled, the rating must be less than 100%. One accepted method for combining disabilities in accordance with these precepts is to apply the Multiple Disabilities Table (MDT). This table is located in the back of the rating schedule and contains full instructions for its use. The table relies on a mathematical process that ensures that an overall rating will not exceed the 100% limit, and that the combination of two or more separate disabilities from a single injury will produce a rating that adequately represents the overall disability sustained. The Multiple Disabilities Table is intended to be a guide as to the overall level of disability from a single injury, but its use is not mandatory.

The rating for an amputation of any extremity represents the maximum labor disabling effect of any other injury to that extremity; for instance, loss of a hand, arm, foot or leg. Therefore, when the employee sustains multiple injuries to a single extremity, the combined rating for all separate disabilities cannot exceed the rating the employee would have received if the extremity had been amputated. A standard mathematical procedure is used to avoid pyramiding in single extremities. First, each disability is rated separately, and the disability producing the highest rating is identified. Next, the ratings for each of the remaining disabilities are added together. The employee receives the full amount of the rating for the greatest disability plus one-half the sum of the rating percentages for all of the lesser disabilities. The result is the combined percentage of disability for the employee's disability, and this percentage will be less than the rating for a complete amputation of the extremity.

When alternative standard ratings apply to a single disability, the correct standard rating is the one that entitles the employee to the highest percentage of disability after modification for age and occupation. For example, the employee may have a fingertip amputation that also causes a loss of motion in the finger and grip loss in the hand. Each of these is a separately-scheduled disability, since each could exist by itself. The employee's disability manifests itself in three ways that the schedule describes differently under three separate disability numbers. In such cases, each disability is rated separately, and the results are compared. The formula that produces the greatest percentage of disability is then deemed to be the correct formula for determining the employee's percentage of disability.

Duplication. The employee cannot receive more than one rating for the same disability or any part thereof that results from a single injury. In the preceding example, the employee is not entitled to receive the sum of the three separate ratings that apply, because this would amount to giving the employee duplicate credit for labor disabling effects of the injury that are fully encompassed within the highest rating. Combining ratings for equivalent factors of disability that are separately stated or described by a physician is referred to as duplication of disability. The goal of the rating is to determine the overall impact of the injury on the employee's ability to compete in the open labor market. This goal is achieved by a rating that considers every separate factor of disability but does not include double credit for any duplicate factors of disability.

Overlapping Disabilities

The term "duplication" refers to one injury that causes multiple disabilities. A Disability Evaluation Specialist has authority to determine all of the nonduplicative factors of disability that are caused by a single injury (see 10.35). The term "overlap" refers to duplication of factors of disability from multiple injuries or conditions. Disabilities overlap when some or all of the factors of disability that are currently present predated the employee's injury. Overlap involves the legal issue of apportionment under LC4750 (see 10.40). If a dispute arises, a judge has authority to determine whether and to what extent any current factors of disability overlap or are attributable to causes other than the industrial injury. The assignation of separate factors of disability to distinguishable causes is a legal, not a rating, issue. However, the expert opinion of a Disability Evaluation Specialist may be relied upon in determining the rating for factors of disability that are judicially determined to result from the current injury.

10.35 DISABILITY EVALUATION UNIT

At most local offices of the WCAB, the Division of Workers' Compensation employs individuals who perform permanent disability ratings. The official title of these individuals is Disability Evaluation Specialists (although, unofficially, they are called "raters"), and the department in which they work is called the Disability Evaluation Unit (DEU) of the Division of Workers' Compensation.

Prior to 1990, LC124 provided this Unit with the statutory duty to "facilitate and expedite the determination of the proper percentage of disability, if any, for injuries." Effective 1990, LC124 instead referred to the duties of this Unit as "those previously performed," and all reference to this unit was deleted from LC124 as of 1994. Reference to the function of this unit is now found solely in administrative regulations. Per CR10150, the Disability Evaluation Unit "will issue permanent disability rating determinations."

Anyone can perform a permanent disability rating. However, Disability Evaluation Specialists perform ratings as their sole job duty. They are considered to be experts in determining the percentage of disability based upon medical factors of disability, and they testify as expert witnesses on the evaluation of permanent disabilities in WCAB proceedings. Disability Evaluation Specialists routinely provide information and assistance on rating principles and procedures and the application of the rating schedule to particular disabilities. Rating formulas on individual cases can also be provided. Ratings are commonly prepared when requested by a Judge or an Information and Assistance Officer, upon the joint request of opposing legal counsel, or after submission of the comprehensive medical-legal report of the treating physician or a Qualified Medical Evaluator (see 7.80).

The employer can perform its own ratings as a basis for estimating its liability for permanent disability benefits. In fact, claimspersons must be competent at rating in order to set appropriate reserves on claim files (see 2.25) and assess the potential settlement value of contested claims. However, no matter how competent or accurate the employer's claims administrator may be at estimating its potential liability, a determination of the employee's permanent disability benefits will not be based upon the employer's self-rating. For the employee's protection, the extent of permanent disability must also be evaluated by the Disability Evaluation Unit or the WCAB.

10.36 SUMMARY RATINGS

Two forms are used to request a summary rating of permanent disability for unrepresented employees: the Employee's Permanent Disability Questionnaire (DEU Form 100) and the Employer's Request for a Summary Rating (DEU Form 101). Both of these forms were revised effective 1/28/94 as were administrative regulations applicable to permanent disability ratings (see CR10160-10166). Summary ratings are not required by LC4061 in cases where the employee is represented by an attorney, but CR10160.5 permits summary ratings to be obtained in such cases. (Note: represented employees are not required to submit a completed questionnaire form to an Agreed or Qualified Medical Evaluator as part of the summary rating process; see 7.79)

Per LC4061, if the employee is unrepresented, the evaluation of the treating physician can be submitted for a rating instead of or in addition to a summary rating based upon an evaluation of a Qualified Medical Evaluator (see 7.75). For 1994 or later injuries, this right represents a major statutory change, and this right applies only to cases where the employee is not represented by an attorney. Per LC4061, either "the unrepresented employee or the employer may submit the treating physician's evaluation for the calculation of a permanent disability rating." This language appears to imply that any party could exercise this right concurrently with a request for a summary rating of an evaluation by a Qualified Medical Evaluator. However, these rights are actually mutually exclusive.

The party who disputes the findings of the treating physician would submit an evaluation of a Qualified Medical Evaluator for a summary rating. A party who accepts the report of the treating physician would submit this report to the

Disability Evaluation Unit for a rating. As of 1/28/94, a request for a rating based upon the findings of the treating physician would constitute a request for a "consultative rating" under CR10166. The employee's age and occupation must be included with a request for a consultative rating (although not required by CR10166, it is unlikely that a consultative rating will be issued for an un-represented employee unless the employee's questionnaire form is also included).

Appeal of Summary Rating

Since 1991, LC4061 only requires permanent disability to be rated by the Disability Evaluation Unit in cases where the employee is not represented by an attorney. For this reason, the right to request reconsideration of a summary rating pursuant to LC4061 applies only to cases involving an unrepresented employee. (When the employee is represented, the parties have the right to request a rating from the Disability Evaluation Unit and/or to commence proceedings and have disputed issues adjudicated by the WCAB.)

The party who is dissatisfied with a summary rating can request the Administrative Director of the Division of Workers' Compensation to "reconsider the recommended rating." An appeal of a summary rating pursuant to LC4061 is limited in scope to a review of the four issues that are listed on the form required for this purpose, a Request for Reconsideration of Summary Rating (DEU Form 103). If an appeal is based upon an improper calculation of the rating, further medical information is not necessary. If deficiencies in the medical evaluation that was rated are the basis for an appeal, the rating will be recalculated when such deficiencies have been corrected. The three deficiencies that are set out in LC4061 include: some relevant issues were not addressed; some medical issues were not completely addressed; or, an evaluation was "not prepared in accord with the procedures of the Industrial Medical Council promulgated" pursuant to LC139.2(j)(2) or (3) (see 7.80). (Note: the employer may concurrently have valid objections to payment for services by a particular physician; see 7.73 and 7.80.)

If reconsideration is granted on a medical basis, the Administrative Director's authority to correct deficiencies is limited by LC4061 and is different for 1991-1993 injuries than for 1994 or later injuries. For 1991-1993 injuries, the Administrative Director may be requested to "obtain additional evaluations from a qualified medical evaluator." Reference is made to evaluations (in the plural) since the employer and the employee may both seek reconsideration of the same report but allege different issues. However, upon granting reconsideration for either party, LC4061 mandates that the Administrative Director "shall return the report to the qualified medical evaluator" whose report was submitted for a summary rating "for appropriate action as the administrative director instructs."

For 1994 or later injuries, the parties may request the Administrative Director to "obtain additional evaluations from the treating physician or medical evaluator," since the employer and/or the employee may have relied upon the findings of the treating physician in lieu of a Qualified Medical Evaluator. As of 1994, upon granting reconsideration, LC4061 mandates that the Administrative

Director "shall return the report to the treating physician or qualified medical evaluator" whose report is being appealed "for appropriate action as the" Administrative Director instructs.

There is no statutory time limit for the Administrative Director to act on a request for reconsideration of a summary rating. Depending upon the grounds asserted, a decision may be made without the need for an amended rating. The Administrative Director may determine that all relevant medical issues were fully addressed by the Qualified Medical Evaluator despite a party's assertions to the contrary. In this case, the parties will receive a written notice that the request for reconsideration is denied. In other cases, the parties will receive an amended summary rating. Amended ratings may be issued after receipt of a supplemental report from a Qualified Medical Evaluator. Alternatively, amended ratings may be issued after recalculation of a previous rating to reflect revised factual information; e.g. after the Administrative Director determines that a prior rating used an incorrect occupational group number or compensation rate.

The employer or the employee can submit a treating physician's report to the Disability Evaluation Unit for a summary rating (along with the employee's questionnaire form which is always required to obtain a rating when the employee is unrepresented.) However, a Qualified Medical Evaluator is required to submit a report directly to the Disability Evaluation Unit and send copies to the parties at the same time. Upon review of its copy, the employer or the employee may identify defects in the physician's report. Depending upon the defects involved, it may be deemed reasonable to request a supplemental report from the same physician; e.g. where necessary measurements are not included or the report fails to mention all body parts that are included on the employee's claim form. The claims administrator will usually assume responsibility for requesting a supplemental report from a Qualified Medical Evaluator in a manner that avoids ex parte communications (communication with an evaluator will be in writing with service on all parties; see 7.79).

Prompt action is required when reports submitted to the Disability Evaluation Unit are deficient in and of themselves or in view of later-received reports from the treating physician. In the optimum situation, a supplemental report would be provided to the Disability Evaluation Unit before a summary rating is issued. However, this is ordinarily not possible because a summary rating will usually issue more quickly than a supplemental report can be obtained. Instead, the employer will request a supplemental medical report, and this report will then be used to support a request for reconsideration of the summary rating — unless the employer's request for a supplemental report was untimely.

Per CR10164, the "Administrative Director shall not accept or consider, as a basis for a request for reconsideration, a supplemental or follow-up evaluation that was requested by a party after a summary rating determination has already been issued to the parties." A report need only be requested, not necessarily obtained, before a summary rating issues in order to protect the employer or employee's rights on appeal. The parties would otherwise retain the right to adjudicate the disputed rating at the WCAB but would lose a valid basis for an administrative appeal.

10.37 PROPOSED RATINGS

For 1994 injuries, LC4065 requires the employer and the employee to submit a "proposed permanent disability rating" to the WCAB in some, but not all, cases where permanent disability benefits are disputed. When submission is required, LC5502 requires proposed ratings to be included in the pretrial conference statement that is filed with the WCAB when "a claim is not resolved at a mandatory settlement conference." (The term "baseball arbitration" has received widespread use in reference to the proposed ratings required by LC4065 despite the fact that this statute has nothing to do with baseball or arbitration.) Proposed ratings are not required by LC4065 in any case where the parties can resolve permanent disability issues without the need for WCAB proceedings; permanent disability issues have been evaluated by an Agreed Medical Evaluator (see 7.78); or, the only opinions in dispute are those of a treating physician. Proposed ratings are required by LC4065 only in cases where:

1. One or both parties dispute the treating physician's determination of permanent disability issues pursuant to LC4061, AND
2. One or both parties have obtained an evaluation of permanent disability from a Qualified Medical Evaluator pursuant to LC4061 (including an evaluation from a panel-QME if the employee is unrepresented), AND
3. One or both parties contest the comprehensive medical evaluation of the opposing party's QME, AND
4. The parties cannot agree informally regarding a permanent disability settlement amount.

Per CR10633, a proposed rating shall include the disability number and standard rating for each body part "resulting in permanent disability" (see 10.32). There is no requirement for a party to support its proposed rating by reference to any particular medical evidence. The employer may propose a rating that is based upon the range of evidence (considering all medical evidence). The employee may propose a rating based upon testimony of disability that the employee intends to present in the case. Although not required, a party may submit alternative ratings. For instance, the employer may concurrently submit a proposed rating before apportionment as well as after apportionment, thus making its proposed rating contingent upon the prerequisite judicial finding on the issue of permanent disability apportionment (see 10.47).

Where LC4065 is silent on specific details regarding proposed ratings, any reasonable efforts of the parties that are intended to facilitate resolution of disputed issues are usually appreciated by the WCAB. For instance, the parties may be able to stipulate to the age and/or occupation to be used for rating purposes yet still dispute the standard rating for the disability sustained (see 10.32), or the parties may stipulate that disability has been sustained to certain body parts but not others.

When the parties are required to submit proposed ratings, the WCAB "shall be limited to choosing between either party's proposed permanent disability rating." A judge has no discretion as to the part of the body or the standing rating. However, LC4065 does not negate nor dilute a judge's authority to issue an award that is based upon proper evidence. For instance, the judge can issue formal instructions to the Disability Evaluation Unit regarding the occupation to be used in a rating formula. The provisions of LC4065 apply solely to cases where the parties have already exercised their right to obtain medical evidence that can support the extent of disability that they propose should be awarded. Furthermore, the WCAB is not required to choose between the parties ratings until after a hearing at which evidence on permanent disability can be presented.

After the WCAB makes its selection between the proposed ratings, the unsuccessful party will owe the costs of the successful party's comprehensive medical evaluation. If the WCAB selects the employer's proposed rating, the employee's award will be reduced. If the employee's proposed rating is selected, the employee's award will be increased by the appropriate amount.

Payment to the Qualified Medical Evaluator whose report was not utilized to resolve the issue of disputed permanent disability is not affected by the provisions of LC4065. The party who selected this evaluator will bear an adverse financial consequence. However, it is possible for the WCAB to reject a proposed rating for reasons unrelated to the quality of medical evidence (e.g. where a proposed rating is outlandish or handwritten and illegible). If multiple contested issues were evaluated, it is entirely possible that issues other than the extent of permanent disability may be resolved based upon this physician's findings (e.g. the issue of "scope of further treatment" under LC4062). Naturally, the party who selects and pays for an evaluation that is not persuasive on the issues addressed is not likely to refer future cases to the same physician.

10.38 CONSULTATIVE RATINGS

In litigated cases where the employee is represented by an attorney, the parties can obtain consultative ratings from a Disability Evaluation Specialist. In cases where the employee is not represented, an Information & Assistance Officer can obtain a consultative rating (usually for the purpose of reviewing the adequacy of a proposed settlement that has been submitted to the WCAB as is required by CR9927). If a summary rating is required by LC4061, a summary rating must be obtained and not a consultative or informal rating (see 10.36).

Consultative ratings (as well as summary ratings) are normally computer-generated at the Disability Evaluation Unit on paper that does not contain any official insignia. The rating will identify the physician's name and the date of the report that is rated. A consultative rating is purely advisory in nature. Consultative ratings are not obtained for the purpose of being admitted as evidence in judicial proceedings, nor are Disability Evaluation Specialists subject to cross-examination regarding such ratings. Generally, the purpose of consultative ratings is to assist in the resolution of disputes regarding the extent of the employee's permanent disability without the need for formal WCAB proceedings to be conducted by a judge on this issue.

A consultative rating can be based on one medical report or any group of medical reports. Sometimes the parties will jointly select the examining physician, and a rating will be requested solely on the basis of factors of disability contained in the report of this Agreed Medical Evaluator. More frequently, opposing parties will request separate ratings on medical reports that each has obtained on its own behalf. The consultative rating procedure provides an expeditious method for obtaining ratings of opposing medical reports in cases where LC4061 does not require a summary rating.

10.39 APPORTIONMENT OF DISABILITY

The employer's liability for permanent disability benefits is limited to payment for disability that results from an industrial injury. Three Labor Code sections provide the employer with a legal basis for apportioning, or subtracting out, factors of disability that are due to some other cause. The employer does not owe compensation for any disability the employee may have that:

1. Existed at the time of the industrial injury (LC4750), OR
2. Is caused solely by the normal progression of a disease process regardless of the occurrence of any industrial injury (LC4663), OR
3. Results solely from a noncompensable injury sustained subsequent to an industrial injury (LC4750.5).

Each of the three Labor Code Sections that is referenced above is based upon the provisions of Article XIV, Section 4 of the California Constitution that limit the employer's liability to payment for disability "sustained by the said workers in the course of their employment" to the extent of "relieving from the consequences of" an industrial injury. The employer owes full compensation for all disability that did not exist at the time of injury and is present at this time because of the effects of the industrial injury. The employer is not required to provide compensation for any portion of the overall disability that would exist regardless of whether the employee has sustained an industrial injury.

Depending upon the circumstances, the employer may seek apportionment under one, two, or even all three of the apportionment statutes on a single claim. The type of evidence that is necessary to meet the employer's burden of proof on this affirmative defense will vary to some extent according to the statute under which apportionment is being claimed. However, in all cases, it will be necessary for a physician to determine the overall factors of disability and specify those factors that are a result of the industrial injury as opposed to factors of disability having some other cause. Each of the separate Labor Code sections on this topic are covered separately in the sections that follow.

10.40 APPORTIONMENT – PREEXISTING DISABILITY

Per LC4750, if the employee is "suffering from a previous permanent disability or physical impairment" at the time the employee sustains an industrial injury, the employer has no liability to compensate the employee for the preexisting permanent disability. This disability cannot be a consequence of the industrial injury since it was present before the industrial injury was sustained. The employer's burden of proof under LC4750 can be summarized as: establishing the existence of objective and/or subjective factors of disability that adversely affected the employee's ability to compete in the open labor market at the time an industrial injury was sustained. Specifically, the employer must establish all of the following facts:

1. The employee incurred a prior permanent disability, AND
2. The previous disability was labor disabling, AND
3. Some or all of the previous disability was present at the time of a later industrial injury, AND
4. The precise factors of objective or subjective disability that were present that affected the employee's ability to compete in the open labor market at the time the industrial injury was sustained.

Disability can result from industrial injuries, nonindustrial injuries, congenital conditions, illnesses, or disease processes. The identity of its source can direct the employer to the location of previous records, available documentation, and medical evidence regarding the nature and extent of the previous disability. For instance, a search of WCAB records would be conducted if the prior disability was sustained in an industrial injury, and a police report that described injuries and the name of the hospital that provided emergency care would be obtained if the employee had an automobile accident. Disabling injuries can occur at home, during recreational or athletic activities, in military service, or while traveling; the possibilities are limitless. An assessment of the employee's interests, hobbies, past endeavors, and general activities can guide an investigation towards identification of potential sources of previous disability.

The fact that the employee was permanently disabled at some past time is not sufficient to support a claim for apportionment. It is a well-established fact that some employees are successful in rehabilitating themselves from the effects of a "permanent" disability through diligent efforts and that some or all of a "permanent" disability may diminish or disappear with the mere passage of time. Therefore, the employer must also prove that some or all of the previously sustained disability was still present and labor disabling at the time of the later industrial injury. The employer must accumulate evidence that establishes that the employee's past and present employment as well as personal activities do not contradict its allegations that the employee was suffering from specific factors of preexisting permanent disability on the date of injury.

The fact that the employee was unaware of a disability does not negate its existence. The employee can suffer from the effects of a labor disabling condition without any previous medical diagnosis, formal notification to the employee or any known effect on the employee's performance of any activity of choice. A preexisting disability need not be apparent on the job where an injury subsequently occurs.

The employee can be fully capable of performing all physical tasks required in the date-of-injury employment but still have a disability that would affect the ability to compete elsewhere in the labor market or even to perform a different job with the same employer. This situation is referred to as a "congenial work setting," in relation to the preexisting permanent disability. For example, the employee may first become aware that his vision is impaired during the course of an examination for a minor industrial eye injury that does not result in any permanent disability. The employee may insist that his vision was perfect prior to the injury. However, medical evidence can confirm both the existence and the nature and extent of the preexisting vision impairment of which the employee had no knowledge.

Generally, the employee will attempt to defeat the employer's claim for apportionment of permanent disability under LC4750 by showing that the employee never sustained any prior disability, did not have any disability on the date of the industrial injury or that the disability was not as great as the employer alleges. In this regard, the employer should be prepared to overcome the following types of allegations:
1. The employee did not sustain any injury in the past.
2. The employee did not sustain any disability as a result of a past injury.
3. The employee did not have any preexisting illness or disease.
4. The employee did not suffer any disability as a result of any preexisting illness or disease process.
5. Any disability that existed in the past was temporary, not permanent, disability.
6. The employee overcame a specified portion of his previous permanent disability.
7. The employee achieved a full recovery or rehabilitation from the effects of his prior permanent disability.
8. The employee was able to perform all of the duties of his employment without restriction or difficulty.
9. The employee had no disability that affected his ability to compete in the open labor market.
10. The employee was unrestricted in any activities of his choosing.

10.41 APPORTIONMENT – PROPHYLACTIC RESTRICTIONS

A prophylactic restriction is a rateable permanent disability and constitutes a valid basis for a workers' compensation permanent disability award. For this reason, the existence of a prophylactic restriction (that was imposed for a prior industrial injury or any cause other than the current industrial injury) constitutes a preexisting disability for purposes of apportionment under LC4750. However, the fact that the employee is at all times physically capable of performing a prophylactically restricted activity creates a dilemma for the employer when it claims apportionment. The employee may or may not have performed the restricted activity, and this fact may or may not negate the existence of a prophylactic disability at the time of an industrial injury.

The employee may have received a prior WCAB award of permanent disability that was based upon a prophylactic restriction. At a future date, the employee may rely upon the fact that he later performed the restricted activity as evidence that he has rehabilitated himself from the previous disability. The employee's point may be well taken where a great deal of time has elapsed since the prophylactic restriction was rendered, or the employee's adjustment to the disability took place gradually, and/or the employee took positive steps toward overcoming the disability such as a course of exercise or medical therapy.

From the employer's perspective, the fact that the employee's physical activities have not exceeded a prior restriction constitutes evidence of the prior disability. Evidence of a preexisting disability would also appear sufficient where the employee does engage in the restricted activities and sustains a later industrial injury upon performance of the precise activity that was restricted. However, a judge will consider it very relevant to know the number of times the activity was performed prior to an injury. The employee may have successfully rehabilitated himself (no apportionment because no preexisting disability) or he may simply have taken the gamble with his health that he was advised against (still suffering from a prior disability).

Evidence of a failure to achieve rehabilitation from a prior disability may consist of proof that an injury occurred upon a first attempt to perform, or actual performance of, the restricted activity. Additional evidence will be required where the employee chooses to repeatedly engage in a prophylactically restricted activity even with full realization of the potential for deleterious results. It is necessary to know the number of times that the activity has been performed, over what period of time (short duration or long-term), how recently the activity has been performed, and under what circumstances. Regardless of the employee's explanation for performing particular activities, the employee's denial of disability can be refuted with evidence that the employee was adversely affected by the performance of the restricted activity. For instance, the employee may have been temporarily disabled for a short time or may have required medical treatment, medication, or special exercises.

In reviewing physician's opinions, the claimsperson must be able to identify a retroactively-applied prophylactic restriction, because this type of restriction does not constitute a preexisting disability and does not provide any basis for apportionment. The physician describes a retroactively-applied restriction when s/he reports the opinion that s/he would have advised the employee not to perform certain work activities if s/he had known in advance that the employee planned to engage in an employment where such activities would be required ("s/he" means "he" or "she").

A retroactively-applied prophylactic restriction is a "hindsight" medical opinion without any value, and the fact that the opinion is based upon objective medical findings such as pre-employment X-rays does not increase its value. The employee cannot be said to be suffering from a preexisting disability where both the employee and the employer are unaware of any disability, and an injury results from engaging in the exact duties that the employee was hired to perform and did perform without difficulty prior to an injury.

When discussing apportionment, careful attention should be given to semantics. A restriction that is retroactively identified as being in place prior to an industrial injury, as opposed to a retroactively applied restriction, can support a claim for apportionment. In the case of a retroactively identified restriction, the employee had a previous disability that was labor disabling, but the disability was first identified and described by a physician after an injury occurred. The employee may not have realized that he suffered from a disability, or its extent, but the disability did in fact exist. In order for the physician's opinion to be valid, the previous disability must be compatible with the employee's employment history, and the restriction (prophylactic or otherwise) must not be contradicted by the employee's unimpaired performance of the restricted activity in his personal or employment environment.

10.42 APPORTIONMENT – PREEXISTING DISEASE

Per LC4663, "in case of aggravation of any disease existing prior to a compensable injury, compensation shall be allowed only for the portion of the disability due to the aggravation of such prior disease that is reasonably attributed to the injury." To support apportionment under this statute, the employer must establish all of the following:

1. The employee has a disease.
2. The disease process commenced prior to the injury.
3. The disease is a type that causes permanent disability.
4. The specific factors that affect the onset of disability from the disease (e.g. passage of time, heredity, diet, or injury).
5. The existence of one or more of the factors that affect the onset of disability from the disease.
6. One of these factors is not the aggravative effect of an industrial injury.
7. The disease did result in permanent disability.
8. Some of the employee's disability resulted from the disease process independently of the aggravative effects of the industrial injury.
9. A portion of the overall disability would exist at this time in the absence of the occurrence of an industrial injury.
10. The precise factors of disability, objective and/or subjective, that are explained solely by the existence of the disease process.

The employer is not required to prove the existence of any disability at the time of injury. Rather, LC4663 requires that the disease process itself predate the injury. At the time that the employee's condition is permanent and stationary, a physician must delineate all of the separate factors that comprise the employee's overall disability into three categories:

A. All disability due solely to the industrial injury is compensable. If all disability falls into this category, there is no basis for apportionment of any of the employee's disability.

B. All disability resulting from the aggravative effects of an industrial injury upon a preexisting disease is also compensable. Per LC4663, this disability is considered to be disability resulting from an industrial injury and therefore compensable.

C. Any additional disability arising solely from the normal progression of the disease process is not compensable (e.g. where an injury causes a flare up of a disease process but the condition resolves with treatment to a preinjury level). Disability in this category is not a result of an industrial injury. This disability is due to a preexisting disease, and this disability would be present even if the employee had not sustained any industrial injury.

Employees can overcome claimed apportionment under LC4663 with proof that all of the employee's disability was either caused by the industrial injury or is due to the aggravative effects of the industrial injury. The employer's reporting physician should prepare to address the following employee allegations that are usually relied upon in medical opinions by the employee's examining physician:

a. The disease was asymptomatic at the time of injury: the employee never suffered any disability until an industrial injury aggravated the disease; ergo, there would not be any disability from the disease if there was no industrial injury.

b. Absent an injury, no disability would be present at this time: the industrial injury resulted in the onset of disability from disease in advance of its normal progression; ergo, all present disability is a result of aggravation of the disease.

c. The industrial injury was serious enough to alter the normal progression of the disease process: a great degree of disability exists after the injury, but the normal progression of the disease would be expected to produce a lesser degree of disability in the time elapsed since the injury. When the employee relies upon this allegation, the validity of apportionment is usually not disputed. Rather, the employee is attempting to increase the portion of the overall disability that is compensable (attributable to the aggravative effects of the injury).

The employer's success in obtaining apportionment for disability caused by a preexisting disease is directly proportionate to the competence of the reporting physician in understanding the provisions of LC4663. Repeatedly, the appellate courts have indicated that the physician must be thoroughly familiar with the nature of the preexisting disease and its normal progression.

When physicians are asked to opine on the disability a particular disease is capable of producing at a particular point in time and under what circumstances, physicians sometimes feel they are asked to give answers to questions that have no answer in the world of medicine. However, physicians are not expected to do the impossible. Physicians are considered to be expert witnesses on medical matters, and as such, they are expected to be able to provide opinions that are stated in terms of reasonable medical probabilities. In every case, a physician is required to support every opinion by appropriate explanation as to the basis for it. Opinions that are speculative or stated as mere possibilities are inadequate as medical evidence on apportionment or any other medical issue.

10.43 APPORTIONMENT – SUBSEQUENT INJURY

Per LC4750.5, where the employee "subsequently sustains an unrelated non-compensable injury," the employee "shall not receive any permanent disability indemnity for any permanent disability caused solely by the subsequent noncompensable injury." This Labor Code section became effective on 1/1/84 and enjoys the rare distinction of stating legislative intent by naming a specific appellate court decision. The purpose of LC4750.5 "is to overrule the decision in Jensen v. WCAB, 136 Cal. App. 3d 1042." However, future judicial interpretation may involve application of this statute to additional fact situations. The stated language of LC4750.5 appears to give the employer the burden of establishing all of the following facts:

1. The employee sustained a compensable industrial injury.
2. Subsequently, the employee sustained a different injury.
3. The subsequent injury is not compensable.
4. The subsequent injury was not proximately caused by the prior industrial injury.
5. The subsequent injury resulted in disability.
6. Those specific factors of objective and/or subjective disability that are solely a result of the later injury.

The subsequent noncompensable injury could be industrial or nonindustrial. The employee may sustain another work-related injury after he returns to work with his previous employer or a new employer. If the later injury is a compensable one, LC4750.5 does not apply (but LC4750 could apply; see 10.40). However, a claim for apportionment would appear to be appropriate if a judge finds that the subsequent industrial injury is noncompensable; for instance, the claim is barred by a statute of limitations, or there is a valid initial physical aggressor defense. In this event, the employer would deny liability for any portion of the employee's overall disability that is attributable solely to the later injury.

A subsequent injury may not be a different injury. If the initial injury is the proximate cause of the subsequent injury, no new injury has occurred. For example, if the employee falls from a hospital bed and fractures a wrist while hospitalized for a previous industrial injury to a leg, the subsequent injury is a consequence of the previous injury. Under such circumstances, no new injury has occurred, and the employer has full liability for disability that may result from the initial injury as well as the subsequent injury that was proximately caused by the initial injury.

The claimsperson should obtain early and continuous medical estimates of the factors of permanent disability that are anticipated to result from the industrial injury. If the employee later sustains a noncompensable injury, the physician is then capable of rendering a credible medical opinion as to the factors of disability that resulted solely from the later injury and can distinguish between the employee's overall disability and that disability that would reasonably result solely from the industrial injury. This type of preparedness will strengthen the potential for a successful claim of apportionment under LC4750.5.

10.44 SUBSEQUENT INJURIES FUND

Per LC4751, the employee can claim permanent disability benefits directly from the state's Subsequent Injuries Fund (SIF) in special circumstances. Claims against the Subsequent Injuries Fund are handled by the Claims Unit of the Division of Worker's Compensation.

The initial qualifying criteria for benefits requires that "an employee who is partially disabled receive a subsequent compensable injury resulting in additional permanent partial disability so that the degree of disability caused by the combination of both disabilities is greater than that which would have resulted from the subsequent injury alone." The second qualifying criteria is that the permanent disability rating for the employee's overall disability must equal or exceed 70%. (Note: if the disability was due solely to an industrial injury, the employee would qualify for a permanent disability life pension). Having met these two criteria, the employee must also meet the criteria that are set forth in either subsection (a) or (b) of LC4751 as explained below.

1. LC4751(a). The standard rating for the prior permanent disability (prior to adjustment for age or occupation) is 5% or more of the overall rating, and both disabilities involve an "opposite and corresponding member" of the body. specifically – the opposite hand, arm, foot, leg or eye, OR
2. LC4751(b). The standard rating for the industrial disability alone (without modification for age or occupation) "is equal to 35 percent or more of the total" rating percentage for the combined or overall disability.

The establishment of the Subsequent Injuries Fund serves two basic purposes. Employees are assured that they will not go uncompensated for any increased disability resulting from the combined effect of their prior disability and an industrial injury for which the employer has no liability. Employers are encouraged to hire individuals with disabilities by knowing that their liability for compensation for injuries will not be greater in the case of a worker with a preexisting disability than for workers without a disability. (Note that an injured worker with a disability is not necessarily a "qualified individual with a disability" as that phrase has meaning for purposes of an employer's compliance with the provisions of the federal Americans With Disabilities Act.)

The combined effect of two disabilities can produce a greater degree of overall permanent disability than is reflected by simple addition of their separate percentages. This increased effect-in-concert is referred to by the term synergism, meaning basically that the sum of the parts can be greater than their mathematical total because of their interaction with one another. This concept is graphically demonstrated by a review of the standard ratings assigned to various disabilities in the *Schedule for Rating Permanent Disabilities.* For example, loss of sight in one eye is assigned a standard rating of 25%; whereas, loss of sight in both eyes receives a standard of 100%, not 50% (25% + 25%). The synergistic effect of a loss of sight in two eyes results in a much more significant disability than that reflected by a 50% rating.

An employee who is totally blind is 100% disabled under the rating schedule. If the industrial injury resulted in a loss of eyesight in only one eye, the employer's liability for compensation is limited by law to payment of disability that results from the industrial injury, or a 25% standard rating. It is the increased disability that is present after (but is not a result of) the industrial injury that provides a basis for a claim for payment from the Subsequent Injuries Fund. Even so, some employees who meet the statutory eligibility criteria of LC4751 will not be entitled to Subsequent Injury Fund payments.

Per LC4753, the Subsequent Injuries Fund is entitled to a credit for any payments the employee may have received for the prior disability "from any source whatsoever" (with some exceptions not covered here). The purpose of the credit provision is to ensure that employees are not doubly compensated for any disability. If the employee's prior disability was compensated by payment of a large civil damage award, it is possible that the Subsequent Injuries Fund would not owe any additional payments or would not owe further payments until some distant time in the future when this credit had been fully applied. In all cases, the credit provision applies to any workers' compensation permanent disability benefits that the employee is entitled to receive or has received in the past.

SAMPLE (a). The employee previously lost his left eye in a skiing accident and was never compensated for this disability. On 4/15/96, the employee sustained an industrial injury and lost the sight in his right eye. The industrial loss of sight produced a rating of 25%. The employee's compensation rate is $400/wk, based upon earnings of $600/wk.

Overall Disability: 100% = $400/wk for life
Industrial Disability: 25% = $164/wk for 95.75 weeks

Payments to employee for first 95.75 weeks:

$164.00	From employer
+236.00	From SIF
$400.00	Total of weekly payments to employee

Payments to employee after first 95.75 weeks:
$400.00/wk for life from Subsequent Injuries Fund

Note: If the employee's loss of sight in the left eye also resulted from an industrial injury, SIF payments would not commence until such time as credit had been taken for the full amount of the prior WCAB award. Credit would be taken at the rate of $236/wk for the first 95.75 weeks and $400/wk thereafter.

SAMPLE (b). The employee previously lost the sight in her left eye after cataract surgery and was never compensated for this nonindustrial disability. On 2/7/97, she sustained an industrial injury and lost the sight in her right eye that produced a rating of 25%. The employee's compensation rate is the maximum rate based upon earnings of $800/wk.

Overall Disability: 100% = $490.00/wk for life
Industrial Disability: 25% = $170.00/wk for 95.75 weeks

Payments to employee for first 95.75 weeks:

$170.00   From employer
+320.00   From SIF
$490.00   Total of weekly payments to employee

Payments to employee after first 95.75 weeks:

$490/wk for life from Subsequent Injuries Fund

A claimsperson's awareness of the provisions of LC4751 can prove advantageous in resolving permanent disability issues with an injured worker. Entitlement to Subsequent Injury Fund payments does not require that the previous disability result from an industrial injury, that the employee was aware of its existence, or that the employee ever received compensation of any kind. An employee with a back injury who has only one arm (due to a congenital defect) may be pleased to learn of potential entitlement to Subsequent Injuries Fund benefits in addition to permanent disability benefits that are owed. The employee will be even more pleased if the claims administrator is willing to assist the employee by requesting and paying for a medical report that contains medical opinions on all issues that are relevant to the employee's eligibility for Subsequent Injuries Fund benefits.

There may not be any medical records concerning the extent of a prior disability from a congenital defect (or other nonindustrial condition or injury). However, the claimsperson will, as a routine matter, obtain a medical determination of the factors of permanent disability that are due to the industrial injury. The same physician who makes this determination can also be asked to report regarding the employee's overall disability and any factors of current disability that have not resulted from the industrial injury claim. By this action, the claimsperson can avoid the possibility that the employee might be deterred from seeking Subsequent Injuries Fund benefits due to the expense of obtaining necessary medical evidence.

10.45 EDD – UNEMPLOYMENT & DISABILITY LIENS

As of 1994, the Employment Development Department (EDD) has statutory authority to seek a lien recovery against the employee's permanent disability benefits. Previously, liens of the Employment Development Department were recoverable only against an award of temporary disability benefits because employees could qualify to receive unemployment compensation benefits from the Employment Development Department concurrently with receipt of permanent disability benefits. An employee who was eligible for unemployment compensation insurance benefits could only receive such benefits if the weekly rate for such benefits exceeded the employee's compensation rate for permanent disability benefits. In such cases, the employee was entitled to the difference from the Employment Development Department.

For 1994 or later injuries, LC4904 provides that the WCAB shall allow the lien of the Employment Development Department "in the amount of benefits which it finds were paid for the same day or days ... for which an award of ... any permanent disability indemnity resulting solely from the same injury or illness or temporary disability indemnity, or both, is made and for which the employee has not reimbursed the" Employment Development Department pursuant to UIC2629.1. Therefore, the amount of Employment Development Department payments of unemployment compensation disability benefits now constitute a valid lien against the employee's permanent disability benefits. The effect of this 1994 change is that procedures that formerly applied to Employment Development Department liens against temporary disability benefits now also apply to liens against permanent disability benefits that are payable to the employee (as explained in 9.37).

(THIS PAGE LEFT BLANK INTENTIONALLY)

[11] REHABILITATION

11.1 REHABILITATION – IN GENERAL

Rehabilitation in general refers to the process of recovery from, and adaptation to, the effects of an injury. Vocational rehabilitation refers specifically to services that provide assistance in overcoming the work-debilitating effects of an industrial injury. There is one reason for workers' compensation rehabilitation benefits: to return the employee to work.

Major changes to the rehabilitation category of workers' compensation benefits apply to employees injured on or after 1/1/94. Employees are generally not entitled to rehabilitation benefits unless their employers do not provide modified or alternative employment that a permanently disabled employee is able to perform (see 11.26). Benefits are subject to a variety of time limits and monetary caps that, collectively, reduce the employer's cost to provide rehabilitation benefits and restrict the scope and duration of benefits for employees. In LC4635.1, the Legislature declares that rehabilitation "provides an important tool for the retraining of injured workers. However, it is equally important that this retraining should be provided in an efficient and cost-effective manner."

11.2 REHABILITATION UNIT – GENERAL DUTIES

The Rehabilitation Unit of the Division of Workers' Compensation is created pursuant to the authority of LC139.5. (Prior to 1990, this unit was known as the "Rehabiliation Bureau," and some forms that are currently required for claims involving injuries occurring prior to 1990 have form numbers that begin with an "RB" designation.) The Rehabilitation Unit is staffed with "Rehabilitation Consultants." The duties of the professional staff of the Rehabilitation Unit are set out in LC139.5 as:

1. "To foster, review, and approve vocational rehabilitation plans developed by a qualified rehabilitation representative" of the employer, employee, or the Rehabilitation Unit.
2. "To develop rules and regulations ... providing for a procedure" that allows for a waiver of "the services of a qualified rehabilitation representative" in cases where an employee's rehabilitation will involve completion of a collegiate program that is already in progress (see 11.11).
3. "To develop rules and regulations ... which would expedite and facilitate the identification, notification, and referral of industrially injured employees to vocational rehabilitation services."
3. "To coordinate and enforce the implementation of vocational rehabilitation plans."
4. "To develop a fee schedule ... governing reasonable fees for services provided."
5. "To develop standards ... for governing the timeliness and the quality of vocational rehabilitation services."

In 1990, an inter-industry advisory committee was established by LC4647 to assist "in recommending forms, procedures, and rules and regulations consistent with the effective administration of this article" (meaning Labor Code Sections 4635-4647). As a result of recommendations of this committee, the Rehabilitation Unit has published standards entitled *California Standards Governing Timeliness and Quality of Vocational Rehabilitation Services*. The contents of this report are advisory or informational in nature and do not supplant any requirements under the Labor Code or the Code of Regulations. These standards are useful to the parties in appraising the reasonableness of various rehabilitation procedures based upon the commonly accepted standards that are described within this report. However, these standards are not binding upon the Rehabilitation Unit since they are advisory in nature rather than required.

The Rehabilitation Unit has been given broad powers to enforce the employer's liability for rehabilitation benefits. General authority for actions of the Rehabilitation Unit will be found in the Labor Code, administrative regulations and case law (and is further clarified by internal procedural guidelines as explained below). The rules and regulations of the Rehabilitation Unit are a matter of public record and published in the Code of Regulations (CR10122-CR10133.4). These rules establish time limits for required actions by the parties, definitions of terms, the use of prescribed forms for various purposes, the content of required employee notices and procedures for the resolution of disputes.

The Rehabilitation Unit itself requires that each Rehabilitation Consultant adhere to so-called "administrative guidelines." (Note: Rehabilitation Unit Consultants are required to adhere to ethical standards that also apply to WCAB judges and auditors; see 1.15). The guidelines are a compilation of separate written policy statements on specific topics. The administrative guidelines are intended to assist Rehabilitation Consultants in the issuance of determinations on specific disputed issues in a uniform and consistent manner on a statewide basis. The guidelines serve an affiliated purpose of providing all parties with the opportunity to determine the Rehabilitation Unit's posture on a variety of issues prior to initiating the dispute resolution process.

The majority of currently applicable administrative guidelines took effect 2/14/97, but revision of these internal guidelines is an ongoing process. Copies of the *Rehabilitation Unit Administrative Guidelines* are available to interested parties upon request. It is anticipated that the administrative guidelines will ultimately meet all criteria that are legally required to officially call such guidelines the "policy and procedure manual" of the Rehabilitation Unit. Meanwhile, the title "administrative guideline" is appropriate when referring to any specific section(s) of this publication. For instance, A.G. 1-10-01 permits deviations from the administrative guidelines only after a Rehabilitation Consultant has obtained approval of the consultant's Area Supervisor.

The Rehabilitation Unit maintains district offices throughout the State, usually in the same buildings as district offices of the Workers' Compensation Appeals Board. Per CR10123, information regarding currently required forms, filing instructions, and venue lists that identify the proper local district office where forms are required to be filed are available from the Rehabilitation Unit, P.O. Box 420603, San Francisco, CA 94142.

Rehabilitation Consultants do not provide rehabilitation benefits or services to injured workers, and they should not be confused with rehabilitation counselors who actually provide rehabilitation services and sometimes refer to themselves as rehabilitation consultants. Rehabilitation Consultants who are employed within the Rehabilitation Unit are considered to be experts regarding workers' compensation rehabilitation matters. They provide information and assistance to interested parties upon request, act in a regulatory capacity to ensure that proper and timely benefits are provided to qualified workers, and have the authority to resolve disputes that arise and issue determinations and orders affecting the rights and duties of employees and employers.

By virtue of a variety of forms that are required to be submitted under various circumstances, the Rehabilitation Unit will receive notification of every case in which the employer either provides or disputes its liability for rehabilitation benefits (see 11.24). The Rehabilitation Unit assigns its own case number to each case that involves some action by this unit. The party who requests the first Rehabilitation Unit action on the case is required to submit a Case Initiation Document (DWC Form RU-101). This form operates to generate assignment of a case number. The form also provides the Rehabilitation Unit with basic identification information including the names, addresses and telephone numbers of the parties involved (that explains the secondary required use of this form for advising the Rehabilitation Unit of any changes in this data; see CR10123).

The Case Initiation Document (CID) must accompany all required documentation to be submitted to the Rehabilitation Unit where a Rehabilitation Unit case number has not yet been assigned. The person submitting this form and/or any other required form is also required to attach copies of all medical and vocational reports that have not previously been submitted to the Rehabilitation Unit and, on the same date, to serve all parties with a copy of any of these documents that have not previously been provided to them. Information regarding specific forms and reporting requirements is detailed in subsequent sections (see CR10123).

11.3 REHABILITATION UNIT – DISPUTES

The Rehabilitation Unit's involvement in disputes arises only after opposing parties admit defeat in attempting to resolve a dispute among themselves. The Rehabilitation Unit's involvement serves the purpose of enabling resolution by a statutorily designated expert without the delays inherent in litigation at the WCAB.

The Rehabilitation Unit has the authority to require a vocational evaluation at the employer's expense. This authority is usually not exercised unless the employer fails to cooperate in providing timely information to the Rehabilitation Unit or unless another opinion is necessary to resolve disputes. (Note: if the treating physician's determination of medical eligibility is disputed, referral to an Agreed or Qualified Medical Evaluator is required by LC4062; see 7.75.) The Rehabilitation Unit can order the employer to provide rehabilitation services or issue a determination that the employee is not entitled to services. Prior to issuing such extreme decisions, the Rehabilitation Unit will make reasonable inquiries to determine the position of the parties.

Per CR10127, either the employer or the employee can request the Rehabilitation Unit to resolve a dispute by submission of a Request For Dispute Resolution (DWC Form RU-103). The Rehabilitation Unit will not make an expert determination based upon incomplete information nor will it consider that a valid dispute exists when one party possesses more information than another. For this reason, the Rehabilitation Unit requires copies of any medical and vocational reports that were not previously provided to be forwarded to an opposing party concurrently with submission to the Rehabilitation Unit. Per CR10127, an opposing party is allowed 15 days from receipt of a Request for Dispute Resolution form to forward its "position with supporting documentation to the Rehabilitation Unit with copies to all parties."

The Rehabilitation Unit favors resolution of disputes with a primary reliance upon a review of written information. The scheduling of a formal conference at the Rehabilitation Unit is disfavored because this manner of resolution is not expeditious, and it is the most time-consuming option for the Rehabilitation Consultant assigned to the case. Before a formal conference is scheduled, the Rehabilitation Unit expects the parties to meet with each other to confer and attempt to resolve a dispute by themselves. This meeting is referred to as an "informal conference." Historically, the parties have met face-to-face, but it is becoming more common for an informal conference to be conducted as a telephone conference call. Even if a dispute cannot be resolved informally, the Rehabilitation Unit may still not grant a formal conference.

Per CR10127, the Rehabilitation Unit "shall either issue its determination based on the record, ask for additional information, or set the matter for formal conference." A determination shall issue within 45 days of "receipt of the original request." Even if a formal conference is scheduled, the parties are not necessarily expected to appear. Per CR10127.1, the parties can request permission to cancel a conference if a dispute is otherwise resolved. Also, "any party unable to attend the conference may submit his/her position, on the issue(s) in writing" to the Rehabilitation Unit.

After a formal conference is held, CR10127.1 requires the Rehabilitation Unit to "issue a determination based on its file, information provided during the conference, and any written positions submitted prior to or at the time of the conference." The Rehabilitation Unit is required to issue its decision within 30 days of the conference date. However, if the Rehabilitation Unit requested additional information at the formal conference, the 30 days runs "from the date of receipt of all further requested information." For instance, if the Rehabilitation Unit orders the employer to obtain a written opinion from an Independent Vocational Evaluator, submission will occur thirty days after receipt of this document.

The procedures above do not apply to expedited conferences under LC4643 that are conducted when the employee objects to the employer's written notice of intent to withhold payment of maintenance allowance benefits. (See 11.9 for an explanation of requirements for expedited conferences.) Also, for 1994 or later injuries when a dispute involves "identification of a vocational goal," CR10127 provides that the Rehabilitation Unit can conduct a telephone conference. If this approach is unsuccessful, then a formal conference will be "held on an expedited basis within 10 days."

Note that CR10127 pertains to an employee who is undisputably entitled to rehabilitation benefits but has not commenced a rehabilitation plan because the parties cannot agree on an appropriate vocational goal for the employee. Expedited services are provided because these cases involve a solitary final issue that is delaying participation in an appropriate rehabilitation plan (11.22).

11.4 SUITABLE GAINFUL EMPLOYMENT

The end result of successful rehabilitation is "suitable gainful employment" (SGE) for the employee. This term is defined in LC4635. The definition enables all parties to ascertain the factors that control the Rehabilitation Unit's approval or disapproval of any particular rehabilitation program (see 11.22 for situations where Rehabilitation Unit approval of a rehabilitation plan is not required). The detail provided in the definition can assist employees in developing realistic expectations of rehabilitation benefits. Employers can direct their efforts appropriately. A proposed rehabilitation plan will receive Rehabilitation Unit approval if it can reasonably result in suitable gainful employment considering all the elements of the definition of this term as explained below.

Suitable gainful employment can be either "employment or self-employment" (for a listing of suitable gainful employment alternatives, see 11.11). The proposed employment must meet each of the following criteria:

    a. It is "reasonably attainable." It must be readily apparent that the employee is capable of completing the program.

    b. It causes the employee to be rehabilitated "as soon as practicable." The sooner the rehabilitation occurs, the more effective it usually is.

    c. It provides an earnings level "as near as possible to maximum self-support." The employee must be able to support himself and his family at the proposed level of earnings.

There may be several alternative programs, all of which could achieve the above goals. The employer may seek Rehabilitation Unit approval for the least costly plan, that usually means the plan that can be completed in the shortest period of time. The employee may request approval of the "best" available plan, that could be the longest program or the most expensive alternative; e.g. the employee might agree on a vocational goal but insist on attending a renowned trade school in another state (see 11.11).

Per LC4635, in determining whether proposed employment is "suitable gainful employment," the Rehabilitation Unit will give "due consideration" to several factors. These factors may warrant approval of one plan versus other proposals, or they may warrant a Rehabilitation Unit determination that the employee is not a qualified injured worker and not entitled to rehabilitation at employer expense.

The five criteria that Rehabilitation Consultants are bound to consider in review-ing a plan are discussed separately below.

1. The "Employee's Qualifications"

It must be apparent that the employee possesses the knowledge and skills needed to perform the proposed work. Knowledge and skills may exist either because of the employee's previous work experience, as a result of vocational training incorporated as part of a proposed plan, or both.

2. "Likely Permanent Disability"

It must be reasonable to anticipate that the employee will be medically capable of performing the physical demands of the prospective employment after the employee has received the maximum benefit from medical treatment. (The employee may commence pre-employment activity such as training before active medical treatment is concluded or the employee's condition is permanent and stationary; see 10.8.)

3. The Employee's "Vocational Interests and Aptitudes"

A plan has potential for success when the employee likes the proposed type of work and is committed to completion of the plan. The employee's lack of interest reduces the potential for successful completion of the proposed plan or any effective long-term rehabilitation into the proposed employment. The employee may not want to work at the moment or any time in the future. If so, no amount of rehabilitation will provide suitable gainful employment. The employee may be motivated by financial gain to participate in a program solely to receive a fraudulent extension of workers' compensation payments. If this fact is verifi-able, the employee is not a qualified injured worker (and a fraud report must be filed with the Department of Insurance; see 2.30).

The only reason the employee works may be to save money for educating his children rather than for self-support. Once this goal is reached, the employee may not have further incentive for continued employment. The employee's reasons for working must be assessed before a suitable gainful employment goal can mesh with these incentives. Ultimately, each case requires a judgment decision as to whether there is a reasonable expectation that the employee intends to pursue the vocational objective of a proposed rehabilitation plan as a new vocation.

The employee's personal preferences and any special talents are relevant only to the extent that they relate to a reasonable employment goal. The rehabilitation category of benefits is not intended to provide employees with the job they have always dreamed of doing at the employer's expense.

Suppose the employee is medically precluded from bowling. The employee may have been a championship bowler whose personal life has long revolved around bowling. Notwithstanding the employee's stated interest in returning to work only in a position where he can utilize his knowledge of bowling, the Rehabilitation Unit will consider the employee's interests and aptitudes only to the extent that they have a direct correlation to a reasonably attainable employment goal (and, see #5 below).

4. "Preinjury Earnings and Future Earning Capacity"

The employer is not obligated to seek out new employment opportunities at an employee's preinjury level of earnings. The reduced physical capacity that qualifies an employee for rehabilitation benefits will usually mean a reduction in the employee's overall earning capacity (if the injury had no adverse effect on the employee's competitiveness for available jobs in the open labor market, the employee would not have a compensable permanent disability and would therefore not qualify for receipt of rehabilitation benefits). Earnings in the employee's occupation at the time of injury may have been much higher than entry level earnings that are presently available in any other occupation that the employee may be physically capable of performing.

The employee may demand a salary that even after training is not available in the local labor market. If the employee demands an unreasonably high level of earnings, the Rehabilitation Unit may decide that the employee is not a qualified injured worker. It may not be possible to achieve the employee's goals through the provision of rehabilitation services. A suitable gainful employment is usually one that will provide the highest level of earnings that the employee is reasonably capable of earning. Anything less than this may be seen as an attempt by the employer to provide inexpensive, rather than effective, rehabilitation.

5. The "Present and Projected Labor Market"

The purpose of rehabilitation is to provide the employee with continued future employment on a long-term basis. After rehabilitation, there must be a job market for the employee's new occupation. If the employee loses the first job, there must be other jobs for which the employee can effectively compete. The employment must not be so highly specialized or competitive that the employee is not likely to hold long-term employment. Economic conditions, particularly in the employee's geographical area, are a pertinent consideration. Occupations that are seasonal, temporary, or especially susceptible to fluctuations in the economy are not suitable gainful employments. A suitable gainful employment is not "a job." It is an occupation that offers continued employment, albeit with different employers, in that portion of the labor market that is realistically accessible to the employee.

Since 1990, LC4638.5 requires the utilization of "occupational supply and demand information from the California Occupational Information System" (as established under UIC10530 et seq.), but only "if the system is available in the labor market area." Per UIC10532, a coordinating committee has the duty to "develop and annually revise a plan for the use of available resources to design and implement a statewide comprehensive labor market and occupational supply and demand information" as required under federal law. This system is currently in its infancy but will ultimately provide access to data that will increase efficiency in matching people seeking jobs with jobs needing to be filled by people in a particular area. Further details regarding supply and demand information available from the State system may be obtained from the California Occupational Information Coordinating Committee, P.O. Box 94422, Sacramento, CA 94244.

11.5 BENEFITS – THREE TYPES

Per LC139.5, there are three, and only three, categories of rehabilitation benefits. Each of these is the topic of following sections. Every payment the employer makes as a rehabilitation benefit will be for one of the following:

1. Maintenance allowance.
2. Additional living expenses.
3. Vocational rehabilitation services.

11.6 MAINTENANCE ALLOWANCE – BASIC DISTINCTIONS

For 1990 or later injuries, employees who are entitled to rehabilitation benefits are entitled to receive a maintenance allowance. This benefit is commonly referred to as a "vocational rehabilitation maintenance allowance" or "VRMA," although the Labor Code refers to this benefit merely as a "maintenance allowance." An understanding of the rehabilitation maintenance allowance category of benefits requires that the following preliminary distinctions be made:

a. Basic Maintenance Allowance: a payment that the employer is required to make under LC139.5 in the "amount the employee would have received as continuing temporary disability indemnity" except that the rate cannot exceed the maximum compensation rate that is specified in LC139.5, and this amount is lower than the maximum rate for temporary total disability benefits (see 9.4).

b. Permanent Disability Supplements: the employee has the right to request and receive advance payments of permanent disability benefits in a weekly amount that is equal to the difference between the employee's compensation rate for temporary total disability benefits (including increases that the employee would be entitled to receive under LC4661.5 if temporary total disability was payable more than two years after the date of injury; see 9.5) and the employee's lower compensation rate for a basic maintenance allowance.

c. Full Maintenance Allowance: a payment that the employer is required to provide in the same weekly amount as temporary total disability benefits would otherwise be payable to the employee with no portion being credited against permanent disability benefits. This payment is required under LC4642 only during periods where the employer is responsible for a delay in the provision of appropriate rehabilitation benefits.

11.7 MAINTENANCE ALLOWANCE – COMPENSATION RATE

Per LC135.9, the compensation rate for a vocational rehabilitation maintenance allowance is computed as "two-thirds of the employee's average weekly earnings at the date of injury." Low wage earners are subject to the same minimum average weekly earnings limits in LC4453 that would apply if temporary total disability benefits were payable to the employee (see 9.4), so these employees' compensation rate will be the same for both categories of benefits. However, the maximum compensation rate for vocational rehabilitation maintenance allowance benefits is lower than that payable for temporary total disability benefits (except where benefits are unreasonably delay as explained below).

The maximum compensation rate for a basic vocational rehabilitation maintenance allowance is the maximum rate that was specified in LC139.5 on the date of the injury (unlike LC4453, LC139.5 specifies a maximum compensation rate, not a maximum earnings amount). From 1990-1997 (and until the next legislative change), LC139.5 specifies $246/wk as the maximum compensation rate for vocational rehabilitation maintenance allowance benefits. This benefit rate is ⅔ of $369/wk.

Any employee injured in 1996 whose average weekly earnings were less than $369 will receive the same compensation rate for rehabilitation indemnity and temporary total disability indemnity benefits, and this rate will be less than $246/wk. The compensation rate for an employee who earned more than $369/wk will ordinarily be $246/wk, and this rate will be less than the employee's compensation rate for temporary total disability benefits (unless a penalty applies under LC4642 as explained below).

SAMPLE (a). Julie earned $300/wk on a part time job when she was injured on 2/2/96, and she was paid $200/wk for temporary total disability benefits. Julie is entitled to receive vocational rehabilitation maintenance allowance benefits from 8/8/96 until 3/13/97.

$$AWE \ \$300 \times ⅔ = \$200/wk \ CR \ for \ TTD \ benefits$$
$$AWE \ \$300 \times ⅔ = \$200/wk \ CR \ for \ VRMA \ benefits$$

SAMPLE (b). Richard earned $366/wk when he was injured on 4/15/96. Temporary total disability benefits were owed at $244/wk, and Richard is entitled to VRMA indemnity payments from 2/9/97 until 6/15/97.

$$AWE \ \$366 \times ⅔ = \$244/wk \ CR \ for \ TTD \ benefits$$
$$AWE \ \$366 \times ⅔ = \$244/wk \ CR \ for \ VRMA \ benefits$$

NOTE: Neither Julie nor Richard above can opt to receive supplemental payments of permanent disability since their compensation rate is less than the maximum rate for rehabilitation indemnity that is set out in LC139.5.

Increase in Rate After Two-Years. Any increase in the statutory maximum average weekly earnings amount that applies to temporary total disability benefits can affect an employee who is entitled to receive rehabilitation indemnity benefits (e.g. the increases under LC4453 that took effect on 7/1/94, 7/1/95, and 7/1/96). If the employer is ordered to pay a maintenance allowance at the same rate as temporary total disability indemnity as a penalty (for the delayed provision of rehabilitation benefits per LC4642), the compensation rate for the maintenance allowance must include each increase that would be required for payments of temporary total disability pursuant to LC4661.5 (see 9.5 and Sample #c below).

In all cases, it is necessary to ascertain the employee's current compensation rate for temporary total disability benefits in order to correctly compute the weekly rate of payment for concurrent permanent disability payments that the employee has opted to receive to supplement his vocational rehabilitation maintenance allowance (see 11.7). As initially established in 1990, the maximum compensation rate for a maintenance allowance was $246/wk. The maximum compensation rate for maintenance allowance benefits has remained the same from 1990 through 1997 (and until the next change).

However, the maximum weekly rate of payment for concurrent permanent disability indemnity that is payable has increased each time the maximum compensation rate for temporary total disability benefits was increased. From 1991-6/30/94, this difference amounted to a maximum of $90/wk (the maximum temporary total disability compensation rate of $336/wk − $246/wk maximum rate for rehabilitation indemnity). The maximum amount payable as a weekly permanent disability supplement is $160 as of 7/1/94, $202 as of 7/1/95, and $244 as of 7/1/96. (Note: permanent disability that is payable concurrently with rehabilitation indemnity is not payable at the same rate as permanent disability indemnity alone would be payable and can in fact exceed the maximum compensation rate for permanent partial disability payments; see 10.9)

SAMPLE (c). David earned $696/wk when injured on 1/13/95. David was paid temporary total disability benefits at the maximum compensation rate of $406/wk until he became eligible to receive VRMA payments commencing on 10/28/96. David is unhappy about the lower weekly rate for VRMA benefits and wants to receive supplemental payments of permanent disability benefits if this is permissible.

(1). Optional PD payments if David is entitled to VRMA from 10/28/96 - 1/12/97 (within two years from the date of injury).

Earnings $696 = $609 AWE × ⅔ $406/wk   CR for TTD benefits
Earnings $696 = $369 AWE × ⅔   −246/wk   CR for VRMA benefits
                        Difference $160/wk   Optional PD payment

(2). Optional PD payments if David is still entitled to VRMA benefits as of 1/13/97 (more than two years after the date of injury; see 9.5).

Earnings $696 = $696 AWE × ⅔ $464/wk   CR for TTD benefits
Earnings $696 = $369 AWE × ⅔   −246/wk   CR for VRMA benefits
                        Difference $218/wk   Optional PD payment

Penalty For Delay. Labor Code 4642 provides that the maximum compensation rate for a vocational rehabilitation maintenance allowance that is specified in LC139.5 does not apply when an employer fails to comply with its statutory requirements for the prompt provision of rehabilitation benefits. Employer-caused delays can result in the employer being ordered to pay vocational rehabilitation maintenance allowance benefits at the employee's temporary disability rate as a penalty. In this event, all payments owed during the period of the delay will be exempt from monetary caps and time limits on rehabilitation benefits that would otherwise apply (see 11.28-11.29).

SAMPLE (d). Brad earned $750/wk when he was injured on 7/22/96. Temporary total disability benefits were payable at the maximum rate of $490/wk. The Rehabilitation Unit determined that the employer unreasonably delayed the provision of VRMA benefits from 11/14/96 - 1/26/97. The employer owes a full maintenance allowance for this period and a basic maintenance allowance thereafter, plus Brad wants to receive optional supplemental payments of his permanent disability benefits (see 11.7).

Earnings $750 = $735 AWE × ⅔	$490/wk	CR for TTD benefits
Earnings $750 = $369 AWE × ⅔	−246/wk	CR for VRMA benefits
Difference	$244/wk	Optional PD payment

Prior to 1/27, $490/wk is owed for VRMA with no credit allowed against PD.
As of 1/27, $246/wk is owed for VRMA.
As of 1/27, $244 is owed for PD supplements.

11.8 MAINTENANCE ALLOWANCE – QUALIFYING CRITERIA

Upon concurrence of the four events that are listed below, temporary disability benefits cease. Effective 1994, LC139.5 provides that the employer is liable for the payment of a basic maintenance allowance and, at the employee's option, may also be liable for the provision of permanent disability supplements when:

1. The employee "is determined to be medically eligible," AND
2. The employee's "medical condition becomes permanent and stationary," AND
3. The employee "chooses to participate in a vocational rehabilitation program," AND
4. The employee makes a "request for vocational rehabilitation services."

A high wage earner may be motivated to delay a medical determination of permanent and stationary status or a decision to participate in a rehabilitation program in order to prolong the payment of temporary disability benefits at a higher compensation rate. Per LC139.5, an employee can supplement lower rehabilitation benefits with optional payments of permanent disability benefits (see examples in 11.7). However, the employee may prefer to prolong the receipt of temporary disability benefits instead of using up any of his permanent disability benefits, or there may be insufficient permanent disability benefits available to supplement a maintenance allowance up to the employee's temporary disability rate for the duration of rehabilitation services. Lump sum payments while temporarily disabled may have provided the employee with all or nearly all permanent disability benefits that are owed for the employee's percentage of disability (see 10.19 regarding WCAB considerations in allowing lump sum payments).

The reason(s) for any delayed acceptance of offered rehabilitation services should be solicited and addressed. However, the employer is not obligated to provide maintenance allowance benefits to employees who do not request vocational rehabilitation benefits after receipt of required notifications. An employee cannot prolong the receipt of temporary disability benefits (usually at a higher rate of payment than a vocational rehabilitation maintenance allowance) by failing to respond to a notice of medical eligibility for rehabilitation.

If an employee whose condition has become permanent and stationary fails to respond to a notice of medical eligibility for rehabilitation benefits, the employer will commence payments of permanent disability benefits only. The employee will not become entitled to maintenance allowance benefits and optional permanent disability supplements unless and until the employee notifies the employer that he wishes to receive rehabilitation benefits (see 11.18). This financial incentive is intended to encourage prompt requests for rehabilitation benefits.

Maintenance allowance benefits are not payable if an otherwise qualified employee does not "choose to participate" and signs a Statement of Decline of Rehabilitation Benefits (DWC Form RU-107A). The employer will also be relieved of liability for maintenance allowance benefits if an employee unreasonably fails to cooperate in the provision of rehabilitation services or if rehabilitation services end before the employee's condition becomes permanent and stationary. Maintenance allowance benefits are not owed if the employee does not sustain a wage loss as a result of participation in a rehabilitation plan, e.g. where the date of injury employer continues full earnings under a salary continuation plan and/or the employee's existing skills enable direct placement in a new job as soon as the employee is no longer temporarily disabled.

11.9 MAINTENANCE ALLOWANCE – PAYMENT ISSUES
During Disputed Medical Eligibility

Temporary disability benefits are payable until the employee's condition becomes permanent and stationary (see 10.8). If "the employer disputes the treating physician's determination of medical eligibility" after the employee's condition is permanent and stationary, the employer is then required by LC139.5 to pay the basic vocational rehabilitation maintenance allowance benefit "pending final determination of the dispute" (but not permanent disability supplements). When either party disputes the treating physician's determination of medical eligibility, a determination by an Agreed or Qualified Medical Evaluator is required by LC4062.

If the employee disputes the treating physician's determination of medical eligibility and "prevails," LC139.5 requires the employer to provide payment of a basic maintenance allowance benefit "retroactive to the date of the employee's request for vocational rehabilitation services." In this event, the claim file payment record must be corrected.

The claimsperson will compute the dollar amount of maintenance allowance benefits that are owed for the number of weeks and days that the dispute was pending. Payments that were made during this period and labeled as "permanent disability" are now deemed to have been payments of maintenance allowance benefits, and an appropriate accounting entry will be made in the claim file payment records. Any remaining unpaid balance of maintenance allowance benefits will be paid to the employee. (Note: the compensation rate for a basic maintenance allowance will be higher than the employee's permanent disability compensation rate except in cases of earnings of $105 or less per week.) The employee must also be provided with a corrected benefit information notice that specifies the amount, rate, and dates of payment for both permanent disability benefits and maintenance allowance benefits.

If the Rehabilitation Unit determines that the employer's refusal to provide benefits was unreasonable, the employer will be ordered to pay a full maintenance allowance retroactive to the date a dispute arose. This Rehabilitation Unit determination could in turn result in assessment of an administrative penalty under LC129.5 (at a dollar amount specified in CR10111.1).

During a Failure to Cooperate

Effective 1994, LC139.5 mandates the adoption of administrative regulations "to ensure that the continued receipt of ... maintenance allowance benefits is dependent upon the injured worker's regular and consistent attendance at, and participation in, his or her vocational rehabilitation program" (see 11.21). Effective 2/21/95, CR10125.1 specifies grounds that constitute an unreasonable failure to cooperate. Such behavior includes "unreasonable failure to attend scheduled meetings and unreasonable failure to follow-up on tasks assigned in the development or implementation of a vocational rehabilitation plan." Usually, it is a Qualified Rehabilitation Representative who will inform the employer of the employee's failure to cooperate in some phase of the provision of rehabilitation services.

Per LC4643, the employer is required to provide the employee with advance written notice when it intends to withhold maintenance allowance payments because "the employee unreasonably fails to cooperate in the provision of vocational rehabilitation services." Effective 1/7/94, CR9813 requires the employer to provide this notice at least 15 days before it ceases payments. The employer will usually send this notice by certified mail, return receipt requested, to obtain evidence of the date received, because the employee has the right to object within 10 days of receiving this notice. If the employee objects, the Rehabilitation Unit is required by LC4643 to conduct an expedited conference and to issue its written determination "within 10 days of receipt of the employee's objection." Effective

1995, LC4643 no longer requires the Rehabilitation Unit to serve its decision by certified mail.

Absent an objection from the employee, the employer can cease payments on the 16th day following the employee's receipt of the written notice of intent to withhold maintenance allowance benefits that is required by LC4643. If the employee objects within the allotted 10-day period, the employer must continue to pay a basic maintenance allowance until receipt of the determination of the Rehabilitation Unit regarding the dispute. It would be cost effective for the employer to obtain this determination by telephone rather than waiting to receive the Rehabilitation Unit's determination in the mail after an expedited conference. If the Rehabilitation Unit's decision is not timely provided by mail or cannot be obtained by phone, the employer will remain legally liable to continue payments after the Rehabilitation Unit has determined that an employee is ineligible to receive such benefits.

Manner & Frequency of VRMA Payments

Maintenance allowance benefits are payable in the same manner as temporary disability benefits (see 9.14). Since 1990, LC4650 has required temporary disability benefits to be paid every 14 days on the day of the week designated with the first payment. Effective 1/1/94, CR10125.1 specifically requires that payments of a vocational rehabilitation maintenance allowance also comply with the 14-day payment schedule established by LC4650. Equivalent benefit information notices are required by LC138.4 and CR9812-CR9813 for both categories of benefits (see 9.15). The employee must be advised in writing of the commencement, termination or any change in the type or amount of benefits that are paid. A major distinction between these two categories of benefits is that a 10% self-imposed increase for late payments under LC4650 does not apply to maintenance allowance payments. However, other statutes do provide financial penalties for the late payment of vocational rehabilitation maintenance allowance benefits.

The employee's compensation rate for a basic maintenance allowance will usually be higher than the employee's permanent disability compensation rate (except when weekly earnings are $105 or less). For 1990 or later injuries, maintenance allowance benefits are payable at the same rate as temporary disability indemnity if the employer "causes any delay in the provision of vocational rehabilitation services" (see 11.7). For 1994 or later injuries, LC4642 further provides that the amount of rehabilitation indemnity benefits that are not timely paid do not count against the overall monetary cap on rehabilitation benefits that is specified in LC139.5. Also, if a delay "is primarily the result of actions of an insurer, any increase in the costs that result shall be charged against the insurer's expenses," as explained below.

Presume a compensation rate of $246/wk for rehabilitation and $348/wk for temporary disability indemnity. If the Rehabilitation Unit determines an insurer unreasonably disputed the employee's vocational feasibility for an 8-week period, rehabilitation indemnity would be payable retroactively at $348/wk, and

$816 ($348 − $246 = $102 × 8 weeks) would be chargeable as a claim expense. If the employer was responsible for an 8-week delay (e.g. by the provision of inadequate or inaccurate information concerning the physical requirements of the employee's preinjury position), the additional $816 that is payable as a penalty for delay is chargeable as a loss (it will be included in the reserve posted to the claim and can therefore affect the employer's insurance premium; see 2.24).

52-Week Limit on VRMA Payments

For 1994 or later injuries, LC139.5 provides that maintenance allowance payments "shall not exceed 52 weeks in the aggregate." The 52-week period is cumulative weeks of payments, not consecutive calendar weeks. Maintenance allowance benefits could be payable more than one year after payments commence if entitlement is intermittent, e.g. if there has been an interruption of services. There are three basic exceptions to the 52-week limit on payments as explained below. Where an exception applies, maintenance allowance payments can exceed the 52-week time limit for payments as well as the overall monetary cap that would otherwise apply.

Per LC139.5, the 52-week limit does not apply to payments of a basic maintenance allowance that the Rehabilitation Unit retroactively determines to have been payable for periods when the employee's medical eligibility was disputed. Per LC4642, if the employer is responsible for any delay in the provision of a basic maintenance allowance or other rehabilitation benefits, the employer shall pay a full maintenance allowance "for the period of the delay" (as a penalty), and such payments "shall not be subject to the overall cap on" rehabilitation benefits.

Lastly, LC4644 allows for exceptions that extend the 52-week limit for maintenance allowance payments where the Rehabilitation Unit determines that the employer is liable for the costs of a second vocational rehabilitation plan. (No more than 52 additional weeks of maintenance allowance benefits will be allowed for a second plan, and the other two exceptions explained here equally apply to initial or second plans.)

Penalty For Delay

Per LC4642, the employer owes a full maintenance allowance, with no portion credited against the employee's permanent disability benefits, during any period when the employer does not timely provide rehabilitation benefits that are due or "causes any delay in the provision of vocational rehabilitation services." This provision of LC4642 has relevance only to employees whose compensation rate is higher for temporary disability than for maintenance allowance benefits (see 9.4). However, LC4642 provides an additional financial penalty for employer delay.

The full amount of any rehabilitation maintenance allowance benefits that are determined to have been unreasonably delayed are owed by the employer over and above the monetary limit that is otherwise established by LC139.5 as the monetary cap on rehabilitation benefits. The employer can be ordered to pay a full maintenance allowance retroactive to the date a dispute arose if the

Rehabilitation Unit determines that rehabilitation benefits were payable and the employer's refusal to provide benefits was unreasonable. This determination could in turn result in the assessment of an administrative penalty under LC129.5 and at a dollar amount set out in CR10111.1.)

11.10 BENEFITS – ADDITIONAL LIVING EXPENSES

"Additional living expenses" are mentioned in LC139.5 but are not explained in the Labor Code. This benefit refers to some item of expense that is not usually contemplated by the provision of temporary disability or maintenance allowance indemnity benefits. Both of these indemnity payments are wage replacement payments that provide for expenses that would ordinarily be paid out of the employee's earnings. Thus, regular temporary disability indemnity provides payment for the employee's usual and customary living expenses. Routine expenses include rent, food, clothing, loan payments, car upkeep, home maintenance, utility bills, and other incidental expenses. "Additional living expenses" refers to living expenses that:

1. Are unique to the provision of rehabilitation benefits: the expense is not incurred during receipt of any workers' compensation benefit except rehabilitation.
2. Would not be incurred if the employee did not participate in vocational rehabilitation services: participation means receipt of services during the development and completion of a Rehabilitation Plan.
3. Arise for the first time on or after the date the employee first receives rehabilitation benefits: the necessity for the expense did not exist previously and will not continue to exist after rehabilitation benefits end.

All reasonable expenses of transportation that are necessitated by the employee's receipt of vocational rehabilitation services are considered to be an additional living expense. In most instances, travel involves a local commute, and the employer is obligated to provide mileage reimbursement at the same rate payable for medical transportation expense (see 7.17). The employee may live in a remote area. If it is necessary for the employee to obtain lodging in a different locality where a rehabilitation program can be provided, the expense of lodging and food over and above the employee's usual expenses for these items is additional living expense.

The employee may be required to purchase uniforms as part of a rehabilitation program. Clothing is an ordinary living expense, but the cost of newly-required uniforms is an additional living expense for the duration of rehabilitation services. Once a rehabilitation program is completed, the ongoing expense of new uniforms or cleaning expenses becomes an ordinary living expense for the employee.

If the employee had to pay for a babysitter while working (or at other times) prior to the injury, then payment for child care expenses during a rehabilitation program is not an "additional living expense." While an employee is receiving temporary disability benefits, payment for babysitting services is undisputably the employee's personal responsibility, e.g. child care services while the employee is hospitalized. The living expenses provided by temporary disability benefits do not discriminate by providing a higher monetary benefit to employees with children versus those without. It is only for purposes of establishing death benefits that the Legislature has deemed it appropriate to provide for increased benefits because the employee has children.

The employee may refuse to participate in a rehabilitation program because the employee refuses to pay for child care expenses. The employee may have grown accustomed to not having to spend money for this expense since the injury, or the employee may be motivated by financial gain with a primary interest in having the employer pay for as many expenses as possible. The employer may object for the reasons mentioned above, or it may take the position that the employee is not interested in rehabilitation services and is using this expense item as an excuse not to participate. The Rehabilitation Unit may view this cost as a minor problem that is preventing the employee from otherwise successful rehabilitation, and it can order the employer to pay for child care expenses.

There are many gray areas. No item of expense can be unique to the provision of rehabilitation services nor "necessitated by" the provision of "vocational rehabilitation services" as required by LC139.5 if the expense would be incurred even if the employee had never been injured and never needed rehabilitation services. However, the employer can anticipate that it may be ordered to pay "minor" expenses (subject to applicable monetary caps) when the Rehabilitation Unit determines that a reluctant employee will participate in a rehabilitation program if further financial incentive is provided.

11.11 BENEFITS – VOCATIONAL SERVICES & TRAINING

A qualified injured worker's right to receive "vocational training" and "vocational rehabilitation services" are mentioned separately in LC139.5, but training is actually one type of service. In LC4635, the term "vocational rehabilitation services" is defined expansively to include training as well as other types of services. This definition recognizes the fact that training cannot be provided without an evaluation process to determine whether training is required and, if so, the type of training that is reasonably required on a particular case. Per LC4635, all rehabilitation services fall into two general categories:

1. Services "to determine if the employee can reasonably be expected to return to suitable gainful employment," (services necessary to make a determination of vocational feasibility) AND
2. Services "to provide an employee with the opportunity to return to suitable gainful employment" (services necessary after a determination of vocational feasibility).

Services from the first category listed above include services to assess the employee's medical eligibility and vocational feasibility for rehabilitation benefits (to determine if the employee is a "qualified injured worker" as defined by LC4635; see 11.14). The employer is only liable for services from the second category when services from the first category establish the employee's vocational feasibility. As of 1991, the reasonableness of the costs of any vocational rehabilitation services that are provided are subject to the Vocational Rehabilitation Fee Schedule (see 11.37).

The distinction that is made between an actual return to work and an "opportunity" to return to work appears to provide the employer with a basis for termination of services in cases where the employee remains unemployed after the provision of all reasonable services by the employer (see 11.26). Also, the word "opportunity" explains the Rehabilitation Unit's position that the employer is obligated to provide undocumented workers with all rehabilitation benefits except job placement services within the United States (where an employer who hires an illegal alien would be guilty of a crime).

According to the definition in LC4635, the provision of "services" that are necessary to establish whether or not the employee is entitled to rehabilitation benefits are deemed to be the provision of a rehabilitation benefit. Although inherently contradictory upon first glance, this situation is comparable to the employer's liability to pay for a medical examination when a medical opinion is required to ascertain whether or not an employee is suffering from a work-related condition and is therefore entitled to receive medical treatment.

Some vocational rehabilitation services are listed in LC4635, but the employer will also be liable for any nonspecified services that are encompassed in one of the general categories listed above. The employer's liability for rehabilitation services will terminate when the employer offers qualifying reemployment (see 11.26). Subject to this exception, LC4635 provides that vocational rehabilitation services "include, but are not limited to" the following items:

  a. **"Medical Evaluation":** a medical examination to determine medical eligibility as a qualified injured worker.
  b. **"Vocational" Evaluation":** a job analysis (see 11.14), work evaluation programs, testing, and other services necessary for a determination of the employee's vocational feasibility (the employee's ability to return to work through the provision of the types of vocational rehabilitation services that are described in items #c-#g below).
  c. **"Counseling":** the professional services of a Qualified Rehabilitation Representative including selection with the worker of an appropriate vocation and a training facility; determination of necessary equipment, tools, and supplies; negotiation of the rehabilitation plan with all interested parties; monitoring of training; development of job placement skills; and continued monitoring of vocational adjustment in a new occupation.
  d. **"Retraining":** the cost of instruction, education, or schooling, including technical or trade schools, correspondence courses or college classes.

Community Colleges. Per LC4635.1 (effective 1994), the Legislature "finds that community colleges can provide a cost-effective alternative" to other types of services "and declares its intent to encourage the implementation of vocational rehabilitation services at community colleges." To this end, LC4635.2 mandates the creation of a task force to create "rehabilitation schooling plans" that "focus on the underutilized potential of the schools to provide ... rehabilitation services in an affordable and cost-effective manner." The task force is to be a joint undertaking of the Administrative Director of the Division of Workers' Compensation and the Chancellor of the Community Colleges. (See also QRR-waiver in 11.13.)

e. **"On-the-Job Training"** (OJT): payment for part of the employee's wages while a prospective employer provides on-site training leading to eventual permanent employment. The employee is rehabilitated by a hands-on approach. As skills improve, earnings increase. The employee ordinarily continues on in permanent employment with the same employer who provides the training, but this is not a mandatory requirement.

f. **"Job Modification Assistance":** short periods of training in new areas where the employee will continue to perform some or most of the tasks that were previously performed in a particular position. This type of rehabilitation service may be provided when a previous employer (not necessarily the employer at the time of injury) is willing to modify the employee's previous job, or create a new job, or has a different job available for the employee. Rehabilitation services provide training only in those new skills that will be required of the employee. (See 11.26 regarding limitations on the employer's liability for rehabilitation benefits when the employer offers to return the employee to modified or alternative work that meets the criteria specified in LC4644.)

g. **"Job Placement Assistance":** services necessary to assist the employee in obtaining employment with new skills, including counseling in personal presentation and job placement skills training. The employee may be provided with specific job leads or payment of fees for professional employment agencies. Services may be provided up to the time the employee receives earnings as long as the employee is making a reasonable effort to obtain employment. Some employees will require more assistance than others to reach an employment goal. However, placement assistance is subject to time and monetary caps (see 11.28-11.29).

Effective 1994, as part of the counseling process, employees will be informed of the estimated cost and time for the provision of various rehabilitation services. The employee's informed consent is a necessary part of the counseling process due to monetary caps and time limits that restrict the extent of the employer's liability for vocational rehabilitation services. In effect, the employee has become a partner in cost considerations. For instance, the employee may be presented with two alternatives. The employee may prefer a four-month on-the-job training program that could be completed within statutory monetary and time limits for rehabilitation rather than a program involving a longer classroom training program if the costs for the schooling program would not be fully paid by the employer.

Out-of-State Services

The employee may request rehabilitation services to be provided outside California. The employee may have moved since the injury or be planning to move. Or, the employee may wish to travel to another state solely for purposes of pursuing a particular vocational goal; e.g. where the employee wishes to receive specialized education or training in another state and then return to California to seek employment.

Effective 1994, LC4644 provides that an "employer shall not be liable to provide vocational rehabilitation services at a location outside the state unless" the employer agrees, with one exception. The employer is liable for the payment of services outside California if the Rehabilitation Unit determines that such services "are more cost-effective than similar services provided in" California (in which case, it appears unlikely that the employer would resist payment).

Conceivably, an argument could be made that it will always be more cost-effective to provide services in another state where the employee resides rather than incurring the cost of the proposed rehabilitation program locally and paying the employee to travel back and forth to participate in the California program. This concept may appear ridiculous at first glance. However, consider the employer's liability for medical treatment when the employee moves to another city, state or country after an injury.

When an injured employee moves, the employer remains liable for payment of all medical expense that is reasonably required to cure or relieve from the effects of the injury. In nearly all cases, it will be more cost-effective for the employer to arrange for medical treatment to be provided locally near the employee's new residence rather than paying for multiple trips to California for necessary treatment. The employer's liability for any and all workers' compensation benefits is subject to a test of reasonableness.

11.12 PROVIDERS OF SERVICES – IN GENERAL

A person who provides workers' compensation vocational rehabilitation services is called a "Qualified Rehabilitation Representative" (QRR). This term is defined in LC4635 to mean "a person capable of developing and implementing the vocational rehabilitation plan, whose experience and regular duties involve the evaluation, counseling or placement of disabled persons." This definition is tantamount to a statement that any person who is capable of providing rehabilitation services is, ergo, qualified to provide such services.

In common practice, Qualified Rehabilitation Representatives are interchangeably referred to as vocational rehabilitation counselors, rehabilitation counselors or simply as counselors (see also Independent Vocational Evaluators in 11.13). Qualified Rehabilitation Representatives may be employed in private practice, or the employer or its insurance company may employ counselors or rehabilitation nurses who provide vocational rehabilitation services (see 11.13 regarding restrictions that apply to the use of in-house counselors). Licensing is not required under California laws, but the generally accepted standards for rehabilitation counselors are outlined in LC4635 and conform to standards set by the California Association of Rehabilitation Professionals (CARP).

Although not required for workers' compensation purposes, some counselors possess professional designations or credentials that are indicative of professional achievement within the field of rehabilitation. These designations include C.R.C. for a Certified Rehabilitation Counselor, C.I.R.C. for a Certified Insurance Rehabilitation Specialist, and C.V.E. for a Certified Vocational Evaluation Specialist. Such credentials are not state-specific and do not reflect any special knowledge of California workers' compensation laws.

Counselors are most often private practitioners, but the State Department of Rehabilitation does have a small group of its counselors assigned to its Program for the Industrially Injured. This State agency is not part of the Division of Workers' Compensation. It exists independently of the workers' compensation system and existed prior to the creation of the Rehabilitation Unit in 1975. The Department's function is to provide rehabilitation services at State expense to persons requiring such services, and eligibility is based on medical disability regardless of whether industrially or nonindustrially incurred. This Department will provide services without cost to an employee, but if the employer is later found to be legally liable for the provision of rehabilitation services under the workers' compensation laws, the employer will be billed for all costs of services provided by the Department.

11.13 PROVIDERS OF SERVICES – SELECTION

Initial Selection of Counselor – QRR

Within 10 days of knowledge that the employee has been determined to be medically eligible for rehabilitation benefits (that can occur during the first 90 days of total disability), LC4637 requires the claims administrator to notify the employee of the right to agree to the selection of the counselor who will assess the employee's vocational feasibility. This right includes the right to receive a preliminary evaluation by one counselor and to request a change of counselors thereafter.

Injured employees are not expected to have any personal knowledge of a particular counselor or any basis for comparing qualifications of counselors. The employee's right to agree to or request a change of the counselor selected by the employer is intended to encourage employers to act wisely in selecting a counselor who is unobjectionable to the employee in relevant areas such as effectiveness, language, or ability to engender confidence. The *California Standards Governing Timeliness and Quality of Vocational Rehabilitation Services* recommend that the employee or the employee's legal representative be provided with a panel containing the names of at least three counselors and allowed a set time period to select one.

In cases where the employer is voluntarily providing rehabilitation services, it behooves the employer to exercise judgment in its selection of a counselor. When the employee is represented by an attorney, it is common practice for the attorney's agreement to be solicited prior to a referral to a counselor, since a mutual selection can avoid a later request for the Rehabilitation Unit to order the employer to pay for services of a different counselor. Mutual considerations of the employer and the employee regarding the selection of a counselor could include:

1. Known ability to establish reasonable employee expectations and to motivate employees to actively cooperate in pursuing a rehabilitation plan.

2. Special knowledge or experience in providing rehabilitation services to employees with equivalent types of disabilities, a very important consideration in cases involving serious disabilities such as amputation of limbs, paraplegia, and organic brain damage.

3. Known ability to respond timely and deal effectively with problems that have arisen in past cases including prompt reporting of problems during completion of an approved plan.

4. Success rate in providing actual placement of employees in the designated suitable gainful employment objective of rehabilitation plans developed in the past.

5. Special abilities such as speaking the employee's native language if other than English.

6. Satisfaction of previously referred employees, e.g. no employee has complained that a counselor was unresponsive to reasonable questions or requests for information.

7. Sufficiency of staffing and ability to adhere to required time limits for action under workers' compensation laws, e.g. preparation of a rehabilitation plan within 90 days of a determination of vocational feasibility as required by LC4638.

8. Geographic location in relation to employee's location.

9. Known ability to recommend and/or to provide effective vocational rehabilitation services within applicable monetary caps and time limits (see 11.28-11.29).

As the entity who will pay for the services that a counselor provides, the employer would also consider all of the following items in its referral of additional cases to a particular counselor:

a. Proposed rehabilitation plans are reasonable; e.g., plans are possibly creative, but they are not unique, outlandish, or extravagant nor intended to comply with the employee's personal desires to the extent that a proposed employment goal will not realistically lead to long-term future employability.

b. All services are reasonable and necessary at the time they are provided; e.g., testing is only performed when necessary, and only necessary tests are performed.

c. No particular service is over-utilized: costly services such as a work hardening program or job analysis are not recommended on every case.

d. Charges for services are reasonable, and any disputes that may arise are handled in a professional manner (see 11.37).

e. The counselor maintains a professional relationship with employees; e.g., the employer and/or the claim administrator is not maligned, and any friendships that may develop do not supplant a professional basis for recommendations or actions by the counselor.

Use of In-House QRR

Effective 1994, LC4635 contains a statement of the Legislature's intent "to allow use of an in-house qualified rehabilitation representative." To facilitate this intent, LC4635 provides that direct communication with a represented employee "shall not constitute a violation of Rule 2-100 of the State Bar Rules of Professional Conduct." This Labor Code provision enables a counselor who is an employee of the claims administrator to converse with an employee outside the presence of the employee's attorney. (Employees can, of course, contact their attorneys anytime that they have questions concerning rehabilitation or any other workers' compensation benefits.)

Any employer, insured or self-insured, can use in-house "QRRs," but insured employers are provided with special protections under the Labor Code. Per LC139.5, it is unlawful for an insurer "to charge against any claim for the expenses of" the provision of rehabilitation services by its own employees "unless those expenses are disclosed to the insured and agreed to in advance." An insurer that offers in-house services can ordinarily provide the employer with historical data that will enable the employer to make an informed decision in this regard.

Proprietary Interests - Counselors & Insurers

Some counselors and insurers either own or have an ownership interest in outside facilities that provide rehabilitation services to injured workers. Owned facilities may provide high quality services that greatly benefit injured workers, and frequent referrals to such facilities may be made by many entities who derive no financial benefit from a referral. However, any referral that generates a financial gain to the referring entity generates concern as to whether a referral would be necessary if the profit motive was removed (see 7.79 for comparable concerns regarding physician referrals). This concern underlies several amendments to LC139.5 that took effect in 1994 as explained below.

Per LC139.5, it is "unlawful for a qualified rehabilitation representative or rehabilitation counselor to refer" injured workers to "any work evaluation facility or to any education or training program" where any proprietary interest exists pursuant to an express or an implied contract with a Qualified Rehabilitation

Representative, a counselor, spouse, employer, coemployee or any other party. For instance, LC139.5 prohibits an informal arrangement whereby a counselor agrees to refer all cases to a spouse-owned facility for vocational testing.

It is also unlawful for an insurer to refer an employee "to any rehabilitation provider or facility" in which the insurer has a proprietary interest, except that such referrals are permissible if "disclosed to the insured and agreed to in advance" (as explained above, and see CR10123.3). An insurer may have a proprietary interest in a Health Care Organization (HCO). Such organizations are required to "provide a program ... to promote ... early return to work for injured employees" as a prerequisite to certification under LC4600.5. Per CR10123.3, prohibitions on referrals to facilities where an insurer has a proprietary interest "shall not be construed to restrict or prohibit return-to-work services provided by" a Health Care Organization that is certified pursuant to LC4600.5.

In-House Supervision of Outside Services

Per LC139.5, any costs for a self-insured employer to supervise outside rehabilitation services do not count against any monetary limits that would otherwise apply to the employee's vocational rehabilitation benefits. Otherwise, the more money it costs the employer to monitor services, the less services the employee would be entitled to receive. Likewise, LC139.5 provides that any "charges by an insurer for the activities of an employee who supervises outside vocational rehabilitation services shall not exceed the vocational rehabilitation fee schedule" nor count against the overall monetary cap for rehabilitation benefits or the separate "limit on counselor's fees" (e.g. $16,000 and $4,500 respectively for a 1996 injury).

Charges for in-house rehabilitation services are deemed to be "expenses and not losses for purposes of insurance rating." Employers and insurers can utilize services of in-house vocational rehabilitation counselors and can monitor outside services as they deem necessary, but LC139.5 ensures that the finite funds that are allowed for an employee's rehabilitation benefits will not be depleted by the cost of such services. In order to accurately measure the cost of benefits provided directly to employees, the monitoring costs of insurers and self-insured employers are treated as an expense rather than a rehabilitation benefit for the purposes of claim file reserves.

Change of Counselor – IVE

If the employer fails to provide timely rehabilitation services, the employee has a right under LC4639 to request that the employer be ordered to provide services by a Qualified Rehabilitation Representative of the employee's choice. This request is made by submission of a Request for Dispute Resolution (DWC Form RU-103). The Rehabilitation Unit is required to "immediately advise the employer of the receipt of this request" (unless the employer is self-insured and self administers its claims, the employer's claims administrator will be provided with this notification and will respond on behalf of the employer).

The employer is allowed 20 days after receipt of this notification to either "agree to provide services or to demonstrate that the employee is not" entitled to services. Otherwise, the Rehabilitation Unit can authorize services by a counselor "of the employee's choice."

The employer or the employee may be dissatisfied with a counselor of the other's selection. Per LC4640, the employer and the employee have a right to agree among themselves to a change of, or a consultation with, a different counselor. Each party also has the right under LC4640 to request the Rehabilitation Unit to assign a counselor to provide services (and the employer is required to do so by CR10127.2 whenever a referral is required but agreement on the selection of a counselor cannot be reached within 15 days).

When the Rehabilitation Unit exercises its authority to refer an employee to a counselor whom it designates, this counselor is called an "Independent Vocational Evaluator" (IVE). This term is defined in LC4635 as a person who meets the definition of a "Qualified Rehabilitation Representative" (see 11.12) and also possesses specified alternatives for minimum educational and experience requirements. Per CR10127.2, the Rehabilitation Unit is required to maintain a list of properly qualified individuals that is "reviewed and revised on a yearly basis, and shall be made available upon request." Appointment of a particular counselor "shall be made in rotation from a panel of all independent vocational evaluators in the geographic area included within the venue of the correct Rehabilitation Unit district office and who meet the language and specialty requirements, if any, of the employee."

Upon "receipt of notification of the IVE appointment," CR10127.2 requires the employer to "forward all medical and vocational reports to the IVE within ten" days. If the appointed counselor cannot meet with the employee within 10 days of receipt of such reports, the Rehabilitation Unit is required "to appoint another IVE" upon being notified of this fact by the employee or the employer (written notice is not required). The employer can respond to requests that are initiated by the counselor, and such requests "shall be confirmed in writing by the IVE." However, the employer cannot otherwise communicate in any manner with the Independent Vocational Evaluator unless directed to do so by the Rehabilitation Unit.

The issuance of a Rehabilitation Unit order for services to be provided by an Independent Vocational Evaluator equates to higher costs for the employer. The fact that the qualifications established for Independent Vocational Evaluators exceed those for Qualified Rehabilitation Representatives transposes into higher charges for services provided by Independent Vocational Evaluators. Services of Independent Vocational Evaluators are only utilized after Rehabilitation Unit intervention has been requested to resolve a dispute, and any action that extends the rehabilitation process ordinarily means that the employer is also liable for payment of a longer period of rehabilitation benefits. Of additional concern for the employer is a lack of active input, since Independent Vocational Evaluators report directly to the Rehabilitation Unit and not to the parties.

Waiver of Qualified Rehabilitation Representative

For 1994 or later injuries, it is possible for an employee to waive the right to the provision of services by a Qualified Rehabilitation Representative. A so-called "QRR waiver" is permissible in one situation only. An injured worker may have "been enrolled and made substantial progress toward completion of a degree or certificate from a community college, California State University, or the University of California." If so, LC139.5 permits a waiver of an otherwise required referral to a Qualified Rehabilitation Representative if the employee desires a plan to complete such degree or certificate. (All plans that are developed without a Qualified Rehabilitation Representative require approval by the Rehabilitation Unit; see 11.22.)

11.14 QUALIFIED INJURED WORKER – DEFINED

Per LC4635, a "qualified injured worker" is defined to mean "an employee who meets both of the following requirements:"

1. **Medical Eligibility:** "The employee's expected permanent disability as a result of the injury, whether or not combined with the effects of a prior injury or disability, if any, permanently precludes, or is likely to preclude, the employee from engaging in his or her usual occupation or the position in which he or she was engaged at the time of injury," called "medical eligibility" (see 11.15), AND

2. **Vocational Feasibility:** "The employee can reasonably be expected to return to suitable gainful employment through the provision of vocational rehabilitation services," called "vocational feasibility" (see 11.19).

Necessary criteria for determining a "qualified injured worker" are discussed in depth in the following sections. Note however that each separate workers' compensation benefit has an intended purpose, and the employee is not entitled to receive any category of benefits unless the intended purpose of such benefit will be achieved. Since the purpose of the rehabilitation category of benefits is to assist a disabled employee to return to employment, an employee will be a "qualified injured worker" under LC4635 when rehabilitation benefits are necessary and can realistically achieve the result of returning the worker to gainful employment.

For 1994 or later injuries, rehabilitation benefits are not deemed necessary and the employee is not entitled to rehabilitation services if the employee is able to return to work with the preinjury employer without such services. Simple logic would support a lack of entitlement to rehabilitation benefits under such circumstances. However, the LC4635 definition of a "qualified injured worker" has previously been liberally construed to entitle an employee to rehabilitation services at a preinjury employer's expense if a disabled employee simply did not wish to return to suitable gainful employment at the same place of employment. As a result, some employers were ordered to pay for rehabilitation services that were intended to lead to employment with a new employer in cases where an employee simply wanted to change jobs for reasons unrelated to an injury; e.g. grudges over work conditions or personality conflicts with supervisors or coworkers.

It was not until 1994 amendments to the Labor Code that the employer was specifically relieved of liability for the provision of rehabilitation benefits under circumstances discussed above. The LC4635 definition of a "qualified injured worker" did not change in 1994. What changed was the statutory basis for termination of the employer's liability for rehabilitation benefits under LC4644. As a result, the employee is not a qualified injured worker (is not eligible for rehabilitation benefits) if the pre-injury employer offers reemployment that meets specific statutory criteria (see 11.26). Where qualifying reemployment is not available or offered, it is then necessary to determine whether the employee is a qualified injured worker and therefore entitled to the provision of rehabilitation benefits.

11.15 MEDICAL ELIGIBILITY – EXPLAINED

Per LC4635, the employee is eligible for rehabilitation benefits on a medical basis when it is determined that the "expected permanent disability as a result of the injury, whether or not combined with the effects of a prior injury or disability, if any, permanently precludes, or is likely to preclude the employee from engaging in his or her usual occupation or the position in which he or she was engaged at the time of injury." There must be a reasonable basis for believing that an employee will be entitled to permanent disability benefits as a result of the industrial injury (although the employer's liability to provide rehabilitation benefits can, and often does, arise before the employee's condition becomes permanent and stationary for purposes of determining the full amount of the employee's permanent disability benefits). Also, the employee must be medically prohibited from returning to work absent the provision of rehabilitation services, as contrasted to the employee's failure to return to work due to economic conditions or personal reasons.

The industrial injury must be a contributing cause of the employee's medical inability to return to work, but the industrial injury need not be the sole cause. The employer may be liable for a minor percent of the employee's overall permanent disability, because it is entitled to apportionment (the employer is not liable for payment of any permanent disability that did not result from the injury; see 10.39). However, per LC4635, the employee is medically eligible when any portion of the disability that permanently precludes the employee's return to work is due to the injury, because LC4635 refers to the effects of the industrial injury "whether or not combined with a prior injury or disability."

The employee's overall permanent disability is compared to his preinjury status. If the industrial injury contributed to the ultimate inability to return to work, the employee can be a qualified injured worker even if the permanent disability resulting from the industrial injury is minor when considered by itself, or the employee is significantly disabled from some other cause. A medical determination of entitlement, or anticipated entitlement, to permanent disability benefits is a prerequisite to qualified injured worker status. However, entitlement to permanent disability benefits does not in and of itself provide automatic entitlement to rehabilitation benefits, because employees can receive permanent disability benefits regardless of whether they ever return to work.

The employee's occupation at the time of injury is all that is used for permanent disability rating purposes (see 10.26), but the employee's entitlement to rehabilitation services is not controlled by the employee's occupation at the moment of injury or even in the employment where the injury was sustained. Per LC4635, the employee can be a qualified injured worker if the effects of his injury preclude a return to either the position he was performing when injured or some other occupation that the employee considers to be his "usual occupation."

The employee may be a mechanic by trade but injured while temporarily employed as a gas station attendant. The employee may be injured during a short-term assignment to a job that he does not ordinarily perform, e.g. a supervisor who was working as a manager during the latter's vacation. Consider the case of an employee who is injured while employed 20 hrs/wk as a law clerk and also worked 40 hrs/wk delivering pizzas for a restaurant. The employee's disability may not prevent a return to part time duties as a law clerk, or the law firm employer may offer to provide continued employment at the same earnings with appropriate modifications to accommodate any permanent effects of the injury (see 11.26). Even so, this employee may be entitled to rehabilitation benefits at the law firm employer's expense if medically precluded from returning to work delivering pizzas. The Rehabilitation Unit may agree with the employee's allegations that the pizza job is the employee's "usual occupation."

This liberal criteria for qualified injured worker status has been difficult for employers to accept. However, the Labor Code clearly establishes the authority of the Rehabilitation Unit to order benefits to be provided at the full expense of the employer who is liable for the provision of all other workers' compensation benefits when:

1. The injury does not preclude the employee's return to all regular duties of a full time employment where the injury occurred (such as the gas station attendant mentioned above who is medically precluded only from a return to work as a mechanic), or

2. The employee can perform all usual or customary duties but not a temporary job that was being performed when injured (e.g. the supervisor in the example above who may assert that performance of short-term managerial duties constitutes an integral part of the supervisor's usual occupation), or

3. The employee rejects an offer to provide modified or alternative work that would satisfy the employer's liability for rehabilitation benefits if the employee had been employed by this employer only (e.g. the pizza delivery worker above who rejects an offer of reemployment with the law firm employer).

11.16 JOB ANALYSIS vs. JOB DESCRIPTION

The physical demands of the employee's occupation must be identified in order to determine whether or not the employee is medically able to return to a preinjury employment. A job description can provide a sufficient basis for this determination. However, some employers (especially small employers) do not have formal job descriptions, or the description they do have is too general, incomplete, inaccurate, out-of-date, or otherwise inadequate. It is sometimes necessary to know the frequency and/or duration of specific work tasks such as lifting or climbing ladders, but a job description does not usually provide this type of information regarding work duties.

A job analysis provides a detailed listing of the physical tasks of a job. This document is prepared by qualified rehabilitation personnel who develop information by contact with employer representatives or coemployees or by direct observation of a job. A formal job analysis can involve several hours of a counselor's time (see CR10132.1), depending upon how much necessary information is readily available and how much needs to be developed. This expense is neither reasonable nor necessary unless there is a specific need for information that is not otherwise readily available.

A physician cannot make an accurate assessment of the employee's medical eligibility for rehabilitation benefits without a clear understanding of the physical demands that are required of the employee in a particular employment. A form developed to assist the physician in this assessment is the Description of Employee's Job Duties (DWC Form RU-91). Per LC4636, this form is "developed jointly by the employee and the employer" and is only required under LC4636 if:

1. "Aggregate total disability continues for 90 days," AND
2. The employee has not yet been identified as medically eligible for rehabilitation benefits.

For some activities, the RU-91 form asks whether or not the activity is performed. For other activities (such as standing, sitting, and lifting), the form requests the approximate number of hours of each workday that the activity is performed. A comments section allows for the addition of other activities that are not specifically listed on the form (e.g. activities relevant to psychiatric disabilities such as tasks involving decision-making without immediate supervision or requiring an ability to influence actions of others).

Conceivably, the RU-91 form could be used on an informal basis where its use is not required. The physician could be asked to review the form after completion by the employer (or by a claimsperson after contact with appropriate employer personnel). However, some employers (small businesses in particular) will be frustrated by the type of detail that is requested by the form, may resent being asked to take the time to ascertain such information, and may refuse to complete the form or provide this information orally at the request of a claimsperson.

Nothing prevents solicitation of the employee's input during the first 90 days of disability. The employee can be asked to review any selected document for accuracy and to provide clarification if necessary. Once agreement is reached, the employee may be asked to sign any document that accurately describes job duties. Such document can then be forwarded to a physician for an opinion as to those specific tasks the employee can and cannot perform. This information has value in assessing the appropriateness of rehabilitation services as well as the nature and extent of any permanent disability.

No complaint will be raised by an employee if a physician who is not provided with a completed RU-91 is otherwise able to determine that the employee is medically eligible for rehabilitation benefits. If a physician is able to make this determination during the first 90 days of total disability, a job analysis would be unreasonable. However, a "representative" job analysis may or may not be needed to determine the employee's ability to perform alternative work with the same employer or the duties of a different employment that is the goal of a proposed rehabilitation plan.

Although not required, many employers have developed written job specifications that are designed to facilitate compliance with antidiscrimination provisions of the Americans With Disabilities Act. Job descriptions or job analyses that identify "essential functions" of a job are now commonplace. Any employee who cannot perform a job function of his or her time-of-injury employment that the employer identifies as an "essential function" will unquestionably be medically eligible for rehabilitation benefits. However, an employee who worked for multiple employers can also be medically eligible for rehabilitation benefits if the injury precludes the employee from performing the essential functions of the employee's other jobs. It is crucial to note that medical eligibility for workers' compensation rehabilitation benefits is determined by completely different and more expansive criteria (see 11.15).

11.17 MEDICAL ELIGIBILITY – DETERMINATION

The employer has a duty to identify those employees who are medically eligible for rehabilitation services. Medical eligibility is ordinarily established by physicians, but a physician's opinion is not always necessary to determine that an employee is medically eligible. In some cases, knowledge of the nature of the employee's injury combined with awareness of the employee's preinjury duties can lead any reasonable person to conclude that the employee will be unable to return to gainful employment without the provision of rehabilitation services. In such cases, medical eligibility may be determined soon after an injury. In other cases, the provisions of LC4636 ensure that where a physician's opinion is necessary, one will be requested after three months of disability.

90 Days – Action Required

Pamphlet and Notice of Potential Rights. For 1994 or later injuries, if there has not been a determination of the employee's medical eligibility for rehabilitation benefits after 90 aggregate days of total disability, the employer is required to immediately (within 10 days per CR9813) provide the employee with a notice of potential rights. Per LC4636, this notice must inform the employee of potential rights of disabled individuals under workers' compensation laws, the Americans with Disabilities Act and the Fair Employment and Housing Act. This notice requirement is satisfied by the provision of a pamphlet, *Help in Returning to Work-94* (see 10133.2) and an accompanying benefit information notice (see CR9813). The separate notice will advise the employee of the current status of the employee's entitlement to rehabilitation benefits and any action required by the employee. (See 11.18.)

Develop Job Description. After 90 days of total disability, LC4636 requires the claims administrator to provide the treating physician with a job description ("developed jointly with the employee and the employer") and other relevant information concerning the "physical requirements of the employee's duties at the time of injury" (see 11.17). Per CR10124, if a job description is not available, the employee will be assisted in the development of one. Commonly, this task will involve completion of the Description of Employee's Job Duties (DWC Form RU-91) by a Qualified Rehabilitation Representative. A narrative description of job duties may be used instead of, or as a supplement to, this form as may a video taping of work tasks or equipment.

Per CR10124, if the parties disagree as to the employee's job duties, the claims administrator is required to submit this dispute to the Rehabilitation Unit to "resolve the dispute on an expedited basis." Sometimes an employee will refuse to participate in the development of a job description. This situation is not considered to be a "dispute." In this situation, "the employer's description shall be presumed to be the joint description" that is required by LC4636.

Medical Progress Reports. A Treating Physician's Report of Disability Status (DWC Form RU-90) is used to report the physician's determination of the employee's medical eligibility for rehabilitation benefits. After the treating physician has been provided with a job description, the claims administrator has a duty to monitor the employee's recovery and seek a determination of medical eligibility from the treating physician.

Per LC4636, the treating physician is required to submit a report at least every 60 days after the initial request. (Note: CR9785 requires treating physicians to submit reports every 45 days or after "12 visits with the physician or a provider prescribed by the physician, whichever occurs first"; see 7.56). Each report must be given to the employee as well as the claims administrator. The 60-day reporting requirement ceases when the treating physician provides a determination of medical eligibility or disability continues for more than one year (in which case medical eligibility is presumed; see below).

365 Days – Presumption of Medical Eligibility

When "aggregate total disability exceeds 365 days and the employee has not previously been identified as being medically eligible for vocational rehabilitation," LC4636 provides that there shall be a rebuttable presumption that the employee is medically eligible for vocational rehabilitation services." Note that this presumption can apply to employees who were previously determined **not** to be medically eligible, e.g. a permanently totally disabled employee with severe brain damage who is in a coma! This presumption is rebuttable, not conclusive. The employer is not required to commence the provision of rehabilitation benefits when it is aware of the existence of evidence sufficient to overcome the presumption, including evidence of facts such as those described below. The employer is however required to provide a notice of potential rights as explained above.

The presumption explained above is rebuttable, not conclusive. Certain information, when it is reported by a physician, will constitute medical evidence that the employee is not a qualified injured worker, including cases involving less than one year of temporary total disability. For instance, the following types of medical facts negate a determination that the employee is medically eligible for rehabilitation benefits.

    a. The employee is medically able to return to work without any rehabilitation services; any permanent disability resulting from an industrial injury will not prohibit the employee's return to work without such services.

    b. The severity of the injury negates the employee's return to any suitable gainful employment in the open labor market.

    c. The injury did not, or is not anticipated to, result in any permanent disability.

    d. The employee's inability to return to work is due to medical problems that are unrelated to the industrial injury.

11.18 MEDICAL ELIGIBILITY – REQUIRED NOTICES

When the treating physician makes a determination of the employee's medical eligibility for rehabilitation benefits, LC4636 requires the employer to provide a copy "to the employee together with notice of the procedure to be followed in contesting this determination." Usually, the claims administrator becomes aware of this determination upon receipt of the Treating Physician's Report of Disability Status (DWC Form RU-90). However, medical eligibility can also be established upon the receipt of "knowledge of a physician's opinion indicating the employee is medically eligible" per LC4637 and by presumption on the 366th day of total disability (see 11.17). Within 10 days of knowledge that the employee is or is not medically eligible, the claims administrator is required to concurrently provide the employee with a:

    a. Copy of the physician's final report of medical eligibility (LC4636).

    b. Notice "of the procedure to be followed in contesting the treating physician's determination" that the employee is or is not medically eligible (LC4636).

    c. Notice of Offer of Modified or Alternate Work (DWC-RU-94) that will inform the employee "whether the employer will be able or unable to offer modified or alternative work" (LC4636) or else an

explanation that the employee will receive this notice within 30 days
after further investigation is conducted (CR9813).

    d. *Help In Returning to Work-94* pamphlet that serves as a comprehen-
sive notice of the employee's potential rights regarding rehabilitation
benefits (see LC4637 and CR10124).

    e. Notice of Potential Eligibility. No particular form is required, but the
contents of this benefit information notice are specified in LC4637
and CR9813. This notice is usually provided in a checklist format
and/or a narrative letter that advises whether the employer accepts or
rejects liability for rehabilitation or an explanation of any delay in
making this decision (e.g. a delay in determining whether the
employer will be able to offer a return to modified work for a
medically eligible employee or a delay pending referral to a Qualified
Medical Evaluator if medical eligibility is disputed).

Notice of Modified or Alternative Work. If medical eligibility is undisputed,
the employee must be provided with specific information regarding the current
availability of modified or alternative work with the preinjury employer. (Note:
the Labor Code refers to "alternative work," but some administrative regulations
and forms refer to "alternate work.") Subject to specific statutory criteria, the
employer's offer to provide certain modified or alternative work will eliminate
further liability for rehabilitation benefits to the employee (see 11.26). The
employee must therefore receive sufficient information to enable the employee
to properly appraise the employer's offer and, should the employee so choose, to
dispute a termination of rehabilitation benefits based upon such offer.

At the time that a notice of medical eligibility is provided (as detailed in
CR9813), an investigation may be necessary to determine the availability of
qualifying reemployment. If so, the employer must notify the employee of this
fact. In this event, CR9813 requires that "a final notice regarding the availability
of modified or alternate work shall be sent within 30 days of the Notice of
Potential Eligibility.

When an employer has qualifying reemployment available, CR10126 requires
the employer to present its offer using a Notice of Offer of Modified or Alternate
Work (DWC Form RU-94). The employee must act affirmatively to accept the
employer's offer, because a lack of response within 30 days of receipt of the
employer's offer is deemed to be a rejection of rehabilitation benefits. Per
CR10126, the 30-day reply period may be "extended by the employer" ("or by
the terms and conditions of a collective bargaining agreement" for some construction industry employers pursuant to LC3201.5).

The employer is required to submit a copy of its Notice of Offer of Modified
or Alternate Work to the Rehabilitation Unit (along with a Case Initiation Document) within 30 days of the employee's response. The form must be filed whether
the employee accepts or rejects the offered employment (including a failure to
respond). In the event of a dispute regarding the employer's offer, either party can
initiate dispute resolution procedures.

Notice of Potential Eligibility. Whether or not the employer offers to provide qualifying reemployment, LC4637 requires that the employee receive specific details regarding potential rights. Such details are only applicable to cases where qualifying reemployment is not offered or not timely offered, but all employees who are medically eligible will receive such details since they are provided as part of the contents of the Help In Returning to Work-94 pamphlet. An employee must receive certain information before the employee can effectively exercise the right to "choose to participate" in a rehabilitation program per LC139.5. A determination of medical eligibility (including by presumption) thus precipitates the LC4637 requirement that the employer immediately provide the employee with a written notice that includes all the following:

1. Notice of the types of "vocational rehabilitation services available to the employee ... and the effect of any delay in the acceptance" of such services.
2. "Instructions as to how the employee may apply for" rehabilitation services; e.g. whether a response may be made by phone, fax or letter and appropriate details to enable a reply to be made.
3. The potential result of "failure to apply within 90 days of receipt of notice of medical eligibility" is termination of entitlement to such services, and the exceptions that extend this 90-day period (e.g. the severity of the employee's medical condition precludes participation in a rehabilitation program at this time, and applicable statutes of limitations; see 6.31).
4. The right to agree upon a counselor and to request a preliminary "evaluation of vocational feasibility prior to any acceptance or rejection" of such services.
5. The fact that "vocational rehabilitation services may not be settled or" paid as a lump sum cash payment (a provision that ensures the employer need not pay for vocational rehabilitation services unless the employee receives such services).

Delay in Determination of Entitlement. The employer may need additional information to decide whether it is liable for the provision of rehabilitation benefits to a medically eligible employee. An investigation may be necessary to assess the viability of a return to work with the same employer. A referral to a Qualified Medical Evaluator may be required if the treating physician's determination of medical eligibility is disputed (see 7.75). Per CR9813, a delay notice must be provided to a medically eligible employee within 10 days after receipt of a medical report containing this determination or "from receipt of the employee's request for services."

Per CR9813, the employee must be notified of the reason for a delayed decision and the anticipated date by which a decision will be made. The employee must thereafter be notified of any extension of this deadline within five days after a previously anticipated deadline. Any subsequent delay notices shall include remedies that are currently available to the employee; e.g. the employee may be advised of the right to voluntarily agree to allow the employer more than 30 days to investigate the viability of reemployment or request the Rehabilitation Unit to resolve a dispute.

Denial of Medical Eligibility. If a physician determines that the employee is not medically eligible, the employer will concurrently notify the employee of potential rights and that rehabilitation benefits are denied. In some cases, benefits will be partially denied and partially accepted. For instance, if the employer disputes the employee's medical eligibility, LC139.5 requires it to pay basic vocational rehabilitation maintenance allowance benefits pending resolution of the dispute. In this case, CR9813 requires the claims administrator to "explain the distinction between the terminated and continuing rehabilitation benefits."

A denial notice is required by CR9813 within 10 days of knowledge of circumstances that provide a proper basis for a denial of rehabilitation benefits (and is required when and if vocational feasibility is denied). As part of a denial notice, the employer must advise the employee of the procedures for contesting the denial. Therefore, CR9813 requires the employee to be provided with a Request for Dispute Resolution and (except where a Rehabilitation Unit case number exists) a Case Initiation Document.

Reminder Notice. After a notice of potential rights is provided, the employee has the right to request the provision of rehabilitation benefits. Since LC4637 provides that a failure to apply within 90 days may terminate the employee's entitlement, CR9813 gives the employer a duty to remind the employee of the employee's "right to vocational rehabilitation services." This duty must be performed within narrow confines of time. Per CR9813, a reminder notice must be tendered "not earlier than 45 nor later than 70 days after the employee's receipt of the Notice of Potential Eligibility." Multiple reminder notices can be provided within the allotted 25-day period.

11.19 VOCATIONAL FEASIBILITY – EXPLAINED

Per LC4635, the second of the two separate requirements for qualified injured worker status, "vocational feasibility," requires a determination that "the employee can reasonably be expected to return to suitable gainful employment through the provision of vocational rehabilitation services." An informal prediction of vocational feasibility can be derived from knowledge of information such as the employee's education, abilities, work history and stated desire to return to work. However, rehabilitation services are provided by vocational rehabilitation counselors, so a formal determination of vocational feasibility is customarily made by such counselors. For 1994 or later injuries, the employee's vocational feasibility will need to be assessed when:

1. The employee has been determined to be medically eligible for rehabilitation benefits, AND
2. The employer does not offer, or timely offer, reemployment in qualifying modified or alternative work, AND
3. The employee has received required notices regarding potential eligibility including instructions on how to apply, AND

4. The employee's medical condition does not preclude participation in rehabilitation services, AND
5. The employee makes a timely request for rehabilitation benefits (usually within 90 days of receipt of a notice of potential eligibility, but exceptions exist).

Pursuant to LC4637, the employer is required within 10 days of knowledge of "a physician's opinion, indicating an employee is medically eligible" to "assign a qualified rehabilitation representative selected in agreement with the employee, to determine" vocational feasibility. If the parties cannot agree, then LC4637 requires the employer to request the Rehabilitation Unit to appoint an Independent Vocational Evaluator pursuant to LC4640. However, the employer is not required to initiate an evaluation of vocational feasibility within 10 days under LC4637 if "the employee's medical condition precludes participation" at that time, or "the employee declines to accept vocational rehabilitation services"; e.g., where the employee signs a formal declination (a DWC Form RU-107A), or the employee fails to request benefits after being informed and reminded of entitlement (see 11.24).

A referral for a determination of vocational feasibility is also required by LC4637 "within 10 days after the employee is" rebuttably presumed to be medically eligible under LC4636 because "aggregate total disability exceeds 365 days" (see 11.15). The reasons listed above that eliminate liability for a vocational evaluation also apply when medical eligibility is presumed by law. As a general rule, the employer is obligated to pay for a vocational feasibility evaluation only when the evaluation is capable of achieving its intended purpose. An exception appears to apply when the employee is medically eligible by presumption. However, in such cases, the employer will have had an entire year to gather evidence to rebut the presumption (and to utilize available dispute resolution procedures).

The goal of any counselor who evaluates vocational feasibility is the same: to assess the employee's ability to benefit from rehabilitation services that can assist an injured employee to obtain employment that is available within the employee's permanent medical restrictions. Some employees will not return to gainful employment due to medical reasons or personal reasons unrelated to the injuries they sustained. Many employees will return to employment without any rehabilitation services. Where vocational rehabilitation services would be meaningless or ineffectual, the employee is not vocationally feasible because such services would not achieve their intended purpose.

The employer is actually providing rehabilitation benefits when an assessment of the employee's vocational feasibility is being conducted. Counseling is one type of vocational rehabilitation service, and an evaluation of the employee's vocational feasibility may also necessitate the provision of other types of services (see 11.9). A determination that the employee is not vocationally feasible therefore means that the employee is not entitled to further vocational rehabilitation services beyond the date of this determination.

Assessment of Modified Work – Who Pays?

A question arises whether rehabilitation benefits are being provided when the employer (not its claims administrator) incurs fees in order to determine if it will be able to offer qualifying modified or alternative work that will constitute grounds for termination of rehabilitation benefits pursuant to LC4644. The Labor Code does not specifically create a liability for payment of such services. A claims administrator will certainly wish to provide any reasonable assistance in this regard in order to control workers' compensation costs. For instance, a timely offer to provide reemployment can avoid or reduce liability for payment of vocational rehabilitation maintenance allowance benefits and also reduce the potential for assessment of penalties for the delayed provision of rehabilitation benefits. However, employers have independent incentives that supersede any financial concerns relative to workers' compensation laws.

Employers have statutory obligations to employees with disabilities other than workers' compensation obligations. Employers need to also be concerned about potential lawsuits for alleged discrimination against disabled employees under other applicable California and federal laws such as California's Fair Employment and Housing Act and (if employing 15 or more employees) the federal Americans With Disabilities Act. (Effective 1994, LC4636 mandates that employees be concurrently advised of potential rights under these laws as well as under the Labor Code.) An assessment of reemployment opportunities will serve several employer interests in avoiding potential liabilities under multiple statutes, not just the Labor Code. This is one reason why an insurer may take the position that costs necessary to determine reemployability with the same employer are the responsibility of the employer and not covered as a rehabilitation benefit under the Labor Code.

For 1994 or later injuries, it is possible for the employer's liability for vocational rehabilitation benefits to cease upon presentation of an offer to return to work under conditions specified in LC4644 (see 11.26). However, it is also possible that rehabilitation services may be necessary to resolve disputes thereafter regarding the employee's ability to perform offered reemployment. For instance, it may be appropriate to perform a job analysis to resolve a dispute as to whether the physical requirements of an alternative position are compatible with the employee's physical capacities. Not to be ignored is the fact that services of a rehabilitation counselor may be utilized to identify alternative positions or facilitate job modifications that then form the basis for an offer of employment that will terminate the employer's liability for further vocational rehabilitation benefits.

Period for Determining Vocational Feasibility.

After a medically eligible employee requests rehabilitation benefits, the Labor Code does not specify a time limit for an evaluation of vocational feasibility to be commenced or concluded. Per LC4637, the employee is allowed 90 days from receipt of a notice of medical eligibility to choose to accept vocational rehabilitation services, and the employee is entitled to an evaluation of vocational feasibility at the employer's expense prior to making this decision. If the counselor does not provide progress information that addresses the anticipated date of a final determination, the claims administrator must assume responsibility for monitoring the progress of a final determination of vocational feasibility.

It is apparently contemplated that a determination of vocational feasibility will ordinarily be concluded within the 90-day period allowed for the employee to request the provision of rehabilitation benefits. However, LC4637 also recognizes circumstances that would warrant a longer evaluation period, e.g. where recovery from surgery precludes immediate participation in rehabilitation services (a type of circumstance that constitutes good cause for an interruption of services; see 11.25).

11.20 VOCATIONAL FEASIBILITY – DETERMINATION

Although medical eligibility is assessed by a physician, it is within the expertise of a vocational rehabilitation counselor to determine whether or not suitable gainful employment will be reasonably available to the employee in view of the employee's physical capacities. Medical information will always be a primary consideration in the formulation of a counselor's opinion of vocational feasibility regardless of other information that is relied upon. For 1994 or later injuries, a determination of whether the employee will be able to return to modified or alternative work with the same employer is also of primary importance.

The employer's offer of qualifying reemployment (within allowable time periods) provides a basis for termination of further liability for counseling services or other rehabilitation benefits (see 11.26). However, a decision regarding potential reemployment may not be made within time periods allowed, or the employer may initially refuse to offer such work but later change its mind. Under these circumstances, but only if the employee so chooses, a determination of vocational feasibility can include an assessment of the viability of modified or alternative work for the same employer. In other cases, it is the employer's failure to timely offer qualifying reemployment or its unequivocal position that reemployment is not possible that will entitle the employee to counseling services for the purpose of determining vocational feasibility for rehabilitation benefits.

Vocational feasibility is determined through an information gathering process. A counselor is expected to know the physical demands of employments that are generally available in the open labor market, the range of available types of vocational rehabilitation services, and the purpose or potential benefit to be derived from such services. Based upon this knowledge, a counselor attempts to determine whether gainful employment is reasonably obtainable for an employee either with or without the provision of rehabilitation services. (If services are not necessary, the employee is not vocationally feasible; e.g. where the employer offers reemployment in qualifying modified or alternative work.)

Sufficient information may be obtained in the counselor's initial interview. If not, further interviews and/or formal methods of assessment such as testing or work evaluation programs may be required. The employee may or may not be the solitary source of the following types of information upon which a counselor could determine that an employee who is medically eligible for rehabilitation benefits is also vocationally feasible:

1. The employee has existing work skills that can be used in a different occupation (transferable skills).
2. The employee has special qualifications, knowledge, licenses or abilities that are in demand in the labor market.
3. The employee has personal interests or hobbies from which the employee has developed skills that are in demand in the labor market.
4. The employee's educational history is indicative of a desire as well as the ability to learn new information.
5. The employee's past work history reflects a pattern of continuous success in learning and performing new job duties.
6. The employee's work history indicates a desire to be employed.
7. The employee possesses basic characteristics that are necessary to seek, obtain and retain desired employments.
8. The employee is presently interested in returning to suitable gainful employment.
9. The employee has realistic expectations of the purpose and potential results of the provision of rehabilitation services.

Positive indications of employability must be assessed in conjunction with any negative indications of future employability that may be revealed in an employee interview or by a review of past employment information. A counselor should assess the potential for recurrence of a past pattern of disciplinary actions, a history of involuntary termination of employments, and/or a history of voluntary resignations from multiple employments.

There are certain minimum criteria that nearly all employers require and without which no person, no matter what else they have to offer, may be reasonably expected to obtain employment. A determination of vocational feasibility must therefore encompass an assessment of any relevant facts such as: offensiveness in personal hygiene; rudeness or antagonism towards others; strange or bizarre mannerisms in speech, dress or habits; inexplicable lack of understanding of normal conversation or simple instructions; admitted or verified alcohol dependency or substance abuse; or, attendance problems during evaluation of feasibility.

The facts above can negate any reasonable expectation that the provision of rehabilitation services can actually result in gainful employment. Additionally, the employee may be determined to be vocationally ineligible for rehabilitation benefits when a vocational evaluation reveals facts such as these:

a. The employee is not interested in employment and does not want to return to work.
b. The employee's lack of availability to participate and/or the employee's failure to cooperate in an evaluation of vocational

feasibility is deemed to be reasonably predictive of an unsuccessful result of any proposed rehabilitation plan.

c. The employee has unrealistic demands or expectations that cannot be met through the provision of reasonable rehabilitation services.

11.21 REHABILITATION PLAN – FORM & CONTENT

A "vocational rehabilitation plan" is defined by LC4635 as meaning "the written description of and rationale for the manner and means by which it is proposed that a qualified injured worker may be returned to suitable gainful employment" (see 11.4). The word "proposed" makes it clear that the plan is not a guarantee of employment. The success of any plan will always be contingent upon the employee's willingness to afford himself or herself of the opportunity for employment that is extended at the employer's expense. A Qualified Rehabilitation Representative will prepare a Vocational Rehabilitation Plan (DWC Form RU-102).

For 1994 or later injuries, LC4635 provides that rehabilitation plans may contemplate "modification of the employee's occupation at the time of injury" or alternative work with a different employer if the employer where an injury occurred "has initially failed or refused to provide modified or alternative work." This language precludes rehabilitation plans that are directed towards a goal of employment with a new employer in cases where the preinjury employer is willing to provide qualifying modified or alternative work (see 11.26). As an ancillary effect, this language may enable some employees to return to a preinjury employment where an employer who initially refused to provide modified work changes its mind after the time allotted for this decision (see 11.18); e.g. where it is confronted with a cost analysis of other options for fulfilling its rehabilitation obligations.

Per LC4635, the plan shall "define the responsibilities of the employee, employer, qualified rehabilitation representative and other parties in implementing the plan." All costs of the plan must be stated as well as who will pay these costs. All active participants in the plan must be listed along with their responsibilities in accomplishing the plan.

For employees with 1994 or later injuries, CR10126 requires that all "plans must contain a description of the level of participation expected of an employee in order to continue to receive maintenance allowance" payments. Per LC4643, the employee's failure to adhere to this agreement provides the employer with the right to file a notice of intent to withhold maintenance allowance payments for the period of the employee's unreasonable failure to cooperate in the provision of rehabilitation benefits pursuant to LC4643 (using procedures specified in CR10127 and CR9813, and see 11.9).

A Vocational Rehabilitation Plan (DWC Form RU-102) is the form that is used to outline a plan. This form is prepared by a Qualified Rehabilitation Representative. It is thereafter reviewed and signed by all parties to indicate their agreement and commitment to the terms specified within the plan. Notwithstanding the agreement of the parties, the appropriateness of all plans that involve unrepresented employees or a waiver of the services of a Qualified Rehabilitation Representative are subject to approval by the Rehabilitation Unit (see 11.22).

Insured Employers

A provision of LC4638 that applies only to insured employers operates to encourage employers to offer qualifying reemployment opportunities by providing a financial incentive to do so. Whenever this special provision applies, all pertinent details should be specified as part of a proposed plan. For instance, the plan should provide that the insurer will "advise the employer of a potential refund as described in" LC4638 "within 60 days of" Rehabilitation Unit approval. Insured employers are entitled to a premium rebate only after an approved rehabilitation plan returns a "worker to modified or alternative work at the employer's place of employment for 12 consecutive months."

The rebate is computed as the actual premium payable for workers' compensation insurance based on the payroll for this one employee for this one-year period. Employers are warned against premeditated termination of employees after receipt of a premium rebate by a reference to the employee's continued protection against "discrimination under LC132a" (that prohibits employment actions that are motivated by the fact of a work injury and treat injured workers in an adverse manner).

11.22 REHABILITATION PLAN – APPROVAL

Per LC4638, the employer's liability to pay for development of a plan arises only when and if "the employee is determined to be a qualified injured worker." This determination occurs on the date vocational feasibility is determined, because that is the date on which the employee will be both medically eligible and vocationally feasible as required by LC4635. However, for 1994 or later injuries, LC4638 does not require a rehabilitation plan to be developed unless the employer has notified a medically eligible employee (in the time allowed) that it will be unable to provide reemployment in qualifying modified or alternative work.

Plan Approval – When Not Required

Effective 1994, LC4638 does not require the employer to submit a plan for Rehabilitation Unit approval unless submission is "required pursuant to Section 139.5." Labor Code 139.5 requires Rehabilitation Unit approval for all plans involving unrepresented employees. Rehabilitation Unit approval is not required for agreed plans when an employee is represented by an attorney, with one exception. A plan that involves a so-called "QRR waiver" (per LC139.5, is "developed without the assistance of" a Qualified Rehabilitation Representative; see 11.13) "must be approved by the" Rehabilitation Unit.

Per CR10126, "offers to provide alternate or modified employment with the employer that meet the criteria of " LC4644 (as explained in 11.26) "do not require a written plan nor approval from the Rehabilitation Unit." Instead, CR10126 requires the claims administrator to "submit a copy of the acceptance or rejection of the reemployment offer to the Rehabilitation Unit within 30 days of" the employee's decision. The employer will ordinarily submit a copy of the Notice of Offer of Modified or Alternative Work (DWC-RU-94) along with a Notice of Termination of Vocational Rehabilitation Services (DWC-RU-105).

Per CR10126, if the employee fails to respond to the "bona fide" written offer "within 30 calendar days of receipt ... the offer is deemed rejected unless the" 30-day "time period for reply is extended by the employer or by the terms and conditions of a collective bargaining agreement." (The alternative provision refers to employees in construction-related employments; see LC3201.5.) Both forms referenced above must be submitted to the Rehabilitation Unit when an offer of reemployment is rejected, whether the employee signs and declines the formal offer of reemployment or simply fails to respond.

Plan Approval – Requirements

In those cases where LC4638 requires a plan to be developed, the employer is required to do one of the following "within 90 days after" a determination of vocational feasibility:

1. Submit an agreed plan to the Rehabilitation Unit for approval (that, besides occurring within the 90-day period above, must additionally be submitted per CR10126 "within 15 days after the employee and employer have agreed to the terms and conditions" of the plan), OR
2. Request dispute resolution by the Rehabilitation Unit (per CR10126, by filing a Request For Dispute Resolution along with "a summary of the informal conference and the results thereof, including iden-tification of issues pending, position of the parties, and the rationale/supporting information for the position(s)").

A rehabilitation plan that is required by LC4638 must be submitted to the Rehabilitation Unit for approval even when the plan is mutually agreed to by all parties. However, approval is not required before the commencement of any rehabilitation plan. For instance, suppose the plan provides for a formal training program that is only offered once a year. It would be unreasonable for an employee to refuse to attend a scheduled program or for the employer to be held liable for the provision of maintenance allowance payments until next year's program merely because the intended training program is scheduled to begin after an agreed plan is submitted but prior to expiration of the 30-day period that CR10126 allows for the Rehabilitation Unit to approve or disapprove a plan.

It is unlikely that the Rehabilitation Unit would disapprove a plan that was agreed to by all parties and is already underway at the time the Rehabilitation Unit first reviews the plan. However, if a plan does not receive Rehabilitation Unit approval, the employer would have wasted its money, because the employer would still be liable for the full expense of some other approved plan.

If the employee does not agree to a rehabilitation plan that is proposed by the employer, the employer can still seek approval of the plan. The Rehabilitation Unit can approve the employer's proposed plan without the employee's agreement (or a plan proposed by the employee without the employer's agreement). This is unlikely but could occur if the employee preferred approval of some other alternative plan that the Rehabilitation Unit considered to be unreasonable. In the event of a dispute, the employer would comply with the dispute resolution procedures mentioned in #2 above, and expedited procedures will apply.

Per CR10127, if "a dispute exists regarding the identification of a vocational goal ... the parties may contact the Rehabilitation Unit for a telephone conference." A Rehabilitation Consultant will attempt to assist the parties in resolving the dispute or, if necessary, "schedule a conference to be held on an expedited basis within 10 days."

Per CR10126, "the Rehabilitation Unit shall approve or disapprove" a proposed plan "within 30 days of receipt." This time period commences when the Rehabilitation Unit receives a plan that is "properly submitted, documented, and signed." In its discretion, the Rehabilitation Unit may make inquiries or request additional information before reaching its decision. When a plan has been properly submitted and there is no communication from the Rehabilitation Unit within 30 days of its receipt of the plan, CR10126 provides that "the plan shall be deemed approved." Most plans are approved, so the Rehabilitation Unit saves time and money by withholding written notices of approval.

Nothing precludes a party from requesting a modification to a plan after it has been submitted for approval, e.g. where notice is received that additional tools must be purchased or that a course sponsor has lengthened a proposed classroom training program by two weeks. Per CR10126, requests for approval of plans and modifications to proposed plans are submitted to the Rehabilitation Unit using the same form, a Vocational Rehabilitation Plan. Requests for approval of modifications to a previously submitted plan will extend the 30-day period for a Rehabilitation Unit decision. The Rehabilitation Unit then has 30 days from receipt of the modified plan to approve or disapprove (and may approve by default by not issuing any decision).

Per LC4638, plans that "utilize an employee's transferable skills and experience shall be preferable to plans that propose training for an occupation in which the employee has no skills or experience." Certain exceptions are set out that prevent an insured employer from fulfilling its rehabilitation obligations by providing employment that is not likely to endure or else utilizes existing skills that would not be readily transferable if the current employment ended.

Employers ordinarily experience the lowest costs through direct placement into modified or alternative work, and such plans have traditionally provided the most expeditious and lasting benefits for injured workers. Since 1990, other factors being equal, such plans are preferred by law for workers' compensation purposes. However, as of 1994, an offer to provide modified or alternative work can terminate any employer's (whether insured or self-insured) liability for the provision of rehabilitation services (see 11.26).

11.23 REHABILITATION PLAN – PROBLEMS DURING

An approved rehabilitation plan may be thought of as a written agreement between the parties that formalizes the commitment of each party to adhere to all responsibilities placed upon them as set forth in the plan. A party's failure to adhere to previously agreed upon commitments is considered to be a breach of this agreement. Breaches may be minor, in which case the parties will probably resolve any problems among themselves without the need for intervention by the Rehabilitation Unit. However, the parties have a right to request Rehabilitation Unit action when a party commits a significant or material breach. A material breach is one that places the success of the entire plan in jeopardy, and this may result from an action or inaction of either the employer or the employee.

The employer's failure to provide funds or any services at the time they are necessary would constitute evidence of a material breach. The potential consequences of a material breach by the employer include liability for costs necessitated by an extension of the agreed upon plan or for a new plan under LC4644. Per LC4642, maintenance allowance payments and "any costs attributable to the delay shall not be subject to the overall cap" on expenditures in LC139.5 (see 11.28). Additionally, the employer would owe payment of a full maintenance allowance under LC4642 "for the period of delay" (see 11.9). No employer wishes to extend its liability beyond the scope of an approved plan. Potential liability for greatly increased costs provides a sufficiently strong financial incentive for an employer to monitor an ongoing plan by whatever means are appropriate to avoid such a result.

A consequence is specified in LC4643 for an employee who "unreasonably fails to cooperate in the provision of vocational rehabilitation services ... implementation of a vocational rehabilitation plan ...or completing an approved" plan. For the duration of the employee's unreasonable failure, the employee is not entitled to receive the basic maintenance allowance benefit otherwise payable under LC139.5 (but can receive permanent disability benefits).

The employer has the burden of proving that the employee's failure to participate is unreasonable. There is no repercussion under LC4643 if the employee's condition is not yet permanent and stationary, since the employee is therefore not yet eligible to receive a maintenance allowance. Otherwise, the employer will comply with the procedures that are prerequisite to a termination of liability for maintenance allowance payments (see 11.7). It is conceivable that an employee's failure to cooperate could be unreasonable on multiple occasions throughout the provision of rehabilitation benefits. One additional remedy is available to the employer. The employer can request approval of a termination of its liability upon a ground specified in LC4644: the "qualified injured worker unreasonably failed to complete an approved vocational rehabilitation plan."

11.24 NOTICE REQUIREMENTS – OVERVIEW

The rehabilitation category of benefits involves an intricate system of required written employee notices, reports to the Rehabilitation Unit utilizing required forms, and time periods for action and reaction to a multitude of circumstances. Virtually every separate aspect of rehabilitation benefits from an initial assessment of the employee's right to receive such benefits through the final payment of benefits precipitates a notice and/or reporting requirement within a specific number of days (as explained under their affiliated topics in the text).

The employer is required to provide two preinjury notices that will advise the employee of a potential right to receive rehabilitation benefits if injured: a posted notice and a time of hire notice. Within five days of the employer's receipt of knowledge that an employee is claiming a work-related injury, the employer is also required by CR9882 to again provide the employee with the same information that was relayed in preinjury notices. Each of these separately-required notifications advise employees of their potential entitlement to all benefits including rehabilitation (see 6.5-6.6).

Some employees will need more specific information at a later time when the rehabilitation category of benefits becomes more relevant to them. A notice of a potential right to rehabilitation benefits is usually provided in a letter format, but a pamphlet describing the nature and extent of this benefit is routinely enclosed to supplement the contents of the employer's notice letter. Such pamphlets are ordinarily obtained from the Rehabilitation Unit or provided by the employer's insurance company. The rehabilitation-specific pamphlet available from the State is titled *Help in Returning to Work-94.*

Multiple pamphlets may be provided to one employee. A notice of potential rights (usually provided by a pamphlet) serves a more general purpose than a Notice of Potential Eligibility (as detailed in 11.18) which is required only if the employee has been determined (or is presumed) to be medically eligible for rehabilitation benefits. A pamphlet is also provided with a notice of medical or vocational noneligibility. A separate pamphlet is used to advise the employee of potential entitlement and the procedure for requesting rehabilitation benefits upon each of the following events:

1. Receipt of knowledge that the employee is medically eligible.
2. Receipt of knowledge that the treating physician (or an agreed or Qualified Medical Evaluator) has determined that the employee is medically eligible.
3. Aggregate total disability payments equal 90 days and medical eligibility is not yet determined.
4. Aggregate total disability payments exceed 365 days and a physician has not previously determined that the employee is medically eligible.
5. Notice of denial of rehabilitation benefits is provided to the employee.

Some rehabilitation notice requirements arise under circumstances that will not necessarily occur in every case. However, all employees who receive notice of the potential right to receive rehabilitation benefits will additionally receive one of the two written documents described below.

1. Denial of Vocational Rehabilitation Services: to notify an employee who is not a qualified injured worker that the employee is therefore not entitled to rehabilitation services, OR

2. Request for Termination of Rehabilitation Services: a copy of this form is provided to an employee at the time the request is submitted to the Rehabilitation Unit.

11.25 INTERRUPTION OF BENEFITS

Per LC4644, there can be a "deferral or interruption of vocational rehabilitation services upon agreement by the employee and employer" (for any period of time) or else "upon a good cause determination" by the Rehabilitation Unit. Examples of reasons that may constitute good cause for interruption of rehabilitation services may include:

1. The employee currently declines vocational rehabilitation services for a specified period of time for a personal reason; e.g., the employee plans to take a vacation or wishes to remain home with his or her children during a school vacation and chooses to receive offered services at a later and/or specific, date.

2. The employee's medical condition has changed, and an accurate evaluation of vocational feasibility is not possible until the employee has received additional medical treatment, surgery or therapy.

3. The employee insists on receiving a specific vocational rehabilitation service that is unavailable at this time, e.g. services from a counselor who is on vacation or ill or otherwise unavailable for a specified period of time.

4. The employee is unavailable for receipt of vocational rehabilitation services, e.g. while the employee is hospitalized for a nonindustrial accident or incarcerated.

For 1994 or later injuries, an interruption of services is applicable only to medically eligible employees to whom the employer has not extended an offer of qualifying reemployment. Per CR10129.1, the employee can request a deferral of rehabilitation benefits after "being advised of medical eligibility for services, but prior to accepting services, only if the employer has not offered to provide alternative or modified work not exceeding the medical restrictions." A bona fide offer of reemployment extinguishes the employer's liability and thus provides a basis for termination, not an interruption, of further rehabilitation benefits from the date of the employee's receipt of the offer.

When a period of interruption is agreeable to the parties, CR9813 requires the employer to provide a confirmation notice to the employee "within 10 days of agreeing to interrupt." The notice will confirm the duration of the interrupted benefits, advise the employee of the applicability of the five-year statute of limitations period in LC5410 (see 11.34), and explain the steps necessary in order for the employee to notify the claims administrator that the employee "is ready to resume participation." The employee must be advised whether a telephone call will suffice or whether a written notice is required and to whom the oral or written notice must be provided; e.g. the employee's attorney or the claims person.

Rehabilitation benefits that are payable to employees with 1994 or later injuries are subject to time limits. Therefore, a request for interruption prior to completion of an approved plan requires an additional notification to the employee. Per CR9813, the employer must "explain that the plan must be completed within 18 months of approval" (see 11.25).

An interruption of rehabilitation services may occur during the provision of services to determine the employee's eligibility for services, while a rehabilitation plan is being developed, or after an approved plan has commenced. Where the employer wants to suspend services but the employee wants services to continue, a Request for Dispute Resolution (DWC Form RU-103) must be filed; this dispute requires a Rehabilitation Unit determination.

11.26 TERMINATION OF BENEFITS – GROUNDS

Per LC4644, "the liability of the employer for vocational rehabilitation services shall terminate" upon the occurrence of any of seven specific events, each of which is explained below. Exceptions to each event exist that will prevent Rehabilitation Unit approval of the employer's request and/or enable rehabilitation services to be reinstated at a future time (see 11.30).

Per CR10131, "when the claims administrator elects to terminate rehabilitation services," the claims administrator is required to submit a Request for Termination of Rehabilitation Services (DWC Form RU-105) and a proof of service to the Rehabilitation Unit within 10 days. Aside from specific time limitations and monetary caps on the provision of rehabilitation benefits (see 11.28-11.29), the employer can terminate liability for rehabilitation benefits to employees with 1994 or later injuries upon the occurrence of any of the seven events explained below. Note that, for 1994 or later injuries, grounds #5, #6, and #7 provide a basis for a termination of liability for rehabilitation benefits with the least cost to the employer.

1. Employee Declines Rehabilitation Benefits.

If the employer does not offer, or timely offer, to provide qualifying reemployment, a medically eligible employee who declines receipt of proffered rehabilitation services must complete a Statement of Decline of Vocational Rehabilitation Benefits (DWC Form RU-107). Rehabilitation Unit approval will not be given, and therefore the employer cannot unilaterally terminate rehabilitation benefits merely because the employee refuses such benefits or refuses to respond in any manner to a notice of medical eligibility. Termination on this basis requires the employee's willingness to sign an Employee Statement of Declination of Vocational Rehabilitation Services.

A procedural exception applies to 1994 or later injuries where the employer offers qualifying reemployment, but the employee refuses to respond within 30 days of receipt of the offer. In such cases, the employer need only submit a copy of its Notice of Offer of Modified or Alternate Work to the Rehabilitation Unit.

2. Employee Completes Plan.

Per LC4644, benefits will terminate after the employee completes "an approved vocational rehabilitation plan." For this reason, the designated completion date of services is an essential plan detail. Even so, an employee who remains unemployed upon plan completion may likely object to a termination of rehabilitation benefits.

3. Unreasonable Failure to Complete Plan.

Per LC4644, the employer can request the termination of rehabilitation benefits on the basis that the employee "unreasonably failed to complete an approved vocational rehabilitation plan." The employer has the burden of proving that the employee's failure to complete an approved plan constitutes an "unreasonable failure." If the employer can prove an unreasonable failure to complete an approved plan, the employer has two available remedies. The employee's failure to cooperate in the provision of any type of rehabilitation services can lead to a termination of maintenance allowance benefits under LC4643 for the period of the failure. Also, the employer can request termination of rehabilitation services under LC4644.

As a rule, the Rehabilitation Unit encourages interruption or deferral of benefits rather than termination. After all, the employee met two eligibility tests for Qualified Injured Worker status before a plan was developed, and (with rare exceptions) all parties agreed to the plan. For instance, consider an example of two employees who are both participating in an on-the-job training program. Unreasonable failure (and possibly fraud) may be established where one employee is missing days from work because he prefers to be doing something else such as engaging in personal hobbies like surfing the internet or socializing with friends. Interruption of services may be deemed more appropriate for another employee whose excessive absenteeism is apparently attributable to a sudden emotional crisis when his live-in girlfriend of many years finds a new boyfriend.

4. Benefits Not Requested in 90 Days

A medically eligible employee may not choose to participate in a rehabilitation program "within 90 days of notification" of medical eligibility. Per LC4644, the employer may request termination of rehabilitation benefits on the basis that the employee did not timely accept proffered rehabilitation services.

The employer cannot request a termination of benefits during the period allowed for the employee to make a decision regarding proffered rehabilitation benefits (90 days from receipt of a Notice of Potential Eligibility form). Additionally, LC4644 provides that rehabilitation services will not be terminated after the 90-day period unless the employer provided the employee with a reminder notice that cannot be sent until the 45th day after the initial notice of medical eligibility was provided but must be sent by the 70th day. Even if one or more reminder notices are timely provided, rehabilitation services cannot be terminated until after expiration of the 90-day period allowed for the employee's decision (on day 91) or the 21st day after the date the reminder notice was provided, whichever is later.

5. Employer Offers Modified Work.

Per LC4644, the employer's liability for rehabilitation benefits shall terminate when the employer offers "modified work lasting at least 12 months." The employer satisfies its liability for the provision of rehabilitation benefits by making this offer whether or not it is accepted by the employee. If the employee does accept the offer but later voluntarily quits, the employer is still not liable for rehabilitation benefits if the offered employment remains available to the employee for a full 12 months.

6. Employer Offers Alternative Work.

Liability for rehabilitation benefits terminates when the employer offers "alternative work meeting all of the" four conditions that are explained below. The employer's bona fide offer satisfies its liability for rehabilitation benefits even if the offer is rejected by the employee. However, the employee is entitled to rehabilitation services if the employer's offer fails to meet any one of these four required conditions:

    a..The "employee has the ability to perform the essential functions of the job" (usually a medical determination, but vocational services such as a job analysis may also be necessary to support an offer).

    b. The "job provided is in a regular position" that is anticipated to last "at least 12 months" (the 12-month requirement is identical to that explained in #1 above; the term "regular position" is defined in CR10122).

    c. The job "offers wages and compensation that are within 15 percent of those paid to the employee at the time of injury" (e.g. if offered work does not include a previously provided company car, it may be necessary to offer higher wages to offset this loss of compensation).

    d. The "job is located within reasonable commuting distance of the employee's residence at the time of injury" (a commute would appear to be reasonable if the employee is not asked to travel a greater distance than the employee's preinjury commute to work).

7. Employer Offers & Employee Accepts Work.

Per LC4644, liability for rehabilitation benefits terminates when the employer offers work that is expected to last at least 12 months which does not meet the conditions that are detailed in either #5 or #6 above but is acceptable to the employee. This situation is a catch-all provision that enables employees to return to work with a preinjury employer under conditions that are mutually agreeable (except that the offered job must last a minimum of 12 months). For instance, the employee may be willing to return to work for greatly reduced wages or with a longer commute in order to continue employment with desirable personnel, job benefits or location.

11.27 TERMINATION – FORMS & PROCEDURES

A Request for Termination of Rehabilitation Services form requests detailed information regarding rehabilitation benefits that have been provided. The form requires an accounting of benefits that includes starting and ending dates for all payments of maintenance allowance benefits and any concurrent advance payments of permanent disability benefits that the employee opted to receive; a listing of specific rehabilitation services that were provided; information as to the type of rehabilitation plan, if any, the goal of the plan, whether or not the plan resulted in employment, and if so, the date of the employee's return to work and the amount of wages received in the new employment. One purpose of the form is to enable the collection of information from which statistical data can be compiled.

When the employer requests termination of rehabilitation benefits, the employee is allowed 20 days after receipt of the employer's request to object by filing a Request for Dispute Resolution. Per CR10131, the starting date of the 30-day period allowed for Rehabilitation Unit action depends upon whether the employee objects to the employer's request. If the employee does not object, the employer's request must either be approved or determined to be inappropriate within 30 days of receipt. Otherwise, the Rehabilitation Unit has 30 days from receipt of the employee's objection to "hold a conference or otherwise obtain the employee's reasons for objection ... and issue its decision."

11.28 TERMINATION – MONETARY CAPS

For 1994 or later injuries, LC139.5 sets a maximum overall cap of $16,000 on the employer's liability for rehabilitation services. This monetary cap is all-inclusive. Included in the $16,000 overall cap is a separate monetary cap of $4500 for counseling fees (see 11.36).

Certain items such as additional living expenses, counseling fees, and a maintenance allowance are specifically mentioned, but LC139.5 provides that all costs and expenses "associated with, or arising out of, vocational rehabilitation services" are included. However, no costs or expenditures are applied against the monetary cap unless they are "incurred after the employee's request for vocational rehabilitation services." Further clarification is provided in CR10125 that specifies that deductions from the $16,000 cap begin after a medically eligible employee has:

1. Been notified of potential eligibility, AND
2. Received a written notice that confirms "the lack of alternate or modified work with the employer," AND
3. "Made a request for services."

There are limited exceptions to the $16,000 cap (and $4500 subcap). The amount of any untimely payments of benefits as well as any penalties that are attributable to employer-caused delays in the provision of rehabilitation benefits are not counted against the $16,000 overall cap. Also, payments for a second rehabilitation plan can exceed this cap (see 11.30).

11.29 TERMINATION – TIME LIMITS

Benefits payable to employees with 1994 or later injuries are subject to a variety of time limits. As a general rule, the employer is relieved from liability for the payment of services that are provided beyond statutorily allotted time periods, but exceptions exist. The most common exception involves employer-caused delays. The employer's liability can exceed otherwise fixed time limits and dollar amounts on rehabilitation benefits if the employer is determined to be responsible for a delay in the provision of rehabilitation services to which the employee is entitled (see also second plans in 11.30). Absent an exception, the employee's entitlement to rehabilitation benefits is limited to:

a. **52 Weeks of VRMA.** Per LC139.5, vocational rehabilitation maintenance allowance payments are limited in duration to a 52-week maximum period (subject to exceptions; see 11.7).

b. **18 Months to Complete Plan.** Per LC4644, rehabilitation "plans shall be completed within an 18-month period after approval of the plan." Per CR10126, if approval of a plan is not required, the 18-month period in LC4644 runs "from the date of plan commencement" (this date should be specified within the plan). Not included in the 18-month period is any period of time while rehabilitation benefits are being provided prior to plan approval or commencement. Benefits may be owed outside of the 18-month and 60-day time periods in limited circumstances; e.g. based upon good cause considerations or where the employee becomes entitled to a second plan.

c. **60 Days for Placement.** Included in the 18-month period for plan completion is a maximum 60-day period for job placement services (see 11.11).

11.30 REINSTATEMENT OF BENEFITS

The employee has a right to request reinstatement of benefits following either an interruption or termination of the employer's liability for the provision of rehabilitation benefits. However, the time and manner in which the employee makes this request and the factors that control the allowance of the employee's request differ for each of these situations, as explained below.

After Interruption of Benefits

The written terms of an agreed interruption or a Rehabilitation Unit determination will advise the employee of the maximum time allowed and the procedures necessary to resume benefits. The employee has the burden of initiating a timely reinstatement of benefits subject to such terms. Per CR10129, if "the claims administrator fails to commence or continue vocational rehabilitation services after receipt of a timely request, the employee can request the Rehabilitation Unit" to resolve the dispute by ordering the provision of services at the employer's expense. If the employee does not request reinstatement of benefits prior to expiration of the specified period of the interruption, the employer may request the Rehabilitation Unit to determine that its liability for rehabilitation benefits has terminated.

After Termination of Benefits

The employee also has a right to request reinstatement of rehabilitation benefits subsequent to a Rehabilitation Unit determination that the employer's liability for benefits was terminated. This right must be exercised timely because neither the Rehabilitation Unit nor the WCAB has jurisdiction to order the employer to provide rehabilitation benefits subsequent to the expiration of the statute of limitations that applies to the employee's claim (see 11.34).

Per CR10130, all requests for reinstatement following a termination of benefits "shall initially be submitted to the claims administrator." Depending upon the reason for the employee's request, the employer may voluntarily reinstate the employee's benefits and provide appropriate services at its expense. If necessary, the employee can thereafter request "a determination of entitlement to further rehabilitation services" by filing a Request for Dispute Resolution (DWC Form RU-103) with "the correct Rehabilitation Unit district office."

Several grounds for reinstatement of benefits derive from some type of failure of an employer's offer to provide modified or alternative work to employees with 1994 or later injuries. For instance, the employee will regain entitlement to rehabilitation benefits where a modified position does not last for 12 months for reasons that are not within the employee's control; e.g. due to job restructuring, a merger, a plant close down, a strike or a deterioration of the employee's medical condition.

Unlike reinstatement following an interruption, a reinstatement of benefits after termination requires the employee to establish that good cause exists for this request. Specific reasons that may constitute good cause for reinstatement of rehabilitation benefits are listed in LC4644. For instance, reinstatement of previously terminated rehabilitation services may be sought after work obtained through direct job placement in modified or alternative work (with the same or a different employer) "terminates, other than for cause, within 12 months," and that "work is unavailable in the labor market."

The employer would resist a request for reinstatement of rehabilitation benefits on the above grounds if the employee was discharged from employment as a result of a bona fide personnel action (such as insubordination, excessive absenteeism, or failure to complete work assignments). Reinstatement on such grounds is possible only when the reason for nonemployment is not within the employee's control; e.g., where the employee's job ends due to outsourcing (the job is no longer performed by employer personnel) or a plant closure. In such cases, the employee has the burden of establishing that employment opportunities for persons possessing comparable skills and duties are not realistically available at a different place of employment.

Second or Additional Rehabilitation Plan

As a general rule, few employees will receive more than one rehabilitation plan at the employer's expense as of 1994. Qualifying criteria for second or additional plans are set out in some detail in LC4644, which also contains a catchall provision. Per LC4644, any employee can receive a second plan if the Rehabilitation Unit "finds that the employee cannot complete" a plan because a "school or other training facility has closed," or the employee's condition under-goes a "sudden and unexpected change in disability that renders the plan inappropriate, or other similar circumstances." Depending upon the employee's reasons for requesting further services, any additional benefits will be subject to the $16,000 overall monetary cap on benefits or may be subject to another $16,000 overall cap.

11.31 ATTORNEY FEES – DEDUCTED FROM BENEFITS

An employee who chooses to be represented by an attorney owes the cost of services rendered by the attorney (with limited exceptions that are not covered herein). Benefits that are otherwise payable to the employee are reduced by the amount of any fee that is owed to the employee's attorney. There is no statutory authority for the exact manner in which attorney fees relating to rehabilitation issues are to be deducted from the employee's benefits. However, a common practice does exist that ensures that a sufficient amount of the employee's compensation will be withheld for anticipated attorney fees (that are not paid until the attorney has requested and received WCAB approval of a specific fee amount after termination of rehabilitation services).

When the employer is aware that the employee is represented by an attorney, the employer will withhold some of the employee's compensation in anticipation that the attorney will seek payment for services rendered (absent the attorney's specific written advice to the contrary). The amount withheld will be the amount the attorney requests or an amount the employer reasonably estimates that the WCAB will ultimately allow for attorney fees in the case. Estimated fees will be based upon a claimsperson's knowledge of the complexity of the legal issues and disputes involved and the range of fees that are customarily allowed in similar cases. It is the attorney's responsibility to advise the employer of any fee that will be requested. The attorney may also specify the category of benefits from which the employer should withhold this amount. The fee is usually stated as a percent-age of the employee's compensation rather than a set dollar amount.

Occasionally, an attorney may waive any fee, e.g. where an initial dispute was resolved in one brief telephone conversation with the claimsperson and no further effort was required beyond routine review of reports or merely monitoring the employer's voluntary provision of rehabilitation benefits. Sometimes, an attor-ney will notify the employer and the employee that a fee for services related to rehabilitation benefits will be requested to be payable out of any permanent disability benefits that may be awarded by the WCAB at a future date. In such cases, the attorney will notify the employer to provide full payment of any temporary disability or maintenance allowance benefits that become due to the employee, e.g. where the compensation rate for maintenance allowance benefits is a low amount and a reduction in weekly payments would cause a financial hardship for the employee.

In all cases, attorney fees related to rehabilitation benefits are payable only in a manner and an amount as directed by the WCAB (see CR10775-CR10778). Per LC4903, the WCAB is precluded from awarding fees for legal services to any "representative who is not an attorney" (except where an Application was filed with the WCAB or else the disclosure statement that is required by LC4906 was filed with the employer prior to 1992; and, see CR10779 regarding disbarred and suspended attorneys).

11.32 JURISDICTION – REHABILITATION UNIT vs. WCAB

The WCAB has exclusive jurisdiction to determine the compensability of the employee's claimed injury. The Rehabilitation Unit lacks authority to determine if the employee has sustained an industrial injury and whether the employee is entitled to compensation under the provisions of the workers' compensation laws. When compensability of an injury is disputed, the WCAB must decide this issue prior to any involvement of the Rehabilitation Unit. The Rehabilitation Unit does not have any authority to order or enforce the provision of rehabilitation benefits in noncompensable cases.

Per LC139.5, the Rehabilitation Unit has jurisdiction to "review, and approve vocational rehabilitation plans" and to "coordinate and enforce the implementation of vocational rehabilitation plans." This jurisdiction exists only when the employee has sustained a compensable industrial injury.

The Rehabilitation Unit's jurisdiction is initial jurisdiction, not exclusive jurisdiction. The WCAB will not render decisions on rehabilitation benefits unless and until the Rehabilitation Unit has first invoked its jurisdiction. Per LC4645, "where the question of entitlement to vocational rehabilitation benefits is first raised before a workers' compensation judge" in a compensable case, the judge shall "refer the question of entitlement to vocational rehabilitation services to the Rehabilitation Unit." The Rehabilitation Unit must provide its recommendations before the judge enters "a finding, decision or award on the issue of vocational rehabilitation."

In many cases the jurisdiction of the Rehabilitation Unit is final without any involvement of the WCAB. Per LC4645, any party can appeal "any determination or recommendation" of the Rehabilitation Unit to the WCAB "within 20 days after service." If no appeal is timely filed with the WCAB, the Rehabilitation Unit's decision is final. If an appeal is timely filed, the WCAB has jurisdiction to make a final determination on the issue of rehabilitation benefits.

Per CR10958, rehabilitation disputes that are submitted to the WCAB "shall be assigned, heard, and determined in the same manner as proceedings instituted for the collection of other compensation except that the burden of proof shall be on the person disputing the finding or determination of the" Rehabilitation Unit (unless mandatory arbitration is required; see below). The parties may present evidence, including witness testimony. The judge's decision may or may not conform to the previous decision of the Rehabilitation Unit. Judges can however be expected to rely upon opinions of Rehabilitation Consultants as expert witnesses. In any event, the judge's decision supersedes any prior administrative decisions that were rendered by the Rehabilitation Unit.

Mandatory Arbitration

Mandatory arbitration of disputed rehabilitation issues is required only when the employee is represented by an attorney. For represented employees, LC4645 provides that "all disputed matters shall be submitted to arbitration," with certain exceptions. Arbitration is not mandatory when LC4643 requires an expedited conference to determine whether maintenance allowance benefits should be terminated for a failure to cooperate in the provision of rehabilitation services. Also, adjudication by the WCAB, not arbitration, is required when the threshold issue of the compensability of an alleged injury is disputed in its entirety.

By agreement, LC5275 permits the parties to submit any disputed issues for arbitration at their option. However, LC5275 requires arbitration of rehabilitation disputes in two circumstances only. Per LC5275, "regardless of the date of injury," a dispute must be submitted for arbitration if:

1. The Administrative Director determines that a request for Rehabilitation Unit dispute resolution "will not be set for conference within 90 calendar days from the date of filing of the request," OR
2. The Presiding Judge at the WCAB determines that an appeal of a determination of the Rehabilitation Unit "will not be set for hearing within 120 calendar days from the date of the filing of the appeal."

11.33 SETTLEMENT OF REHABILITATION BENEFITS

Settlement Ordinarily Prohibited

Per LC5100.6, the "appeals board shall not permit the commutation or settlement of compensation or indemnity payments or other benefits to which the employee is entitled under rehabilitation." If the employee is a qualified injured worker, the total value of rehabilitation benefits cannot be paid in a lump sum. Once the money is paid, no one can effectively control how the employee spends the money. The employer could provide the full cost of a rehabilitation program, but the employee might not ever undergo the program.

For the reasons discussed above, lump sum payments by settlement or otherwise are prohibited by LC5100.6 and, since 1990, by LC4646. This prohibition inures to the benefit of the employer as well as the employee. An employee who is a qualified injured worker is assured of receipt of rehabilitation benefits and services. When an employer is obligated to provide rehabilitation benefits, it will only owe the cost of benefits that the employee actually receives.

Settlement Permissible in Disputed Cases

"Settlement or commutation of vocational rehabilitation services" is prohibited by LC4646 (and under LC5100.6) with one exception. Rehabilitation benefits can be settled or paid as a lump sum if a judge makes a finding "that there are good faith issues which, if resolved against the employee, would defeat the employee's right to all compensation" (see CR10870). Upon such finding, the

WCAB can approve a Compromise and Release settlement under which the employer is ordinarily released from liability to provide any further benefits including rehabilitation, and the employee receives payment of a lump sum.

Raising an issue in "good faith" means raising an issue that the employer appears capable of supporting with evidence. Examples of issues that, if successfully proven, can result in a "take nothing" award include initial physical aggressor, statute of limitations or intoxication. The Labor Code only prohibits the settlement of any rehabilitation benefits that are payable to an employee in a compensable case (as a general rule, a compensable case is any case where the employer voluntarily pays benefits).

The employee may request rehabilitation benefits after approval of a Compromise and Release settlement. If the WCAB made a specific finding that there was a good faith issue as to compensability, the Rehabilitation Unit will rely on this finding to issue a decision that the employee is not entitled to benefits. When this finding is requested as part of a Compromise and Release agreement, the employer should give careful review to the wording of an Order of Approval. If this finding is omitted inadvertently, immediate steps can be taken to obtain a corrected order (including filing a Petition for Reconsideration to appeal the Judge's decision). If there is no such finding in the WCAB's Order of Approval of the Compromise and Release, the Rehabilitation Unit could determine the employee's request on its merits. The employer could still dispute the compensability of the injury, but this issue would have to be adjudicated by the WCAB.

A WCAB hearing can be conducted on the issue of compensability subsequent to approval of a Compromise and Release. This can only be done in cases where the claim is not yet barred by a statute of limitation. The judge may find the claim to be compensable. If so, the case will then be referred back to the Rehabilitation Unit for a separate determination on the employee's entitlement to rehabilitation benefits. Within five years from the date of injury, a Compromise and Release can be set aside for good cause under LC5803, and the employer can be ordered to provide full benefits on any compensable claim. After expiration of this five-year period, the WCAB's jurisdiction will be limited to an award of rehabilitation benefits only (see 11.34). Even if the claim is found to be compensable, the employee cannot be awarded any other benefits except rehabilitation.

11.34 STATUTES OF LIMITATIONS

Statutes of limitations on rehabilitation benefits restrict the time in which a party can adjudicate entitlement issues (as opposed to time limits that merely restrict the duration of the employee's entitlement to particular subcategories of rehabilitation benefits; see LC4644 and 11.29). Separate statutes of limitations for rehabilitation benefits are found in LC5405.4, LC5410, and LC5803.

Per LC5405.5, the employee has a right to "request vocational rehabilitation benefits" within one year from "the date of last finding of permanent disability by the appeals board" or "the date the appeals board approved a compromise and release of other issues," subject to exceptions provided in LC4644 and LC5410.

The WCAB makes a "finding of permanent disability" when it issues a finding, decision, award or order on the employee's entitlement to permanent disability benefits. The issue of permanent disability may be adjudicated more than once. The final finding of permanent disability can be made by issuance of any of the following:

a. A Findings and Award (F&A) conforming to the oral stipulations of the parties or approving a Stipulations With Request for Award settlement document.

b. A Findings and Order (F&O) or a Findings and Award (F&A) after formal proceedings whereby the WCAB makes a written finding on the existence and extent of permanent disability. A finding may be that no disability has resulted from an injury, or a finding may specify a percent of disability.

c. A findings, order, decision or award that provides a determination of issues raised by the timely filing of a Petition to Reopen a previously final award of permanent disability under LC5410 or LC5803 (see 6.23-6.28).

d. A decision rendered after the timely filing of an appeal of a final finding of permanent disability, e.g. a Decision and Order of the Appeals Board following timely filing of a Petition for Reconsideration or a decision of the Court of Appeal or the Supreme Court.

e. An Order Approving Compromise and Release (C&R) by which the WCAB approves of the settlement amount an employer is willing to pay as being adequate compensation for permanent disability benefits (and usually all other benefits) that would otherwise be due to an employee.

The date of approval of a Compromise and Release settlement is the date shown on the Order of Approval. In effect, the Order is a "finding" that the employee is being paid a fair and adequate amount of compensation for all benefits encompassed within the terms of the settlement document. A Compromise and Release settlement can be a partial settlement; approval can release the employer from liability to provide further temporary disability benefits and/or medical expense without any reference to permanent disability benefits. The statute of limitations begins to run from the date a settlement is approved that disposes of the entire case or disposes of the issue of permanent disability benefits.

As amended effective 1990, LC5410 enables the employee to request rehabilitation benefits within five years from the date of injury if the employee can establish that "the provision of rehabilitation services has become feasible because the employee's medical condition has improved or because of other factors not capable of determination at the time the employer's liability for vocational rehabilitation services otherwise terminated" (e.g. the employee's condition got worse). The employer's defense to claims for rehabilitation benefits under LC5410 will parallel defenses that could be used to defend claims for any other type of new and further disability (see 6.25).

If an informal request for the employer to provide benefits is not successful, LC5410 permits the employee to institute WCAB proceedings by filing an Application for Adjudication of Claim or a Petition to Reopen within five years from the date of injury. (An Application is the correct document if one has not previously been filed or was previously filed but dismissed; a Petition to Reopen is used to seek modification of a prior WCAB award.) This Labor Code section applies only to employees and does not provide the employer with any right to institute WCAB proceedings regarding disputed rehabilitation benefits.

An additional ground for seeking adjudication of disputed rehabilitation benefits is provided in LC5803. This statute only applies to claims where a WCAB case is already on file, and a judge has issued a previous decision in the case. Per LC5803, the WCAB has jurisdiction to "rescind, alter, or amend" any "decisions and orders of the rehabilitation unit." However, the jurisdiction of the WCAB is limited by LC5804 to a period of five years from the date of injury.

Unlike LC5410, LC5803 provides equal rights for the employer and the employee. Either party can file a Petition to Reopen for Good Cause pursuant to LC5803 within five years from the date of injury. Either party must establish "good cause" why the previous Rehabilitation Unit decision should be changed. The employee can show good cause by establishing a current need for rehabilitation services. The employer could establish good cause by showing fraud on the part of the employee in receipt of previous or current rehabilitation benefits.

A review of the provisions of LC4644 (that are referenced in LC5410) reveals that for every time limitation that is set out in LC4644, there is at least one exception. The net effect of LC4644 is to restrict the time in which rehabilitation benefits may be requested by employees who are not medically eligible or have no interest in receiving rehabilitation benefits. Close reading of LC4644 reveals sufficient grounds for any employee who has a compensable claim and is in need of rehabilitation benefits to request and receive rehabilitation benefits at any time notwithstanding any provisions of LC5405.5 or LC5410 to the contrary.

11.35 FAIR EMPLOYMENT AND HOUSING ACT

The employer's duties differ regarding treatment of disabled persons under the California Labor Code and the Fair Employment and Housing Act. The Fair Employment and Housing Act (FEHA)is a state law that contains provisions that are intended to preclude work-related harassment and discrimination against persons with disabilities (and other types of discrimination not covered herein.)

Effective 1994, LC4636 requires that an employee who is advised of medical eligibility for workers' compensation benefits must concurrently be provided with a "notice of rights under the Americans with Disabilities Act" (see below) "and the provisions of the Fair Employment and Housing Act relating to individuals with a disability." This notice requirement is met by providing the employee with a *Help In Returning to Work-94* pamphlet. The pamphlet informs the employee that this California law is administered by the Department of Fair

Employment and Housing and provides a telephone number to contact this State agency (1-800-884-1684).

11.36 AMERICANS WITH DISABILITIES ACT

An employer's obligations to disabled employees under state workers' compensation laws do not always coincide with obligations under certain federal laws or even other California laws. The duty to provide rehabilitation benefits to qualified injured workers (QIWs) under California workers' compensation laws varies in significant detail from duties owed to qualified individuals with disabilities (QIDs) under the federal Americans with Disabilities Act (ADA). (This Act was applicable as of 7/26/92 to employers of 25 or more employees and 15 or more employees as of 7/26/94.)

Full compliance with workers' compensation obligations does not eliminate the employer's exposure to liabilities arising from civil suits based upon violations of antidiscrimination provisions of other applicable laws. For instance, the employee's willingness to participate in a proposed rehabilitation plan that provides direct job placement with a new employer may fulfill all workers' compensation obligations without relieving the employer from any concurrent obligation under the Americans with Disabilities Act to provide a reasonable accommodation if this employee would thereby be able to perform all of the essential functions of the preinjury job assignment.

Uncertainties exist as to whether some conditions that constitute compensable disabilities for workers' compensation purposes also constitute disabilities under the Americans with Disabilities Act; for instance, a work restriction that is prophylactic in nature (see 10.41). There are many gray areas where decisions should be made based upon sound legal advice. In the optimum situation, a workers' compensation claimsperson should strive to become aware of and comply with the employer's concurrent state and federal obligations to disabled workers to the fullest extent possible without exceeding statutory requirements for the provision of workers' compensation benefits.

Information on the provisions of the Americans with Disabilities Act is available from the federal government. The *Help In Returning to Work-94* pamphlet advises employees that they may obtain information by calling the Equal Employment Opportunity Commission at 1-800-USA-EEOC (1-800-872-3362). This agency also disseminates other publications, mostly free of charge, that are designed to assist employers in complying with their obligations under the Americans with Disabilities Act.

11.37 VOCATIONAL REHABILITATION FEE SCHEDULE

Per LC139.5, the Administrative Director of the Division of Workers' Compensation is required to "develop a fee schedule ... governing reasonable fees for vocational rehabilitation services." Per CR10132.1, adjustments to the Vocational Rehabilitation Fee Schedule are required to be reviewed by the Administrative Director "on an annual basis."

A brief perusal of the fee schedule will provide an overview of the nature and extent of different vocational rehabilitation services, as well as their comparative costs. (This perusal can provide the claims administrator with information that is relevant to the establishing of claim file reserves; see 2.25). Rehabilitation providers and employers can agree to rates higher than fee-scheduled amounts. However, CR10132 requires that all such agreements must be "made in writing prior to the provision of such rehabilitation services." Documentation of the parties agreement should avoid any future need to invoke the dispute resolution services of the Rehabilitation Unit pursuant to CR10132 regarding the application of the fee schedule.

The Vocational Rehabilitation Fee Schedule is set out in CR10132.1. This regulation provides that "all billings for casework are to be itemized in tenths of an hour and submitted using the service code" numbers shown in the schedule. Some services are assigned a specific dollar amount as being payable per service, per day or as a maximum limit (dependent upon actual time spent). Other services are billable at a specified hourly rate for actual time with some being designated as "not to exceed" a specified amount of time. For instance, the fee deemed reasonable for preparation of a job analysis is expressed as "actual time, not to exceed 5 Hours."

Some items are specified to be "non-billable costs." Per CR10132.1, these "non-billable costs include: postage, clerical services, photocopies, in-house waiting time, attempted telephone contacts, and in-house staffing." With the exception of non-billable costs, "all billings from vocational rehabilitation service providers are due and payable within sixty days of receipt pursuant to" CR10132. This regulation relieves the employer from its obligation to provide payment if, within the 60-day period allotted, it files an objection "contesting the billing or any portion thereof." If the employer contests only part of the billing, uncontested amounts are required to be paid within the 60-day period. Per CR10132, the employer's failure to pay or file an objection within the 60-day period can result in assessment of an administrative penalty (see 2.27).

Effective 1994, LC139.5 requires the Administrative Director of the Division of Workers' Compensation to establish "maximum aggregate permissible fees" for three categories of counseling activities, subject to a $4500 overall cap. As initially established, the maximum permissible fees for counseling services include: $1200 for the evaluation of vocational feasibility, $2500 for plan development, and $2000 for job placement. Overall counseling fees for 1994 or later injuries are limited to $4500 by LC139.5 despite the fact that the cumulative total of fees allowed for different types (or phases) of counseling services exceed $4500 in the Vocational Rehabilitation Fee Schedule, as set out in CR10132.1.

The monetary cap on counseling fees that is specified in LC139.5 applies only to injuries that occur on or after 1/1/94. However, CR10132 provides that the current limits on counseling fees "shall be presumed reasonable for services to employees who are determined medically eligible on or after 1/1/94." Even so, it is difficult to imagine how a counselor could justify higher fees where the solitary difference between two employees who received the same service on the same day is the date of injury. (Note: the fee schedules for medical treatment expense and medical-legal expenses apply to services rendered on or after the effective date of any revisions.)

11.38 REHABILITATION UNIT FORMS – LISTING

Since 1994, CR10123.1 provides that all forms required by the Rehabilitation Unit may be submitted on white paper (color coding of forms was previously required by the Rehabilitation Unit). Copies of the *Help in Returning to Work-94* benefit information pamphlet, required forms and instructions for the completion and submission of required forms to the correct venue (correct district office) are available from the Rehabilitation Unit, Headquarters, P.O. Box 420603, San Francisco, CA 94142.

A list of the forms and notices that are prescribed by the Rehabilitation Unit is provided as a handy reference below. In common practice, each form is referred to by its number rather than its lengthier official title. For instance, the Treating Physician's Report of Disability Status is usually referred to simply as the "RU-90."

DWC Form RU-90: Treating Physician's Report of Disability Status.
DWC Form RU-91: Description of Employee's Job Duties.
DWC Form RU-94: Notice of Offer of Modified or Alternate Work
DWC Form RU-101: Case Initiation Document.
DWC Form RU-102: Vocational Rehabilitation Plan.
DWC Form RU-103: Request for Dispute Resolution.
DWC Form RU-104: (see note below)
DWC Form RU-105: Request for Termination of Rehabilitation
    Services.
DWC Form RU-106: (see note below)
DWC Form RU-107: Statement of Decline of Vocational Rehabilitation
    Benefits.
DWC Form RU-120: Initial Evaluation Summary.
DWC Form RU-121: Vocational Rehabilitation Progress Report.

Note: There is no currently used form numbered RU-104 or RU-106.

[12] DEATH

12.1 DEATH BENEFITS – OVERVIEW

There are two types of death benefits: burial benefits and dependency benefits. The burial benefit provides reimbursement for a specific expense. Dependency benefits provide a wage replacement benefit (an indemnity benefit) to certain qualified persons who were dependent upon the employee's earnings for their own financial support. Death may result instantaneously or after a lengthy period of disability. There is no offset of indemnity benefits against death benefits. Per LC4702, death benefits are payable by the employer in addition to any disability indemnity benefits that may have been paid to the employee prior to death.

12.2 DATE OF INJURY vs. DATE OF DEATH

There are two important dates in a death case: the date of injury (DOI) and the date of death (DOD). Except where a spousal presumption of dependency applies (see 12.7), the following matters are all evaluated as of the date of the injury that resulted in death:

    a. The amount of the death benefit that is payable.
    b. The compensation rate for payment of benefits.
    c. The amount of the burial benefit.
    d. Who is or is not a dependent of the employee.
    e. Whether dependency is total or partial.
    f. The extent (percentage) of partial dependency.

Both the date of injury and the date of death are utilized when determining the applicable statute of limitations that applies to a claim for death benefits (see 12.31). There is only one situation where a factual matter relative to death benefits is controlled exclusively by the date of death without regard to the date of the injury resulting in death. For 1990 or later injuries, the date of death is used to determine certain facts pertaining to a presumption of spousal dependency (but not the presumption of dependency applicable to certain children; see 12.6). Except for the issue of presumed spousal dependency and the issue of whether a statute of limitations bars a claim, all other issues relating to death benefits are determined according to facts existing at the time of injury.

12.3 BURIAL EXPENSE

Per LC4701, the employer is liable for "reasonable expenses of the employee's burial" up to a specified maximum amount (e.g., $5,000 for 1991 or later injuries and until the next increase). The full burial expense in LC4701 is not always owed. If actual burial expenses are less than the statutory benefit amount, the employer owes the amount incurred. When an employee is not survived by any dependents or heirs, LC4706 provides that the "appeals board may order the burial expense ... paid to the proper person."

12.4 DEPENDENCY – DEFINED

Per LC4701, dependency benefits are payable "when the employee leaves any person dependent upon him for support." For workers' compensation purposes, dependency means financial dependency. Dependents are persons who relied upon the employee's income for their own support. The employee's death adversely affects the dependents' ability to maintain their customary standard of living or to obtain life necessities such as food, clothing or shelter.

12.5 DEPENDENCY – TOTAL OR PARTIAL

Total dependents have one source of support: the employee's earnings. The dollar amount of the employee's contributions is irrelevant. Since they have no other source of income, these persons are financially 100% dependent upon the employee. Total dependents lose their entire source of support when the employee's income ceases upon his death. Occasionally, a person who is totally dependent on the date of the injury may become self-supporting prior to the employee's death. This person is still a total dependent under the Labor Code, because financial dependency is assessed as of the date of injury (with one exception that applies to a spouse; see 12.7).

Partial dependents rely in part on the employee's earnings, but they have at least one other source of income. For instance, the partial dependent may also receive support from other persons, wages from other employment(s), investment income or payments under state or federal assistance programs. Part of the dependent's income, not all of it, is lost with the employee's demise. Any dependent who is less than 100% financially dependent upon the employee is a partial dependent.

12.6 DEPENDENCY PRESUMED – CHILD

Since 1990, there are two presumptions of dependency in the Labor Code. One presumption applies exclusively to certain children of a deceased employee. Another applies to a surviving spouse (see 12.7). Some children of a "deceased employee-parent" are "conclusively presumed to be wholly dependent for support." A child who meets one of three criteria specified in LC3501 is treated as a total dependent without any proof of actual financial contributions. For purposes of this presumption, all facts necessary for application of the presumption are determined as of the date of injury. A child is automatically considered to be a total dependent if "at the time of the injury resulting in death of the parent":

1. The child is a minor AND living with the employee. The child must be under the age of 18, and his residence address must be the same as the employee, OR

2. The child is over "the age of 18 years" AND "physically or mentally incapacitated from earning" (when employability is medically precluded, the child is deemed to be a total dependent whether or not the child is a minor or resides with the employee; e.g., the child could be mentally retarded, 25 years old, and living at home or in an institution), OR

3. The employee-parent was "legally liable" for the child's maintenance, AND there is no "surviving totally dependent parent."

The third criterion is the most confusing. The presumption of dependency does not apply if the child's other parent is alive and qualifies as a total dependent (the child can still qualify as a total dependent but would have to prove this with evidence). When the deceased employee is the child's only parent, the child's residence location need not be determined. It is only necessary to determine whether the employee was legally liable for the child's support, e.g. under a court decree or under general provisions of California laws.

The amount of the employee's contributions is irrelevant because LC3501 does not specify any particular amount. If the employee provided financial support, the child is presumed to be totally dependent regardless of whether support was partial or total. In fact, the presumption can apply when the employee did not provide any support at all. A child's benefits will not be jeopardized in any manner by the fact that a parent who was legally liable for support refused or neglected to pay court-ordered support payments or was willing but financially unable to provide necessary support.

12.7 DEPENDENCY PRESUMED – SPOUSE

For 1990 or later injuries, a second presumption of dependency exists (besides the presumption of dependency that applies to certain children of a deceased employee; see 12.6). The second presumption applies exclusively to a spouse (but not every deceased employee's spouse), and all facts necessary for application of this presumption are determined as of the date of death, not the date of injury.

Per LC3501, "a spouse to whom a deceased employee is married at the time of death shall be conclusively presumed to be wholly dependent for support" if the spouse's earnings were $30,000 or less in the one-year period immediately preceding the date of the employee's death. For purposes of this presumption, a spouse means a person who is legally married to the employee, a fact that may be disputed and is subject to proof. (Note: if the presumption does not apply, a nonmarital partner can still qualify for total or partial dependency by proving financial support: see 12.9). A spouse is not required to prove that he or she resided with the employee, only the validity of the marriage.

Both of the required criteria (marital relationship and earnings) are determined as of the date of death, not as of the date of injury. Some experts anticipate that the Legislature intended the facts that are required for application of the spousal presumption to be determined as of the date of the employee's injury rather than the date of death and that future legislation will make this change. Absent a legislative change, the claimsperson should be aware of the potential for fraud in cases where there is an extended period between the date of the injury and the date of death. For instance, a person may wed the employee after the date of injury and/or a spouse may quit a job to ensure that earnings will not exceed $30,000 in the year prior to the employee's death. Also, employees (and/or their intended heirs) may be astonished to learn that an estranged spouse is entitled to receive a substantial financial benefit if the employee dies prior to the date that a divorce becomes final (up to $125,000 for an injury in 1997!).

12.8 QUALIFICATIONS FOR DEPENDENTS

Some children and spouses can qualify as total dependents by meeting the criteria required for application of the statutory presumptions of dependency that are set out in LC3501. Per LC3502, "in all other cases, questions of entire or partial dependency and questions as to who are dependents and the extent of their dependency shall be determined in accordance with the facts as they exist at the time of the injury" (not facts that exist on the date of the employee's death).

An initial qualification is found in LC4701 that provides that dependency benefits are payable when the employee "leaves any person dependent upon him or her for support." Persons claiming dependency benefits are required to provide proof of receipt of financial support from the employee. However, some persons who were financially dependent upon a deceased employee will not be entitled to dependency benefits because there is a separate and additional qualification for dependents. Per LC3503, "no person is a dependent of any deceased employee unless" the person, on the date of injury, bore one of the following relationships to the employee:

1. The person was one of the specific relatives of the employee who are listed in LC3503 (related by blood, marriage or adoption), OR
2. The person was a "good faith member of the family or household of the employee."

12.9 DEPENDENT – RELATIVE OF EMPLOYEE

Some relatives may be dependents while others are not. In LC3503, relatives who are eligible to receive workers' compensation dependency benefits are listed according to their relationship to the employee as follows:

a. Husband or wife.
b. Child, adopted child, stepchild, grandchild, and posthumous child (one born after the employee's death).
c. Mother, mother-in-law, grandmother, father, father-in-law, and grandfather, .
d. Brother, brother-in-law, sister, and sister-in-law.
e. Uncle, nephew, aunt, and niece.

The above relationships must be proven; legal documents such as birth certificates, marriage licenses, and divorce papers will suffice as evidence. These relatives may reside with the employee, in their own home, or anywhere else. However, they are only entitled to death benefits if they were financially dependent upon the employee for their support.

A dependency relationship is not created each time money changes hands between relatives. The amount, frequency or duration of payments to relatives is pertinent but not controlling. The reason why the employee provided money must be examined. Common reasons for providing money or items of value to non-dependent relatives (and nonrelatives) would include:

a. Gifts, e.g. cash enclosed in a holiday greeting card to a niece, taking an uncle out to dinner to celebrate a job promotion or purchasing all the food for a family barbecue.
b. Business relationships, e.g. the employee makes a monthly payment in return for a room and meals in the home of an aunt-landlord, he leaves tips for his mother as a customer at the restaurant where she works as a waitress, or he employs and pays a stepchild to babysit or paint his house.
c. Emergency financial assistance, e.g. short-term provision of money or food to a sister who has recently lost her job where there is no intention to continue assistance on a long-term basis.
d. Debtor-creditor relationships, e.g. payments to a nephew are repayments of money loaned to the employee. There is usually a time limit

on loan payments but not on support contributions to a dependent, and loan payments are made under a contractual obligation (that need not be written). The outstanding loan balance as of the date of the employee's death is a claim against the employee's estate.

e. Family closeness, e.g. allowing grandparents to reside in the employee's home rent-free while their home is being rebuilt after a fire (yet another example of short-term assistance).

12.10 DEPENDENT – GOOD FAITH MEMBER OF FAMILY

Per LC3503, any family members residing with the employee can qualify as dependents, even a relative who is not specifically listed in LC3503. The person could be a cousin or great-uncle, or the person could be related to the employee's spouse rather than the employee himself, e.g. the spouse's aunt or grandmother. Indeed, the person need not be a relative of anyone in the employee's home. Per LC5303, any "good faith" member of the employee's "family or household" can qualify as a dependent. The person may be a nonmarital partner whose status is comparable to that of a spouse under a marriage contract, or the person may be a close friend (such as a godmother) who is treated as a relative. The person must receive financial support in order to qualify as the employee's dependent. In general, the person must receive similar treatment financially to all other family members in the employee's home.

Persons residing with the employee can be treated as members of the family but not be financial dependents. A tenant may take meals with the family and enjoy the use of the employee's home — this relationship is one of landlord-tenant, not dependency. A live-in maid, nurse, tutor or babysitter may be treated as one of the family — these are employer-employee relationships in that money is expended in exchange for performance of services. The employee may entertain out-of-town guests by providing food, shelter, and entertainment. This is a gratuitous relationship with courtesies being extended on a short-term basis. Even if the guests make regular annual visits to the employee's home, the regularity of the situation does not change the relationship — these persons are guests, not dependents. In general, financial dependency is not demonstrated by short-term periods of financial assistance.

12.11 ANNUAL SUPPORT – CLAIMED BY DEPENDENT

Partial dependents must prove the amount they received as support in the one-year period preceding the date of injury. The death benefit payable to a partial dependent is computed based upon the annual amount of the employee's contributions (see 12.20). Allegations of support without documentation are susceptible to exaggeration and inaccuracies. Witness statements may be plentiful but self-serving rather than realistic. The claimsperson should be alert to "puffery" of statements regarding the amount of support payments and should always seek documentation of contributions. Documentation of support may take the form of income tax returns, bank statements, canceled checks, letters, credit applications, legal documents or cash receipts.

Unless the employee's contributions are replaced, there should be a demonstrable effect on the dependent's standard of living after the employee's death. Certain affiliated information can assist in determining the viability of claimed support contributions. The dependent's total income from all other sources can be determined. Next, the dependent's normal living expenses can be assessed. A monetary gap between the person's financial needs and the ability to provide these needs without the alleged contributions from the employee lends credence to a claim of support payments within this range. However, concurrent unrelated events might also have had an adverse financial impact on the dependent, e.g. a rent increase or the loss of a part-time job. It is still necessary for the dependent to present evidence supporting the precise amount of the employee's contributions.

All claimed amounts of support are subject to verification. Payments made directly to a third person can be confirmed by this source, e.g. a landlord or housekeeper. Undocumented cash contributions present problems, but the legitimacy of their receipt can be realistically appraised. The claimsperson must evaluate the validity of the amount claimed in view of its intended purpose. An alleged contribution of $1500 a month for rent could be shown to be a gross exaggeration by presenting evidence that the actual rent was a lesser amount, e.g. a copy of the lease, receipts retained by the landlord or statements of other renters at the same location.

When housing or other items are provided directly to the dependent, the reasonable cash value of such items must be assessed; e.g., free meals have a cash value equal to the amount the dependent would otherwise have to pay for food, and free rent is equivalent to the fair rental value of similar housing to any nondependent. The employee's contributions to partial dependents must always be stated as a dollar amount regardless of the method of providing financial support.

12.12 ANNUAL SUPPORT – PROVIDED BY EMPLOYEE

Support claimed by partial dependents must be realistic when compared to the amount of earnings that the employee actually had available to use for this purpose. If the employee also had total dependents, some of the employee's income was utilized for their support. Even if there were no total dependents, the employee's gross income cannot be presumed to measure the support provided to partial dependents. An employee does not receive the full amount of gross annual earnings. The greatest amount of accessible income is the employee's net earnings after state and federal taxes are deducted. From the remainder, some portion of the employee's earnings will be used for the employee's self-support: providing life necessities to himself or herself. The employee's gross earnings must be reduced by the amount of taxes, self-support (that includes support shared with total dependents), and any exclusively personal expenditures. The reduced earnings figure will represent the maximum earnings that the employee had available to use for support of all partial dependents.

Some expenses are entirely personal. The purchased item is used or consumed entirely by the employee, or the employee has a personal legal obligation for payment of the expense. Examples of entirely personal expenses of the employee could include:

1. Food consumed by the employee, e.g. the cost of meals away from home or all food if the employee lives alone.
2. Payments of legal obligations, e.g. credit card charges, college loans or other personal debts.
3. Clothing, including laundry and dry cleaning expense.
4. Medical expenses, e.g. examinations, treatment, braces and prescription medications.
5. Work related expenses, e.g. uniforms, briefcases, equipment, tools or union dues.
6. Transportation, e.g. bus fare or car payments, maintenance and insurance.
7. Entertainment expense, e.g. sports such as skiing, bowling, golf, and fishing, recreational vehicles or vacations by oneself.
8. Club memberships, e.g. health spas, athletic facilities or private clubs.
9. Hobbies, e.g. sports car racing, stamp or coin collecting.
10. Shelter, e.g. rent or house payments and maintenance costs.
11. Investments, e.g. real estate, stocks or bonds, retirement fund contributions or profit sharing plans.
12. Insurance, e.g. medical, disability or auto.
13. Donations, e.g. to religious, political or charitable organizations.

When partial dependents reside outside the employee's home, all of the above expenses should be deducted from the employee's earnings. When partial dependents reside in the employee's home, certain ordinarily personal expenses, such as the residence itself, may be shared in such a way as to be inseparable. When the benefit derived from a particular expenditure is shared with a partial dependent in an inseparable manner, the expense is considered to be support provided to the partial dependent (for additional examples of communal expenses, see 12.13).

12.13 ANNUAL SUPPORT – PROVIDED TO SPOUSE

The most common example of a partial dependent residing with the employee is a partially dependent spouse (meaning a spouse who does not qualify for the spousal presumption of total dependency under LC3502; see 12.7). The cost of food or clothing or other expenses that were incurred for the employee's personal use cannot reasonably be considered to be an amount devoted to the support of a partial dependent. Annual support provided to a spouse will include all of the employee's earnings that were devoted to the direct support of the spouse. Additionally, appellate courts have indicated that the full amount of fixed expenses that are incurred for the communal benefit of both spouses or to maintain the general standard of living enjoyed by both members of the marital community will also be considered as earnings donated to the support of the dependent spouse, not personal expenses of the employee.

If an employee paid the full monthly house payment, it is not necessary to determine the exact square footage of the couple's home that was used personally by the employee as opposed to that used by the spouse. If an employee paid insurance premiums for the couple's vehicle, it is not necessary to determine the number of miles driven by each spouse. Likewise, when the employee paid for a swimming pool maintenance service, it is not necessary to determine the percentage of time the pool was used by the employee versus the spouse. It would be ludicrous to require a separation of these fixed communal expenses based upon exact usage for each resident, and the courts are not interested in this type of exact and overly-personal detail. The full amount of the communal expense is considered to be support provided to a partially dependent spouse.

Fixed expenses that are deemed to provide a communal benefit to both spouses are those expenses that will continue to be incurred by the spouse after the employee's death but without the benefit of contributions from the employee's earnings. Some examples of fixed and recurrent communal expenses that would appear to clearly meet the criteria established by the courts as contributions to the support of the dependent spouse are listed below.
   a. Rent or indebtedness for a home loan and insurance for the dwelling and/or its contents.
   b. Maintenance of the residence, e.g. gardener, maid or swimming pool service.
   c. Utility bills, e.g. gas, water, electricity, and recurrent basic monthly charges for telephones or a cable television service.
   d. Communal vehicles, e.g. insurance and loan payments where the couple share one car.

Workers' compensation dependency benefits provide a partial wage replacement benefit, and the benefit payable to a partial dependent is based on four times the amount of the employee's annual earnings that were used for the dependent's support. The California Constitution limits the employer's liability to "the extent of relieving from the consequences of injury or death." Mislabeling the employee's personal expenses as being communal expenses will therefore result in a prohibited provision of a wage-replacement benefit for a wage loss that was not sustained; and, in fact, provision of a quadruple financial profit or a windfall benefit equivalent to four times the value of the personal expense.

Disputes will arise as to whether various expenditures should be categorized as personal (not annual support to spouse) or communal (annual support to spouse). A dispute regarding any specific expense can be resolved by ascertaining the extent, if any, of the financial consequence to the spouse as a result of the loss of the employee's earnings. The four possible financial consequences for a partially dependent spouse are explained below:
   1. No Financial Consequence because the expense will not be incurred after the employee's death. The employee may have paid for an

annual family membership at a health club that the spouse never utilized and will now cancel. Expenses the employee incurred for union dues, tools, clothing, and any other expenses necessitated by the employee's employment will neither continue to be owed nor be paid by the spouse.

2. **No Financial Consequence** because the expense will be incurred after the employee's death but by someone other than the spouse. The employee may have paid operational expenses for a personal vehicle that was never used by the spouse because the spouse does not like the vehicle. If the vehicle is sold, future operational expenses will be paid by the new owner.

3. **A Partial Financial Consequence** because the expense will continue to be incurred by the spouse but in a reduced amount. A membership at the yacht club may be continued at the reduced annual fee payable for a single person. The spouse may not be on speaking terms with the employee's brother who the employee called long distance on a frequent basis; the spouse will continue to incur basic telephone service charges but not the toll charges previously incurred for calls to the brother.

4. **A Full Financial Consequence** because the spouse will continue to incur the expense in the same amount. For examples of expenses that may continue to be payable entirely by the spouse, refer to the listing of communal expenses shown in (a) - (d) above.

12.14 COMPENSATION RATE

Per LC4702, the death benefit "shall be paid in installments in the same manner and amounts as temporary total disability indemnity would have to be made to the employee, unless the appeals board otherwise orders." The compensation rate for death benefits payable to dependents is computed in the same manner as the employee's compensation rate for temporary total disability would be computed (see 9.4), except that a different and higher minimum compensation rate applies to death benefits.

The maximum compensation rate is the same for temporary disability and for death benefits. However, LC4702 requires use of a different (and higher) minimum compensation rate for death benefits. For 1990 or later injuries, the compensation rate at which death benefits are payable to dependents cannot be less than the minimum compensation rate specified in LC4702 on the date of the employee's injury, regardless of the fact that the employee's compensation rate for temporary disability benefits would have been a lesser amount. Per LC4702, "no payment shall be made at a weekly rate of less than" the amount specified in this section (effective 1990 and until the next change, this amount is $224/wk, that is $2/3$ of average weekly earnings of $336/wk).

In past practice, death benefits have often been awarded at the maximum temporary disability rate regardless of whether the injured employee would be entitled to receive a lower rate if currently temporarily disabled (or in fact had actually been awarded temporary disability benefits at a lower rate). The only Labor Code provision that addresses the compensation rate for death benefits is LC4702, and this statute does not require payments at the maximum temporary disability rate that exists on the date of injury.

If the employee was paid temporary disability, dependents must be paid at the same rate or the payments will not meet the statutory requirement that they be "the same ... amounts as" temporary disability payments (with the exception that a different minimum compensation rate is used for death benefits for 1990 or later injuries). However, the language "unless the appeals board otherwise orders" has been construed by some judges to sanction WCAB awards of death benefits at the maximum temporary disability rate regardless of the deceased employee's temporary disability rate.

12.15 PAYMENTS – MANNER & FREQUENCY

Per LC4702, death benefits are payable to dependents in the same manner as the employer would otherwise pay temporary total disability benefits. A review of statutory requirements for payments of temporary total disability benefits leads to a requirement, by implication, that a qualified dependent should receive a first payment of death benefits within 14 days of concurrence of the employer's knowledge that a work-related death has been sustained and that a person who claims dependency benefits is qualified to receive such benefits. (Alternatively, it may be appropriate to provide a notice of delay or denial of death benefits; see 6.8-6.9.)

There is no waiting period before commencement of death benefits. If death is immediate as of the date of injury, death benefits are also payable immediately (14 days after notice of the injury and death).

For a 1990 or later date of injury (not date of death), it appears that payments subsequent to an initial payment to dependents should be made every 14 days on the day of the week that is designated with the first payment. Otherwise, payments to dependents will not be made "in the same manner" as temporary disability benefits as required by LC4702. (Note: the employer is also required to provide notice of any delay or denial regarding provision of benefits to dependents, including payment of temporary or permanent disability benefits that are accrued on the date of the employee's death; see 9.29, and 10.17.)

12.16 MAXIMUM DEATH BENEFIT

For injuries on or after 7/1/94, four separate maximum amounts are set out in LC4702. The maximum benefit that applies to a particular dependent will be determined by whether dependency is total or partial and whether there are other persons who are total dependents. For convenience, the following chart shows the injury dates that control the benefit amounts in effect, the four maximum amounts, and how the maximum amounts apply to different types and numbers of dependents. (Note: benefits payable to a totally dependent minor continue until age 18 despite maximum benefit limits that otherwise apply; see 12.18.)

DATE OF INJURY	Statutory Benefit Amount TOTAL DEPENDENTS 3 or More — 2 or More — Only One	Maximum Benefit Amount PARTIAL DEPENDENTS Any Number
01/01/91	$115,000	–0–
to	or $95,000 and	⟶ $20,000
06/30/94	or	$95,000
07/01/94	$150,000 vs. $135,000	–0–
to	or $115,000 and	⟶ $10,000
06/30/96	or	$115,000
07/01/96	$160,000 vs. $145,000	–0–
to	or $125,000 and	⟶ $20,000
Next Chg.	or	$125,000

The above chart graphically illustrates some confusing language of LC4702. Referring to the chart, note the following:

    a. LC4702(a): If there are two or more total dependents, no benefits are payable to any partial dependents.

    b. LC4702(b): If there is one total dependent, the maximum benefit payable for any number of partial dependents is $20,000 ($10,000 for injuries occurring between 7/1/94 and 6/30/96).

    c. LC4702(a-b): The second-level benefit amount only applies when there is more than one dependent, AND one of the dependents is a total dependent, e.g. two totals or one total and one partial.

    d. LC4702(d): Where there are no total dependents, the maximum benefit payable for any partial dependents is the same amount that would be paid to one total dependent.

    e. LC4702(d): If there are no total dependents, the maximum benefit amount for partial dependents is not affected by the number of partial dependents.

12.17 BENEFIT – ADULT TOTAL DEPENDENT

A total dependent is automatically entitled to receive the statutory benefit amount that is specified in LC4702 for the date of injury involved. It is not necessary to ascertain the actual amount of financial support provided by the employee. It is only necessary to verify that the dependent qualifies as a total dependent by proof or by presumption.

When it is determined that a person is a total dependent, the amount of the dependency benefit is stated in LC4702. If the only dependent of the employee is a total dependent, a reserve for dependency benefits can be established on a claim file solely on the basis of identifying the statutory benefit amount stated in LC4702 (except where the total dependent is a minor; see 12.18).

12.18 BENEFIT – MINOR TOTAL DEPENDENT

For 1990 or later injuries, LC4703.5 requires dependency benefits to continue to be paid to a totally dependent minor (at the appropriate weekly rate; see 12.14) until the child is 18 years old. The special continuation benefits are not payable to minor children who qualify for partial dependency benefits. In the event of a fatal injury occurring after 1989, the amount of the death benefit payable to a totally dependent minor child is the sum of:

1. The statutory benefit amount that is payable to the totally dependent minor (see 12.14), AND
2. The dollar value of the weeks and days remaining, if any, between the date that the statutory benefit amount is paid in full and the date of the child's 18th birthday.

The steps shown below can be used to determine if a totally dependent minor will be entitled to receive continuation benefits after payment of the statutory benefit amount (the likelihood of receipt of such benefits decreases as age increases). The number of weeks in each step should be determined as of the same date, ordinarily the date that payment of death benefits commence. As a reference point, note that 18 years of age is equivalent to 936 weeks (18 × 52 wks/yr = 936 wks).

  a. Compute the number of weeks it will take to pay out the statutory benefit amount: divide the statutory benefit amount owed by the weekly rate payable to the minor (see 12.14).
  b. Compute the number of weeks between the date death benefits commence and the minor's 18th birthday (that cannot exceed 936 weeks). In determining the number of weeks until the minor's next birthday, it is easiest to use reference tables that show the number of days between any two dates rather than manually counting days.
  c. If (b) computes to fewer weeks than (a), no continuation benefits are payable (because the dependent will not be a minor when payments of the statutory benefit amount end).
  d. If (b) computes to more weeks than (a), continuation benefits will be payable. The dollar value of continuation benefits is computed by multiplying the applicable compensation rate times the number of weeks remaining to age 18.

SAMPLE (a). The only dependent is a totally dependent minor child with a 10/1/80 date of birth (DOB). This child is 15 years and 14 days old when death benefits commence on 10/15/95. The date of injury is 6/20/95. The statutory benefit that is payable to one total dependent for a 6/20/94 injury is $115,000. The employee's earnings produce a compensation rate of $406/wk (the maximum for a 6/20/95 injury).

17 years + 365 days	18 years (stated as years and days)
−15 years − 14 days	Age of minor at start of payments
2 years + 351 days	Remaining to age 18

$115,000 ÷ $406/wk = 283.2512 wks to pay out $115,000
2 × 365 = 730 + 351 = 1081 days ÷ 7 days/wk = 154.4285 wks to age 18
283 wks exceeds 154 wks to age 18, so no continuation benefits are owed.

In example (a), a quick appraisal is all that is really necessary to determine that continuation benefits will not be owed to this dependent. Dividing the 283.2512 weeks shown above by 52 wks/yr reveals that it will take 5.447 years to pay the statutory benefit amount. Since a 15 year old will attain age 18 in 3 years at the most, no purpose is served by computing the exact number of weeks remaining until this minor's 18th birthday.

SAMPLE (b). The only dependent is a totally dependent minor child who is 2 years old (DOB 2/14) when death benefits commence on 10/15/95. The statutory benefit payable to one total dependent for a 6/20/95 injury is $115,000. Based upon the employee's earnings, the compensation rate is $406/wk.

        17 years + 365 days 18 years (stated as years and days)
        −2 years − 243 days Age of minor at start of payments
        15 years + 122 days Remaining to age 18

15 × 365 = 5475 + 122 = 5597 days ÷ 7 days/wk = 799.5714 wks to age 18
        $115,000 ÷ $406/wk = 283.2512 wks to pay out $115,000

799.5714 wks − 283.2512 = 516.3202 wks of continuation benefits at $406/wk
        516.3202 wks × $406/wk = $209,626.00
        $115,000 + $209,626.00 = $324,626.00 Death benefit

SAMPLE (c). The only dependent is a totally dependent minor child who is 8 years old (DOB 10/31) when death benefits commence on 10/15/95. The statutory benefit payable to one total dependent for a 6/20/95 injury is $115,000. Based upon the employee's earnings, the compensation rate is $406/wk.

        17 years + 365 days 18 years (stated as years and days)
        −8 years − 349 days Age of minor at start of payments
        9 years + 16 days Remaining to age 18

9 × 365 = 3285 + 16 = 3301 days ÷ 7 days/wk = 471.5714 wks to age 18
        $115,000 ÷ $406/wk = 283.2512 wks to pay out $115,000

471.5714 − 283.2512 wks = 188.3202 wks of continuation benefits at $406/wk
        188.3202 wks × $406/wk = $76,458.00
        $115,000 + $76,458.00 = $191,458.00 Death benefit.

NOTE: The claimsperson should do two things prior to issuance of the last payment of continuation benefits to a minor: look at a calendar to see what day the 18th birthday will be, and determine the daily compensation rate for death benefits (weekly rate divided by 7). These actions are necessary to ensure that the last check provides payment for the number of days remaining unpaid up to, but not including, the minor's 18th birthday (and to avoid an underpayment or overpayment of death benefits).

12.19 BENEFIT – MULTIPLE TOTAL DEPENDENTS

When there are two or more total dependents, LC4702 specifies a statutory benefit amount, and this amount is ordinarily used as the claim file reserve for dependency benefits (see 2.25). The solitary exception applies to cases where one or more of the total dependents is still under the age of 18 years after the statutory benefit amount has been paid out. In this event, but only for a 1990 or later injury, continuation benefits may also be payable to the minor (see 12.18).

Per LC4703, if there is more than one total dependent, "the death benefit shall be divided equally among them." All total dependents are equally affected by the employee's demise, since each loses his/her entire source of income. Therefore, the Labor Code provides for distribution of the maximum benefit amount on an equal-shares basis. The number of total dependents is divided into the maximum benefit set by law to produce the amount payable to each total dependent. Each dependent will receive the same dollar amount of benefits, and this amount will decrease as the number of dependents increases.

NOTE: In the samples that follow and elsewhere in this chapter, it is sometimes necessary to round off decimals in an arbitrary fashion. The rounding-off process should never affect the total amount of the death benefit that is owed by the employer.

SAMPLE (a). There are three total dependents on the date of injury, 6/20/95: a 15 year old whose DOB is 10/1; an 8 year old whose DOB is 10/31; and, a 2 year old whose DOB is 2/14. Death benefits are payable commencing on 10/15/95. The maximum death benefit for three or more dependents is $150,000. Based upon the employee's earnings, the weekly rate of payment is $406. (The number of weeks for which any continuation benefits may be payable to a minor is determined by the process shown in 12.15.)

1. Death Benefit For Three Total Dependents

$$\$150,000 \div 3 = \$50,000$$

$ 50,000.00	Statutory benefit payable to 15 year old
50,000.00	Statutory benefit payable to 8 year old
+ 50,000.00	Statutory benefit payable to 2 year old
$150,000.00	Statutory benefit payable on claim

2. Weekly Payments – Compensation Rate

$406/wk ÷ 3 = $135.33/wk compensation rate for each dependent

$135.33	Statutory benefit payable to 15 year old
135.33	Statutory benefit payable to 8 year old
+135.34	Statutory benefit payable to 2 year old
$406.00	Weekly benefit payable on claim

Note: the benefit payable to the 2 year old is automatically increased by one penny because 3 × $135.33/wk does not total $406/wk. The employer cannot pay less than $406/wk. Judgment dictates which dependent(s) receives the benefit of this arbitrary adjustment that in this example was given to the youngest child.

3. Amount Of Last Payment Of $150,000 Payable For Week #370

$50,000.00 ÷ $135.33/wk = 369.4672 weeks of payments each

$135.33/wk × 369 weeks = 49,936.77
$135.34/wk × 369 weeks = 49,940.46

$ 50,000 −	49,936.77 =	$ 63.23	Balance owed to 15 yr. old
50,000 −	49,936.77 =	63.23	Balance owed to 8 yr. old
+ 50,000 −	49,940.46 =	+ 59.54	Balance owed to 2 yr. old
$150,000 −	149,814.00 =	$186.00	Balance remaining

4. Amount Of Continuation Benefits Payable For Week 370

$406/wk − $186 = $220 continuation benefits in wk 370 ÷ 2 = $110

Last check, 15 yr. old (now 18)	$ 63.23
Owed to 8 yr. old ($63.23 + $110.00)	173.23
Owed to 2 yr. old ($59.54 + $110.00)	+169.54
Payable for week 370	$406.00

Note: The $63.23 payment to the 15 yr old for week #370 is a final payment since this child is will have previously reached age 18. The employer owes a total of $406/wk for week #370 because the weekly rate of payment is continuous for the duration of payment of death benefits. Therefore, it is necessary to compute the amount of this weekly rate that is payable to the two remaining minor dependents as payment of continuation benefits. The initial $220 payment of continuation benefits ($406 − $186) is evenly split between the 8 and 2 year olds because benefits payable to multiple total dependents are divided equally.

5. Continuation Benefits Owed For Week #371 And Until 8 Year Old Turns 18

$406/wk ÷ 2 = $203/wk payable to each minor until 8 yr old is 18

6. Continuation benefits payable for week of 8 year old's 18th birthday. A normal payment period is a Thursday through a Wednesday, and the 8 year old turns 18 on a Monday. The daily rate of $58 ($406/wk ÷ 7 days/wk) is payable to the 2 year old for each day after, as well as the day of, the 8 year old's 18th birthday.

Thu-Sun	4 days × $58 = $232 ÷ 2 =	$116.00	Last check to 8 yr old
Thu-Sun	4 days × $58 = $232 ÷ 2 =	116.00	Owed to 2 yr old
Mon-Wed	3 days × $58	+174.00	Owed to 2 yr old
		$406.00	Total payable this week

7. Continuation Benefits Until 2 Year Old is 18: Now Payable at $406/wk

SAMPLE (b). On the date of injury, 6/14/97, there are five total dependents: a mother and four minor children. A death benefit of $160,000 is payable at $438/wk (⅔ of the employee's earnings). All of the children will be 18 years or older when the $160,000 is paid in full after 365.2968 weeks of payments.

Benefit Amount: $160,000 ÷ 5 = $ $32,000 each
Weekly Payments: $438/wk ÷ 5 = $87.60/wk each
$32,000 ÷ $87.60/wĸ = 365.2968 wks of payments each

Benefit to be paid	$32,000.00	$31,974.00
365 wks @ $87.60	−31,974.00	+ 26.00
Last check	$ 26.00	$32,000.00

Claim File Reserves. Effective 7/1/94, LC4702 provides a separate higher benefit amount if there are three or more total dependents than if there are only two total dependents or only one total dependent (see 12.14). Once the number of total dependents is identified, the benefit amount in LC4702 is ordinarily used as the claim file reserve for dependency benefits (see 2.24). The solitary exception applies to cases where one or more of the total dependents is still under the age of 18 years after the statutory benefits amount has been paid out. In this event, but only for a 1990 or later date of injury, continuation benefits may also be payable to the minor (see 12.15).

12.20 BENEFIT – COMPUTED FOR PARTIALS

Per LC4702, the death benefit is "four times the amount annually devoted to the support" of partial dependents. However, if this amount exceeds the applicable maximum benefit limit contained in LC4702, the partial dependent is instead entitled to receive the applicable statutory benefit amount. The following steps are used to determine the amount of the death benefit that is payable to one partial dependent:

1. Determine if there are two total dependents. If there are, partial dependents are not eligible for benefits. If there are no total dependents or just one, go to step two.
2. Determine the amount annually contributed to support of the partial dependent.
3. Multiply the amount of annual support by four.
4. Compare this figure to the maximum amount in LC4702 that applies to the type and number of qualified dependents in a particular case, e.g. for a 1997 injury, $20,000 if there is also one total dependent or $125,000 if there are dependents only.
5. Determine the amount the partial dependent is entitled to receive. The amount of the dependency benefit will be the lesser of:
   a. Four times the amount annually contributed to support, OR
   b. The maximum limit that applies per LC4702 (see 12.14).

12.21 BENEFIT – MULTIPLE PARTIAL DEPENDENTS

When there are multiple partial dependents, the first step is to compute four times the annual support for each dependent. Next, add all of these amounts together. If this sum is less than the maximum payable benefit, each is to be paid the amount so determined. If this sum exceeds the maximum benefit amount that was specified in LC4702 on the date of the employee's injury, special procedures are necessary.

Per LC4703, the "death benefit shall be divided among" all persons who are "partially dependent in proportion to the relative extent of their dependency." This language requires the partial dependents to share the allowable death benefit in direct proportion to the loss of income each sustained. The amount of annual support that the employee provided to a dependent represents the extent of his/her dependency. The relative extent of dependency means the ratio of financial dependency, or the comparative degree to which the employee's income was relied upon, or the comparative percentage of support received when compared to other partial dependents.

The Labor Code does not contain any mathematical formula for computing the proportionate share of benefits for partial dependents. Any mathematical approach that results in an equitable distribution of benefits can be used. Three commonly used methods are illustrated in the samples that follow. The employer can select any method of preference, since the death benefit paid by the employer is unaffected by the distribution among multiple dependents. Sometimes a particular dependent may prefer one method over another because the amount payable to each dependent can vary, although only in small amounts, under different methods.

SAMPLE COMPUTATIONS - GENERAL RULES

1. **Convenience:** Decimal numbers are sometimes converted to whole numbers in the first step of multistep computations. Accuracy may or may not be affected; double-check by comparing results obtained using an alternate method.

2. **Accuracy:** When multiplying or dividing using decimal numbers, the greatest accuracy will be achieved by using a minimum of four decimal positions and by rounding off decimals only when converting them to a dollar amount.

3. **Arbitrary Adjustments:** When converting decimal numbers to percentage figures or dollars-and-cents amounts, increases from the rounding up of decimals are distributed among dependents according to the amount of support received, in decreasing order.

METHOD ONE - FORMULA
RELATIVE EXTENT OF DEPENDENCY

$$\frac{\text{Annual support to each dependent}}{\text{Annual support to all dependents}} = \text{Relative extent of dependency}$$

Multiply relative extent of dependency times maximum benefit

SAMPLE (A1). The employee had two partial dependents, The DOI was 7/7/97. The maximum benefit is $125,000, and the compensation rate is $490/wk. A mother received $32,000 and a sister received $6,000 in annual support.

```
Mother   4 × $32,000 =   $128,000
Sister   4 × $ 6,000 =   + 24,000
                         $152,000 (exceeds $125,000 maximum)
```

(A1.1). Apply formula: Use Method One Formula

```
Mother  $32,000  ÷ $38,000 = .8421 = .84  × 100 =    84%
Sister  + 6,000  ÷ $38,000 = .1578 = +.16 × 100 =   +16%
        $38,000                      1.00           100%
```

(A1.2). Benefit Payable to Each ($125,000 maximum)

```
Mother  .84 × $125,000 =  $105,000
Sister  .16 × $125,000 =  + 20,000
                          $125,000
```

(A1.3). Weekly Benefit Rate ($490 maximum)

```
Mother  84% = .84 × $490 = $411.60
Sister  16% = .16 × $490 = + 78.40
                           $490.00
```

(A1.4). Weeks of Payments ($125,000 ÷ $490/wk = 255.1020 wks)

```
Mother   255 wks × $411.60 =  $104,958.00     $105,000.00
              Last check +         42.00      −104,958.00
                              $105,000.00      $      42.00

Sister   255 wks × $78.40 =   $19,992.00      $20,000.00
              Last check +          8.00      −19,992.00
                              $20,000.00       $      8.00
```

METHOD TWO - FORMULA
RELATIVE EXTENT OF DEPENDENCY

$$\frac{4 \times \text{Annual support each dependent}}{4 \times \text{Annual support to all dependents}} = \text{Relative extent of dependency}$$

Multiply relative extent of dependency times maximum benefit

SAMPLE (A2). Use Same Situation As Sample (A1) – Apply Different Formula.

(A2.1). Apply Formula: Use Method Two Formula

Mother	$32,000 × 4 =	$128,000	÷ $152,000 =	.8421 =	84%
Sister	$ 6,000 × 4 =	+ 24,000	÷ $152,000 =	.1578 =	+16%
		$152,000			100%

(A2.2)-(A2.4). Remaining steps and results: same as shown in (A1.2)-(A1.4).

METHOD THREE - FORMULA
RELATIVE EXTENT OF DEPENDENCY

$$\frac{\text{Amount of maximum death benefit}}{\text{Sum of } 4 \times \text{support to all dependents}} = \text{Percent Payable to Each}$$

Multiply percent of dependency times 4 × support to each dependent

---

NOTE: A drawback to Method Three is the potential for obtaining divergent results in the weekly rate and/or the benefit amount payable to each dependent when different persons apply the same formula but use a different mathematical approach. For instance, rounding off .822368 in step (A3.1) below to .8223, .823, or .82 will produce divergent results for all subsequent steps shown. Such variances can affect the compensation rate and the number of weeks it will take to pay benefits to a particular dependent (that is why a particular dependent might favor the use of this formula) but will not affect the amount the employer owes overall.

SAMPLE (A3). Use same situation as Sample (A1). There are two partial dependents. The DOI was 7/7/97. The maximum benefit is $125,000, and the compensation rate is $490/wk. A mother received $32,000 and a sister received $6,000 in annual support.

(A3.1). Apply Formula: Use Method Three Formula

Mother	$32,000 × 4 =	$128,000
Sister	$ 6,000 × 4 =	+ 24,000
	$125,000 ÷ $152,000	= .822368 (or 82.2368%)

(A3.2). Benefit Payable to Each: 4 × support to each × percentage payable

Mother	$128,000 × .822368 =	$105,263.10 + .07 =	$105,263.17
Sister	$ 24,000 × .822368 =	+ 19,736.83	+ 19,736.83
		$124,999.93	$125,000.00

The employer owes a total payout of $125,000 on this case, not $24,999.83. Therefore, an additional seven cents was arbitrarily added to the benefit amount that will be paid to the mother because she received the greatest amount of financial support. The seven cents is a one-time payment that should be included in the last check paid to the mother.

(A3.3). Weekly Benefit Rate: Compute Percentage And Apply to $490/wk

Mother	$105,263.17 ÷ $125,000 =	.8421	=	.84	=	84%
Sister	$ 19,736.83 ÷ $125,000 =	+.1579	=	+.16	=	+16%
		1.0000		1.00		100%

Mother $490 × .84 = $411.60
Sister $490 × .16 = + 78.40
                                $490.00

This step illustrates another drawback to the use of the Method Three Formula. More separate mathematical steps are involved than would be necessary if either the Method One Formula or the Method Two Formula were used.

(A3.4). Weeks Payable to Each Dependent

($125,000 ÷ $490/wk = 255.10 wks, but see note below)

Mother $105,263.17 ÷ $411.60/wk = 255.74 wks
Sister $ 19,736.83 ÷ $ 78.40/wk = 251.75 wks

NOTE: Decimal numbers that represent fractional weeks of payments are not used to compute the amount of the last check that is owed to a dependent. In sample (A3.4), it will take 255.10 weeks to pay $125,000 at a weekly rate of $490. The decimal number 255.10 represents 255 full weeks of payments at $490 and the decimal .10 indicates that the final payment is owed in week 256. The decimal .10 is not multiplied times the weekly rate at which death benefits are payable. The final payment to each dependent is computed by subtracting the amount of death benefits previously paid from the full amount of the death benefit that was awarded to that dependent (except continuation benefits to a minor child are computed as $1/7$ of the minor's weekly rate for each day remaining before age 18; see 12.18).

(A3.5) Final Payment to Each Dependent

(a). Compute the amount of death benefits that are owed through the last full week of payments for the dependent who will receive the fewest weeks of payments. In this example, only a partial week remains unpaid to the sister after week #251.

Mother $411.60/wk × 251.00 wks = $103,311.60
Sister $ 78.40/wk × 251.00 wks = $ 19,678.40

(b). Compute the amount of the last check to the sister in week 252 and the mother's weekly rate for this week only. Thereafter, the mother will receive a weekly compensation rate of $490 until her benefit amount has been fully paid.

Sister   Week 252: $19,736.83 − $19,678.40 = $ 58.43
Mother Week 252: $490.00/wk − $58.43 = $431.57

(c). Compute the balance payable to the mother after week 252.

Paid to week 252 $103,311.60   Total Owed $105,263.17
        Week 252 +   431.57   Paid −103,743.17
                 $103,743.17 Remaining $ 1,520.00

$1,520.00 ÷ $490/wk = 3.10 wks left to pay
−1,470.00 ($490 × 3 for wk 253, 254, 255)
$ 50.00 Last check to mother in week 256

(A3.6) Verify Payout of Death Benefits to Each Dependent

Mother $105,263.17 ÷ $411.60/wk = 255.74 wks

255 wks × $411.60 = $104,958.00 $105,263.17
Last check (.74 wks +.07) +   305.17   −104,958.00
Includes $.07 from step (A3.2) $105,263.17 $ 305.17

Sister $19,736.83 ÷ $78.40/wk = 251.75 wks

251 wks × $78.40 = $19,678.40 $19,736.64
Last check (.75 wks) +   58.24   −19,678.40
                 $19,736.64 $ 58.24

Total benefit payout is $125,000 ($105,263.17 + $19,736.64).

SAMPLE (B1). The DOI is 6/6/96. There were three partial dependents. The maximum benefit is $115,000, and the weekly rate is $345 based upon the employee's earnings at the time of injury. Annual support was provided as follows: $22,000 to a father, $12,000 to a brother, and $5,000 to a niece ($39,000 × 4 = $156,000 that is over the maximum benefit limit of $115,000).

(B1.1). Apply Formula - Use Method One Formula (see A1)
Father $22,000 ÷ $39,000 = .5641 =   .56 =   56%
Brother   12,000 ÷ $39,000 = .3076 =   .31 =   31%
Niece   + 5,000 ÷ $39,000 = .1282 = +.13 = +13%
           $39,000   1.00   100%

(B1.2). Benefit Payable to Each ($115,000 maximum)
Father $115,000 × .56 = $ 64,400
Brother $115,000 × .31 =   35,650
Niece $115,000 × .13 = + 14,950
                             $115,000

(B1.3). Weekly Benefit Rate ($345/wk)
Father $345 × .56 = $193.20
Brother $345 × .31 = 106.95
Niece $345 × .13 = + 44.85
                        $345.00

(B1.4). Weeks of Payment ($115,000 ÷ $345 = 333.33 weeks)

Father	333 wks @ $193.20 =	$64,335.60	$64,400.00
	Last check	+ 64.40	−64,335.60
		$64,400.00	$ 64.40

Brother	333 wks @$106.95 =	$35,614.35	$35,650.00
	Last check	+ 35.65	−35,614.35
		$35,650.00	$ 35.65

Niece	333 wks @ $44.85 =	$14,935.05	$14,950.00
	Last check	+ 14.95	−14,935.05
		$14,950.00	$ 14.95

NOTE: When the cost to process the last check exceeds the amount being paid, the employer will usually save money by including this amount in the next-to-last payment, e.g. the niece would be paid $59.80 ($44.85 + $14.95) in the 333rd week.

SAMPLE (B2). Use same situation as Sample (B1). The DOI is 6/26/96. There are three partial dependents. The maximum benefit is $115,000, and the weekly rate is $345. Annual support was provided as follows: $22,000 to a father, $12,000 to a brother, and $5,000 to a niece.

(B2.1). Apply Formula - Use Method Two Formula (see A2)

Father	$22,000 × 4 =	$ 88,000	÷ $156,000 = .5641 =	.56 =	56%
Brother	$12,000 × 4 =	48,000	÷ $156,000 = .3076 =	.31 =	31%
Niece	$ 5,000 × 4 =	+ 20,000	÷ $156,000 = .1282 =	+.13 =	+13%
		$156,000		1.00	100%

(B2.2)-(B2.4). Remaining steps and results are same as Sample (B1).

SAMPLE (B3). Use same situation as Sample (B1): The DOI is 6/6/96. There are three partial dependents. The maximum benefit is $115,000, and the weekly rate is $345. Annual support was provided as follows: $22,000 to a father, $12,000 to a brother, and $5,000 to a niece. ($39,000 × 4 = $156,000 that exceeds the maximum benefit limit of $115,000.)

(B3.1). Apply Formula - Use Method Three (see A3)

Father	$22,000 × 4 =	$ 88,000
Brother	$12,000 × 4 =	48,000
Niece	$ 5,000 × 4 =	+ 20,000
	$115,000 ÷ $156,000	= .737179

(B3.2). Benefit Payable to Each ($115,000 maximum)

Father	$88,000 × .737179 =	$ 64,871.75	+.08	=	$ 64,871.83
Brother	$48,000 × .737179 =	35,384.59		=	35,384.59
Niece	$20,000 × .737179 =	+ 14,743.58		=	+ 14,743.58
		$114,999.92	+.08		$115,000.00

Note: The employer owes a death benefit of $115,000, not $114,999.92. Eight cents was arbitrarily given to the father since he received the greatest amount of financial support. Also note the use of .737179 rather than .7371 (a four-place decimal) or .7372 (.73717 rounded-off to a four-place decimal). As a preliminary step, it was necessary to determine which mathematical equivalent of .737179 would produce a total overall payout close to $115,000. It was necessary to use the decimal .737179 for greatest mathematical precision.

(B3.3). Weekly Benefit Rate ($345/wk maximum)

Father	$ 64,871.83	÷ $115,000 = .5641 =	.56	× $345 =	$193.20
Brother	35,384.59	÷ $115,000 = .3076 =	.31	× $345 =	106.95
Niece	+ 14,743.58	÷ $115,000 = .1282 =	+.13	× $345 =	+ 44.85
	$115,000.00		1.00		$345.00

12.22 BENEFIT – TOTAL & PARTIAL DEPENDENTS

Per LC4703, if there are two or more total dependents, no partial dependency benefits will be paid. When there is only one total dependent, any number of partial dependents can also receive benefits. The maximum benefit amount for each partial dependent is computed (see examples in 12.21). Next, the proportional extent of dependency of every dependent is computed. This computation is necessary to determine how the weekly benefits will be paid out or distributed.

SAMPLE (C). The DOI is 9/9/96. There is one totally dependent adult child and two partial dependents. A spouse received $24,000 and an uncle received $2,000 annually. The death benefit for the total dependent is $125,000; the maximum benefit for the partials is $20,000; and, the weekly compensation rate for death benefits is $490.00.

(C1). Compute Benefit Owed to Partial Dependents

$24,000 × 4 =	$ 96,000	÷ $104,000 =	.92	× $20,000 =	$18,400
$ 2,000 × 4 =	+ 8,000	÷ $104,000 =	+.08	× $20,000 =	+ 1,600
	$104,000		1.00		$20,000

(C2). Compute Benefit Owed to All Dependents

Child	$125,000	Total dependent (see chart in 12.14)
Spouse	18,400	Partial dependent - benefit computed in (C1)
Uncle	+ 1,600	Partial dependent - benefit computed in (C1)
	$145,000	

(C3). Weekly Benefit Rate: Apply Weekly Benefit Formula

FORMULA
WEEKLY BENEFIT – MULTIPLE DEPENDENTS

$$\frac{\text{Benefit payable to each dependent}}{\text{Benefit amount payable to all dependents}} = \text{Decimal} (\times \ 100 \ = \ \text{percentage})$$

Multiply decimal obtained times employee's weekly compensation rate

---

Child	$125,000	÷ $145,000 =	.8620 =	.86	× $490 =	$421.40
Spouse	18,400	÷ $145,000 =	.1268 =	.13	× $490 =	63.70
Uncle	+ 1,600	÷ $145,000 =	.0110 =	+.01	× $490 =	+ 4.90
	$145,000			1.00		$490.00

NOTE: As a general rule, decimal numbers should always be rounded-up from the fourth position (with the exception that decimal positions beyond the third decimal position are ignored when rounding off to a dollars and cents amount in the final step of a computation).

(C4). Weeks of Payments Will Vary For Each Dependent

Child	$125,000	÷ $421.40 =	296.63 weeks of benefits
Spouse	18,400	÷ $ 63.70 =	288.85 weeks of benefits
Uncle	+ 1,600	÷ $ 4.90 =	326.53 weeks of benefits
	$145,000		

(C5). Compute the amount of the final payment for the dependent who will receive the fewest weeks of payments.

Spouse	$ 63.70 for 288.85 wks	$18,400.00
	$ 63.70 for 288.00 wks	−18,345.00
	Owed for wk #289	+ 54.40

Note: The final payment of $54.40 is owed in week #289. However, in this example, the final payment is being paid a week in advance. This example demonstrates a common practice of including final, partial payment in the next to last check.

After 288 Weeks, the following amounts will have been paid out:

Spouse	$ 63.70 for 288.85 wks	$ 18,400.00
Child	$421.40 × 288.00 wks =	121,363.20
Uncle	$ 4.90 × 288.00 wks =	+ 1,411.20
		$141,174.40

(C6) Remaining unpaid as of week 289 (after spouse has been paid in full):

Child	$125,000 − $121,363.20	paid to date =	$3,636.80 Remaining
Uncle	$ 1,600 − $ 1,411.20	paid to date =	+ 188.80 Remaining
			$3,825.60

After the spouse is paid in full, depending upon the wording of a court award of benefits, either:

   a. The remaining dependents will continue to receive their weekly rate until the full amount of the death benefit payable to each is paid, OR

   b. The formula above (see C3) is again applied to the remaining dependents, and the maximum amount of $490/wk is redistributed among them. This will not be necessary unless a judge orders the employer to pay a set weekly amount each week such as $490 rather than a fixed rate for each dependent for a fixed number of weeks.

(C7). Recompute Weekly Benefit Rate - $490/wk (maximum)

Child	$125,000	÷	$126,600	=	.9873	=	.99	×	$490	=	$485.10
Uncle	+ 1,600	÷	$126,600	=	.0126	=	+.01	×	$490	=	+ 4.90
	$126,600						1.00				$490.00

(C8). Recompute Number of Weeks of Payments Remaining

Child	$3,636.80	Remaining	÷	$485.10	=	7.50 weeks
Uncle	+ 188.80	Remaining	÷	$ 4.90	=	38.53 weeks
	$3,825.60					

After 7.50 weeks, the child's benefit of $125,000 will be paid in full. Thereafter, the weekly payment to the uncle would be readjusted, and he would receive $490/wk until he was paid his full benefit of $1,600.

NOTE: Computations of future redistributions of benefits should be done at the same time that the initial payments to the dependents are made, and the claim file should be diaried for the date the redistribution(s) will occur. Required increases in weekly rates of payment must be made timely to avoid assessment of a 10% penalty under LC5814 for an unreasonable delay in the provision of benefits at the proper rate of payment (and assessment of administrative penalties under LC129 and LC1295.).

12.23 BENEFIT – REASSIGNMENT TO DEPENDENT

Per LC4704, the appeals board may "reassign the death benefit to any one or more of the dependents in accordance with their respective needs and in a just and equitable manner, and may order payment to a dependent subsequent in right, or not otherwise entitled thereto." The initial distribution of benefits may become inequitable in view of changes in the financial circumstances of the dependents. For instance, one dependent may establish an urgent need for a lump sum payment of his portion of the award. The WCAB can order the award to this dependent commuted to a lump sum payment under LC5100-5101 but paid in installments for remaining dependents.

A partial dependent may be precluded from an award because there are two total dependents. If one total dependent dies, the appeals board could award the benefits that are allowable for one total and one partial dependent thereby providing the partial dependent with benefits he would not otherwise be entitled to receive.

When benefits are awarded to multiple dependents and one of them dies, the remainder of the deceased dependent's award can be redistributed among the remaining surviving dependents as dependents subsequent in right. For example, three total dependents might be awarded a weekly rate of one-third of $490/wk. Upon the death of one dependent, the award could be revised to provide a weekly rate of one-half of $490/wk for the two surviving dependents.

SAMPLE (D1). The DOI was 4/15/97. A totally dependent spouse and a totally dependent mother were jointly awarded $145,000 payable at $224/wk ($112/wk to each). A partially dependent adult son received $4,000 in annual support, but no death benefit was payable because there were two total dependents. Otherwise, the adult child would have received a death benefit of $16,000 (4 × $4,000). Both total dependents are killed in a vehicle accident after only a portion of the death benefit payable to each has been paid.

(D1.1). Paid Before Total Dependents Die - After 100 Weeks

Benefit Awarded	$145,000	÷ $224/wk	=	647.32 wks
Benefits Paid	− 22,400	÷ $224/wk	=	−100.00 wks
Remaining Unpaid	$122,600			547.32 wks

(D1.2). Benefit to Partially Dependent Son if Only Dependent

$4,000 × 4 = $16,000 at $224/wk

(D1.3). Reassignment of Death Benefit to Son

$16,000 is less than $122,600 (amount of award not paid)
Payable to son: $16,000 ÷ $224/wk = 71.43 wks

(D1.4). Amount Employer Will Pay - Reduced by Reassignment

To son	71 wks × $224.00 =	$15,904.00	$16,000.00
Last check	.43 wks @ $119.00	+ 96.00	−15,904.00
		$16,000.00	$ 96.00

(Refer to note in (A3.4) regarding computation of the last check for .43 wks.)

(D1.5). Employer's Liability Reduced By Reassignment

Original obligation for payments	$145,000	for	647.32 wks
Liability after reassignment	− 38,400	for	−171.43 wks
Savings to employer	$106,600		475.89 wks

$22,400 was paid to the two total dependents prior to their deaths and $16,000 was owed to the adult child thereafter for a total of $38,400 after the reassignment of death benefits.

SAMPLE (D2). Same situation as Sample (D1): The DOI was 4/15/97. A totally dependent spouse and a totally dependent mother were jointly awarded $145,000 payable at $224/wk ($112/wk to each). A partially dependent adult son received $4,000 in annual support, but no death benefit was payable because there was more than one total dependent. Otherwise, the son would have received a death benefit of $16,000 (4 × $4,000).

(D2.1). Benefits Paid Before Spouse And Mother Die After 600 Weeks

Benefit Awarded	$145,000	÷ $224/wk =	647.32 wks
Benefits Paid	−134,400	÷ $224/wk =	−600.00 wks
Remaining Unpaid	$ 10,600		47.32 wks

(D2.2). Benefit Payable to Son - If Only Dependent

Son $4,000 × 4 = $16,000 ÷ $224/wk = 71.43 wks

(D2.3). Reassignment of Death Benefit to Son

$16,000 exceeds $10,600 (amount of award not paid)
Payable to son: $10,600 ÷ $224/wk = 47.32 wks

(D2.4). Full Amount Employer Will Pay

To totals	600.00 wks	× $224 =	$134,400	
To partial	47.00 wks	× $224 =	10,528	$10,600
Last check	+ .32 wks		+ 72	−10,528
	647.32 wks		$145,000	$ 72

(D2.5). Employer's Liability Unaffected by Reassignment

The employer's original and final obligation for payments is $145,000 for 647.32 weeks. The employer will not pay more than $145,000, because this is the maximum amount under 1997 law for two total dependents or else for one total dependent and one partial dependent.

SAMPLE (E). The DOI is 9/9/96. The employee left a totally dependent child and three partial dependents: $10,000 support to spouse, $5,000 support to brother, and $2,000 annual support to father. The maximum benefit was awarded as follows: $125,000 to the total dependent and $20,000 among all partial dependents payable at $490/wk. If there was no total dependent, the partial dependents would have been entitled to their pro rata share of the $125,000 benefit amount.

(E1). Benefit Per Partial Dependent Under Award ($20,000 maximum)

Spouse	4 × $10,000 =	$40,000	÷ $68,000 =	.59	× $20,000 =	$11,800
Brother	4 × $ 5,000 =	20,000	÷ $68,000 =	.29	× $20,000 =	5,800
Father	4 × $ 2,000 =	+ 8,000	÷ $68,000 =	+.12	× $20,000 =	+ 2,400
		$68,000		1.00		$20,000

(E2). Weekly Benefit Rates Under Initial Award ($490/wk maximum)

Child	$125,000	÷ $145,000 =	.86 =		× $490 =	$421.40
Spouse	11,800	÷ $145,000 =	.08 =		× $490 =	39.20
Brother	5,800	÷ $145,000 =	.04 =		× $490 =	19.60
Father	+ 2,400	÷ $145,000 =	.02 =		× $490 =	+ 9.80
	$145,000					$490.00

(E3). Benefits Allowed If Child Dies ($125,000 maximum)

All benefits previously paid to the child would be deducted from the $125,000 maximum allowed for partial dependents in cases where there is no total dependent. This adjusted benefit amount would be used instead of $125,000 below.

Spouse	.59 × $125,000 =	$ 73,750	.59 × $490 =	$289.10/wk
Brother	.29 × $125,000 =	36,250	.29 × $490 =	142.10/wk
Father	.12 × $125,000 =	+ 15,000	.12 × $490 =	+ 58.80/wk
		$125,000		$490.00/wk

(E4). Benefits Payable if Brother Dies ($125,000/20,000)

Note: All benefits previously paid to the brother would be deducted from the $20,000 maximum otherwise allowed for partial dependents. This adjusted maximum benefit amount would be used in place of $20,000 in the computations below.

Spouse	4 × $10,000 =	$40,000	÷ $48,000 =	.83	× $20,000 =	$16,600
Father	4 × $ 2,000 =	+ 8,000	÷ $48,000 =	+.17	× $20,000 =	+ 3,400
		$48,000		1.00		$20,000

Child	$125,000	÷ $145,000 =	.86 × $490 =	$421.40/wk
Spouse	16,600	÷ $145,000 =	.12 × $490 =	58.80/wk
Father	+ 3,400	÷ $145,000 =	+.02 × $490 =	+ 9.80/wk
	$145,000		1.00	$490.00/wk

(E5). Benefits Allowed if Spouse Dies ($125,000/20,000).

Compute the same as shown in (E4) but with the maximum benefit amount of $20,000 reduced by all payments previously paid to spouse.

(E6). Benefits Allowed if Father Dies ($125,000/20,000)

Compute the same as shown in (E4) but with the maximum benefit amount of $20,000 reduced by all payments previously paid to father.

12.24 DEATH OF DEPENDENT

When a dependent dies, death benefits can be reassigned among remaining dependents under LC4704. However, there may not be any other dependents. Per LC4706, "at the time of death of the sole remaining dependent" any death benefits that are "accrued and payable" shall be paid "to the heirs of the dependent." If the dependent has no heirs, the payment is made to "the heirs of the deceased employee."

The executor of the employee's or dependent's estate could provide the names of any heirs. If there are no heirs, the employer does not owe any further payment. Otherwise, the accrued benefits are payable "without administration." Upon request, a judge can issue an order directing payment to the proper person as full satisfaction of the employer's obligations under the prior award. Unless there is some dispute regarding the proper payee, there is no necessity for any court proceedings.

12.25 PAYMENT TO STATE – NO DEPENDENT

If the employee sustains a compensable injury resulting in death but does "not leave surviving any person entitled to a dependency death benefit," the employer owes a payment to the State of California. Per LC4706.5, the employer owes the Department of Industrial Relations the commuted value of the maximum death benefit for one total dependent. The employer is entitled to a 3% interest credit because the payment is required to be made in a lump sum rather than installments. The employer can "voluntarily make the payment" without any court order to do so. The payment is due and payable "when, after a reasonable search, the employer concludes that the deceased employee left no one surviving who is entitled to a dependency death benefit and concludes that the death was under such circumstances as to entitle the employee to compensation benefits."

Installment payments of temporary or permanent disability may be accrued and unpaid when the employee dies following a compensable injury. Per LC4700, all compensation "accrued and unpaid" up to the date of the employee's death "shall be paid" to the "dependents" or the "personal representative" or heirs of the employee "without administration." If no such persons exist, LC4706.5 requires the employer to make payment to the State of California. The accrued compensation is payable regardless of whether the cause of death is the industrial injury for which benefits were being provided or any unrelated injury or condition. If disability payments were being made voluntarily, the employer can pay the appropriate person or the State and close its file. Where payments were owed under a WCAB order or award, the employer should request an order directing payment to the proper payee and terminating its liability upon such payment.

The money the State collects in nondependent death cases is used to fund the Subsequent Injuries Fund (see 10.44). The Non-Dependent Death Unit of the Division of Workers' Compensation is staffed by attorneys (who are physically located within the Claims Unit of the Division of Workers' Compensation). These attorneys represent the State's interests in collecting monies for deposit to the Subsequent Injuries Fund. Per CR10501, service upon the Non-Dependent Death Unit is required when an application or a compromise and release settlement agreement "is filed in a death case ... except where the deceased employee left a surviving minor child" (see 12.27).

12.26 PAYMENT FROM STATE – DEPENDENT FOUND

After the employer makes payment to the State in a nondependent death case, a dependent may be located, or the WCAB may decide a person is a qualified dependent although the employer disputed this person's entitlement to benefits. If the appeals board makes a finding that some person "is entitled to a dependency death benefit," per LC4706.5, "all payments which have been made shall be forthwith returned to the employer" or its insurance carrier (whoever made the payment). The employer is protected from duplicate payments, since it has a right to be repaid any sums the State was not entitled to receive.

12.27 EMPLOYERS' REPORTING REQUIREMENTS

Three separate notices are required by three different State agencies for three different purposes. All employers must file an Employer's First Report of Work Injury with the Division of Labor Statistics and Research in every case of an industrially related death. This agency compiles statistical data from information contained in reports submitted by all employers in the state (see 2.22). Also, LC6409.1 requires that "a report shall be made immediately by the employer to the Division of Occupational Safety and Health by telephone or telegraph." This State agency is interested in being advised of hazards in the workplace that may cause serious injuries and that can and should be immediately eliminated through appropriate safety precautions.

Additionally, the Division of Workers' Compensation requires submission of a Notice of Employee Death (Form DWC510). Per CR9900, this notice must be filed "within 60 days of the employer's notice or knowledge of the employee death." If the employer is insured, it forwards the completed notice to its insurance carrier who then files the form with the State. The notice is required "regardless of the cause of death" or whether or not the employer believes it to be work-related. Per CR9900, the only instance where this notice is not required is when "the employer has actual knowledge or notice that the deceased employee left a surviving minor child." In this instance, it is clear that the employer will owe death benefits to a dependent. In all other cases, the State wants notice so that it can collect benefits that are payable to the State in nondependent death cases.

12.28 SETTLEMENT PRIOR TO DEATH

Pursuant to LC5000, the employee can enter into a settlement that releases his dependents' right to seek death benefits should the employee later die. The dependents need not sign the settlement or be parties to it. The standard language of the Compromise and Release form used for a disability (as opposed to a death) claim is not sufficient to effect a release of death benefits even though the printed language on the form states "approval of this agreement RELEASES ANY AND ALL CLAIMS OF APPLICANT'S DEPENDENTS TO DEATH BENEFITS RELATING TO INJURY OR INJURIES COVERED BY THIS COMPROMISE AGREEMENT." This language is prefaced by "unless otherwise expressly provided herein" since death benefits will not be released every time this settlement form is used; e.g., the probability of death from a fingertip amputation injury is unlikely to warrant a settlement of potential death benefits.

The back of the Compromise and Release form (DWC WCAB Form 15) contains specific instructions. In order for the parties to release death benefits, "they must indicate in clear language that they have considered the release of death benefits in arriving at their agreement and direct the attention of the workers' compensation judge to that fact."

The required information can be provided on the settlement document or in an addendum. It must be clear to the judge that the employee understands he is releasing any and all rights his dependents might otherwise have and that the settlement amount provides adequate compensation for the injury sustained and the release of all future rights. If so, the wording of the judge's Order Approving Compromise and Release will confirm the fact that death benefits are released. Absent a clearly worded statement to this effect, approval of the settlement releases the employee's future rights to compensation but does not release the rights of his dependents.

12.29 CAUSE OF DEATH – AUTOPSY

An autopsy may be necessary to determine the exact cause of death and whether death resulted from industrial or nonindustrial causes. Per LC5706, the appeals board can "require an autopsy" to be performed, designate physicians to be present at an autopsy performed by the coroner, or designate physicians to perform an additional autopsy or reexamination. The employer will owe the expenses incurred in performing an autopsy, except "no fee shall be charged by the coroner for any service, arrangement, or permission given by him."

When an autopsy is requested, time is usually of the essence. Per CR10342, an order directing an autopsy or exhumation can only be issued by "the Appeals Board or a member thereof." The term "Appeals Board" is defined in CR10301 to mean "the commissioners and deputy commissioners" of the WCAB, and LC110 provides that "a member of the board is a 'commissioner'." Therefore, a petition for such an order must be filed with the Appeals Board in San Francisco. A judge cannot issue this type of order, so it would create an entirely unnecessary delay to file these petitions with a district office of the WCAB.

An appeals board order for an autopsy or exhumation for the purpose of performing an autopsy is subject to the dependents' acquiescence. Per LC5707, if a majority of the employee's dependents "refuse to allow the autopsy, it shall not be performed." However, exercising this right of refusal can inure to their detriment in meeting their burden of proof on the issue of industrial causation. Upon such refusal, LC5707 provides "it is a disputable presumption that the injury or death was not due to causes entitling the claimants to benefits." The dependents can overcome the presumption with other evidence of industrial causation, but the employer will not owe any benefits unless a judge determines that the supplemental evidence suffices to refute the presumption against compensability.

12.30 APPORTIONMENT OF DEATH BENEFIT

The sole basis for relieving the employer from payment of death benefits is a determination that the employee's injury/death was not compensable. Dependents will be entitled to receive either the death benefit set by law or no benefits at all. The fact that the death was also due to nonindustrial causes will not reduce the dependents' benefits in a proportionate amount. For instance, if medical evidence reveals that death was a result of equally contributory industrial and nonindustrial causes, the employer owes full death benefits, not one-half. Whenever the employment is a contributing cause without which the death would not have occurred, the employer owes death benefits in the amount established by the Labor Code.

Liability for the payment of the industrial death benefit is apportionable between employers. For instance, two or more employers could be jointly liable for benefits if death results from a work-related disease process that spans multiple employments. In cumulative injury cases, liable employers or carriers ordinarily share liability for benefits in proportion to their periods of coverage. The dependents might receive payment from one employer who then requests reimbursement from the others for their pro rata share, or the dependents might receive separate checks from each liable employer. Liability for payments can only be apportioned if two or more employers are jointly liable for the injury that was the proximate cause of the employee's death.

A claim for contribution from another employer must be made timely. Per LC5500.5, a party claiming contribution must institute WCAB proceedings within one year of the WCAB's award of compensation benefits "in connection with an occupational disease or cumulative injury." If a claim is timely pursued, the WCAB can determine the appropriate apportionment of liability and direct the manner of contribution among employers who are jointly responsible for payment of workers' compensation benefits. (Note: contribution differs from subrogation which refers to recovery of monies from nonemployer third parties whose negligence or partial negligence resulted in an injury; see 3.15.)

12.31 STATUTE OF LIMITATIONS

Proceedings for death benefits are commenced by filing an Application for Adjudication of Claim – Death Case (but proceedings will not be scheduled until a Declaration of Readiness is also filed). The statute of limitations for death benefits is the period within which this form must be filed with the WCAB. For all other benefits, WCAB proceedings are commenced by filing an Application for Adjudication of Claim (DWC WCAB Form 1). The distinction between the forms is important. Failure to file an application for death benefits can bar the right to receive this category of benefits even if an application for disability benefits was timely filed with the WCAB for the same injury. (See also 6.18.)

Per LC5406, there are alternative statute of limitations periods for death cases. The time period in which a dependent can file a timely application for death benefits in a particular case is controlled by these three factors:

a. Whether the employee received other categories of workers' compensation benefits prior to death, AND
b. The time elapsed since the date of injury, AND
c. The time elapsed since the date of death.

There are two time limits that apply to every claim. Per LC5406, no proceedings for death benefits "may be commenced":

1. "More than one year after the date of death," NOR
2. "More than 240 weeks from the date of injury."

By this language, it appears that a claim is barred by statute if the claim is filed within 240 weeks from the injury but more than one year after the date of death. Likewise, a claim is not timely if it is filed within one year from the date of death but more than 240 weeks after the date of injury.

The shortest statute of limitations for death benefits will apply to cases where no benefits have been furnished prior to the employee's death. An employee may choose not to pursue a valid claim and not report an injury, or the employer may have formally denied a claimed injury that the employee then chose not to appeal by filing a timely application with the WCAB. Where no compensation has been provided, the statute of limitations for death benefits is stated in LC5406(a). The claim must be filed within one year from the date of injury or one year from the "date of death where death occurs within one year from the date of injury." If the death occurred on the date of injury, the maximum time limit would be one year from this date. If the employee dies any time within one year from the date of injury, the one-year time period would run from the date of death.

The longest statute of limitations for death benefits will apply to cases where workers' compensation benefits have been provided prior to the employee's death. In these cases, there are two alternate time limits, and the greatest time period applies (subject to a maximum period of 240 weeks from the date of injury). Per LC5406, a death claim is timely if it is filed within one year from:

1. The "date of last furnishing of any benefits," OR
2. The "date of death."

One year from the date of the death would appear to be a longer time period than one year from the last date that benefits were provided. However, the "benefits" that are referred to in LC5406 include death benefits that the employer may provide to dependents after the employee's death. A dependent has one year from the last day that benefits were provided to commence WCAB proceedings, even if the last day of this time period is more than one year after the employee's death. However, in all cases, an Application for Adjudication of Claim – Death Case must be filed with the WCAB within 240 weeks from the injury (except where the dependent is a minor, see 6.30).

INDEX

INDEX TO CODE SECTIONS
(See Referenced Text Sections)